P9-CIU-688

DRYDEN

THE DRAMATIC WORKS

PREFATORY NOTES · INTRODUCTION · CHRONOLOGY

OF DRAMATICK POESIE · THE WILD GALLANT

THE RIVAL LADIES · THE INDIAN QUEEN

THE INDIAN EMPEROUR

NOTES

IN SIX VOLUMES · VOLUME I

EDITED BY MONTAGUE SUMMERS

GORDIAN PRESS

NEW YORK

1968

Originally published 1932
by the Nonesuch Press
in an Edition of 1000 Sets
Reprinted 1968
by Gordian Press

Library of Congress Catalog Card Number 68-15208

Published by Gordian Press, Inc.
by Arrangement with Nonesuch Press

TO

HECTOR STUART-FORBES

THIS EDITION OF JOHN DRYDEN

Οὐ γὰρ ἐν μέσοισι κεῖται
δῶρα δυσμάχητα Μοισᾶν
τὠπιτυχόντι φέρειν.

Bacchylides.

THE CONTENTS

PREFATORY NOTE

IT has more than once been emphatically remarked, and particularly perhaps has it been repeated during the past quarter of a century, that no English author stood so badly in need of editorial attention as John Dryden. There has been no adequate, no reliable reprint of Dryden, and the Plays especially have, until quite recent years, been entirely—one might almost say ostentatiously—neglected and forgotten.

More than one hundred and thirty years ago Edmond Malone published his edition, "The Critical And Miscellaneous Prose Works of John Dryden Now First Collected," in three volumes, 1800, of which Volume I is divided into two Parts. The First Part consists of "Some Account Of The Life And Writings Of John Dryden," a biography which is written in the full flower of Malone's wide scholarship, all annotated with amplest excursuses and most careful illustrative matter. Unfortunately, Malone in his reprint modernized the text, and it is sad to use in Bodley's Library the original quartos which he has altered and changed by his pencilled marginalia for the printer's direction.

In 1808 Sir Walter Scott issued in eighteen volumes *The Works of John Dryden Now first collected*; second edition, eighteen volumes, 1821. The genius of Scott, confessedly, did not lie in the direction of editorship, and however excellent his criticisms and literary appreciation of Dryden, his presentation of the text and his glosses thereon—although indeed these often contain points of great interest—are hardly adapted to modern norms and requirements of scholarship. It was inevitable that there should be many errors and many omissions.

Three-quarters of a century passed and the Scott edition of Dryden was reprinted, "Revised And Corrected By George Saintsbury," eighteen volumes, 1882–1893. The "Editor's Preface to Dramas," Vol. II, commences: "To an editor of Dryden at the present day, the Dramas supply the most troublesome and perhaps the most thankless, but also the most considerable, part of his task." Mr. Saintsbury then sets forth in detail the lines upon which he presents Dryden's plays. Instead of "taking the latest version which may pretend to some authority, and correcting by the first editions," he prefers "to take the first editions and correct, if necessary, by the latter," apparently meaning that the standard is to be such worthless reprints as could most easily be obtained. Accordingly we are not surprised to find that punctuation, the use of italics (so important and so thoroughly systematized), spelling, nay, very phrasing itself, are all thrown completely overboard, whilst there is throughout a wild and random rewriting of stage directions, a violent insertion of scene divisions and the like, utterly destructive of the dramatic technique, which is ever so careful and so adroitly designed, since Dryden was pre-eminently a man of the theatre. In fact I have no hesitation in saying that this reprint of 1882–1893 is the worst edition of any considerable English author I know. There are blunders which a scholar may make: ill-health, weariness, failing eyesight, the inability to read proofs with precision, will all play sad tricks with one's work. But there are blunders no scholar can make, and in these latter Mr. Saintsbury's recension is extremely prolific. We have notes which are the merest guess-work, the idlest hazard; flat assertions demonstrably untrue; we have readings which occur in no edition of Dryden that can be traced and glosses to bolster up the error; worst of all we have a fudge title-page, that of *The State of Innocence* which, relying on a mistake of Malone, is presented as 1674. The first quarto was 1677.

In 1900 (Second Impression, 1926) Professor W. P. Ker collected certain Essays of Dryden in two volumes, Clarendon Press, Oxford. Professor Ker was reputed, and I believe justly reputed, a scholar of no mean attainment, but his Dryden is not among his higher achievements.

The edition of Dryden's *Poems* edited by John Sargeaunt, Oxford University Press, 1910, must be used with much caution. The work is incomplete; there are gravest inaccuracies, and what is worse, unpardonable abridgements and deliberate excisions.

Of Dramatick Poesie was edited with very copious and useful notes by T. Arnold, Oxford, 1889, second edition, 1896; new edition revised by W. T. Arnold, Oxford, 1903. Various other reprints would seem to be adapted to school purposes and therefore hardly call for comment.

Of Dramatick Poesie was reissued in a fine format, 1928, by Frederick Etchells and Hugh Macdonald, *The Haslewood Books*, but the edition was not helped by an unnecessary trifling dialogue which intruded as prefatorial matter.

It is hardly an exaggeration to say that since the days of Malone the only purely critical work of any value that has been done upon Dryden is that by the late Mr. G. Thorn-Drury, K.C., whose notes, however, originally appearing in *The Review of English Studies* (Vol. I, Nos. 1, 2 and 3, January, April and July, 1925) as collected are only twelve in number, and of these but two directly concern the plays. My late friend was keenly interested in this present edition of Dryden, and I am particularly grateful to him for the gift of a large paper copy of the folio *Comedies, Tragedies, and Operas*, 2 vols., 1701.

The late Sir Edmund Gosse not infrequently discussed with me the Nonesuch edition of Dryden's plays, and I am very sure that it has suffered no greater disadvantage than the being deprived of his generous sympathy, his illuminating criticism, his ready help, the loan of many a treasure from his library, now dispersed. It is perhaps even yet hardly realized how intimate was his knowledge of the Restoration drama, and it has been remarked by not a few that this side of his scholarship was unfortunately ignored, or at least but barely touched upon, in the Memoir which has recently appeared. It may be that I shall publish the correspondence, extending over a large number of years, which passed between us, and in his letters will be found many of his literary appreciations of these authors, expressed as only he knew how to convey.

The task of editing Dryden has proved very onerous. Of immense assistance to me has been *A Dryden Library*, 1930, a complete and most amply annotated bibliography by Mr. T. J. Wise, whom I have to thank for his gift of a work that has in no small degree lightened my labours. To the student this Bibliography is not merely of incalculable value, it is an essential companion.

I have to thank Mr. William Andrews Clark, Jr., for presenting me with his privately printed *All For Love*, 1929, a superb edition, embellished with thirteen Plates produced in colour of a rare excellence. In addition to a modernized text this fine book also furnishes a photographic facsimile reprint of the Bridgewater copy of the 4to, 1678.

Of the encyclopædic learning of Professor Bensly, who never wearied in answering my questions and was indefatigable in tracing down the obscurer quotations for which Dryden too often trusted to memory, I have taken fullest advantage.

Without many years of research at the British Museum and at the Bodleian, and indeed in many other libraries, it would not be possible to undertake such a work as the editing of Dryden.

I am sincerely grateful to the Librarians and other officials of these our two great libraries for their invariable courtesies and prompt assistance, which I record with deep appreciation as having extended over a period of well-nigh four decades.

Nor must I neglect gratefully to mention the Cambridge University Library, and the Libraries of Christ Church and Worcester Colleges, Oxford. I have to thank the Librarians and several authorities for the facilities which they so ungrudgingly afforded me.

To the Master, Fellows and Librarian of Trinity College, Cambridge, are due my best thanks for their courtesy in allowing me to collate the MS. of *The Indian Emperour*.

I would make particular acknowledgement of the kindness of the President and Fellows of Harvard University in permitting me to collate the MS. *The Fall of Angels and Man in Innocence* (*The State of Innocence*), which is among their chiefest treasures. I also have to thank Mr. R. P. Blake, Director of the Harvard Library, and the Librarian, Mr. A. C. Potter, for the trouble they were at to supply me with a rotograph of this important script.

Several of the notes upon Purcell's music to Dryden's plays were given to me in past years by that great authority, the late Mr. W. Barclay Squire.

To correspondents who have in their letters elucidated particular points, local, topographical and technical, I wish to express my thanks, although they would not have me name them individually and in more specific fashion.

Above all I am indebted to Mr. Hector Stuart-Forbes without whose ungrudging help, sympathy and constant encouragement this edition of Dryden would scarcely now be completed.

M. S.

NOTE AS TO THE TEXT

THE sole authoritative text of Dryden's plays is that of the first quartos, and this has been here exactly given, having been duly collated with all issues that appeared during the author's lifetime, as also with the folio "The Comedies, Tragedies, and Operas Written by John Dryden, Esq; now first Collected together, and Corrected from the Originals. In Two Volumes. London, Printed for Jacob Tonson . . . MDCCI." In some copies, it may be noted, the Second Volume adds the Secular Masque (with a variant title-page), but more often this piece does not appear. This edition, which neither includes *The Mistaken Husband*, 4to, 1675, nor *The Vindication of the Duke of Guise*, 4to, 1673, is the latest which textually has any possible value, although occasionally in order to illustrate the introduction or permanence of an error, or some similar point, I have made reference to a reading in the so-called Congreve edition, six volumes, 1717.

How far the Folio, 1701, may actually claim to be the first Collected Edition is open to question inasmuch as during Dryden's life there was a considerable demand for his collected "Works," and Tonson met this by binding together in various volumes the quarto plays of several dates as also the poems. Naturally when Dryden wrote a new piece an extra item had to be added to these "Works."

In such a case as that of *Tyrannick Love; or The Royal Martyr*, of which play the Second Edition was expressly "review'd by the Authour," particular attention has been given to the readings of the second quarto, 1672. In the first edition, 1673, in the quarto 1691, and the folio 1701, of *Amboyna* certain scenes and speeches, especially in Acts IV and V, are plainly blank verse, and are indeed set as such in the 12mo Dryden of 1735, "Printed for Jacob Tonson in the *Strand*." This arrangement I have ventured to follow. The third quarto, 1690, of *The Spanish Fryar* adds to the text four passages of some significance. These I have duly inserted, remarking them in the notes. In the first quarto, 1680, of *The Kind Keeper; or, Mr. Limberham* (and once or twice in other plays) we have VV for W and vv for w. Thus in *The Kind Keeper*, quarto, 1680, on p. 18 and on p. 41 both *Wood. and VVood.* occur as speech-prefixes, whilst on p. 17 we have "my Son *VVoodall*" in the text with "*Enter* Woodall" seven lines below. This edition does not aim at being a photographic facsimile, and I have judged it better consistently to keep to W and w throughout.

Mr. T. J. Wise in his *A Dryden Library*, 1930 (p. 57), writes: "The First Issue of the First Edition of *Amphitryon* is an extremely uncommon book. Its title-page is dated 1690, and it is the last of the Plays included in the second volume of Dryden's Works advertised upon signature 12. The three volumes there announced were composed of remainders of the separate editions of most of the plays and poems, arranged in three volumes, provided with collective title-pages. These title-pages were no doubt dated 1690, but no example of this first collected edition of Dryden's Works is at present available. In 1693 there appeared an edition in four volumes." A copy of Dryden's "Works" in a single volume with title-page dated 1691 is known. The Third Volume of the "Works" with title-page, 1693, usually contains: *The Spanish Fryar*, third edition, 1690; *The Duke of Guise*, 1687; *The Vindication*, 1683; *Albion and Albanius*, 1691; *Don Sebastian*, 1692; *Amphitryon*, 1691; *King Arthur*, 1691; *Cleomenes*, 1692.

"Mr. Dryden's Plays" were collected in two volumes with general title-page, 1694.

"The Second Volume of the Works of Mr. John Dryden," which is in my own library, with general title-page 1695, contains: *Marriage A-la-mode*, 1691; *Love in a Nunnery*, The Third Edition, 1692; *Amboyna*, 1691; *State of Innocence*, 1695; *Aurenzebe* (*Aureng-Zebe*), 1694; *All for Love*, M DC XCVI (this is possibly a later insertion); *Limberham*, 1690; *Oedipus*, The Fifth Edition, n.d., [1694?]; *Troilus and Cressida*, 1695; *Spanish Fryar*, 1695.

It may be noted that the Fifth Edition of *Oedipus* is sometimes assigned to 1696, but this would appear to be an error, and 1694 may be taken as the correct date.

"The Dramatick Works of Mr. John Dryden," Vol. III, with general title-page, 1695, contains: *Duke of Guise*, 1687; *The Vindication*, 1683; *Albion and Albanius*, 1691; *Don Sebastian*, M DC XC II; *Amphitryon*, The Second Edition, 1694; *King Arthur*, 1695; *Cleomenes*, 1692; *Love Triumphant*, 1694.

In his *John Dryden Bibliographical Memoranda*, 1922, pp. 7 and 8, Mr. P. J. Dobell describes what is apparently a unique copy of *Sr. Martin Mar-all*, retaining a cancelled leaf C2 (pp. 11–12) which carries a page of conversation between Moody and Sir John Swallow. This is reproduced in an Appendix to the monograph, p. 30.

As is remarked in the particular notes upon the text of the various pieces, certain of Dryden's plays, *The Wild Gallant*, 4to, 1669; *Sr Martin Mar-all*, 4to, 1668; *An Evening's Love*, 4to, 1671; present bibliographical problems as to separate issues or editions of the same year, but these questions have now all been acutely and authoritatively resolved by the vast and intimate knowledge of my most ingenious friend Mr. Wise, than whom no man is more learned in these things.

In the case of *The Indian Emperour* I have given *The Defence of an Essay of Dramatick Poesie*, a piece of extreme interest, which, however, only appears in some copies of the Second Edition, 4to, 1668, of that tragedy, since it was suppressed by the author.

The final paragraph, added by Dryden to the Preface of *Tyrannick Love*, Second Edition, 4to, 1672, will also be found in its due position.

It has been stated that there is only one known manuscript of any of Dryden's plays, the Harvard MS., "The Fall of Angels and Man in Innocence," of *The State of Innocence*, 4to, 1677. This, however, is not correct, since MSS. of the same play are also to be found in the British Museum and Bodleian libraries. The MS. of *The Indian Emperour* which is preserved in the library of Trinity College, Cambridge, has hitherto been entirely overlooked. It is none the less of great importance, and is to be dated 1665, the play itself not appearing in print until 1667. All these MSS. have been collated for the present edition.

NOTE AS TO THE TEXT

"Memorandos litterarum partus, quos sapientissimi magistri depurata mens olim profudit, ac insequens aetas partim invidiosa offudit tenebris, partim confusa serie, preloque impolito immodice corrupit, succollante divinae gratiae praesidio, quae suaviter dat omne bonum velle, et fortiter perficere, typis emaculatioribus, atque usui plurimorum daturus, ex destinati ratione consilii futurorum existimabam, si praemitterem quae vitae statum, gradum, tempusque auctoris contingunt, et circumstant: Maioris notitiae, in quantum pro tempore assequi datum fuit, ac clarioris famae argumentum. Praenosse siquidem, in quam, quisque scriptor aetatem inciderit, quae patria, qui natales obtigerint: quam nactus societatem, quam vivendi normam professus, quo dignitatis gradu sublimatus, legentis atque amantis interest plurimum." *Prolegomena de Vita Magistri Adami, dicti Anglici, Ordinis Præmonstratensis;* ii.

Under favour, I may say in conclusion that not the least difficult part of my labours has been the endeavour to present a complete and accurate text of the Plays, and that this is in effect the first time any such attempt has been made. There is certainly no author of the first order who presents in every direction such intricate and baffling problems as John Dryden, but the work must needs be essayed. That my success has been perfect, final and complete it were too much to expect; that I have spared neither time, patience, long and toilsome research, I will even add health itself in the inquiry, it is not too much to assert and faithfully affirm.

INTRODUCTION

DURING that rich and glowing half-century from the Restoration to the death of Queen Anne, there stands out one pre-eminent figure, admirable beyond all others, whether it be for the ample measure of his actual work, his eight-and-twenty plays—the industrious output of thirty years—and the astonishing breadth and sureness of his range, or for the majesty and sweet melody of his verse, the wit and infinite humour of his comic scenes. Beyond all these excellencies is added yet another quality, the fact that there was, perhaps, no poet of his own day, few before, and since fewer still, who possessed so keen and felicitous a sense of the theatre as John Dryden. This rare talent can only be fully discerned and appreciated by those minds which have acquired some practical knowledge of the stage and the technical requirements of the scene. Not merely familiarity with the script but a certain particular training is required in order to be able to visualize an acted play, in order exactly to estimate the nice points of a playwright's skill, the more delicate subtleties of his craft. This all-important matter was for many a long year completely ignored, so the academics, the professors of crowded book-shelves and library arm-chairs, fell unrestrained upon Shakespeare, who, it was clean forgotten, was an actor as well as a writer, who made his plays for the boards, not for grammarians, philomaths, and pedants to smother his scenes with the dust of arid commentaries. It is no pleasing reflexion when we consider the vast amount of erudition and lifelong research which has been thrown away upon William Shakespeare, thrown away and wasted because so hopelessly misdirected, because those who were the most painstaking in their efforts, the most unremitting in their study, did not possess even the primary qualifications essential for dealing intelligently with the work of a man who was an actor and a dramatist.

The theatre of Dryden has been treated in similar fashion by those who were incapable of recognizing this peculiar aptness for the stage which is the quintessence and the hall-mark of dramatic genius. But Dryden has suffered, not from a plethora of injurious meddlesomeness, but from a severe and almost unexampled neglect. His plays have never yet been examined and appreciated with understanding. On all hands they were universally disregarded and contemned. Scott, it is true, now and again ventured a few words of commendation, but even the theatrical historians as well as the professed biographers of Dryden follow Scott very half-heartedly whilst with apologies and anæmic excuse they dismiss as soon as may be these brilliant dramas to the appreciation of which they bring neither knowledge nor sympathy. Yet when *Marriage-à-la-Mode* was revived, after an interval of two hundred years, in February, 1920, a crowded house rose in enthusiasm at Dryden's comedy, and the critics became lyrical in their eulogies.

To account for this long neglect and misliking of Dryden is not, I think, altogether difficult. Dryden was above all things a man of his age. Not only was he moulded by his time, but he also, in his turn, moulded his time. Perhaps in all literature it would be difficult to find so complete an instance of interaction and reaction between a writer and his era. The years from 1660 to 1700 when John Dryden was the supreme influence in literature were

b

essentially full-blooded years, years of swift and vital changes, restoration and revolution, political chaos, civil war, systematic plotting and villainies wellnigh unparalleled in English history; yet they were years which glittered with the most brilliant British court that ever patronized and was keenly interested in things literary, whose king was himself a critic, whose wildest rakes were dramatists of considerable parts and lyric poets of bewildering beauty, whose factions fought not only with the sword but with the pen, a weapon hardly less sharp than cold steel and which dealt wounds far more enduring. It was a time when literature and life were inextricably mingled, and he who was master in the one might bid fair to be a master of the other.

In order to appreciate the genius of John Dryden, in order, truly, to estimate his rightful place and position amongst English writers, it is necessary to consider him in relation to the age in which he lived, to study not only the man but the period. And the more we know of the forty years from 1660 to 1700 the more capable are we of recognizing his greatness.

In himself Dryden summed up the whole province of literature. He is a poet of the highest order. He is the most discerning and constructive of English critics. His prose is unsurpassed for clarity and purity. It is not too much to point out that with the exception of fiction—a notable exception, I grant, but the novel was then hardly born—there is no part of English literature which is not to be found at perfection among the works of John Dryden. The great poet will say things which have often been said before, which have often been repeated since, but he will say them with a felicity of thought and a faculty of words that throughout all time cannot be bettered or improved. And often it is no profound meditation or startling image which he thus delivers, but merely some simple truth expressed in some simple way upon which he has conferred a serene immortality. There are few poets who have had this power in a more marked degree than Dryden. What are commonplaces in the verse of others, in his numbers shine with that rare significance we call perfection.

However exquisite a singer's harmony, however sweet his verse, however graceful and gracious his conceptions, there must be something more than even the extremest endeavour of technical accomplishment if he is to rank among the finest. The great poet must make the things of eternity his theme. Fair as is the loveliness of this world, the springtide flowers and the autumn tilth, the country garden and the wide savannah, the laughing rill and the mountain cataract, fair as are the thousand landscapes nature paints in ever-varying colours, ever new, the poet must lift Nature's veil and, like the patriarch of old, essay his vision of Nature's God face to face. Herein lies the difference between Catullus and Ovid, between Wordsworth and Waller. Although at one time, as he confesses in the Preface to *Religio Laici* (1682), "naturally inclin'd to Scepticism in Philosophy," Dryden, both in this poem, whilst he was so to speak groping his way, and yet more completely in the fuller, more logical, more stable *The Hind and The Panther* (1687), has in his own fashion and along his own lines treated of the eternal verities. He is not afire with faith and inspiration as were Crashaw and Francis Thompson, but he is none the less whole-hearted, convinced and intellectually sincere. *The Hind and The Panther* for its force of clear sequential reasoning is Duns Scotus in magnificent verse.

INTRODUCTION

It is hardly my province to give a discursive and critical biography here, especially since this I have provided in another place. None the less it will be necessary briefly to remind ourselves of the main outlines of Dryden's life, for without some such summary the plays which we have to consider in detail would be disjointed and unrelated productions, whereas they reflect and are in many cases the direct outcome of forces, literary and political, which served to fashion and develop the poet's artistic creed; and more, practically to shape and regulate the actual conduct of his days.

John Dryden was the eldest son of Erasmus Driden[1] who had married Mary, the daughter of the Reverend Henry Pickering, younger son of Sir Gilbert Pickering, who in spite of the fact that he was a zealous and indeed an intemperate puritan, stood high in favour with James I. The Reverend Henry Pickering was born in 1564, and in 1597 he was presented by his kinsman John Pickering, to whom the advowson then belonged, to the living of Aldwinkle All Saints, Northamptonshire, which ministry he served for forty years, dying in 1637.

The industry of Malone has traced a great many interesting circumstances concerning both the Pickerings and the Dridens, but actually of the poet's father Erasmus, less is known than of almost any other of his relations. Erasmus Driden, the third son of Sir Erasmus Driden of Canons Ashby,[2] *comitatu* Northants, the first baronet of that ancient house, was himself the father of fourteen children, four sons and ten daughters, of whom some few unimportant particulars have been preserved, such for example as that Erasmus, the second son, who was long in trade and resided in King Street, Westminster, succeeded very late in life to the family title and estates upon the death of his cousin, Sir John Driden, and died at his seat of Canons Ashby on 3 November, 1718, leaving one daughter and five grandsons; that Henry, the third brother, went to Jamaica where he died, leaving one son, Richard; that James, the fourth son, was a tobacconist in London; that Frances, the youngest child, married Joseph Sandwill, a tobacconist in Newgate Street, and died 10 October, 1730, at the advanced age of ninety, having survived her eldest brother the poet about thirty years.

There can be little doubt that Erasmus Driden was an obstinate and fanatical

[1] Both Sir Erasmus, the grandfather, and Erasmus the father of the poet wrote *Driden*. In the marriage register of Pilton *die* 21 October, 1630, the name is spelled *Dreydon*. *Driden* is the spelling of John Dryden's surname in the Register of Trinity College, Cambridge, and in the University Register. He was the first to write *Dryden*, and this form is printed on the title-page of *Three Poems Upon the Death of his late Highnesse Oliver* Lord Protector, 4to, 1659. *Astræa Redux*, folio, 1660, has "By *John Driden*"; *To His Sacred Maiesty*, folio, 1661, has "*By* John Dryden"; *To My Lord Chancellor*, folio, 1662, has "By *J. Driden.*" The title-page to *The Rival Ladies* 4to, 1675, has "Written by *John Driden* Esquire," and the Dedication is signed "John Driden." The same spelling occurs in 4to, 1693, of the play. There are, of course, other variants of the name.

[2] Canons Ashby was an ancient but unimportant house of Black Canons, Augustinians. The date of foundation is uncertain, but it seems to have been earlier than the reign of Henry II.

sectary since he acted as a Justice of Peace[1] for the county of Northampton during the Usurpation, and his elder brother, with whom he was on excellent terms, Sir John Driden, "was never noted for Ability or Discretion; was a *Puritan* by Tenure, his House (Canons Ashby) being an ancient College, and his Lands the Revenues of the College, where he possessed the Church, and abused most part of it to prophane Uses. . . ."[2] Erasmus Driden fully shared these abominable opinions, and indeed if he had not the old Genevan, Henry Pickering, would never have accepted him as son-in-law.

It seems highly probable that Erasmus Driden was even a Committee-man.

There can be no doubt then that Dryden's earliest days were passed in a home of sourest fanaticism, and this being no secret furnished his later opponents with an unworthy occasion to jeer and heck at a circumstance for which he was certainly not responsible and which he could neither alter nor avoid.

The earliest reference to the fact that Dryden was employed by Sir Gilbert Pickering and that his father was a committee-man would seem to be made in "A letter from a Gentleman[3] to the Honourable Ed. Howard, Esq.; Occasioned By a *Civiliz'd Epistle* of Mr. Dryden's Before his Second Edition of his *Indian Emperour*," 4to, 1668, when it is said: "His (Dreyden's) fortune and that of the honourable gentleman (Sir Robert Howard) are different for the Squire (Dreyden) mistakenly charges him that the corruption of a poet was the generation of a statesman; but on the contrary, the Squire (Dreyden) having been imployed as a Puny Statesman under his Father a Zealous committee-man, and *Sir Gilbert Pickering* a crafty Privy Counceller in the late times, it may more properly be applied to the Squire, that the corruption of a Statesman is the generation of a Poet Laureat."

It has been worth while just briefly to remark upon influences which should, it might appear, powerfully have moulded Dryden's character and qualities, and we must often bear in mind the arid home atmosphere and Genevan principles, the glum social intercourse and bigot manners of pietism in which his earliest and most susceptible years were passed.

Dryden's suspicion and severe judgement of the clergy are undeniable, and his old mistrust he derived (I think) from his very childhood, not indeed from the rancorous abuse and angry strictures with which he must so often have heard ecclesiastics disparaged and defamed—his nature was too generous and too fair for that—but rather from the daily parade of hypocrisy, cant, sham and pharisaism which the sectarian pastors and their vessels of election so signally exhibited and aroused. Upon a young and reflective mind such impression would have been most permanent and extremely discomposing.

[1] Malone notes that in one of the vestry books of Aldwinkle S. Peters is an order made by Erasmus Driden in 1653, by which he gives his sanction, as a Justice of the Peace, to the appointment of a parish officer.

[2] "An account of the Northamptonshire Committee of Sequestration" by the Rev. Jeremiah Stephens, Rector of Wotton cum Quinton, Northants, as printed from the manuscript by Walker in his *Sufferings of the Clergy*, folio, 1715, Part 1, p. 91.

[3] The writer was "R.F." who was thought by Cunningham to be Richard Flecknoe, *The Gentleman's Magazine*, December, 1850. This would certainly explain Dryden's supreme contempt for and dislike of Flecknoe.

INTRODUCTION

Erasmus and Mary Driden were married at the Church of Our Lady and All Saints,[1] Pilton, which is some three miles from Aldwinkle, on 21 October, 1630, and John, their eldest son, was born on 9 August, 1631, at the rectory house, Aldwinkle All Saints.[2] The rectory is a plain but extremely picturesque two-story building of rubble and plaster, long and rather low, with a thatched roof. It dates in part from the sixteenth century, but the windows have unfortunately been modernised and the house otherwise altered. A window over the door is said to have lighted the chamber where Mary Driden was actually brought to bed, but the interior has been considerably changed.

John Dryden was born the fifth hour, the thirty-third minute, and the sixteenth second of the afternoon of 9 August, 1631. These very precise details are to be ascertained from a horoscope of John Dryden, calculated by Elias Ashmole and contained in a MS. volume of horoscopes and cognate astrological matter preserved in the Bodleian Library, Ashmole MS. 243 (p. 209). The horoscope, which is in Ashmole's hand, is inscribed "Mr Dridens [Nat. *erased*] the poet his Nat:."

Erasmus Driden possessed property in Titchmarsh, a village which lies off the main road from Northampton to Peterborough, about two and a half miles from Thrapston. It was at Titchmarsh that John Dryden received the first rudiments of his education, for it was here that his family resided, as we are informed by the monument which was erected to the poet's memory in the Church of Our Lady S. Mary, Titchmarsh, by Mrs. Elizabeth Creed in 1722.

There is a tradition that John Dryden received part of his education at Oundle Grammar School.[3] The head master of Oundle in Dryden's school-days was Thomas Johnson, who commenced his duties on 3 February, 1636. There were then seventy boys, arranged in eight classes. The scholars seemed to remain on an average about three years.

It was no doubt from Oundle that John Dryden was admitted a King's Scholar at Westminster, as Malone conjectures "probably about the time of the Civil War's breaking out, when he was near eleven years old."[4] Here he came under the tuition of an English Orbilius, the celebrated Dr. Richard Busby,[5] who had been appointed provisional Master of Westminster in 1638, in the place of Lambert Osbolston whom Archbishop Laud ejected from the post. Busby was confirmed in his office in 1639 and died Master of the school 6 April, 1695, at the age of eighty-eight.

[1] The earliest dedication seems to have been All Saints only.

[2] This is the constant tradition and may be accepted. Unfortunately the registers of Aldwinkle All Saints, and Aldwinkle S. Peters of this date are lost. Malone and Scott after him, were somewhat exercised whether Dryden's birthplace could be correct, as through an error in reading an inscription on his tomb it was supposed that the Rev. Henry Pickering was not appointed minister of All Saints, Aldwinkle, until 1647. This mistake was corrected by the Rev. H. Ward, Rector of S. Peter's Church.

[3] See *English Schools at the Reformation* (p. 153), 1896, by A. E. Leach, M.A., F.S.A.

[4] The earliest extant Register of elections to Westminster School commences in 1663.

[5] Born in 1607; student of Christ Church, Oxford, in 1624; proceeded M.A. in 1631.

In the "Argument of the Third Satyr" of Persius in his translation, folio, 1693, Dryden remarks: "I remember I translated this Satyr, when I was a *Kings-Scholar* at *Westminster* School, for a *Thursday* Nights *Exercise*, and believe that it, and many other of my *Exercises* of this nature, in *English Verse*, are still in the hands of my *Learned Master*, the Reverend Doctor *Busby*." I imagine that there are very few public-school boys of to-day—so degenerate and idle is the race become—who would care to be set to turn a satire of Persius into English verse for their homework, or who could tackle it even if such a task were appointed. Dryden always regarded his old Head Master with great respect, and the two letters[1] addressed by him to Dr. Busby, which have been preserved, are written in a strain of marked personal deference. This is sufficiently noticeable as one of these missives concerns an injustice which seems to have been done to Charles, the poet's eldest son, and of which as a father he very properly makes complaint.[2]

It is interesting to note that a form on which Dryden's name is cut in large letters is still carefully preserved at Westminster. Yet whatever else Busby taught Dryden, and there can be no doubt both from the Master's learning[3] and the pupil's ability that the future great scholar was well and widely grounded in the classics, one important detail was omitted. Busby did not train Dryden to verify his citations and to quote with exactitude from his originals. Almost inevitably Dryden paraphrases rather than reproduces the sentences of his Greek and Latin author. The sense is never perverted; the application is always just, illuminating and pertinent; but the phrase is varied. Felton remarks that "Dr. *Busby* strictly forbad the use of Notes, and for our *Greek* and *Latin* authors we had nothing but the plain Text in a correct and chaste edition."[4]

During the last year of his residence at Westminster Dryden contributed an Elegy to "*Lachrymae Musarum. The Tears of the Muses:* Exprest in Elegies By divers Persons of Nobility and Worth, upon the death of the most hopefull Lord *Hastings*, Onely Sonn of the Right Honourable Ferdinando Earl of *Huntingdon* Heir-generall of the high-born Prince George, Duke of *Clarence*, Brother to King Edward the fourth. *Collected and set forth by R.B.*"[5], 1649, an octavo whose title-page is bordered with heavy black rules of most lugubrious aspect. Herein are collected thirty-five memorial pieces lamenting the untimely death from small-pox of his schoolfellow Henry, Baron Hastings of Ashby-de-la-Zouch. Aston Cokain, Herrick, Denham, Marvell, Charles Cotton and many well-known poets are represented in this volume.

On 11 May, 1650, John Dryden was admitted as a Westminster Scholar at

[1] Malone dates these 1682.

[2] There is also extant a letter (1682) from Lady Elizabeth Dryden to Dr. Busby whom she addresses as "Honnord Sir," subscribing herself "Your remembrancer, and allwayes, Honnord Sir, Your humble Servant."

[3] "Doctissimus Busbeius . . . vir in Linguae Græcæ tum cognitione tum institutione omnibus ævi sui ac præteriti forsanque & futuri magistris longè superior," is the inflated praise of Maittaire, *Stephanorum Historia*, 1709, vol. I, part II, p. 358.

[4] *Dissertation on reading the Classics and forming a just Style*, 1718, pp. 41–2.

[5] Dryden's poem occupies pp. 88–92. Other Westminster scholars, Montague, Adams, Campion, and Wyche, contributed poems in Latin and very good they are.

Trinity College, Cambridge, under the tuition of the Rev. John Temple, and here he matriculated on the following 6 July.

In 1650 John Hoddesdon published his *Sion and Parnassus, or, Epigrams on several Texts of the Old and New Testament*, octavo, prefixt to which is a copy of commendatory verses *To his Friend the Authour, on his Divine Epigrams*, signed J. Dryden of Trin. C. The compliment is gracefully turned, and these six-and-twenty lines already afford indication of more than ordinary poetical powers.

Of Dryden's College career at Cambridge nothing is known save that quite early in his third year of residence he was guilty of some trifling breaches of discipline and in consequence incurred a routine punishment of no very serious nature. In the Books of Trinity College there occurs the following entry: "April 23. 1655. At the election of Scholars Wilford is chosen into Dreyden's place."

At Cambridge he continued in residence until 1655. Elkanah Settle seems to allude to a seven years' residence in his *Notes and Observations on the Empress of Morocco Revised*,[1] an answer to the *Notes And Observations On The Empress of Morocco*, 4to, 1674, a pamphlet in which Dryden, Shadwell and Crowne combined to attack that tragedy then so greatly in vogue and loudly applauded both by the Court and Town. It will readily be remembered that the dramatists had been particularly nettled by the publication of *The Empress of Morocco*, 4to, 1673, embellished "With Sculptures." Settle particularly jeers Dryden for his "smart Quibbles in his Cambridge Dialect" (p. 5); and also impugns his arguments with "Now for Mr. *Drydens Logick*. . . . The poorest Freshman in the University would be sconced for half so great a *blunder*, but Mr. *Dryden* is a great *professor* of Learning, if ye'l believe himself or his flatterers, and so cannot sin" (p. 11). . . . "But such is the *Reasoning* of a man of Seven years standing in *Cambridge*, and twice as many in *Covent-Garden Coffee-House*" (p. 31). This period of seven years has, as we shall note, been traditionally accepted, and indeed Dryden may have continued to live in Cambridge, although the tenure of his scholarship had lapsed in its own due course.

In June, 1654, Erasmus Driden, being then about sixty-six years old, died after a short illness and upon the 18th of that month was buried at Titchmarsh. This naturally proved a considerable interruption to the studies of John Dryden, who as the eldest son was obliged to leave Cambridge for a while in order both to take possession of his inheritance and to see to the decent and seemly settlement of his father's affairs. By the Will of Erasmus Driden, which was made on 30 December, 1652, and proved by his widow and executrix, 23 January, 1654–5, John Dryden succeeded to a small estate—a house and a few "yardlands" at a little village named Blakesley,[2] about three miles from Canons Ashby. Two-thirds of this property, which in all was worth about sixty pounds a year, were devised to the testator's son, and the other third during the term of her life to his wife, who was also his residuary legatee. Upon the death of

[1] 418, 1674; *Term Catalogues*, Hilary (15 February), 1675.

[2] Blakesley, a village and civil parish, lies in well-wooded and pleasant country some five miles west from Towcester. In 1921 the population was 632 in the ecclesiastical, and 432 in the civil parish.

Mary Driden this third was to revert to the poet, as came about in the year 1676. To his several children Erasmus Driden had bequeathed portions of varying amounts.

In a letter which is addressed from Cambridge on 23 May, 1655,[1] to his cousin-german Honor Driden, the young poet who had received the gift of a silver standish from the lady, replies in a strain of the most elegant and admired gallantry. That his admiration expressed with the most rococo compliment, conceits such as enraptured Cathos and Madelon, and contrived with no little ingenuity, need be read as a serious courtship I take leave to doubt, for Madam Honor Driden, to whose fair hands the letter craved admittance, was not a celebrated beauty although she enjoyed what was for that time no inconsiderable fortune.[2] She was born about the year 1637, and having remained single all her life, died a little later than 1707. Dryden's letter concludes with eight lines of poetry, harmonious numbers, embroidered much in the style of Cowley.

It has been remarked that Dryden "stayed in Cambridge seven years, that being then the usual length of the course for Orders in the Church of England, but he did not take Orders, nor proceed to his M.A. degree."[3] In order to account for a long residence at Cambridge the suggestion that Dryden was preparing for Anglican Orders, yet for some reason unknown eventually decided not to adopt a clerical career is extremely ingenious. There are, however, fatal objections to any such theory. In the first place, Episcopacy had been crushed by the tyranny of Cromwell and utterly forbidden. The Bishops, abused, outcast and persecuted, were no longer suffered to exercise their functions. It is hardly likely that a young man, having his way to make in life, who came of an extreme Puritan stock, whose relations were prominent and active republicans, high in favour with the usurper, would commence his career by taking Anglican Orders,[4] when probably he could only have accomplished this by a trip to the Continent, and in any case we are sure he could not have prepared for the ecclesiastical state at either University, at Cambridge possibly least of the two.

It is curious that later there was a constant report that Dryden had more than once seriously contemplated taking Holy Orders. We find it bruited quite early as it is alluded to in that violent attack, "A Letter from a Gentleman to the *Honourable* Ed: Howard Esq.; Occasioned By a *Civiliz'd Epistle* of Mr. Dryden's Before his Second Edition of his *Indian Emperour*," 4to, 1668. It again crops up in Settle's *Absalom Senior*, folio, 1682:

> For which religiously no change he miss'd
> From commonwealth's-man to royalist;
> Nay, would have been his own loath'd thing, call'd priest:
> Priest, whom with so much gall he doth describe,
> 'Cause one unworthy thought of *Levi's* tribe.

[1] See Malone, *op. cit.*, Vol. I, Part 2, p. 3 *n*.

[2] Sir John Driden, her father, who died in 1658 left her £2500.

[3] A. W. Verrall, *Lectures on Dryden*, 1914, p. 13.

[4] "My Father wisely bad me be a Clerk," so runs a line in the *Satyr to His Muse*. But this lampoon of Shadwell's carries no weight.

Shadwell too, in the *Satyr to his Muse*, 4to, 1682, jeers thus:

> Baudy in Prologues, Blasphemous in Plays,
> So lewd, thou mad'st me for the Church unfit,
> And I had sterv'd but for a lucky hit.

Langbaine when reviewing *The Spanish Fryar* sneers: "One truth is ever since a certain Worthy Bishop refus'd Orders to a certain Poet, Mr. *Dryden* has declar'd open defiance against the whole Clergy." However, in his Preface to the *Fables* Dryden denies the canard: "If I had taken to the Church (as he (Milbourne) affirms but which was never in my Thoughts) I should have more Sense, if not more Grace."

Had Dryden whilst at Cambridge, and even after his father's death, contemplated Anglican Orders, as Professor Verrall suggests, he must have broken with his Puritan family, and this he did not do, as is most conclusively shown by the fact that when in 1657 he removed from Cambridge to London, owing to the influence of his friends and relatives, every door was opened to him for a successful and lucrative career. Moreover, among those patrons upon whom he might confidently rely for countenance and support the principal undoubtedly was Sir Gilbert Pickering, who stood related to him in a double connexion, being not only cousin-german to the poet but also to his mother. Sir Gilbert Pickering, son of Sir John Pickering of Titchmarsh, by Susannah, daughter of Sir Erasmus Driden, was born in 1613. He was admitted to Gray's Inn on 6 November, 1629, and at some date, which is uncertain, he was created a baronet of Nova Scotia. In the Short Parliament of 1640 and during the Long Parliament he represented the county of Northampton. At the outbreak of the Civil War he zealously threw in his lot with the rebels and fanatics, so there was none more whole-hearted as an abettor of Cromwell's tyranny and usurpation, none who showed himself more painfully active in the Good Old Cause, as sedition and murder were euphemistically termed. He "Was first a *Presbyterian*, then an *Independent*, then a *Brownist*, and afterwards an *Anabaptist:* He was a most furious, fiery, implacable Man; was the principal Agent in casting out most of the Learned Clergy; a great Oppressor of the County; got a good Mannor for his Booty of the E. of *R.*; and a considerable Purse of Gold, a Plunder at *Lyn* in *Norfolk*."[1] We are not at all surprised to learn that such a roaring Tamerlane was appointed one of the King's judges, but master fox knew a trick worth two of that, since with cunning prudence he attended only a couple of sittings of the so-called court, and did not sign the death-warrant of his sovran. Nevertheless, none was higher in favour with Cromwell. Accordingly he was a member of each of the five councils of state of the Commonwealth; of the small council set up by the army on 29 May, 1653; and of that nominated in December, 1653. He cut a great figure too in the "Little Parliament" of 1653, and in the two parliaments called by Cromwell as Protector. On 12 July, 1655, Pickering was elected one of the Committee for the advancement of trade. In December, 1657, he was summoned to Cromwell's mock House of Lords, and about the same time, writes a contemporary

[1] Walker, *Sufferings of the Clergy*, p. 91.

pamphleteer, "is become High Steward of Westminster; and being so finical, spruce, and like an old courtier, is made Lord Chamberlain of the Protector's Household or Court."[1]

In those bad days there could have been no more powerful patron for a young man than Sir Gilbert Pickering, and Dryden began his career in London as his clerk or secretary.

We must always bear in mind and make some allowance for Dryden's upbringing in his father's house. The early influences of a home are often not easily to be dismissed in later life. As we may suppose, Dryden's enemies did not forget to search into and keep green this brief period of his career. One specimen of this malice will amply serve. Shadwell in *The Medal of John Bayes*, 4to, 1682, after a venomous reference to Cambridge and some poorly invented scandal, continues with sour spite:

> The next step of Advancement you began,
> Was being Clerk to *Nolls* Lord *Chamberlain*,
> A Sequestrator and Committee-man.
> Then all your wholesome Morals you suckt in;
> And got your Gentile Gayety and Meen.
> Your Loyalty you learn'd in *Cromwel's* Court,
> When first your Muse did make her great effort.
> On him you first shew'd your Poetick strain,
> And prais'd his opening the Basilick Vein.[2]

It may be remarked that this jobation comes admirably indeed from Shadwell, than whom none was more republican, more factious and disloyal.

After the death of the usurper, Pickering signed the proclamation declaring Richard Cromwell his father's successor, and he continued to act as one of the Council of Fourteen and Lord Chamberlain under Tumble Down Dick. Yet he was shrewd enough, it seems, to scent the coming turn and obtained leave of absence in 1659. However, when the army quarrelled with the Parliament he suffered himself to be drawn back for a little to active life.

At the Restoration he owed his escape, and that immunity from the retribution which he had so amply earned, to the influence of his brother-in-law Edward Montagu, Earl of Sandwich. Pickering's name had been very justly inserted in the list of persons excepted by the Commons from the Act of Indemnity (12 Car. II. c. xi.) for penalties not reaching to life, but upon the earnest intercession of Montagu he obtained a pardon, was not so exempted, and was but punished by perpetual incapacitation from office of any kind. He thereupon retired to his native county, to Titchmarsh, and here he made an end, 18 October, 1668, after "being long expected to die, having been in a lethargy long."[3]

It is hardly surprising that, circumstanced as he was, Dryden upon the death

[1] *A Second Narration of the Late Parliament*, 4to, 1658.

[2] " See his Poem upon Oliver.—*And wisely he essay'd* to stanch the Blood by breathing of a Vein." Shadwell's note

[3] Pepys, 21 October, 1668.

of the usurper at Whitehall, 3 September, 1658, should have gratified his patron by a copy of verses on this event, *Heroick Stanzas Consecrated to the Memory of His Highness, Oliver, Late Lord Protector of this Commonwealth, &c. Written after the Celebration of his Funeral.*[1] These seven-and-thirty quatrains first appeared in "Three Poems Upon the Death of his late Highnesse Oliver Lord Protector of *England, Scotland, and Ireland.* Written By Mr. Edm Waller. Mr. Jo Dryden. Mr. Sprat, of *Oxford*," 4to, 1659. Dryden's poem commences the book,[2] although Waller's name precedes his on the title-page.

It has often been stated, and was until quite recently maintained, that Dryden's poem first appeared as a pamphlet, 4to, 12 pp.; that this was his earliest separate publication;[3] and that afterwards the *Heroick Stanzas* were included in the *Three Poems*. This, however, as Mr. T. J. Wise has shown in his *A Dryden Library*,[4] pp. 6, 7, is an error. The little volume bears the date 1659, but "the pamphlet was actually printed in order that the poem might take its place in the fourth volume of Dryden's gathered works of 1693, the original *date* being retained upon the separate title-page. . . . This was not done with any intention to mislead, but was in conformity with a custom which at one time widely obtained."

At the moment the *Heroick Stanzas* seem to have attracted little attention—men's interests were all absorbed by the swift changes in contemporary political life—and after the Restoration Dryden was very well content that his quatrains, firm as they are, judged purely from a literary point of view, should swiftly fall into oblivion, from which they were only retrieved by his angry opponents of twenty years later. Shadwell and Settle, Pordage, Robert Gould, Edmund Hickeringill, Tom Brown, and others with wearisome reiteration are ever battologizing charges of apostacy and inconsistence, angrily throwing in Dryden's teeth such phrases as "His Grandeur he Derived from Heav'n alone"; "And naturally all Souls to his did bow"; "His Name a great example stands to show"; and above all the unfortunate, most regrettable, "To stanch the Blood by breathing of the Vein," a line so easily wrested to signify approval of the murder of Charles I, although actually it intends no such meaning. In 1681 some envenomed Whig, incensed beyond all bounds, reprinted the piece as "An Elegy on the Usurper O.C., by the author of Absalom and Achitophel published to show the loyalty and integrity of the poet."

For a few months, at least, when politics were as variable as a vane, life must have seemed all out of kelter to the young poet bent upon winning fame and place in the world of letters. His intimate connexion with Sir Gilbert Pickering, who was himself standing in imminent peril, could hardly have been to his advantage, the best service that fanatic could render a juvenal at

[1] The obsequies of Oliver Cromwell, originally fixed for 9 November, 1658, owing to the extraordinary magnificence of the preparations were not performed until the 23 November. It is said that no less a sum that £60,000 was wickedly wasted in this riot of extravagant sepulture.

[2] It occupies B 1 recto to C 1 recto.

[3] It is so presented with a reduced facsimile title-page of the print (as editio princeps in Sergeaunt's very unreliable and incomplete *Poems of John Dryden*, Oxford, 1910.

[4] London. Printed for Private Circulation Only. 1930.

the opening of his career was to disguise and sever as far as possible all such ties, either of blood or of business.

Malone, Scott and Verrall are unwilling to believe that Dryden was at all hard pressed, but it seems clear he had something of a struggle and he must indeed have been awkwardly placed for a while, although truly it were easy to exaggerate the difficulties with which he had to contend, and concerning which his enemies in later years were wont to discourse with all the vigour and vehemence that ill-intentioned rancour and a truculent desire to injure could invent or dictate.

In his spleenful, and sometimes profane, lampoon *The Reasons of Mr. Bays Changing his Religion*, 4to, 1688, Tom Brown makes Bays say: "In the first place, after some years spent in the University, I quitted all my preferment there to come and reside at the Imperial City, because it was likely to prove a Scene of more advantage and business. . . . At first I struggled with a great deal of persecution, took up with a lodging which had a Window no bigger than a Pocket-Looking-glass, Dined at a Three-penny Ordinary enough to starve a Vocation Taylor, kept little Company, went clad in homely Drugget, and drunk Wine as seldom as a *Rechabite*, or the *Grand Seignior*'s Confessor. Much about this time Mr. *Crites*, as you may very well remember, I made my first addresses in Panegyric to *Oliver Cromwell*, and that puissant Usurping *Phocas*[1] had certainly conferr'd the Title of Oecumenical Universal Poet upon me, if a Tempest had not hurried him out of the World before his Time.[2] . . . Being unfortunately disappointed of my hopes in this place, I tack'd about with the times." There is a peck of malice, and a grain of truth in all this.

Shadwell, also, in 1682,[3] bespatters Dryden with rancorous abuse:

> But he being dead, who should the slave prefer,
> He turn'd a Journey-man t'a Bookseller;
> Writ Prefaces to Books for Meat and Drink
> And as he paid, he would both write and think.
> Then by th' assistance of a Noble *Knight*
> Th' hadst plenty, ease, and liberty to write.
> First like a *Gentleman* he made thee live;
> And on his Bounty thou didst amply thrive.
> But soon thy Native swelling Venom rose,
> And then didst him, who gave thee Bread, expose.
> 'Gainst him a scandalous Preface didst thou write,
> Which then didst soon expunge, rather than fight.
> (When turn'd away by him in some small time)
> You in the Peoples ears began to chime,
> And please the Town with your successful Rime.

Shadwell took care to annotate his own lines, and on the word "Bookseller" he supplies a gloss: "Mr. Herringman, *who kept him in his House for that purpose.*"

[1] The Byzantine tyrant who ruled from 602 to 610, having risen to the throne from the position of a groom.

[2] Actually a violent storm raged at the hour of Cromwell's death.

[3] *The Medal of John Bayes.*

Upon "*Noble Knight*" we have: "*Sir R.H. who kept him generously at his own House.*"

Incidentally it should be remarked that the "scandalous Preface" of Shadwell's vapourings alludes to Dryden's answer, the *Defence of an Essay of Dramatique Poesie*, to the Preface which Sir Robert Howard has printed before his tragedy *The Great Favourite; or The Duke of Lerma*, 4to, 1668. The Defence was prefixed to the second edition of *The Indian Emperor*, 4to, 1668. Dryden, however, withdrew this, and it was not reissued until after his death. It deals with purely literary matters, and will be considered later. Both poets are warm in their opinions, but Shadwell's "scandalous" is, of course, absurd.

That Dryden should occupy himself with literary work, and that at first this should have been of the kind Shadwell so coarsely and roughly disparages I see no reason to doubt. I have yet to learn that any reproach attaches to the post of a publisher's reader and adviser, and it is this position (or very nearly) which Dryden appears to have filled. When the great Erasmus in 1508 was superintending the re-impression of his *Adagia* by Aldo Manuzio at Venice he conveniently sojourned with the printer and they set to the task together in Aldo's workshop. "Together we attacked the book," says Erasmus, "I writing, while Aldo gave my copy to the press." I imagine such another picture at the Blue Anchor, New Exchange, where Henry Herringman lived, and it was quite natural that Dryden should be boarded in the same house. Mr. Wheatley's suggestion[1] that Herringman's home was elsewhere than in the New Exchange is without foundation, and not borne out by what we know of the manners and customs of the day when it was something very singular and exceptional if a man did not reside at his place of business.

During the time that Dryden had been employed as secretary to Sir Gilbert Pickering he had become friendly with Herringman. Accordingly when the new order of things deprived Dryden of his political patrons, Herringman was ready, nay more, he was eager to supply his recruit with work and to launch him, as it were, on his literary career.

Among those who liked to look in at Herringman's and linger there was a very important figure, an "ingenious Person . . . equally conspicuous for the lustre of his birth, and the Excellency of his Parts."[2] Robert Howard,[3] son of Thomas Howard, the first Earl of Berkshire, by Elizabeth, daughter of William Cecil, who was afterwards second Earl of Exeter, was born in 1626, and, according to Antony à Wood, he proceeded whilst quite young to Magdalen College, Oxford.[4] At the outbreak of the Great Rebellion Howard enlisted in

[1] *Dryden's Publishers.* " A Paper read before the Bibliographical Society, December 20, 1909." London, 1912, p. 8.

[2] Langbaine, *An Account of the English Dramatick Poets*, 1691, p. 276.

[3] As I have already given an ample account of Sir Robert Howard in another place it seems necessary only to rehearse here an outline of his life so far as he is connected with Dryden. See my Introduction to Shadwell's *Works*, 1927, pp. xli-li.

[4] Wood, cf. Bliss, Vol. IV, *s.n.* Cole, *Athenae Cantabrigienses*, states that Sir Robert Howard was of Magdalene, Cambridge, but this apparently is a mistake, and the dramatist is being confused with his namesake and uncle, the Cantab., Sir Robert Howard.

the Royalist forces, and so distinguished himself by his bravery that although only eighteen years old he was knighted by the King upon the field of Cropredy Bridge, 29 June, 1644. During the Commonwealth Sir Robert was imprisoned in Windsor Castle, when he was regarded as so dangerous a malignant and "a favourer of Roman Catholicks" that he narrowly escaped out of the usurper's hands with his life. Whilst in captivity Sir Robert Howard had consoled his tedious hours with the courtship of the Muses.

These poems—"there is not any of them that have not layn by me these many years (two or three copies of Verses onely excepted)," writes Howard—he entrusted upon his release to Herringman for publication, whence it was Dryden's business in the ordinary course of events to look through the sheets. Inevitably some few details presented themselves for discussion, and this gained him a nearer acquaintance with the author, an intercourse of mutual tastes, which soon ripened into friendship and a close intimacy.

In his address "To The Reader" Sir Robert acknowledges Dryden's suggestions: "I confesse my Interest prevail'd with me though, not wholly to neglect the Reader, since I prevail'd with a worthy Friend to take so much view of my blotted Copies, as to free me from grosse Errors."[1]

The complimentary verses "*To my Honored Friend Sr* Robert Howard, On His Excellent Poems," signed John Driden, may be esteemed a model of their kind, courteous without fulsomeness, elegant without prettiness and trifling.

At the Restoration Sir Robert Howard was created a Knight of the Bath, returned member for Stockbridge in Hampshire, and appointed Secretary to the Commissioners of the Treasury.

After his connexion with the Puritan party, the friendship of so famous a loyalist, one who stood high in the King's good graces, must have been of infinite service to Dryden, who naturally enough was quick to celebrate the monarch's return.

"Astræa Redux. A Poem On the Happy Restauration and Return of His Sacred Majesty Charles the Second. By *John Driden*," folio, 1660, was published by Herringman, who issued in the following year "To His Sacred Majesty, A Panegyrick On His Coronation. *By* John Dryden," folio. Since we are not concerned to review Dryden's poetry, it will suffice to say that both are extremely vigorous pieces, abounding in passages of rare beauty and most felicitous images, both immensely removed from the pæans which men of no small talents, and it may be even of genius, have written upon similar occasions.

In 1662 Herringman published an "encomiastick poem" "To My Lord Chancellor. Presented on New-Years-day, by J. Driden," folio.

In the summer of the same year Dryden prefixed to Dr. Walter Charleton's[2] *Chorea Gigantum, or, The most Famous Antiquity of Great Britain, Vulgarly called Stone-Heng, Standing on Salisbury Plain, Restored to the Danes*, 4to, 1663,[3] a copy of verses "*To my Honour'd Friend*, Dr. Charleton, *on his learned*

[1] *To the Reader, Poems* (unnumbered page), A 4.

[2] 1619–1707.

[3] Imprimatur. *Ex Æd. Sat.*, 11 *Sept.*, 1662. The Dedication to the King is dated *April* the 27th, 1662.

and careful Works; and more particularly this of Stone-Heng, *by him restored to the true Founders.*"

Already in 1662 Dryden was something of a celebrity in the world of letters,[1] and had indeed achieved so considerable a degree of reputation that on Wednesday, 12 November of that year, he was by Dr. Walter Charleton proposed for membership in the Royal Society. The poet was duly elected on Saturday, 15 November, and admitted on Wednesday, 26 November following.[2] On 30 March, 1664, the whole membership of the Society was apportioned to various standing committees, and it is interesting to note that Dryden was a member of two such bodies, one the business of which was to undertake "collecting all the phænomena of nature hitherto observed, and all experiments made and recorded"; the second "for improving the English language."

On 26 February, 1665–6, it was found necessary to empower the "collector to the treasurer of the Royal Society" to repair to the several members who had not paid subscriptions with a request for the fees due. Eight names are given of members, and among these are Waller and Dryden. After the intermission caused by the Great Plague it was decided that the names of members who could not or did not care to pay their subscriptions must be struck off the roll of the Society. Six names are given on 16 November, 1667, among which is that of Dryden, from whom is claimed £9 19s. Now Dryden had been admitted as a Fellow on 26 November, 1662, and from that date his dues (an entrance fee of forty shillings and a weekly subscription of one shilling) would have amounted to this sum, whence it appears that he had paid neither fee nor subscription to the Society. So Sprat's *History of the Royal Society*, 1667,[3] which gives a list of Fellows does not include Dryden's name.

Dramatic work had begun to claim all Dryden's activities. Save for the small income accruing from his little patrimony, he was obliged to depend upon the labours of his pen for a livelihood, and thus "his becoming a writer of plays was a necessary consequence."[4] "He applied, therefore, to dramatick poesy, as soon as any benefit could be derived either to himself or others from such an exercise of his talents."[5] It is common knowledge that in spite of the amplest Puritan legislation, in particular the crushing Ordinance of September, 1642, which prohibited any acting while "these sad causes and set-times of humiliation do continue," the stern confirmation of this measure "for the better suppression of Stage-Playes," Interludes, and Common Players, on 22 October, 1647, and

[1] It is a bad blunder to say of Dryden that "before he had won any notice by his writing at all, in 1662, he was made a member of the newly chartered Royal Society." This error is made by Mr. Mark Van Doren in his *The Poetry of John Dryden*, New York, 1920, pp. 18–19.

[2] The Election of Fellows shall be made by way of Ballet: and this Admission by a solemn Declaration made by the President of their Election. Spratt, *History of the Royal Society*, p. 145.

[3] pp. 431–433. In the official list of the Fellows of the Royal Society issued 30 November, 1663, is the name *John Driden Esq*. In the list issued 30 November, 1667, the name no longer occurs.

[4] Scott, *Life of John Dryden* (*Works*), Vol. I, Section II, p. 65. Ed. 1821.

[5] Malone, *The Life of Drydeu* (*Prose Works*), Vol. I, Part I, p. 52, 1800.

the Draconian statute of 9 February, 1648—surreptitious performances had been taking place at various theatres.

In a well-known passage James Wright[1] relates how the players in Oliver's time "used to Act privately, three or four miles, or more, out of Town, now here, now there, sometimes in Noblemens Houses, in particular *Holland-house* at *Kensington*," and "At *Christmas* and Bartlemew fair, they used to Bribe the Officer who Commanded the Guard at Whitehall, and even thereupon therefore connived at to Act for a few Days, at the Red *Bull;* but they were sometimes notwithstanding disturb'd by Soldiers."

It was hardly likely that under conditions such as these any new tragedies or comedies would be required by the actors, and indeed had a poet provided them with fresh fare for their obreptitious performances the company who were glad enough when their audience "used to make a purse for them" had not the wherewithal to pay any budding dramatist.

Almost immediately after the return of Charles II, however, there were at least three independent companies acting in London. John Rhodes was manager of a young troupe at the Cockpit; Major Michael Mohun was the leading man of the older players at the Red Bull; whilst yet another band occupied Salisbury Court under William Beeston. Much difficulty and many legal complications were already arising with regard to the exact status of these theatres, a situation further embarrassed by the energies and autocracy of Sir Henry Herbert, who was zealously reasserting his authority as Master of the Revels, and claiming wellnigh unlimited powers over dramatic entertainments of whatsoever kind.

It is not necessary here to enter into all details, suffice to say that Sir William Davenant and Thomas Killigrew came to a mutual agreement by which they planned a joint monopoly, that each should be empowered to build his own theatre and form a company to the exclusion and indeed suppression of all rival forces. Great instance was made to the King, and upon 21 August, 1660, a royal grant was obtained which entirely satisfied their wishes. Killigrew for his part took over the Mohun company and brought it from the Red Bull to Gibbons' Tennis Court, the last house of the Elizabethan kind, that is to say a platform stage with arras, and here they opened on Thursday, 8 November, 1660, with Shakespeare's *King Henry IV*. A tennis court was chosen as being the type of building most easily convertible into a theatre.[2] The main entrance of Gibbons' Tennis Court was from Vere Street, which ran into Clare Market on the south-east. Therefore this theatre is most appropriately termed the Theatre Royal, Vere Street.

As it is with the Theatre Royal that Dryden was most intimately connected for wellnigh fifteen years, it may be as well to remark here that Killigrew's company went from Vere Street to the Theatre Royal, Bridges Street, where they opened with *The Humorous Lieutenant* on Thursday, 7 May, 1663, and here for the first time they employed painted scenery.

[1] *Historia Historica*, 8vo., 1699.

[2] "In Paris, from 1620 onwards, most of the troupes had been installed in playhouses fitted up in tennis-courts." W. J. Lawrence, *The Elizabethan Playhouse*, Second Series, p. 141.

Under his patent Davenant chose the younger company which had been mustered by Rhodes. He was constituted the sole "Master or Superior," and his actors forthwith began to give performances at Salisbury Court. Meanwhile he was transforming Lisle's Tennis Court, which stood between Lincoln's Inn Fields and Lesser Lincoln's Inn Fields and of which he had already taken a lease, into the Duke of York's theatre.

The Union of the two Companies took place in 1682, when the one troupe opened at Drury Lane on 16 November of that year.

Sir Robert Howard had already, and quite permanently, established himself as a most important and influential figure in the Thespian world since he alone it was who furnished a full quarter of the money needed for the building of the new Theatre Royal, a house to be erected between Drury Lane and Bridges Street. Thus he held nine shares of the total six-and-thirty.

The actors were beginning to make money, and were able to afford to pay for those fresh pieces they were eager to obtain from new writers, so that Dryden, who was closely in touch with all literary movements and not least with the reviving theatre, and who could moreover confidently rely upon the warmest encouragement and most powerful assistance from Howard, at once set to work to meet the demand.

No explanation has been offered, but some surprise has been expressed that there should seemingly have ensued considerable delay after the actual Restoration of King Charles in 1660 and the appearance of new authors upon the stage, since in the summer of 1660 there were no less than three companies giving several performances—at least for a time—in London. Yet apparently the first new play was not produced at Vere Street until 3 March, 1662; whilst Davenant was satisfied with the attraction of *The Siege of Rhodes* and other of his work in addition to the revived pieces. None the less it is easy to understand why during these months the actors were content to rely upon their older favourites. In the first place we will remind ourselves that the legal position of the theatre, so long under a ban and subject to severest prosecutions, must be stabilized and authoritatively recognized, no simple problem amid the quarrels and conflicts of hotly contentious and competitive parties, each one demanding a preference and aiming at a monopoly. Moreover, it was necessary that the managers and actors should be in a position adequately to remunerate new talent, poets who would depend for their livelihood upon their earnings, their "third days." A new piece meant money too for costumes and properties; no new writer was ever willing to make his bow in an old suit with grandam trimmings; and above all there loomed large the eagle-eyed Sir Henry Herbert with his unlimited rapacity for fees and vails, his self-assertive dominion over new plays, the greedy squeamish censor of plots and scripts, with his morbid itch to snuff out "oathes, prophaness, & publick Ribaldry."

In the actual year of the Restoration, indeed, Dryden with his almost uncanny flair for political parallels had already drafted a tragedy, *The Duke of Guise*, "as the fairest Way, which the *Act of Indemnity* had then left us, of setting forth the *Rise* of the *Late Rebellion;* and by *Exploding* the Villainies of it upon the *Stage*, to *precaution Posterity* against the like Errors." Upon the careful advice of friends, however, he thought it better to lay his copy aside. No doubt it would have been unwise just then to have raked the fires of puritan resentment, and the Scene of the Duke of Guise's return to Paris, against the King's positive command, although transcribed almost *verbatim* from Arrigo Caterino Davila's great work, *Delle Guerre Civili di Francia*, published at Venice in 1630,[1] might by wilful misunderstanding and misuse have fanned the smouldering passions of the sectaries and rebels. Two-and-twenty years later the poet made good use of these passages, which he had kept by him in manuscript, when he joined with Lee[2] to write that fine drama *The Duke of Guise*, produced at the Theatre Royal, Drury Lane, 30 November, 1682.

Since Dryden's tragedy had met with some discouragement, although merely from private critics and for reasons purely accidental, he determined to essay the sock rather than the buskin, and accordingly during the later months of 1662 he busied himself with his first comedy, *The Wild Gallant*, which was produced at the Vere Street Theatre on Thursday, 5 February, 1662–3.

The Wild Gallant was not a success in the public theatre, and for my part I am puzzled to account for the failure of this comedy, which certainly amused the King and found a patroness in Lady Castlemaine. There are, it is true, some awkwardnesses of construction, but these again may, in the piece as we have it, be due to the revision of the scenes.

It were, perhaps, too speculative to inquire what form the alterations took and how far they extended. In the Prologue to the Reviv'd play Dryden certainly hints that an intrigue between Loveby and Mrs. Bibber, which in the comedy as we have it is hardly suggested save in raillery, formed a not unimportant episode in the original version. The introduction of Lady Du Lake and her covey of cyprians in Act IV appears to be an addition, and is a satire upon Lady Bennet,[3] one of the most notorious procuresses of the day. It has been said that the appearance of Lady Constance "habited like Fortune" and her marriage to Loveby who is conducted to her presence by Setstone "Antickly habited" as a Genius is a little too fantastic, but this objection hardly seems valid. We allow the entrance of Hymen saffron-clad and garlanded with marjoram at the close of *As You Like It*, nor are the Satyr, the mock Fairies, the hobgoblin and Herne the Hunter at all out of place in the forest glades of *The Merry Wives of Windsor*. Exception has further been taken to the scene in the fourth act of *The Wild Gallant*, where old Lord Nonsuch is persuaded that he is enceinte as being too absurdly farcical. Dryden, however, is broadly satirizing a circumstance much talked of at the time, and which is thus related

[1] An edition of Davila's works, edited by Apostolo Zeno was issued at Venice in 1730.

[2] It is interesting to note that Lee inserted in *The Duke of Guise* two scenes from his tragedy, *The Massacre of Paris*, then in manuscript, but afterwards acted at Drury Lane in November 1689, and published quarto, 1690, *The Term Catalogues*, Michaelmas (November), 1689.

[3] She is mentioned by Pepys, 22 September, 1660, as "the Lady Bennet (a famous strumpet)," and again 30 May, 1668, as "my Lady Bennet." It will be remembered that Wycherley in a strain of most biting satire dedicates *The Plain-Dealer* "To my Lady *B*——," who in *The Tatler*, No. 84, is spoken of as "the celebrated Mother Bennet." Dryden again refers to her in *Sr Martin Mar-all*, Act IV.

by Stevens in his notes upon *A Yorkshire Tragedy*,[1] as a fact "which may afford gratification to innocent curiosity." Having quoted from *The Rape of the Lock* Pope's line,"Men prove with Child, as pow'rful Fancy works,"[2] he continues: "The fanciful person here alluded to, was Dr. Edward Pelling, one of the chaplains to K. Charles II, James II, William III, and Queen Anne. He held the livings of Great S. Helen's and Ludgate, a prebend of Westminster, &c. Having studied himself into the disorder of mind vulgarly called the hyp (for he rarely quitted his study except during dinner-time,) between the age of forty and fifty he imagined himself to be pregnant, and forebore all manner of exercise, lest motion should prove injurious to his ideal burden. Nor did the whim evaporate till his wife had assured him she was really in his supposed condition. This lady was masculine and large-bon'd in the extreme; and our merry monarch Charles being told of the strange conceit adopted by his chaplain, desired to see her. He did; and, as she quitted his presence, he exclaimed with a good round oath, that "if any woman could get her husband with child, it must be Mrs. Pelling." I received this narrative from one of the doctor's grand-daughters,who is still alive,and remembers that the line of Pope already quoted, was always supposed to have reference to the story."[3]

It can hardly be denied that several of the incidents, laughable enough in the mere reading of *The Wild Gallant*, upon the boards must have proved exquisitely entertaining. However, a preliminary damp did not at all discourage the author, that is to say to any greater extent than the inevitable disappointment he experienced at finding his play miscarry. He realized that he had begun with "the most difficult part of *Dramatique Poetry*," Comedy; and he set himself forthwith to essay another *genre*. During the year 1663 he was engaged upon his romantic tragi-comedy *The Rival Ladies*, and also much occupied in collaboration with Howard in the composition of *The Indian-Queen*. Although actually his independent work, *The Rival Ladies*, was not produced until after *The Indian-Queen* it will be more convenient to consider it here before passing on to the question of the heroic drama, of which the latter play is so remarkable and so important an example.

The Rival Ladies was given at the Theatre Royal, Bridges Street, in the early summer of 1664, probably in May. Unfortunately, the cast has not been preserved.[4]

Although it is quite untrue to say that this piece borrows anything from Beaumont and Fletcher's *Love's Pilgrimage*, there are similar situations and parallel passages, which is hardly to be wondered at since both derive suggestions from the same source, a novella of Cervantes, *Las Dos Doncellas*.

It is not to be disputed, I think, that Dryden knew both Jean Rotrou's

[1] "Supplement to the Edition of Shakespeare's Plays Published in 1778 by Samuel Johnson and George Steevens," 1780, Vol. II, p. 660.

[2] Canto IV, l. 53.

[3] For a not dissimilar, but terrible and tragic history see the Chronicle of Hugh, Abbot of Flavigny, *sub anno* 1100. *Monumenta Germaniae historica*, edente Georg. Henr. Pertz. VIII, p. 496.

[4] No epilogue was printed with the play. The Prologue is given in a Bodley MS., but the epilogue which follows this belongs to another piece.

dramatization of Cervantes, *Les Deux Pucelles*, and Quinault's *Les Rivales*. From Quinault indeed he may be said to have taken something. No very exact phrase or prominent incident, perhaps, yet as one reads the two plays echoes of *Les Rivales* now and again strike through the poetry of *The Rival Ladies*. It is a question of that intangible quality, atmosphere. Dryden has caught and deployed the heroic, rather rococo romance of Quinault.

The locale of *Love's Pilgrimage* is Barcelona, and although the scene of *The Rival Ladies* lies at Alicant, there is mention of Barcelona more than once.[1] The story of *The Rival Ladies* is sufficiently entangled when we find Honoria and Angellina, both concealed in page's attire under the names of Hippolito and Amideo; both in love with Don Gonsalvo de Peralta, who for his part is enamoured of Julia, for whose hand Don Rhodorigo de Sylva is a suitor. The play opens with a robbery in a wood, and presently there is a duello in a street at twilight, some mistaking of persons of many counter-mistakes. This is all pure Lope de Vega, Alarcon, and de Castro. There is then introduced a Masque, The Rape of Proserpine, during which Rhodorigo, who personates Pluto, endeavours to carry off Julia but is foiled in the attempt. In the end, however, he wins her hand, whilst Gonsalvo frankly confesses: "I by Conquest am Honoria's," and Angellina acknowledges that in time she may be persuaded to accept Don Manuel. The adventures with pirates also must not be forgotten. In spite of so intricate an intrigue Dryden tells his tale with consummate skill, and the action, always interesting, if complicated, is never confused. Pepys on several occasions pronounced *The Rival Ladies* to be "a very innocent and most pretty witty play," "a most pleasant and fine writ play," "a very pretty play," and we may whole-heartedly concur in his judgment. *The Rival Ladies* is notable as being the first of Dryden's plays wherein he employs heroic verse, and the Dedication to the Earl of Orrery, a prolegomenon written in his own masterly style, discusses with great acumen the use and advantages of rhyme. This romantic tragi-comedy seems to have been occasionally revived during the next decade. It was printed quarto, 1664, being entered at Stationers' Hall on 27 June of that year.

There is extant a letter from Sir Andrew Henley, first Baronet of Bramshill, Hants (and of Henley, Somerset), which is addressed to Sir Robert Howard and runs thus:

Sr.

I had as ill luck as yor self in missing you one munday whe[n] I made sure of being one the guard or at Wincester sessions, I rode Directly thither and in that Confidence Answered not yor Letters nor Excused my not meeting at yor Rendezvous, All which must now be Remidyed all the wayes I can: for my part had I not missed you I had not beene at Sessions yor request to us had not rec[d] such Dispatch as now it Did, The objections are not weighty Enough to be Delybred in a Letter but soe strong that they had hindred yo[r] satisfactione; next the business of the house must be mencôned in which all y[t] I can say is that for the serge Bed Mr Dreidon useth that bed you lye in and the little green serge furniture I shall use at Bramshill as the pewter, All the other

[1] See my Note on the Source of this Play.

things I desire may be valued and that by one of yor and another of my Choosing, And I hope you will Think what I put in new into the house when you Came to it little the worse for using and all that I can I will take for my owne use thereof And besides particularly the furniture of the Dyning Roome but for the tyme I referr that to yor owne Conveniency, In this and all other transactions I desyre to appeare under no other Character then of

Bramshill 8″

8 ber 1663 — Yor most affectionat friend

For Sr. Robert Howard
In Lincols In feilds the sixth — & very humble servant,
Doore from Turnstyle Holborne Row
London these — Andrew Henley.

This letter[1] then shows us that Howard and Dryden were living together at the former's house in Lincoln's Inn Fields, and during the year 1663 under these convenient conditions they collaborated in the composition of *The Indian-Queen.* Dryden also, as we have seen, was working on an independent play, *The Rival Ladies.*

This latter, when printed, was dedicated to Roger Boyle, Earl of Orrery, under whose notice, as I think there can be no question, Dryden was instantly brought by Howard, and whose patronage the poet assiduously cultivated. For as he himself tells us, when Orrery was residing in Ireland between 1661 and 1664 he was not slow in submitting scenes and detached passages for his patron's approbation and critique. He boasts of "*the kindness your Lordship has continually shown to all my Writings. You have been pleas'd my Lord, they should sometimes cross the* Irish *Seas to Kiss your Hands; which passage (contrary to the Experience of others) I have found the least dangerous in the World. Your favour has shone upon me at a remote distance, without the least knowledge of my Person; and (like the Influence of the Heavenly Bodies) you have done good without knowing to whom you did it.*" There was no compliment which Orrery would have better tasted, no acknowledgement by which he would have been more highly gratified. It was not indeed until 1664 upon his return to London in the June of that year that he was to meet the Author who had burned this sweet incense at his shrine, the poet who—if only he had known it then—was to dispossess him in his own discovered domain.

It should further be remarked that ties of kinship existed between Sir Robert Howard and Orrery, who had married Margaret Howard, daughter of Theophilus Howard, Earl of Suffolk, who was brother to Thomas Howard, Earl of Berkshire. Thus the Countess of Orrery and Sir Robert Howard were first cousins. Nay, further, Dryden himself was to become a relative of the Earl of Orrery by his marriage with the Lady Elizabeth Howard, the sister of Sir Robert.

The Indian-Queen, the joint composition of Howard and Dryden, was the first heroic play to be produced upon the London stage. It was not, however,

[1] Sloane MS. 813, f. 71. This was, I believe, first printed by Mr. W. S. Clark in *Modern Language Notes*, vol. XLII (pp. 16–20); January, 1927.

the first heroic play to be acted in the Three Kingdoms. The earliest heroic play actually to be seen in the theatre was given at Smock Alley, Dublin, and was *The General*, written by the Earl of Orrery, "the pioneer and a prominent purveyor of heroic tragedy."[1]

Late in December, 1660, the Earl of Orrery[2] crossed to Ireland after having been in residence for several months at Whitehall, where he was now an important figure, a trusted and intimate friend of the King. On 23 January, 1661/2, he wrote to the Duke of Ormonde who was then in London, but in July crossed to Ireland as the new Lord-Lieutenant:[3]

May it please your Grace,When I had the honour and happiness the last time to kiss his majesty's hand, he commanded me to write a play for him. I did not scruple therein to evidence my great weakness, since thereby I did evidence the greater obedience; and therefore, some months after, I presumed to lay at his majesty's feet a tragi-comedy, all in ten feet verse and rhyme. I writ it in that manner upon two accounts; first, because I thought it was not fit a command so extraordinary should have been obeyed in a way that was common; secondly, because I found his majesty relished rather the French fashion of plays, than the English. I had just grounds to believe, at least fear, that my play would have been thought fitter for the fire than the theatre; but his Majesty's Mercy having condemned it only to the latter, and then giving it to be acted by Mr. Killegrew's company, my old friend Will. D'Avenant appeared so displeased his company missed it, that nothing could reconcile me to him, but to write another purposely for him. Therefore the last and this week, having gotten some few hours to my self from my public duties, I dedicated them to please my particular friend, and wrote this unpolished draught of two acts. I know no man can better discover faults, or will sooner forgive them, than your grace; and therefore, upon both these scores I humbly present you with what I have wrote, and as cheerfully and as rationally choose you for my judge. The plot is such, that I wish you could but as much like the rest of the play, as I flatter myself you will like that, when by the finishing of what is begun, you will know it. And that your grace may have some guess at it, I will tell you now, that Acorces is Romira in disguise. In the speeches and discourses of duel, honour, jealousy, revenge, love and envy, I have carefully declined saying any thing I had ever heard or read on any of the subjects, that if the conceptions of them should not please you, the newness of them might. The humour of Hilas,[4]

[1] Orrery's "The Tragedy of Zoroastres," *Essays in Petto* (1928), by Montague Summers.

[2] " His lordship was now created Earl of Orrery, and sworn privy counsellor of England and Ireland, and was at last of his Majesty's cabinet council; and after these honours had been conferred upon him, his lordship retired into Ireland, to look after his affairs there, and secure all things for the interest of his majesty." *Memoirs of Roger, Earl of Orrery*, by the Rev. Thomas Morrice, *A Collection of the State Letters of the Right Honourable Roger Boyle, Earl of Orrery*, folio, London, 1742, chapter VI, p. 32.

[3] *Ibid.*, pp. 38, 39.

[4] Mr. F. W. Payne discussing in a very amateurish and indeed inexact paper "Dryden and the Earl of Orrery," *The Review of English Studies*, vol. I, No. 2, April,

of which your grace will see some touches in the beginning of the second act, shall be interwoven, if your grace dislike it not, in every one of the remaining; though I despair to make my Hilas as famous on the theatre as the marquis of Urfe has made his in the romance; for besides his genius being exceedingly above mine, his Hilas was not limited to number and rhyme, as mine is.

But though I shew my weaknesses to your grace, yet I humbly beg this may be seen by none but you, who, I hope, will believe I conceal nothing from you, since they are by choice exposed now to your sight by

May it please your grace,

Your grace's most humble, most faithful,
and most affectionate devoted servant,
ORRERY.

Actually there is no play by Orrery extant which contains a character Romira who is disguised under the name Acorces; nor does Hilas appear in any of his plays as we now have them. We can only suppose that the author for some reason, perhaps because of a criticism by Ormonde, did not complete the piece in question, or at any rate completely altered it. We know that his first drafts were apt to be very rough, and quite another thing from their final and polished revision. Thus *The Tragedy of Zoroastres*, which is without Prologue and Epilogue, contains some good matter which could be effectively worked up, but which certainly needs a power of rehandling. Orrery's dramas were often printed long after they were penned, and he continually modified his scripts before they went to press. The *Tragedy of Zoroastres*[1] has never yet been printed; *Herod the Great*, first called *Mariamne*, and written in 1672, was not printed until 1694, in folio; *Mr. Anthony*, acted at Dorset Garden in 1670–1, first appeared quarto, 1690; *Guzman*, produced at Lincoln's Inn Fields in 1673, was issued folio, 1693; *King Saul* (which is certainly his), 4to, 1703. It may be noted with regard to the incident of Romira disguised, that in *The Black Prince* we have Valeria disguised as her brother. *The Black Prince* is a Theatre Royal play. The heroic drama which Orrery eventually wrote for his old friend Davenant was *Henry V*, produced at Lincoln's Inn Fields on Saturday, 13 August, 1664.

On 25 February, 1662–3, King Charles wrote a letter with his own hand from Whitehall to Orrery, and after having graciously expressed his appreciation of Orrery's services, he concluded: "I will now tell you, that I have read your first play, which I like very well, and do intend to bring it upon the stage, as soon as my company have their new stage in order, that the scenes may be worthy the words they are to set forth. For the last I have only seen in my lord lieutenant's hands, but will read it as soon as I have leisure."[2] From this

1925 (pp. 173–181), does not seem to appreciate that Hylas is a famous and typical character in Honoré d'Urfé's *Astrée*, by whom was, it is said, represented the Duc de Mayenne, not the Duc de Maine as Patru writes by a slip.

[1] Sloane MSS., 1828. This play was first described by the present writer in an article *Modern Language Review*, January, 1917, Vol. XII, No. 1, pp. 24–32; reprinted in *Essays in Petto*, 1928.

[2] *Ibid.*, p. 65.

correspondence it is plain that Orrery had at the King's suggestion written a tragi-comedy in rhyme during the year 1661, and that this piece was sent to the King, who handed it to Killigrew, bidding him produce it so soon as the "new stage" should be ready. This "new stage" was the Theatre Royal in Bridges Street, which opened on Thursday, 7 May, 1663.

"We have little doubt," wrote Sir Walter Scott, "that the heroic tragedies were the legitimate offspring of the French romances of Calprenède and Scudéry," and although of late years there have been dissentients from this view it is, I conceive, quite obvious that those who seek other sources and acclaim the heroic play of the Restoration as derived from Beaumont and Fletcher; or as "fostered by that other Elizabethan strain which took its rise in Marlowe's Tamburlaine"; or, more vaguely yet, from "the romantic plays of the early Stuarts," are in fact delivering judgement upon a subject concerning which they are not qualified to speak. An essential preliminary for the consideration of the Heroic Play of the Restoration is an intimate knowledge of the Heroic Romance. He who has not read at least his *Polexandre*, *Cassandre*, *Cléopatre* and *Faramond*, his *Ibrahim*, *Artamène*, *Clélie*, and *Almahide*, whether in the original or in the English translations, to which the dramatists so frequently turned, is simply neither equipped nor competent to write upon the Restoration theatre.

Some survey of the heroic romance must therefore be attempted. At best it can be nothing more than a slight and (I fear) inadequate summary of an absorbing subject; a study which, however, it would require volumes rather than pages to treat with the detailed attention and full analyses which it most certainly deserves. To exaggerate the permeating influence and the continued popularity of the heroic romance is wellnigh impossible. It is a vast mistake to believe that La Calprenède and Madeleine de Scudéry had lost their fascination and altogether disappeared by the middle of the eighteenth century, so often and so superficially presumed.

As late as 1752 *The Female Quixote* by Mrs. Lennox, a novel the humour of which it is impossible to appreciate without acquaintance with the heroic romances, was very favourably received, and it is to be supposed that the readers of this work took the point when Arabella dismissed her lover "who, if he had read a single page, would have known that Orontes and Oroondates was the same person," or else when the same fair heroine conjectured that her charms could "work as powerful effects as those of Olympia, princess of Thrace, whose brother was passionately enamoured of her."

And even now, if only one can be retired, in summer time in some old-world garden, quiet and reposeful, with its quaint clipped hedges, sundials, and smooth lawns; or it may be at a winter fireside in a well-furnished library, far from the penetrating jar of crowds, there are few more pleasurable hours than those which may be spent with Oroondate and Cassandre, with Ibrahim, or our own English Parthenissa.

The heroic romances are, primarily, in large part descended from the older romances of chivalry, from Amadis and Palmerin. It is true that dragons, enchantments, magic castles, aged wizards, giants, and griffins have all vanished away; but the flames and raptures, the feats of arms and derring-do persist.

The only change as far as the main elements are concerned lies in this point, which is of itself far from unimportant, as it indeed deorientates the psychology of the work. In the romances of chivalry love seems in some sense subordinate to valorous achievement; but with the heroic romances love is the ruling passion, and the glory of the tourney and the field takes a second place. It may be said that glory inspires the romance of chivalry and love the heroic romance. "L'amour doit etre le principal sujet de Roman," wrote the Abbé Lenglet. Many other influences, too, went to inform and fashion the heroic romance. Especially important are the Greek stories of Heliodorus, Longus, and Achilles Tatius; the Ephesiaca; the *Chaereas and Callirrhöe* of Chariton, the *Hysmine and Hysminias* of Eustathius, also many more, all of which served as models in various ways, and in their adventures were often pretty closely followed and imitated. La Calprènede certainly used the *Argenis* (1621) of John Barclay, a narrative of which it has been said "There appears little to distinguish the *Argenis* from the common heroic romance." In "Au lecteur" prefixed to *Artamene ou le Grand Cyrus* which appeared under the name of Georges de Scudéry, the author frankly avows: "Je vous diray donc seulement que i'ay pris et que ie prendray touiours pour mes vniques Modelles, l'immortel HELIODORE, et le Grand VRFE, Ce sont les seuls Maistres que i'imite, et les seuls qu'il faut imiter: car quiconque s'ecartera de leur route, s'egarera certainement puis qu'il n'en est point d'autre qui soit bonne: que la leur au contraire est assurée: et qu'elle mene infalliblement où l'on veut aller: ie veux dire, Lecteur, a la Gloire."[1] This "Gloire" Scudéry hastens to qualify by assuring his readers that he bestowed upon his heroic Cyrus "beaucoup d'amour."

The first de Scudéry romance, *Ibrahim, ou l'Illustre Bassa,* seems at least to have been suggested by Jacques Yver's *Printemps* (1572).

A very important source for the heroic romance was that most famous of all pastorals, "L'Astrée de Messire Honoré D'Urfé." Premiere (Seconde) Partie, 1610.[2] A Paris, 8vo. The third part was issued 8vo, Paris, in 1619; the fourth part 8vo, 1626–7, *cura* Balthazar Baro, who also from the ample notes which D'Urfé had left issued *La Conclusion et derniere partie d'Astrée* (8vo, Paris) in 1628. *L'Astrée . . . Cinquiesme partie* (Paris, 8vo), 1626 (5), and *L'Astrée . . . Sixiesme partie* (Paris, 8vo), 1626, both probably printed in Holland, are the work of Borstal, sieur de Gaubertin. It may be noted that the original edition of the First Part of the *Astrée* was printed at Paris in 1607,[3] 8vo, chez Joussainets Du Bray. It was this which Henry IV was wont to have read to him whilst he lay sleepless at night suffering from the tortures of gout.

In some six thousand pages D'Urfé relates the loves of Céladon and Astrée, and tells how the shepherd was thrown into the depths of wanhope by the

[1] *Artamène ou Le Grand Cyrus,* Second Edition, Ten vols. Paris, 1650–1654, Vol. I (1650), "Au Lecteur" (unnumbered pages).

[2] The "Achevé d'imprimer pour la premiere fois" is dated 15 Feb., 1610.

[3] Only one exemplar is known. This was discovered at Augsburg in 1869, and is now in the library of Baron James de Rothschild. See Picot's Catalogue of this Library, Paris, 1887, Vol. II, p. 197, No. 1527. The *privilège* is dated 18 August, 1607. For a full bibliography of *L'Astrée* see Reuse's "Notice Bibliographique de Astrée," *La Vie et Oeuvres d'Honoré d'Urfé,* Paris, 1910, pp. 216–223.

cruelty and disdain of his shepherdess, how he was raised to heights of happiness by the reward of her affection. When L'Astrée commences "l'amoureux Berger s'estant levé fort matin pour s'entretenir ses pensées . . . s'alla asseoir sur le bord de la tortueuse riviere de Lignon," into which stream he presently precipitates himself—"il se jetta les bras croisez dans la riviere"—upon the occasion of an unjust suspicion and slight from Astrée, who chides him as "perfide et desloyal Berger . . . trompeur et mechant." He is rescued by the Nymphs of the stream, Galathée and her two attendants, by whom he is borne to the palace of Isoure, and forthwith commence a seemingly infinite number of interlacing stories: Alcippe and Amarillis; Corylas and Stelle; the amours of Hylas; Beleride and Célize; Madonthe and Damon; Euric, Daphnide and Alcidon, and many many more—I have counted forty such, and the tale is by no means complete—all reticulated with the adventures of the secondary figures in the romance, such as Lycidas, Laonice, Alcidon, Doris, Palemon, with the narrative of Diane and Silvandre, conjoining with the main theme. As M. Bochet well says, there are "histoires sentimentales, histoires romanesques, histoires chevaleresques, nouvelles historiques," and other episodes which flow into and disembogue from the main flood.

One point of extraordinary fascination for contemporaries which we must to-day perforce miss was that under pastoral names D'Urfé drew well-known and living figures. Thus Euric, King of the Visigoths, was Henry IV; Daphnide, Gabrielle d'Estrée; Alcidon, le duc de Bellegarde; Clarinte, Louise-Marguerite de Lorraine, princesse de Conti; Filandre, Anne d'Urfé, the author's brother, and so on. Similarly, in *Artamène ou le Grand Cyrus* contemporaries recognized that Cyrus was the Prince de Condé; Mandane, the Duchesse de Longueville; Crésus, the Archduke Leopold; Mazare, the Maréchal de Grammont; Cléandre, Cinq-Mars; Amestris, the Princesse d'Harcourt; la princesse de Salamis, la Marquise de Sablé; Élise, Mlle Paulet; le mage de Sidon, Mgr Godeau, Bishop of Grasse and Vence; Aristée, Chapelain; Sapho, Mlle Scudéry herself; the Egyptians, the Lorrains; the town Artaxate, Paris; the battle of Thybarra, the battle of Lens; and the siege of Cumes, the siege of Dunkirk,[1] both of which are exactly described. These and a thousand other such strokes gave, of course, the pages an engrossing interest which to-day has lost its savour.

In England Sir Philip Sidney's *Arcadia*, commenced in 1580, but which appeared after his death, 4to, 1590, rivalled the popularity in France of *L'Astrée*. This "vain amatorious poem," as Milton[2] dubbed it, was reprinted times out of number, extracts and abridgements were extremely popular, persisting throughout the eighteenth century. The adventures of Argalus and Parthenia circulated up and down the country as a chap-book. In 1624 Badouin translated the *Arcadia* into French, *L'Arcadie de la Comptesse de Pembroke*, 3 vols., Paris, 8vo.

A very important, perhaps the most important, feature in *L'Astrée* is the theory of, with discussions upon, Platonic love. "Dans cette encyclopédie

[1] Thus La Calprenède in his "Epistre" prefixed to *Cassandre*, III Partie, says: "ie dresseray le Plan du siege de Babilone sur celui de Graveline."

[2] *Iconoclastes*. Prose Works, 1806, vol. II, p. 408.

Romanesque de l'amour on peut distinguer quatre choses: des théories abstraites sur la beauté et l'amour, des controverses sur l'amour, des histoires d'amour, et des procès d'amour.

"La métaphisique platonicienne de la beauté et de l'amour est la partie la plus obscure de l'*Astrée*. Adamas, assis au pied d'un arbre avec Céladon, par une claire nuit d'été, lui révéla la genèse du pur amour: 'Toute beauté procède de cette souveraine bonté que nous appellons Dieu, et c'est un rayon qui s'eslance de luy sur toutes les choses créées. Et comme le soleil esclaire l'eau, et la terre du mesme rayon, ce soleil éternel embellit aussi l'âme raisonnable et la matière; mais la clarté de Dieu est très plus belle en l'âme raisonnable qu'en la matière.'

"Or l'amour est un désir de beauté; le tout est d'aimer ce qui est digne d'amour. Si, dans l'objet aimé, nous ne cherchons que la perfection des formes du corps, notre amour sera inférieur, grossier et matériel comme le corps. C'est donc l'âme qu'il faut aimer, et l'amour ainsi entendu est la 'Vraye et naturelle action de l'homme. . . .' "[1]

This is all pure Dryden, and in *The Indian Emperour*, *The Indian-Queen*, *Tyrannick Love*, *The Conquest of Granada* and *Aureng-Zebe*, these ideas of an etherialized sentimentalism are poised, discussed, disputed again and again from every outlook, from every vantage of the mind. "Des théories abstraites sur la beauté et l'amour, des controverses sur l'amour"; le Chanoine Reuse might be writing of Dryden's heroic tragedies.

Commenting upon the exquisite yet artificial days passed by these shepherds and shepherdesses in that imaginary lotus-land where the Lignon flows,[2] M. Bochet writes: "C'est bien l'amour qui les préoccupe tous, et qui, à lui seul remplit la vie." "Ainsi c'est mourir en soi pour revivre en autrui . . . c'est une volonté de se transformer s'il se peut, entièrement en la chose aimée,"[3] so says Céladon, a phrase which might be exactly matched in the mystical raptures of S. Catherine of Siena, S. Teresa, or S. John of the Cross. This statement would shock le Chanoine Reuse not a little,[4] but it is none the less literally true.

There is much of Céladon and Silvandre in Dryden's Porphyrius, Almanzor, Abdelmelech, Osmyn, and Aureng-Zebe. Berenice, Almahide, Indamora, and

[1] *La Vie et les Oeuvres de Honoré D'Urfé* par le Chanoine O.-C. Reuse, Paris, 1910, pp. 243–244.

[2] " Des bergers oisifs . . . qui passent les jours et les nuits uniquement occupés à faire l'amour," Bernardin de St. Pierre calls them in the *Preambule* de l'Arcadie, and it almost shames one to add in a note the comments of Rousseau: "Apropos des bergers du Lignon, me dit-il, j'ai fait une fois le voyage du Forez, tout exprès pour voir le pays de Céladon et d'Astrée, dont D'Urfé nous a fait de si charmants tableaux. Au lieu de bergers amoureux, je ne vis, sur les bords du Lignon, que des maréchaux, des forgerons, et des taillandiers.

Comment ! dans un pays si agréable ?

Ce n'est qu'un pays de forges. Ce fut ce voyage de Forez qui m'ôta mon illusion. Jusqu'à ce temps là, il ne passait point d'année qui je ne relusse l'*Astrée* d'un bout à l'autre ; j'étais familiarisé avec tous ses personnages. Ainsi la science nous ôte nos plaisirs." *Oeuvres de Saint-Pierre*, Paris, 1840, vol. I, p. 608.

[3] *L'Astrée*, III, 9, p. 878, ed. 1630.

[4] *Op. cit.*, p. 244. See also Fortunat Strowski, *Saint François de Sales*, Paris, 8vo, 1898.

Aſtrée frequently all take the same tone with their lovers, and enforce the philosophy that love is of the soul, and of the soul alone; Traxalla, Maximin, Morat show themselves gross, carnal, material because theirs is a physical passion and desire. Nay more, there is the very spirit of Hylas in Dryden's Celadon (*Secret Love*) and Palamede; I will go further, in Wildblood and Woodall.

Lorsque j'aime une fois, c'eſt d'un amour extrême.
Cet amour, j'en conviens, passe rapidement;
Mais rien ne peut durer qui soit si vehement.
Et c'eſt, vous le sçavez, un arrêt du sort même.

J'abhorre ces amours si conſtamment gardées;
Eſt-il rien de si doux qu'une jeune beauté?
Quel eſt enfin le prix de la fidelité?
D'insipides amours, et des beautés ridées.

Le temps qui détruit tout, rend la beauté moins belle.
Et pourquoi retrancher à nos foibles plaisirs?
Changeons donc chaque jour l'objet de nos désirs;
Pour jouir chaque jour d'une beauté nouvelle.

So lightly sings Hylas,[1] and is this not the very beſt spirit of Celadon with Florimel, and Palamede with Doralice? Could not young George Aldo have echoed this ſtrain and have lived up to its peccant philosophy?

Again, we may take the thirteen articles agreed upon between Hylas and Stelle, of which number one runs: "Que l'un n'usurpera point sur l'autre cette autorité que nous appellons tyrannie"; three: "Que notre amour sera éternellement sans contrainte"; four: "Que nous aimerons tant qu'il nous plaira"; five: "Que qui voudra cesser d'aimer, le pourra sans aucun reproche d'infidelité"; seven: "Que la jalousie et les plaintes seront bannis d'entre nous, comme incompatibles avec notre parfaite amitié." Well might Silvandre declare "je voudrais encore ajouter une condition. Laquelle? demanda Hylas. Que vous n'en observerez aucune, reprit Silvandre."[2] This is exactly the contract of Celadon and Florimel at the conclusion of *Secret Love*, an episode which was adversely criticized, as it was felt such badinage ought not to have been suffered in the presence of the Queen.

Dryden borrowed much from *L'Aſtrée*, but what he conveyed he has with rareſt genius made all his own. The sentimental Platonism, highly metaphysical, but perhaps not so unreal as some have supposed, which informs his heroic tragedies, and traces of which are by no means absent from other of his plays, came to him mainly through the romances of La Calprenède and Mlle de Scudéry, who themselves moſt directly derived this philosophy of love from D'Urfé.

When we consider how vaſt was the eagre of heroic tragedy in the English theatre, and when, moreover, we bear in mind that these heroic ideals and sentimental gallantries are the leitmotiv of many another play of this kind, although

[1] *L'Astrée*, III Partie, livre cinquième. Ed. Paris, 1733, Tome III, pp. 183–184.
[2] *Ibid.*, III Partie, livre neuvième, pp. 422–423.

the scenes may not happen actually to be written in rhyme, it appears wellnigh impossible to overestimate the importance of the heroic romance in its relations to our dramatists, and in particular to Dryden, the greatest of his age, the man who not only was moulded by, but also moulded and directed the taste and culture of England.

It was, of course, his very genius as a dramatist that manifested itself in Dryden's masterly handling of his material, his selection and juxtaposition of incident. When he read Mlle de Scudéry's *Almahide, ou l'esclave reine* he at once saw which episodes were to be discarded and which situations were to be wrought up to a keener pitch, concentrated and conserved. He alchemized the metal of the romances, and transmuted their endless pages into his five acts of purest gold.[1]

Dryden has frequent speeches, and indeed scenes in his tragedies which are informed by platonic sentimentality and interpret the whole gospel of metaphysical cicisbéism. Each exquisite heroine and her cavaliere-servente are thoroughly versed in the subtile sigmate code and the nicest practice of heroic gallantry, and are ready one and all to poise and counterpoise with rhyming couplets of rarest beauty, such argument and long debate of quintessential eroticism as would have delighted the trouvères who sang *l'amour courtois* and are crowned with myrtle or with bay at some Provençal judiciary of love.

There are also, of course, directer borrowings from the romances. Langbaine, before he penned his review of *The Conquest of Granada*, carefully went through Mlle de Scudéry's *Almahide* with tireless quill, most meticulously jotting down any thought, any turn which might, by however strained a gesture, have been reflected from the pages of that romance. The consequence is that he declares *The Conquest of Granada* to be a very patchwork, a thing mitred and morticed from a thousand pieces. He is sadly to seek. Never was play conceived and written in such a fashion.

The Indian-Queen was suggested by the episode of Zelmatide in *Polexandre*, whilst for *The Indian Emperour* Dryden turned to the actual historians, de Gómara, Bernal Diaz del Castillo, Sahagun, Torquemada, Durán, Ixtlilxochitl, J. B. Pomar, and the rest. Naturally, he interwove against the historical background a romantic drama of rivalry and love, a tangle of circumstances, and jostle of passion which might be fairly closely paralleled in *Cassandre* and *Cleopâtre*.

Of all heroic romances De Gomberville's *Polexandre* most nearly approaches the Amadis and Palmerin, or rather the Agesilan of Colchos and Felixmarte of Hyrcania, type; for in its extravagances it is nearer akin to the scions of the romances of chivalry than is it a graft of the older stock. We have a vast

[1] Mr. W. S. Clark having entirely refuted Miss Lynch's article and demonstrated the falsity of her position in a note "*The Platonic Element in the Restoration Heroic Play*," P.M.L.A., vol. xlv, 2; June, 1930, pp. 623–4, the lady replied (pp. 625–6) with a further note which plainly implied that she was not at all clear as to her own premises, and these indeed seem too vague and unreal to discuss profitably or with intelligence. It may be added that Miss Lynch's *Social Mode of Restoration Comedy* (1926) showed that she had made no adequate study of the Restoration stage; and what is more unfortunate yet, that she continually relied upon and echoed the opinions of the least dependable and most superficial writers on the subject.

geography—Morocco, the Canary Isles, Senegal, the gulf of Benin, Tombut, Mexico, the Antilles, Tartary, Cashmire, and many more—; giants, tourneys, naval engagements, dragons of a particularly horrible and monstrous kind ("il sortit des déserts de Zarfara un prodigieux serpent"),[1] fellest chimaeras that desolate and ravin whole kingdoms; a vessel steered by enchantment to "*les Isles inaccessibles*" where dwells Alcidiane, the fairest princess in the whole world, who is beloved by Polexandre, King of the Canaries.[2]

J'ai lu vingt et vingt fois celui de *Polexandre*,[3]

says La Fontaine; le grand Condé used to turn these pages "à toute heure"; Sorel praises the "hautes et magnifiques" adventures of Gomberville and admires in him "le savoir et l'art"; Segrais valued his style; Chapelain wrote "Il parle très purement sa langue"; Boileau, it is significant, never once rallies his books; but La Harpe, who confessed he had never read De Gomberville, speaks of *Polexandre* as "ce terrible ouvrage"; and a later critic, Victor Fournel, wrote, "*Polexandre* est certainement un des livres les plus enchevêtrés que nous ayons dans la langue française." This is very modern and severe. In its day at least the romance was so greatly admired that it "attayned to speake an elegant English phrase" as "The History of Polexander: In Five Bookes. Done into English by *William Browne*, Gent. For the Right Honourable Philip, Earle of Pembroke and Montgomery, &c. London, Printed by Tho: Harper, for Thomas Walkley, and are to be sold at his shop at the Golden Pestle and Mortar betweene Yorke House and Charing Crosse. 1647." The copy I have used has a duplicate title-page with date 1648.[4]

In the history of the English heroic play *Polexandre* is very important, as it may be generally remarked that hence are derived the romantic episodes of Mexican and Peruvian history upon which both Dryden and Howard's *The Indian-Queen* and Dryden's sequel *The Indian Emperour* are based. The scenario and other details seem to be suggested by "*The History of* Zelmatida, *heire to the Empire of the* Incas, *and of the Princesse* Isatida." This is related by Garruca, the servant of Zelmatida, one of those faithful old retainers who having "no pleasure equall to that of publishing the vertues of the King his Master," and then amply obtaining his chance in one of those criss-cross digressions that interlace the heroic romances, is by no means sparing of his glowing periods and verbal ornatures.

The dramatists have, of course, used their material with much freedom, and from the extraordinary variety of incidents and adventures at their command they were, of course, able to select but one or two particulars which had to be developed on the lines of a five-act tragedy, not upon the lines of a five-volume

[1] Troisième partie, livre 2.

[2] Amongst other romances, they figure in *Tirante el Blanco* and in the eleventh and twelfth books of *Don Florisel de Niquea*. The Canary Isles discovered began to be well known in Europe about 1405. Tradition told many extravagant tales of their size and marvels.

[3] La Ballade des romans.

[4] Esdaile, *English Tales and Romances* (p. 259), describes this as another edition, which is hardly exact.

romance. Montezuma in *The Indian-Queen* corresponds to the son of Inca Guira Capa, Zelmatida, supposed an orphan, the Peruvian Prince who gains triumphant victories for King Quasmez, a monarch "whose Empire extends it self from the territories of Mexico to those of the Inca's," and who takes prisoner the Prince of Mexico, whom he "entertayn'd . . . as his brother, and sent him presents, which absolutely gain'd him, and made him resolve to love his vanquisher." Here, I think, we have more than a hint for Acacis.

In *The History of Zelmatida* Montezuma is absent for a while. It is from the romance that the extraordinary, and of course entirely unhistorical and perplexing connexion of Mexican and Peruvian affairs which forms the theme of *The Indian-Queen* is taken. Zempoalla has something of "the invincible Telesman a Queene of the warlike virgins," *Polexander*, Part I, Book IV (pp. 104–107), but in her circumstances she more closely, perhaps, corresponds to Queen Hismalita "who in the absence of Montezuma did performe all the royall offices" of Mexico, and whom Zelmatida, "concealing his condition and Countrey," and making "himselfe taken for a kinsman of the last Cacique that Montezuma had brought under his obedience," serves as her general. He now falls in love with the young princess Isatida, who in her turn becomes enamoured of the handsome stranger. The lady, however, is a high platonic and lays down rules and regulations of love: "It behooves you to have an asseduitie without example, that your respects goe even to Idolatry, and that Death it selfe be not powerfull enough to breake your silence, And more, take it for most certayne that you lose me for ever, if ever your love comes not only to the knowledge of the Queene my Mother, but to any person else whatsoever."

The name Zempoalla is taken from a province conquered by Montezuma, "the Estates of the Cacique of Zampoallan," and Traxalla is from the Traxallan-Indians whom Dryden in the "*Connexion of the* Indian Emperour, *to the* Indian Queen" calls "*Taxallan-Indians*." In *Polexander* Garruca, who narrates all these adventures, is the faithful servant of Zelmatida; in *The Indian-Queen* Garrucca is "*a faithful Subject to* Amexia," the lawful Queen of Mexico. Ismeron, "*one of their Prophets, a Conjurer*," was suggested by Gomberville's "great Prophet Tisnatidez" and in name at least by "the learned Habul Ismeron, who is the oracle of kings, and the still watchful eie of the Kingdom of Morocco" and who appears in the Third Part of *Polexander* (The first Book). The name Orazia seems a variation of that of the incomparable Princess Coriza in the romance.

In the original French romance the "Histoire de Zelmatide heritière de l'Empire des Incas, et de la Princesse Izatide" commences on p. 238, Vol. I, 8vo, 1641, and extends to p. 397. There it is interrupted, to be resumed on p. 429, "Suite des Adventures de Zelmatide et d'Izatida" (English translation, *The continuance of the adventures of* Zelmatida, *and* Isatida, p. 63), to break off at p. 564. It is taken up once more on p. 589 by Garruca, who concludes on p. 772 with "Voila la principale partie des aventures du roi. J'ai passé pas dessus mille particularités, excellentes, et terni l'éclat de cette vie héroique par la simplicité de ma narration. Mais vous avez les yeux assez clairvoyants pour découvrir la splendeur des actions de mon maître, au travers de l'obscurité de mes paroles."

With regard to actual characters, too, the stock types appear in the heroic tragedy, as in the La Calprenède and De Scudéry romances, as in real life. The heroines, whether of the main story or of the underplot, are gentle and divinely fair—sometimes they are by honour tied to a tyrant or a rawly jealous husband, Berenice and Almahide; sometimes this dream of love is crossed by rivalry and a father's interdict, Indamora, Orazia, Benzayda. The hero is all aflame with love and honour, Montezuma (*The Indian-Queen*), Porphyrius, Almanzor, Ozmyn, Aureng-Zebe. An ageing monarch, caught with love, dotes upon some fair beauty, Montezuma (*The Indian Emperour*); Maximin Cæsar; the old Emperor (*Aureng-Zebe*). There are generous rivals, Acacis; unscrupulous and powerful rivals, Traxalla, Zulema, Morat. Almeria, again, Lyndaraxa, and Nourmahal resemble, as one jealous woman, imperious and proud, resembles another, Roxane in *Cassandre;* Salomé, the sister of Herod in *Cleopâtre*, and Tullie in *Clélie*.

This is very foolishly jeered by Martin Clifford, who in his *Notes upon Mr. Dryden's Poems in Four Letters*, 4to, 1687, a virulent and abusive attack, rails thus: "I am strangely mistaken if I have not seen this very *Almanzor* of yours in some disguise about this Town, and passing under another Name. Prithee, tell me true, was not this Huff-cap once the Indian Emperour, and at another time did he not call himself Maximine? Was not *Lyndaraxa* once called *Almeria*, I mean under *Montezuma* the Indian Emperour? I protest, and vow they are either the same, or so alike, that I can't for my heart distinguish one from the other. You are therefore a strange unconscionable Thief, that art not content to steal from others, but do'st rob thy wretched Self too" (p. 7).

Secret Love, *or The Maiden Queen*, was, as Dryden himself tells us, suggested by the "Histoire de Cleobuline,"[1] Reine de Corinthe, in *Le Grand Cyrus*, Septiesme Partie, Livre Second. Celadon is not without a smack of Hylas in *L'Astrée*. If *The Mock Astrologer's* adventure is similar to that of the lively Marquis de Touraine in *L'Illustre Bassa*, Thomas Corneille has his *Le Feint Astrologue* and Calderon *El Astrólogo Fingido*. In *Tyrannick Love* the "platonisme passionel" of Berenice largely directs the conduct of events. *The Conquest of Granada*, it is allowed, has many suggestions from *Almahide*, but more from Perez de Hita; and the episode of Osmyn and Benzayda is modelled upon the story of Osmin and Alibech in *L'Illustre Bassa*. No doubt the serious romance of *Marriage A-la-Mode* was suggested by the story of Sesostris and Timarète, *Le Grand Cyrus*, Sixième Partie, Livre Second. Whether Palamede and Rhodophil have a shadowy original in the episode of Timarète and Parthenie, *Le Grand Cyrus*, Sixièsme Partie, Livre Premier, I more than question; whilst I feel sure that the death of Morat in *Aureng-Zebe*[2] is not a copy from the expiring King of Assyria to whom Mandane shows some small kind courtesies.

With regard to the somewhat extravagant flights and florid bravuras of the

[1] Cleobuline is Christina of Sweden. So Dryden's *Secret Love* may be said to be founded upon the actual events of history.

[2] The point is a small one, but Holzhausen in his *Dryden's Heroisches Drama* (*Englische Studien*, xiii, 414–445; xv, 13–52; xvi, 201–229) has misunderstood Dryden's Epistle Dedicatory to *Aureng-Zebe* when he says that one episode of the plot is taken from de Scudéry.

heroic tragedy, "Language, lofty and becoming the Grandeur of the Illustrious Personages that speak,"[1] which has been superficially supposed to be a heritage from the earlier Elizabethan drama, this also is the very tone of the magnificos and ladies of great quality in heroic romance. There is no harking back to Marlowe and his peers. Indeed, I would emphatically say that Marlowe had no shadow of influence upon the Restoration drama. He who cannot discern the essential difference between the swelling rants of Tamberlaine and the ermined altiloquence of Maximin is a sorry critic and an ignorant to boot. Again let us stress the fact that there is no link—not even here—between the heroic tragedy and the Elizabethans, no tradition descended.

The explanation of many of these errors and fallacies with regard to the heroic drama in Charles the Second's day lies in the fact that writers have been misled in the first place by Dryden himself. They have unquestioningly accepted —and this indeed was the poet's aim—Dryden's *Of Heroique Playes. An Essay* as a "critical recipe,"[2] that is to say a scholarly and deliberate quasi-Aristotelian treatise in which he sums up and sets forth the theories and rules by which he was governed and to which he adhered in the composition of his heroic tragedies. Nothing could be further from the fact. *Of Heroique Playes* is prefixed to *The Conquest of Granada*,[3] 4to, 1672, and this Essay was largely an answer to the burlesque *The Rehearsal*, which had been produced at the Theatre Royal on 7 December, 1671, a satire upon Dryden himself in particular and the heroic tragedy in general.

It is obvious that Dryden dare not immediately reply to so high-placed, powerful and entirely unscrupulous a personage as the Duke of Buckingham, who fathered the new piece at which all London was laughing its loudest, but he could securely defend the heroic tragedy along the lines of Castelvetro, the Prefaces (A qui lit) of Georges de Scudéry, the *Discours* and *Examens* of Corneille. *Of Heroique Playes* is imprimis Dryden's vindication of *The Conquest of Granada*, which had been one of the chief butts of ridicule. It is difficult to see how this could have escaped intelligent notice since he himself says that his Essay is in fine a "particular Defence" of the play before which it is printed. None of his other plays in heroic verse are so much as mentioned. *Aureng-Zebe*, of course, had not then been written, and it may be argued that he would leave any reply that concerned *The Indian-Queen* to Howard; but he has no word to say for either *The Indian Emperour* or *Tyrannick Love*, two plays of immense importance and popularity, both of which are severely enough handled in *The Rehearsal*.

It is true that Dryden affects to regard *The Siege of Rhodes* as the first heroic drama to be seen upon the English stage, yet although Davenant himself used the term *heroique plays* in his Dedication to the Earl of Clarendon, first printed (before the Second Part) in the third quarto, 1663, it is not at all certain that he attached the later meaning to this phrase, that he understood it in the special

[1] "The Address to the Reader," prefixed to the English translation of *Le Grand Cyrus*, folio, 1653.

[2] B. J. Pendlebury, *Dryden's Heroic Plays* (1923), a slight and inadequate monograph.

[3] It is printed before the First Part, but both Parts were published together.

sense in which it is now generally accepted. "The story represented," he writes, ". . . is heroical." Valour and conjugal love displayed amid "the continual hurry and the heroic agitations of a hot siege," thus he sums up his theme, and this description would equally well fit *The Conquest of Granada*. Yet we must not, I think, press Dryden's assertion that *The Siege of Rhodes* was the first heroic play. The term was at any rate ill-defined and vague in its application, and *Of Heroique Plays* was written when Dryden had just read the Preface to Davenant's *Gondibert*, "An Heroick Poem" (1650),[1] a discourse which reflects Chapelain's preface to the *Adone*, Scudéry's preface to *Ibrahim, ou l'Illustre Bassa*, Tasso's *Discorsi del Poema Eroico* translated into French (1638) by Jean Baudoin, *Traité du Pöeme épique de T. Tasso*, and Scaliger's *Poetices*. Davenant is considering the heroic poem, in fact he distinguishes the "Heroicks" (Homer, Vergil, Statius, Tasso, Spenser) from the "Dramaticks." Dryden is dealing with heroic tragedy, but so closely does he follow Davenant as sometimes almost to seem to paraphrase from him with the result that many of the expositions in the *Of Heroique Plays* are really concerned with the epic rather than with the stage. This he must have appreciated, and to cover his tracks and save himself from a charge of impertinence he ingeniously proclaimed that Davenant's own piece, the operatic *The Siege of Rhodes*, must be regarded as the first heroic play.

It must be plain that Dryden's five rhyming tragedies—and these are strictly his heroic plays—*The Indian-Queen, The Indian Emperour, Tyrannick Love, The Conquest of Granada* (the two parts of which may be conveniently regarded as one drama of ten acts) and *Aureng-Zebe*, are not composed according to any defined and determinate "critical recipe," but, in spite of certain common characteristics, are so varied and individual that they do not follow and adhere to a system of set formularies and fully developed ideas.

Dryden's use of actual incident and character from the heroic romances is comparatively not important although far from negligible; his creation of atmosphere and the philosophy of love he takes thence is extremely remarkable and of essential significance. He was by far the greatest exponent of heroic drama, but without covering the whole field it may be well to mention here a few of the more important plays of other dramatists who followed his lead in this kind, and who had recourse to the French romances.

Cassandre was drawn upon by John Weston in his unacted tragi-comedy *The Amazon Queen; or, The Amours of Thalestris To Alexander the Great*, 4to, 1667; by Lee in *The Rival Queens, or the Death of Alexander the Great*, produced at the Theatre Royal, January, 1676–7; by John Banks in his imitation *The Rival Kings, or The Loves of Oroondates and Statira*, produced at the Theatre Royal in the early summer of 1677; by Samuel Pordage in his *The Siege of Babylon*, Dorset Garden, autumn of 1677; by Edward Cooke in his *Love's Triumph; or The Royal Union*, 4to, 1678, unacted; by Crowne in his *Darius, King of Persia*, Theatre Royal, April, 1688; from *Cleopatre* Pordage took *Herod and Mariamne*, Dorset Garden, October, 1673; Lee took *Gloriane*,

[1] The Preface to *Gondibert* was published separately at Paris, *chez Matthieu Guillemot*, 1650, as *A Discourse upon Gondibert, An heroick Poem, written by Sr William D'Avenant, With an Answer to it by Mr. Hobbs*. This was reprinted the following year in London prefixed to the Poem itself.

or The Court of Augustus Cæsar, Theatre Royal, January, 1676; Mrs. Behn, *The Young King, or, The Mistake*,[1] Dorset Garden, spring of 1679; and Lord Orrery, his unacted *Herod the Great*, folio, 1694; from *Faramond* Lee took *Theodosius, or, The Force of Love*, Dorset Garden, autumn of 1680. De Scudéry's *Ibrahim, ou l'Illustre Bassa* supplied Lord Orrery with the plot of *The Tragedy of Mustapha, Son of Solyman the Magnificent*, Lincoln's Inn Fields, April, 1665; and Elkanah Settle dramatized episodes from the same romance as *Ibrahim the Illustrious Bassa*, Dorset Garden, 1676. From *Le Grand Cyrus* Banks derived his *Cyrus the Great, or The Tragedy of Love*, which Downes calls *The Grand Cyrus*. It was produced at Lincoln's Inn Fields in December, 1695, although written long before. *Clélie* provided Lee with the romantic and most important scenes in his *Lucius Junius Brutus, Father of his Country*, produced at Dorset Garden in December, 1680, and almost immediately prohibited by Arlington on account of "very scandalous expressions and reflections vpon ye Government."[2]

The plot of Lee's *Sophonisba, or, Hannibal's Overthrow*, produced at Drury Lane in April, 1675, is taken from Orrery's famous romance *Parthenissa*, "The Story of Izadora and Perolla."[3] The First Part, Book IV. The first five parts of *Parthenissa* were published in 1654. The Sixth Tome appeared 4to, 1669, and the romance "compleat"—that is to say as far as Orrery went, for the adventures were never finished—folio, 1676. It is an ornate, finely panached piece of work, very closely modelled upon La Calprenède, but to my mind it lacks something—a je ne sais quoi—that I find in the French writers. Dorothy Osborne's critique is just; the stories and episodes have "nothing new and *surprenant* in them; the ladies are all so kind they make no sport."

Perhaps a word should be given here to what is, I believe, the only other English venture in this kind, Crowne's *Pandion and Amphigenia; or, the History of the Coy Lady of Thessalia*.[4] Although he asserts he will not imitate "that ceremonious nation," the French, he certainly copies de Scudéry, but he lacks the wit and polish, I will venture to say, the interest of *Le Grand Cyrus* and *Clélie*, he has little or no psychology, and his conceits rather resemble rockets huzzing tantivy through the sky than flowers, sweet if gay, set in a formal parterre.

It were interesting to follow the exotic sentiment and rococo ideals of heroic tragedy, its subjectivity, love of the picturesque, and reactionary spirit in their variations and influence throughout the eighteenth century, to note how their luxuriance was seemingly pruned only to blossom out with richer efflorescence, to mark the reappearance of emotions long since discarded, and an outlook long since despised, as the romantic revival of Gothicism and Chivalry which were made fashionable by Strawberry Hill and popular by *Otranto*. Surprise

[1] *The Rival Queens* (save for some speeches); *The Young King; Theodosius; Cyrus the Great; Lucius Junius Brutus;* are not in rhyme.

[2] See also the Preface to Charles Gildon's *The Patriot, or The Italian Conspiracy*, 4to, 1703, an adaptation from *Lucius Junius Brutus*.

[3] Colley Cibber's tragedy *Perolla and Izadora*, produced at Drury Lane, 3 December, 1705; 4to, 1706; is founded upon this same story.

[4] Adorned with sculptures, London, 8vo, 1665.

has been expressed at the admiration felt by Gray for Dryden. Nothing could be more logical, nothing could be more inevitable. However fascinating the theme, it must suffice to say that there are essential qualities which link the heroic tragedies with the romances of Ann Radcliffe.

The production of *The Indian-Queen* naturally brought Dryden into prominent notice, and although when this tragedy was published it appeared in the folio volume 1665 *Four New Plays*,[1] as written by the Honourable Sir Robert Howard without a hint of collaboration in any one piece, there can be no doubt that the wits were very well aware that the greatest share in the most successful of this mournival of plays must be ascribed to Dryden.

For many reasons Dryden may have deemed it far more diplomatic not to press his claim. In fact he does not even include *The Indian-Queen* among his works in the list of his plays and poems which he gave upon the reverse of the half-title of *King Arthur, or, The British Worthy*, 4to, 1691 (Both First and Second Issue), and this tragedy was not printed under the joint names of Sir Robert Howard and John Dryden until the collected edition of 1717. It is not included in the folio, 1701, although Sir Robert had then been dead some three years.[2]

On 1 December, 1663, Dryden married the Lady Elizabeth Howard, and he fully appreciated that his brother-in-law was an exceedingly tetchy and tender person, especially so far as points of literary reputation were concerned.[3] Accordingly, with rare modesty the only reference he makes to his share in *The Indian-Queen* occurs in the paper "*Connexion of the* Indian Emperour, *to the* Indian Queen," "part of which Poem," he says, "was writ by me." This paper was distributed among the audience in the theatre, and is also printed in the quartos of *The Indian Emperour*.

As might have been expected, the poet's enemies in later days did not forget to assail the Lady Elizabeth Dryden with bawdy railings, and openly declared that she was a notorious whore both before and after wedlock. Thus Shadwell in *The Tory-Poets*, 1682, has some coarsely abusive lines:

> His *Muse* was prostitute upon the Stage,
> And'*s Wife* was Prostitute to all the age:
> The Wife is Rich although the Husband Poor,
> And he not honest, and she is a Whore.

The *Satyr to his Muse*, 4to, 1682, also by Shadwell, commences:

> Hear me dull Prostitute, worse than my Wife,
> Like her the shame and clog of my dull Life. . . .

[1] Imprimatur *March* 7, 166⁴⁄₅. *Roger L'Estrange*.

[2] He died 3 September, 1698.

[3] This susceptibility of Sir Robert Howard was severely satirized by Shadwell in *The Sullen Lovers; or, The Impertinents*, Lincoln's Inn Fields, May, 1668, in the character of Sir Positive At-all and his challenging two clerks who sat in the eighteen-penny gallery the first day of his new play *The Lady in the Lobster* and railed at his scenes.

and proceeds to specific charges:

> Against my Will I Marry'd a rank W——,
> After two Children and a Third Miscarriage,
> By Brawny Brothers hector'd into Marriage. . . .
> To writing bred, I knew not what to Say,
> With Scolding Wife and Starving Chits Beset. . . .

The two children have never been heard of, and I believe never existed. The miscarriage is a thing impossible to prove, and one might have thought, as it would have hardly been bruited abroad, impossible to know save through treachery or some extraordinary indiscretion. The canard that Dryden was hector'd into marriage by the lady's brother is clearly an echo of the story told of De Grammont, who was fetched back from Dover by Miss Hamilton's brother to marry their sister, when about to cross to France. The Grammont adventure is said to have suggested to Molière *Le Mariage Forcé*.[1]

It is apparently upon this foundation and from some second-hand gossip or vague memories of ancient dowagers and aunts that Malone has conceived an ill opinion of the temper and reputation of the Lady Elizabeth, yet such evidence surely seems very slender for assuming an unhappy union, quarrels and domestic vexations. Dryden was on excellent terms with his wife's family. During the Great Plague of 1666 he stayed at Charlton in Wiltshire, the seat of his father-in-law the Earl of Berkshire, and here his eldest son Charles was born, at 3 p.m., 6 September, 1666.[2] There was no break in his friendship with Sir Robert Howard. True, the brother-in-law grew warm in a purely literary discussion, as authors will, and Dryden prefixed a critical preface that has a dry bob or two at Howard to the second quarto, 1668, of *The Indian Emperour*, but he withdrew this almost immediately and did not suffer it to be reprinted. Indeed, it has been removed from many examples of the 1668 edition.[3] Yet his enemies alleged that not venturing to caricature Sir Robert Howard openly, he did so by a subtle shift. It was said that the character of Sir Positive At-all, a notorious burlesque of Howard, in Shadwell's *The Sullen Lovers; or, The Impertinents*, produced at Lincoln's Inn Fields, 2 May, 1668, was actually written by Dryden, by whom it was given to Shadwell to be inserted in that dramatist's new comedy. This is more than hinted at in a University lampoon, where the writer, after attacking *The Assignation; or, Love in a Nunnery*, continues: "But however, if he were taken for no good Comick-Poet, or Satyrist; he had found a way of much easier License, (though more remarkable in the sense of some) which was, not only to Libel mens persons, but to represent them on the Stage too: . . . Besides, that he

[1] We must remember the Marriage of Panurge, Rabelais, III, ch. xxxv. *Le Mariage Forcé* was given at the Louvre in three acts with a ballet, 29 January, 1664; and in one act at the Palais Royal on the 15 February following.

[2] The horoscope is in Ashmole MS. 243 (p. 209), Bodleian Library.

[3] As, for example, the copy in the Bodleian, which was duly received from Stationers' Hall with *A Defence of an Essay of Dramatique Poesie* deliberately and carefully removed.

had been so frankly obliging as (where he could not use a Character, or apprehended the License) to assign it to some other Poet of his Cabal, or exchange one part for another, it may be *Club Wit* too, the better to set men forth: That this was a *Sir Positive Truth* Mr. Dryden had not the fore-head enough to denie." *The Friendly Vindication of Mr. Dryden*, Cambridge, 1673 (p. 8). Shadwell's vituperation of Dryden, malicious and unconfirmed, goes for nothing. Indeed, there is an old proverb about people who dwell in glass-houses. Thus Tom Brown in *The Late Converts Exposed* (Part the second), 4to, 1690, whilst he has a cast at Dryden, does not forget Og's own domestic irregularities: "You are plagued with an odd sort of *Latitudinarian* creature at home (which they say is your own misfortune, Mr. *Bays*, as well as Mr. *Sh-dw-ll's*).[1]

Assuredly there needs no scandalous explanation of the marriage of Dryden and the Lady Elizabeth Howard; there was in fact no such disparity in their respective stations as has been supposed.[2] Lady Elizabeth showed herself a loving and careful mother to her children.[3]

That he was not a model of conjugal fidelity we are bound to allow, inasmuch as his name was notoriously connected with the beautiful Anne Reeve (or Reeves) of the Theatre Royal, and since we are mainly considering Dryden as a dramatist some account of his liaison with this fascinating actress, the only woman whom he tenderly loved, will not be impertinent here.

The name of the lovely Anne Reeve appears very infrequently in the printed casts. We find her as Esperanza in *The Conquest of Granada* (Part I, December), 1670; (Part II, January), 1671; and to this character Bayes' "*bel esperansa de ma vie*" in *The Rehearsal* undoubtedly alludes. Buckingham's famous satire was produced 7 December, 1671, and it is clear that Mrs. Reeve played Amaryllis. The theatre of Charles II was none too delicate for such a situation however personal and shameless the attack. It is true that recently it has been questioned whether Mrs. Reeve could actually have played Amaryllis, but so far as I am aware only one scholar has raised this doubt, and that upon no evidence save the very creditable feeling of the indecorum of such an impersonation. But the Restoration theatre was not so nice. The dialogue in *The Rehearsal* is pointed and plain, and unless Amaryllis were taken by Mrs. Reeve it becomes meaningless and flat. Moreover, the old tradition which finds its place in Briscoe's *Key to the Rehersal*, 1704, cannot be lightly discarded, and that upon no grounds beyond a certain disrelish for so broad and, if you will, so brutal a fleer.

About Easter, 1672, at Lincoln's Inn Fields, Mrs. Reeve played Philotis in *Marriage A-la-Mode*, and later in the same year she undertook the male rôle of Ascanio, the page, in *The Assignation*. She had, it may be noted, a few months previously acted a man when *The Maiden Queen* was given "by the

[1] Page 11.

[2] "On his marriage to Lady Elizabeth Howard . . . her father, the Earl of Berkshire, I believe, settled upon them a small estate in Wiltshire, the exact value of which I have not been able to ascertain ; but it probably was not less than sixty pounds a year." Malone, *Life of Dryden*, p. 447.

[3] See her letter to Dr. Busby, Ascension Day, 1682.

Women only," and also delivered the Epilogue. Her name has not been traced in any other parts, and in the spring of 1675 she disappeared from the stage to take the veil in a foreign convent.[1] A very pointed reference occurs in the Prologue to *Every Man Out Of His Humour*, "Spoken by Mr. Hayns, July 1675." (Duffett's *Poems*, 1676, p. 73):

> So Crack enjoy'd, the queazy Gallants slight,
> And she, though still her beauty's in its height
> In rage turns Nun and goes to Heav'n in spight.

This is also glanced at in the Epilogue to Otway's *Don Carlos*, produced at Dorset Garden in 1676, probably June. The speaker, a girl, says:

> But now, if by my Suit you'l not be won,
> You know what your unkindness oft has done:
> I'le e'n forsake the Play-House, and turn Nun.

Rochester, too, in his *A Trial of the Poets for the Bays* did not fail to recall this incident:

> In the head of the Gang, *John Dryden* appear'd,
> That ancient grave Wit so long lov'd and fear'd,
> But *Apollo* had heard a story in Town,
> Of his quitting the *Muses*, to wear the Black Gown;
> And so gave him leave now his Poetry's done,
> To let him turn Priest since *Reeve* is turn'd Nun.

Mrs. Reeve had more beauty than talent. The rôles she essayed were small, and as an actress she met with little success. Possibly she owed her appearance on the boards to her lover, as she chiefly performed in his plays. That Dryden's amour with her was common town talk there can, I think, be no doubt. Contemporary verse and long-continued tradition couple the poet's name with that of Mrs. Reeve in a way the persistence of which would have been utterly vapid and pointless had not the fact of the intrigue been public property.

Thomas Shadwell, the author of *The Medal of John Bayes*, 4to, 1682, in his "Epistle to the Tories" prefixed to that satire writes: "*His prostituted Muse will become as common for hire as his Mistress* Revesia *was, upon whom he spent so many hundred pounds; and of whom (to shew his constancy in Love) he got three Claps, and she was a Bawd. Let all his own* Romantick *Playes shew so true and so Heroick a Lover*." A further allusion to Mrs. Reeve in the satire itself is very gross.

The oft-quoted passage from the letter, purporting to be penned by an old doddle of some seven-and-eighty years, published in *The Gentleman's Magazine*, February, 1745 (p. 99), *On the Poets and Actors in King* Charles II'*s Reign*, signed W.G., is more than suspect. It can be clearly shown that this letter is a mere rifacimento from various sources of which Otway's *The Poet's Complaint Of His Muse*, 4to, 1680, is not the least considerable, and moreover the writer in some instances misunderstood and misused his authorities. He says: "I remember plain *John Dryden* (before he paid his court with success to the great,)

[1] "She died a religious." *Gentleman's Magazine*, February, 1745, p. 98.

in one uniform cloathing of *Norwich* drugget. I have eat tarts with him and Madam *Reeve* at the *Mulberry-garden* when our author advanced to a sword, and chadreux wig." This anecdote, however untrue, has at least one value: it serves to demonstrate the persistence of a long-enduring tradition with regard to the relations between Dryden and Anne Reeve. In the same number of *The Gentleman's Magazine* it is interesting to note that another writer breaks out into verse when he recalls the actors who made *Marriage A-la-Mode* (Easter, 1672) so brilliant a success:

> *Cibber* will smile applause: and think again
> Of *Hart*, of *Mohun*, and all the female train,
> *Coxe*, *Marshall*, *Dryden's Reeve*, *Bet. Slade*, and *Charles's* reign.

Although Sir Robert Howard has almost consistently been vastly underrated, he showed himself no mere dilettante or amateur, but a dramatist of parts and a critic of ideas.[1] *The Committee*, for example, is a capital comedy; "the characterization is admirable. Mr. and Mrs. Day are worthy to be named in the same breath as some of the minor characters of Dickens." I would add that the exquisite satire upon bureaucracy is as pungent and pointed in this very Year of Grace as ever it was wellnigh three centuries ago when the play first trod the boards. In his romantic and more serious plays Howard's verse is nervous and facile, of superior quality to that of such dramatists as Tatham, Sir Aston Cokain, Cosmo Manuche, or Porter, and comparing very favourably with the diction of Davenant himself. But his rhyming scenes, although by no means wanting in felicitous passages, are often broken by some awkwardness or clumsy handling of words, as though his talent could not for long together sustain that evenness without insipidity and ease without monotony which we find in the one master of this metre. Probably he recognized this defect, and here, no doubt, we have the reason why his tragedy *The Vestal Virgin, or, The Roman Ladies* and that fine drama *The Great Favourite; or, The Duke of Lerma* alternate between blank verse and rhyme. There is a noteworthy sentence

[1] No man was more abreast of his time. It is ridiculous to write, "Howard too was out of touch, not only with the tragedy of his day, but with the whole outlook of his day as well." It can only be said that such was not the case. This amazing sentence occurs in Mr. D. D. Arundell's *Dryden & Howard*, 1929, a book which reprints the Essay *Of Dramatick Poesie*, *The Indian Emperour*, and *The Great Favourite*. "The texts are taken from the first editions." As regards the *Of Dramatick Poesie* and *The Indian Emperour* this assertion is simply incorrect. I do not know whence the text of *The Indian Emperour* is taken, but I imagine it must be from some very late and very worthless reprint. On the reprinted text of *The Great Favourite* I cannot pronounce as I have not examined it. At a somewhat hasty glance it seems to me very suspect and shows signs of having been tinkered at not a little. A sophisticated and faulty script is even further vitiated by an erratic system of new punctuation and a peppering of diacritical dots, maddening to the ordinary reader, interpolations to make a scholar's gorge rise. The book was "made up" because the King Edward VII Professor of English Literature in the University of Cambridge was pleased when *The Great Favourite* was first read to him. This I frankly do not understand. It is impossible that the King Edward VII Professor of English Literature in the University of Cambridge should not have read so celebrated a piece as Sir Robert Howard's play.

in the address "To The Reader" prefixed to *The Great Favourite* which bears directly upon this point and seems to speak clearly enough. "I will not," declares the author, "therefore pretend to say, why I write this *Play*, some *Scenes* in blank Verse, others in Rhime, since I have no better a Reason to give than Chance, which waited upon my present Fancy, and I expect no better a Reason from any ingenious Person, than his Fancy for which he best relishes." A very sound and sensible piece of criticism. Later, in the same preface, Howard continues: "I had almost forgot one Argument, or observation, which that Author [Dryden] has most good fortune in; it is in his *Epistle Dedicatory*, before his *Essay of Dramatick Poesie*, where, speaking of Rhyme in Plays, he desires it may be observed, That none are violent against it, but such as have not attempted it, or who have succeeded ill in the attempt; which as to my self and him I easily acknowledge; for I confess that none has written in that way better than himself, nor few worse than I." This is, of course, exaggerated to emphasize the point, for there are many heroic plays far inferior to these of Sir Robert Howard.

The versification of *The Indian-Queen* flows with such vigour, and so many of the chiming couplets are not without great beauty, that it seems obvious Dryden must have pretty freely rehandled the whole. The character of Montezuma and Zempoalla are most certainly his, as is also the lyric Incantation Scene, in later years to be so exquisitely set by the genius of Henry Purcell.

Encouraged by the extraordinary success of *The Indian-Queen*, Dryden ventured upon that hazardous thing, a sequel, and in the spring of 1665 he produced at Drury Lane *The Indian Emperour: or, The Conquest of Mexico by the Spaniards*. This proved to be one of those rare cases in which the sequel falls no whit short of, but is rather beyond, its antecessor and begetter. The triumph of *The Indian Emperour* eclipsed even the popularity of *The Indian-Queen*, nor is there any reason for surprise, seeing that now Dryden has become stronger and more sure of his ground his rhyme rings clearer with music that is more subtly sweet, the motives of heroic honour and passionate love are debated with the analytic skill and fervid rhetoric of a master.

It is interesting to remark that in his original script Dryden had appropriately (if not very correctly) distinguished the Mexican High Priest by the name of Caliban, which he afterwards deleted, although he calls the aerial spirit Kalib.[1] This would seem merely to be an abbreviation of Caliban, and has no connexion with the Hindoo Witch divinity, the blood-thirsty Durga or Kali, Queen of Hell. The derivation of the word Caliban[2] is disputed, nor is it of consequence here, but it is significant that Dryden was already paying some attention to Shakespeare's *The Tempest* whence, no doubt, he borrowed for very uncouthness sake this vocable.

In the first draft the Christian Priest was particularized as a Jesuit father. Good taste changed this; better taste might have eliminated the scene, effective

[1] In history Kalib was that King of Assyria known to Greek historians as Elesbaan or Hellesthaios.

[2] It is sometimes considered to be a metathesis of Canibal, *i.e.*, Caribee, in which case Shakespeare's source was Florio's *Montaigne*, 1603, Book I, c. 30 *Of the Caniballes;* it is sometimes derived from the Gipsy *cauliban*, "blackness."

as it must be allowed to be. Some amends, however, have been made in *Tyrannick Love.*

The Indian Emperour greatly pleased Charles II, and in the Lord Chamberlain's records there are notes of Dryden's drama having been played before him at the theatre upon several occasions. It was no less popular with the public.

The play was entered at Stationers' Hall, 26 May, 1665, but not published (quarto, *for H. Herringman*) until 1667. The delay was due to the outbreak of the pestilence, so that when Elizabeth Puckering Newton was anxious to read the new play of which all London was talking a fair copy was made from the script and sent down to the Priory, Warwick, for the lady.[1] This MS. is now preserved in the library of Trinity College, Cambridge, to which it was presented with a noble gift of other MSS. and books, in fact the bulk of his library, by Sir Henry Puckering Newton in 1691. The MS. in question consists of forty-two folio sheets, and is very neatly written on both sides of the paper between red rules. It is elegantly bound, and bears the owner's name inscribed in her own hand, Eliz. Puckering Newton, 1665.

The second edition of *The Indian Emperour* followed in 1668, and to this was prefixed the *Defence of an Essay of Dramatique Poesie* which is more particularly considered a little later.

Of Dramatick Poesie, An Essay, is written in an easy and simple style whose native elegance admits both of scholarship and vigour. This, together with the apt and witty arguments, the just yet nicely weighed appreciations, particularly of Shakespeare and Ben Jonson, render the treatise one of the finest pieces of English prose our literature can boast, as well as of prime importance and authority in the history of dramatic criticism. It is composed in the form of a dialogue, an agreeable method of presentation, which, since its revival from classical times by Poggio, Lorenzo Valla, Pontano, Cristoforo Landino, Erasmus, and other great Renaissance scholars, had been largely made use of by French, Spanish, and Italian authors. The interlocutors are four in number, "Three of them Persons whom their Wit and Quality have made known to all the Town," Eugenius (Lord Buckhurst), Crites (Sir Robert Howard),[2] Lisideius (Sir Charles Sedley), and Neander (Dryden himself). A valuable and definite realism—a certain unity and solid verisimilitude as it were—is adroitly supplied by the exactness of the opening sentences: "It was that memorable day, in the first Summer of the late War, when our Navy ingag'd the *Dutch*," Saturday, 3 June, 1662, when the Dutch were defeated off Harwich and Admiral Opdam's ship blown up with all on board. Hardly less admirable is the skilful passage which so cleverly leads us from the descriptive introduction to the critical discussion: "*Crites*, a person of a sharp judgment, . . . said, smiling to us, that if the concernment of this battel had not been so exceeding great, he could scarce have wish'd the Victory at the price he knew he must pay for it, in

[1] Lady Puckering Newton was Elizabeth, daughter of Thomas Murray, Provost of Eton, and sister to Lady Anne Halkett.

[2] There is a novel and altogether unfounded suggestion that Crites was not designed for Sir Robert Howard, but that some other, perhaps Roscommon, is intended. The old tradition, however, is correct.

being subject to the reading and hearing of so many ill verses, as he were sure would be made upon it."

So much is said in this *Essay* concerning the "rule of the Unities" that a few words should be said upon this subject here. It was dogmatically laid down by sixteenth and seventeenth-century critics that "the rule of the Three Unities"—definitely propounded by "le régent de Parnasse" Boileau,[1] by Réné le Bossu, Father Rapin, S.J., and others, and more or less acknowledged and obeyed by Corneille—is to be explicitly, if not verbally, found in Aristotle's *Poetics*, which is a treatise upon tragedy written about a century later than the golden age of Sophocles and Euripides. It was asserted, moreover, that in practice the ancient tragedians meticulously followed these principles, from the observance of which in their works Aristotle formulated his directions.

But this theory, which seems to have hypnotized and held in thraldom the critics and dramatists for more than two centuries, and the Aristotelian basis of which is often accepted and vouched for even to-day, is as a matter of fact the emptiest assumption, originated by a confusion of ideas which arises from an impossible attempt to fit the general, but by no means universal, practice of the ancient drama to certain preconceived laws certainly disregarded by, because as such unknown to, Sophocles and Euripides.

Aristotle in the *Poetics* is quite explicit concerning the relevance and connexion of scenes, and he lays down with perfect judgement that the worst fault a tragedy can have is to be interrupted and held up by detached scenes introduced without probable or necessary sequence. It is not suggested that the scenes should be continuous in supposed time one with another. On the Athenian stage such mechanical continuity would, even if desired—which it was not—have been impossible owing to the intervention of the chorus and choric song.

The essential error of Renaissance critics who, at first at any rate, were writing theoretically rather than practically, consisted in a misunderstanding of the nature of dramatic representation. Aristotle's definition of tragedy commences thus: "Tragedy is the imitation of an action that is serious, complete." And upon imitation "μίμησις" he insists. There must be "imitation of nature." Even if there are introduced upon the stage purely imaginary beings such as the good fairies, demons, ogres, in a Victorian pantomime, they must act as is the nature of good fairies, demons, and ogres to do. The Renaissance critics through their fusion of mistaken ideas, thought that what Aristotle demanded when he said "imitation" is the production in the spectator of a fancy that he is actually present at the place and during the time of the dramatic action. Accordingly from this false premiss they logically deduced various far-reaching conclusions, in fine, the whole Draconian legislature and incubus of the Three Unities. It is obvious that the attempted observance of the first of these rules, the Unity of Time, must at once create difficulties, contradictions, and even absurdities.

[1] Mais nous, que la raison à ses règles engage,
Nous voulons qu'avec art l'action se ménage,
Qu'en un lieu, qu'en un jour, un seul fait accompli
Tienne jusqu'à la fin le théatre rempli.

Art Poétique, ch. III.

Strictly, the supposed time of a play's action should exactly equal the time required for its performance from the rise to the fall of the curtain. In practice this could not be maintained; three, or at most four, hours proved too short a period for the business of a play, and accordingly the ancient "day" had to be granted the poets. But if we are to extend the three hours during which the spectator is in the theatre to twenty-four hours, why not extend three hours to forty-eight hours, a week, a fortnight? Such a prolongation is easy, and indeed inevitable, once it is granted that three hours in the theatre may upon the stage include more than three hours by the watch. It is true that in so rare an instance as *The Double-Dealer* the time is "from Five a Clock to Eight in the Evening,"[1] but this proves nothing. *Love for Love* occupies the whole of two days. And nobody has even dreamed of a rule disallowing the time of a play's action to be coincident with that of performance. We merely object to the undeviating law which rigidly prescribes this so-called Unity.

With regard to the Unity of Place, it is obvious that the introduction of scenery and the advent of the picture-stage did much to nullify its authority and influence.

The Unity of Action which was soon narrowed down to the exclusion of any secondary plot whatsoever, never obtained upon the English stage. There are, indeed, many examples of plays which would entirely satisfy this definition, as *All for Love*, *The Orphan*, *The Siege of Damascus*, *The Revenge*, *Fatal Curiosity*, *Tancred and Sigismunda*, *Irene*, *Barbarossa*, *Douglas*, *The Mysterious Mother*, but the reason why these tragedies are so constructed is merely because the story they relate is best told by simple concentration upon one only theme. Dryden himself never showed the slightest indication of wishing to obey the ruling of this Renaissance fiction, as witness *Secret Love*, *Marriage A-la-Mode*, *Don Sebastian*, *Love Triumphant*, whilst in the Epistle Dedicatory before *The Spanish Fryar* he plainly writes: "*There are evidently two Actions in it: but it will be clear to any judicious man, that with half the pains I could have rais'd a Play from either of them: for this time I satisfied my own humour, which was to tack two Plays together; and to break a rule for the pleasure of variety. The truth is, the Audience are grown weary of continu'd melancholy Scenes: and I dare venture to prophesie, that few Tragedies except those in Verse shall succeed in this Age if they are not lighten'd with a course of mirth. For the Feast is too dull and solemn without the Fiddles.*" From this we can see that he was ill content to be bound by the fallacies of the French school, which none the less he frequently accepts in his critical dissertations, and by his complaisance he not unseldom involves himself in a curious imbroglio.

It were superfluous to trace the neglect and ultimate dismissal of the Three Unities in the eighteenth century, and it is hardly necessary to do more than refer to Dr. Johnson's famous attack upon these formalities with his defence of tragi-comedy (1765). Yet it is surprising how long the catch-word "Unities" lingered in circles that plumed themselves upon being literary and theatrical, who were the patrons rather than the lovers of the drama. As late as 1838 Mr.

[1] In Colley Cibber's second comedy, *Womans Wit: Or, The Lady in Fashion*, 4to, 1697, we have: "The Scene St. *James's*, and the Time of Action, Five Hours," but this is a mere accident. Cibber cared nothing for the Three Unities.

Curdle upon hearing of a new play could ask the author, "I hope you have preserved the unities, sir?" And when informed that the forthcoming piece was distinguished by abundance of incident, sprightly dialogue, strongly marked characters, and other qualities, he returned: "All unavailing without a strict observance of the unities, sir. The unities of the drama, before everything."

The latter part of *Of Dramatick Poesie, An Essay*, is occupied with Dryden's masterly defence of the use of rhyme in plays. The earliest blank verse, such as was employed by Sackville in *Gorboduc*, by Hughes and the Senecan school of tragedians, is a vehicle of extraordinary stiffness and unpliable to a degree. Even if the sense does not actually terminate with a line there is always evident a perceptible pause; there is no *enjambement;* and the result becomes a dull jog-trot, indescribably heavy and hobbling. Marlowe taught blank verse flexibility and supple strength, he gave it beauty; rare qualities eminently preserved by Jonson, Shakespeare, Beaumont, Webster, and Ford. The fertile Fletcher with his free distinction of pauses in the verse, his feminine endings, and characteristic redundancy of some emphatic monosyllable which cannot be slurred, added yet a new grace to the line, howbeit his example sanctioned, though it did not warrant, the beginnings of that careless ease which so swiftly and so readily degenerated into slackness and slipsloppery. In the hands of lesser men blank verse disintegrated. At the Restoration the flaccid and nerveless metre employed by writers such as Edward Howard, Sir William Lower, Meriton, Sir William Killigrew, and the author of *The Feign'd Astrologer*, has become completely inorganic. It is neither blank verse nor passable prose.

It was necessary that some constriction should promptly be imposed upon dramatic verse, and this was found in the restraint of rhyme. It is hard to see how any other course could have been adopted.

Dr. Johnson, writing with unfailing sound common sense, remarks in his *Life of Dryden* (1779): "Rhyme has been so long banished from the theatre that we know not its effects upon the passions of an audience." Happily this is no longer true, and at the production of *Marriage A-la-Mode* in 1920 the rhymed love-scenes between Leonidas and Palmyra, heroic couplets of exquisite beauty, delivered with sweetest harmony by a silver-tongued actor and actress,[1] enraptured the audiences with the spell of their lovely cadences and charm, amply proving that in practice upon the stage there is no verse more pleasing than the melody of dramatic rhyme.[2]

In 1668 when Sir Robert Howard published his drama *The Great Favourite; or, The Duke of Lerma*,[3] (quarto), in the address To the Reader, a most admirable and finely written piece of criticism, he found occasion to take a little notice of the "great pains the Author of an Essay of Drammatick Poesie has

[1] Mr. Murray Kinnell and Miss Rita Thom.

[2] It is perhaps worth noting that throughout a great part of the nineteenth century two of the most popular stage-forms were in rhyme ; the pantomime, and the burlesques of such prolific writers as William Brough, H. J. Byron, and Burnard. The fact is significant, although such inadequate and eccentric versifying must not be linked with Dryden's poetry. Nor is it permissible to do more than mention the fairy extravaganzas of Planché in this connexion.

[3] Produced at the Theatre Royal, Thursday 20th February, 1667–8.

taken, to prove Rhime as natural in a serious Play and more effectual than blank Verse." Howard's remarks upon the Three Unities are exceedingly sensible and most aptly to the point. He explains quite clearly "upon what ill grounds they dictate Lawes for *Dramatick Poesie*," and makes it evident "that there's no such thing as what they all pretend; for if strictly and duely weigh'd, 'tis as impossible for one stage to present two Houses, or two Roomes, truly, as two Countreys or Kingdomes; and as impossible that five houres, or four and twenty houres should be two houres and halfe as that a thousand houres or yeares should be less than what they are." The tone he adopts throughout is one of urbane sarcasm, and it must be confessed that the writer is quite emphatic that "I intend not to trouble myself nor the World any more in such subjects, but take my leave of these my two long acquaintances," which seems perhaps a little supercilious as if he were treating of trifles beneath his notice. Dryden, who was nettled by so perfunctory a tone, promptly retaliated with a vigorous, not to say incisive, *A Defence of an Essay of Dramatique Poesie, being an Answer to the Preface of the Great Favourite, or the Duke of Lerma*, which appeared in the second edition of *The Indian Emperour*, 1668. It was omitted, however, from all subsequent issues of the play,[1] and even if for the moment there was some slight personal friction between himself and his brother-in-law, the coolness was quite temporary.

In the last week of November, 1666, the theatres were reopened after their long silence, due to the terrible visitation of the Great Plague.

On Saturday, 2 March, 1666–7, was produced at the Theatre Royal, Bridges Street, Dryden's comedy *Secret Love: or, The Maiden Queen*.

The play proved a brilliant success, and here we have for the first time in full flower the pair of gay witty lovers, already adumbrated in Loveby and Lady Constance, a motif which Dryden was so happily to repeat in many an excellent comedy.[2] Primarily, it was, no doubt, owing to the inimitable acting of Hart and Nell Gwyn—whose comely face it may be remarked is precisely described in Act I, Scene 2—that *Secret Love* enraptured the Town, and these buoyant episodes have on all hands won unstinted praise, somewhat, it is to be feared, at the expense of the romantic scenes, which are truly beautiful, but which have scarcely been yet accorded their proper meed of admiration. The character of the Queen herself, in whose bosom royal dignity strives with hot human passion, finally stifled but not altogether overcome, has pathos and simple loveliness. Dryden well brings out the lonely grandeur and friendless sovereignty of the woman whose heart is breaking, and the scene where she reveals her passion to Philocles whilst he mistakes, thinking she speaks of Candiope, is managed with exquisite art.

[1] The Third Edition was quarto, 1670.

[2] In *The Censure of the Rota*, Oxford, 1673, is roughly jeered an incident which Dryden himself allows to be a little theatrical in its contrivance, "that indecency, committed in his *Mayden Queen*, when the *Queen* and Courtiers stand still, to hear *Celadon* and *Florimell* with a great deal of cold mirth absurdly *usurp* the Queens Prerogative in making new Marriage-Laws." This is absurdly and unfairly put, but he were a poor producer who could not most adroitly handle the situation, and make it very effective and without a jar upon the stage.

The plot, as Dryden points out in his Preface, "is founded on a Story of *Cyrus*, which he calls the *Queen of Corinth*, in whose character, as it has been affirm'd to me, he represents that of the famous *Christina*, Queen of *Sweden*."

In *Covent Garden Drolery*, 1672, there is printed an Epilogue, spoken by Nell Gwyn to a revival at the Theatre Royal (1669–70) of *The Knight of the Burning Pestle*, which commences:

> The Prologue durst not tell, before 'twas seen,
> The Plot we had to swinge the *Mayden Queen*.
> For had we, then, discover'd our intent,
> The Fop, who writ it, had not giv'n consent.

It is clear that there had been introduced (without Dryden's knowledge) some burlesque of *Secret Love* into the Beaumont and Fletcher revived play. I have no doubt the jest was good-humoured enough since the actors would never have been so foolish as to pasquin save in lightest mood one of the best pieces in their repertory.

From the time that he commenced dramatist Dryden had been intimately connected with the King's Company; he signed contracts and agreements on their behalf alongside Killigrew, Hart, Mohun, Lacy, Kynaston and other leading actors, as representing the government of their theatres;[1] he had indeed been specially engaged by them to provide three new plays a year, in consideration of which he "was admitted and continued as a sharer in the King's Playhouse for diverse years, and received for his share and a quarter three or four hundred pounds, *communibus annis*."[2]

However, his next play, *Sr Martin Mar-all, or The Feignd Innocence*, appeared at the rival theatre, Lincoln's Inn Fields, where it was produced on Thursday, 15 August, 1667. This was owing to the fact that *Sr Martin Mar-all* is to some extent based upon, or rather was suggested by, a bare translation of *L'Etourdi; ou, les Contre-Temps*, given to Dryden by William, Duke of Newcastle, a particular and most powerful patron of the Lincoln's Inn Fields Company, to whom he entrusted both of his post-Restoration plays, *The Humorous Lovers*[3] and *The Triumphant Widow*.[4] *Sr Martin Mar-all* is actually entered at Stationers' Hall (24 June, 1668) as the work of Newcastle, and it was not printed with Dryden's name on the title-page until the quarto of 1691.[5] Downes expressly says that the Duke gave his draft from Molière[6] to Dryden by whom it was adapted for the stage, and Pepys, who saw the second performance, notes "The Feign Innocence, or Sir Martin Marr-all; a play made by my Lord Duke of Newcastle, but, as every body says, corrected by Dryden." In reading this comedy, moreover, Dryden's hand, both in dialogue and method,

[1] Fitzgerald's *A New History of the English Stage*: 1882, vol. I, p. 139.
[2] Malone's *Life of Dryden*; Prose Works of John Dryden, vol. I, Part I, 1800, pp. 73–75.
[3] Acted at Lincoln's Inn Fields, March, 1667.
[4] Acted at Dorset Garden, November, 1674.
[5] The quartos have neither dedication nor preface.
[6] The "Famous *French* Poet *Monseur Moleire*," Downes.

is obvious throughout every scene, and it is only just to class it as wholly his work.

L'Etourdi[1] is founded upon an excellent comedy, *L'Inavvertito, overo Scappino Disturbato e Mezzettino Travagliato* by Nicolo Barbieri detto Beltrame, produced at Venice in the spring of 1629, and received with universal applause. It was printed in the summer of that year, "Per Angelo Salvadori Libraro a S. Moisè," and a second edition was called for in 1630. The dedication, dated 6 July, is addressed to Christine de France, Madame Royale, the daughter of Henri IV and Marie di Medici, who at thirteen years old was married in 1619 to Vittore Amedeo, Prince of Piedmont.[2] *L'Inavvertito*, which is in five acts, partakes largely of the *commedia dell' arte*. The scene is laid at Naples, the home of fantastic intrigue, and among the characters we have Pantalone, his son Fulvio; Scappino; Mezzettino, the slave merchant; and the typical braggadocio, the Sicilian Capitano Bellorofonte Martelione.[3] Molière's Lélie, however, is very different from Sir Martin Mar-all. As Emile Faguet pertinently remarks "Le principal personnage tient de l'étourdi proprement dit et du généreux, ce qui le rend très sympathique tout en le laissant plaisant . . . un personnage à la fois comique et digne d'affection, dont on rit et que l'on aime." Lélie is a gentleman and a gallant lover,[4] Sir Martin is a coxcomb and a clown. The reason why this character was broadened in its humour lies in the fact that Dryden wrote it for the celebrated low comedian James Nokes, whose performance in the part proved inimitable.[5]

Sir Martin Mar-all proved immensely popular,[6] and it is without doubt an excellent comedy. The quick yet natural succession of incident, the amusing battle of wits, the mistakes and counter-mistakes are contrived with exquisite felicity, and upon the stage these scenes assuredly act with extraordinary verve and spirit. Nor must Dryden's skill in having so completely anglicized his material be passed over without notice and our meed of admiration.

In Act V of *Sir Martin Mar-all* mention is made of Cambridge, and *Dorothy Draw-water*, the vintner's daughter at the *Rose*. To-day we lunch—and fare vastly well to boot—at the Hop Pole, Tewkesbury, and drink a glass, bottle ale, Madeira or port, to Mr. Pickwick, or maybe we spend a night at the Great White Horse, Ipswich, half expecting to meet Mr. Peter Magnus in a corridor or to stumble anon into the chaste chamber of Miss Witherfield, and it touches a warm sympathetic chord to find that Mr. Pepys and his party

[1] It would seem to owe little or nothing to *La Emilia* of Luigi Groto, 'icieco d Hadria" (1541–85), a French translation of which was published at Paris in 1619. Molière, however, seems to have taken a few hints from *Angelica*, a comedy of the Neapolitan poet Fabritio de Fornaris, which was published at Paris in 1585.

[2] She was left a widow on 7 October, 1637, and died at Turin 27 December, 1663.

[3] Molière at first played Mascarille in a black mask, and the very name is derived from *Maschera*. Later he preferred Sganarelle.

[4] In spite of Anselme's purse, and "S'il est ainsi, j'ai tort."

[5] "He Adapted the Part purposely for the Mouth of Mr. *Nokes*, and curiously Polishing the Whole." Downes.

[6] Downes emphasizes the fact that it was an outstanding financial success. "This, and Love in a Tub, got the Company more Money than any preceding Comedy."

visiting Cambridge on Tuesday, 8 October, 1667, "did take up at the Rose, for the sake of Mrs. Dorothy Drawwater, the Vintner's daughter, which is mentioned in the play of Sir Martin Mar-all."

Sir Martin Mar-all was printed quarto, 1668, and it is evident that alterations were made whilst the copy was passing through the press. The original leaves C1, C2, and H4 were cancelled, although there still exists a copy (possibly a unique exemplar)[1] which retains the original leaf C2 (pp. 11–12), carrying a page of conversation between Moody and Sir John Swallow, which shows that in the original version Moody made his appearance towards the conclusion of the first act (as we now have the play he does not enter until Act III). Sir Martin has offended the old Swashbuckler by a modish phrase, "Pardon me,"[2] and Sir John is at some pains to pacify the crusty Elizabethan.

It cannot but have been extremely mortifying to the King's House, especially after the great success of *Sr Martin Mar-all*, that yet another play in which Dryden had a considerable share should also have been produced at the rival theatre.

However, when he assisted Sir William Davenant in their famous alteration of *The Tempest*, this piece was naturally given at Lincoln's Inn Fields, the première being Thursday, 7 November, 1667.

Modern literary censure may regard this alteration of *The Tempest* decidedly askew, but theatrically it proved extremely effective. With some slight modifications indeed it kept the stage until well within the nineteenth century, and it was not until 13 October, 1838, that Macready, at Drury Lane, presented his sumptuous production "from the text of Shakespeare."[3]

In the provinces the alterations lingered till a still later date. Professor Dent in his *Foundations of English Opera*, 1928 (p. 147), writes: "I am indebted to the kindness of Mr. Bridges Adams for a copy of a playbill dated 23 July, 1845, announcing a performance of *The Tempest* in the Theatre at Southwell, in which not only Hypolito [*sic*] and Dorinda appear in the list of characters, but also Rosebud and Bluebell, two spirits whose names suggest that they belong to the same century as the performance."

No doubt much of the original popularity of *The Tempest, or The Enchanted Island*, was due to the music, the effects, the scenery and costumes.

The text of the Davenant and Dryden comedy was printed quarto, 1670, and it must be noted that there are two issues. It again reappears with some variants in the folio Dryden, 1701.

When Betterton looked around for a hand to transform *The Tempest, or The Enchanted Island*, into an opera, he fixed his choice upon Thomas Shadwell,

[1] In the possession of Mr. P. J. Dobell. I have not had access to this copy, and therefore I must refer the reader to *John Dryden Bibliographical Memoranda* by Percy J. Dobell, 1922, pp. 7–8. The cancelled passage is given on p. 30 as an appendix.

[2] Thus in *The Rehearsal*, acted 1671, II, 2, the Second King, who speaks French to show his breeding, exclaims: "Sweet, Sir, *Pardonnes moy*."

[3] None the less he omitted the words of the first scene on shipboard and gave a moving picture to open the play. Charles Kean in his production of *The Tempest*, 1 July, 1857, followed this example. The spectacle of the vessel foundering in the storm is said to have been very effective.

who was one of the principal dramatists attached to Dorset Garden, where his comedy *Epsom Wells* had been produced in December, 1672, with very great success. It was obvious that Dryden himself could not be approached to undertake the alteration as he was a Theatre Royal dramatist, and since *The Tempest* had been so largely the work of Davenant it was the property of the Duke's House, whilst the rivalry between the two companies continued unpeaceful and mistrusting. Shadwell, moreover, was a musician; he prided himself upon his mastery of the lute;[1] he was a close friend and eager pupil of the admired Pietro Reggio. Accordingly with much advertisement and lavish expenditure *The Tempest, or The Enchanted Island*, made into an opera by Mr. *Shadwell*, was produced at Dorset Garden, 30 April, 1674. I have, in another place, discussed the difficulties and discrepancies in connexion with this operatic version of *The Tempest* in amplest detail.[2]

To these vexed questions attention was first drawn by Dr. W. J. Lawrence in his article "Did Thomas Shadwell write an Opera on *The Tempest?*", *The Elizabethan Playhouse and other Studies* (I), and they have been discussed in detail by Dr. Lawrence, the late Mr. G. Thorn-Drury, and myself. It is now generally accepted that the quarto, 1670, represents the Dryden-Davenant alteration of the play *The Tempest, or, The Enchanted Island*, which was produced at Lincoln's Inn Fields on Thursday, November 7, 1667; whilst the quarto of 1674, which (except in the folio, 1701) has been included among Dryden's dramatic works, is indeed the operatic version of *The Tempest, or, The Enchanted Island* due to Shadwell.

This was emphatically the view of the late Mr. W. Barclay-Squire, one of the most learned and cautious of investigators, who has often expressed to me his wish that the problem of *The Tempest* might be laid to rest. However, the late Mr. Thorn-Drury held that Dryden himself was responsible for the operatic version of *The Tempest*, although he allowed that Shadwell may have lent a hand "as it proceeded on its successful career." Dr. Lawrence and myself, accepting Downes' explicit statement, argue that the operatic version is by Shadwell.

The author of *The Touch-Stone*[3]—said to be James Ralph[4]—writing in 1728 says in his first essay "Of Musick": "*Dryden* (who was one of our greatest criticks, as well as poets, and who has given us three *English* Operas in

[1] One of the sharpest hits in D'Urfey's *Sir Barnaby Whigg; or, No Wit Like a Woman's*, Drury Lane, early autumn of 1681, is when Benedick says of Sir Barnaby (Shadwell): "If I mistake not this fellow values himself extremely by playing on the Musick." "Oh, Yes," answers Wilding, "but the Town of late has us'd him so unkindly, that he has left it off, and now sets up for a grand Politician." In a satirical piece, "A Dialogue Between a *Yorkshire-Alderman* and *Salamanca-Doctor*, at the *Devil* by *Temple-Bar*. About Swearing," broadside, 1683, the company so fell by the ears that it was thought Satan had got among them, "but *Shad—ll* came in with his Lute, and allayed the Evil Spirit."

[2] In *Shadwell's Works*, by the present writer, Fortune Press, 1927, Vol. I; Introduction, pp. civ–cix.

[3] 8vo, 1728.

[4] 1705 (?)–1762.

a different taste) owns he could not, by the nicest scrutiny get any just Light, either as to the time, or the first Inventers of Operas."[1] Later, he speaks of the introduction, after the Restoration, of "Drammatick Operas, which were indeed regular Stage-Plays larded with pieces of occasional Musick, vocal and instrumental, proper to the Fable. . . . These were likewise embellished with scenes, Machines, *French* Dancing-Masters, long trains, and Plumes of feathers; of this sort were the *Faerie Queen and Tempest* alter'd from *Shakespeare; Dioclesian* and *Island Princess*, from *Beaumont* and *Fletcher;* Dryden's *Fall of Man;* never acted, and King *Arthur; D'Avenant's Circe; Granville's British Enchanters; Dennis's Rinaldo* and *Armida;* and *Durfey's Kingdom of the Birds*. These I believe were the principal if not the whole that appeared upon our Stages of this kind of Dramma; and, as I remember, during their Possession of the Stage, nothing was admitted in any other musical way, excepting *Dryden's Albion* and *Albanius;* which consisted altogether of Musick in Recitation and Airs; tho' I believe more after the *French* than *Italian Gou;* being set to Musick by a *Frenchman*."[2]

This passage is interesting, and although not of first importance is at least contributory evidence, since *The Tempest*, an Opera, is mentioned, but not ascribed to Dryden, who is regarded as the composer of three English Operas, *The State of Innocence; Albion and Albanius;* and *King Arthur*.

It has not, I think, before been remarked in this connexion that Sir John Hawkins, *A General History of Music*, Vol. IV (1776), Book IV, Chapter 2 (p. 394), definitely ascribes the operatic *Tempest* to Shadwell, and says that it was the success of this piece which inspired him to engage upon *Psyche*.

Sir William Davenant died at his house adjoining the Lincoln's Inn Fields' theatre, on Tuesday, 7 April, 1668, and on 13 April, six days later, was issued a "warrant for a grant to John Dryden of the Office of Poet Laureate, void by the death of Sir William Davenant."[3] On 19 May, 1668, Aubrey writes to Anthony à Wood, "Sir William was Poet Laureate,[4] and Mr. John Dryden hath his place." On 18 August, 1670, the post of historiographer royal was combined with the poet laureateship, the patent then issued conferring the one and confirming the other. "In consideration," runs one clause, "of the many good and acceptable services by John Dryden, Master of Arts and eldest sonne of Erasmus Dryden of Tichmarsh in the County of Northton Esquire to vs heretofore done and performed, and taking notice of the learning and eminent abilityes of him the said John Dryden and of his great Witt and elegant Style both in Verse and prose and for divers other good causes and consideracōns . . . (wee) doe nominate constitute declare and appoint him . . . our Poett Laureate and Historiographer Royall." The emolument for the two offices was "one

[1] *The Touch-Stone*, p. 3.

[2] *Ibid.*, p. 10.

[3] *Cal. State Papers, Dom.*; 1667–8, vol. viii, p. 341.

[4] It were superfluous here to inquire nicely into Davenant's exact official position. When the folio edition of Davenant was published in 1673, Herringman writes: "My Author was Poet Laureat to two Great Kings." Langbaine, *English Dramatick Poets*, Oxford, 1691 (p. 106), describes Davenant as "Poet *Laureat* to Two Kings." But after the Restoration Davenant received no salary from Charles II.

Annuity or yearely Pencon of two hundred pounds" together with "one butt or Pype of the best Canary Wyne."[1] It will be noted that the office of historiographer royal was not conferred upon Dryden until he had been laureate for more than two years, and it should be remarked that actually the pension of £200 was attached to the post of historiographer royal, whilst the laureateship was unsalaried. Since, however, he had held this office for two years without fees, the pension was in a Treasury Warrant of 1671 made retroactive to the date of his first appointment, in April, 1668. Later the usual pension of £100 a year, as paid to Jonson and Davenant,[2] was granted to Dryden. When this pension was confirmed by King James II, the prejudiced Macaulay asserted that the fees of the laureateship were a new bribe to induce the poet to declare himself a Papist.

The *Annus Mirabilis* had more than sufficiently demonstrated the abilities of our greatest poet laureate to fill that office, and indeed his two masterpieces of political satire, *Absalom and Achitophel* and *The Medal*, both written at the express desire of Charles II,[3] were certainly composed in the service of his royal master. Rightly considered, both *Tyrannick Love* and *The State of Innocence* could well be regarded as "official" plays. *Amboyna*, again, is certainly "official." Even these two magnificent poems, *Religio Laici* and *The Hind and the Panther*, might be held to be in some sense indicative of, although by no means inspired or dictated by, the poet's position. With regard to his responsibilities as historiographer royal, there could be no more vigorous exposure of the King's enemies than *The Duke of Guise*, and the subsequent *Vindication*, upon which followed the honour of His Majesty's command to translate Maimbourg's *History of the League*, 8vo, 1684.[4] We may also in this connexion remark his translation of *The Life of St. Ignatius*, 8vo, 1686,[5] and his *Defence of the Papers written by the late King of Blessed Memory, and Duchess of York*, 4to, 1686.[6] There are also, of course, the poems which are ostensibly panegyric, *Threnodia Augustalis;* "A Funeral-Pindarique Poem sacred to the Happy Memory of King Charles II," 4to, 1685, and *Britannia Rediviva;* "A Poem on the Birth of the Prince," folio, 1688.[7] Of their kind these are admirable,

[1] Patent Rolls, 21, Charles II, No. 3119, No. 6.

[2] Under Charles I, before the outbreak of the Great Rebellion.

[3] Tate tells us that it was Charles II who suggested *Absalom and Achitophel*; for *The Medal* see Spence's *Anecdotes*.

[4] Louis Maimbourg, S.J., 1610–86. Unfortunately this celebrated historian was tainted with Gallicanism, and in 1681 he was expelled from the Society of Jesus. Louis XIV, however, granted him a pension. His works, remarkable for the elegant style, were collected at Paris, 1686. Dryden's translation is advertised in *The Observator*, No. 172, Monday, 24 November, 1684, and also in *The London Gazette*, 4–8 December, 1684.

[5] *La Vie de St. Ignace*, Paris, 1679, by Dominique Bonhours, S.J., 1632–1702. Father Bonhours taught rhetoric at Paris, Tours, and Rouen.

[6] The book was published "By Command."

[7] The quarto edition with date, 1688, which is sometimes said to be a First Edition was, as a matter of fact, printed in 1691 to form part of Dryden's collected Works.

and inspired by the genius of a master celebrating momentous happenings in history.[1]

It was some satisfaction no doubt to Killigrew that the first play written by Dryden since his appointment as Poet Laureate should be given at the Theatre Royal, where, on 12 June, 1668, was produced that excellent comedy, *An Evening's Love; or The Mock Astrologer*, which was received with great favour. Curiously enough, the new piece was not much liked either by Pepys or by Evelyn; although the former was obliged to confess "the World commends" it. Mrs. Pepys told her husband that the intrigue of *An Evening's Love*, or, at least, that part of it which concerns Bellamy's passing as an astrologer, was taken from de Scudéry's *Ibrahim ou l'Illustre Bassa*, "the famous episode of the Marquis François," in the English translation, the second part, the second book, *The History of the Feigned Astrologer*. One Saturday Pepys went to the theatre, and the next afternoon when dinner was cleared away his wife read to him from *l'Illustre Bassa*, "the plot of yesterday's play, which is most exactly the same." Nevertheless, de Scudéry had only borrowed from the same source as Dryden, that is to say, from Calderon's *El Astrólogo Fingido* a *comedia* in three *jornadas*. Thomas Corneille turned Calderon's piece with a great deal of humour, retaining the title *Le Feint Astrologue*,[2] and this had already been translated into English as *The Feign'd Astrologer*, 4to, 1668, a somewhat arid version, which was almost certainly not performed in the theatre.

In Ariosto's *Il Negromante*, composed for the Roman Carnival of 1520, Maestro Jachelino, who holds the threads of the whole intrigue, is a quack and swindler, but he styles himself the Astrologer *par excellence:*

> Faccia professione di Philosopho,
> D'Alchimista, di Medico, di Astrologo,
> Di Mago, e di scongiurator' de spiriti.[3]

Again in Giordano Bruno's *Candelaio*,[4] the scene of which is laid at Naples, Scaramurè feigns himself an astrologer to further his plans.

Tauro Rafaele of the Infiammati, a literary Academy of Bitonto, wrote a *Falsa Astrologia Ovvero Il Sognar vegghiando*, which was published at Bitonto, 1669, second edition Naples, 1690, but this is from *La Vida es Sueño* not from *El Astrólogo Fingido*, whence, however, were derived *Il finto Astrólogo*, a comedy printed at Narni towards the end of the seventeenth century, and a second but different version, *Il finto Astrólogo*, 1763. Both these are anonymous.

Dryden was himself a profound student of the Astrological sciences, and he was accordingly able to turn his technical knowledge to good account in this play. In a letter, 3 September, 1697, written to his sons Charles and John, who

[1] To write "that one of the chief functions of the poet laureate was to compose masques and such-like pieces to be acted by the court" (Saintsbury, *Life of Dryden*, *English Men of Letters*, p. 69) is, of course, mere ignorance.

[2] *El Astrólogo Fingido* had previously been drawn upon by d'Ouville in *Jodelet Astrologue*, 1646.

[3] I quote from the Venice edition of *Il Negromante*, 1535.

[4] Printed Paris, 12mo, 1582.

were then at Rome, Dryden says: "Towards the latter end of this month, September, Charles will begin to recover his perfect health, according to his Nativity, which casting it myself, I am sure it is true, and all things hitherto have happened accordingly to the very time that I predicted them: I hope at the same time to recover more health, according to my age." Oldys in a MS. note upon this copy of Langbaine, further mentions that Dryden had great confidence in oneirocriticism. Many years after, Mrs. Elizabeth Thomas, whom Dryden had once dubbed Corinna, took advantage of her six months' acquaintance with the great poet to weave for Curll a romance around his memory. In the course of her imaginative lucubrations she has many wonderful things to tell of Dryden's trust in judicial astrology, his planetary schemes, and studies in the Almagest.[1]

An Evening's Love is a comedy full of situations which are intricate, yet coherent and never involved; of incidents which are vastly amusing, without once trenching upon the divertissement of farce. The dialogue is always elegant and easy; often brilliantly witty and humorous. The interest is not merely sustained, but rises until the very conclusion of the fifth act. It is, in fact, a lively piece of extraordinary merit. Henry Herringman, the bookseller, told Pepys that Dryden himself called it "but a fifth-rate play." This may be mere gossip, and it is altogether at variance with what he says in his Preface.[2]

It had more than once been suggested to Dryden that some compliment to Queen Catherine of Braganza would be very well received in the highest quarters, and indeed as England's poet laureate, he was in a sense by courtesy obliged to pay his respectful homage to the consort of his royal master. That the history of S. Catherine of Alexandria should have suggested itself is truly happy, although at the time this particular subject could hardly have failed to appeal to the imagination of the poet as extremely idoneous and appropriate. James Huysman, the celebrated "picture drawer," had painted a portrait of the Queen as S. Catherine, and it became the rage for ladies to pose for their portraits with the wheel and palm of martyrdom, the particular attributes of the Saint. Thus John Hales painted Lady Peters, Mrs. Pepys, and many more.[3] The Queen's Chapel at S. James's, which the Capuchin Fathers served, was much frequented;

[1] Although the technical terms may not be generally familiar, judicial astrology is still so widely believed in that one of the most popular Sunday newspapers devotes week by week considerable space to "What the Stars Tell," and this is not the least eagerly read portion of that journal.

[2] In Adam Elliot's *A Modest Vindication of Titus Oates . . . An Essay To Demonstrate Him only Forsworn in several Instances*, folio, 1682, the author gives some account of his captivity in Morocco, and this narrative contains an interesting allusion (p. 12), which shows how popular were those delightful songs which Dryden introduces into his comedies. Elliot writes: "I sat down with the Company, and compos'd my self to be as merry and agreeable as possibly I could; I sung several *English* Songs to them, particularly I remember *Calm was the Evening*, &c. in the *Mock-Astrologer*, which was new when I left *England;* they were wonderfully affected with it, and were very desirous to have me translate *ha ha ha*, &c. into *Spanish*, which made me laugh more heartily than I sung."

[3] Pepys, *Diary*, Thursday, 15 February, 1665-6.

by many, I fear, out of idle curiosity; and here the Feast of S. Catherine was observed with great solemnity.[1]

Dryden was a frequent attendant at the S. James' Chapel, and he would certainly have visited it on the twenty-first of November, the Queen's festa. The dramatic possibilities of the history of S. Catherine must have struck him forcibly, so he may have glanced at de Saint Germain's *Sainte Catherine* (1644), and he tells us he looked through *Le Martyre de Sainte Caterine*, a tragedy in prose (1643) by that extraordinary creature, Puget de La Serre,[2] the most prolific and most ridiculous of French dramatists, of whom it was said that books only cost him "la peine de les escrire ou de les dicter."[3] His facts Dryden derived from Symeon Metaphrastes, Συμεὼν ὁ μεταφράστης,[4] who is to be identified with Symeon Magister the Logothete,[5] the author of a chronicle under Nicephorus Phocas (963–69).[6] Symeon Metaphrastes, one of the most famous of Greek medieval writers, is the principal compiler of the lives of the Saints in the *Menologia* of the Byzantine Church.[7]

Some who heard the title of Dryden's new tragedy *Tyrannick Love*, at once jumped to the conclusion that he was going to give an alteration of Georges de Scudéry's famous *L'Amour Tyrannique* acted at Paris in 1638; 4to, 1639; which had been put forward as a rival to *Le Cid.*[8] Dryden had never even seen the play, and as I show in my Note upon the Source of *Tyrannick Love*, *L'Amour Tyrannique* differs in every respect from the English tragedy.

Our author tells us that he employed no more than seven weeks upon his Poem, a feat which if not unparalleled is at least extraordinary.

It would appear that Dryden was occupied in writing *Tyrannick Love; or, The Royal Martyr*, in February and March, 1669, and immediately delivered

[1] The Queen's actual birthday, 15 November, was *seculari modo* made the occasion of "fine fireworks" and "an extraordinary appearance of gallantry at Whitehall." See Evelyn, *Diary*, *s.d.* 15 November, *ann.* 1668, 1672, 1684.

[2] This hack was born, according to the Frères Parfaict (VI, 150), at Toulouse "*vers* 1600"; according to his own account, in 1593 or 1594. After much adventuring he was appointed librarian to Gaston d'Orléans. He died in 1665. Guéret, *Le Parnasse reformé*, Paris, 1671 (p. 47), avers he wrote more than 100 volumes; Tallemant, *Historiettes*, VI (240–244), says 60 volumes. In an amusing burlesque of the *Cid*, the *Chapelain décoiffé*, de la Serre as Chimène's father boasts:

> Chaque heure, chaque instant, fait sortir de ma plume
> Cahiers dessus cahiers, volume sur volume.

Yet Richelieu assisted three times at his *Thomas Morus* (published 1642), and the crowd at the first performance was so vast that four door-keepers were crushed to death (Guéret). Puget de la Serre wrote entirely in prose, save for a few copies of occasional verse.

[3] *Pompe funèbre de Scarron*, Paris, 1660 (p. 21).

[4] μετάφρασις; compilation.

[5] A Secretary of State, with the title *Magister*.

[6] Ehrard, *Symeon Metaphrastes u. die griechische Hagiographie*, in the *Röm. Quartalschrift* (1897), 531–53.

[7] There is an important Latin translation from Metaphrastes by Lippomannus, *Vita SS. priscorum Patrum*, Venice, vols. v-vii, 1556–58.

[8] *L'Amour Tyrannique* followed the *Sentiments de l'Academie sur le Cid.*

the script to the actors, but as he tells us in the Preface to the printed play his tragedy was "afterwards hindered by many accidents from a speedy Representation." What one—and not the least—of these accidents which caused such delay happened to be is known from an interesting Chancery suit which has been printed by Mr. Hotson.[1]

Tyrannick Love, we learn, was produced at the Theatre Royal in the last week of June 1669, and proved a tremendous success, crowding the house for fourteen days, a most notable run.

The Old Batchelour had a run of fourteen successive nights, and that was accounted phenomenal. In a satirical play, *The Female Wits; or A Triumvirate of Poets at Rehearsal,*[2] Calista (Mrs. Trotter) proclaims that in her opinion the new play she has written will be acted for fifteen or sixteen nights. "Why, Madam," exclaims Mrs. Wellfed (Mrs. Pix), "that will be a night longer than *The Old Batchelour.*" In 1695 *Love for Love* "being extraordinary well acted took 13 days successively." "*The Mourning Bride* had such success, that it continu'd acting uninterrupted 13 days together."

In forty years there is recorded only one play, a revival of *King Henry VIII*, which drew packed houses on account of the elaborate production, the crowds, the dresses, the scenes, which ran longer than *Tyrannick Love*, and that was but one day; there is recorded only one play, *The Old Batchelour*, the run of which equalled that of *Tyrannick Love.* It is well to insist upon this point, as the immense and deserved popularity of Dryden's plays is often slurred or forgotten.

Of the Prologue and the Epilogue, Dryden was the completest master, and perhaps there are few epilogues more famous in the English Theatre than that which he furnished to *Tyrannick Love.* Valeria, the Emperor's daughter, acted by Nell Gwyn,[3] had killed herself for love, and when the curtain descended at the conclusion of the Fifth Act she lay on the apron, when according to the custom of the day, presently appeared the bearers to carry the body within. Leaping to her feet she saluted one of these gentry with a box o' the ear, and announced her intention of speaking the epilogue. In Buckingham's *Works*, 1714, Vol. II, is an excellent illustration of the scene, which I reproduced in my edition of *The Rehearsal*, 1914. This sudden turn enraptured the audience, and many are the allusions to this resuscitation. Thus the Epilogue to *Piso's Conspiracy*, produced at Dorset Garden in the winter of 1675, 4to, 1676, and spoken by Poppea, whom Nero has killed in Act IV, commences:

> *It is a trick of late grown much in vogue,*
> *When all are killed, to raise an epilogue,*
> *This some pert Rhymer wittily contriv'd,*
> *For a surprize, whilst the Arch Wag believed;*
> *'Twould please you to see Pretty* Miss *revived.*

[1] *The Commonwealth and Restoration Stage*, 1928; pp. 250–253; and Appendix, pp. 348–355. See further the Theatrical History prefixed to the play.

[2] 4to, 1704; but acted some six or eight years earlier.

[3] Mr. Saintsbury, who apparently had not read the play, speaks of "The part of St. Catherine (very inappropriately allotted to Mrs. Eleanor Gwyn)." *Dryden, English Men of Letters*, 1881, p. 44.

But, Gentlemen, the case is alter'd now,
We may be dead,—and Damned too for all You:
And therefore, just as my poor Ghost came down,
All the Elizian *Shades began to frown;*
Told me that I must there expect no Grace,
Till I return'd to you, and made my Peace.

The great success of *Tyrannick Love* naturally encouraged Dryden to essay a tragedy of the same kind, that is a drama written in heroic verse, and for his subject he was most happily inspired to select the siege and conquest of Granada, an event of the first importance in European history. Such a chronicle would afford the poet every opportunity of introducing those conflicts of love and honour, those romantic episodes of chivalry and knightly arms, those quick variations of fortune and chance, which both sustain the quick eager interest of gallant pageantry and admit of the tense devotion and amorous idolatries of lovers to whom their flames are more than sceptres. In fact, *The Conquest of Granada* proved so fruitful and procreant a theme that Dryden was led to write his play in two parts;[1] which resemble the *journées* of French *tragi-comédie.*

The genius of Dryden never blazed brighter than in *The Conquest of Granada*, and he who cannot appreciate and admire these scenes can have no conception of Dryden's poetic powers, can form no worthy opinion of Dryden as a dramatist.

It should be remarked with what skill Dryden has presented the character of Mohammed Boabdelin; he wins our sympathy, and in spite of a jealousy which is weak, capricious, and, once at least, entirely despicable, the unhappy king, whose throne is fast tottering to its ruin, who loves deeply where he knows he is not loved again, where cold duty and not affection rules, is a figure that awakes our compassion, a compassion he would fiercely reject, so helpless is he, in spite of his royal state, so destined and doomed to humiliation he did not deserve but cannot avoid. Almahide, radiantly beautiful in her tender womanhood, walks through the play with gentle grace; whilst the lovers, Osmyn and Benzayda, have the fragrance and the charm of a day in early spring, when the breath of woodland flowers and new life is in the air. So delicate and ingenuous are they that the superb and traitorous wanton, Lyndaraxa, almost overshadows them as she weaves her subtle schemes; evil, fickle, and siren fair. Chaste, coldly chaste she is no doubt, since she knows that virginity has its price in the mart, nor will she let her jewel lightly go, but her mind is that of a harlot, who auctions for the highest bid, and she games for no less than a sovran diadem. Her last words as she falls stabbed by her lover's hand, are sublime in their thirst for power, ambition even death can neither quench nor quell.

Almanzor is magnificently audacious. He is a hero of the realms of romance.

[1] This was imitated by Crowne in his *The Destruction of Jerusalem by Titus Vespasian.* Two parts, 4to, 1677. In a letter prefixed to the *Works of the Earls Of Rochester, Roscommon, and Dorset, Etc.*, London, 2 vols., 1731, and supposed to have been written to the Duchess of Mazarin by St. Evremond, it is said that "Mr. *Crowne's Destruction of Jerusalem* . . . met with as wild and unaccountable success as Mr. Dryden's *Conquest of Granada*" (II, p. 218).

His splendid arrogance justifies itself; at least it is justified by Dryden's peerless verse. His stature surely fits Moorish Granada, and the ideal chivalry of Catholic Spain, albeit his speech is blazoned with many quarterings.

The first part of *The Conquest of Granada* was produced at the Theatre Royal very shortly before Christmas, 1670.

The second part followed on Tuesday, 9 January, 1671, as we learn from a letter addressed by Lady Mary Bertie to her niece, Katharine Noel, then at Exton. 1670 (–71), January 2. Westminster. . . .[1], "There is lately come out a new play writ by Mr. Dreyden who made the *Indian Emperour*. It is caled the *Conquest of Grenada*. My brother Norreys tooke a box, and carry'd my Lady Rochester and his mistresse and all us to(o), and on Tuesday we are to goe see the second part of it which is then the first tim acted. I am suere you would bee with us if wishes could bring you. My sister Osborne and all heare are well and all my brothers. Here was the Duke of Buckingham and a grate deale of company din'd here to-day." In Lady Bertie's last previous letter, 10 December, 1670, no mention is made of Part I.

Mrs. Evelyn, in a letter written in the spring of 1671 to Dr. Ralph Bohun, Fellow of New College, Oxford, who had recently gone into residence, proffers some silly remarks on Dryden's piece: "since my last to you, I have seen 'The Siege of Granada,' a play so full of ideas that the most refined romance I ever read is not to compare with it; love is made so pure, and valour so nice, that one would imagine it designed for an Utopia rather than our stage. I do not quarrel with the poet, but admire one born in the decline of morality should be able to feign such exact virtue; and as poetic fiction has been instructive in former ages, I wish this the same event in ours. As to the strict law of comedy, I dare not pretend to judge: some think the division of the story not so well as if it could have been comprehended in the day's actions: truth of history, exactness of time, possibilities of adventures, are niceties the ancient critics might require; but those who have outdone them in fine notions may be allowed the liberty to express them their own way, and the present world is so enlightened that the old dramatic must have no sway." The lady seems to hanker after the unities which she acknowledges she does not understand; and her Critique, such as it is, has many symptoms of feminine contrariety. The letter none the less is interesting if only as evidence of the immense popularity of *The Conquest of Granada*, since so starch and precisian a huswife as Madam Evelyn had sufficient curiosity to assist at a performance.

It was, further, played by amateurs of quality, of whose buskin'd attempts there is no detailed record. But in *Thomas Shipman's Carolina, or Loyal Poems*, 1683, we find (p. 190): "The Huffer, 1677, spoken by Ant. Eyre, Esquire, *and dedicated to the right Honourable, the Lady* Roos, *when he acted* Almanzor *in the* Granada, at Belvoir; *in way of Prologue*," also another poem (p. 191), "The Representation, 1677. *Upon the Honourable Mrs.* Bridget Noel, *acting the Part of* Almahide, in Dryden'*s* Granada, *at Belvoir*."

The prologue to the First Part of *The Conquest of Granada* is especially famous. It was "Spoken by Mris. *Ellen Guyn* in a broad-brim'd hat, and wastbelt," a head-gear and cincture which ridiculed an extravagant costume

[1] Hist. MSS., Com. XII, App. 5 (Rutland), p. 22.

worn by Nokes of the Duke's House, when he played Sir Arthur Addle in Caryl's *Sir Salomon, or the Cautious Coxcombe*, at Dover, during the visit to the brother of Madame, the Duchess of Orleans. Downes in his *Roscius Anglicanus* thus relates the event: "our company were commanded to *Dover*, in *May*, 1670. The King with all his court, meeting his sister, the Duchess of *Orleans* there. This Comedy, *The Sullen Lovers*, and *Sir Solomon Single*, pleased Madam the Dutchess, and the whole Court extremely. The *French* wearing then Excessive short Lac'd Coats; some scarlet, some Blew, with Broad wast Belts; Mr. *Nokes* having at that time one shorter than the *French* Fashion, to Act Sir *Arthur Addle* in; the Duke of *Monmouth* gave Mr. *Nokes* his sword and belt from his Side, and Buckled it on himself, on purpose to ape the *French:* That Mr. *Nokes* lookt more like a Drest up ape, than Sir *Arthur:* Which upon his first Entrance on the Stage, put the King and Court to an Excessive laughter; at which the *French* look'd very shaggrin, to see themselves Ap'd by such a buffoon as Sir *Arthur:* Mr. *Nokes* kept the Dukes Sword to his dying day."

The tables, however, were completely turned when Nell Gwyn appeared in a hat whose brim had the circumference of a cart-wheel, and a cestus as wide as Sahara. In an unpublished lampoon,[1] "Horace Lib. I, The Second Satyr," occurs the following allusion to this celebrated hat:

> Who Noke's Wheel broad brim deride,
> Cock up their own, scarce half-crown wide,
> If Penthouse Hat more wit excess,
> Too narrow's comical no less.

As might have been expected, the great success of *Tyrannick Love*, followed by the equally enthusiastic reception of *The Conquest of Granada*, stirred up the meanest jealousies of the smaller fry.

At Oxford in 1673 was printed "The Censure of The Rota *On* Mr. Dryden's *Conquest of Granada*," a dull diatribe of one-and-twenty pages. When the writer has dragged up the "Elegy on Oliver," jeered at the "representation of *big-bellied Men*" in the *Wild Gallant*—"that incomparable clenching comedy;" condemned the use of the supernatural in poetry; asserted that the descriptions are "borrowed from *Statius and Montaign's* Essays, the Reason and Politicall Ornaments from *Mr. Hobs*, and the Astrologicall (and if need be the Language too) from *Ibrahim*, or the Illustrious Bassa," he appears to think that hiccus doccius! presto! he has done the trick.

The authorship of this lampoon has been ascribed to Richard Leigh, a younger son of Edward Leigh, of Rushall, Staffs. Leigh entered Queen's College, Oxford, in Lent term, 1666, and proceeded B.A. on 19 June, 1669. He is said later to have become an actor at the Duke's House, but this I believe to be an error. In any case his heavily-shod prose plouters with neither wit nor elegance to imp its wing.

A few weeks after this Oxford quiz had vented his puny spleen there was published "A Description Of The Academy of The Athenian Virtuosi: With *A* discourse *held there in Vindication of Mr.* Dryden's Conquest of Granada;

[1] Bodleian; Rawl. MS. Poet. 159; No. 67.

Against the Author of the Censure of the Rota," London, 4to, 1673. The writer very agreeably rallies the *Censure of the Rota*, "which," says he, "I lightly read over, for it deserv'd little consideration. Indeed I was surpriz'd at the indiscretion of the Author to venture his poor thinn Off-spring to seek its Fortune in cold winter weather, but especially in such a dangerous time, when there was great need of wast Paper. . . . Poor Author he imagin'd no harm, he only made use of the *Saturnalia*, as Servants used to doe, make bold with his betters, and so forth." Without entering into any detailed examination of this clever little pamphlet it is perhaps sufficient to say that here we have a complete answer to the silly squib which occasioned it.

"The Friendly Vindication of Mr. Dryden From the Censure of the Rota By His Cabal of Wits," Cambridge, 4to, 1673, would from the title also purport to be a reply to *The Censure of the Rota*, but in fact it is an equally ungenerous and scurril attack upon the poet. Here not only *The Conquest of Granada* but also *Marriage A-la-Mode* and *The Assignation* are lewdly censured: "As for his Comedy, it was objected by some, that it was as great an offence to good Morality, as his *Maximin* was to Christianity. That his *Marriage A la Mode*, and his *Love in a Nunnery*, were most excellent Collections of *Bawdery*. . . . But perhaps Mr. *Dryden* conceives of the success of Plays, as *Martial* did of some Licentious Writings of his:

Non possunt sine mentula placere,[1]

or which is all one, the *Dildo* of Mr. *Drydens* Muse, so neatly applied to the females of the Town."

To this buffoon banter Charles Blount, the deist, smartly retaliated with "Mr. *Dreyden* vindicated in a Reply to the Friendly Vindication of Mr. *Dreyden*," 4to, 1673, an admirable defence of Dryden, which, published anonymously, administered a severer jobation than the wit-worms could willingly stomach or sustain.

It will not be unfitting here to give a few words to the most famous attack upon heroic plays in general and upon Dryden in particular. There was at the court of Charles II a literary cabal of the strictest Jonsonians, centring round the Duke of Buckingham, who "it seems, conversed with Ben when his Grace was a boy of about thirteen, and the poet was near his grand climacterique, and thence conceived such a veneration for him, that it never left him afterwards."[2] It was they who crowded the playhouses to applaud every line of Jonson, to admire each scene. Their ideal tragedies were *Sejanus* and *Catiline*, and they could hardly bear that any other poet should attempt to wear the buskin. It was owing to their efforts that a very expensive and very splendid revival of *Catiline* was staged at the Theatre Royal on Friday, 18 December, 1668. "The Duke of Buckingham and Lord Dorset were admirers of Jonson to a degree of idolatry; it is very probable that by liberal promises, they encouraged the actors to bring forward this forgotten tragedy."[3] To them "the most severe of Johnson's sect" the heroic drama with its romance and its ideals must have appeared

[1] I, XXXVI, 5.
[2] Davies, *Dramatic Miscellanies*, 3 vols, 1783; vol. II, p. 94.
[3] *Ibid.*, p. 88.

wellnigh a negation of all they held most sacrosanct in the theatre and in literature. The Master had in his *Poetaster* flagellated the writers of his day, who were not of his school, and Buckingham also determined to arraign the contemporary dramatists, to ridicule and blast them in a "Comicall Satyre."

In consequence, on 7 December, 1671, at the Theatre Royal, was produced *The Rehearsal*,[1] in which Dryden was caricatured as the central figure, the poetaster, Mr. Bayes. It is hardly necessary to enter into a detailed history of the first conception of this burlesque, how at first Sir Robert Howard was to have been scarified as Robert Bilboa, and how when, after the Great Plague had hindered and delayed the original production, Bilboa became Bayes, the laureate, the most important figure in the world of letters, whose genius was so largely devoted to heroic tragedy.

It would, however, be paying Buckingham far too high a compliment to suppose that *The Rehearsal* came from his pen alone. Thomas Sprat, afterwards Dean of Westminster and Bishop of Rochester, Martin Clifford, afterwards Master of the Charterhouse; and it is said Butler, Waller, and Cowley, all lent their aid. It skills not to inquire here exactly which points in the parody may be due to Butler; which scene may be traced to Clifford, which to Sprat. Various lampoons, of which several may be found in the collection conveniently called *Poems on Affairs of State*, speak of the heterogeneous authorship of *The Rehearsal* as well known and undisguised; thus one ballad has:

> With help of Pimps, plays, and table chat,
> And the advice of his own canonical *Sprat*,
> And his family scribe antichristian *Mat*,
>
> With transcribing of these and transversing those,
> With transmitting of Rhyme and transversing Prose,
> He has dressed up his Farce with other mens Cloathes.

Another writer says:

> I confess the Dances are very well writ,
> And the Time and the Tune by *Haines* are well set.

In *The Duke of Buckingham's Litany* the following petition occurs:

> From owning twenty other men's Farce,
> *Libera Nos.*

Of the original actors in *The Rehearsal* we only know that Cartwright doubled Thunder (in the mock Prologue) and the Second King of Brentford; Kynaston played Volscius;[2] and Mrs. Reeve, Amaryllis; whilst Lacy, specially

[1] See *The Rehearsal*, by the present editor. The Shakespeare Head Press, 1914.

[2] The speech of Volscius in *The Rehearsal*, Act III, 5, occurs in a MS. with the heading: "On the humour in Mr Howards Play, where Mr Kinaston disputes his staying in, or going out of Town, as he is pulling on his Boots. In Imitation of the Earle of Orrery." (Bodley MS. Eng. poet. e. 4.) The play in question by James Howard is *The English Mounsieur*.

trained by Buckingham, created Bayes. Not only are Dryden's plays caricatured; the turn of his speech and his phrases are reproduced, there are frequent references to his own personal tastes, such as his liking for stewed plums, his fondness for snuff, and, as we have already remarked, even his amour with Ann Reeve is alluded to in very unmistakeable terms. Theatrical tradition has it that Lacy made up closely to resemble the laureate, whose tones and gait he mimicked, dressing the character in a suit of black velvet, such as Dryden chiefly affected.

Spence in his *Anecdotes* (ed. 1820, pp. 102–103) reports from Lockier, "It is incredible how much pains he (Buckingham) took with one of the actors to teach him to speak some passages in Bayes's part in *The Rehearsal* right. The vulgar notion of that play's being hissed off the first night is a mistake."

"I have heard, indeed," writes Davies,[1] "that the Duke of Buckingham and the Earl of Dorset prevailed on Dryden to accompany them, in the boxes, on the first night of acting the Rehearsal; and placed the poet between them to enjoy the feelings of his mind during the exhibition of his own picture. The peculiarities of Dryden, when he instructed the players, seem to be strongly marked throughout the piece."[2]

The fact that *Marriage A-la-Mode*, which was produced about Easter, 1672, is plainly parodied in *The Rehearsal*, 4to, 1672; but first performed December, 1671, has caused some confusion. Yet there is no difficulty here. When *The Rehearsal* was originally given there could not, of course, have been any allusion to *Marriage A-la-Mode*, but the script of the burlesque was in a fluid state, that is to say modifications were constantly being allowed and additions made. *The Rehearsal* is entered in the *Term Catalogues*, Trinity, 24 June, 1672, and thus there would be ample opportunity before the quarto was published for Buckingham to have written in a bob or two at Dryden's latest play, and this indeed is exactly what happened; just as he wrote in some crude satire of *The Assignation*, parody which first occurs in the third (and best) Edition of *The Rehearsal* "with amendments and large Additions by the Author," 4to, 1675.[3]

Dryden did not immediately reply to the attack. It would have been impolitic, not to say highly dangerous, to have retaliated, for that blackguard libertine, His Grace of Buckingham, was more than capable of a riposte from which the poet might deem himself lucky if he escaped with life and limb. The revenges taken by these fine gentlemen, and ladies too if vexed at some disrespect or biting scomm, were notorious.

[1] *Dramatic Miscellanies*, 1783, vol. III, pp. 289–90.

[2] With regard to the theatrical history of *The Rehearsal*, Lacy was succeeded by Joe Haines. The mimic Estcourt, Theophilus Cibber, and Foote were much admired in this rôle. Colley Cibber even excelled Garrick, in the opinion of Walpole who judged that the Bayes of Garrick was "Entertaining, but it was a Garreteer-bard. Old Cibber preserved the solemn coxcomb; and was the caricature of a great poet, as the part was designed to be." The place of Buckingham's farce has been largely usurped by Sheridan's tamer copy. But "the water of *The Critic* is a mean thing to place beside the strong wine of *The Rehearsal*."

[3] Actually in *The Defence of the Epilogue* that follows *The Conquest of Granada*, Part II, 4to, 1672, Dryden compliments Buckingham upon his excellent alteration of *The Chances*.

INTRODUCTION

It was His Grace of Buckingham who killed the Earl of Shrewsbury in a duel at which Lady Shrewsbury was present in the disguise of a page. When her husband fell, the lady rushed forward and embraced the Duke all clotted and spattered with the poor cuckold's blood. Truly Dryden did well to wait, even if he winced under *The Rehearsal.*

His opportunity, however, was to come, and more than amply did he repay Buckingham by the portrait of Zimri in *Absalom and Achitophel*, drawn with the fullest power of his brilliant genius. In the Dedication to his *Juvenal*, 1693 (p. lii), Dryden himself remarks: "The Character of *Zimri* in my *Absalom*, is, in my Opinion, worth the whole Poem: 'Tis not bloody, but 'tis ridiculous enough. And he for whom it was intended was too witty to resent it as an injury."

It is true that *Political Reflections On A Late Poem Entituled, Absalom and Achitophel, by a Person of Honour*, folio, 1682, is generally ascribed to Buckingham,[1] but actually is certainly not from his pen. Wood, whose views on the authorship of similar pieces are very erroneous, seems to be the authority for this ascription, but his statement is vague and ambiguous. "However it was, sure I am that the Duke of Bucks did not cause him (Dryden) to be beaten, but wrote, or caused to be wrote, *Reflections on the said Poem called Absalom and Achitophel*, which being printed on a sheet of paper,[2] was, tho' no great matter in it, sold very dear."[3]

As to the name Bayes, Dryden did not value the banter a rush; it stuck to him, and in some sense he even recognised it, writing in the Epilogue to *All for Love; or, The World Well Lost*, 4to, 1678:

For our poor wretch, he neither rails nor prays,
Nor likes your wit just as you like his plays;
He has not yet so much of Mr. Bays.

In the *Vindication of the Duke of Guise*, 4to, 1683 (p. 22), he says: "Much less am I concerned at the noble name of *Bayes;* that's a *Brat* so like his own *Father*, that he cannot be mistaken for any other body." In the Dedication to the *Juvenal*, folio, 1693 (p. iv), he further remarks, "I answer'd not the *Rehearsall*, because I knew the Author sate to himself when he drew the Picture, and was the very Bays of his own Farce."

Dean Lockier is the authority for the following, related in Spence's *Anecdotes.*[4] Dryden allowed *The Rehearsal* to have a good many strokes in it "though so severe (added he) upon myself; but I can't help saying that Smith and Johnson are two of the coolest, most insignificant fellows I ever met with on the stage."

"The greatness of Dryden's reputation," said Dr. Johnson, "is now the only

[1] e.g. by Malone; *Life of Dryden*, vol. I, 1800, p. 157, by Sir Walter Scott (*Life of John Dryden,* Works, vol. I, seconded 1821, pp. 253–4) and Lady Burghclere (*George Villiers*, 1903, pp. 266.)

[2] This is incorrect. It is a folio, 9 leaves.

[3] A copy exists with a contemporary inscription "By Esquire Howard," and it is probable Edward Howard was the author.

[4] Edition 1820: Arranged with notes by Malone.

principle of vitality which keeps the duke of Buckingham's play from putrefaction."[1]

It cannot be too strongly and persistently emphasized that although London laughed at and applauded *The Rehearsal*, although Buckingham's burlesque held the stage until the beginning of the nineteenth century, and, as we have seen, not a few actors of the first rank—Haines, Estcourt, Colley Cibber, Garrick, Foote, Henderson, King, Farren—strutted and mimicked and gagged as Mr. Robert Bayes, actually this travesty so far from inflicting a death-blow upon the heroic play, as has ineptly been pretended, entirely failed if its object was seriously to damage and to scuttle the heroic drama. Men shook with mirth one night at Drawcansir, the two Kings of Brentford and Lardella's funeral, but the next night they sat in rapt attention to hear Almanzor and Almahide, jealous Boabdelin, Lyndaraxa, and her lovers twain.

The Indian-Queen was drawing crowded houses five-and-twenty years after the production of *The Rehearsal*, and was being played at least as late as 1715; *The Indian Emperour* kept the stage with unbated popularity, and had a great success at Goodman's Fields in January, 1734; *Tyrannick Love* remained in the theatrical repertory for at least thirty years; *The Conquest of Granada* was frequently acted during the reign of Queen Anne, but it must be remembered that a play in two parts presents especial difficulties, and so elaborate a production entailed great expense; Wilks and Mrs. Oldfield were sustaining Aureng-Zebe and Indamora at Drury Lane in December, 1721. Even if we turn to the heroic plays of other writers we shall find that they were long received with great favour. Thus Crowne's *The Destruction of Jerusalem*, Part II, was revived at Drury Lane by the summer company in July, 1712; Lee's *Sophonisba, or Hannibal's Overthrow*, which draws its plot from Orrery's *Parthenissa* rather than from history, and enjoyed frequent revivals, was acted at Lincoln's Inn Fields in March, 1735; at Drury Lane in July, 1708, Booth (Crimalhaz) and Mrs. Porter (Morena) were appearing in Settle's famous *Empress of Morocco*; Otway's *Don Carlos*, also at this House in the same year, drew large audiences to applaud the Carlos of Booth and the Queen of Mrs. Porter.

In no way did *The Rehearsal* minify the popularity and prestige of the heroic play.

Unhappily, a most disastrous accident now went near to ruin the fortunes of Killigrew's Company, and proved in effect their final undoing. Between seven and eight o'clock on Thursday evening, 25 January, 1671–2, a fatal fire broke out destroying the Theatre Royal, Bridges Street, and causing terrible damage.[2] The conflagration, which began under the stairs at the back of the house, burned down at least half the building together with the entire stock of scenery and costumes. Thence the flames spread swiftly to the adjacent houses, and before they could be checked by demolishing with gunpowder a portion of

[1] *Anecdotes of the late Samuel Johnson, LL.D.*, by Hesther Lynch Piozzi (1786): ed. Cambridge, 1925 (p. 39).

[2] *Reliquiae Baxterianæ*, folio, 1696, Part III, pp. 89–90 (198): "And this *Jan.* 1671. The King's Play-house in *Drury Lane* took Fire, and was burnt down, but not alone, for almost fifty or sixty Houses adjoyning, by Fire and blowing up, accompanied it." Cf. also Hist. MSS. Commission, Second Report (1871), Appendix, p. 22.

Russell Street and Vinegar Yard, damage more than £20,000 was done. Young Richard Bell, a most promising and talented actor, perished.[1]

The company, in great distress, was now obliged to seek a temporary home at Lincoln's Inn Fields (the Lisle's Tennis Court theatre), which some eleven weeks previously had been vacated by the Duke's men upon their removal to a new and splendid house at Dorset Garden. Here Hart and his fellows with borrowed costumes and make-shift scenes commenced under the most pitiful conditions on 26 February, 1671–2, when *Wit without Money* was very appropriately given. The King made a point of being present, and Michael Mohun, who acted Valentine, spoke a Prologue[2] written for the occasion by Dryden. And here the hapless players perforce remained until their new Theatre Royal had been built, where they opened on 26 March, 1674.

It was necessary that any and every novelty which might attract audiences should be essayed. None the less, they were obliged largely to depend upon revivals, and in order to lend a piquancy to this fare several favourite pieces, including *Philaster* and *Secret Love*, were acted by the women alone. Meanwhile Dryden was hard at work upon a new play, which luckily was to prove a triumphant success, and thus went far to recover their fallen fortunes and cheer their drooping spirits. It was suggested by Sir Walter Scott[3] that the more serious episodes of Dryden's *Marriage A-la-Mode*, which is described in the first quarto, 1673[4] as "A Comedy," may have originally been intended for a heroic drama, but that the poet, writing in the full flush of the effect of Buckingham's burlesque, chequered the verse romance with those sparkling scenes of brilliant wit penned in prose. This is certainly very ingenious, but I hardly think it at all likely. Already in *Secret Love*, an extremely successful and admired play, Dryden had given a lighter background, so to speak, to the heroic theme which is but nearly removed from tragedy. He repeated the experiment and the success.

Marriage A-la-Mode, the first original piece the King's actors gave at Lincoln's Inn Fields, was produced about Easter, 1672, and achieved none other than a triumph. It is, indeed, one of the best of all Dryden's plays. The romantic scenes are of the rarest and most exquisite beauty. Than the dialogue between Leonidas and Palmyra which concludes Act I nothing lovelier has ever been spoken upon the stage, the words melt into a divine music. Dryden has further shown himself a supreme master of light and gallant intrigue, whilst as a *bonne bouche* he has given us two melodious and magnificent songs, *Why should a foolish Marriage Vow* and the voluptuous *Whilst Alexis lay prest*.[5]

On 17 January, 1745, there was acted at Drury Lane an operatic trifle, *The*

[1] He was buried in S. Paul's, Covent Garden, 27 January, 1671–2.

[2] Printed in *Covent Garden Drolery*, 1672.

[3] *The Works of John Dryden*, Second edition, 1821; vol. I, *Life of John Dryden*, pp. 143–44.

[4] In the *Stationers' Register*, 18 March, 1672–3, the play was entered as *Amorous Adventures; or Marriage A-la-Mode*.

[5] The first song was set by Robert Smith; *Whilst Alexis lay prest* by Nicholas Staggins. On the occasion of the Phœnix revival, February, 1920, these were sung by Irma Valentini.

Temple of Dullness, sometimes ascribed to Colley Cibber. In the following month *The Gentleman's Magazine* published a poetical address "*To* Mrs. Sybilla *on her acting the* Goddess of Dullness and *persuading her to attempt* Melantha *in* Dryden's Marr. Alamode."

In the same number was printed a letter signed W.G., a contributor who furnished intimate details concerning many dramatic poets of the reign of Charles II and who, moreover, declared that he well remembered the original production of *Marriage A-la-Mode* seventy-three years before, saying: "This comedy, acted by his majesty's servants at the theatre royal, made its first appearance with extraordinary lustre. Divesting my self of the old man, I solemnly declare that you have seen *no* such acting, no not in *any* degree, since." That the letter is genuine it does not seem possible to believe; that it represents a very definite tradition is almost certain. *Marriage A-la-Mode* was, as we have seen, produced about Easter, 1672, and if W.G. were then a mere lad of eighteen or twenty years he must have attained the great age of three-and-ninety when he entrusted his communication to *The Gentleman's Magazine*. It seems far more probable that the letter was written by a man who had often heard his father talk of the glories of those bygone years, and himself was almost persuaded that he had lived in the past and applauded Hart, Mohun, Mrs. Boutell and the superb Marshall.

The most brilliant pages of Cibber's *Apology* are those which give a critical analysis of the part of Melantha as played by Susanna Mountfort, Mrs. Boutell's successor in this rôle.

For some quite incomprehensible reason Sir Walter Scott pronounced Dryden's next comedy, *The Assignation: or Love in a Nunnery*, to be both "indifferently conducted" and lacking in liveliness, since when every writer who found occasion to mention this play has echoed "dull." Such placid herd-like unanimity breeds the suspicion that *The Assignation* has not been read. At any rate, if read, it has not been visualized. For it requires but little dramatic experience and technical judgement to appreciate that upon the stage these scenes would act most brilliantly, and the conduct of the business throughout is that of a complete master. So far from being "dull" the interest never sags for a moment, and the broadly humorous episodes of blundering Benito are agreeably diversified with the frank and honest love of Camillo and Violetta, the romantic passion of Prince Frederick and Lucretia.

"The scene is laid in Rome, and although there are topical allusions, 'Meeting the Vertuosi'; Donato Bramante's Cortile di Belvedere; the House of 'the *Colonne*'; the Olivetan *nobili dame* of S. Francesca Romana's convent in the Forum, the Tor de' Specchi, where indeed several important incidents take place; yet for all this adroit local colour it is the Rome of romance and the stage, the Rome of carnival and serenades, of rendezvous at night in nunnery gardens, of twanging guitars and old French songs—Eveillez-vous, Belles Endormies—of visors, dark lanthorns, the duello in the dark, plashing fountains, starlight and kisses."

Yet *The Assignation*, which was produced at Lincoln's Inn Fields late in October, 1672, "succeeded ill in the representation," but this was "against the opinion of many of the best Judges of our Age." "Whether the fault," writes

Dryden in his Epistle Dedicatory to Sir Charles Sedley, "was in the Play itself, or in the lameness of the Action, or in the number of its Enemies, who came resolved to damn it for the Title, I will not now dispute." There can be no doubt that the truth lies in this last suggestion. *Love in a Nunnery* must have vastly excited salacious minds, whilst the plot of the play would have bitterly disappointed them.

It may be remarked that Congreve has drawn upon *The Assignation* for his pleasing novel, *Incognita*, published February, 1691–2.

In 1783 was published 8vo *Intrigue in a Cloyster*, "A Farce Of Two Acts. By Thomas Horde, jun. Esq. . . . Oxford: Printed For And Sold By The Author: Sold also by the Oxford Booksellers, and by Turner of Witney." *Intrigue in a Cloyster* is a very indifferent compression of *The Assignation, Or Love in a Nunnery*. The Duke of Mantua, Ascanio, Hippolita, and some other characters are omitted; and there are ridiculous changes in the names of the rest, Prince Frederick, for example, becoming Baretti, Son to the Duke of Savoy; the Abbess Sophronia, Donna Miletta; Laura, Amarillis. The speeches have been re-written and entirely spoiled, whilst curiously enough there occur borrowings verbatim from Congreve, Farquhar, and Sheridan. Although a Prologue and an Epilogue are duly supplied there is, I think, no record that *Intrigue in a Cloyster* was ever acted. According to the *Biographia Dramatica*, ed. 1812, Vol. I, Part I, p. 366, Thomas Horde "was a teacher in the grammar school at Stow on the Wold, Gloucestershire."

On 4 July, 1672, was produced at Dorset Garden Edward Ravenscroft's *The Citizen turn'd Gentleman*, printed 4to, 1672, and reissued 4to, 1675, as *Mamamouchi*. This comedy is cleverly made up from Molière, *Monsieur de Pourceaugnac* being grafted on to *Le Bourgeois gentilhomme*. Old Jorden was played with broadest humour by Nokes, who fairly delighted the King and Court in this buffo rôle. Downes tells us that *The Citizen Turn'd Gentleman* "was look't upon by the Criticks for a Foolish Play, yet it continu'd acting 9 days with a full House."

In the Dedication to Prince Rupert, 4to, 1672, Ravenscroft says that the play was performed thirty times, mostly with the Prince present. (This does not mean thirty times successively.) The quarto also has a "Prologue spoken at the Middle Temple." Dryden who, as he himself declared, nourished no great liking for comedy, especially if it trenched upon farce, appears to have taken umbrage at this popular hit, and in the Prologue to *The Assignation* he has some very sharp bobs at Ravenscroft's success.

You must have Mamamouchi, such a Fop
As would appear a Monster in a Shop:
Hee'l fill your Pit and Boxes to the brim,
Where, Ram'd in Crowds, you see your selves in him.
Sure there's some spell our Poet never knew
In hullibabilah da, and Chu, chu, chu;
But Marabarah sahem most did touch you,
That is: Oh how we love the Mamamouchi!
Grimace and habit sent you pleas'd away:
You damn'd the Poet, and cry'd up the Play.

Marabarah sahem (Ah how much in love am I!) *Hula baba la chou, ba la baba la da*, and *Chou, chou, chou*, are all phrases in the jargon spoken by the feigned Turks when Old Jonathan Jorden is made an illustrious *Mamamouchi;* and are, of course, borrowed from the lingua franca of *Le Bourgeois Gentilhomme.*

Ravenscroft did not fail to notice the allusions, and in the Prologue to *The Careless Lovers*, produced at Dorset Garden in March, 1673, he retaliates in kind, having a bob at *The Conquest of Granada* and making great capital out of the failure of *The Assignation:*

> *They that observe the Humors of the* Stage,
> *Find* Fools *and* Heroes *best do please this Age,*
> *But both grown so extravagant, I scarce*
> *Can tell,* if Fool *or* Hero *makes the better farce:*
> *As for Example, take our* Mamamouchi,
> *And then* Almansor, *that so much did touch ye;*
> *That Bully* Hero, *that did kill and slay,*
> *And conquer ye* Ten Armies *in one day: . . .*
> *An* Author *did to please you, let his Wit run*
> *Of late much on a* Serving-Man *and* Cittern,
> *And yet you would not like the* Cerenade,
> *Nay, and you Damn'd his* Nunns *in* Masquerade.
> *You did his* Spanish *Sing-Song too abhor,*
> Ayeque locura con tanto rigor.
> *In fine, the whole by you so much was blam'd,*
> *To act their Parts, the* Players *were asham'd;*
> *Ah! how severe your Malice was that Day,*
> *To Damne at once, the* Poet *and his* Play;
> *But why, was your Rage just at that time shown,*
> *When what the* Poet *writ, was all his own?*
> *Till then he borrow'd from* Romance, *and did Translate,*
> *And those* Playes *found a more Indulgent Fate.*

Ravenscroft was a bold man thus to launch charges of plagiarism. In *The Careless Lovers* De Boastado is a close copy of Monsieur de Porceaugnac, whilst the scene in the Fourth Act, where Mrs. Breedwell and Mrs. Clapham enter with their children, as they pretend, is a lively paraphrase from the episode of Nenine (feinte Picarde) and Lucette (feinte Gasconne) in Molière's comedy, II, 8, 9, and 10. Moreover, he filches from Dryden himself; for with their provisos when entering upon matrimony, Careless and Jacinta have plainly taken the hint from Celadon and Florimel.

In his Preface, however, to the printed play he jests lightly on the matter, and tells the Reader that the Prologue "was Written in Requital to the *Prologue*, before the *Assignation, or Love in a Nunnery* and not without Provocation, *Laesit prius:* But Devils of Wit are not very dangerous, and so we both sleep in whole Skins. If you are Inquisitive to know why there are such continual Picques amongst the *Poets*, I can give you no other Reason than what one Whore told the other—*Two of a Trade can seldom agree.*" It was wellnigh impossible seriously to quarrel with one who laughingly thus turned off the matter.

A more important dispute was that which brought a lean and wizened immortality to Dryden's opponent, erstwhile even (as it seemed) his rival. Elkanah Settle, who had been born at Dunstable on 9 February, 1647–8, was admitted a King's Scholar at Westminster in 1663, and matriculated on 13 July, 1666, at Trinity College, Oxford, was beginning to put himself forward as the leader and choragus of the heroic dramatists, a usurpation Dryden would not tolerate for a moment. As Tonson once said,[1] "Even Dryden was very suspicious of rivals," and in the year of grace 1673 it really might have seemed to a contemporary as if for a while Dryden's position were seriously threatened. Settle, who did not proceed to a degree at Trinity, nevertheless had a play in his pocket, when he left Oxford. In January, 1671, *Cambyses, King of Persia*,[2] his first heroic tragedy, was produced at Lincoln's Inn Fields and proved a tremendous attraction, which indeed was not undeserved from a theatrical point of view. There was a very strong cast, including Betterton and his wife, Harris, Smith, Crosby, Sandford, Mrs. Long, Mrs. Jennings, Mrs. Dixon, and a number of Persians, Magicians, Villains, Ghosts, Spirits, Masquers, Executioners, *et hoc genus omne* to make it "thick and slab." Vastly inflated by his success, Settle now assumed fine airs and openly aimed at the dictatorship of Parnassus. He occupied himself very busily with a new heroic play, which he offered to the Theatre Royal. It was accepted, put into rehearsal, and a pretty pother ensued. It seemed that Settle had bound himself to write his next play for the Duke's Company, who had newly migrated to Dorset Garden, and Betterton was not slow to press his claims.

In *A Narrative Written by E. Settle*, folio, 1683, that very unfortunate individual turns cat-in-pan, and informs "His Honour'd Friend Sir Thomas Taylor, Baronett," who accepted the Dedication of the piece: "About ten years since I writ a Play call'd, *The Empress of Morocco*, and some time after I carryed it to His *Majesties Theatre*, where in the height of Mr. *Harts* Health and Excellence, I flatter'd my self with assurance of wonderful success from the performance of then so able a Company: but upon former Treaties with His Highnesses Servants, they made a complaint to their *Royal Master*, got the Play commanded back again to their own Play-House, where tho' His *Royal Highness*, upon condescending to hear his Servants in so humble a Cause, upon the Circumstances against me, did nothing but the highest Peice of Justice, yet Self-justification and my defeated Vanity begat that malignant resentment, that *manet alta mente repostum*, and engendered that unhappy Gall, that above Seven Years could not remove. . . This I declare was the true Cause that misled me into so much Spleen and Venome, of which I heartily repent and am ashamed, and humbly implore Pardon at the Feet of that Royal Prince for all these accumulated wrongs I have done both against his Honour and Vertue."[3]

[1] Spence's *Anecdotes*, ed. 1820; p. 106.

[2] It was much liked by the Duchess of Monmouth and when printed it was dedicated to that lady. *Cambyses*, in which Settle is said to have been helped by a fellow-collegian, William Buller Fyfe, ran into four editions (1671, 1672, 1687, 1698) before the end of the century.

[3] He particularly alludes to his scandalous libel *The Character of a Popish Successor*, 4to, 1681

Settle's recantation gives rise to some very satirical reflections, such as *Remarks upon E. Settle's Narrative*, folio, 1683,[1] in which it is interesting to note he is flouted as "a *Bartholomew-Fair Booth-man*, a *Strowller* about the Country with *Farces*," and he is told that the Postscript to his *Narrative* "is like the Fools Part in a *Fortune-Playhouse-Comedy* to make the sixpenny Gallery Sport." A letter to Mr. Settle (signed W.S.), folio, 1683, caustically jeers the pretext that his animosity against the Duke of York was "nothing else but that (as you pretend in your *Epistle Dedicatory*) Illustrious Princes remanding back from the *Kings-house* your *Play* to be Acted by His own Servants, according to your Contract and Treaty made with them. A wonderful Affront indeed! No less than the fall of a Great Prince, and National Inflamings, were judged to be Sacrifice enough to expiate the guilt of making the great *Settle* and his Empress appear in so mean a place as the *Duke's Royal Theatre*."

It is, of course, possible that Settle's literary vanity was seriously hurt, and that like the good wife in *Tam O'Shanter* he nursed his spleen and kept it warm. It is only too true that among authors some such petty vexation and rebuff will be morbidly dwelt upon and worried until it becomes a grievous wrong to be avenged with all the violence slander and malice can inspire.

However that may be, he was certainly for some years to come much misliked at the Theatre Royal, although in fairness the balk was none of his. Nor were Hart and Mohun any better pleased when *The Empress of Morocco*, produced with great splendour at Dorset Garden on 3 July, 1673, became the rage of the Town. It had been cast and rehearsed with considerable care, and with such actors as Betterton, Smith, Harris, supported by Mrs. Betterton, Mrs. Mary Lee, and Mrs. Johnson, the artistic presentation must have indeed been superb. In the preface to *Dennis's Remarks upon Mr. Pope's Translation of Homer* (1717) Settle's tragedy is said to have run a month together, which can hardly mean upon successive days, but is none the less a tradition of an altogether exceptional and extraordinary triumph. Indeed, *The Empress of Morocco* is a most effective melodrama; and, as I have written elsewhere, "Settle's verse, always fluent and facile, which even Dryden was bound to allow, not infrequently is vigorous and within measure of some inspiration."

Owing to the influence of the Earl of Norwich *The Empress of Morocco* had already been acted at Whitehall, the Prologue on the first night being written by the Earl of Mulgrave, and on the second by the Earl of Rochester. "*You gave it a noble Education, when you bred it up amongst Princes, presenting it in a* Court Theatre, *and by persons of such Birth and Honour, that they borrow'd no greatness from the Characters they acted*," wrote Settle in the Epistle Dedicatory to the Earl of Norwich, when the play was published 4to, 1673, "With Sculptures. The like never done before." Upon the title-page Settle dubbed himself "Servant to His Majesty," he reflects upon Dryden in the Dedication, and the laureate's wrath was unbounded. Nor was he at all unreasonably displeased; for, as Dennis says, "Now Settle was a formidable rival to Mr. Dryden." Accordingly he joined with Crowne and Shadwell in a pamphlet, "*Notes And Observations On The Empress of Morocco*, Or, Some few *Erratas* to be Printed

[1] Before June of that year.

instead of the Sculptures with the Second Edition of that Play," 4to, 1674, a pamphlet of seventy-two pages, which dissects and anatomizes Settle's tragedy line by line, almost word by word, and sometimes fairly, sometimes by a quibble, succeeds in making fine nonsense of the whole. The piece was published anonymously, but the authorship can have been no secret at the time. At any rate, Settle scented the triple alliance, and was not slow to riposte early in 1675 with a quarto pamphlet of ninety-five pages, *Notes and Observations on the Empress of Morocco Revised with some few Erratas to be Printed instead of the Postscript with the next Edition of the Conquest of Granada.* Valueless as criticism, the pamphlet has a certain accidental interest, since it admirably illustrates the method of prose attack employed by Settle and his peers. This was largely imitative, and as one might suppose was vehemently laced with personal obloquy and abuse.

It is unnecessary to trace Settle's harlequin career; his swift purveyance of plays to the theatre, *The Conquest of China*, *Ibrahim*, both heroic tragedies; *Pastor Fido*, a rhyming pastoral; a scandalous *The Female Prelate*; and many more; his violent and foolhardy rush into politics; his outrageous Whiggism with its infamous "pope-burning" pageantry; his shiftless tergiversation; his city laureateship; his Bartholomew Fair motions; and then a final retreat to the Charterhouse, when he died, a poor brother, on 12 February, 1723–4. Doeg's last feeble attack upon Dryden was a quarto *Reflections upon Several of Mr. Dryden's Plays*, 1687, which is in fine nothing more than a reprint of the *Notes and Observations on the Empress of Morocco Revised* of 1674, but he had already been annihilated in the Second Part of *Absalom and Achitophel*, published in November, 1682, and was now as flat as any flounder. The laureate in *The Vindication of The Duke of Guise*, 4to, 1683, has a contemptuous cast at his old antagonist, who in truth ere long was so damaged with every party as to be a somewhat stale and sorry butt for the caustic shafts of satire.

On 17 March, 1672, at a decisive meeting of the Cabinet war was declared against Holland; and an ecclesiastical fast was ordered by the Anglican Church to invoke the protection of Heaven. The English policy is well summed up by Arlington, who, in a letter to Gascoyne then at Innsbruck, declares that England must have "a short war," an idea which was dispelled by the battle of Solebay, 28 May. By 12 June, however, Louis, Condé, and Turenne had overrun with their armies five Dutch provinces. Charles himself, relying on the Treaty of Dover, was for insisting upon the absolute humiliation of the Dutch, but the French alliance made the war suspect in some quarters. The Commons, still leavened with Puritan bigotry, were unresponsive and cold. The recently-created Earl of Shaftesbury in his new Chancellor's robes was thundering forth "Delenda est Carthago," and as the campaign dragged on through 1673 it was inevitable that the laureate, who had always had a singular detestation for the Dutch, should employ his powerful pen to inflame popular feeling against these enemies of England. Dryden then aptly took as his subject this atrocious outrage which had been perpetrated just half a century before, and though deeply resented by King James I, was in the end left unavenged.

As Mr. Keith Feiling has well written, "*Amboyna* was the word of shame, the Fontenoy or the Khartum for that generation of Englishmen, evoking that passion for revenge which dies last and hardest in international relations."[1] In the Dutch war of 1664–1666, *Amboyna* "was on all lips, and the suffering of British Seamen, bound in misery and iron and half-starved on rice and water, which had been commended to King James, rose from oblivion with cries to his grandson for vengeance."[2] In 1623 the Dutch traders among the Spice Islands of the Indian Archipelago, upon the pretext of a plot having been formed against the influence and commercial ascendancy of The Hague, seized upon a number of English merchants and settlers in the Molucca Islands, and ruthlessly tortured and put to death ten Englishmen, a Portuguese, and eleven Japanese. The English were pointedly reminded of this massacre, which was indeed attended by circumstances of the most treacherous and horrid cruelty, by Henry Stubbe in his *A Further Justification of the Present War against the United Netherlands*,[3] published in the winter of 1672, with date 1673. The book sold like wild-fire, and a second edition, which was immediately called for, appeared early in February, 1673,[4] at the enhanced price of four shillings, the original issue costing only half a crown. As detailed consideration of this will be found in the note on the Source of the play, it is not necessary to relate the piteous story here again. *Amboyna; or, The Cruelties of the Dutch to the English Merchants* follows the historical facts with commendable accuracy.

A topical tragedy, "contriv'd and written in a Month," it was produced by the King's Company at Lincoln's Inn Fields in the summer of 1673. Although it has undeservedly met with some very unfair criticism the scenes are vigorous and interesting, the catastrophe well managed, piteous, and terrible; the persons—even of such minor characters as the English woman, Towerson's page, and the ship-boy,—drawn with spirited and distinguishing strokes. Ysabinda, the Indian lady, a convert to Christianity,[5] is a beautiful figure, and her rescue by Towerson after young Harman's rape is a situation of most poignant pathos.

The Tragedy, which contains an exquisite Epithalamium, and that long-popular ballad, *The Sea Fight*, proved extraordinarily successful.

Dryden's *Amboyna* was not the first play which had the "late accident at Amboyna"—to use a phrase of The Hague diplomatists—as its theme. In February, 1625, Dutch residents in London were extremely afraid that a popular rising might endanger their lives and property, and they complained to the Lords of the Council that in addition to the pamphlets which were scattered broadcast, a play was to be publicly acted exhibiting the sufferings of the English, and a great picture had been painted, "lively, largely, and artificially" of the tortures and executions. This play was never given.[6]

Here may conveniently be considered a couple of plays both of which have

[1] *British Foreign Policy*, 1660–1672: 1930, p. 101.

[2] *Ibid.*, p. 96.

[3] Illustrated with Sculptures. In Quarto. Price, sticht, 2s. 6d. *Term Catalogues*. Michaelmas, (21st November) 1672.

[4] *Term Catalogues*. Hilary (7th February), 1673.

[5] In January, 1546, S. Francis Xavier visited the Molucca Islands, and for the space of a year and a half he preached in Amboyna, Ternato, Baranura, and many lesser islands.

[6] Calendar of State Papers. *East Indies*, 1625–1629. Pars. 61 and 63.

been ascribed to Dryden. In the one case it can definitely be shown that the comedy in question was none of his; whilst in scenes of the second he most probably had a finger at least, if not a hand. On Tuesday, 15 September, 1668, Pepys went "to the King's playhouse, to see a new play, acted but yesterday, a translation out of French by Dryden, called '*The Ladys à la Mode*': so mean a thing as, when they come to say it would be acted again to-morrow, both he that said it, Beeson, and the pit fell a-laughing, there being this day not a quarter of the pit full." This inaccuracy on the part of Pepys, just the silly draff of pit gossip which no doubt fathered the play on Dryden of malice prepense, and which he jotted down without much heed, has given rise to a good deal of superfluous discussion. Sir Edmund Gosse, although he in later days at all events held quite the contrary, had once suggested that the play seen by Pepys was *The Mall: Or, The Modish Lovers*, "*Acted by his Majesties Servants*," and published 4to, 1674. But *The Mall* was given at Lincoln's Inn Fields, and the name does not in the least resemble *The Ladys a la Mode*.[1] The Epistle Dedicatory "*To William Whitcomb, Junior, Esq.*," is signed J.D., who may be confidently identified with John Dover. *The Roman Generalls: or the Distressed Ladies*, a tragedy by Dover, was published 4to, 1667, and à Wood tells us he wrote two or three more dramatic pieces.

The play seen by Pepys was none other than Richard Flecknoe's *The Damoiselles A La Mode*, which was printed 12mo, 1667. "This *Comedy*," says the author, "is taken out of several Excellent pieces of *Moliere*. The main plot of the *Damoiselles* out of his *Pretieusee's Ridiculee's*; the Counterplot of *Sganarelle*, out of his *Escole des Femmes*, and out of the *Escole des Marys*, the two *Naturals*; all of which like so many *Pretieuse* stones, I have brought out of *France*; and as a Lapidary set in one Jewel to adorn our *English Stage*." One is not surprised to know that this curious amalgam or "posy" as the author prefers to term it, was at first refused by the Theatre Royal, whereupon Flecknoe determined the public should be able to read his play in the closet even if they could not see it in the theatre. Eventually by dint of much importunity and some influence Flecknoe secured the production of *The Damoiselles A La Mode* at the Theatre Royal on Monday, 14 September, 1668, and since we know from the Lord Chamberlain's accounts that the King was present, the identity of Flecknoe's play and Pepys' *The Ladys a la Mode* is definitely established.

In 1675 Magnus and Bentley published, quarto, *The Mistaken Husband*, "A Comedie, As it is Acted by His Majesties Servants At the Theatre-Royall, *By a Person of Quality*." In a note *to the Reader* Bentley says: "*This Play was left in Mr. Dryden's hands many years since. The Author was unknown to him, and return'd not to claim it. After twelve years expectation Mr. Dryden gave it to the Players, I have heard him say, that finding a scene wanting, he supply'd it.*" This seems a very plain statement of fact. *The Mistaken Husband* bears every mark of revision by Dryden, and nothing could be more likely than that considering the difficult position of the King's company after the burning down of

[1] The *Biographia Dramatica*, 1812, vol. III, p. 12, noticing *The Mall* says: "This play has been ascribed to Dryden: but its style and manner bear little resemblance to those of that author; and therefore it is reasonable to imagine it the work of some more obscure writer."

the Theatre, Dryden, who was their house dramatist, would most willingly undertake such a piece of work in order to assist and do them a service with the attraction of a new play. That afterwards he should discard the piece, and formally dismiss it as none of his is equally probable and easily to be understood. *The Mistaken Husband* is a lively comedy of considerable merit, and I have not hesitated to give it a place among Dryden's work, although but sponsored for a while and embellished by him.

There were few events which caused greater discussion in contemporary England, and which in the end had more far-reaching results than the ceremony that took place in Italy on 30 September, 1673, when the Princess Mary Beatrice Eleanora d'Este of Modena was married by proxy, the Earl of Peterborough, to His Royal Highness James, Duke of York and Albany. Already there had been political complications. The Bishop of Modena, Mgr. Roberto Fontana, declined to officiate, and it was an English Dominican, Father White, O.P., who celebrated the nuptials in that exquisite Romanesque duomo beneath the shadow of la Ghirlandina. Five days later the Duchess of York celebrated her fifteenth year. The journey to her new country was long and difficult; she arrived at Dover on the evening of 21 November, and was warmly welcomed by her husband. A few hours later Dr. Nathaniel Crewe, then Bishop of Oxford, translated to Durham in 1674, joined them with the Anglican rite, taking care, none the less, to emphasize that the marriage by proxy was sacred, lawful, and secure. Next they proceeded by slow stages towards London, and on 26 November, the King received his new sister-in-law at Gravesend. Charles was wholly delighted with this rare Italian beauty, and knowing by sad experience how estranged and forlorn her heart must be in a strange court, he exerted himself to the utmost to entertain and recreate the girl bride. In after years she often spoke warmly of his kindness during those first months, his affectionate consideration, always a grateful and gracious memory. Balls, banquets, galas, divertissements of every kind, were the order of the day. Nor must it be supposed that theatrical representations would be omitted. An English comedy or tragedy to celebrate the nuptials would have been a little unfitting perhaps as the bride could as yet understand little of her husband's tongue, and accordingly, with rare good taste, a French opera after the Italian mode was selected.

On 5 January, 1673–74, Evelyn noted in his Diary: "I saw an Italian Opera in musiq, the first that has been in England of this kind." As Professor Dent points out by an "*Italian Opera*" is meant "not an Opera in the Italian language, and by an Italian composer, but simply a dramatic performance set to music."[1] There can be no question that this was a court performance for the celebration of the royal marriage, and that the opera in question (sung in French) was *Ariane, ou le Mariage de Bacchus*,[2] an altered version of an earlier French Opera by Pierre Perin, set to music by Cambert, and now rearranged

[1] *Foundations of English Opera*, chapter 6, p. 108.

[2] The libretto was published both in English and French, "Ariadne or the Marriage of Bacchus, an Opera or a Vocal Representation: First Compos'd by Monsieur P. P. Now put into Musick by Monsieur Grabut, Master of his Majesties Musick. And acted by the Royall Academy of Musick, at the Theatre Royal in Covent Garden. In the Savoy, Printed by Tho. Newcombe. 167¾."

by Louis Grabu, the Master of the King's music. When published a frontispiece, representing the prologue, the scene being a prospect of London Bridge and the Thames viewed from Whitehall, was engraved and thus supplied an illustration of the stage setting of the Court Theatre at Whitehall.[1]

This prologue introduces three Nymphs, the Thames, the Seine and the Tiber, who sing various chansons, after which they are joined by a Nymph of the Po, who trills in courtly compliment to Mary Modena "la Divine" and her spouse, a "Demidieu,"

> Soufre, que je vienne en ces Lieux,
> Malgré les Destins et l'Envie,
> Joindre ma Divine Marie
> Au plus Grand de tes Demidieux.

The second Theatre Royal in Bridges Street opened on 26 March, 1674, the Prologue and Epilogue being specially written by Dryden for the occasion. The first play given was an old favourite, *The Beggar's Bush*, but this was followed four days later by *Ariane*, the first public production, for which the court scenery was lent to the Theatre. The opera season appears to have lasted some three weeks, until about 23 April.

Although Dryden certainly had not the apprehension of a laureate's duties as they were conceived by Eusden, Colley Cibber, or Pye who ground out Birthday Odes and New Year's Odes with relentless regularity, it may seem surprising that he should have let pass so memorable an occasion as the marriage of his royal patron, the Duke of York and Albany, without some epithalamium or other poetic recognition of so happy an event. Nor, in fact, did he so; for there can, I think, be no doubt that *The State of Innocence, and Fall of Man* was composed in the winter (probably November) of 1673 to be presented at the splendid wedding festivities which were to celebrate the arrival in England of Mary Beatrice. Upon the title-page of the printed Opera, 4to, 1677, is very significantly emblazoned "And Dedicated to Her *Royal Highness*, The Dutchess. By *John Dryden*, Servant to His Majesty." It is, if I am not mistaken, unique to find upon a title the announcement of the Patron to whom a Dramatic piece is inscribed, and this denotes something extremely particular. There, at any rate, we have the clue.

Moreover, in "The Author's Apology for Heroique Poetry" Dryden quite definitely states that his Opera was composed "*at a Month's warning, in which time, 'twas wholly Written, and not since Revis'd.*" This points clearly enough to a Court command somewhat hastily issued to the Poet Laureate, who as in duty bound at once fulfilled the official behest, but when his work was not utilized for the purpose in view was not at the trouble to polish and perfect it.

It has been frequently repeated, chiefly in reliance upon an opinion expressed by Scott,[2] "that *The State of Innocence* could not be designed for the stage."

[1] For a detailed discussion, see "A Restoration Opera Problem," W. J. Lawrence, "The Times Literary Supplement," Thursday, 26 November, 1929.

[2] Malone, *Life of Dryden* (*Prose Works of John Dryden*, Vol. I, Part I, 1800), p. 109, had written that "the State of Innocence, which was published in 1674, could not have been intended for a stage-exhibition." But it is chiefly Scott to whom deference is made on this point.

Nothing is further from the truth. Dryden's Opera was unmistakably and beyond all question written for representation. The very completeness and practicality of the stage-directions sufficiently demonstrate this. The machinery is the regular elaborate stage machinery of a Restoration Opera. Nor, indeed, was there any reason why this Opera should not have been performed. The subject was no bar; and in any case it is treated with great reticence and decorum. Scott argues that the costumes, or rather lack of costumes, in the case of Adam and Eve must have presented unsurmountable difficulties. Yet in Eve's dream, III, I, a woman appears "habited like *Eve*." Our first mother, then, was visualized by Dryden as wearing even before the Fall, for stage purposes, some kind of habit. This would offer no difficulty, nay rather it would afford great scope to the costumier, paradox as it may seem.

In the famous *Ordo repraesentationis Adae*,[1] concerning which scholars dispute whether it is to be assigned to the twelfth or the thirteenth century, there are very full stage-directions, and we are instructed that the Saviour must be clothed in a dalmatic, whilst "Adam is to wear a red tunic and Eve a woman's robe of white with a white silk cloak." After the Fall, Adam "must now be out of sight of the people, and shall put off his solemn raiment, and put on poor raiment sewn together of fig leaves."

Warton wrote: "In these Mysteries I have sometimes seen gross and open obscenities. In a play of *The Old and New Testament*, Adam and Eve are both exhibited on the stage naked, and conversing about their nakedness: this very pertinently introduces the next scene, in which they have coverings of fig leaves."[2] Undoubtedly there is a stage direction in the Chester plays "Statim nudi sunt . . . Tunc Adam et Eva cooperiant genitalia sua cum foliis."[3] Warton was right. Sir E. K. Chambers argues that "a too literal interpretation of the stage-directions" must not be assumed. This is an error; stage-directions must be literally followed. They are direct workaday formulas, written there to say what is intended, and if some illusion or piece of stagecraft is designed such is invariably suggested. Jordan's stage-direction in his *Creacion of the Worlde* (1611),[4] that Adam and Eve are to be "aparlet in whyte lether" proves this very point. No doubt at the performance of *The State of Innocence* some similar device would have been adopted.

Again Dryden in his *Apology* declares that to satisfy the Readers, "I think myself oblig'd to render them a Reason, why I publish an Opera which was never acted." This, if it means anything, certainly conveys that a production was contemplated. There is a somewhat striking confirmation of this in a second version of the well-known story, for which Aubrey[5] is the authority, that Dryden visited Milton to ask permission "to tagge his verses." *The Monitor*,

[1] *Tours MS.*, 927. Ed. V. Lazarche, Tours, 1854; K. Grass, Halle, 1891; and other editions.

[2] *History of English Poetry*. Edited by W. E. Hazlitt, 4 vols, 1871, II, p. 223.

[3] *The Chester Plays*, ed. H. Deimling (*Early English Text Society*), Part I, p. 30.

[4] *MS. Bodl.* 219. *The Creation of the World*, ed. (from *Harl.* 1867) by Davies Gilbert, 1827.

[5] *Brief Lives*, ed. Clark, ii. 72.

Vol. I, No. 17,[1] related "a Passage told a Gentleman of our Society almost Forty years since by Mr. *Dryden*, who went with Mr. Walker in Company to make a visit to Mr. Milton and desire his leave for putting his Paradise Lost into Rhime for the Stage." (Milton's reply is then given much as Aubrey has it, with ample detail.) Here it is definitely asserted that *The State of Innocence* was intended for the stage.

Yet another point which clearly indicates that Dryden wrote for theatrical production may be discerned in his handling of the theme, as has been hinted above. It should be observed—and this is very important—that the poet nowhere represents the Deity, to whom all reference is in the most reverent and indeed guarded terms. The Archangel S. Raphael executes "Heav'n's Care" and the will of Heaven. The term "Heaven" is continually employed for the Godhead, even in places where Deity or God would be more appropriate, and there is design in this. When guilty man has eaten of the apple, it is S. Raphael who enters to announce the punishment. Moreover Dryden wholly omits the Redemption. It would have been very indecent to discuss the most sacred and profoundest truths of Christianity in a stage play; in fact, such a suggestion must have prohibited any performance. Dryden's great art is herein apparent. Milton, it is true, does not admit the Christian Scheme; but this was from a very different reason.

Since then it was preferred officially to celebrate the royal nuptials with *Ariane* rather than with Dryden's Heroic Opera, the poet decided at any rate to lay the printed copy at the feet of the Duchess of York for whom it was originally intended, and he was, moreover, resolved to emphasize the occasion. This he effectually did by inditing an Epistle Dedicatory which is so entirely in the Italian manner that his homage has been hitherto much misunderstood, and even misrepresented as bordering almost on the profane, whereas nothing was further from the poet's mind as he penned those baroque and elegant periods of truly renaissance compliment and celestial courtesy.

If we ask why *The State of Innocence* was not given, it can be sufficiently conjectured that a foreign opera was felt to be more appropriate and more agreeable to, as better understood by, the Italian Princess. Thus no slight was put upon the laureate when *Ariane* was selected. Naturally the expense of mounting Dryden's opera would have been very great, and Killigrew was quite unable to undertake so elaborate a presentation without extraneous assistance. Had the piece been given, as intended first, at Whitehall, the public theatre could have availed itself of the Court scenery and costumes (as actually happened in the case of *Ariane*), a loan which would have solved this very practical and initial difficulty.

Dryden has amply made reference to Milton; but the Fall of Man was treated as a Drama long before *Paradise Lost*, and it may pertinently be remembered that Milton first contemplated a "Tragedy" on the subject of Adam. His earliest draft gives a list of Dramatis Personae amongst whom appear S. Michael; Lucifer; Adam, Eve, with the Serpent; a chorus of Angels; and various personifications such as Conscience, Labour, Discontent, Faith, Hope

[1] From Monday, April 6, to Friday, April 10, 1713.

and Charity. In another draft his scheme is divided into five Acts, and Moses προλογιζει. Yet again he suggests *Adam Unparadized* as a possible name for his theme. The epic itself seems actually to have been begun in 1658. Moreover there can be little question that Milton had borrowed much of the original suggestion from the *Adamo*[1] of Giovanni Battista Andreini, the Italian poet (1578–1652). The *Adamo* was published at Milan, 4to in 1613; where a second edition appeared, 4to 1617; a third edition 12mo was printed at Perugia in 1641; and a fourth at Modena, 12mo, 1685. It was, then, a well-known and admired work, and was doubtless familiar to the Duchess of York. *Adamo* has amongst other Interlocutori the Padre Eterno, Arcangelo Micaele, Adamo, Eva, Lucifero, Sathan, Belzebu, il Serpe, and a Cherubino, "Custode d'Adamo." There are choruses of Seraphim and Angels; Spirits and Foletti. This *Sacra Representatione* of which I have used the Second Edition, 4to, 1617, with exquisitely beautiful plates of Cesare Bassano, is an exceedingly fine and intensely religious poem.

Incidentally mention must also be made of the *Adamo Caduto*, a drama, by the Franciscan, Fra Serafino della Salandra, printed at Cosenza in 1647.[2] *Paradise Lost* is largely a paraphrase, philosophically distorted but often literally verbal, from the Italian.

Dryden, in fine, has borrowed no more from Milton than the older poet himself took without acknowledgement from Salandra and Andreini.

Meanwhile, however, the publisher having safeguarded the piece by registration at Stationers' Hall it was temporarily laid aside. Many hundred copies of it began to circulate through the Town and were sent into the country for perusal. Naturally as transcripts were being quickly made at third and fourth hand innumerable errors soon appeared, and almost as it were in self-defence Dryden resolved to publish his Poem. Of these MSS. at least three have come down to us; one exemplar, the most important, as having corrections in the author's own hand, is now in Harvard College Library;[3] a second is in the Bodleian,[4] and a third in the British Museum.[5]

By some quite exceptional error Malone wrote that *The State of Innocence* was first published in 1674, a mistake he repeats twice quite definitely.[6] Scott

[1] There were also French plays of the seventeenth century on the subject of Adam. For example, about 1617 Cousturier published at Rouen a duodecimo collection of eight tragedies, of which only two are dated, one in 1612, the other in 1614. In this volume is a brief *Tragédie de la Naissance ou Création du Monde*, "où se void de belles descriptions des Animaux, Oiseaux, Poissons, Fleurs et autres choses rares, qui virent le iour à la naissance de l'Vniuers." The piece, which is in four acts, was written by Ville Toustain. It extends beyond the Creation and Fall of Man to the murder of Abel and branding of Cain. There are some curious turns, as when Adam asks what Apelles wrought Paradise. The apple, when he eats it, sticks " au milieu de la gorge." In fact, we have the awkwardness, but not the simplicity, of a mediaeval guild-play.

[2] See Norman Douglas, *Old Calabria*; xxi, "Milton in Calabria."

[3] Now first collated for the present edition. See further the Textual Notes upon the play.

[4] Rawl. C. 146. 103.

[5] Add. MS. 37158, folio 1.

[6] *Life of Dryden* (*Dryden's Prose Works*, 1800, vol. I, Part I), pp. 109 and 219.

fell into the trap,[1] and Geneſt also went aſtray.[2] Masson in his *Life of Milton* by further misunderſtanding emphasized and enlarged upon the falsity.[3] A. W. Ward, in his *English Dramatic Literature* (New ed., 1899), Vol. III, p. 368, followed Scott; and W. C. Ward repeated the blunder.[4]

Relying upon all this mass of unreliable evidence Saintsbury not being able to find a quarto, 1674, of *The State of Innocence*, fudged a title-page. I am sorry to use the expression, but the fact remains. There the thing is and it speaks for itself.

[The State of Innocence and Fall of Man, an Opera, written in Heroic Verse, and dedicated to Her Royal Highness the Duchess, by John Dryden, Servant to His Majeſty.

————Utinam modo dicere possem
Carmina digna deâ: Certe eſt dea carmine digna.

OVID. MET.

London: Printed by T. M. for Henry Herringman, at the Anchor in the Lower Walk of the New Exchange, 1674.—ED.] This is given on p. 94, Vol. V of *The Works of John Dryden*, edited by Sir Walter Scott, Bart., "Revised and Corrected by George Saintsbury," Edinburgh, 1883. There was a little (and it is difficult not to believe deliberate) juggling with the correct title-page of the Firſt Quarto, 1677. ("Heroic" inſtead of "Heroique" and "Duchess" for "Dutchess" may pass as that unscholarly modernization which Mr. Saintsbury affects. But no amount of modernization will account for 1674 inſtead of 1677.) The 1677 title-page has "Ovid. Metam."; above we read "OVID. MET."; originally we have "Printed by *T. N.* for *Henry Herringman*"; above we read, "Printed by T. M for Henry Herringman"; differences slight but sufficient. In fact, the thing is a flam, and we had beſt leave it at that.[5] Mr. T. J. Wise, *A Dryden Library*, p. 26, gives a full description of 4to, 1677, with a facsimile title-page and writes "The *Firſt Edition*." Nothing more remains to be said.[6]

That *The State of Innocence* was widely read and admired is shown by the fact that there are quartos of 1678; 1684; 1690; 1692; and 1695.

It was doubtless this popularity which inspired Edward Eccleſtone's curious rhyming Opera, *Noah's Flood; or, The Deſtruction of the World*, published quarto, 1677, with a dedication to the Duchess of Monmouth, to whom incidentally Dryden had inscribed his sacred drama, *Tyrannick Love*. There are commendatory verses by Richard Saunders, John Leanerd, and John Norton. Beside Noah and his family, we have Abaddon and Agon, "*two Monstrous*

[1] *Works of Dryden*, London and Edinburgh, 1808; vol. V, p. 94.

[2] *Hiſtory of the English Stage*, 1832, Volume I, page 161.

[3] *Life of Milton*, VI, p. 710.

[4] *Wycherley's Plays*, ed. W. C. Ward (Mermaid Series), Vizetelly; 1888, p. 364.

[5] When Mr. Saintsbury was asked where a copy of this 1674 quarto could be seen, he merrily turned off the inquiry by saying that this edition "is probably a Boojum!"

[6] W. C. Hazlitt, *Manual of Old English Plays*; and Halliwell, *Dictionary of Plays*, speak of a 1676 4to, for which there is absolutely no evidence.

Gyants," good and bad Angels, Sin, Death and other mysterious figures, whilst the whole concludes with the destruction of the Town of Babel, "*with bellowing Thunder and flakes of Lightning*." In 1685 this Opera was reissued with a series of plates under the new title, *The Cataclysm; or, General Deluge of the World*. In 1690 it again appeared as *The Deluge; or The Destruction of the World*, and finally in 1714 there was published a duodecimo edition as *Noah's Flood: or the History of the General Deluge. An Opera being the sequel to Mr. Dryden's Fall of Man*. This is embellished with a frontispiece divided into four compartments, comprising a set of designs different from the illustrations in the quarto, 1685. In his *Epistle to the Reader* Ecclestone says: "Mr. Dreydon's State of Innocency and Fall of Man, *is of the same Nature with this, from whose incomparable Piece I drew the rugged draught*." Richard Saunders congratulates Ecclestone with the following conceits:

> Dryden will grieve to hear thy Couplets Chime,
> And yield he's foyl'd at his own Weapon, *Rhime;*
> While ev'ry Page such sweetness does distill,
> Thy *Noah's Ark* rests on Parnassus Hill.

Whilst Norton not to be outdone declares:

> In every individual Line of thee,
> We plainly see,
> *Milton* and *Dreydon in Epitome*.

As we have noted, the second Theatre Royal in Bridges Street, a house which cost more than £4,000, was opened on 26 March, 1674, when the King and Queen were present in state. It might have been expected that Dryden would have furnished this house with a new play during that year, but such was not the case. Perhaps he was dissatisfied with the internal conditions of the theatre which, largely owing to Killigrew's mismanagement and quarrels with his company, were beginning to be in a very unsatisfactory condition. It appears that certain of his actors were wont suddenly to throw up their parts without a minute's warning, or what was even worse, they adopted the plan of transferring their services to the rival house. As early as 16 May, 1674, two months after the opening of the Theatre Royal, the Lord Chamberlain issued a very strongly worded order forbidding these changes and caprices and enjoining that in the case of any retirement or the like three months' warning must be lodged with the Manager. Later in the year Killigrew was again at loggerheads with his principals, and accused them of taking money which was due to himself. In January, 1674–5, Kynaston, Mohun, Lacy, Burt, Shatterel, Wintershal, and Cartwright were bidden to attend at Whitehall so that the Lord Chamberlain might go into the matter of dispute, and meantime they were to continue acting without any disturbance.

When we hear this long tale of dissension it is hardly surprising that Dryden should hesitate and not be over eager to provide the actors with a new piece. He was at work upon a heroic play—his last in that kind as it proved—and in November, 1675, *Aureng-Zebe* was produced at the Theatre Royal. Albeit

INTRODUCTION

Aureng-Zebe[1] (Aurang Zeb—Throne-ornament) was actually a living potentate, who came into contact with and disliked English pioneers in Hindustan; he must have been as visionary a figure to most Englishmen as Montezuma, Maximin, and even Almanzor. Although the scene is still laid in a far Oriental court, and we have a background of assaults and battles, a prisoned hero, a peerless captive queen, an amorous and passionate empress, mutes, daggers, and poisoned bowls, there is a marked difference between the conduct of this tragedy and that of the earlier heroic dramas. The plot is by no means as intricate as formerly, nor is it so interwoven with accidents and the intrigues of various characters. It is simpler, more concentrated, more direct. "The personages are imperial; but the dialogue is often domestick, and therefore susceptible of sentiments accommodated to familiar incidents."[2] Nevertheless the language is exceedingly beautiful and singularly moderated in tone. Particularly remarkable is the constant tendency towards *enjambement*, which breaking down the closer control of the couplet certainly points in the direction of blank verse. It is important to notice an unusual feature which may be missed—the entire absence of all supernatural machinery, those sorcerers and apparitions who had no small part in *Tyrannick Love* and *The Conquest of Granada*. Whether this is an improvement or no will, I suppose, be differently decided by diverse judgements. It is, moreover, sufficiently plain from the Epistle Dedicatory to the Earl of Mulgrave that these alterations were conscious and deliberate. Actual history in *Aureng-Zebe* is very closely followed on the surface so to speak, and Dryden has also constructed an intrigue, the motif of which probably owes some slight suggestion to Racine's *Mithridate*,[3] acted and printed two years before; whilst in his Epilogue he very unmistakably asserts his regard for the serious decorum of the French theatre. *Aureng-Zebe* was a great favourite with Charles II, to whom it was shown whilst yet in manuscript by Lord Mulgrave. It would even appear that the King condescended to give Dryden valuable advice with regard to the conduct of the scenes.[4] It would not seem that Indamora's conduct upon the death of Morat was actually suggested by that well-known episode in *Le Grand Cyrus*, IX, 1, where Mandane sits down beside and comforts the expiring King of Assyria, Philidaspe. Dryden's reference in his Epistle Dedicatory has been a little misunderstood. *Aureng-Zebe* was very successful, and kept the stage for about fifty years.

In *The European Magazine*, Vol. LXIII, May and June, 1808, was printed a melodrama in two acts by Joseph Moser[5] entitled *Nourmahal, Empress of*

[1] Born 4 November, 1618; ascended the throne of Delhi in July 1658; died at Ahmednuggar, 3 March, 1707.

[2] Dr. Johnson.

[3] It is altogether an exaggeration to go as far as Holzhausen, "Über Dryden's heroisches Drama," *Englische Studien*, xv, p. 15, and assert that Xiphares corresponds to Aureng-Zebe, Pharnace to Morat, and Monimie to Indamora.

[4] Epistle Dedicatory to Mulgrave: "You were likewise pleased to recommend it to the King's perusal, before the last Hand was added to it, when I receiv'd the Favour from him, to have the most considerable Event of it modell'd by his Royal Pleasure."

[5] 1748–1819. This gentleman's talent seems to have lain in the direction of supplying the deficiencies of other authors. Thus in 1807 he wrote an additional scene for

Hindostan. This, which is a mixture of verse and prose, was never performed, and indeed it is wholly unsuited for the Stage, although furnished with a Prologue "Spoken by Mr. . . ." and an Epilogue. There is a silly reference to Dryden in the former:

> Chamelion *Dryden's* works too every hue,
> The rainbows varied tints the zenith's blue,
> Some pieces strangely *warp'd*, some shot with fable:
> This mixture aptly answers white and sable,
> And shows his fickle shuttle oft inclin'd
> To imitate the *panther* or the *hind*.

The Scene of *Nourmahal* is laid in Agra, and the play was no doubt suggested by *Aureng-Zebe*, although it widely differs from Dryden's tragedy in every respect.

Lord Mulgrave's patronage of Dryden, however profitable and honourable, was to cost the poet dear, for when in November, 1679, the *Essay on Satire*, which Mulgrave says was first written in 1675, began to circulate in MS. about the town, gossip at once had it that Dryden was the author.[1] It is probable indeed that he had given the original draft a few of his inimitable touches. In the course of this poem there are some pretty severe but very true reflections on Rochester, who, forwarding a copy to Henry Savile on 21 November, 1679, writes: "I have sent you herewith a Libel, in which my own share is not the least . . . the Author is apparently Mr. D[ryden], his patron my L[ord] M[ulgrave], having a Panegyrick in the Midst." In another letter dispatched very shortly after Rochester plainly acknowledges to Savile: "You write me word, that I'm out of favour with a certain Poet. . . . If he falls upon me at the *Blunt*, which is his very good Weapon in Wit, I will forgive him if you please, and leave the Repartee to *Black Will*, with a Cudgel." The result was a blackguardly assault upon Dryden, an outrage notoriously instigated by Rochester. As the poet was returning from Will's Coffee House to his home in Gerrard Street about 8 o'clock on the night of 18 December he was attacked by three stalwart hooligans, and so violently beaten that for some days his life was considered in danger. The King was furiously angry, but it proved impossible to bring the guilt sufficiently home to the aggressor. However, His Majesty caused an advertisement to be inserted in *The London Gazette*, No. 1472, 18–22 December, in which it stated that any person who made discovery of the gang to a justice of peace was to receive fifty pounds, "which is deposited in the hands of Mr. Blanchard, Goldsmith, next door to Temple Bar for the said purpose," and moreover, upon his declaring his hirer and accomplices he should receive the royal pardon.[2] Rochester apparently bribed higher still, for the criminals remained undiscovered.

Murphy's *The Upholsterer*; in 1808 he paid the same tribute to Vanbrugh's *Æsop*; in 1809 he obliged both Shakespeare and Jonson with fresh scenes for *As You Like It* and *The Alchemist* respectively. Other plays received similar attention at his hands.

[1] Thus Shadwell, *The Tory-Poets, A Satyr*, 1682: "And *Mul——ve* is a Wit because I taught him."

[2] The same advertisement appeared on 26 December in *Domestick Intelligence or News from both City and Country*.

The affair naturally caused a tremendous sensation and was the talk of every coffee house in Town. It is constantly alluded to by contemporaries and long remained in men's memories. As Scott remarks: "The Rose-Alley ambuscade became almost proverbial." Otway in his Epilogue to *Venice Preserv'd*, Dorset Garden, 9 February, 1681–2, speaks with deserved contempt of the Ruffians and Rascals who set "*a Rose-Alley cudgel Ambuscade.*"[1] "It will certainly be admitted, that a man, surprised in the dark and beaten by ruffians, loses no honour by such a misfortune," yet as might have been expected, Dryden's antagonists did not fail to jeer the poet to their own lasting discredit, but not to his. Thus Settle in the Prologue to his *The Heir of Morocco with the Death of Gayland*, Theatre Royal, 11 March, 1681–2, has:

No fear of cudgells when there's hope of Bread:
A well-fill'd Panch forgets a broken Head.

Shadwell in *The Tory Poets*, 1682, has:

After *Rose-alley* drubs he'd ne're use weapon more.

But it were as disgusting as it were impertinent to cite more examples of the coarse-fibred folly of Dryden's enemies.

It cannot have been without a certain misgiving that Dryden in the autumn of 1677 entrusted the tragedy which he wrote after *Aureng-Zebe* to the Theatre Royal. On 22 February of that year Charles Killigrew had replaced his father as Master of that house, but the actors seem soon to have found as just cause of complaint against the son as they had against their first manager. On 30 July the King expressed himself so dissatisfied with the government of the Players that he resolved to let them rule their own commonwealth. Moreover, the migration of actors to the other theatre, apparently at their own sweet will, continued unchecked. In the spring, 1677, for example, two leading ladies of Killigrew's company, Mrs. Marshall and Mrs. Hughes, were playing in D'Urfey's *A Fond Husband; or, The Plotting Sisters* at Dorset Garden.[2] Nevertheless *All For Love: or, The World well Lost*, which it is interesting to note was also known as *Anthony and Cleopatra*, was produced at the Theatre Royal on Wednesday, 12 December, 1677.

It has been said that *All For Love* is "a direct imitation of Shakespeare's *Antony and Cleopatra*."[3] Nothing could be further from the truth. There is no more diffuse and panoramic play than *Anthony and Cleopatra;* the action and interests are dissipated over half the globe. It is indeed "the most spacious of the plays."[4] In *All For Love* we are shown the last stages and catastrophe of the story; the crisis actually is over, although the actors do not know it, and it is this very point which lends such infinite poignancy to all their sleeveless endeavours.

1 See Otway's *Works* by the present editor, Nonesuch Press, 1926, III, p. 83 and note on that passage.

2 Mrs. Marshall, Maria; Mrs. Hughes, Cordelia.

3 Verrall, *Lectures on Dryden*, 1914; Chapter IX, p. 238.

4 H. Granville-Barker, *Prefaces to Shakespeare* (Second Series), 1930; p. iii.

INTRODUCTION

Anthony and Cleopatra was a difficult tragedy even on the Elizabethan stage. Difficult, not from the task set the players or producers, but from the point of view of the audience. The whole Roman Empire is the locale, and we pass from place to place with unrelated celerity. "The events, of which the principal are described according to history, are produced without any art of connection or care of disposition," this is the sentence of Dr. Johnson. It is easy to assert that the action swings effectively to and fro; unfortunately, too much is lost in the mere shifting movement. In the hands of modern editors, with whom Act III has eleven scenes and Act IV thirteen, the whole thing is beyond all imagination bewildering to read.

Anthony and Cleopatra is on too vast a plan; it is not the grandeur of dignity which must have proportion; it is gargantuan. Technically, it is not a good play, not even as judged through Elizabethan eyes; technically, *All For Love* is flawless, judged by any standard, even by that of the precise and rigorous Ibsen. It would have been wellnigh impossible for Shakespeare's spectators to have appreciated that at the commencement of Act II—I use, for convenience sake in reference, the deplorable "scene-divisions"—they were in Syria; and after three dozen or so lines in Rome; thence to Alexandria (although here Cleopatra gives the cue); then to Athens; back to Rome again; next to Actium, and so on through the many unfolding episodes. The two great figures round whom centres the fortune of the whole world give the play unity, it is true; but magnificent as they are, we are apt to stray in the wake of that crowd of "Friends to Cæsar" and "Friends to Anthony" who distract the stage with their marching. In a word, the piece is patchy. Yet the whole is redeemed by those superb passages which the rapture of love inspires.

In *All For Love*, it has been said, "many traits of the heroic plays still survive."[1] "The influence of the heroic drama is powerful in this play."[2] It is extraordinary to find that sound critics can go so far afield, and apparently read into a drama some preconceived notion theyexpect to find there. *All For Love* in diction, in characterization, in acting, in technique obviously represents that definite detachment from the heroic play which Dryden was at some pains (seemingly in vain) to emphasize. One of the extraordinary qualities of the supreme genius of Dryden is that in his development from strength to strength his work is so incessantly alive with new beauty and new expression, creations proceeding indeed from what went before, a natural and orderly progression, but in themselves entirely unoriginate and new. There are few writers of whom it can be affirmed, as can be so certainly said of Dryden, that there is no trace of weariness, no faltering throughout his work.

To attempt a comparison between *All For Love* and Shakespeare's *Anthony and Cleopatra* seems to me too singularly unintelligent an inquiry to pursue. The question must be asked, however, what did Dryden mean by "A Tragedy . . . Written in Imitation of *Shakespeare*'s Stile"? To regard *All For Love* as

[1] G. R. Noyes, *Selected Dramas of John Dryden*, 1910, Introduction, p. xcvii.

[2] Hazleton Spencer, *Shakespeare Improved*, 1927, p. 221. In another writer we have such trivial rubbish as: "In *All For Love* Antony is made a brother of Almanzor, Cleopatra the sister of Almahide, Dolabella the image of Acacis." In another place this writer says: "*All for Love* is a classicised specimen of the heroic school!"

an adaptation from Shakespeare is, of course, too preposterously silly for any serious consideration. Dryden himself, moreover, has exactly informed us what he intended: "In my Stile I have profess'd to imitate the Divine *Shakespeare;* which that I might perform more freely, I have dis-incumber'd my self from Rhyme."

All For Love was regarded by Dryden himself with particular affection. Perhaps the full quality of the work, the concentration, the especial economy which only genius at its height could have wrought, can best be appreciated when this tragedy is given in the theatre. Other beauties are apparent, exquisitely apparent, in the reading; but I doubt whether this mastery and easy manipulation of supreme technique does not perhaps a little escape notice in the closet. In some degree it must, I suppose, strike everyone. Yet a new Zoilus has been so bat's-eyed as to declare that *Anthony and Cleopatra* "would furnish forth half a dozen *All For Loves.*"

When *All For Love* was given in March, 1922, being produced by Edith Craig, with Edith Evans as Cleopatra and Ion Swinley, Marc Anthony, the sweet luminous music of Dryden's verse was spoken with such undercurrent of emotion, with such an ecstasy that not one but felt that Love was indeed worth all, that not merely Anthony and Cleopatra, great protagonists in the world's history as they were, stood there to meet the shock of fate, serene in all save when some accident should seem to fleck their love, but rather that the man and woman were symbolic figures, expressive of some deep mystic elemental passion which sways the heart resistlessly, older than time, wider than space.

All For Love was the last play Dryden wrote for the King's players, with whom he had so long and so intimately been connected. There can be no doubt that the quarrels and disagreements among the actors, which went from bad to worse, caused him to sever his old connexion, for the company was now in a condition of hopeless disorganisation. Moreover, Charles Hart and Michael Mohun were growing elderly and had for some time been in fast failing health. Hart was greatly afflicted with the stone and gravel, whilst Mohun was a martyr to gout.[1]

The Dorset Garden company on the other hand was wellnigh at its fullest strength. It was admirably managed by Betterton; and it boasted such excellent actors as Smith, Joseph Williams, Henry Harris, and Underhill, with two notable comedians, James Nokes and Anthony Leigh. Among the ladies were Mrs. Betterton, Mrs. Mary Lee, Mrs. Barry, Mrs. Betty Currer, and for broader effects Mrs. Elinor Leigh and Mrs. Norris. We can hardly be surprised that Dryden should have preferred to place his new comedy with Betterton at Dorset Garden. At this house, then, on 11 March, 1677–8, was produced *The Kind Keeper; or, Mr Limberham.* Unhappily, as Dryden himself tells us, this

[1] Thus the Prologue to Crowne's *The Ambitious Statesman; or, The Loyal Favourite,* Theatre Royal about March, 1679, candidly avows:

> *In our poor Play-house fallen to the ground,*
> *The Times Neglect, and Maladies have thrown*
> *The two great Pillars of our Play-house down.*

excellent comedy, "an honest Satyr against our crying Sin of Keeping... was permitted to be acted only thrice. The Crime for which it suffer'd was ... that it express'd too much of the Vice which it decry'd." Yet it is difficult to suppose that *The Kind Keeper* was prohibited entirely on account of its libertine zest and frolic freedom. Aphra Behn is certainly as wanton in her scenes; one may mention for example *Sir Patient Fancy* and *The Luckey Chance;* Shadwell is far coarser in his language, and profane to boot. An audience that applauded Crowne's ruttish *The Countrey Wit*, that thronged *Friendship in Fashion* and *The Souldiers Fortune*, was not to take exception at Dryden's raillery. The comic scenes of Lee's *The Princess of Cleve* are far more rampant and unabashed; the incontinence of *The Relapse* more brutal and lubrique.

Langbaine remarks of *The Kind Keeper*: "In this Play (which I take to be the best Comedy of his) he so much expos'd the keeping part of the Town, that the Play was stop't, when it had but thrice appear'd on the Stage; but the Author took a becoming Care, that the things that offended on the Stage were either alter'd or omitted in the Press. One of our modern Writers in a short *Satyr against Keeping* concludes thus:

> Dryden *good man thought* Keepers to *reclaim*,
> *Writ a Kind* Satyr, *call'd it* Limberham.
> *This all the Herd of* Letchers *straight alarms*,
> From Charing-Cross *to* Bow *was up in Arms*,
> *They damn'd the Play all at one fatal Blow*,
> *And broke the Glass that did their Picture Show*."

It seems probable that the satire was more particular than general. Malone says: "I have, I think, somewhere read, that the author in the character of Limberham, had Lord Shaftesbury particularly in view; whose partisans were probably highly offended, and joined heartily in its condemnation."[1] Another tradition has it that the person aimed at was the Earl of Lauderdale, who by his great interest obtained the immediate suppression of the play. Both these peers were extremely licentious in their private lives, and although it has been objected that the feckless cully, Mr. Limberham, could not have portrayed the dark and dangerous Achitophel it is quite possible that Dryden hardly ventured to limn his portrait too like, and therefore of intent fitted Shaftesbury's lewdness to a cuckoldy poltroon. In the figure of the hypocritical and precisian Mrs. Saintly is exposed Mrs. Cresswell, the notorious procuress, who, after the decease of Mother Moseley, ministered so energetically to the carnal requirements of the quondam Chancellor. This goodly matron was indeed extensively patronized by the Whigs whose party she greatly affected. "It is well

[1] Malone, *Life of John Dryden* (*Prose Works*, 1800 *ut cit.*), p. 117. The villainous Shaftesbury was, of course, not infrequently brought upon the stage as by Dryden himself in *Albion and Albanius*. He is also glanced at under the name of Benducar in *Don Sebastian*. Otway exposed his vices as Antonio in *Venice Preserv'd* and his political intrigues as Renault in the same play. See *The Works of Thomas Otway* by the present editor, Nonesuch Press, 1926, vol. III, pp. 277–79.

known, I kept as good orders in my house as ever was observed in a nunnery; I had a church bible always lay open upon my hall table, and had every room in my house furnish'd with the *Practice of Piety*, and other good books for the edification of my family . . . and tho' I say it, I had a parcel of as honest, religious girls about me, as ever pious Matron had under her tuition at a *Hackney* boarding school. I always did every thing in the fear of the Lord, and was, I thank my Creator, so happy in my memory, that I had as many texts of scripture at command as a presbyterian parson. . . . Never neglect public prayers twice a day, hear two sermons every *Sunday*, receive the sacrament twice a month, but let this be done at a church where you are unknown; and be sure read the scriptures often, and be sure fortify your tongue with abundance of godly sayings, let them drop from you in strange company, as thick as ripe fruit from the tree in a high wind; and whenever you have a design upon the daughter, be sure of the mother's faith, and ply her closely with religion, and she will trust her beloved abroad with you, in hopes she may edify; for you must consider, there is no perfect bawd without being a true hypocrite."[1] In this strain does Tom Brown make Mother Cresswell write to Moll Quarles, and the satire—if truth be satire indeed—is the very accent of Mrs. Saintly.

It may be noted that the name Limberham seems to have been in use to represent a sapless keck-dry type even before Dryden made it famous. Thus in *The Country-Wife*, Theatre Royal, January, 1674–5, Sir Jasper Fidget declares that there can be no more scandal for a woman to be seen with Mr. Horner, who is supposed a eunuch, than if she were "with Mr. *Tatle*, or Master *Limberham*." In Southerne's *The Maid's Last Prayer; or, Any, Rather than Fail*, Theatre Royal, January, 1692–3, III, Lord Malapert banters Siam with "but had not you twins six months after you were marry'd, tho?" only to be taken up by "No, *Limberham:* nor will you get half a one, in six years after you are marry'd." "I drolled upon the City Do-littles to tickle the *Covent-Garden Limberhams*" Bayes is made to say (p. 24) in *The Reasons for Mr. Bays changing his Religion*, 4to, 1688.

Since the printed play, as we have it, 4to, 1680, has been maltreated and cut about, we can but judge *The Kind Keeper; or, Mr. Limberham* at a great disadvantage. There are obvious gaps in the action; loose threads and ends left hanging where the waft has been slashed by the censor's scissors.[2] Even so, it remains a comedy which of its kind (although this be domestic and even bourgeois, if you will) must be placed in the foremost rank. The humours of the boarding-house are drawn by no faltering hand, and many of the strokes are

[1] *The Second Volume of The Works of Mr. Thomas Brown*. The Eighth Edition, 1744. Letters from the Dead and The Living: "*From Madam* Cresswell of pious Memory, *to her Sister in Iniquity* Moll Quarles *of* known Integrity," pp. 259 and 261. Courtine in Otway's *The Souldiers Fortune*, Dorset Garden, 1680, Act V, cries: "But where the Devil am I? Sincerely in a Bawdy-House: Fogh! what a smell of sin is here! Let me look about; if there be even a *Geneva* Bible or a Practice of Piety in the room, I am sure I have guest right."

[2] And Mr. Flecknoe tells us in his *Discourse of the English Stage:* "A good Play shou'd be like a good stuff, closely and evenly wrought, without any breakes, thrums or loose ends in 'um."

exquisitely happy. The situation where the two amorous ladies who have resorted to Woodall's bedchamber are severally concealed, but at the entry of the landlady, only to be surprised and discovered by her too energetic overtures to their gallant, is vastly amusing and mirthful. The ineffable conceit of Brainsick is well done; and father Aldo is brisk and vivacious albeit a lewd old Turk.

It is true that the gaiety is somewhat heartless, but then the fair cyprians, married or mistress, and their wanton amoroso are (as they themselves entirely recognize) but playing a game, and the skill with which they manage their intrigues and criss-cross rendezvous counts in their eyes almost as much as the actual consummation and enjoyment. There must be adventure to spice the amour, else the affair were dull indeed. So when Master Woodall is too eager Tricksy rebuffs him: "Your Friend was unconscionable if he desired more Favours at the first Interview." A gallant must be witty as well as handsome to satisfy these ladies. There is something of the intellect in their liaisons, but nothing of sentiment.

That the manuscript should have perished is extremely exasperating, the more so as we know that Malone examined either the original or a direct copy. In a MS. notes on *The Kind Keeper* in his *Biographia Dramatica*, Vol. II, p. 178,[1] he has: "In an original MS. of this play, corrected by Dryden's own hand, which had once belonged to Pope, and is now in the possession of Revd. Dr. Wilson, Senior Fellow of the College of Dublin, instead of *Woodall*, *Stains* is found passim. In one place these words are found; thus corrected: A punk of two descents. Mrs. Tricksey—Damaris. Act IV. *Stains*. Twill ~~Very punk of very punk~~,
be time to marry at three score when I have enough but for one woman: to engage before, would be the direct way to sin. I cannot confine my appetite to Manna yet. *Ger*. And then you will be past tasting it. *Staines*. I warrant thee. Our family is good winter fruit: Were bon Chretien: my father's an example of it. Marry me now, and I shall beget an offspring of young rouges [*sic*] to supplant my pleasure as I do his."

It would seem that the scriptural allusions gave offence, and the echo of a phrase from the Symbolum of Nicaea. I well remember that many years ago, when some young witling at Oxford composed what he was pleased to call his literary credo, "The Creed of a Despairing Decadent," in some sort of parody of the Credo of Nicaea, there was immense scandal in the University. But now that academic divines have outgrown the formularies of a mere Creed, I imagine the thing would pass unnoticed. It was in any case silly enough. I do not doubt that the modern stage too would consider these phrases which a Restoration audience misliked, very pap for an up-to-date palate.

Although it is not to be supposed that the Theatre Royal company exactly relished the production of a play by Dryden at the rival house, since this piece proved so unfortunate they did not concern themselves beyond a private remonstrance, but when their poet in collaboration with Nat Lee, of whose tragedies also, till now, they had had the monopoly, composed an *Oedipus* which the author gave to Betterton, they felt some very definite steps must be taken and accordingly they formulated their grievance in the following petition,

[1] Bodley, Malone 156.

which was doubtless addressed to Lord Arlington, The Lord Chamberlain—the actual superscription is lost:

"Whereas upon Mr. Dryden's binding himself to write *three plays* a yeere, he, the said Mr. Dryden, was admitted and continued as a Sharer in the King's Playhouse for diverse years, and received for his share-and-a-quarter, three or four hundred pounds, *communibus annis;* but though he received the moneys, we received not the playes, not one in a yeare. After which, the house being burnt, the Company in building another contracted great debts, so that the shares fell much short of what they were formerly. Thereupon Mr. Dryden complaining to the Company of his want of proffit, the Company was so kind to him, that they not only did not presse him for the playes which he so engaged to write for them, and for which he was paid beforehand, but they did also, at his earnest request, give him a third day for his last new play, called All for Love; and at the receipt of the money of the said third day, he acknowledged it as a guift, and a particular kindnesse of the Company. Yet notwithstanding this kind proceeding, Mr. Dryden has now, jointly with Mr. Lee (who was in with us to the last day of our playing, and shall continue,) written a play called Oedipus, and given it to the Duke's Company, contrary to his said agreement, his promise, and all gratitude, to the great prejudice and almost undoing of the Company, they being the only poets remaining to us. Mr. Crowne, being under the like agreement with the Duke's House, writ a play called The Destruction of Jerusalem, and being forced by their refusal of it to bring it to us, the said Company compelled us after the studying of it, and a vast expence in scenes and cloathes, to buy off their clayme, by paying all the pension he had received from them; amounting to one hundred and twelve paid by the King's Company, besides neere forty pounds he the said Mr. Crowne paid out of his owne pocket.

These things considered, if, notwithstanding Mr. Dryden's said agreement, promise, and moneys freely given him for his said last new play, and the many titles we have to his writings, this play be judged away from us, we must submit.

(Signed) Charles Killigrew.
Charles Hart.
Rich. Burt.
Cardell Goodman.
Mic. Mohun."[1]

This petition may be assigned to the winter, November or December, 1678, as *Oedipus* is already in rehearsal by Betterton. The case seems fairly stated. On the other hand, the dramatists argued that the condition of the Theatre Royal was such that it was almost impossible to rely upon the production of a new play by that Company, and that in any case it would not be set off to the best advantage. The result of the actors' petition we can pretty certainly surmise from the fact that Dryden's next two plays (before the Union) *Troilus and Cressida* and *The Spanish Fryar*, were both given at Dorset Garden.

Nathaniel Lee, whose first piece, *The Tragedy of Nero, Emperour of Rome*, was produced at the Theatre Royal in May, 1674, had since that beginning

[1] Printed by Malone, *Life of Dryden, op. cit.*, pp. 73–75.

furnished Killigrew's house with four tragedies in succession, all of which were —as indeed they deserved—mightily well received by the town; *Sophonisba, or Hannibal's Overthrow* (1675); *Gloriana, or the Court of Augustus Cæsar* (1675–6); *The Rival Queens, or the Death of Alexander the Great*, which had given Hart one of his great rôles (1676–7);[1] and *Mithridates, King of Pontus*, (1677–8). The epilogue to this last piece, a "Lady's Play,"[2] had been written by Dryden, who also furnished the Prologue for the Oxford production of *Sophonisba*.

When *The State of Innocence and Fall of Man* was published early in 1677,[3] prefixed to the Opera there appeared a copy of complimentary verses by Lee, and later in the same year, Dryden in turn addressed the author of *The Rival Queens* in a poem "*To Mr.* Lee, *on his* Alexander," which was duly printed with that tragedy, quarto, 1677.[4]

> *The Blast of common Censure cou'd I fear,*
> *Before your Play my Name shou'd not appear;*
> *For 'twill be thought, and with some colour too,*
> *I pay the Bribe I first receiv'd from You:*
> *That mutual Vouchers for our Fame we stand,*
> *To play the Game into each other's Hand. . . .*

thus Dryden commences his fine panegyric of "*the mighty Merit of your Play*." It was almost inevitable that the idea of collaboration should have suggested itself to the two poets, with the result of the most admirable tragedy, *Oedipus*.

"Having offered some observations elsewhere upon this play, and the mode in which its celebrated theme has been treated by the dramatists of different nations, I need not here resume the subject,"[5] and it will suffice to note that it was produced at Dorset Garden in January, 1678–9, and that being "Admirably well *acted;* especially the Parts of *Oedipus and Jocasta:* One by Mr. *Betterton*, the other by Mrs. *Betterton;* it took prodigiously, being *Acted* 10 days together."[6]

Dryden himself has informed us of the exact partition of the labours of the two writers, since he says: "I writ the first and third acts of *Oedipus* and drew the *Scenery* of the *whole play*."[7] Even by contemporary critics attention was

[1] When Hart, although ill and on the eve of retirement, played Alexander "the House was fill'd as at a New Play, he acting that with such Grandeur and Agreeable Majesty, that one of the Court was pleas'd to Honour him with this Commendation; That *Hart* might teach any King on Earth how to comport himself." Downes; *Roscius Anglicanus*.

[2] Prologue; concluding line.

[3] *Term Catalogues*, Hilary (12 February), 1677.

[4] *Term Catalogues*, Michaelmas (26 November), 1677.

[5] I quote Scott, *Life of John Dryden* (*Works*, Second Edition, 1821; vol. I, p. 222), whose very phrase fits extraordinarily here.

[6] *Roscius Anglicanus*.

[7] *The Vindication of the Duke of Guise*. It may be remarked that Downes blunders, for he ascribes "the first two *Acts*" to Dryden, and "the 3 last" to Lee.

drawn to the occasional extravagances which flare out in Lee's contributions to this tragedy. In particular the couplet:

> May there be not a glimpse, one starry Spark,
> But Gods meet Gods, and jostle in the Dark;

was well roasted and burlesqued.[1]

About this time Dryden was much occupied in work for the theatre, since whilst he was collaborating with Lee, he also had in hand his second Shakespearean adaptation,[2] *Troilus and Cressida; or Truth found too Late*, which was produced at Dorset Garden at no very long interval after *Oedipus*, that is to say during the spring of 1679.

In the Preface to that masterly piece of literary analysis, the "Grounds of Criticism in Tragedy" which is prefixed to the printed play, quarto, 1679, the poet himself states the reason why he undertook to alter Shakespeare's *Troilus and Cressida*, and he further sets out the lines upon which he directed his revision. The preliminary remarks are a tribute to the genius of Shakespeare, and the just foundation of that reverence in which his name is held. Dryden then discusses four main points. First, he remarks that in this particular play we have an exceptional number of obsolete, ungrammatical, coarse and obscure expressions. Secondly, the folio supplies no division into acts and scenes. This is purely a practical matter affecting the theatre, but none the less it is for him a very important consideration. And, indeed, when this tragedy is given, unless it be upon an Elizabethan platform—from which the Restoration theatre had just escaped, a throw-back to which would not have been for a moment tolerated in 1679—it seems essential that the producer should make out some scheme of acts and scenes.[3] This has even been done by modern editors who have far less excuse for their innovations and interference, yet who have not been able to refrain from slicing piecemeal the finish of the play. It was necessary, then, that the tragedy should be shaped to the exigencies of the picture stage. Thirdly, "the latter part of the Tragedy is nothing but a Confusion of Drums, and Trumpets, Excursions and Alarms." That is to say, the end fritters away in a chaotic and incoherent turmoil of clamour and war. Dryden's own *mêlée* is a different matter. It is purposeful, conclusive, and is not confused. Lastly, "The Persons, who give name to the Tragedy, are left alive: *Cressida* is false, and is not punished." This was the most fundamental change of all the four. It entailed viewing the Story from a new angle, setting the incidents in a fresh

[1] Radcliffe in his *News from Hell* jeers:

> A sixth, whose lofty Fancy towers
> 'Bove Fate, Eternity, and Powers:
> Rumbles i' th' Sky, and makes a bustle;
> So Gods meet Gods i' th' dark and justle.

See also Dennis in *The Impartial Critick* (1693); *The Spectator*, No. 40.

[2] In *A Collection of Plays by Eminent Hands*, MDCCXIX, vol. I, was included *The Tragedy of Julius Cæsar . . . alter'd by Sir William Davenant and John Dryden*. The alterations are worthless, and there is no authority for the ascription which may safely be ignored.

[3] The fewer the better. I once saw a performance of *Troilus and Cressida* in Five Acts and twenty-four scenes!

light. The Greek chieftains, Achilles, Ajax, and the rest who, in Shakespeare's *Troilus and Cressida*, showed themselves so ignoble, so braggart, so incredibly sottish and debased for all their muscles and brawn, ay, even perhaps because of that very animal strength, their cynicism and salaciousness as they neighed like fed horses in the morning, in fine the wholy filthy fester and stagnation of camp-life must be edulcorated and effectually deterged; further the heroes must be nobled and drawn in statelier guise; Troilus, himself, no less amorous, but his green-sickness gone, must be spiritualized, as it were, to match the heroine, peerless and true, who was to die for love.

That Dryden's *Troilus and Cressida, Or, Truth Found too Late* is a better play than Shakespeare's original *Troilus and Cressida* is not open to question. Structurally the fundamental technique of *Troylus and Cressida*, whether judged from an Elizabethan, Restoration, or modern point of view is chaotic, nor, as sometimes happens in the earlier seventeenth-century plays, does any such order or design evolve from the imbroglio, as permits us almost to echo the immoral saw: The end justifies the means. Dryden manages the separation of Troilus and Cressida—and this is the turning-point of the whole history—far more pathetically and far better than Shakespeare, the reason for which perhaps is that whilst Shakespeare's Cressida is a heartless coquette, a depraved Millamant in fact, Dryden's Cressida is a loving tender woman.[1] It is not without significance that so great an actress as Miss Edith Evans should have shown supremely admirable in Cressida and in Millamant. In Shakespeare there is no conclusion to the play. Hector is slain, but beyond a tame ranting speech by Troilus nothing more comes of it; and Pandarus wanders on to the battlefield—how or why is not explained—to deliver some moralizing tags addressed to the pimps and procuresses in the audience, which gentry are less likely to be edified than are the rest to be entertained. Dryden's conclusion, on the other hand, is admirably planned. It may not read well, but it would act most convincingly. We could wish that Dryden had retained Cassandra, howbeit the eerie prophetess would have been an intrusion upon the pathetic simplicity of the parting of Hector and Andromache, a scene which may be read not without emotion even after Homer.

Thersites is but little changed. We miss one or two caustic scomms of the original, which might well have been left in his mouth. Pandarus is more unctuous, more oily, more rubicund and comfortable, a completer cock-bawd.

The technical alterations, then, consist for the most part of condensation, and some admit rearrangement in view of stage requirements; of verbal changes and improvements; and the shaping of the whole to a more natural period.

That Dryden used the Folio is shown by his inclusion of certain passages which do not occur in the Quarto, *The Famous Historie of Troylus and Cresseid*, 1609. There are also some readings in Dryden that follow the Folio which differs from the Quarto text.[2]

[1] Thus Pandarus does not talk too smuttily before her. In *Troylus and Cressida*, folio, 1623, "How now, how now? how goe maiden-heads?" cries Pandarus. Dryden, *Troilus and Cressida*, III, 2, "How now, how now, how go Matters?"

[2] See Delius: *Shakespeare Jahrbuch*, IV, 23, 24; and Zenke, *Dryden's Troilus and Cressida im Verhältnis zu Shakespeare's Drama*, p. 15. Rosbund erroneously supposes Dryden employed the Quarto, *Dryden als Shakespeare-Bearbeiter*, pp. 10–14.

INTRODUCTION

Having given two plays in quick succession a year now passed before Dryden produced his next comedy. *The Spanish Fryar, Or, The Double Discovery,* which was first acted at Dorset Garden on 8 March, 1679–80, has very generally been esteemed the best of his lighter work, and certainly he has drawn no one comic character with such full strokes as Father Dominic. This worthy Jacobin may take his place secure in the world's immortal gallery of humorous creations. Without him *The Spanish Fryar* were an excellent play; Lorenzo is brisk and virile; Elvira a fascinating minx; Gomez an amusing old hunks with his "and the times had not been hard, my Billet should have burnt too"; but sheer genius comes in and goes out with the Friar. The scenes in which he plays his part must be ranked among the most mirthful in all English literature. In comedy they are certainly unsurpassed. By what an easy slip, just one false jar, the character might have become dangerous if not actually disgustful! But how skilfully does the author avoid and even seem to ignore any such element. Dryden, I suppose, determined that poetical justice must be done, but who can help feeling sorry when the rabble push Dominic off and Gomez jeers. Nevertheless, I, for one, am content. I am very sure that the Friar was never "stript of his Habit, and dis-order'd"; that he never walked the streets of Saragossa in quirpo. No; he might be seen there, I will vouch, for many a year, very dignified and portly in his white habit and his *cappa nigra*, a little more irritable perhaps, a little less inclined to befriend young people in their affairs.

How this rôle was acted by that inimitable comedian Anthony Leigh, has been described for us by Colley Cibber in one of his best portraitures.

In his Dedication of *The Spanish Fryar* to Lord Haughton, Dryden not without reason draws notice to the construction of this work: "*I us'd the best of my endeavour, in the management of two Plots, so very different from each other, that it was not perhaps the Tallent of every Writer, to have made them of a piece.*" The serious and comic episodes of the play are indeed very adroitly combined and developed.

It was in the winter of 1681, or early in 1682, that Nathaniel Lee claimed from Dryden the fulfilment of a promise made whilst the two authors were at work upon *Oedipus*, namely, that they should collaborate in another play. In 1680–81 Lee taking his cue from the turbulence of Oates' plot had designed and written a "Protestant Play,"[1] *The Massacre of Paris*, no doubt in the first place suggested by "A Relation of the barbarous and bloody Massacre of about a hundred thousand Protestants begun at *Paris*, and carried on all over *France* by the Papists, in the year 1572: collected out of Mezerey, Thuanus, and other approved authors," 4to, 1678,[2] an outrageous boutefeu polemic from the pen of the unscrupulous Burnet. Naturally enough, a license was refused to an inflammable tragedy which concludes with highly-coloured tableaux of S. Bartholomew's Eve, 1572. Lee then employed himself very deedily with a somewhat chaotic *The Princess of Cleve*,[3] "a Revenge for the refusal of the other,"

[1] *The Reasons of Mr. Joseph Hains Conversion* (1690), Part III, p. 28: "There were more weeping eyes in the Church, than there were at the first acting of Mr. *Lee's* Protestant Play, *The Massacre of Paris.*"

[2] *Term Catalogues*, Michaelmas (6 December), 1678.

[3] Not printed until 1689.

which did not, Downes tells us, have any great success. Accordingly, when in December, 1680, *Lucius Junius Brutus, Father of his Country*, was prohibited,[1] and the actors required "Not to Act ye said play again" on account of "very scandalous expressions and reflections vpon ye Government," Lee may well have felt sadly in need of some helping hand and sober guidance. To none better could he turn than to his friend the laureate and the most opportune assistance was such as he could ask with a perfect good grace.

Dryden, who had been extremely occupied with *Absalom and Achitophel*, Part I, would have been glad, as he himself tells us, to enjoy a little well-earned leisure, but Lee was so earnest and eager in his request that out of sheer good nature he consented to continue at his desk without respite or break, no doubt with a full understanding of the circumstances of the case. He turned then, to various unfinished pieces and suggestions of scenes which he had by him, and among them there was the MS. of a play upon the subject of the Duke of Guise, written twenty years before, and left incomplete. It is true that he had been considering a tragedy upon the subject of the Sicilian Vespers.[2] But since he had some scenes already in hand, the Duke of Guise would mean far less labour, moreover, Lee could utilize matter from the banned *Massacre of Paris*, whilst the whole story might be treated in extremely topical fashion. Incontinently the two poets set to work.

The Duke of Guise was put into rehearsal at the end of June, 1682, but, as might have been supposed, in spite of every precaution, all sorts of rumours began to be bruited up and down the coffee-houses. The original date of production was fixed for 18 July, but writing on the 26 of that month from London to the Duke of Queensberry in Scotland, the Hon. John Drummond, Secretary of State for Scotland, says: "There is a play hear to be acted that makes a great business, for the Duke of Munmouth has complained of it, and they say that notwithstanding it is to be acted sometime next week. They call it The Duke of Guise, but in the play the true story is cheinged to the plott time hear."[3] Three days later a newsletter reports: "A play by Mr. Dryden, termed *The Duke of Guise*, wherein the Duke of Monmouth is vilified and great interest is being made for the acting thereof, but coming to His Majesties' knowledge is forbid, for though His Majesty be displeased with the Duke, yet he will not suffer others to abuse him."[4] In *The London Mercury*, Num. 34, Friday, 28 July to Tuesday, 1 August, 1682, is announced: "A play, being supposed to be made by Mr. *Dryden*, termed *The Duke of Guise*, and it being judged to have reflections on his Grace the Duke of *Monmouth*, tho it was much endeavoured by some that the same should be acted, yet coming to His Majesties' Knowledge it is forbid."

The chief complaint was that a scene in the play, Act IV, Scene I, when the

[1] The order is dated 11 December, 1680.

[2] *Bayes* . . . expressed then an intention of writing the story of the *Sicilian Vespers*." Shadwell's *Some Reflections Upon . . . The Play Called The Duke of Guise*, 4to, 1683.

[3] Hist. MSS. Comm. Buccleuch II (1903), Second Section, p. 108.

[4] Hist. MSS. Comm. *Somerset, Ailesbury, and Puleston*, XV Report, Appendix, Part VII (1898), p. 108.

Duke of Guise presents himself in Paris against the King's express wish and command, was obviously suggested by the unexpected return to London in November, 1679, of the Duke of Monmouth, who it was known had not the royal permission to come back to England from his exile.

Dryden's reply was both practical and unanswerable. He waited upon the Lord Chamberlain, and submitted Sir Charles Cotterel's *History of the Civil Wars of France*, a translation from the Italian of Enrico Caterino Davila, whence the incident was taken, to his Lordship for inspection. Nothing had been added. The authors had merely dramatized an event which did actually take place one hundred years before, and the episode in the tragedy was little more than a paraphrase from the original historian. However, the script was returned after some two months without a word of direction or command. The Whigs, scenting how matters might go then, raised a mighty clamour that Charles II was presented as the effeminate Henri III; that the throne of England was insulted, an end which had in fact been their most anxious study for many a decade past. All this was so transparently ridiculous and untrue that so mischievous an insinuation carried no weight. In fine, after some months of anxious waiting the prohibition was withdrawn.

Meanwhile there had taken place a very important theatrical event which had long been pending, the Union of the Two Patents. Circumstances indeed mark this matter not of choice but of necessity, especially so far as the actors of the Theatre Royal[1] were concerned, with whom their rivals, fully cognizant of their low estate and difficulties, drove a very advantageous bargain. The joint Companies commenced acting on 16 November, 1682, at the Theatre Royal, which house was preferred since it was more convenient and accessible than Dorset Garden.

The Duke of Guise was produced at the Theatre Royal on 30 November, 1682, with Betterton, who was now clearly the leading actor of the day, in the title rôle. The play, Dryden writes, "succeeded beyond my very *Hopes*, having been frequently Acted, and never without a considerable Audience."

Almost immediately began the pelting of pamphlets and snarl of satires. The Whig faction, furious on every account that *The Duke of Guise* was produced at all in the first place, that it was being given to thronged houses, that it was applauded to the echo, that it was an excellent play, that it was so admirably acted, in fine, desperate with baffled rage, at once launched an attack by every means that lay in their power, that is to say by foul means, by lies, insult and abuse. The vollies opened feebly enough with "The True History of The Duke of Guise. Extracted out of *Thuanus*, *Mezeray*, Mr. *Aubeny's Memoirs*, and the *Journal* of the *Reign* of *Henry* the third of *France*. *Published for the undeceiving such as may perhaps be imposed upon by* Mr. Dryden's *late* Tragedy *of the* Duke of Guise. Together with some *Remarks* upon the same." London, "Printed and are to be sold by *R. Baldwin*." This is a quarto pamphlet of thirty pages with an address "To The Reader" commencing: "*Tis a mad World my Masters! The fiery Crape-Gowns vex the Pulpit, and the hot brain'd*

[1] Actually the King's company had been dissolved in April, 1682. Davenant's company were playing regularly at Dorset Garden until their move to the Theatre Royal.

Poets wrest prophane History. For certainly the Tragedy of the Duke of Guise, was a Thing *set on foot merely to try how far the limits of* Poetica Licentia *might extend. Whether it might be lawful for a man to give an ill Character of his Sovereign in Verse, and to parallel a vertuous Prince, and belov'd of his subjects with a Prince Disesteem'd and almost forsaken by his People, for the ill management of his Government; because it is a hanging matter to do it in Prose. Or whether it might be lawful for a Poet to expose the Majesty of his Royal parallel and bring him in upon the Stage of a publick Play-house, Courting and kneeling to his Rebell's Mistress in Verse, which could have hardly enter'd into the thought of the most vile* Associated *Ribald to have done in prose.*" The pamphlet, which is some thirty pages, is written to insist upon the very points which Dryden's enemies knew he had not intended. All the opponents of *The Duke of Guise* repeat with wearisome reiteration that it is treasonable to represent the King of England as Henri III of France. But this was never designed, and it was never done. As a matter of fact the author of the *True History of the Duke of Guise* gives his whole case away with both hands when he says of the play: "*And then 'twas a cursed mistake to bring the King in, so passionately courting a woman, whom all Histories report to be another way inclin'd. He had his* Quelus's, *his* D'Os, *his* Villequiers, *and his* Valette's, *and a peculiar way of hampering the Refractory by letting down the lid of a great chest upon their reins, while they were stooping and searching by Command for what was known to be never there.*"[1] The sexual life of Charles II of England and the sexual life of Henri III of France were so widely dissimilar that no comparison or juxtaposition is possible. And if it is "a cursed mistake" to represent Henri III, enamoured of Marmoutiere, as Dryden has done, then it is altogether impertinent to discuss the historical Henri III since in the play he is on this showing quite another person. It is true that Dr. Von Römer[2] has asserted that Charles II was a pseudo-homosexual, a figment which Dr. Johannes Prinz[3] seems to favour. But these inept vagaries we justly dismiss with no small impatience.

Then came a blustering bludgeon onslaught, "Some Reflections Upon The Pretended Parallel In The Play Called The Duke of Guise. In a Letter to a Friend," 4to, 1683, which is so violent and impetuous, so rough and clumsy

[1] "Prendre le lièvre au collet." This adventure happened to Saint-Luc. See Jean Hervez, *Mignons et Courtisanes au XVIème Siècle*, Paris, 1908, ch. 11, pp. 51–52.

[2] *Rochester's Sodom*, "Herausgegeben nach dem Hamburger Manuscript, mit einer Einleitung, von L.S.A., M. v. Römer." Amsterdam, Paris, 12mo, 1904. (Reprinted in κρυπτάδια, Paris, 1883–1911, vol. IX.) Unfortunately this edition is worthless. It is not too much to say that the editor had no acquaintance with the work of Rochester, and the various problems, bibliographical and critical, that are involved. As there is such uncertainty concerning the authorship of *Sodom* it may be worth remarking that a contemporary MS. satire, unprinted, in Bodley definitely ascribes this piece to Rochester.

[3] *John Wilmot, Earl of Rochester, His Life and Writings.* Leipzig, 1927, pp. 168–169. This monograph must be used with caution and reserve. The bibliographical details are very ample and show evidence of assiduous research, but Dr. Prinz has not the general knowledge of the period necessary for such a study. Many of his literary and critical judgements can be gravely impugned, and he has omitted important authorities from his pages, whilst too often relying upon indifferent writers.

withal, that the King of Basan may be spelled in every line. Shadwell goes several times to see *The Duke of Guise* and flies out at once with: I was "extreamly incensed at the wicked and barbarous Design it was intended for," and when Og was incensed there followed foul words and such swindging sentences of damnation as might have made Muggleton himself turn livid with envy at so rich and rare a vein.

Some Grub-street rhymester also rushed into print with a copy of verses—if they may so be termed—but the rarity of the broadside is its only merit, as may be carefully judged by the following specimen. A sounding name was bestowed on the thing, and it is interesting to note the bob at Dryden's well-known belief in judicial astrology. The piece is dubbed "*Sol* in opposition to *Saturn*. Or Aa [*sic*] short return to a late Tragedy call'd The Duke of Guise" which commences:

> Hail Royal Prince! our happy Morning Star;
> The Genius of our Peace, the Soul of War:
> High by descent, by vertue higher yet,
> Which makes the people crovvd to kiss thy feet.
> Fame blow thy Trumpet! and let the mighty sound,
> Of *Monmouth*, from the *Antartick* Pole rebound.

And so on for another ninety-three lines. There is singularly little to do with *The Duke of Guise* in this doggerel save we are told of the Poet "His Plot doth Item what sport he'd be at."

In 1683 was published (broadside) "An Epode to his worthy Friend Mr. John Dryden, To Advise him not to Answer Two Malicious Pamphlets against his Tragedy called *The Duke of Guise*."

This piece, which has considerable merit—there is a real swing and force in the stanzas and the metre is used with uncommon mastery—has been ascribed to Nat Lee, which seems most unlikely. In the first place the manner and diction of the poem are both utterly unlike Lee. Secondly, it is hardly probable that he would allude to *The Duke of Guise* as the work of Dryden alone.

Dryden, however, felt that these attacks, which were something more than merely personal, could not be passed over in silence, and accordingly he was at the pains to confute the Whiggish scribblers in his *Vindication of The Duke of Guise*.[1] Nothing could have been more galling, nothing could have been more unanswerable than the disdain with which he dismisses his assailants. His own position he establishes beyond all cavil with the most transparent sincerity; their sham castle of lies and vituperation crumbles into dust at the play of his native wit and relentless scorn. Even as a piece of English prose, taken without any relation to the occasion which demanded this reply, *The Vindication* is one of the finest pieces of controversy in the language.

Dryden probably received a hint from the Court to the effect that the scurril allegations of Hunt, Shadwell and the rest should be finally rebutted, and in any case Charles very plainly showed that he thoroughly approved his laureate's argument and attitude by enjoining upon him to undertake a version of Louis

[1] Thus the head-lines of the 4to, 1683, each verso being headed *The Vindication of* and each recto *The Duke of Guise*.

Maimbourg's[1] *Histoire de la Ligue* (Paris, 4to, 1683; and 2 vols. 12mo, 1684), which appeared demy octavo, 1684, as "The History of the League. Written in *French* by Monsieur *Maimbourg*. Translated into *English* according to His Majesty's Command." This is dedicated to the King himself in a strain of decent loyalty, which is neither fulsome nor exaggerated. The postscript also is very well worth attention, as much for the matter as for the style.

Shadwell, Settle, and others now found themselves regarded with marked disfavour, and it must be acknowledged that they had done their utmost to earn such reprobation. In those days, too, Og and Doeg were particularly unpopular at the theatre. Betterton had by no means relished the difficulties and disorders particularly which attended the production of *The Lancashire Witches* in the autumn of 1681, and Shadwell found that Dorset Garden wanted no more of his ware. "By God, my Lord," he complained to the Earl of Dorset, "those Tory Rogues will act none of my Plays." As for Settle, his tergiversation had discredited him with all parties. Dryden, whose influence with Betterton was paramount, with reason objected to the production of disloyal and malcontent dramas, and Tom Brown in "The Reason of Mr. Bays Changing his Religion, considered in a Dialogue between *Crites*, *Eugenius* and Mr. *Bays*," has set out the situation with some malice and a good deal of truth. Here after ridiculing "the fierce *Elkanah*" "and a fat old gouty Gentleman, commonly called the King of *Basan*, who had almost devoured the stage with free-quarter for his men of Wit, and humourists," Bayes continues "to prevent all infection of their errors, I direct my Monitory Letters to the Sieur *Batterton*, advising him to keep no correspondence, either directly or indirectly, with these aforesaid Apostates from Sense and Reason, adding, that in case of neglect, I would certainly put the theatre under an interdict."[2]

When *The Prophetess: or, The History of Dioclesian*, an opera, was produced at Dorset Garden in June, 1690, Dryden had furnished a Prologue which contained some spice of political allusion. "This Prologue was forbidden to be spoken the second night of the representation of the *Prophetess*. Mr. Shadwell was the occasion of its being taken notice of by the Ministry in the last Reign. He happen'd to be at the House on the first night, and taking the beginning of the Prologue to have a *double meaning*, and that meaning to reflect on the *Revolution*, he told a gentleman, *He would immediately put a stop to it*. When that gentleman ask'd, Why he would do the Author such a disservice? He said, *Because while Mr.* Dryden *was Poet Laureate, he would never let any Play of his be Acted*."[3] It is pretty well established that *Bellamira, or The Mistress*, which passes under Sedley's name, is by Shadwell; and that had not Sir Charles fathered this comedy it could not have been produced in May, 1687.

As for Settle, after his *The Heir of Morocco*, produced at the Theatre Royal in 1682, it was not until an interval of more than eight years had passed that he

[1] 1610–1686. Maimbourg was a prolific historical writer, and a sound opponent of Jansenism. His pages are remarkable for their elegant diction, but unfortunately he had imbued Gallican ideas, and of his writings some were even placed on the Index as having given great offence to the Ven. Innocent XI.

[2] 4to, 1688, p. 16.

[3] *The Muses Mercury: or, Monthly Miscellany*, Vol. I, Number 1, January, 1707.

could obtain a hearing upon the stage with *Distress'd Innocence, or The Princess of Persia.*

During the latter part of the year 1684 and January, 1685, Dryden was engaged upon an Opera designed to celebrate in allegory the triumph of order and justice over anarchy and rebellion. The music was composed by Louis Grabu,[1] whose work Charles II extremely admired. The piece was already in rehearsal, and the King himself had been graciously pleased that on more than one occasion it should be given before him even in its incomplete state and without the final touches, when as all was well in train for a most brilliant première His Majesty was struck down by a sudden apoplexy and after some four days died on 6 February, 1685.

There are, perhaps, few accidents more fatal to the success of a production than postponement, and a postponement in such melancholy circumstances was almost inevitably bound to spell failure. Alterations naturally must have been made in the "*Fabrick of* the Opera," and although Dryden talks lightly enough of these one conceives that more changes were involved than he cared to admit to the public. It is candidly acknowledged in the Preface that this libretto "was originally intended as a Prologue to a Play, of the Nature of The *Tempest*," that is actually to the play which afterwards became *King Arthur*. Ill luck pursued the piece, for the first performance took place at Dorset Garden[2] on Saturday, 6 June, 1685, and the sixth performance was on the Saturday following, 13 June, which very morning word reached Whitehall of the landing of the Duke of Monmouth at Lyme in Dorsetshire some thirty hours before.

The news was communicated to the House of Commons by a message from the King, which was delivered by the Earl of Middleton. Having voted and drawn up an address to His Majesty, desiring him to take care of his sacred person, they adjourned until four o'clock, in which interval they went to Whitehall, presented their address, and then met again. It may be supposed, therefore, that the news got abroad about this time, and soon reached the theatre where the audience were assembled at the representation of the opera.

It is remarked in *The Touch-Stone*[3] that *Albion and Albanius* "consisted

[1] Louis Grabu, Master of the King's Music, had composed the score to the English Version of Perrin's *Ariane et Bacchus* (*Ariadne, or, The Marriage of Bacchus*), produced in celebration of the marriage of James, Duke of York, with Mary of Modena. He also composed the settings for songs and entertainments in several other plays, notably the music for Shadwell's *Timon of Athens*, produced in Dorset Garden early in January, 1677–8, or possibly even in December, 1677. The "Warrant to Edward, Earl of Manchester, to swear in —— Grabu as Master of the English Music" is dated 12 November, 1666, and Pepys, Wednesday, 20 February, 1666–7, notes: "They Talk also how the King's viallin, Bannister, is mad that the King hath a Frenchman come to be chief of some part of the King's musique." On Friday, 15 November, 1667, Pelham Humphreys, laughing at the King's music, boasted to Pepys "that Grebus, the Frenchman, the King's master of the musick, how he understands nothing, nor can play on any instrument, and so cannot compose : and that he will give him a lift out of his place."

[2] Since this was a larger house than the Theatre Royal and better adapted for magnificent and imposing spectacles.

[3] 1728; p. 10.

altogether of Musick in Recitative and Airs; tho' I believe more after the *French* than *Italian Gou;* being set to musick by a *Frenchman;*" but it differs in several important features from *Ariane, ou le Mariage de Bacchus* to which Grabu had written music eleven years before.[1] Between the acts in *Ariane* occur *intermèdes* (interludes), each of which consists of one or two *entrées de ballet* (Mask-Entries). In *Albion and Albanius* each Act concludes with a scenic spectacle and choruses naturally arising out of and serving as a climax to the preceding action.

The Decorations and the Inventions of the Ornaments, largely the work and care of Betterton who had expended large sums upon this part of the Entertainment, were primarily suggested by the *décorations* of Corneille's *Andromède*, produced in January, 1650,[2] as of course also by the Operas which in their turn followed upon the lines thus chalked out for their machinery and effects. The machines of *Andromède* were the work of Jacopo Torelli, who was born at Fano in 1608. Mazarin invited him to Paris, where from his skill he was known as "le grand sorcier." In 1663 he returned to Italy and built a magnificent theatre at Fano, his native town. Here he died in 1678. The machine drawn by peacocks in *Albion and Albanius* was a hint from Act V, Scene VII of *Andromède*, where "Jupiter déscend du ciel dans un trône tout éclatant d'or et de lumières, infermé dans un nuage qui l'environne. A ses deux côtés, deux autres nuages apportent jusqu'à la terre Junon et Neptune . . . ils se déploient en rond autour de celui de Jupiter, et occupant toute la face du théâtre, ils font le plus agréable spectacle de toute cette représentation." The second scene of Act II in *Albion and Albanius*, the prospect of London, is figured much on the same lines as the *décoration* of *Andromède*, I, 1, "la ville capitale du royaume de Céphée, ou plutôt la place publique de cette ville. Les deux côtés et le fond du théâtre sont des palais magnifiques tous différents de structure, mais qui gardent admirablement l'égalité et les justesses de la perspective." Apollo appears in *Albion and Albanius* drawing the chariot of the sun, and holding the reins of his horses in his hand. In the Prologue to *Andromède:* "On voit le Soleil s'avancer dans un char tout lumineux, tiré par les quatre chevaux, qu' Ovide lui donne."[3] In the English Opera Neptune arises from the sea with Rivers, Tritons, and Nymphs in attendance; thus in *Andromède*, III, 4, "trois Néréides s'élèvent du milieu de flots," and then appears Neptune, "dans un char formé d'une grande conque de nacre, et tiré par deux chevaux marins," the great scallop-shell richly adorned, and "drawn by Dolphins" wherein are seen Venus and Albanius (Act III). There is an allusion to the prologue of *Andromède* in Dryden's line:

Le plus grand Roy du Monde, is always ringing.

In the French Opera, Le Soleil and Melpomène sing a duetto in which occurs the refrain, "Louis est le plus jeune et le plus grand des rois."

[1] The original music to which Pierre Perrin's libretto was set had been composed by Robert Cambert. *Ariane* wa given privately at Paris in April 1669.

[2] The machines of *Andromède* were pictured in six copper-plates (folio) engraved by Chauveau.

[3] *Metamorphoseon* II, 153–155. See also Hyginus, *Fabularum Liber*, 183.

The Poetical Hell of *Albion and Albanius* with which Act II opens is a common operatic property. A "dismal Hell" was shown in IV, 1, in the *Descent of Orpheus into Hell*, "Presented by the French Comedians at the Cock-Pit in Drury Lane" in 1661. Shadwell's *Psyche*, Dorset Garden, February, 1674–5, Act V, commences with Hell with Prometheus, Sisyphus, Pluto, the Furies, and other denizens of the mythological underworld.[1]

So extremely fine is Dryden's libretto that the allegory seems scarcely to have faded even to-day. The metrical effects are varied with great propriety and great beauty, whilst in the more satirical passages there is a force which none but the pen that wrote *Absalom and Achitophel* and *Mac Flecknoe* could achieve. The short sharp lines which sum up the infamies of Oates are unforgettable in their vigour. They have all the compelling energy of quick taps on a drum, resonant and wellnigh electric, as they stamp and seal the truth.

It is indeed unfortunate that Purcell did not set Dryden's words. We might then have possessed a masterpiece of English Opera. Dis aliter visum. As it is, with regard to Louis Grabu's music Professor Dent writes as follows: "Grabu's recitatives are a caricature of Lulli's Paradeschritt. The perpetual changes from bars of four beats to bars of three and *vice versa* are additionally destructive to the natural flow of the words, and this is made worse by perpetual ill accent owing to Grabu's very inadequate knowledge of English. Even when he accents the syllables rightly, he often makes nonsense out of a sentence by an unsuitable melodic outline. . . .

"The instrumental and lyric parts are indescribably dull. Grabu deserves praise for his idea of the great *chaconne* at the end of Act II, but the music itself is of the poorest quality. There can, however, be little doubt that Purcell studied the score with discriminating attention for there are a few passages that can often and easily be paralleled in the English composer's Operas. We may quote the dance and song of the nereids and tritons who rise from the sea to comfort Albion at the beginning of Act III. . . . Grabu's tune effectually destroys all Dryden's delicate variation of the hackneyed rhythm.

"The air for the Graces and Loves shows a certain charm and variety of treatment; and lastly, attention should be called to the air for Fame, or as Grabu prefers to call her, 'The Renown,' which is obviously the model for the air of Fame in Purcell's *The Indian Queen*."[2]

Albion and Albanius failed, and this failure was due not so much to the impropriety of Grabu's music, indifferent though this be, as to the fact that this magnificently mounted Opera had the ill-luck to appear at that anxious moment when a restless pretender, a second Perkin, had been foolhardy and criminal enough to invade English soil. "The Nation being in a great Consternation, it was perform'd but Six times, which not Answering half the Charge they were at, involv'd the Company very much in Debt."[3] Dryden's enemies, although they dare not venture so far as formerly, were not slow to jeer and taunt him

[1] A Classical Hell is shown in a masque, Settle's *The Empress of Morocco*, Dorset Garden, 1673, also in Powell's *Brutus of Alba*; *or, Augusta's Triumph*, I, 1 and 2, Dorset Garden, 1696.

[2] *Foundations of English Opera*, 1928, chapter VIII, pp. 166–168.

[3] Downes; *Roscius Anglicanus*.

with their pasquils and pistolets of song. The following parody is among the best of these political squibs:

From Father *Hopkins*, whose vein did inspire him,
Bayes sends this raree-show, to publick view;
Prentices, fops, and their footmen admire him,
Thank patron, painter, and Monsieur *Grabu*.

Each actor on the stage his luck bewailing,
Finds that his loss is infallibly true;
Smith, *Nokes*, and *Leigh* in a Feaver with railing,
Curse poet, painter, and Monsieur *Grabu*.

Betterton, *Betterton*, thy decorations,
And the machines were well written we knew;
But all the words were such stuff, we want patience,
And little better is Monsieur *Grabu*.

Damme, says *Underhill*, I'm out of two hundred
Hoping that Rainbows and Peacocks would do;
Who thought infallible *Tom* could have blunder'd,
A plague upon him and Monsieur *Grabu*.

Lane thou hast no applause for thy capers,
Tho all without thee would make a man spew;
And a month hence will not pay for the tapers,
Spite of *Jack* Laureat and Monsieur *Grabu*.

Bayes thou wouldst have thy skill thought universal,
Tho thy dull ear be to musick untrue;
Then whilst we strive to confute the *Rehearsal*,
Prithee learn thrashing of Monsieur *Grabu*.

With thy dull Prefaces still wouldst thou treat us,
Striving to make thy dull bauble look fair;
So the horn'd herd of the city do cheat us,
Still most commending the worst of their ware.

Leave making Operas and writing Lyricks,
'Till thou hast ears and canst alter thy strain;
Stick to thy talent of bold Panegyricks,
And still remember the breathing the vein.

Yet if thou thinkest the Town will extol 'em,
Print thy dull notes, but be thrifty and wise;
Instead of angels subscrib'd for the volume,
Take a round shilling, and thank my advice.

In imitating thee this may be charming,
Gleaning from Laureats is no shame at all;
And let this Song be sung next performing,
Else ten to one but the prices will fall.

Very shortly after the accession of King James II, Dryden, as the logical outcome of his philosophical and intellectual development, was received into the Catholic Church. It should be clear to any reader of his works that this step was the inevitable and ultimate solution of the various debates he argues so acutely from so many points of view. To suspect his sincerity is to show oneself not merely ungenerous but lacking in perception. Macaulay wrote: "Finding that, if he continued to call himself a Protestant, his services would be overlooked, he declared himself a Papist. The King's parsimony immediately relaxed. Dryden was gratified with a pension of a hundred pounds a year, and was employed to defend his new religion both in prose and verse."

To quote Dryden's own words on another occasion: "Now there are three damn'd lyes crowded together in a very little room." A Treasury warrant of 6 May, 1684, directs the payment to Dryden of certain arrears since 1680 on a pension of £200 a year, and of further arrears since the same date on "an additionall annuity." This latter was continued by James II, and it is this which is declared to be a first bestowal as the price of apostacy. Dr. Johnson, Malone and Scott have very rightly recognised that Dryden was entirely sincere.

It is clear that the questions of religion incessantly occupied his mind. He may put them on one side; he may even jest, as he essays temporarily to avoid them; but they obtrude; he is compelled to appreciate their eternal significance, his own awful responsibility. Yet the keenly logical mind is fearful. May it not be some emotionalism? Can reason decide?

Happily it is not necessary to do more than pass by, with the briefest and most contemptuous mention, the swarm of virulent libels which sought to blacken the poet upon his conversion. There was hardly a pestiferous pamphleteer in Town who had not his quota of mud to throw, who did not smutch some sheet of paper with his sluttish and reasty doggerel. The more libertine clowns penned profane and dull dialogues; jeering even those things which men of every persuasion by common consent hold sacred and which are respected by men of no persuasion at all. The pasquils were of the poorest. Even Aphra Behn forgot her wonted good-nature and peppered "*Mr.* Dryden, *Renegate*" with a copy of verses, the weakest and ugliest thing she ever penned. Tom Shadwell roared like a Bedlamite possessed.

Indeed, his opportunity soon came, for there were evil forces at work; as has been well said; "a company of men perhaps as destitute of honour and as God-forsaken as any of which history has record—the politicians who were to make the revolution of 1688." Swiftly the whole bad business was engineered. The Prince of Orange arrived at Torbay on 5 November, 1688; and three months later his wife, the Princess Mary, landed at Whitehall stairs. The Revolution incontinently deprived Dryden of his two official posts, the laureateship and the position of historiographer royal. It was impossible that he should take the oaths of allegiance, supremacy and abjuration, and accordingly among the Lord

Chamberlain's records we find: "A warrant to sware Thomas Shadwell, Esqr., into the place and quality of poet-Laureat to His Matie, March 9, 1688–9."[1]

The Earl of Dorset had been appointed Lord Chamberlain on February, 1688–9, and we may well believe that, in spite of the fact that he was Shadwell's patron, he was extremely reluctant to render vacant the posts of poet-laureate and historiographer royal, which had been held so long and filled so worthily by his old friend. Nevertheless, it was not in his power to continue Dryden in these important offices. As a Catholic, to Prince William, the poet would have been an object of aversion and mistrust, whilst Mary of Orange soon showed herself only too ready to seize the slightest occasion of persecuting and harassing her father's laureate with every vexation and circumstance of displeasure that petty spite and inveterate malice could dictate. Dorset himself, with rare liberality, although obliged by his authority to sunder Dryden's connexion with the Court, made the poet "a most bountiful present," and to this Dryden refers in terms of heartfelt gratitude in the Dedication to his *Juvenal*[2] (A Discourse concerning the Original and Progress of Satire), which is most suitably inscribed to that generous nobleman. It is traditionally said that Dorset, although compelled to deprive his friend, supplied from his private purse the annual salary carried by the forfeited offices.

Moreover, the poet had the satisfaction of knowing that many who had been most warm in their welcome of the Dutchman very soon repented of their treacherous desertion of King James, and amongst these his reputation stood very high as one who had not wavered when others were tripped and fell. Immediately after the revolution, Dryden, who during the past four years had ceased his dramatic activities, turned once more to the theatre as his mainstay and chief resource. It is generally disputed whether *Don Sebastian, King of Portugal*, produced at Dorset Garden, November, 1689, or *All for Love* is to be esteemed the highest effort of his genius.

It is interesting to remark how Dryden in the Preface to *Don Sebastian*, which was published quarto, 1690, acknowledges that either through a long disuse of writing for the stage, or else because he wished to crowd too many characters and incidents into his scenes, he clean forgot the usual compass of a play, and the action at the first performance proved unduly drawn out and protracted. Betterton, however, soon remedied this defect and the tragedy was received with that applause it so thoroughly deserves. *Don Sebastian* must indeed be rated very highly. No more romantic figure could have been chosen for a hero than that of *Don Sebastian*, who so mysteriously disappeared from mortal ken after the battle of Alcazar. Since I have in the note upon the Source given with appropriate quotation the various traditions that arose, and were widely believed, concerning the fate of this monarch, a true knight of Christian chivalry, there is no need to repeat the tale here, and it will suffice to say that Dryden is perfectly justified in directing the events as he chose.

In his choice of Barbary as the locale of his play Dryden showed himself the practised man of the theatre. The scene of the slave-market is full of life and movement, and the mingling of Spanish and Oriental costumes must have made

[1] Public Records, LC., 5149, p. 99.

[2] Folio, 1693.

a fine display. It would appear that particular attention was paid to these Moorish robes, always most effective upon the stage.[1] Their magnificence and varied colouring became almost traditional. This is jeered at in *The Female Wits: Or, The Triumvirate of Poets at Rehearsal*, 4to, 1704, but acted some eight years before, Act II, the play-house scene where Mrs. Cross says: "The *Morocco* dresses, when new formerly for *Sebastian*, they say enliven'd the Play as much as the Pudding and Dumpling Song did *Merlin*."

In spite of Dorset's bounty it was necessary that Dryden should not relax his efforts, and the loyalty of his later years unluckily did not bring that independence and sufficient provision which he had a right to expect might have been his lot. A reading of Plautus or a reading of Molière suggested that a story which had employed the fancy both of the Roman and the French dramatists, might well be fitted to suit the London Stage. *Amphitryon, or the Two Socia's* was produced at the Theatre Royal in September, 1690.[2] This delightful comedy proved a triumphant success, and at once passed into the theatrical repertory, never failing to draw a crowded and enthusiastic audience. When we contrast *Amphitryon* with Dryden's earlier plays, the lighter episodes of *Secret Love* and *Marriage A-la-Mode* or *An Evening's Love* and *The Assignation*, a difference of style and technique may be immediately remarked. *Amphitryon* has more humour than wit; we smile and are deliciously amused at Celadon and Florimel; we laugh right out at the high-flavoured speech of Mercury and Phaedra. Upon the stage *Amphitryon* is perhaps the most broadly comical of all Dryden's plays; one can only make a possible exception in the case of *Sr. Martin Mar-all*. *The Spanish Fryar* stands as it were between the plays of the 'sixties and the plays of the 'nineties. Amusing as is the Latin tragicomoedia, and elegant as is the French *comédie*, *Amphitryon* stands far above even Plautus and Molière. The comic vigour of Dryden is at its broadest and its merriest here. Well did Granger write: "There was a native fire in this great poet which poverty could not damp, nor old age extinguish."[3] The fun, sheer fun, sparkles and sparkles, soon to burst into a blaze.

Lady Mary Wortley Montagu has so joyous and characteristic a description of an *Amphitryon* which she saw in Vienna in 1716 that it assuredly must be quoted in full. She writes to Pope on 14 September[4]: "But if their operas are thus delightful, their comedies are in as high a degree ridiculous. They have but one playhouse, where I had the curiosity to go to a German comedy, and was very glad it happened to be the story of Amphitrion. As that subject has already been handled by a Latin, French, and English poet, I was curious to see what an Austrian author would make of it. I understand enough of that language to comprehend the greatest part of it; and besides, I took with me a lady, who had

[1] This was fully appreciated by the Elizabethans. Shakespeare in *The Merchant of Venice*, has the stage-direction: "*Enter Morochus a tawny Moore all in white, and three or foure followers accordingly*." One may compare the figure of Othello so distinguished amid the Venetians and Cypriots.

[2] Publication is announced in the *London Gazette*, October 30–November 3, 1690.

[3] *Biographical History of England*. Fifth Edition, 1824, vol. V, p. 241.

[4] *Letters and Works of Lady Mary Wortley Montagu*, ed. by Lord Wharncliffe. Three volumes, 1837. Vol. I, pp. 284–285.

the goodness to explain to me every word. The way is, to take a box, which holds four, for yourself and company. The fixed price is a gold ducat. I thought the house very low and dark; but I confess, the comedy admirably recompensed that defect. I never laughed so much in my life. It began with Jupiter's falling in love out of a peep-hole in the clouds, and ended with the birth of Hercules. But what was most pleasant, was the use Jupiter made of his metamorphosis; for you no sooner saw him under the figure of Amphitrion, but, instead of flying to Alcmena, with the raptures Mr. Dryden puts into his mouth, he sends for Amphitrion's taylor, and cheats him of a laced coat, and his banker of a bag of money, a Jew of a diamond ring, and bespeaks a great supper in his name; and the greatest part of the comedy turns upon poor Amphitrion's being tormented by these people for their debts. Mercury uses Sosia in the same manner. But I could not easily pardon the liberty the poet has taken of larding his play with, not only indecent expressions, but such gross words, as I don't think our mob would suffer from a mountebank. Besides, the two Sosias very fairly let down their breeches in direct view of the boxes, which were full of people of the first rank, that seemed very well pleased with their entertainment, and assured me this was a celebrated piece.

"I shall conclude my letter with this remarkable relation, very well worthy the serious consideration of Mr. Collier."

During the first week of June, 1690, was given at Dorset Garden, now definitely the house of the larger and more spectacular productions, "*The Prophetess*, or *Dioclesian* an Opera, wrote by Mr. *Betterton;* being set out with Coastly Scenes, Machines and Cloaths: The Vocal and Instrumental Musick, done by Mr. *Purcel;* and Dances by Mr. Priest; it gratify'd the Expectation of Court and City; and got the Author a great Reputation."[1]

The Prophetess: or, The History of Dioclesian, is a slight alteration from the *Prophetess*, licensed May 14, 1622, which is ascribed by Oliphant to Fletcher and Massinger. The *Gazette*, 16 June, 1690, advertises the quarto; the score followed in 1691. Mr. E. J. Dent, *Foundations of English Opera*, says: "Betterton did little more than elaborate the scenes where the original authors simply indicated 'music and song.' The musical scenes are, however, very long, and a proportionate curtailment of the original dialogue was necessary."

Langbaine in his review of Fletcher's plays has: "*Prophetess*, a Tragical History, which has lately been reviv'd by Mr. *Dryden*, under the title of *The Prophetess, or The History of Dioclesian*, with Alterations and Additions after the manner of an *Opera*, represented at the Queen's Theatre [Dorset Garden], and printed 4to, Lond., 1690."

Curiously enough Langbaine omits Betterton from his *An Account of The English Dramatick Poets,* and he is almost certainly mistaken in ascribing this version from Fletcher to Dryden. All other authorities agree that it is Betterton's work, whilst Langbaine was misled owing to the fact that Dryden furnished the famous prologue which was promptly forbidden on account of the political allusions, and not printed with the play in 1690. This address was first given, anonymously, in *Poems on Affairs of State*, *Part III*, 1698. Its second

[1] Downes: *Roscius Anglicanus.*

appearance in print was in *The Muses Mercury, or Monthly Miscellany*, January, 1707, Vol. I, Number I. It next found a place also in the 1708 edition of the *Miscellany Poems.*[1] It is, of course, probable that Dryden assisted Betterton with a few hints, but in no sense can *The Prophetess* be claimed to be his work.

The great success, however, of this Opera suggested to the acute manager that an Opera in which Dryden, Purcell and Josiah Priest combined could not fail to be a supreme attraction. Betterton opened his mind to the poet, and Dryden was found willing enough to agree, the more especially no doubt since by this means he would be able to pay a well-deserved and judicious compliment to Henry Purcell, whom he had somehow seemed to slight in the Preface to *Albion and Albanius*, half a dozen years before, when acting under the instructions of Charles II, he had preferred Louis Grabu to an English composer.

Dryden had for some time been pondering an epic poem, and in the Epistle Dedicatory, addressed to Lord Mulgrave, which is prefixed to *Aureng-Zebe*, 4to, 1676, he talks of making "*the World some part of amends, for many ill Plays, by an Heroique Poem.*" In the Preface to his *Juvenal*, folio, 1693, he tells us further: "This too, I had intended chiefly for the Honour of my Native Country, to which a Poet is particularly oblig'd: Of two Subjects, both relating to it, I was doubtful, whether I should chuse that of King *Arthur*,[2] Conquering the *Saxons;* which being farther distant in Time, gives the greater Scope to my Invention: or that of *Edward* the Black Prince in subduing *Spain*, and restoring to it the Lawful Prince, though a Great Tyrant, *Don Pedro* the Cruel." It would appear that he had decided to take Edward the Black Prince as his hero, and accordingly he made King Arthur the subject of a Dramatick Opera *King Arthur: Or, The British Worthy*, which was produced at Dorset Garden in April-May, 1691.[3] When we read Dryden's play we must not look for "le Roy Artur," or for the Arthur of Malory, even less, perhaps, for "the faultless King, That passionate perfection" of Tennysonian Idylls, but we have an Arthur such as Tasso would have drawn. Dryden's Opera is a delightfully rococo fantasy; Italianate rather than English, but none the worse for that. Upon the stage, wedded to Purcell's music, one could desire no more exquisite entertainment. The magic wood has charms which ensorcel not only the royal lover of fair Emmeline. The song of the Sirens and the song which is sung during the dance of Nymphs and Sylvans are of the rarest lyric beauty.

It might be supposed that King Arthur would have been a favourite hero with native dramatists, but such has not proved the case, and the Arthurian legends have never occupied in the English national mind a position similar to

[1] Whence it was reprinted by Scott. In his very faulty and inexact *Poems of John Dryden*, Clarendon Press, 1910, Sargeaunt gives an ambiguous note "1690." But then his edition is abridged.

[2] Sir Richard Blackmore's Epic *Prince Arthur*, " An Heroick Poem, in Ten Books," folio, 1695, writ "*to the Rumbling of his Coaches Wheels,*" ran into two editions. Blackmore himself in the Preface says that this Poem for the greatest part "*was written in* Coffee-houses, *and in passing up and down the Streets.*" This was followed by *King Arthur*, "An Heroick Poem in Twelve Books," folio, 1697. "*Tho' the* Hero *be the same, yet 'tis another entire Poem, distinct from the former,*" Blackmore is careful to tell us.

[3] Publication is announced in the *London Gazette*, 4–8 June, 1691.

the myths which supplied the great Attic masters with matter for their tragedies. Justice Shallow in Shakespeare's *II Henry IV*, iii, 2, recalls: "I was then Sir Dagonet in Arthur's show," some masque or interlude, and *Uterpendragon* was being acted in 1597. *The Misfortunes of Arthur* by Thomas Hughes (and others) was given before Queen Elizabeth at Greenwich in 1588. *The Birth of Merlin, or The Childe hath found his Father* when published by Kirkman in 1662, was curiously enough alleged to be the joint work of Shakespeare and Rowley. *King Arthur*, a play in verse by Comyns Carr, was produced at the Lyceum Theatre, London, 12 January, 1895, with Henry Irving as Arthur; Forbes Robertson, Lancelot; Sidney Valentine, Merlin; Genevieve Ward, Morgan le Fay; and Ellen Terry, Guinevere. There is an unacted *Arthur, Monarch of the Britons*, printed 8vo, 1776, by William Hilton of Newcastle-upon-Tyne; and Ralph Macleod Fullerton, Q.C., published *Merlin, a Dramatic Poem*, 1890.

There are also the burlesques such as William Brough's *King Arthur, or The Days and Nights of the Round Table*, produced at the Haymarket in 1863, and W. M. Akhurst's *King Arthur; or, Lancelot the Loose, Gineva the Square, and the Knights of the Round Table and other Furniture*. A more modern parody of Arthurian legend proved incredibly vapid and tedious in performance.

It is certain that Dryden's *King Arthur* is the only English play upon this legend of poetic value. The rest, for the most part, are mere curiosities.

Those who were privileged to see the very pleasing amateur production of *King Arthur* at the New Theatre, Cambridge, in February, 1928, will perhaps best appreciate the extraordinary merit of Dryden's work.

In spite of failing health, Dryden was obliged to continue his literary exertions, and in addition to his poetical output—for in these years he produced some of his finest work—he was ever employed upon the composition of pieces for the theatre. During the summer of 1691 he was devoting his energies to a tragedy upon the subject of Cleomenes; but as the winter came he was obliged to entrust his script for completion to his young friend, Thomas Southerne, already well known as the author of some excellent dramas, although he had not as yet reached his fullest maturity, which was to shine in *The Fatal Marriage* and *Oroonoko*.

The Wives Excuse; Or, Cuckolds Make Themselves, Theatre Royal, December, 1691, is a remarkably good comedy with some extremely pungent satire and capital characterization. It is as brisk and witty as anything in Sheridan, and has far more literary quality than that very derivative dramatist could ever attain. Yet it was received, if not with coldness, at least with a polite unconcern for which the audiences justly received a severe rebuke from Dryden, who paid Southerne an immortal compliment in verse.

It will be remembered that Dryden's prologue to *The Prophetess* had been forbidden after the first night, and Mary of Orange, who learned of this incident, expressed her displeasure at Dryden's raillery in very warm and lively terms.[1] Jealous eyes were kept upon his movements, and his poems were scanned with inquisitorial precision. *Cleomenes, The Spartan Heroe*, had been carefully rehearsed, and was to have been acted in April, 1692, when it was

[1] Miss Strickland, *Queens of England*, 1847, Vol. XI, p. 277.

suddenly prohibited on the eve of production.[1] It was alleged that the figure of Cleomenes in exile at Alexandria might be too lively a reminder of King James at Saint Germains, and among other objectors Shadwell did not fail strongly to urge this parallel to Dorset.

In *The Gentleman's Journal* for April, 1692, Peter Motteux writes: "I was in hopes to have given you in this Letter an account of the acting of Dryden's *Cleomenes:* it was to have appeared upon the stage on Saturday last, and you need not doubt but that the Town was full of the expectation of the performance; but orders came from her Majesty to hinder its being acted; so that none can tell when it shall be played." In the following month the same writer adds: "I told you in my last that none could tell when Mr. Dryden's *Cleomenes* would appear. Since that time, the innocence and merit of the play have raised it several eminent advocates, who have prevailed to have it acted; and you need not judge but it has been with great applause." The fact was that Lord Dorset had sent for a copy of the play, and when he had read it with some care returned it to Dryden, of whose genius he was, as is very well known, a great admirer, affirming that in his opinion there was nothing to prevent its appearance on the stage. The Earl of Rochester, also, to whom the tragedy was dedicated when it was issued from the press, 4to, 1692, spoke very warmly on Dryden's behalf; whilst Antony, Viscount Falkland, informed Queen Mary that to his certain knowledge Dryden had sketched out a rough plan of the play some seven or eight years before, and had for so long a time entertained the idea of treating this subject. As was inevitable, the postponement, and the reasons for the postponement, being very widely discussed, only served to rouse new interest in the drama, which, when it came upon the stage, was received by crowded houses with those thunders of applause it so entirely merited and deserved. Accordingly the malice of Dryden's enemies only added to the lustre of his reputation.

It is unpleasing to relate that the dramatic career of Dryden closed, as it had begun, with bad success. *Love Triumphant, Or, Nature will Prevail*, a tragi-comedy, is announced in the *Gentleman's Journal*[2] for 1693 as being a play of the same kind with *The Spanish Fryar*, but it by no means achieved the popularity of that excellent comedy. *Love Triumphant* confessedly is not so good a play; it has no such figure as Father Dominic, nor indeed so lively a portraiture as Gomez. Yet Lopez and Dalinda with their rich show and beggarly home, where "the Dining Room plays the Hypocrite for all the House," and "there's neither Sheet nor Shirt in the whole Family" are clear cut as figures of Mateo Aleman or Quevedo. Actually Carlos and Dalinda are not so wittily conceived as Lorenzo and Elvira, but this is not to say that *Love Triumphant* is an indifferent or even an unequal piece of work. In the second rank it may deservedly occupy a considerable place. Its lighter pages can be read with amusement; and upon the stage these comic episodes would, I am assured, be found vastly entertaining. The romantic scenes of the play are always interesting and often powerful to a degree. The whole atmosphere of the Spanish court with its secrets and its intrigues, is admirably conveyed. The tyranny of Veramond,

[1] See Luttrell's *Brief Relation*, Vol. II, pp. 413 and 422; 9 and 16 April, 1692.

[2] November 1693, p. 374. "We are impatiently expecting a Play by Mr. *Dryden*; 'tis of the Nature of his *Spanish Fryar*."

who in some sense dominates the plot, seems to me finely observed and carefully wrought, nor do I imagine that his change of will, although contrary to the Aristotelian canon, is at all unnatural or obscure.

Some adversary of the poet, whom he is pleased to dub "huffing Dryden," writing to a friend in the country on 22 March, 1693–4, reflects very severely upon this piece. "The second play," he says, "is Mr. Dryden's called *Love Triumphant; or, Nature Will Prevail.* It is a tragi-comedy, but in my opinion one of the worst he ever writt, if not the very worst: the comical part descends beneath the style and shew of a Bartholomew-Fair Droll. It was damned by the universal cry of the town, *nemine contradicente* but the conceited poet. He says in his Preface, that this is the last the town must expect from him; he had done himself a kindness had he taken his leave before."[1] This attack seems the outcome of personal and political rancour, and is a good example of the malevolence against which Dryden had ceaselessly to contend.

As early as March, 1694, Motteux in the *Gentleman's Journal* had expressed a hope that Dryden would oblige the world with a translation of Vergil and, occupied in so laborious, if so splendid an undertaking, Dryden would no longer have the time to devote to dramatic composition. Indeed, as has already been remarked, he definitely asserted that *Love Triumphant* was the last Poem which he intended for the theatre. Moreover, there had been considerable changes in the theatrical world, and a state of unrest prevailed, a situation of which a younger man might have made no account, but which was decidedly not an encouragement to the older poet. There was a division in the playhouse and continual differences, a crisis which could only be relieved by the secession of Betterton and a number of the best actors. These formed a new company, which opened at Lincoln's Inn Fields on Monday, 29 April, 1695, whilst Rich and the patentees ruled the Theatre Royal, Drury Lane.

It may be presumed that Dryden drew certain fees from such of his plays as continued in the repertory, as well as from those pieces which were given at any special revival. In his Epistle prefixed before Lord Lansdowne's tragedy, *Heroick Love*,[2] 4to, 1698, Dryden has some pretty reflections upon the state of the theatre:

> Thine be the Lawrel then; thy blooming Age
> Can best, if any can, support the Stage:
> Which so declines, that shortly we may see,
> Players and Plays reduc'd to second Infancy.
> Sharp to the World, but thoughtless of Renown,
> They Plot not on the Stage, but on the Town,
> And in Despair their Empty Pit to fill,
> Set up some Foreign Monster in a Bill:
> Thus they jog on; still tricking, never thriving;
> And Murd'ring Plays, which they miscal Reviving.
> Our Sense is Nonsense, through their Pipes convey'd;

[1] The letter is preserved by Malone, *The Plays and Poems of Shakespeare*, 8vo, 1790, Vol. I, part ii, p. 141.

[2] Published 19 February, 1697–8. *London Gazette*, No. 3368.

Scarce can a Poet know the Play He made;
'Tis so disguis'd in Death: Nor thinks 'tis He
That suffers in the Mangled Tragedy.
Thus *Itys* first was kill'd, and after dress'd
For his own Sire the Chief Invited Guest.

This was probably intended for, and seems particularly to have annoyed, George Powell, Betterton's rival, and the principal actor at the Theatre Royal. In the preface to *The Fatal Discovery, or Love in Ruines*, a tragedy which he ushered on to the stage, and which was printed, 4to, 1698, he girds at Dryden with some profanity, and the most indecent violence: "Here I am afraid he makes but a course Compliment, when this great Wit, with his Treacherous Memory, forgets, that he had given away his Lawrels upon Record twice before, *viz.* once to Mr. *Congreve* and another time to Mr. *Southern.* Prithee, old *Œdipus*, expound this Mystery: Dost thou set up thy own *Transubstantiation* Miracle in the Donation of thy Idol Bays, that thou hast 'em Fresh, New, and whole, to give 'em three times over? . . . For the most mortal stroke at us, he charges us with downright *Murdering of Plays, which we miscall Reviving.* I will not derogate from the merit of those Senior Actors of both Sexes, at the other House, that shine in their several Perfections, in whose lavish praises he is so highly Transported; But, at the same time, he makes himself but an Arbitrary Judge on our side, to condemn unheard, and that under no less a Conviction than Murder; when I cannot learn (for a fair Judgement upon us) that his Reverend Crutches have ever brought him within our doors since the division of the Companies [1695]. 'Tis true, I think, we have revived some pieces of *Dryden*, as his *Sebastian, Maiden Queen, Marriage A-la-Mode, King Arthur*, &c. But here let us be Try'd by a Christian jury, the Audience, and not receive the Bow-string from his *Mahometan* Grand Seigniorship. 'Tis true, his more particular pique against us, as he has declared himself, is in Relation to our Reviving his *Almanzor.* There, indeed, he has reason to be angry, for our waking that sleepy Dowdy, and exposing his nonsense, not ours; and if that Dish did not please him, we have a Scottish Proverb for our Justification, *viz. Twas rotten roasted, because, &c.* and the World must expect, 'twas very hard crutching up what *Hart* and *Mohun* before us could not prop. I confess he is a little severe when he will allow our best Performance to bear no better Fruit than a *Crab-Vintage;* Indeed, if we young Actors spoke but half as sourly, as his Old Gall scribbles, we should be all Crab all over." From this pleasant Billingsgate tirade it would appear that the actors of the Theatre Royal had revived *The Conquest of Granada* but neglected to pay the author's dues.

Attacks on the theatre had, of course, long been common, before Jeremy Collier wrote that, "*Being convinced that nothing has gone farther in Debauching the Age than the Stage Poets, and Play-house, I thought I could not employ my time better than in writing against them.*"[1]

Collier's book I have analysed in detail; and there is no need to rehearse the

[1] *A Short View of the Immorality And Profaness Of The English Stage*, 1698. Preface.

narrative again.[1] Since, however, there seems to persist the extraordinary error that Collier's attack was ineffective, I would emphasize that so far from this being the case the results were both immediate and far-reaching. "It is almost possible in English dramatic literature to draw a line of demarcation between the plays written before and the plays written after the spring of 1698." It is altogether untrue to say that "the old repertory remained unchanged in the theatres." Material and drastic alterations were made, the language was severely amended, oaths were deleted, luscious situations glozed or omitted. Another and chaster spirit informed the theatre both before and behind the curtain. Here *A Short View* only interests us as far as it concerns Dryden. And Dryden, although a principal, perhaps the chief, object of censure, curious as it may seem, it concerned hardly at all. He was too weary of dispute to enter into the arena, and the few words he has to say in the Preface to the *Fables*, 1700, together with his epilogue to *The Pilgrim*, are his answer to an opponent whom he justly disdained to encounter.

Dryden had indeed finished his work for the theatre when Collier wrote, and there was nothing for him to say. His last piece was a Prologue, Epilogue, Dialogue and Masque which he composed for a revival of Fletcher's *The Pilgrim*, "now very much Alter'd" by Vanbrugh, and produced at the Theatre Royal, Drury Lane, on 29 April, 1700. On 30 April, *The Postboy* announced that "John Dryden, Esq. the famous poet, lies a-dying." On the third night, 1 May, Dryden died, and the profits accordingly went to his son, Charles. "Yesterday morning at three of the clock, John Dryden, Esq., departed this life, who for his poetry, &c. excelled all others this age produced." *The Postboy*, Tuesday, 30 April–Thursday, 2 May, 1700.

It will, perhaps, be well if I remark at this place that I have throughout this Introduction aimed at considering Dryden as a dramatist alone. It is not, of course, possible, and it were certainly very inequitable to separate his poems and prose from his dramas in any consideration of his genius, but I have purposely refrained from giving an account of such pieces as were not written for the theatre, wherefore the reader must not be surprised to find the barest mention of such masterpieces of satire as *Absalom and Achitophel* and *MacFlecknoe*, whilst *Annus Mirabilis*, *Religio Laici*, *The Hind and The Panther* are passed over very cursorily, and the *Odes upon S. Cecilia's Day*, *Eleonora*, the Translations, the *Fables*, may seem to be ignored.

It remains briefly to sum up the qualities of Dryden as a playwright and in so doing to establish his just position among our dramatists. Whilst reading his plays one is struck by the extraordinary sureness of their technique. In this respect he showed himself a complete master. None of his pieces, either tragedy or comedy, so far as I can recall, exhibits an awkward situation. All is natural, and yet not too artificially smooth and correspondent. Of his tragedies, *All for Love*, *Don Sebastian*, and I will add, in their kind, the heroic plays, must be put

[1] *Congreve's Works*, by the present editor, Nonesuch Press, 1923, Vol. I. Introduction, pp. 30–54.

in the very first rank. In tragi-comedy, as witness *Secret Love, Marriage a-la-Mode*, and *The Spanish Fryar*, he is supreme. Not less happy is he in the broader scenes of *Sr. Martin Mar-all* or with the baroque fantasy of *Amphitryon*. Whatever I read of Dryden I am entirely satisfied. I cannot conceive that anything of his could be better done.

There are other poets, perhaps, who have vision now and again to equal heights, but there are few indeed who have been able to sustain, apparently without effort, but by sheer force of genius so rare a degree of undeviating excellence. This is all the more remarkable on account of the extent of his achievement. He is certainly the greatest of English critics, nor has the lucidity and beauty of his prose ever been surpassed. There is no English satirist who is worthy to be mentioned in the same breath as John Dryden, nay, hardly one whom we may deem second.

In *Don Sebastian*, and in the figure of S. Catherine, whom Tiepolo should have painted, as she walks in radiant beauty through *Tyrannick Love*, I find a certain quality which only the greatest poets of all time possess. The delicious episodes of Celadon and Florimel, of Rhodophil and Doralice, Melantha and Palamede, are flawless and fair as a picture of Watteau or Fragonard. They bow and bend, they sink in graceful curtsies, and set to partners in their minuets of love through the sultry heat of long summer afternoons—moonlight were too romantic here; the gallants cock their hats, and the ladies flutter fans; there is a rustle of silk, and a scent of marèchale; they compliment and caress; and sometimes one will find that his heart, of which he took no account, stirs a little faster than he desires, whilst a new light glances in his mistress' eyes and her breath comes a little quicker than her wont.

But Dryden can give us more even than these precious fragile things. Dryden was the father of the true English Poetry, and the most universal of all Poets—Chaucer, Shakespeare, Dryden: these are the three names which in English literature tower high above all the rest, poets in whose immortality there is, as it were, something greater, something divine.

I have now discharged the duty of an editor to my best judgement, and I can but conclude a long and arduous task with the words of Dr. Johnson:

"The expectation of ignorance is indefinite, and that of knowledge is often tyrannical. It is hard to satisfy those who know not what to demand, or those who demand by design what they think impossible to be done. I have indeed disappointed no opinion more than my own; yet I have endeavoured to perform my task with no slight solicitude. Not a single passage in the whole work has appeared to me corrupt, which I have not attempted to restore; or obscure, which I have not endeavoured to illustrate. . . . I am now to stand the judgment of the publick. . . . Every work of this kind is by its nature deficient, and I should feel little solicitude about the sentence, were it pronounced only by the skilful and the learned."

MONTAGUE SUMMERS

Oxford—Paris, 1931

A NOTE ON
PURCELL'S MUSIC

THE INDIAN QUEEN

The operatic version of *The Indian-Queen* was never printed, but the libretto and the whole of the music, partly in Purcell's autograph, are to be found in a MS. preserved in the British Museum (Ad. MS. 31449). The Masque of Hymen with which the opera concludes was set by Daniel Purcell, and since Henry Purcell died in November, 1695, it is probable that the work he was prevented by illness from completing was finished by his brother. "The Songs in the Indian Queen: As it is now Compos'd into an Opera. By Mr. *Henry Purcell*, Composer in Ordinary to his Majesty, And one of the Organists of his Majesty's Chapel-Royal" appeared in a pirated edition in 1695. Ismeron's song, the famous "You twice Ten Hundred Deities," was given in Book IV of *Deliciæ Musicæ*, 1696; and, together with several of the other songs, was included in *Orpheus Britannicus*.

The songs from Daniel Purcell's "Masque of Hymen" were printed in the "First Book of the Second Volume" of *Deliciæ Musicæ*, of which the title-page announces that it contains "The Additional Musick to the *Indian Queen*, by Mr. *Daniel Purcell*, as it is now Acted at *His Majesties Theatre*." The publication of this book is advertised in the *Post-Boy*, 29 Feb.–3 March, 1695–6.

THE INDIAN EMPEROUR

Kalib's song in Act II, scene 1, *I look'd and saw within the Book of Fate*, was set by Henry Purcell for the revival of this tragedy in January, 1691–2. This music was printed in the sixth book of *The Banquet of Music*, licensed 17 February, 1691–2.

The song, *Ah fading joy, how quickly art thou past?* Act IV, scene 3, was set (as a song with three-part chorus) by Pelham Humphrey, and this appeared in Playford's *Choice Ayres, Songs, and Dialogues*, 1675.

THE TEMPEST

It was once supposed that the music of Banister and Pelham Humphreys was written for the Dryden and Davenent comedy, but actually this is the score of Shadwell's opera. Pepys, Thursday, 7 November, 1667, speaks of Ferdinand's song as "a curious piece of musique in an echo of half sentences, the echo repeating the former half, while the man goes on to the latter; which is mighty pretty." The idea of "echo songs" goes back to classical times. Poliziano brought it into vogue by his *Pan ed Eco* (*Le Stanze*, ed. Carducci, Florence, 1863, p. 231), and this was imitated by Guarini and Tasso. H. Körting, *Geschichte des Französischen Romans im XVII Jahrhundert*, 1886, Vol. I, p. 109, n. 3, says that du Bellay wrote the first French "echo song." There is one in the *Astrée*, which Sorel did not forget to ridicule in *Le Berger extravagant*. There is also a famous "echo song" in Mlle de Scudéry's *Clélie* (1660, Vol. I, p. 316), which is sung by Horace (Coclès), an episode which is well laughed at by Boileau in his dialogue *Les Héros de Roman*. "Horatius Coclès chantant à l'écho!" cries Minos; "il est vrai que la chose est assez nouvelle," Pluto agrees.

In Book III of *Deliciæ Musarum*, 1696 (but published at the close of 1695), was printed "Dear pretty youth," "A New Song in the *Tempest*, sung by Miss Cross to her Lover, who is supposed dead. Set by Mr. *Henry Purcell*." This song is also given in *Orpheus Britannicus*, and there exists an early single-sheet version of it as "A Song sung by the Girl in the Tempest. Set by Mr. H. Purcell and exactly engrav'd by Thos: Cross." This song, introduced by Miss Cross as Dorinda, belongs to Shadwell's opera rather than to the Dryden and Davenant comedy.

TYRANNICK LOVE

In a MS. volume preserved in the British Museum (Ad. MS. 19759), which is dated 9 June, 1681, is contained an anonymous setting of *Hark, my* Damilcar, *we are call'd below!* entitled "Song by Spirits in Tyrannick love." This was originally sung by Mrs. Knepp (Nakar) and Mrs. James (Damilcar). For a revival of *Tyrannick Love* Purcell set the same song (the words commencing *Hark, my* Damilcar), and also Damilcar's *Ah how sweet it is to love*, which was originally sung by Mrs. James. These were published in *Deliciæ Musarum*, Book I, licensed 23 April, 1695. Purcell's duet was sung by Mrs. Ayliff and Bowman, and the song by Mrs. Ayliff.

THE CONQUEST OF GRANADA

How unhappy a Lover am I, Part II, Act IV, was set by Nicholas Staggins, and is given in *Choice Songs and Ayres*, 1673. It is also extant in various MSS.; British Museum Add. MSS. 29396, and (as "Staggin's Jig") 29371. There was introduced into a revival of this play a song by D'Urfey, *Celemene, pray tell me*, of which an engraved copy *circa* 1694 has "A Dialogue in the Second Part of the Conquest of Granada. The words by Mr. Tho. D'Urfey. Set by Mr. Henry Purcell. Sung by the Boy and the Girl and exactly engrav'd by Tho. Cross." The Boy and the Girl were Jemmy Bowen and Miss Cross. (MS. copy of song, British Museum, Ad. MS. 31448.)

This song had originally been sung in Southerne's *Oroonoko*, produced in the autumn of 1695. It is printed in *Deliciæ Musicæ*, Book IV, 1696, as "A Dialogue Sung in Oroonoko, by the Boy and Girl. Sett by Mr. *Henry Purcell*."

MARRIAGE A-LA-MODE

The song, *Why should a foolish Marriage Vow*, in Act I was set by Robert Smith; the song *Whilst* Alexis *lay prest* in Act IV by Nicholas Staggins.

AURENG ZEBE

A song, *I see she flies me*, was given in *Comes Amoris: or the Companion of Love. Being a Choice Collection of the Newest Songs now in use*, Book V, 1694. It also appeared in *Orpheus Britannicus*, 1698, but without any title; although in the second (1706) and third (1721) editions it is termed "A Single Song."

NOTE ON THE MUSIC

In the British Museum is a collection of single-sheet songs, and among these may be found *I see she flies me* as "A Song in the Play call'd *Oranzebe* set to Musick by Mr. *Henry Purcell* and sung by Mrs. *Ayliff*." There are two other later editions of this song with the same heading, one of which was used by Walsh in his *Orpheus Britannicus*. *I see she flies me* was introduced into a revival of 1693.

Some half-a-dozen years later there was introduced into a revival of *Aureng Zebe* Courteville's *The Charms of bright Beauty*, a copy of which is in the Francis Horton collection, and headed "A Song the words by Capt. Walker, Sung in Oren-sebe by Mrs. Hodgson."

OEDIPUS

The original music of *Oedipus* has not survived. Dr. Burney tells us that Purcell wrote music for the Incantation Scene for a revival of 1692. This complete setting exists, and a song from it, *Hear, ye sullen Pow'rs below*, was first printed in *Orpheus Britannicus*, Book II. Purcell's *Oedipus* music is judged to be among his finest work.

THE SPANISH FRYAR

For the original production of *The Spanish Fryar* music was written by John Eccles.

A song, *Whilst I with grief*, exists in a single sheet headed "A new Song Sung in the Spanish Fryar, set by Mr. Henry Purcell Engraver for I. Walsh." This also appeared in *Deliciæ Musarum*, Book I, 1695 (licensed 3 April, 1695), and then entitled "A Song on Mrs. Bracegirdle's Singing (I burn &c) in the 2nd Part of *Don-Quixote*." It is included with the same title in *Orpheus Britannicus*.

The revival of *The Spanish Fryar* when *Whilst I with grief* was introduced may be dated 1694 or early 1695.

AMPHITRYON

See the Theatrical History to this play.

KING ARTHUR

The music to this play has generally been regarded as Purcell's dramatic masterpiece. Unfortunately, the complete score has not survived, and the music to the first part of Act III seems wanting, although much has been ingeniously pieced together from various MSS. The music was published under the care of Professor Taylor for the Musical Antiquarian Society in 1843, and the opera has more recently been edited by Mr. G. E. P. Arkwright (Cary), 1889; Mr. Fuller-Maitland (Boosey), 1897; Mr. W. H. Cummings (Novello), 1897; and for the Purcell Society in 1928 by Mr. D. D. Arundell, who in his Preface describes a number of MSS., printed selections and other publications. Professor E. J. Dent's *Foundations of English Opera*, Chapter X, 1928, should be consulted for further details concerning Purcell's score.

NOTE ON THE MUSIC

CLEOMENES THE SPARTAN HEROE

The song in Act II, scene 2, *No no, poor suff'ring Heart no Change endeavour*, was set by Purcell, and of this the melody was published in *Joyful Cuckoldom* as "A New Song, in the Play called, the Tragedy of Cleomenes, the Spartan Heroe. Sung by Mrs. *Butler*." The song also appeared, with voice part and bass, in *Comes Amoris*, Book IV, 1693. No trace of the rest of the music required for *Cleomenes* has apparently come down to us.

LOVE TRIUMPHANT

The three songs have been preserved. The "Song of *Jealousie*," *What State of Life can be so blest*, Act III, scene 1, was set by John Eccles and sung by Mrs. Hodgson. It is printed in *Thesaurus Musicus*, Book II, 1694. The "Song: By Mr. *Congreve*," *How Happy's the Husband, whose Wife has been try'd!* in Act V was set by Purcell, and is given in *Thesaurus Musicus*, Book II; "A Song in the last new Play call'd Love Triumphant, &c. Set by Mr. *H. Purcell*, and sung by Mrs. *Ayliff*." With a similar heading the melody is given in *Joyful Cuckoldom. How Happy's the Husband* is also given in D'Urfey's *Wit and Mirth: Or Pills to Purge Melancholy*, Vol. VI (1720), pp. 72–73, as "*A* Song *Sung by Mrs.* Ayliff *in the Play call'd* Love Triumphant: *Or,* Nature will Prevail, *Sett by Mr.* Henry Purcell."

The "Song for a Girl," *Young I am, and yet unskill'd*, Act V, was set by Eccles, whose music is printed in *The Gentleman's Journal*, January–February, 1693–4.

THE SECULAR MASQUE

Malone (*Life of John Dryden*, Vol. I, Part I, of *Prose Works of John Dryden*, 1800, p. 322, n. 6,) has the following: "The name of the original composer of this Masque is not recorded; but probably [certainly] Daniel Purcell was employed on this occasion. At a subsequent period, as Dr. Burney mentions, it was set to musick by Dr. Boyce, and performed, in still life at either the Castle Concert or Hickford's Great Room in Brewer-street. In 1749 [rather on 30 October, 1750,] it was performed at Drury-Lane Theatre with great success; and the Song sung by Diana, beginning—'With horns and with hounds I waken the day,' continued long a popular air."

CHRONOLOGY

TITLE	THEATRE	ENTERED	PUBLISHED
The Wild Gallant.	Theatre Royal, Vere Street, 5 February, 1662–3. Revived (and revised) Theatre Royal, Bridges Street, 1669.	7 August, 1667.	4to, 1669.
The Indian-Queen (with Sir Robert Howard).	Theatre Royal, Bridges Street, January, 1663–4.		Folio, 1665, in *Four New Plays.*
The Rival Ladies.	Theatre Royal, Bridges Street, April–May, 1664.	27 June, 1664.	4to, 1664.
The Indian Emperour; or, The Conquest of Mexico by the Spaniards. Being the Sequel of *The Indian Queen.*	Theatre Royal, April, 1665.	26 May, 1665.	4to, 1667.
Secret-Love; or, The Maiden-Queen.	Theatre Royal, late February, 1666–7.	7 August, 1667.	4to, 1668.
S^r. Martin Mar-all; or, The Feign'd Innocence.	Lincoln's Inn Fields, 15 August, 1667.	24 June, 1668.	4to, 1668.
The Tempest; or, The Enchanted Island (with Sir William Davenant).	Lincoln's Inn Fields, 7 November, 1667.	8 January, 1669–70.	4to, 1670.
An Evening's Love; or, The Mock-Astrologer.	Theatre Royal, 12 June, 1668.	20 November, 1668.	4to, 1671.
Tyrannick Love; or, The Royal Martyr.	Theatre Royal, last week in June, 1669.	14 July, 1669.	4to, 1670.
The Conquest of Granada By The Spaniards.	Theatre Royal, Part I. Between 10 December, 1670, and the New Year. Part II. Tuesday, 9 January, 1670–1.	20 February, 1670–1.	4to, 1672.
Marriage A-la-Mode.	Lincoln's Inn Fields, About Easter, 1672.	18 March, 1672–3.	4to, 1673.
The Assignation; or, Love in a Nunnery.	Lincoln's Inn Fields, November, 1672.	18 March, 1672–3.	4to, 1673.
Amboyna (*or, The Cruelties of the Dutch to the English Merchants*).	Lincoln's Inn Fields, May, 1673.	26 June, 1673.	4to, 1673.

CHRONOLOGY

TITLE	THEATRE	ENTERED	PUBLISHED
The State of Innocence, And Fall of Man.	Unacted; written late in 1673.	17 April, 1674.	4to, 1677.
The Mistaken Husband. By a Person of Quality.	(The second) Theatre Royal, 1675. (Possibly produced at Lincoln's Inn Fields before Midsummer, 1673).		4to, 1675.
Aureng-Zebe.	(The Second) Theatre Royal, November, 1675.	29 November, 1675.	4to, 1676.
All For Love; Or, The World well Lost.	Theatre Royal, 12 December, 1677.	31 January, 1677–78.	4to, 1678.
The Kind Keeper; or, Mr. Limberham.	Dorset Garden, 11 March, 1677–78.		4to, 1680.
Oedipus.	Dorset Garden, November–December, 1678.		4to, 1679.
Troilus and Cressida, or, Truth Found too Late.	Dorset Garden, February–March, 1679.	14 April, 1679.	4to, 1679.
The Spanish Fryar or The Double Discovery.	Dorset Garden, 8 March, 1679–80.		4to, 1681.
The Duke of Guise.	Theatre Royal, 30 November, 1682. By the United Companies. The play was prepared for July, 1682, but prohibited.		4to, 1683.
Albion and Albanius.	Dorset Garden, 6 June, 1685.		Folio, 1685.
Don Sebastian, King of Portugal.	Theatre Royal, November, 1689.	17 December, 1689.	4to, 1690.
Amphitryon; or, The Two Socia's.	Theatre Royal, September, 1690.		4to, 1690.
King Arthur: or, The British Worthy. A *Dramatick* Opera.	Dorset Garden, April–May, 1691.		4to, 1691.
Cleomenes, The Spartan Heroe.	Theatre Royal, April, 1692.		4to, 1692.
Love Triumphant, or, Nature will Prevail.	Theatre Royal, January, 1694.		4to, 1694.

OF

DRAMATICK POESIE

AN ESSAY

Fungar vice cotis, acutum
Reddere quæ ferrum valet, exors ipsa secandi.

Horat. De Arte Poet.

OF DRAMATICK POESIE

To the Right Honourable

CHARLES Lord BUCKHURST

My Lord,

AS I was lately reviewing my loose Papers, amongst the rest I found this Essay, the writing of which in this rude and indigested manner wherein your Lordship now sees it, serv'd as an amusement to me in the Country, when the violence of the last Plague had driven me from the Town. Seeing then our Theaters shut up, I was engag'd in these kind of thoughts with the same delight with which men think upon their absent Mistresses: I confess I find many things in this discourse which I do not now approve; my judgment being a little alter'd since the writing of it, but whither for the better or the worse I know not: Neither indeed is it much material in an Essay, where all I have said is problematical. For the way of writing Playes in verse, which I have seem'd to favour, I have since that time laid the Practice of it aside, till I have more leisure, because I find it troublesome and slow. But I am no way alter'd from my opinion of it, at least with any reasons which have oppos'd it. For your Lordship may easily observe that none are very violent against it, but those who either have not attempted it, or who have succeeded ill in their attempt. 'Tis enough for me to have your Lordships example for my excuse in that little which I have done in it; and I am sure my Adversaries can bring no such Arguments against Verse, as the fourth Act of Pompey *will furnish me with, in its defence. Yet, my Lord, you must suffer me a little to complain of you, that you too soon withdraw from us a contentment, of which we expected the continuance, because you gave it us so early. 'Tis a revolt without occasion from your Party, where your merits had already rais'd you to the highest commands, and where you have not the excuse of other men that you have been ill us'd, and therefore laid down Armes. I know no other quarrel you can have to Verse, then that which* Spurina *had to his beauty, when he tore and mangled the features of his Face, onely because they pleas'd too well the lookers on. It was an honour which seem'd to wait for you, to lead out a new Colony of Writers from the Mother Nation: and upon the first spreading of your Ensignes there had been many in a readiness to have follow'd so fortunate a Leader; if not all, yet the better part of Writers.*

Pars, indocili melior grege; mollis & expes
Inominata perprimat cubilia.

I am almoſt of opinion, that we should force you to accept of the command, as sometimes the Prætorian *Bands have compell'd their Captains to receive the Empire. The Court, which is the beſt and sureſt judge of writing, has generally allow'd of Verse; and in the Town it has found favourers of Wit and Quality. As for your own particular, My Lord, you have yet youth, and time enough to give part of it to the divertisement of the Publick, before you enter into the serious and more unpleasant business of the world. That which the French Poet said of the Temple of Love, may be as well apply'd to the Temple of the Muses. The words, as near as I can remember them, were these:*

Le jeune homme a mauvaise grace,
N'ayant pas adoré dans le temple d'Amour:
Il faut qu'il entre, & pour le sage
Si ce n'eſt pas son vray sejour
C'eſt un giſte sur son passage.

I leave the words to work their effeƈt upon your Lordship in their own Language, because no other can so well express the nobleness of the thought; And wish you may be soon call'd to bear a part in the affairs of the Nation, where I know the world expeƈts you, and wonders why you have been so long forgotten; there being no person amongſt our young Nobility, on whom the eyes of all men are so much bent. But in the mean time your Lordship may imitate the course of Nature, who gives us the flower before the fruit: that I may speak to you in the language of the Muses, which I have taken from an excellent Poem to the King.

As Nature, when she fruit designes, thinks fit
By beauteous blossoms to proceed to it;
And while she does accomplish all the Spring,
Birds to her secret operations sing.

I confess I have no greater reason, in addressing this Essay to your Lordship, then that it might awaken in you the desire of writing something, in whatever kind it be, which might be an honour to our Age and Country. And me thinks it might have the same effeƈt upon you, which Homer *tells us the fight of the Greeks and Trojans before the Fleet, had on the spirit of* Achilles, *who though he had resolved not to ingage, yet found a martial warmth to ſteal upon him, at the sight of Blows, the sound of Trumpets, and the cries of fighting Men. For my own part, if in treating of this subjeƈt I sometimes dissent from the opinion of better Wits, I declare it is not so much to combat their opinions, as to defend my own, which were firſt made publick. Sometimes, like a Schollar in a Fencing-School I put forth my self, and show my own ill play, on purpose to be better taught. Sometimes I ſtand desperately to my Armes, like the Foot when deserted by their Horse, not in hope to overcome, but onely to yield on more honourable termes. And yet, my Lord, this war of opinions, you well know, has fallen out among the Writers of all Ages, and sometimes betwixt Friends. Onely it has been prosecuted by some, like Pedants, with violence of words, and manag'd by others like Gentlemen, with candour and ciuility. Even* Tully *had a Controversie with his dear* Atticus; *and in one of his Dialogues makes him sustain the part of an Enemy in Philosophy, who in his Letters is his confident of State, and made privy to the most weighty affairs of the Roman Senate. And the same respect which was paid by* Tully *to* Atticus, *we find return'd to him afterwards by* Cæsar *on a like occasion, who answering his Book in praise of* Cato, *made it not so much his business to condemn* Cato, *as to praise* Cicero. *But that I may decline some part of the encounter with my Adversaries, whom I am neither willing to combate, nor well able to resist; I will give your Lordship the Relation of a Dispute betwixt some of our Wits upon this subject, in which they did not onely speak of Playes in Verse, but mingled, in the freedom of Discourse, some things of the Ancient, many of the Modern wayes of writing, comparing those with these, and the Wits of our Nation with those of others: 'tis true they differ'd in their opinions, as 'tis probable they would: neither do I take upon me to reconcile, but to relate them: and that as* Tacitus *professes of himself,* Sine studio partium, aut ira: *without Passion or Interest; leaving your Lordship to decide it in favour of which part you shall judge most reasonable, and withall, to pardon the many errours of,*

Your Lordships most obedient humble Servant,

JOHN DRYDEN.

TO THE
READER

THE drift of the ensuing Discourse was chiefly to vindicate the honour of our English Writers, from the censure of those who unjustly prefer the French before them. This I intimate, least any should think me so exceeding vain, as to teach others an Art which they understand much better then my self. But if this incorrect Essay, written in the Country without the help of Books, or advice of Friends, shall find any acceptance in the world, I promise to my self a better success of the second part, wherein the Vertues and Faults of the English Poets, who have written either in this, the Epique, or the Lyrique way, will be more fully treated of, and their several styles impartially imitated.

AN

ESSAY

OF

Dramatick Poesie

IT was that memorable day, in the first Summer of the late War, when our Navy ingag'd the Dutch: a day wherein the two most mighty and best appointed Fleets which any age had ever seen, disputed the command of the greater half of the Globe, the commerce of Nations, and the riches of the Universe. While these vast floating bodies, on either side, mov'd against each other in parallel lines, and our Country men, under the happy conduct of his Royal Highness, went breaking, by little and little, into the line of the Enemies; the noise of the Cannon from both Navies reach'd our ears about the City: so that all men, being alarm'd with it, and in a dreadful suspence of the event, which we knew was then deciding, every one went following the sound as his fancy led him; and leaving the Town almost empty, some took towards the Park, some cross the River, others down it; all seeking the noise in the depth of silence.

Amongst the rest, it was the fortune of *Eugenius*, *Crites*, *Lisideius* and *Neander*, to be in company together: three of them persons whom their witt and Quality have made known to all the Town: and whom I have chose to hide under these borrowed names, that they may not suffer by so ill a relation as I am going to make of their discourse.

Taking then a Barge which a servant of *Lisideius* had provided for them, they made haste to shoot the Bridge, and left behind them that great fall of waters which hindred them from hearing what they desired: after which, having disingag'd themselves from many Vessels which rode at Anchor in the *Thames*, and almost blockt up the passage towards *Greenwich*, they order'd the Watermen to let fall their Oares more gently; and then every one favouring his own curiosity with a strict silence, it was not long ere they perceiv'd the Air break about them like the noise of distant Thunder, or of Swallows in a Chimney: those little undulations of sound, though almost vanishing before they reach'd them, yet still seeming to retain somewhat of their first horrour which they had betwixt the Fleets: after they had attentively listned till such time as the sound by little and little went from them; *Eugenius* lifting up his head, and taking notice of it, was the first who congratulated to the rest that happy Omen of our Nations Victory: adding, we had but this to desire in confirmation of it, that we might hear no more of that noise which was now leaving the English Coast. When the rest had concur'd in the same opinion, *Crites*, a person of a sharp judgment, and somewhat too delicate a taste in wit, which the world have mistaken in him for ill nature, said, smiling to us, that if the concernment of this battel had not been so exceeding great, he could scarce have wish'd the Victory at the price he knew he must pay for it, in being subject to the reading and hearing of so many ill verses as he was sure would be made upon it; adding, that no Argument could scape some of those eternal Rhimers, who watch a Battel with more diligence then the Ravens and birds of Prey; and the worst of them surest to be first in upon the quarry, while the better able, either out of modesty writ not at all, or set that due value upon their Poems, as to let them be often call'd for and long expected! There are some of those impertinent people you speak of, answer'd *Lisideius*, who to my knowledg, are already so provided, either way, that they can produce not onely a Panegirick upon the Victory, but, if need be, a funeral elegy upon the Duke: and after they have crown'd his valour with many Lawrels, at last deplore the odds under which he fell; concluding that his courage deserv'd a better destiny. All the company smil'd at the conceipt of *Lisideius*; but *Crites*, more eager then before, began to make particular exceptions against some Writers, and said the publick Magistrate ought to send betimes to forbid them; and that it concern'd the peace and quiet of all honest people, that ill Poets should be as well silenc'd as seditious Preachers. In my opinion, replyed *Eugenius*, you pursue your point too far; for as to my own particular, I am so great a lover of Poesie, that I could wish them all rewarded who attempt but to do well; at least I would not have them worse us'd then *Sylla* the Dictator did one of their brethren heretofore: *Quem in concione vidimus* (says *Tully* speaking of him) *cum ei libellum malus poeta de populo subjecisset, quod epigramma in eum fecisset tantummodo alternis versibus longiuculis, statim ex iis rebus quas tunc vendebat jubere ei præmium tribui, sub ea conditione ne quid postea scriberet.* I could wish with all my heart, replied *Crites*, that many whom we know were as bountifully thank'd upon the same condition, that they would never trouble us again. For amongst others, I have a mortal apprehension of two Poets, whom this victory with the help of both her wings will never be able to escape; 'tis easie to guess whom you intend, said *Lisideius*; and without naming them, I ask you if one of them does not perpetually pay us with clenches upon words and a certain clownish kind of raillery? if now and then he does not offer at a Catecresis or Clevelandism, wresting and torturing a word into another meaning: In fine, if he be not one of those whom the French would call *un mauvais buffon*; one that is so much a well-willer to the Satire, that he spares no man; and though he cannot strike a blow to hurt any, yet ought to be punish'd for the malice of the action; as our Witches are justly hang'd because they think themselves so; and suffer deservedly for believing they did mischief, because they meant it. You have described him, said *Crites*, so exactly, that I am affraid to come after you with my other extremity of Poetry: He is one of those who having had some advantage of education and converse, knows better then the other what a Poet should be, but puts it into practice more unluckily then any man; his stile and matter are every where alike; he is the most calm, peaceable Writer you ever read: he never disquiets your passions with the least concernment, but still leaves you in as even a temper as he found you; he is a very Leveller in Poetry, he creeps along with ten little words in every line, and helps out his Numbers with *For to*, and *Unto*, and all the pretty Expletives he can find, till he draggs them to the end of another line; while the Sense is left tir'd half way behind it; he doubly starves all his Verses, first for want of thought, and then of expression; his Poetry neither has wit in it, nor seems to have it; like him in *Martiall*:

Pauper videri Cinna vult, & est pauper.

He affects plainness, to cover his want of imagination: when he writes the serious way, the highest flight of his fancy is some miserable *Antithesis*, or seeming contradiction; and in the Comick he is still reaching at some thin conceit, the ghost of a Jest, and that too flies before him, never to be caught; these Swallows which we see before us on the *Thames*, are the just resemblance of his wit: you may observe how near the water they stoop, how many proffers they make to dip, and yet how seldome they touch it: and when they do, 'tis but the surface: they skim over it but to catch a gnat, and then mount into the ayr and leave it. Well Gentlemen, said *Eugenius*, you may speak your pleasure of these Authors; but though I and some few more about the Town may give you a peaceable hearing, yet, assure your selves, there are multitudes who would think you malicious and them injur'd: especially him who you first described; he is the very *Withers* of the City: they have bought more Editions of his Works then would serve to lay under all their Pies at the Lord Mayor's *Christmass*. When his famous Poem first came out in the year 1660, I have seen them reading it in the midst of Change-time; nay so vehement they were at it, that they lost their bargain by the Candles ends: but what will you say, if he has been received amongst the great Ones? I can assure you he is, this day, the envy of a great person, who is Lord in the Art of Quibbling; and who does not take it well, that any man should intrude so far into his Province. All I would wish, replied *Crites*, is, that they who love his Writings, may still admire him, and his fellow Poet: *qui Bavium non odit, &c.* is curse sufficient. And farther, added *Lisideius*, I believe there is no man who writes well, but would think himself very hardly dealt with, if their Admirers should praise any thing of his: *Nam quos contemnimus, eorum quoque laudes contemnimus.* There are so few who write well in this Age, said *Crites*, that me-thinks any praises should be wellcome; they neither rise to the dignity of the last Age, nor to any of the Ancients; and we may cry out of the Writers of this time, with more reason than *Petronius* of his, *Pace vestra liceat dixisse, primi omnium eloquentiam perdidistis*: you have debauched the true old Poetry so far, that Nature, which is the soul of it, is not in any of your Writings.

If your quarrel (said *Eugenius*) to those who now write, be grounded onely upon your reverence to Antiquity, there is no man more ready to adore those great Greeks and Romans than I am: but on the other side, I cannot think so contemptibly of the Age I live in, or so dishonourably of my own Countrey, as not to judge we equal the Ancients in most kinds of Poesie, and in some surpass them; neither know I any reason why I may not be as zealous for the Reputation of our Age, as we find the Ancients themselves in reference to those who lived before them. For you hear your *Horace* saying,

Indignor quidquam reprehendi, non quia crasse
Compositum, illepideve putetur, sed quia nuper.

And after,

Si meliora dies, ut vina, poemata reddit,
Scire velim, pretium chartis quotus arroget annus?

But I see I am ingaging in a wide dispute, where the arguments are not like to reach close on either side; for Poesie is of so large extent, and so many both of the Ancients and Moderns have done well in all kinds of it, that, in citing one against the other, we shall take up more time this Evening, than each mans occasions will allow him: therefore I would ask *Crites* to what part of Poesie he would confine his Arguments, and whether he would defend the general cause of the Ancients against the Moderns, or oppose any Age of the Moderns against this of ours?

Crites a little while considering upon this Demand, told *Eugenius* he approv'd his Propositions, and, if he pleased, he would limit their Dispute to *Dramatique Poesie*; in which he thought it not difficult to prove, either that the Antients were superiour to the Moderns, or the last Age to this of ours.

Eugenius was somewhat surpriz'd, when he heard *Crites* make choice of that Subject; For ought I see, said he, I have undertaken a harder Province than I imagin'd; for though I never judg'd the Plays of the Greek or Roman Poets comparable to ours; yet on the other side those we now see acted, come short of many which were written in the last Age: but my comfort is if we are orecome, it will be onely by our own Countreymen: and if we yield to them in this one part of Poesie, we more surpass them in all the other; for in the Epique or Lyrique way it will be hard for them to show us one such amongst them, as we have many now living, or who lately were so: they can produce nothing so courtly writ, or which expresses so much the Conversation of a Gentleman, as Sir *John Suckling*; nothing so even, sweet, and flowing as Mr. *Waller*; nothing so Majestique, so correct as Sir *John Denham*; nothing so elevated, so copious, and full of spirit, as Mr. *Cowley*; as for the Italian, French, and Spanish plays, I can make it evident, that those who now write, surpass them; and that the *Drama* is wholly ours.

All of them were thus far of *Eugenius* his opinion, that the sweetness of English Verse was never understood or practis'd by our Fathers; even *Crites* himself did not much oppose it: and every one was willing to acknowledge how much our Posie is improv'd, by the happiness of some Writers yet living; who first taught us to mould our thoughts into easie and significant words; to retrench the superfluities of expression, and to make our Rime so properly a part of the Verse, that it should never mis-lead the sence, but it self be led and govern'd by it.

Eugenius was going to continue this Discourse, when *Lisideius* told him it was necessary, before they proceeded further, to take a standing measure of their Controversie; for how was it possible to be decided who writ the best Plays, before we know what a Play should be? but, this once agreed on by both Parties, each might have recourse to it, either to prove his own advantages, or discover the failings of his Adversary.

He had no sooner said this, but all desir'd the favour of him to give the definition of a Play; and they were the more importunate, because neither *Aristotle*, nor *Horace*, nor any other, who writ of that Subject, had ever done it.

Lisideius, after some modest denials, at last confess'd he had a rude Notion of it; indeed rather a Description then a Definition: but which serv'd to guide him in his private thoughts, when he was to make a judgment of what others writ: that he conceiv'd a Play ought to be, *A just and lively Image of Humane Nature, representing its Passions and Humours, and the Changes of Fortune to which it is subject; for the Delight and Instruction of Mankind.*

This Definition, though *Crites* rais'd a Logical Objection against it; that it was onely *a genere & fine*, and so not altogether perfect; was yet well received by the rest: and after they had given order to the Watermen to turn their Barge, and row softly, that they might take the cool of the Evening in their return; *Crites*, being desired by the Company to begin, spoke on behalf of the Ancients, in this manner:

If Confidence presage a Victory, *Eugenius*, in his own opinion, has already triumphed over the Ancients; nothing seems more easie to him, than to overcome those whom it is our greatest praise to have imitated well: for we do not onely build upon their foundation; but by their modells. *Dramatique Poesie* had time enough, reckoning from *Thespis* (who first invented it) to *Aristophanes*, to be born, to grow up, and to flourish in Maturity. It has been observed of Arts and Sciences, that in one and the same Century they have arriv'd to a great perfection; and no wonder, since every Age has a kind of Universal Genius, which inclines those that live in it to some particular Studies: the Work then being push'd on by many hands, must of necessity go forward.

Is it not evident, in these last hundred years (when the Study of Philosophy has been the business of all the *Virtuosi* in *Christendome*) that almost a new Nature has been reveal'd to us? that more errours of the School have been detected, more useful Experiments in Philosophy have been made, more Noble Secrets in Opticks, Medicine, Anatomy, Astronomy, discover'd, than in all those credulous and doting Ages from *Aristotle* to us? so true it is that nothing spreads more fast than Science, when rightly and generally cultivated.

Add to this the more than common emulation that was in those times of writing well; which though it be found in all Ages and all Persons that pretend to the same Reputation; yet Poesie being then in more esteem than now it is, had greater Honours decreed to the Professors of it; and consequently the Rivalship was more high between them; they had Judges ordain'd to decide their Merit, and Prizes to reward it: and Historians have been diligent to record of *Eschylus*, *Euripides*, *Sophocles*, *Lycophron*, and the rest of them, both who they were that vanquish'd in these Wars of the Theater, and how often they were crown'd: while the Asian Kings, and Grecian Common-wealths scarce afforded them a Nobler Subject then the unmanly Luxuries of a Debauch'd Court, or giddy Intrigues of a Factious City. *Alit æmulatio ingenia* (says *Paterculus*) & *nunc invidia, nunc admiratio incitationem accendit*: Emulation is the Spur of Wit, and sometimes Envy, sometimes Admiration quickens our Endeavours.

But now since the Rewards of Honour are taken away, that Vertuous Emulation is turn'd into direct Malice; yet so slothful, that it contents it self to condemn and cry down others, without attempting to do better: 'Tis a Reputation too unprofitable, to take the necessary pains for it; yet wishing they had it, is incitement enough to hinder others from it. And this, in short, *Eugenius*, is the reason, why you have now so few good Poets; and so many severe Judges: Certainly, to imitate the Antients well, much labour and long study is required: which pains, I have already shown, our Poets would want incouragement to take, if yet they had ability to go through with it. Those Ancients have been faithful Imitators and wise Observers of that Nature which is so torn and ill represented in our Plays, they have handed down to us a perfect resemblance of her; which we, like ill Copyers, neglecting to look on, have rendred monstrous and disfigur'd. But, that you may know how much you are indebted to those your Masters, and be ashamed to have so ill requited them: I must remember you that all the Rules by which we practise the *Drama* at this day, either such as relate to the justness and symmetry of the Plot; or the Episodical Ornaments, such as Descriptions, Narrations, and other Beauties, which are not essential to the Play; were delivered to us from the Observations that *Aristotle* made, of those Poets, which either liv'd before him, or were his Contemporaries: we have added nothing of our own, except we have the confidence to say our wit is better; which none boast of in our Age, but such as understand not theirs. Of that Book which *Aristotle* has left us περὶ τῆς Ποιητικῆς, *Horace* his Art of Poetry is an excellent Comment, and, I believe, restores to us that Second Book of his concerning Comedy, which is wanting in him.

Out of these two have been extracted the Famous Rules which the French call, *Des Trois Unitez*, or, The Three Unities, which ought to be observ'd in every Regular Play; as namely, of Time, Place, and Action.

The unity of Time they comprehend in 24 hours, the compass of a Natural Day; or as near it as can be contriv'd: and the reason of it is obvious to every one, that the time of the feigned action, or fable of the Play, should be proportion'd as near as can be to the duration of that time in which it is represented; since therefore all Playes are acted on the Theater in a space of time much within the compass of 24 hours, that Play is to be thought the nearest imitation of Nature, whose Plot or Action is confin'd within that time; and, by the same Rule which concludes this general proportion of time, it follows, that all the parts of it are to be equally subdivided; as namely, that one act take not up the suppos'd time of half a day; which is out of proportion to the rest: since the other four are then to be straightned within the compass of the remaining half; for it is unnatural that one Act, which being spoke or written, is not longer than the rest, should be suppos'd longer by the Audience; 'tis therefore the Poets duty, to take care that no Act should be imagin'd to exceed the time in which it is represented on the Stage, and that the intervalls and inequalities of time be suppos'd to fall out between the Acts.

This Rule of Time how well it has been observ'd by the Antients, most of their Playes will witness; you see them in their Tragedies (wherein to follow this Rule, is certainly most difficult) from the very beginning of their Playes, falling close into that part of the Story which they intend for the action or principal object of it; leaving the former part to be delivered by Narration: so that they set the Audience, as it were, at the Post where the Race is to be concluded: and, saving them the tedious expectation of seeing the Poet set out and ride the beginning of the Course, you behold him not, till he is in sight of the Goal, and just upon you.

For the Second Unity, which is that of place, the Antients meant by it, That the Scenc ought to be continu'd through the Play, in the same place where it was laid in the beginning: for the Stage, on which it is represented, being but one and the same place, it is unnatural to conceive it many; and those far distant from one another. I will not deny but by the variation of painted Scenes, the fancy (which in these cases will contribute to its own deceit) may sometimes imagine it several places, with some appearance of probability; yet it still carries the greater likelihood of truth, if those places be suppos'd so near each other, as in the same Town or City; which may all be comprehended under the larger Denomination of one place: for a greater distance will bear no proportion to the shortness of time, which is allotted in the acting, to pass from one of them to another; for the Observation of this, next to the Antients, the French are to be most commended. They tie themselves so strictly to the unity of place, that you never see in any of their Plays, a Scene chang'd in the middle of an Act: if the Act begins in a Garden, a Street, or Chamber, 'tis ended in the same place; and that you may know it to be the same, the Stage is so supplied with persons that it is never empty all the time: he that enters the second has business with him who was on before; and before the second quits the Stage, a third appears who has business with him.

This *Corneille* calls *La Liaison des Scenes*, the continuity, or joyning of the Scenes; and 'tis a good mark of a well contriv'd Play when all the Persons are known to each other, and every one of them has some affairs with all the rest.

As for the third Unity which is that of Action, the Ancients meant no other by it then what the Logicians do by their *Finis*, the end or scope of any action: that which is the first in Intention, and last in Execution: now the Poet is to aim at one great and compleat action, to the carrying on of which all things in his Play, even the very obstacles, are to be subservient; and the reason of this is as evident as any of the former.

For two Actions equally labour'd and driven on by the Writer, would destroy the unity of the Poem; it would be no longer one Play, but two: not but that there may be many actions in a Play, as *Ben. Johnson* has observ'd in his *Discoveries*; but they must be all subservient to the great one, which our language happily expresses in the name of under-plots: such as in *Terences Eunuch* is the difference and reconcilement of *Thais* and *Phædria*, which is not the chief business of the Play, but promotes the marriage of *Chærea* and *Chremes's* Sister, principally intended by the Poet. There ought to be but one action, says *Corneille*, that is one compleat action which leaves the mind of the Audience in a full repose: But this cannot be brought to pass but by many other imperfect ones which conduce to it, and hold the Audience in a delightful suspence of what will be.

If by these Rules (to omit many other drawn from the Precepts and Practice of the Ancients) we should judge our modern Playes; 'tis probable, that few of them would endure the tryal: that which should be the business of a day, takes up in some of them an age; instead of one action they are the Epitomes of a mans life; and for one spot of ground (which the Stage should represent) we are sometimes in more Countries then the Map can show us.

But if we will allow the Ancients to have contriv'd well, we must acknowledge them to have writ better; questionless we are depriv'd of a great stock of wit in the loss of *Menander* among the Greek Poets, and of *Cæcilius*, *Affranius* and *Varius*, among the Romans: we may guess of *Menanders* Excellency by the Plays of *Terence*, who translated some of his, and yet wanted so much of him that he was call'd by *C. Cæsar* the Half-*Menander*, and of *Varius*, by the Testimonies of *Horace*, *Martial*, and *Velleius Paterculus*: 'Tis probable that these, could they be recover'd, would decide the controversie; but so long as *Aristophanes* in the old Comedy, and *Plautus* in the new are extant; while the Tragedies of *Eurypides*, *Sophocles*, and *Seneca* are to be had, I can never see one of those Plays which are now written, but it encreases my admiration of the Ancients; and yet I must acknowledge further, that to admire them as we ought, we should understand them better then we do. Doubtless many things appear flat to us, whose wit depended upon some custome or story which never came to our knowledge, or perhaps upon some Criticism in their language, which being so long dead, and onely remaining in their Books, 'tis not possible they should make us know it perfectly. To read *Macrobius*, explaining the propriety and elegancy of many words in *Virgil*, which I had before pass'd over without consideration, as common things, is enough to assure me that I ought to think the same of *Terence*; and that in the purity of his style (which *Tully* so much valued that he ever carried his works about him) there is yet left in him great room for admiration, if I knew but where to place it. In the mean time I must desire you to take notice, that the greatest man of the last age (*Ben. Johnson*) was willing to give place to them in all things: He was not onely a professed Imitator of *Horace*, but a learned Plagiary of all the others; you track him every where in their Snow: If *Horace*, *Lucan*, *Petronius Arbiter*, *Seneca*, and *Juvenal*, had their own from him, there are few serious thoughts which are new in him; you will pardon me therefore if I presume he lov'd their fashion when he wore their cloaths. But since I have otherwise a great veneration for him, and you, *Eugenius*, prefer him above all other Poets, I will use no farther argument to you then his example: I will produce Father *Ben.* to you, dress'd in all the ornaments and colours of the Ancients, you will need no other guide to our Party if you follow him; and whether you consider the bad Plays of our Age, or regard the good ones of the last, both the best and worst of the Modern Poets will equally instruct you to esteem the Ancients.

Crites had no sooner left speaking, but *Eugenius* who waited with some impatience for it, thus began:

I have observ'd in your Speech that the former part of it is convincing as to what the Moderns have profitted by the rules of the Ancients, but in the latter you are careful to conceal how much they have excell'd them: we own all the helps we have from them, and want neither veneration nor gratitude while we acknowledge that to overcome them we must make use of the advantages we have receiv'd from them; but to these assistances we have joyned our own industry; for (had we sate down with a dull imitation of them) we might then have lost somewhat of the old perfection, but never acquir'd any that was new. We draw not therefore after their lines, but those of Nature; and having the life before us, besides the experience of all they knew, it is no wonder if we hit some airs and features which they have miss'd: I deny not what you urge of Arts and Sciences, that they have flourish'd in some ages more then others; but your instance in Philosophy makes for me: for if Natural Causes be more known now then in the time of *Aristotle*, because more studied, it follows that Poesie and other Arts may with the same pains arrive still neerer to perfection, and, that granted, it will rest for you to prove that they wrought more perfect images of humane life then we; which, seeing in your Discourse you have avoided to make good, it shall now be my task to show you some part of their defects, and some few Excellencies of the Moderns; and I think there is none among us can imagine I do it enviously, or with purpose to detract from them; for what interest of Fame or Profit can the living lose by the reputation of the dead? on the other side, it is a great truth which *Velleius Paterculus* affirms, *Audita visis libentius laudamus; & præsentia invidia, præterita admiratione prosequimur; & his nos obrui, illis instrui credimus*: That praise or censure is certainly the most sincere which unbrib'd posterity shall give us.

Be pleased then in the first place to take notice, that the Greek Poesie, which *Crites* has affirm'd to have arriv'd to perfection in the Reign of the old Comedy, was so far from it, that the distinction of it into Acts was not known to them; or if it were, it is yet so darkly deliver'd to us that we cannot make it out.

All we know of it is from the singing of their Chorus, and that too is so uncertain that in some of their Playes we have reason to conjecture they sung more then five times: *Aristotle* indeed divides the integral parts of a Play into four: First, The *Protasis* or entrance, which gives light onely to the Characters of the persons, and proceeds very little into any part of the action: 2ly, The *Epitasis*, or working up of the Plot where the Play grows warmer: the design or action of it is drawing on, and you see something promising that it will come to pass: Thirdly, the *Catastasis*, or Counterturn, which destroys that expectation, imbroyles the action in new difficulties, and leaves you far distant from that hope in which it found you, as you may have observ'd in a violent stream resisted by a narrow passage; it runs round to an eddy, and carries back the waters with more swiftness then it brought them on: Lastly, the *Catastrophe*, which the Grecians call'd λύσις, the French *le denouement*, and we the discovery or unravelling of the Plot: there you see all things setling again upon their first foundations, and the obstacles which hindred the design or action of the Play once remov'd, it ends with that resemblance of truth and nature, that the audience are satisfied with the conduct of it. Thus this great man deliver'd to us the image of a Play, and I must confess it is so lively that from thence much light has been deriv'd to the forming it more perfectly into Acts and Scenes; but what Poet first limited to five the number of the Acts I know not; onely we see it so firmly establish'd in the time of *Horace*, that he gives it for a rule in Comedy; *Neu brevior quinto, neu sit productior actu*: So that you see the Grecians cannot be said to have consummated this Art; writing rather by Entrances then by Acts, and having rather a general indigested notion of a Play, then knowing how and where to bestow the particular graces of it.

But since the Spaniards at this day allow but three Acts, which they call *Jornadas*, to a Play; and the Italians in many of theirs follow them, when I condemn the Antients, I declare it is not altogether because they have not five Acts to every Play, but because they have not confin'd themselves to one certain number; 'tis building an House without a Modell: and when they succeeded in such undertakings, they ought to have sacrific'd to Fortune, not to the Muses.

Next, for the Plot, which *Aristotle* call'd τὸ μῦθος and often τῶν πραγμάτων σύνθεσις, and from him the Romans *Fabula*, it has already been judiciously observ'd by a late Writer, that in their Tragedies it was onely some Tale deriv'd from *Thebes* or *Troy*, or at least some thing that happen'd in those two Ages; which was worn so thred bare by the Pens of all the Epique Poets, and even by Tradition it self of the Talkative Greeklings (as *Ben. Johnson* calls them) that before it came upon the Stage, it was already known to all the Audience: and the people so soon as ever they heard the Name of *Oedipus*, knew as well as the Poet, that he had kill'd his Father by a mistake, and committed Incest with his Mother, before the Play; that they were now to hear of a great Plague, an Oracle, and the Ghost of *Laius*; so that they sate with a yawning kind of expectation, till he was to come with his eyes pull'd out, and speak a hundred or two of Verses in a Tragick tone, in complaint of his misfortunes. But one *Oedipus*, *Hercules*, or *Medea*, had been tollerable; poor people they scap'd not so good cheap: they had still the *Chapon Bouillé* set before them, till their appetites were cloy'd with the same dish, and the Novelty being gone, the pleasure vanish'd: so that one main end of *Dramatique Poesie* in its Definition, which was to cause Delight, was of consequence destroy'd.

In their Comedies, the Romans generally borrow'd their Plots from the Greek Poets; and theirs was commonly a little Girle stollen or wandred from her Parents, brought back unknown to the same City, there got with child by some lewd young fellow; who, by the help of his servant, cheats his father, and when her time comes, to cry *Juno Lucina, fer opem*; one or other sees a little Box or Cabinet which was carried away with her, and so discovers her to her friends, if some God do not prevent it, by coming down in a Machine, and take the thanks of it to himself.

By the Plot you may guess much of the Characters of the Persons. An Old Father that would willingly before he dies, see his Son well married; his Debauch'd Son, kind in his Nature to his Wench, but miserably in want of Money; a Servant or Slave, who has so much wit to strike in with him, and help to dupe his Father, a Braggadochio Captain, a Parasite, and a Lady of Pleasure.

As for the poor honest Maid, whom all the Story is built upon, and who ought to be one of the principal Actors in the Play, she is commonly a Mute in it: She has the breeding of the Old *Elizabeth* way, for Maids to be seen and not to be heard; and it is enough you know she is willing to be married, when the Fifth Act requires it.

These are Plots built after the Italian Mode of Houses, you see thorow them all at once; the Characters are indeed the Imitations of Nature, but so narrow as if they had imitated onely an Eye or an Hand, and did not dare to venture on the lines of a Face, or the Proportion of a Body.

But in how straight a compass soever they have bounded their Plots and Characters, we will pass it by, if they have regularly pursued them, and perfectly observ'd those three Unities of Time, Place, and Action: the knowledge of which you say is deriv'd to us from them. But in the first place give me leave to tell you, that the Unity of Place, how ever it might be practised by them, was never any of their Rules: we neither find it in *Aristotle*, *Horace*, or any who have written of it, till in our age the French Poets first made it a Precept of the Stage. The unity of time, even *Terence* himself (who was the best and most regular of them) has neglected: His *Heautontimoroumenos* or Self-Punisher takes up visibly two dayes; therefore, sayes *Scaliger*, the two first Acts concluding the first day, were acted over-night; the three last on the ensuing day: and *Eurypides*, in tying himself to one day, has committed an absurdity never to be forgiven him: for in one of his Tragedies he has made *Theseus* go from *Athens* to *Thebes*, which was about 40 English miles, under the walls of it to give battel, and appear victorious in the next Act; and yet from the time of his departure to the return of the *Nuntius*, who gives the relation of his Victory, *Æthra* and the Chorus have but 36 Verses; that is not for every Mile a Verse.

The like errour is as evident in *Terence* his *Eunuch*, when *Laches*, the old man, enters in a mistake the house of *Thais*, where betwixt his Exit and the entrance of *Pythias*, who comes to give an ample relation of the Garboyles he has rais'd within, *Parmeno* who was left upon the Stage, has not above five lines to speak: *C'est bien employer un temps si court*, sayes the French Poet, who furnish'd me with one of the observations; And almost all their Tragedies will afford us examples of the like nature.

'Tis true, they have kept the continuity, or as you call'd it, *Liaison des Scenes* somewhat better: two do not perpetually come in together, talk, and go out together; and other two succeed them, and do the same throughout the Act, which the English call by the name of single Scenes; but the reason is, because they have seldom above two or three Scenes, properly so call'd, in every act; for it is to be accounted a new Scene, not every time the Stage is empty, but every person who enters, though to others, makes it so; because he introduces a new business: Now the Plots of their Plays being narrow, and the persons few, one of their Acts was written in a less compass then one of our well wrought Scenes, and yet they are often deficient even in this: To go no further then *Terence*, you find in the *Eunuch Antipho* entring single in the midst of the third Act, after *Chremes* and *Pythias* were gone off: In the same Play you have likewise *Dorias* beginning the fourth Act alone; and after she has made a relation of what was done at the Souldiers entertainment (which by the way was very inartificial to do, because she was presum'd to speak directly to the Audience, and to acquaint them with what was necessary to be known, but yet should have been so contriv'd by the Poet as to have been told by persons of the *Drama* to one another, and so by them to have come to the knowledge of the people) she quits the Stage, and *Phaedria* enters next, alone likewise: He also gives you an account of himself, and of his returning from the Country in *Monologue*, to which unnatural way of narration *Terence* is subject in all his playes: In his *Adelphi* or *Brothers*, *Syrus* and *Demea* enter after the Scene was broken by the departure of *Sostrata*, *Geta* and *Canthara*; and indeed you can scarce look into any of his Comedies, where you will not presently discover the same interruption.

But as they have fail'd both in laying of their Plots, and managing of them, swerving from the Rules of their own Art, by mis-representing Nature to us, in which they have ill satisfied one intention of a Play, which was delight, so in the instructive part they have err'd worse: instead of punishing Vice and rewarding Virtue, they have often shown a Prosperous Wickedness, and an Unhappy Piety: They have set before us a bloudy image of revenge in *Medea*, and given her Dragons to convey her safe from punishment. A *Priam* and *Astyanax* murder'd, and *Cassandra* ravish'd, and the lust and murder ending in the victory of him that acted them: In short, there is no indecorum in any of our modern Playes, which if I would excuse, I could not shaddow with some Authority from the Ancients.

And one farther note of them let me leave you: Tragedies and Comedies were not writ then as they are now, promiscuously, by the same person; but he who found his genius bending to the one, never attempted the other way. This is so plain, that I need not instance to you, that *Aristophanes*, *Plautus*, *Terence*, never any of them writ a Tragedy; *Æschylus*, *Eurypides*, *Sophocles* and *Seneca*, never medled with Comedy; the Sock and Buskin were not worn by the same Poet: having then so much care to excel in one kind, very little is to be pardon'd them if they miscarried in it; and this would lead me to the consideration of their wit, had not *Crites* given me sufficient warning not to be too bold in my judgment of it; because the languages being dead, and many of the Customes and little accidents on which it depended, lost to us, we are not competent judges of it. But though I grant that here and there we may miss the application of a Proverb or a Custom, yet a thing well said will be wit in all Languages; and though it may lose something in the Translation, yet, to him who reads it in the Original, 'tis still the same; He has an Idea of its excellency, though it cannot pass from his mind into any other expression or words then those in which he finds it. When *Phaedria* in the *Eunuch* had a command from his Mistress to be absent two dayes; and encouraging himself to go through with it, said; *Tandem ego non illa caream, si opus sit, vel totum triduum? Parmeno* to mock the softness of his Master, lifting up his hands and eyes, cryes out as it were in admiration; *Hui! universum triduum!* the elegancy of which *universum*, though it cannot be rendred in our language, yet leaves an impression of the wit upon our souls: but this happens seldom in him, in *Plautus* oftner; who is infinitely too bold in his Metaphors and coyning words; out of which many times his wit is nothing, which questionless was one reason why *Horace* falls upon him so severely in those Verses:

Sed Proavi nostri Plautinos & numeros &
Laudavere sales, nimium patienter utrumque,
Ne dicam stolidè.

For *Horace* himself was cautious to obtrude a new word upon his Readers, and makes custom and common use the best measure of receiving it into our writings.

Multa renascentur quæ nunc cecidere, cadentq;
Quæ nunc sunt in honore vocabula, si volet usus,
Quem penes arbitrium est, & jus, & norma loquendi.

The not observing this Rule is that which the world has blam'd in our Satyrist *Cleveland*; to express a thing hard and unnaturally, is his new way of Elocution: 'Tis true, no Poet but may sometimes use a *Catachresis: Virgil* does it;

Mistaque ridenti Colocasia fundet Acantho.

In his Eclogue of Pollio, and in his 7th *Æneid*,

—Mirantur & undæ,
Miratur nemus insuetum fulgentia longe
Scuta virum fluvio pictasq; innare carinas.

And *Ovid* once so modestly, that he askes leave to do it;

Si verbo audacia detur
Haud metuam summi dixisse Palatia cœli.

Calling the Court of *Jupiter* by the name of *Augustus* his Pallace, though in another place he is more bold, where he sayes, *Et longas visent Capitolia pompas.* But to do this alwayes, and never be able to write a line without it, though it may be admir'd by some few Pedants, will not pass upon those who know that wit is best convey'd to us in the most easie language; and is most to be admir'd when a great thought comes drest in words so commonly receiv'd that it is understood by the meanest apprehensions, as the best meat is the most easily digested: but we cannot read a verse of *Cleveland's* without making a face at it, as if every word were a Pill to swallow: he gives us many times a hard Nut to break our Teeth, without a Kernel for our pains. So that there is this difference betwixt his *Satyres* and Doctor *Donns*, That the one gives us deep thoughts in common language, though rough cadence; the other gives us common thoughts in abstruse words: 'tis true, in some places his wit is independent of his words, as in that of the Rebel *Scot*:

Had Cain been Scot God would have chang'd his doom;
Not forc'd him wander, but confin'd him home.

Si sic, omnia dixisset! This is wit in all languages: 'tis like Mercury, never to be lost or kill'd; and so that other;

For Beauty like White-powder makes no noise,
And yet the silent Hypocrite destroyes.

You see the last line is highly Metaphorical, but it is so soft and gentle, that it does not shock us as we read it.

But, to return from whence I have digress'd, to the consideration of the Ancients Writing and their Wit, (of which by this time you will grant us in some measure to be fit judges,) Though I see many excellent thoughts in *Seneca*, yet he, of them who had a Genius moſt proper for the Stage, was *Ovid*; he had a way of writing so fit to ſtir up a pleasing admiration and concernment, which are the objects of a Tragedy, and to show the various movements of a Soul combating betwixt two different Passions, that, had he liv'd in our age, or in his own could have writ with our advantages, no man but muſt have yielded to him; and therefore I am confident the *Medea* is none of his: for, though I eſteem it for the gravity and sententiousness of it, which he himself concludes to be suitable to a Tragedy, *Omne genus scripti gravitate Tragædia vincit*, yet it moves not my soul enough to judge that he, who in the Epique way wrote things so near the *Drama*, as the Story of *Myrrha*, of *Caunus* and *Biblis*, and the reſt, should ſtir up no more concernment where he moſt endeavour'd it. The Maſter-piece of *Seneca* I hold to be that Scene in the *Troades*, where *Ulysses* is seeking for *Aſtyanax* to kill him; There you see the tenderness of a Mother, so represented in *Andromache*, that it raises compassion to a high degree in the Reader, and bears the neareſt resemblance of any thing in their Tragedies to the excellent Scenes of Passion in *Shakespeare*, or in *Fletcher*: for Love-Scenes you will find few among them, their Tragique Poets dealt not with that soft passion, but with Luſt, Cruelty, Revenge, Ambition, and those bloody actions they produc'd; which were more capable of raising horrour then compassion in an audience: leaving Love untoucht, whose gentleness would have temper'd them, which is the moſt frequent of all the passions, and which being the private concernment of every person, is sooth'd by viewing its own image in a publick entertainment.

Among their Comedies, we find a Scene or two of tenderness, and that where you would leaſt expect it, in *Plautus*; but to speak generally, their Lovers say little, when they see each other, but *anima mea, vita mea*; ζωὴ καὶ ψυχή, as the women in *Juvenal's* time us'd to cry out in the fury of their kindness: then indeed to speak sense were an offence. Any sudden guſt of passion (as an extasie of love in an unexpected meeting) cannot better be express'd than in a word and a sigh, breaking one another. Nature is dumb on such occasions, and to make her speak, would be to represent her unlike her self. But there are a thousand other concernments of Lovers, as jealousies, complaints, contrivances and the like, where not to open their minds at large to each other, were to be wanting to their own love, and to the expectation of the Audience; who watch the movements of their minds, as much as the changes of their fortunes. For the imaging of the firſt is properly the work of a Poet, the latter he borrows of the Hiſtorian.

Eugenius was proceeding in that part of his Discourse, when *Crites* interrupted him. I see, said he, *Eugenius* and I are never like to have this Question decided betwixt us; for he maintains the Moderns have acquir'd a new perfection in writing, I can onely grant they have alter'd the mode of it. *Homer* describ'd his Heroes men of great appetites, lovers of beef broild upon the coals, and good fellows; contrary to the practice of the French Romances, whose Heroes neither eat, nor drink, nor sleep, for love. *Virgil* makes *Æneas* a bold Avower of his own virtues,

Sum pius Æneas, fama super æthera notus;

which in the civility of our Poets is the Character of a Fanfaron or Hector: for with us the Knight takes occasion to walk out, or sleep, to avoid the vanity of telling his own Story, which the trusty Squire is ever to perform for him. So in their Love Scenes, of which *Eugenius* spoke last, the Ancients were more hearty, we more talkative: they writ love as it was then the mode to make it, and I will grant thus much to *Eugenius*, that perhaps one of their Poets, had he liv'd in our Age,

Si foret hoc nostrum fato delapsus in ævum (as *Horace* says of *Lucilius*)

he had alter'd many things; not that they were not as natural before, but that he might accommodate himself to the Age he liv'd in: yet in the mean time we are not to conclude any thing rashly against those great men; but preserve to them the dignity of Masters, and give that honour to their memories, (*Quos libitina sacravit;*) part of which we expect may be paid to us in future times.

This moderation of *Crites*, as it was pleasing to all the company, so it put an end to that dispute; which, *Eugenius*, who seem'd to have the better of the Argument, would urge no farther: but *Lisideius* after he had acknowledg'd himself of *Eugenius* his opinion concerning the Ancients; yet told him he had forborn, till his Discourse were ended, to ask him why he prefer'd the English Plays above those of other Nations? and whether we ought not to submit our Stage to the exactness of our next Neighbours?

Though, said *Eugenius*, I am at all times ready to defend the honour of my Countrey against the French, and to maintain, we are as well able to vanquish them with our Pens as our Ancestors have been with their swords; yet, if you please, added he, looking upon *Neander*, I will commit this cause to my friend's management; his opinion of our Plays is the same with mine: and besides, there is no reason, that *Crites* and I, who have now left the Stage, should re-enter so suddenly upon it; which is against the Laws of Comedie.

If the Question had been stated, replied *Lysideius*, who had writ best, the French or English forty years ago, I should have been of your opinion, and adjudg'd the honour to our own Nation; but since that time, (said he, turning towards *Neander*) we have been so long together bad Englishmen, that we had not leisure to be good Poets; *Beaumont*, *Fletcher*, and *Johnson* (who were onely capable of bringing us to that degree of perfection which we have) were just then leaving the world; as if in an Age of so much horror, wit and those milder studies of humanity, had no farther business among us. But the Muses, who ever follow Peace, went to plant in another Countrey; it was then that the great Cardinal of *Richlieu* began to take them into his protection; and that, by his encouragement, *Corneille* and some other Frenchmen reform'd their Theatre, (which before was as much below ours as it now surpasses it and the rest of *Europe*;) but because *Crites*, in his Discourse for the Ancients, has prevented me, by touching upon many Rules of the Stage, which the Moderns have borrow'd from them; I shall onely, in short, demand of you, whether you are not convinc'd that of all Nations the French have best observ'd them? In the unity of time you find them so scrupulous, that it yet remains a dispute among their Poets, whether the artificial day of twelve hours more or less, be not meant by *Aristotle*, rather than the natural one of twenty four; and consequently whether all Plays ought not to be reduc'd into that compass? This I can testifie, that in all their *Drama's* writ within these last 20 years and upwards, I have not observ'd any that have extended the time to thirty hours: in the unity of place they are full as scrupulous, for many of their Criticks limit it to that very spot of ground where the Play is suppos'd to begin; none of them exceed the compass of the same Town or City.

The unity of Action in all their Plays is yet more conspicuous, for they do not burden them with under-plots, as the English do; which is the reason why many Scenes of our Tragi-comedies carry on a design that is nothing of kinne to the main Plot; and that we see two distinct webbs in a Play; like those in ill wrought stuffs; and two actions, that is, two Plays carried on together, to the confounding of the Audience; who, before they are warm in their concernments for one part, are diverted to another; and by that means espouse the interest of neither. From hence likewise it arises that the one half of our Actors are not known to the other. They keep their distances as if they were *Mountagues* and *Capulets*, and seldom begin an acquaintance till the last Scene of the Fifth Act, when they are all to meet upon the Stage. There is no Theatre in the world has any thing so absurd as the English Tragi-comedie, 'tis a *Drama* of our own invention, and the fashion of it is enough to proclaim it so; here a course of mirth, there another of sadness and passion; a third of honour, and fourth a Duel: Thus in two hours and a half we run through all the fits of *Bedlam*. The French affords you as much variety on the same day, but they do it not so unseasonably, or *mal a propos* as we: Our Poets present you the Play and the farce together; and our Stages still retain somewhat of the Original civility of the *Red-Bull;*

Atque ursum & pugiles media inter carmina poscunt.

The end of Tragedies or serious Playes, sayes *Aristotle*, is to beget admiration, compassion, or concernment; but are not mirth and compassion things incompatible? and is it not evident that the Poet must of necessity destroy the former by intermingling of the latter? that is, he must ruine the sole end and object of his Tragedy to introduce somewhat that is forced in, and is not of the body of it: Would you not think that Physician mad, who having prescribed a Purge, should immediatly order you to take restringents upon it?

But to leave our Playes, and return to theirs, I have noted one great advantage they have had in the Plotting of their Tragedies; that is, they are always grounded upon some known History: according to that of *Horace*, *Ex noto fictum carmen sequar*; and in that they have so imitated the Ancients that they have surpass'd them. For the Ancients, as was observ'd before, took for the foundation of their Playes some Poetical Fiction, such as under that consideration could move but little concernment in the Audience, because they already knew the event of it. But the French goes farther;

Atque ita mentitur, sic veris falsa remiscet,
Primo ne medium, medio ne discrepet imum:

He so interweaves Truth with probable Fiction, that he puts a pleasing Fallacy upon us; mends the intrigues of Fate, and dispenses with the severity of History, to reward that vertue which has been rendred to us there unfortunate. Sometimes the story has left the success so doubtful, that the Writer is free, by the priviledge of a Poet, to take that which of two or more relations will best sute with his design: As for example, the death of *Cyrus*, whom *Justin* and some others report to have perish'd in the *Scythian* war, but *Xenophon* affirms to have died in his bed of extream old age. Nay more, when the event is past dispute, even then we are willing to be deceiv'd, and the Poet, if he contrives it with appearance of truth, has all the audience of his Party; at least during the time his Play is acting: so naturally we are kind to vertue, when our own interest is not in question, that we take it up as the general concernment of Mankind. On the other side, if you consider the Historical Playes of *Shakespeare*, they are rather so many Chronicles of Kings, or the business many times of thirty or forty years, crampt into a representation of two hours and a half, which is not to imitate or paint Nature, but rather to draw her in miniature, to take her in little; to look upon her through the wrong end of a Perspective, and receive her Images not onely much less, but infinitely more imperfect then the life: this, instead of making a Play delightful, renders it ridiculous.

Quodcunque ostendis mihi sic, incredulus odi.

For the Spirit of man cannot be satisfied but with truth, or at least verisimility; and a Poem is to contain, if not τὰ ἔτυμα, yet ἐτύμοισιν ὁμοῖα, as one of the Greek Poets has express'd it.

Another thing in which the French differ from us and from the Spaniards, is, that they do not embarass, or cumber themselves with too much Plot: they onely represent so much of a Story as will constitute one whole and great action sufficient for a Play; we, who undertake more, do but multiply adventures; which, not being produc'd from one another, as effects from causes, but barely following, constitute many actions in the Drama, and consequently make it many Playes.

But by pursuing close one argument, which is not cloy'd with many turns, the French have gain'd more liberty for verse, in which they write: they have leisure to dwell upon a subject which deserves it; and to represent the passions (which we have acknowledg'd to be the Poets work) without being hurried from one thing to another, as we are in the Playes of *Calderon*, which we have seen lately upon our Theaters, under the name of Spanish Plotts. I have taken notice but of one Tragedy of ours, whose Plot has that uniformity and unity of design in it which I have commended in the French; and that is *Rollo*, or rather, under the name of *Rollo*, The Story of *Bassianus* and *Geta* in *Herodian*; there indeed the Plot is neither large nor intricate, but just enough to fill the minds of the Audience, not to cloy them. Besides, you see it founded upon the truth of History, onely the time of the action is not reduceable to the strictness of the Rules; and you see in some places a little farce mingled, which is below the dignity of the other parts; and in this all our Poets are extreamly peccant, even *Ben. Johnson* himself in *Sejanus* and *Catiline* has given us this Oleo of a Play; this unnatural mixture of Comedy and Tragedy, which to me sounds just as ridiculously as the History of *David* with the merry humours of *Golia's*. In *Sejanus* you may take notice of the Scene betwixt *Livia* and the Physician, which is a pleasant Satyre upon the artificial helps of beauty: In *Catiline* you may see the Parliament of Women; the little envies of them to one another; and all that passes betwixt *Curio* and *Fulvia*: Scenes admirable in their kind, but of an ill mingle with the rest.

But I return again to the French Writers; who, as I have said, do not burden themselves too much with Plot, which has been reproach'd to them by an *ingenious person* of our Nation as a fault, for he says they commonly make but one person considerable in a Play; they dwell upon him, and his concernments, while the rest of the persons are onely subservient to set him off. If he intends this by it, that there is one person in the Play who is of greater dignity then the rest, he must tax, not onely theirs, but those of the Ancients, and which he would be loth to do, the best of ours; for 'tis impossible but that one person must be more conspicuous in it then any other, and consequently the greatest share in the action must devolve on him. We see it so in the management of all affairs; even in the most equal Aristocracy, the ballance cannot be so justly poys'd, but some one will be superiour to the rest; either in parts, fortune, interest, or the consideration of some glorious exploit; which will reduce the greatest part of business into his hands.

But, if he would have us to imagine that in exalting of one character the rest of them are neglected, and that all of them have not some share or other in the action of the Play, I desire him to produce any of *Corneilles* Tragedies, wherein every person (like so many servants in a well govern'd Family) has not some employment, and who is not necessary to the carrying on of the Plot, or at least to your understanding it.

There are indeed some protatick persons in the Ancients, whom they make use of in their Playes, either to hear, or give the Relation: but the French avoid this with great address, making their narrations onely to, or by such who are some way interessed in the main design. And now I am speaking of Relations, I cannot take a fitter opportunity to add this in favour of the French, that they often use them with better judgment and more *a propos* then the English do. Not that I commend narrations in general, but there are two sorts of them; one of those things which are antecedent to the Play, and are related to make the conduct of it more clear to us, but, 'tis a fault to choose such subjects for the Stage which will inforce us upon that Rock; because we see they are seldome listned to by the Audience, and that is many times the ruin of the Play: for, being once let pass without attention, the Audience can never recover themselves to understand the Plot; and indeed it is somewhat unreasonable that they should be put to so much trouble, as, that to comprehend what passes in their sight, they must have recourse to what was done, perhaps, ten or twenty years ago.

But there is another sort of Relations, that is, of things hapning in the Action of the Play, and suppos'd to be done behind the Scenes: and this is many times both convenient and beautiful: for, by it, the French avoid the tumult, which we are subject to in *England*, by representing Duells, Battells, and the like; which renders our Stage too like the Theaters, where they fight Prizes. For what is more ridiculous then to represent an Army with a Drum and five men behind it; all which, the Heroe of the other side is to drive in before him, or to see a Duel fought, and one slain with two or three thrusts of the foyles, which we know are so blunted, that we might give a man an hour to kill another in good earnest with them.

I have observ'd that in all our Tragedies, the Audience cannot forbear laughing when the Actors are to die; 'tis the most Comick part of the whole Play. All *passions* may be lively represented on the Stage, if to the well-writing of them the Actor supplies a good commanded voice, and limbs that move easily, and without stifness; but there are many *actions* which can never be imitated to a just height: dying especially is a thing which none but a Roman Gladiator could naturally perform upon the Stage when he did not imitate or represent, but naturally do it; and therefore it is better to omit the representation of it.

The words of a good Writer which describe it lively, will make a deeper impression of belief in us then all the Actor can perswade us to, when he seems to fall dead before us; as a Poet in the description of a beautiful Garden, or a Meadow, will please our imagination more then the place itself can please our sight. When we see death represented we are convinc'd it is but Fiction; but when we hear it related, our eyes (the strongest witnesses) are wanting, which might have undeceiv'd us; and we are all willing to favour the sleight when the Poet does not too grosly impose upon us. They therefore who imagine these relations would make no concernment in the Audience, are deceiv'd, by confounding them with the other, which are of things antecedent to the Play; those are made often in cold blood (as I may say) to the audience; but these are warm'd with our concernments, which are before awaken'd in the Play. What the Philosophers say of motion, that when it is once begun it continues of it self, and will do so to Eternity without some stop put to it, is clearly true on this occasion; the soul being already mov'd with the Characters and Fortunes of those imaginary persons, continues going of its own accord, and we are no more weary to hear what becomes of them when they are not on the Stage, then we are to listen to the news of an absent Mistress. But it is objected, That if one part of the Play may be related, then why not all? I answer, Some parts of the action are more fit to be represented, some to be related. *Corneille* sayes judiciously, that the Poet is not oblig'd to expose to view all particular actions which conduce to the principal: he ought to select such of them to be seen which will appear with the greatest beauty, either by the magnificence of the show, or the vehemence of passions which they produce, or some other charm which they have in them, and let the rest arrive to the audience by narration. 'Tis a great mistake in us to believe the French present no part of the action upon the Stage: every alteration or crossing of a design, every new sprung passion, and turn of it, is a part of the action, and much the noblest, except we conceive nothing to be action till they come to blows; as if the painting of the Heroes mind were not more properly the Poets work then the strength of his body. Nor does this any thing contradict the opinion of *Horace*, where he tells us,

Segnius irritant animos demissa per aurem,
Quam quæ sunt oculis subjecta fidelibus.—

For he sayes immediately after,

——————————*Non tamen intus*
Digna geri promes in scenam; Multaq; tolles
Ex oculis, quæ mox narret facundia præsens.

Among which many he recounts some.

Nec pueros coram populo Medea trucidet,
Aut in avem Progne mutetur, Cadmus in anguem, &c.

That is, those actions which by reason of their cruelty will cause aversion in us, or by reason of their impossibility unbelief, ought either wholly to be avoided by a Poet, or onely deliver'd by narration. To which, we may have leave to add such as to avoid tumult, (as was before hinted) or to reduce the Plot into a more reasonable compass of time, or for defect of Beauty in them, are rather to be related then presented to the eye. Examples of all these kinds are frequent, not onely among all the Ancients, but in the best receiv'd of our English Poets. We find *Ben. Johnson* using them in his *Magnetick Lady*, where one comes out from Dinner, and relates the quarrels and disorders of it to save the undecent appearing of them on the Stage, and to abreviate the Story: and this in express imitation of *Terence*, who had done the same before him in his *Eunuch*, where

Pythias makes the like relation of what had happen'd within at the Souldiers entertainment. The relations likewise of *Sejanus's* death, and the prodigies before it are remarkable; the one of which was hid from sight to avoid the horrour and tumult of the representation; the other to shun the introducing of things impossible to be believ'd. In that excellent Play the *King And No King*, *Fletcher* goes yet farther; for the whole unravelling of the Plot is done by narration in the fifth Act, after the manner of the Ancients; and it moves great concernment in the Audience, though it be onely a relation of what was done many years before the Play. I could multiply other instances, but these are sufficient to prove that there is no errour in choosing a subject which requires this sort of narrations; in the ill managing of them, there may.

But I find I have been too long in this discourse since the French have many other excellencies not common to us, as that you never see any of their Playes end with a conversion, or simple change of will, which is the ordinary way our Poets use to end theirs. It shows little art in the conclusion of a Dramatick Poem, when they who have hinder'd the felicity during the four Acts, desist from it in the fifth without some powerful cause to take them off; and though I deny not but such reasons may be found, yet it is a path that is cautiously to be trod, and the Poet is to be sure he convinces the Audience that the motive is strong enough. As for example, the conversion of the Usurer in *The Scornful Lady*, seems to me a little forc'd; for being an Usurer, which implies a lover of Money to the highest degree of covetousness, (and such the Poet has represented him) the account he gives for the sudden change is, that he has been dup'd by the wilde young fellow, which in reason might render him more wary another time, and make him punish himself with harder fare and courser cloaths to get it up again: but that he should look upon it as a judgment, and so repent, we may expect to hear of in a Sermon, but I should never indure it in a Play.

I pass by this; neither will I insist upon the care they take, that no person after his first entrance shall ever appear, but the business which brings him upon the Stage shall be evident: which, if observ'd, must needs render all the events in the Play more natural; for there you see the probability of every accident, in the cause that produc'd it; and that which appears chance in the Play, will seem so reasonable to you, that you will there find it almost necessary; so that in the exits of their Actors you have a clear account of their purpose and design in the next entrance: (though, if the Scene be well wrought, the event will commonly deceive you) for there is nothing so absurd, sayes *Corneille*, as for an Actor to leave the Stage, onely because he has no more to say.

I should now speak of the beauty of their Rhime, and the just reason I have to prefer that way of writing in Tragedies before ours in Blanck-verse; but because it is partly receiv'd by us, and therefore not altogether peculiar to them, I will say no more of it in relation to their Playes. For our own I doubt not but it will exceedingly beautifie them, and I can see but one reason why it should not generally obtain, that is, because our Poets write so ill in it. This indeed may prove a more prevailing argument then all others which are us'd to destroy it, and therefore I am onely troubled when great and judicious Poets, and those who are acknowledg'd such, have writ or spoke against it; as for others they are to be answer'd by that one sentence of an ancient Authour.

Sed ut primo ad consequendos eos quos priores ducimus, accendimur, ita ubi aut præteriri, aut æquari eos posse desperavimus, studium cum spe senescit: quod, scilicet, assequi non potest, sequi desinit; . . . . præteritoq; eo in quo eminere non possumus, aliquid in quo nitamur, conquirimus.

Lisideius concluded in this manner; and *Neander* after a little pause thus answer'd him.

I shall grant *Lisideius*, without much dispute, a great part of what he has urg'd against us; for I acknowledg the French contrive their Plots more regularly, and observe the Laws of Comedy, and decorum of the Stage (to speak generally) with more exactness then the English. Farther I deny not but he has tax'd us justly in some irregularities of ours which he has mention'd; yet, after all, I am of opinion that neither our faults nor their virtues are considerable enough to place them above us.

For the lively imitation of Nature being in the definition of a Play, those which best fulfil that law ought to be esteem'd superiour to the others. 'Tis true, those beauties of the French-poesie are such as will raise perfection higher where it is, but are not sufficient to give it where it is not: they are indeed the Beauties of a Statue, but not of a Man, because not animated with the Soul of Poesie, which is imitation of humour and passions: and this *Lisideius* himself, or any other, however byassed to their Party, cannot but acknowledg, if he will either compare the humours of our Comedies, or the Characters of our serious Playes with theirs. He that will look upon theirs which have been written till these last ten years or thereabouts, will find it an hard matter to pick out two or three passable humours amongst them. *Corneille* himself, their Arch-Poet, what has he produc'd except *The Lier*, and you know how it was cry'd up in *France*; but when it came upon the English Stage, though well translated, and that part of *Dorant* acted to so much advantage by Mr. *Hart*, as I am confident it never receiv'd in its own Country, the most favourable to it would not put it in competition with many of *Fletchers* or *Ben. Johnsons*. In the rest of *Corneilles* Comedies you have little humour; he tells you himself his way is first to show two Lovers in good intelligence with each other; in the working up of the Play to embroyle them by some mistake, and in the latter end to clear it up.

But of late years *de Moliere*, the younger *Corneille*, *Quinault*, and some others, have been imitating of afar off the quick turns and graces of the English Stage. They have mix'd their serious Playes with mirth, like our Tragicomedies since the death of Cardinal *Richelieu*, which *Lisideius* and many others not observing, have commended that in them for a virtue which they themselves no longer practice. Most of their new Playes are like some of ours, deriv'd from the Spanish Novells. There is scarce one of them without a vail, and a trusty *Diego*, who drolls much after the rate of the *Adventures*. But their humours, if I may grace them with that name, are so thin sown that never above one of them comes up in any Play: I dare take upon me to find more variety of them in some one Play of *Ben. Johnsons* then in all theirs together: as he who has seen *The Alchymist*, *The Silent Woman*, or *Bartholmew-Fair*, cannot but acknowledge with me.

I grant the French have performed what was possible on the ground-work of the Spanish Playes; what was pleasant before they have made regular; but there is not above one good Play to be writ upon all those Plots; they are too much alike to please often, which we need not the experience of our own Stage to justifie. As for their new way of mingling mirth with serious Plot I do not with *Lysideius* condemn the thing, though I cannot approve their manner of doing it: He tells us we cannot so speedily recollect our selves after a Scene of great passion and concernment as to pass to another of mirth and humour, and to enjoy it with any relish: but why should he imagine the soul of man more heavy then his Sences? Does not the eye pass from an unpleasant object to a pleasant in a much shorter time then is requir'd to this? and does not the unpleasantness of the first commend the beauty of the latter? The old Rule of Logick might have convinc'd him, that contraries when plac'd near, set off each other. A continued gravity keeps the spirit too much bent; we must refresh it sometimes, as we bait upon a journey, that we may go on with greater ease. A Scene of mirth mix'd with Tragedy has the same effect upon us which our musick has betwixt the Acts, and that we find a relief to us from the best Plots and language of the Stage, if the discourses have been long. I must therefore have stronger arguments ere I am convinc'd, that compassion and mirth in the same subject destroy each other; and in the mean time cannot but conclude, to the honour of our Nation, that we have invented, increas'd and perfected a more pleasant way of writing for the Stage then was ever known to the Ancients or Moderns of any Nation, which is Tragicomedie.

And this leads me to wonder why *Lisideius* and many others should cry up the barrenness of the French Plots above the variety and copiousness of the English. Their Plots are single, they carry on one design which is push'd forward by all the Actors, every Scene in the Play contributing and moving towards it: Ours, besides the main design, have under plots or by-concernments, of less considerable Persons, and Intrigues, which are carried on with the motion of the main Plot: just as they say the Orb of the fix'd Stars, and those of the Planets, though they have motions of their own, are whirl'd about by the motion of the *primum mobile*, in which they are contain'd: that similitude expresses much of the English Stage: for if contrary motions may be found in Nature to agree; if a Planet can go East and West at the same time; one way by virtue of his own motion, the other by the force of the first mover; it will not be difficult to imagine how the under Plot, which is onely different, not contrary to the great design, may naturally be conducted along with it.

Eugenius has already shown us, from the confession of the French Poets, that the Unity of Action is sufficiently preserv'd if all the imperfect actions of the Play are conducing to the main design: but when those petty intrigues of a Play are so ill order'd that they have no coherence with the other, I must grant *Lisideius* has reason to tax that want of due connexion; for Co-ordination in a Play is as dangerous and unnatural as in a State. In the mean time he must acknowledge our variety, if well order'd, will afford a greater pleasure to the audience.

As for his other argument, that by pursuing one single Theme they gain an advantage to express and work up the passions, I wish any example he could bring from them would make it good: for I confess their verses are to me the coldest I have ever read: Neither indeed is it possible for them, in the way they take, so to express passion, as that the effects of it should appear in the concernment of an Audience: their Speeches being so many declamations, which tire us with the length; so that instead of perswading us to grieve for their imaginary Heroes, we are concern'd for our own trouble, as we are in the tedious visits of bad company; we are in pain till they are gone. When the French Stage came to be reform'd by Cardinal *Richelieu*, those long Harangues were introduc'd, to comply with the gravity of a Churchman. Look upon the *Cinna* and the *Pompey*, they are not so properly to be called Playes, as long discourses of reason of State: and *Polieucte* in matters of Religion is as solemn as the long stops upon our Organs. Since that time it is grown into a custome, and their Actors speak by the Hour-glass, as our Parsons do; nay, they account it the grace of their parts: and think themselves disparag'd by the Poet, if they may not twice or thrice in a Play entertain the Audience with a Speech of an hundred or two hundred lines. I deny not but this may sute well enough with the French; for as we, who are a more sullen people, come to be diverted at our Playes; they who are of an ayery and gay temper come thither to make themselves more serious: And this I conceive to be one reason why Comedy is more pleasing to us, and Tragedies to them. But to speak generally, it cannot be deny'd that short Speeches and Replies are more apt to move the passions, and beget concernment in us then the other: for it is unnatural for any one in a gust of passion to speak long together, or for another in the same condition, to suffer him, without interruption. Grief and Passion are like floods rais'd in little Brooks by a sudden rain; they are quickly up, and if the concernment be powr'd unexpectedly in upon us, it overflows us: But a long sober shower gives them leisure to run out as they came in, without troubling the ordinary current. As for Comedy, Repartee is one of its chiefest graces; the greatest pleasure of the Audience is a chase of wit kept up on both sides, and swiftly manag'd. And this our forefathers, if not we, have had in *Fletchers* Playes, to a much higher degree of perfection then the French Poets can arrive at.

There is another part of *Lisideius* his Discourse, in which he has rather excus'd our neighbours then commended them; that is, for aiming onely to make one person considerable in their Playes. 'Tis very true what he has urged, that one character in all Playes, even without the Poets care, will have advantage of all the others; and that the design of the whole *Drama* will chiefly depend on it. But this hinders not that there may be more shining characters in the Play: many persons of a second magnitude, nay, some so very near, so almost equal to the first, that greatness may be oppos'd to greatness, and all the persons be made considerable, not onely by their quality, but their action. 'Tis evident that the more the persons are, the greater will be the variety of the Plot. If then the parts are manag'd so regularly that the beauty of the whole be kept intire, and that the variety become not a perplex'd and confus'd mass of accidents, you will find it infinitely pleasing to be led in a labyrinth of design, where you see some of your way before you, yet discern not the end till you arrive at it. And that all this is practicable, I can produce for examples many of our English Playes: as *The Maids Tragedy*, *The Alchymist*, *The Silent Woman*; I was going to have named *The Fox*, but that the unity of design seems not exactly observ'd in it; for there appear two actions in the Play; the first naturally ending with the fourth Act; the second forc'd from it in the fifth: which yet is the less to be condemn'd in him, because the disguise of *Volpone*, though it suited not with his character as a crafty or covetous person, agreed well enough with that of a voluptuary: and by it the Poet gain'd the end he aym'd at, the punishment of Vice, and the reward of Virtue, which that disguise produc'd. So that to judge equally of it, it was an excellent fifth Act, but not so naturally proceeding from the former.

But to leave this, and pass to the latter part of *Lisideius* his discourse, which concerns relations, I must acknowledge with him, that the French have reason when they hide that part of the action which would occasion too much tumult upon the Stage, and choose rather to have it made known by narration to the Audience. Farther I think it very convenient, for the reasons he has given, that all incredible actions were remov'd; but, whither custome has so insinuated it self into our Country-men, or nature has so form'd them to fierceness, I know not; but they will scarcely suffer combats & other objects of horrour to be taken from them. And indeed, the indecency of tumults is all which can be objected against fighting: For why may not our imagination as well suffer it self to be deluded with the probability of it, as with any other thing in the Play? For my part, I can with as great ease perswade my self that the blowes which are struck are given in good earnest, as I can, that they who strike them are Kings or Princes, or those persons which they represent. For objects of incredibility I would be satisfied from *Lisideius*, whether we have any so remov'd from all appearance of truth as are those of *Corneilles Andromede?* A Play which has been frequented the most of any he has writ. If the *Perseus*, or the Son of an Heathen God, the *Pegasus* and the Monster were not capable to choak a strong belief, let him blame any representation of ours hereafter. Those indeed were objects of delight; yet the reason is the same as to the probability: for he makes it not a Ballette or Masque, but a Play, which is to resemble truth. But for death, that it ought not to be represented, I have besides the Arguments alledg'd by *Lisideius*, the authority of *Ben. Johnson*, who has forborn it in his Tragedies; for both the death of *Sejanus* and *Catiline* are related: though in the latter I cannot but observe one irregularity of that great Poet: he has remov'd the Scene in the same Act, from *Rome* to *Catiline's* Army, and from thence again to *Rome*; and besides, has allow'd a very inconsiderable time, after *Catilines* Speech, for the striking of the battle, and the return of *Petreius*, who is to relate the event of it to the Senate: which I should not animadvert upon him, who was otherwise a painful observer of τὸ πρέπον, or the decorum of the Stage, if he had not us'd extream severity in his judgment upon the incomparable *Shakespeare* for the same fault. To conclude on this subject of Relations, if we are to be blam'd for showing too much of the action, the French are as faulty for discovering too little of it: a mean betwixt both should be observed by every judicious Writer, so as the audience may neither be left unsatisfied by not seeing what is beautiful, or shock'd by beholding what is either incredible or undecent. I hope I have already prov'd in this discourse, that though we are not altogether so punctual as the French, in observing the lawes of Comedy; yet our errours are so few, and little, and those things wherein we excel them so considerable, that we ought of right to be prefer'd before them. But what will *Lisideius* say if they themselves acknowledge they are too strictly ti'd up by those lawes, for breaking which he has blam'd the English? I will alledge *Corneille's* words, as I find them in the end of his Discourse of the three Unities; *Il est facile aux speculatifs d'estre severes, &c.* "'Tis easie for speculative persons to judge severely; but if they would produce to publick view ten or twelve pieces of this nature, they would perhaps give more latitude to the Rules then I have done, when by experience they had known how much we are bound up and constrain'd by them, and how many beauties of the Stage they banish'd from it." To illustrate a little what he has said, by their servile observations of the unities of time and place, and integrity of Scenes, they have brought upon themselves that dearth of Plot, and narrowness of Imagination, which may be observ'd in all their Playes. How many beautifull accidents might naturally happen in two or three dayes, which cannot arrive with any probability in the compass of 24 hours? There is time to be allowed also for maturity of design, which amongst great and prudent persons, such as are often represented in Tragedy, cannot, with any likelihood of truth, be brought to pass at so short a warning. Farther, by tying themselves strictly to the unity of place, and unbroken Scenes, they are forc'd many times to omit some beauties which cannot be shown where the Act began; but might, if the Scene were interrupted, and the Stage clear'd for the persons to enter in another place; and therefore the French Poets are often forc'd upon absurdities: for if the Act begins in a chamber all the persons in the Play must have some business or other to come thither, or else they are not to be shown that Act, and sometimes their characters are very unfitting to appear there; As, suppose it were the Kings Bed-chamber, yet the meanest man in the Tragedy must come and dispatch his business there rather then in the Lobby or Courtyard (which is fitter for him) for fear the Stage should be clear'd, and the

Scenes broken. Many times they fall by it into a greater inconvenience; for they keep their Scenes unbroken, and yet change the place; as in one of their newest Playes, where the Act begins in the Street. There a Gentleman is to meet his Friend; he sees him with his man, coming out from his Fathers house; they talk together, and the first goes out: the second, who is a Lover, has made an appointment with his Mistress; she appears at the window, and then we are to imagine the Scene lies under it. This Gentleman is call'd away, and leaves his servant with his Mistress: presently her Father is heard from within; the young Lady is affraid the Servingman should be discover'd, and thrusts him in through a door which is suppos'd to be her Closet. After this, the Father enters to the Daughter, and now the Scene is in a House: for he is seeking from one room to another for this poor *Philipin*, or French *Diego*, who is heard from within, drolling and breaking many a miserable conceit upon his sad condition. In this ridiculous manner the Play goes on, the Stage being never empty all the while: so that the Street, the Window, the two Houses, and the Closet, are made to walk about, and the Persons to stand still. Now what I beseech you is more easie than to write a regular French Play, or more difficult then to write an irregular English one, like those of *Fletcher*, or of *Shakespeare*?

If they content themselves as *Corneille* did, with some flat design, which, like an ill Riddle, is found out e're it be half propos'd; such Plots we can make every way regular as easily as they: but when e're they endeavour to rise up to any quick turns and counterturns of Plot, as some of them have attempted, since *Corneilles* Playes have been less in vogue, you see they write as irregularly as we, though they cover it more speciously. Hence the reason is perspicuous, why no French Playes, when translated, have, or ever can succeed upon the English Stage. For, if you consider the Plots, our own are fuller of variety, if the writing, ours are more quick and fuller of spirit: and therefore 'tis a strange mistake in those who decry the way of writing Playes in Verse, as if the English therein imitated the French. We have borrow'd nothing from them; our Plots are weav'd in English Loomes: we endeavour therein to follow the variety and greatness of characters which are deriv'd to us from *Shakespeare* and *Fletcher*: the copiousness and well-knitting of the intrigues we have from *Johnson*, and for the Verse it self we have English Presidents of elder date then any of *Corneille's* Playes: (not to name our old Comedies before *Shakespeare*, which were all writ in verse of six feet, or *Alexandrin's*, such as the French now use) I can show in *Shakespeare*, many Scenes of rhyme together, and the like in *Ben. Johnsons* Tragedies: In *Catiline* and *Sejanus* sometimes thirty or forty lines; I mean besides the

Chorus, or the Monologues, which by the way, show'd *Ben.* no enemy to this way of writing, especially if you look upon his *Sad Shepherd* which goes sometimes upon rhyme, sometimes upon blanck Verse, like an Horse who eases himself upon Trot and Amble. You find him likewise commending *Fletcher's* Paſtoral of *The Faithful Shepherdess*; which is for the moſt part Rhyme, though not refin'd to that purity to which it hath since been brought: And these examples are enough to clear us from a servile imitation of the French.

But to return from whence I have digress'd, I dare boldly affirm these two things of the English *Drama*: Firſt, That we have many Playes of ours as regular as any of theirs; and which, besides, have more variety of Plot and Characters: And secondly, that in moſt of the irregular Playes of *Shakespeare* or *Fletcher* (for *Ben. Johnson's* are for the moſt part regular) there is a more masculine fancy and greater spirit in all the writing, then there is in any of the French. I could produce even in *Shakespeare's* and *Fletcher's* Works, some Playes which are almoſt exactly form'd; as *The Merry Wives of Windsor*, and *The Scornful Lady*: but because (generally speaking) *Shakespeare*, who writ firſt, did not perfectly observe the Laws of Comedy, and *Fletcher*, who came nearer to perfection, yet through carelesness made many faults; I will take the pattern of a perfect Play from *Ben. Johnson*, who was a careful and learned observer of the Dramatique Lawes, and from all his Comedies I shall select *The Silent Woman*; of which I will make a short Examen, according to those Rules which the French observe.

As *Neander* was beginning to examine *The Silent Woman*, *Eugenius*, looking earneſtly upon him; I beseech you *Neander*, said he, gratifie the company and me in particular so far, as before you speak of the Play, to give us a Character of the Authour; and tell us franckly your opinion, whether you do not think all Writers, both French and English, ought to give place to him?

I fear, replied *Neander*, That in obeying your commands I shall draw a little envy upon my self. Besides, in performing them, it will be firſt necessary to speak somewhat of *Shakespeare* and *Fletcher*, his Rivalls in Poesie; and one of them, in my opinion, at leaſt his equal, perhaps his superior.

To begin then with *Shakespeare*; he was the man who of all Modern, and perhaps Ancient Poets, had the largeſt and moſt comprehensive soul. All the Images of Nature were ſtill present to him, and he drew them not laboriously, but luckily: when he describes any thing, you more than see it, you feel it too. Those who accuse him to have wanted learning, give him the greater commendation: he was naturally learn'd; he needed not the spectacles of Books to read Nature; he look'd inwards, and found her there. I cannot say he is every where alike; were he so, I should do him injury to compare him with the greateſt of Mankind. He is many times flat, insipid; his Comick wit degenerating into clenches, his serious swelling into Bombaſt. But he is alwayes great, when some great occasion is presented to him: no man can say he ever had a fit subjeƈt for his wit, and did not then raise himself as high above the reſt of Poets,

Quantum lenta solent inter vibvrna cupressi.

The consideration of this made Mr. *Hales* of *Eaton* say, That there was no subjeƈt of which any Poet ever writ, but he would produce it much better treated of in *Shakespeare*; and however others are now generally prefer'd before him, yet the Age wherein he liv'd, which had contemporaries with him, *Fletcher* and *Johnson* never equall'd them to him in their eſteem: And in the laſt Kings Court, when *Ben's* reputation was at higheſt, Sir *John Suckling*, and with him the greater part of the Courtiers, set our *Shakespeare* far above him.

Beaumont and *Fletcher* of whom I am next to speak, had with the advantage of *Shakespeare's* wit, which was their precedent, great natural gifts, improv'd by ſtudy. *Beaumont* especially being so accurate a judge of Playes, that *Ben. Johnson* while he liv'd, submitted all his Writings to his Censure, and 'tis thought, us'd his judgement in correƈting, if not contriving all his Plots. What value he had for him, appears by the Verses he writ to him; and therefore I need speak no farther of it. The firſt Play which brought *Fletcher* and him in eſteem was their *Philaſter*: for before that, they had written two or three very unsuccessfully: as the like is reported of *Ben. Johnson*, before he writ *Every Man in his Humour*. Their Plots were generally more regular then *Shakespeare's*, especially those which were made before *Beaumont's* death; and they underſtood and imitated the conversation of Gentlemen much better; whose wilde debaucheries, and quickness of wit in reparties, no Poet can ever paint as they have done. Humour which *Ben. Johnson* deriv'd from particular persons, they made it not their business to describe: they represented all the passions very lively, but above all, Love. I am apt to believe the English Language in them arriv'd to its higheſt perfeƈtion; what words have since been taken in, are rather superfluous then necessary. Their Playes are now the moſt pleasant and frequent entertainments of the Stage; two of theirs being aƈted through the year for one of *Shakespeare's* or *Johnsons:* the reason is, because there is a certain gayety in their Comedies, and Pathos in their more serious Playes, which suits generally with all mens humours. *Shakespeares* language is likewise a little obsolete, and *Ben. Johnson's* wit comes short of theirs.

As for *Johnson*, to whose Character I am now arriv'd, if we look upon him while he was himself, (for his last Playes were but his dotages) I think him the most learned and judicious Writer which any Theater ever had. He was a most severe Judge of himself as well as others. One cannot say he wanted wit, but rather that he was frugal of it. In his works you find little to retrench or alter. Wit and Language, and Humour also in some measure we had before him; but something of Art was wanting to the *Drama* till he came. He manag'd his strength to more advantage then any who preceded him. You seldome find him making Love in any of his Scenes, or endeavouring to move the Passions; his genius was too sullen and saturnine to do it gracefully, especially when he knew he came after those who had performed both to such an height. Humour was his proper Sphere, and in that he delighted most to represent Mechanick people. He was deeply conversant in the Ancients, both Greek and Latine, and he borrow'd boldly from them: there is scarce a Poet or Historian among the Roman Authours of those times whom he has not translated in *Sejanus* and *Catiline*. But he has done his Robberies so openly, that one may see he fears not to be taxed by any Law. He invades Authours like a Monarch, and what would be theft in other Poets, is onely victory in him. With the spoils of these Writers he so represents old *Rome* to us, in its Rites, Ceremonies and Customs, that if one of their Poets had written either of his Tragedies, we had seen less of it then in him. If there was any fault in his Language, 'twas that he weav'd it too closely and laboriously in his serious Playes: perhaps too, he did a little too much Romanize our Tongue, leaving the words which he translated almost as much Latine as he found them: wherein though he learnedly followed the Idiom of their language, he did not enough comply with ours. If I would compare him with *Shakespeare*, I must acknowledge him the more correct Poet, but *Shakespeare* the greater wit. *Shakespeare* was the *Homer*, or Father of our Dramatick Poets; *Johnson* was the *Virgil*, the pattern of elaborate writing; I admire him, but I love *Shakespeare*. To conclude of him, as he has given us the most correct Playes, so in the precepts which he has laid down in his *Discoveries*, we have as many and profitable Rules for perfecting the Stage as any wherewith the French can furnish us.

Having thus spoken of the Authour, I proceed to the examination of his Comedy, *The Silent Woman*.

EXAMEN OF *The Silent Woman*.

To begin first with the length of the Action, it is so far from exceeding the compass of a Natural day, that it takes not up an Artificial one. 'Tis all included in the limits of three hours and an half, which is no more than is requir'd for the presentment on the Stage. A beauty perhaps not much observ'd; if it had, we should not have look'd upon the Spanish Translation of five hours with so much wonder. The Scene of it is laid in *London*; the latitude of place is almost as little as you can imagine: for it lies all within the compass of two Houses, and after the first Act, in one. The continuity of Scenes is observ'd more than in any of our Playes, excepting his own *Fox* and *Alchymist*. They are not broken above twice or thrice at most in the whole Comedy, and in the two best of *Corneille's* Playes, *The Cid* and *Cinna*, they are interrupted once apiece. The action of the Play is intirely one; the end or aim of which is the setling *Moroses's* Estate on *Dauphine*. The Intrigue of it is the greatest and most noble of any pure unmix'd Comedy in any Language: you see in it many persons of various characters and humours, and all delightful: As first, *Morose*, or an old Man, to whom all noise but his own talking is offensive. Some who would be thought Criticks, say this humour of his is forc'd: but to remove that objection, we may consider him first to be naturally of a delicate hearing, as many are to whom all sharp sounds are unpleasant; and secondly, we may attribute much of it to the peevishness of his Age, or the wayward authority of an old man in his own house, where he may make himself obeyed; and this the Poet seems to allude to in his name *Morose*. Besides this, I am assur'd from diverse persons, that *Ben. Johnson* was actually acquainted with such a man, one altogether as ridiculous as he is here represented. Others say it is not enough to find one man of such an humour; it must be common to more, and the more common the more natural. To prove this, they instance in the best of Comical Characters, *Falstaffe*: There are many men resembling him; Old, Fat, Merry, Cowardly, Drunken, Amorous, Vain, and Lying: But to convince these people, I need but tell them, that humour is the ridiculous extravagance of conversation, wherein one man differs from all others. If then it be common, or communicated to many, how differs it from other mens? or what indeed causes it to be ridiculous so much as the singularity of it? As for *Falstaffe*, he is not properly one humour, but a Miscellany of Humours or Images, drawn from so many several men; that wherein he is singular is his wit, or those things he sayes, *præter expectatum*, unexpected by the Audience; his quick evasions when you imagine him surpriz'd, which as they are extreamly diverting of themselves, so receive a great addition from his person; for the very sight of such an unwieldy old debauch'd fellow is a Comedy alone. And here having a place so proper for it I cannot but enlarge somewhat upon this subject of humour into which I am fallen. The

Ancients had little of it in their Comedies; for the τὸ γελοῖον, of the old Comedy, of which *Aristophanes* was chief, was not so much to imitate a man, as to make the people laugh at some odd conceit, which had commonly somewhat of unnatural or obscene in it. Thus when you see *Socrates* brought upon the Stage, you are not to imagine him made ridiculous by the imitation of his actions, but rather by making him perform something very unlike himself: something so childish and absurd, as by comparing it with the gravity of the true *Socrates*, makes a ridiculous object for the Spectators. In their new Comedy which succeeded, the Poets sought indeed to express the ἦθος, as in their Tragedies the πάθος of Mankind. But this ἦθος contain'd onely the general Characters of men and manners; as old men, Lovers, Servingmen, Courtizans, Parasites, and such other persons as we see in their Comedies; all which they made alike: that is, one old man or Father; one Lover, one Courtizan so like another, as if the first of them had begot the rest of every sort: *Ex homine hunc natum dicas*. The same custome they observ'd likewise in their Tragedies. As for the *French*, though they have the word *humeur* among them, yet they have small use of it in their Comedies, or Farces; they being but ill imitations of the *ridiculum*, or that which stirr'd up laughter in the old Comedy. But among the *English* 'tis otherwise: where by humour is meant some extravagant habit, passion, or affection; particular (as I said before) to some one person: by the oddness of which, he is immediately distinguish'd from the rest of men; which being lively and naturally represented, most frequently begets that malicious pleasure in the Audience which is testified by laughter: as all things which are deviations from common customes are ever the aptest to produce it: though by the way this laughter is onely accidental, as the person represented is Fantastick or Bizarre, but pleasure is essential to it, as the imitation of what is natural. The description of these humours, drawn from the knowledge and observation of particular persons, was the peculiar genius and talent of *Ben. Johnson*; To whose Play I now return.

Besides *Morose*, there are at least 9 or 10 different Characters and humours in *The Silent Woman*, all which persons have several concernments of their own, yet are all us'd by the Poet, to the conducting of the main design to perfection. I shall not waste time in commending the writing of this Play, but I will give you my opinion, that there is more wit and acuteness of Fancy in it then in any of *Ben. Johnson's*. Besides, that he has here describ'd the conversation of Gentlemen in the persons of *True-Wit*, and his Friends, with more gayety, ayre and freedom, then in the rest of his Comedies. For the contrivance of the Plot 'tis extream elaborate, and yet withal easie; for the λύσις, or untying of it, 'tis so admirable, that when it is done, no one of the Audience would think the Poet could have miss'd it; and yet it was conceald so much before the last Scene, that any other way would sooner have enter'd into your thoughts. But I dare not take upon me to commend the Fabrick of it, because it is altogether so full of Art, that I must unravel every Scene in it to commend it as I ought. And this excellent contrivance is still the more to be admir'd, because 'tis Comedy where the persons are onely of common rank, and their business private, not elevated by passions or high concernments as in serious Playes. Here every one is a proper Judge of all he sees; nothing is represented but that with which he daily converses: so that by consequence all faults lie open to discovery, and few are pardonable. 'Tis this which *Horace* has judiciously observ'd:

Creditur, ex medio quia res arcessit, habere
Sudoris minimum; sed habet Comedia tanto
Plus oneris, quanto veniæ minus.———

But our Poet, who was not ignorant of these difficulties, had prevail'd himself of all advantages; as he who designes a large leap takes his rise from the highest ground. One of these advantages is that which *Corneille* has laid down as the greatest which can arrive to any Poem, and which he himself could never compass above thrice in all his Playes, *viz.* the making choice of some signal and long expected day, whereon the action of the Play is to depend. This day was that design'd by *Dauphine* for the setling of his Uncles Estate upon him; which to compass he contrives to marry him: that the marriage had been plotted by him long beforehand is made evident by what he tells *True-wit* in the second Act, that in one moment he had destroy'd what he had been raising many months.

There is another artifice of the Poet, which I cannot here omit, because by the frequent practice of it in his Comedies, he has left it to us almost as a Rule, that is, when he has any Character or humour wherein he would show a *Coup de Maistre*, or his highest skill; he recommends it to your observation by a pleasant description of it before the person first appears. Thus, in *Bartholomew Fair* he gives you the Pictures of *Numps* and *Cokes*, and in this those of *Daw*, *Lafoole*, *Morose*, and the *Collegiate Ladies*; all which you hear describ'd before you see them. So that before they come upon the Stage you have a longing expectation of them, which prepares you to receive them favourably; and when they are there, even from their first appearance you are so far acquainted with them, that nothing of their humour is lost to you.

I will observe yet one thing further of this admirable Plot; the business of it rises in every Act. The second is greater then the first; the third then the second, and so forward to the fifth. There too you see, till the very last Scene, new difficulties arising to obstruct the action of the Play; and when the Audience is brought into despair that the business can naturally be effected, then, and not before, the discovery is made. But that the Poet might entertain you with more variety all this while, he reserves some new Characters to show you, which he opens not till the second and third Act. In the second, *Morose*, *Daw*, the *Barber* and *Otter*; in the third the *Collegiat Ladies*: All which he moves afterwards in by-walks, or under-Plots, as diversions to the main design, least it should grow tedious, though they are still naturally joyn'd with it, and somewhere or other subservient to it. Thus, like a skilful Chest-player, by little and little he draws out his men, and makes his pawns of use to his greater persons.

If this Comedy, and some others of his, were translated into French Prose (which would now be no wonder to them, since *Moliere* has lately given them Playes out of Verse which have not displeas'd them) I believe the controversie would soon be decided betwixt the two Nations, even making them the Judges. But we need not call our Hero's to our ayde; Be it spoken to the honour of the English, our Nation can never want in any Age such who are able to dispute the Empire of Wit with any people in the Universe. And though the fury of a Civil War, and Power, for twenty years together, abandon'd to a barbarous race of men, Enemies of all good Learning, had buried the Muses under the ruines of Monarchy; yet with the restoration of our happiness, we see reviv'd Poesie lifting up its head, & already shaking off the rubbish which lay so heavy on it. We have seen since His Majesties return, many Dramatick Poems which yield not to those of any forreign Nation, and which deserve all Lawrels but the English. I will set aside Flattery and Envy: it cannot be deny'd but we have had some little blemish either in the Plot or writing of all those Playes which have been made within these seven years: (and perhaps there is no Nation in the world so quick to discern them, or so difficult to pardon them, as ours:) yet if we can perswade our selves to use the candour of that Poet, who (though the most severe of Criticks) has left us this caution by which to moderate our censures;

————*Ubi plura nitent in carmine, non ego paucis offendar maculis.*

If in consideration of their many and great beauties, we can wink at some slight, and little imperfections; if we, I say, can be thus equal to our selves, I ask no favour from the French. And if I do not venture upon any particular judgment of our late Playes, 'tis out of the consideration which an Ancient Writer gives me; *Vivorum, ut magna admiratio, ita censura difficilis*: betwixt the extreams of admiration and malice, 'tis hard to judge uprightly of the living. Onely I think it may be permitted me to say, that as it is no less'ning to us to yield to some Playes, and those not many of our own Nation in the last Age, so can it be no addition to pronounce of our present Poets that they have far surpass'd all the Ancients, and the Modern Writers of other Countreys.

This, my Lord, was the substance of what was then spoke on that occasion; and *Lisideius*, I think was going to reply, when he was prevented thus by *Crites*: I am confident, said he, the most material things that can be said, have been already urg'd on either side; if they have not, I must beg of *Lisideius* that he will defer his answer till another time: for I confess I have a joynt quarrel to you both, because you have concluded, without any reason given for it, that Rhyme is proper for the Stage. I will not dispute how ancient it hath been among us to write this way; perhaps our Ancestors knew no better till *Shakespeare's* time. I will grant it was not altogether left by him, and that *Fletcher* and *Ben. Johnson* us'd it frequently in their Pastorals, and sometimes in other Playes. Farther, I will not argue whether we receiv'd it originally from our own Countrymen, or from the French; for that is an inquiry of as little benefit, as theirs who in the midst of the great Plague were not so sollicitous to provide against it, as to know whether we had it from the malignity of our own air, or by transportation from *Holland*. I have therefore onely to affirm, that it is not allowable in serious Playes; for Comedies I find you already concluding with me. To prove this, I might satisfie my self to tell you, how much in vain it is for you to strive against the stream of the peoples inclination; the greatest part of which are prepossess'd so much with those excellent Playes of *Shakespeare*, *Fletcher*, and *Ben. Johnson*, (which have been written out of Rhyme) that except you could bring them such as were written better in it, and those too by persons of equal reputation with them, it will be impossible for you to gain your cause with them, who will still be judges. This it is to which in fine all your reasons must submit. The unanimous consent of an Audience is so powerful, That even *Julius Cæsar* (as *Macrobius* reports of him) when he was perpetual Dictator, was not able to ballance it on the other side. But when *Laberius*, a *Roman* Knight, at his request contended in the *Mime* with another Poet, he was forc'd to cry out, *Etiam favente me victus es, Laberi.* But I will not on this occasion, take the advantage of the greater number, but onely urge such reasons against Rhyme, as I find in the

Writings of those who have argu'd for the other way. First then I am of opinion, that Rhyme is unnatural in a Play, because Dialogue there is presented as the effect of sudden thought. For a Play is the imitation of Nature; and since no man, without premeditation speaks in Rhyme, neither ought he to do it on the Stage; this hinders not but the Fancy may be there elevated to an higher pitch of thought then it is in ordinary discourse: for there is a probability that men of excellent and quick parts may speak noble things *ex tempore*: but those thoughts are never fetter'd with the numbers or sound of Verse without study, and therefore it cannot be but unnatural to present the most free way of speaking, in that which is the most constrain'd. For this Reason, says *Aristotle*, 'Tis best to write Tragedy in that kind of Verse which is the least such, or which is nearest Prose: and this amongst the Ancients was the Iambique, and with us is blank verse, or the measure of verse, kept exactly without rhyme. These numbers therefore are fittest for a Play; the others for a paper of Verses, or a Poem. Blank verse being as much below them as rhyme is improper for the *Drama*. And if it be objected that neither are blank verses made *ex tempore*, yet as nearest Nature, they are still to be preferr'd. But there are two particular exceptions which many besides my self have had to verse; by which it will appear yet more plainly, how improper it is in Playes. And the first of them is grounded upon that very reason for which some have commended Rhyme: they say the quickness of repartees in argumentative Scenes receives an ornament from verse. Now what is more unreasonable then to imagine that a man should not onely light upon the Wit, but the Rhyme too upon the sudden? This nicking of him who spoke before both in sound and measure, is so great an happiness, that you must at least suppose the persons of your Play to be born Poets, *Arcades omnes, & cantare pares, & respondere parati*: they must have arriv'd to the degree of *quicquid conabar dicere*: to make Verses almost whether they will or no: if they are any thing below this, it will look rather like the design of two then the answer of one: it will appear that your Actors hold intelligence together, that they perform their tricks like Fortune-tellers, by confederacy, The hand of Art will be too visible in it against that maxime of all Professions; *Ars est celare artem*, That it is the greatest perfection of Art to keep it self undiscover'd. Nor will it serve you to object, that however you manage it, 'tis still known to be a Play; and consequently the Dialogue of two persons understood to be the labour of one Poet. For a Play is still an imitation of Nature; we know we are to be deceiv'd, and we desire to be so; but no man ever was deceiv'd but with a probability of truth, for who will suffer a gross lie to be fasten'd on him? Thus we sufficiently understand that the Scenes which represent Cities and Countries to us, are not really such, but onely painted on boards and Canvass: But shall that excuse the ill Painture or designment of them; Nay rather ought they not to be labour'd with so much the more diligence and exactness to help the imagination? since the mind of man does naturally tend to, and seek after Truth; and therefore the nearer any thing comes to the imitation of it, the more it pleases.

Thus, you see, your Rhyme is uncapable of expressing the greatest thoughts naturally, and the lowest it cannot with any grace: for what is more unbefitting the Majesty of Verse, then to call a Servant, or bid a door be shut in Rhime? And yet this miserable necessity you are forc'd upon. But Verse, you say, circumscribes a quick and luxuriant fancy, which would extend it self too far on every subject, did not the labour which is requir'd to well turn'd and polish'd Rhyme, set bounds to it. Yet this Argument, if granted, would onely prove that we may write better in Verse, but not more naturally. Neither is it able to evince that; for he who wants judgment to confine his fancy in blank Verse, may want it as much in Rhyme; and he who has it will avoid errours in both kinds. Latine verse was as great a confinement to the imagination of those Poets, as Rhime to ours: and yet you find *Ovid* saying too much on every subject. *Nescivit* (sayes *Seneca*) *quod bene cessit relinquere*: of which he gives you one famous instance in his Discription of the Deluge.

Omnia pontus erat, deerant quoque Litora Ponto.

Now all was Sea, Nor had that Sea a shore. Thus *Ovid's* fancy was not limited by verse, and *Virgil* needed not verse to have bounded his.

In our own language we see *Ben. Johnson* confining himself to what ought to be said, even in the liberty of blank Verse; and yet *Corneille*, the most judicious of the *French* Poets, is still varying the same sence an hundred wayes, and dwelling eternally upon the same subject, though confin'd by Rhyme. Some other exceptions I have to Verse, but being these I have nam'd are for the most part already publick; I conceive it reasonable they should first be answer'd.

It concerns me less then any, said *Neander*, (seeing he had ended) to reply to this Discourse; because when I should have prov'd that Verse may be natural in Playes, yet I should alwayes be ready to confess, that those which I have written in this kind come short of that perfection which is requir'd. Yet since you are pleas'd I should undertake this Province, I will do it, though with all imaginable respect and deference both to that person from whom you have borrow'd your strongest Arguments, and to whose judgment when I have said all, I finally submit. But before I proceed to answer your objections,

I must first remember you, that I exclude all Comedy from my defence; and next that I deny not but blank verse may be also us'd, and content my self onely to assert, that in serious Playes where the subject and characters are great, and the Plot unmix'd with mirth, which might allay or divert these concernments which are produc'd, Rhyme is there as natural, and more effectual then blank Verse.

And now having laid down this as a foundation, to begin with *Crites*, I must crave leave to tell him, that some of his Arguments against rhyme reach no farther then from the faults or defects of ill rhime, to conclude against the use of it in general. May not I conclude against blank verse by the same reason? If the words of some Poets who write in it, are either ill chosen, or ill placed (which makes not onely rhime, but all kind of verse in any language unnatural;) Shall I, for their vitious affectation condemn those excellent lines of *Fletcher*, which are written in that kind? Is there any thing in rhyme more constrain'd than this line in blank verse? *I Heav'n invoke, and strong resistance make*, where you see both the clauses are plac'd unnaturally; that is, contrary to the common way of speaking, and that without the excuse of a rhyme to cause it: yet you would think me very ridiculous, if I should accuse the stubbornness of blank Verse for this, and not rather the stifness of the Poet. Therefore, *Crites*, you must either prove that words, though well chosen, and duly plac'd, yet render not Rhyme natural in it self; or, that however natural and easie the rhyme may be, yet it is not proper for a Play. If you insist upon the former part, I would ask you what other conditions are requir'd to make Rhyme natural in it self, besides an election of apt words, and a right disposing of them? For the due choice of your words expresses your sence naturally, and the due placing them adapts the rhyme to it. If you object that one verse may be made for the sake of another, though both the words and rhyme be apt; I answer it cannot possibly so fall out; for either there is a dependance of sence betwixt the first line and the second, or there is none: if there be that connection, then in the natural position of the words, the latter line must of necessity flow from the former: if there be no dependance, yet still the due ordering of words makes the last line as natural in it self as the other: so that the necessity of a rhime never forces any but bad or lazy Writers to say what they would not otherwise. 'Tis true, there is both care and Art requir'd to write in Verse; A good Poet never concludes upon the first line, till he has sought out such a rhime as may fit the sense, already prepar'd to heighten the second: many times the close of the sense falls into the middle of the next verse, or farther off, and he may often prevail himself of the same advantages in English which *Virgil* had in

Latine, he may break off in the *Hemystich*, and begin another line: indeed, the not observing these two last things, makes Playes which are writ in verse so tedious: for though, most commonly, the sence is to be confin'd to the Couplet, yet nothing that does *perpetuo tenore fluere*, run in the same channel, can please alwayes. 'Tis like the murmuring of a stream, which not varying in the fall, causes at first attention, at last drowsiness. Variety of cadences is the best rule, the greatest help to the Actors, and refreshment to the Audience.

If then Verse may be made natural in it self, how becomes it improper to a Play? You say the Stage is the representation of Nature, and no man in ordinary conversation speaks in rhime. But you foresaw when you said this, that it might be answer'd; neither does any man speak in blank verse, or in measure without rhime. Therefore you concluded, that which is nearest Nature is still to be preferr'd. But you took no notice that rhime might be made as natural as blank verse, by the well placing of the words, *&c.* all the difference between them when they are both correct, is the sound in one, which the other wants; and if so, the sweetness of it, and all the advantage resulting from it, which are handled in the Preface to *The Rival Ladies*, will yet stand good. As for that place of *Aristotle*, where he sayes Playes should be writ in that kind of Verse which is nearest Prose; it makes little for you, blank verse being properly but measur'd Prose. Now measure alone in any modern Language, does not constitute verse; those of the Ancients in Greek and Latine, consisted in quantity of words, and a determinate number of feet. But when, by the inundation of the *Goths* and *Vandals* into *Italy* new Languages were brought in, and barbarously mingled with the Latine (of which the *Italian*, *Spanish*, *French*, and ours, (made out of them and the *Teutonick*) are Dialects:) a new way of Poesie was practis'd; new, I say in those Countries, for in all probability it was that of the Conquerours in their own Nations. This new way consisted in measure or number of feet and rhyme. The sweetness of Rhyme, and observation of Accent, supplying the place of quantity in words, which could neither exactly be observ'd by those *Barbarians* who knew not the Rules of it, neither was it suitable to their tongues as it had been to the Greek and Latine. No man is tied in modern Poesie to observe any farther rule in the feet of his verse, but that they be dissylables; whether *Spondee*, *Trochee*, or *Iambique*, it matters not; onely he is obliged to rhyme: Neither do the *Spanish*, *French*, *Italian* or *Germans* acknowledge at all, or very rarely any such kind of Poesie as blank verse amongst them. Therefore at most 'tis but a Poetick Prose, *a Sermo pedestris*, and as such most fit for Comedies, where I acknowledge Rhyme to be improper. Farther, as to that quotation of

Aristotle, our Couplet Verses may be rendred as near Prose as blank verse it self, by using those advantages I lately nam'd, as breaks in a Hemistick, or running the sence into another line, thereby making Art and Order appear as loose and free as Nature: or not tying our selves to Couplets strictly, we may use the benefit of the Pindarique way, practis'd in *The Siege of Rhodes*; where the numbers vary and the rhyme is dispos'd carelessly, and far from often chymeing. Neither is that other advantage of the Ancients to be despis'd, of changing the kind of verse when they please with the change of the Scene, or some new entrance: for they confine not themselves alwayes to Iambiques, but extend their liberty to all Lyrique numbers, and sometimes, even to Hexameter. But I need not go so far to prove that Rhyme, as it succeeds to all other offices of Greek and Latine Verse, so especially to this of Playes, since the custome of all Nations at this day confirms it: All the *French*, *Italian* and *Spanish* Tragedies are generally writ in it, and sure the Universal consent of the most civiliz'd parts of the world, ought in this, as it doth in other customs, to include the rest.

But perhaps you may tell me I have propos'd such a way to make rhyme natural, and consequently proper to Playes, as is unpracticable, and that I shall scarce find six or eight lines together in any Play, where the words are so plac'd and chosen as is requir'd to make it natural. I answer, no Poet need constrain himself at all times to it. It is enough he makes it his general Rule; for I deny not but sometimes there may be a greatness in placing the words otherwise; and sometimes they may sound better, sometimes also the variety it self is excuse enough. But if, for the most part, the words be plac'd as they are in the negligence of Prose, it is sufficient to denominate the way practicable; for we esteem that to be such, which in the Tryal oftner succeeds then misses. And thus far you may find the practice made good in many Playes; where you do not, remember still, that if you cannot find six natural Rhymes together, it will be as hard for you to produce as many lines in blank Verse, even among the greatest of our Poets, against which I cannot make some reasonable exception.

And this, Sir, calls to my remembrance the beginning of your discourse, where you told us we should never find the Audience favourable to this kind of writing, till we could produce as good Playes in Rhyme, as *Ben. Johnson*, *Fletcher*, and *Shakespeare*, had writ out of it. But it is to raise envy to the living, to compare them with the dead. They are honour'd, and almost ador'd by us, as they deserve; neither do I know any so presumptuous of themselves as to contend with them. Yet give me leave to say thus much, without injury to their Ashes, that not onely we shall never equal them, but they could never equal themselves, were they to rise and write again. We acknowledge them our Fathers in wit, but they have ruin'd their Estates themselves before they came to their childrens hands. There is scarce an Humour, a Character, or any kind of Plot, which they have not blown upon: all comes sullied or wasted to us: and were they to entertain this Age, they could not make so plenteous treatments out of such decay'd Fortunes. This therefore will be a good Argument to us either not to write at all, or to attempt some other way. There is no bayes to be expected in their Walks; *Tentanda via est, qua me quoque possum tollere humo.*

This way of writing in Verse, they have onely left free to us; our age is arriv'd to a perfection in it, which they never knew; and which (if we may guess by what of theirs we have seen in Verse, as *The Faithful Shepherdess*, and *Sad Shepherd*:) 'tis probable they never could have reach'd. For the Genius of every Age is different; and though ours excel in this, I deny not but that to imitate Nature in that perfection which they did in Prose, is a greater commendation then to write in verse exactly. As for what you have added, that the people are not generally inclin'd to like this way; if it were true, it would be no wonder, that betwixt the shaking off an old habit, and the introducing of a new, there should be difficulty. Do we not see them stick to *Hopkins* and *Sternholds* Psalmes, and forsake those of *David*, I mean *Sandys* his Translation of them? If by the people you understand the multitude, the *οἱ πολλοί*. 'Tis no matter what they think; they are sometimes in the right, sometimes in the wrong; their judgment is a meer Lottery. *Est ubi plebs recte putat, est ubi peccat. Horace* sayes it of the vulgar, judging Poesie. But if you mean the mix'd audience of the populace, and the Noblesse, I dare confidently affirm that a great part of the latter sort are already favourable to verse; and that no serious Playes written since the Kings return have been more kindly receiv'd by them, then *The Siege of Rhodes*, the *Mustapha*, *The Indian Queen*, and *Indian Emperour*.

But I come now to the inference of your first Argument. You said the Dialogue of Playes is presented as the effect of sudden thought, but no man speaks suddenly, or *ex tempore* in Rhyme: And you inferr'd from thence, that Rhyme, which you acknowledge to be proper to Epique Poesie cannot equally be proper to Dramatick, unless we could suppose all men born so much more then Poets, that verses should be made in them, not by them.

It has been formerly urg'd by you, and confess'd by me, that since no man spoke any kind of verse *ex tempore*, that which was nearest Nature was to be preferr'd. I answer you therefore, by distinguishing betwixt what is nearest to the nature of Comedy, which is the imitation of common persons and ordinary speaking, and what is nearest the nature of a serious Play: this last is indeed the representation of Nature, but 'tis Nature wrought up to an higher pitch. The Plot, the Characters, the Wit, the Passions, the Descriptions, are all exalted above the level of common converse, as high as the imagination of the Poet can carry them, with proportion to verisimility. Tragedy we know is wont to image to us the minds and fortunes of noble persons, and to portray these exactly, Heroick Rhime is nearest Nature, as being the noblest kind of modern verse.

Indignatur enim privatis & prope socco
Dignis carminibus narrari cœna Thyestæ. (Sayes *Horace*.)

And in another place,

Effutire leveis indigna tragædia versus.

Blank Verse is acknowledg'd to be too low for a Poem, nay more, for a paper of verses; but if too low for an ordinary Sonnet, how much more for Tragedy, which is by *Aristotle* in the dispute betwixt the Epique Poesie and the Dramatick, for many reasons he there alledges, ranck'd above it.

But setting this defence aside, your Argument is almost as strong against the use of Rhyme in Poems as in Playes; for the Epique way is every where interlac'd with Dialogue, or discoursive Scenes; and therefore you must either grant Rhyme to be improper there, which is contrary to your assertion, or admit it into Playes by the same title which you have given it to Poems. For though Tragedy be justly preferr'd above the other, yet there is a great affinity between them as may easily be discover'd in that definition of a Play which *Lisideius* gave us. The Genus of them is the same, a just and lively Image of humane nature, in its Actions, Passions, and traverses of Fortune: so is the end, namely for the delight and benefit of Mankind. The Characters and Persons are still the same, *viz.* the greatest of both sorts, onely the manner of acquainting us with those Actions, Passions and Fortunes is different. Tragedy performs it *viva voce*, or by action, in Dialogue, wherein it excels the Epique Poem which does it chiefly by narration, and therefore is not so lively an Image of Humane Nature. However, the agreement betwixt them is such, that if Rhyme be proper for one, it must be for the other. Verse 'tis true is not the effect of sudden thought; but this hinders not that sudden thought may be represented in verse, since those thoughts are such as must be higher then Nature can raise them without premeditation, especially to a continuance of them even out of verse, and consequently you cannot imagine them to have been sudden either in the Poet, or the Actors. A Play, as I have said, to be like Nature, is to be set above it; as Statues which are plac'd on high are made greater then the life, that they may descend to the sight in their just proportion.

Perhaps I have insisted too long upon this objection; but the clearing of it will make my stay shorter on the rest. You tell us *Crites*, that rhyme appears most unnatural in repartees, or short replyes: when he who answers, (it being presum'd he knew not what the other would say) yet makes up that part of the verse which was left incompleat, and supplies both the sound and measure of it. This you say looks rather like the confederacy of two, then the answer of one.

This, I confess, is an objection which is in every ones mouth who loves not rhyme: but suppose, I beseech you, the repartee were made onely in blank verse, might not part of the same argument be turn'd against you? for the measure is as often supply'd there as it is in Rhyme. The latter half of the Hemystich as commonly made up, or a second line subjoyn'd as a reply to the former; which any one leaf in *Johnson's* Playes will sufficiently clear to you. You will often find in the Greek Tragedians, and in *Seneca*, that when a Scene grows up into the warmth of repartees (which is the close fighting of it) the latter part of the Trimeter is supply'd by him who answers; and yet it was never observ'd as a fault in them by any of the Ancient or Modern Criticks. The case is the same in our verse as it was in theirs; Rhyme to us being in lieu of quantity to them. But if no latitude is to be allow'd a Poet, you take from him not onely his license of *quidlibet audendi*, but you tie him up in a straighter compass then you would a Philosopher. This is indeed *Musas colere severiores*: You would have him follow Nature, but he must follow her on foot: you have dismounted him from his *Pegasus*. But you tell us this supplying the last half of a verse, or adjoyning a whole second to the former, looks more like the design of two then the answer of one. Suppose we acknowledge it: how comes this confederacy to be more displeasing to you then in a Dance which is well contriv'd? You see there the united design of many persons to make up one Figure: after they have seperated themselves in many petty divisions, they rejoyn one by one into a gross: the confederacy is plain amongst them; for chance could never produce any thing so beautiful, and yet there is nothing in it that shocks your sight. I acknowledg the hand of Art appears in repartee, as of necessity it must in all kind of verse. But there is also the quick and poynant brevity of it (which is an high imitation of Nature in those sudden gusts of passion) to mingle with it: and this joyn'd with the cadency and sweetness of the Rhyme, leaves nothing in the soul of the hearer to desire. 'Tis an Art which appears; but it appears onely like the shadowings of Painture, which being to cause the rounding of it, cannot be absent; but while that is consider'd they are loſt: so while we attend to the other beauties of the matter, the care and labour of the Rhyme is carry'd from us, or at leaſt drown'd in its own sweetness, as Bees are sometimes bury'd in their Honey. When a Poet has found the repartee, the laſt perfection he can add to it, is to put it into verse. However good the thought may be; however apt the words in which 'tis couch'd, yet he finds himself at a little unreſt while Rhyme is wanting: he cannot leave it till that comes naturally, and then is at ease, and sits down contented.

From Replies, which are the moſt elevated thoughts of Verse, you pass to the moſt mean ones: those which are common with the loweſt of houshold conversation. In these, you say, the Majeſty of Verse suffers. You inſtance in the calling of a servant, or commanding a door to be shut in rhyme. This, *Crites*, is a good observation of yours, but no argument: for it proves no more but that such thoughts should be wav'd, as often as may be, by the address of the Poet. But suppose they are necessary in the places where he uses them, yet there is no need to put them into rhime. He may place them in the beginning of a Verse, and break it off, as unfit, when so debas'd, for any other use: or granting the worſt, that they require more room then the Hemyſtich will allow; yet ſtill there is a choice to be made of the beſt words, and leaſt vulgar (provided they be apt) to express such thoughts. Many have blam'd Rhyme in general, for this fault, when the Poet, with a little care, might have redress'd it. But they do it with no more juſtice, then if English Poesie should be made ridiculous for the sake of the Water Poet's Rhymes. Our language is noble, full and significant; and I know not why he who is Maſter of it may not cloath ordinary things in it as decently as the Latine; if he use the same diligence in his choice of words.

Delectus verborum Origo eſt Eloquentiæ.

It was the saying of *Julius Cæsar*, one so curious in his, that none of them can be chang'd but for a worse. One would think "unlock the door" was a thing as vulgar as could be spoken; and yet *Seneca* could make it sound high and lofty in his Latine.——

Reserate clusos Regii poſtes Laris.

But I turn from this exception, both because it happens not above twice or thrice in any Play that those vulgar thoughts are us'd; and then too (were there no other Apology to be made) yet the necessity of them (which is alike in all kind of writing) may excuse them.

Besides that the great eagerness and præcipitation with which they are spoken makes us rather mind the substance then the dress; that for which they are spoken, rather then what is spoke. For they are alwayes the effect of some hasty concernment, and something of consequence depends upon them.

Thus, *Crites*, I have endeavour'd to answer your objections; it remains onely that I should vindicate an Argument for Verse, which you have gone about to overthrow. It had formerly been said, that the easiness of blank verse, renders the Poet too luxuriant; but that the labour of Rhyme bounds and circumscribes an overfruitful fancy, the sence there being commonly confin'd to the couplet, and the words so order'd that the Rhyme naturally follows them, not they the Rhyme. To this you answer'd, that it was no Argument to the question in hand, for the dispute was not which way a man may write best; but which is most proper for the subject on which he writes.

First, give me leave, Sir, to remember you that the Argument against which you rais'd this objection, was onely secondary: it was built upon this *Hypothesis*, that to write in verse was proper for serious Playes. Which supposition being granted (as it was briefly made out in that discourse, by showing how verse might be made natural) it asserted, that this way of writing was an help to the Poets judgment, by putting bounds to a wilde overflowing Fancy. I think therefore it will not be hard for me to make good what it was to prove: But you add, that were this let pass, yet he who wants judgment in the liberty of his fancy, may as well show the defect of it when he is confin'd to verse: for he who has judgment will avoid errours, and he who has it not, will commit them in all kinds of writing.

This Argument, as you have taken it from a most acute person, so I confess it carries much weight in it. But by using the word Judgment here indefinitely, you seem to have put a fallacy upon us: I grant he who has Judgment, that is, so profound, so strong, so infallible a judgment, that he needs no helps to keep it alwayes pois'd and upright, will commit no faults either in rhyme or out of it. And on the other extream, he who has a judgment so weak and craz'd that no helps can correct or amend it, shall write scurvily out of Rhyme, and worse in it. But the first of these judgments is no where to be found, and the latter is not fit to write at all. To speak therefore of judgment as it is in the best Poets; they who have the greatest proportion of it, want other helps than from it within. As for example, you would be loth to say, that he who was indued with a sound judgment had no need of History, Geography, or Moral

Philosophy, to write correctly. Judgment is indeed the Master-workman in a Play: but he requires many subordinate hands, many tools to his assistance. And Verse I affirm to be one of these: 'Tis a Rule and line by which he keeps his building compact and even, which otherwise lawless imagination would raise either irregularly or loosly. At least if the Poet commits errours with this help, he would make greater and more without it: 'tis (in short) a slow and painfull, but the surest kind of working. *Ovid* whom you accuse for luxuriancy in Verse, had perhaps been farther guilty of it had he writ in Prose. And for your instance of *Ben. Johnson*, who you say, writ exactly without the help of Rhyme; you are to remember 'tis onely an aid to a luxuriant Fancy, which his was not: As he did not want imagination, so none ever said he had much to spare. Neither was verse then refin'd so much to be an help to that Age as it is to ours. Thus then the second thoughts being usually the best, as receiving the maturest digestion from judgment, and the last and most mature product of those thoughts being artful and labour'd verse, it may well be inferr'd, that verse is a great help to a luxuriant Fancy, and this is what that Argument which you oppos'd was to evince.

Neander was pursuing this Discourse so eagerly, that *Eugenius* had call'd to him twice or thrice ere he took notice that the Barge stood still, and that they were at the foot of *Somerset* Stairs, where they had appointed it to land. The company were all sorry to separate so soon, though a great part of the evening was already spent; and stood a while looking back upon the water, which the Moon-beams play'd upon, and made it appear like floating quick-silver: at last they went up through a crowd of French people who were merrily dancing in the open air, and nothing concern'd for the noise of Guns which had allarm'd the Town that afternoon. Walking thence together to the *Piazze* they parted there; *Eugenius* and *Lysideius* to some pleasant appointment they had made, and *Crites* and *Neander* to their several Lodgings.

FINIS.

THE
WILD GALLANT
A COMEDY

THE WILD GALLANT

SOURCE

SINCE Dryden expressly says, "The Plot was not Originally my own; but so alter'd, by me (whether for the better or worse, I know not) that, whoever the Author was, he could not have challeng'd a Scene of it," it would be labour vain to attempt conclusively to trace parallel incidents that lurk in some one of the myriad tangling *comedias* of Spain. The supplying of Loveby with fairy money by a practised entremetteur, a Jeweller, who is disguised in antic habit as a Genius or familiar; the appearance of Constance *habited like Fortune* (in Gravelot's charming engraving to the Dryden of 1735 she is seen with wheel and cornucopia complete); and some other fantastic turns clearly seem the foil of the Spanish original. To me, at any rate, they smack of de Solis, Augustin Moreto, Luis Coello, Francisco de Rojas, Godinez, Alarcon, Guillen de Castro, and the many other dramatists who so finely spun web after web of reticulated intrigue.

Dryden, too, emphasizes the fact that he has entirely anglicized both the characters and conduct of his comedy, thus masking still more completely their original.

It should, perhaps, just be noted that it has been suggested the line *To be indanger'd by a* Spanish *Plot* might refer to the success of Tuke's *The Adventures of Five Hours* (*Los Empeños de Seis Horas*) produced at Lincoln's Inn Fields in January, 1662–3, and *This Play is English, and the growth your own* then points to a native source. Such a line of argument, superficially possible from one or two isolated expressions, would rudely wrest and even distort the general meaning. The poet, perhaps, has not delivered himself very clearly, but this apparently was of intent.

Lope de Vega has a play *El Galán escarmentado*, but as that great Spanish scholar, the late James Fitzmaurice Kelly, wrote to me in a private letter: "Lope's *Galán escarmentàdo* is unprinted: it is a MS. which so far has not been traced. It is mentioned in the 1603 list of plays attached by Lope to his *Peregrino*, and was probably written some time before 1602. Of the 219 plays in this list, only 103 survive either in print or in manuscript. The possibilities as regards Dryden are infinite: it would be equally dangerous to say that he could, or that he could not, have seen the play in MS. form."

The Scene at the end of Act I when Trice *is discovered playing at Tables by himself*, and the Scene at the commencement of Act IV when Trice plays at piquet, imagining Loveby to be his opponent, and discoursing for two persons, are both very much improved from a suggestion in Jonson's *Every Man out of His Humour* (1599), Act V, where Carlo Buffone, in a room at the Mitre, sets two cups of wine on the table, drinks with the one, and pledges with the other, speaking for each of the cups, and swigging alternately. Eventually the supposed companions quarrel; wine, pot, cups, and all are overturned to the floor. *Every Man out of His Humour* was one of the plays of which Killigrew held the monopoly. It had been produced at Vere Street between 1660 and May 1663. In July 1675, Jonson's comedy was revived at the Theatre Royal, when a new prologue by Duffett was spoken.

The incident when old Lord Nonsuch is actually persuaded to believe himself pregnant might be considered too farcical, were it not for the delusion of Dr. Pelling, which was much talked of at the time, and, however extravagant, the circumstance is therefore legitimately used in broad comedy. This has already been dealt with in the Introduction.

In her admirable comedy *The Luckey Chance, or An Alderman's Bargain*, produced at Drury Lane late in the winter of 1686, probably in December, Mrs. Behn has laid *The Wild Gallant* under ample contribution. It is only fair to say that she has employed her borrowings most excellently well. But 'tis a close copy, and when she actually echoes Dryden's words something more. Lady Fulbank, by the hands of Bredwel, who is disguised as a devil, sends money to her poor lover, Gayman, a lodger in Alsatia. The scene between Gayman and Gammer Grime, his landlady, is written with the utmost spirit and verve, although it owes something to Fletcher's *The Chances*. Sir Cautious Fulbank misses his gold amongst which are "some remarkable pieces" he will be able to recognize. His study lock was picked, and Bearjest, speaking of Gayman, declares: "I saw him once open a Lock with the Bone of a Breast of Mutton." So Failer falsely relates Loveby's burglarious exploits: "I gad he opens me all the Locks with the Blade-bone of a Breast of Mutton." Many other passages might be thus closely compared.

THEATRICAL HISTORY

THE original version of *The Wild Gallant* was produced on Thursday, 5 February, 1662–3, at the Theatre Royal, Vere Street (Gibbons' Tennis Court, by Clare Market), an oblong roofed theatre, being the last constructed house of the Elizabethan order, which was opened by Killigrew, November, 1660, and closed April, 1663. This is apparent from the Prologue as it was first acted, and Evelyn notes that he was present at the performance: "5 February, 1663. I saw *The Wild Gallant*, a comedy." On 23 February, the play was seen by Pepys at Court. "To Court, and there got good places, and saw 'The Wilde Gallant,' performed by the King's house, but it was ill acted, and the play so poor a thing as I never saw in my life almost, and so little answering the name, that from beginning to end I could not, nor can at this time, tell certainly which was the Wild Gallant. The King did not seem pleased at all, all the whole play, nor any body else, though Mr. Clerke whom we met here did commend it to us. My Lady Castlemaine was all worth seeing to-night and little Steward."

When Dryden had made no inconsiderable name as a poet and dramatist *The Wild Gallant* was revived with alterations and additions in 1667 at the

Theatre Royal, Bridges Street, which for convenience' sake is loosely known as the first Drury Lane. None the less this comedy, both in its original and its revised form, was received with ill favour. That it was more than once seen at Court was due to the influence of Lady Castlemaine, to whom Dryden has addressed some famous lines *upon Her incouraging his first Play*, where he pays her the pretty compliment

> But you have done what *Cato* cou'd not do,
> To chuse the Vanquish'd, and restore him too.

There is no record of any revival, and the fact that Mrs. Behn used so much of Dryden's material in her *The Luckey Chance*, acted late in 1686, would seem to show that by then *The Wild Gallant* had for some while fallen out of the theatrical repertory.

PREFACE

IT would be a great Impudence in Me to say much of a *Comedy*, which has had but indifferent success in the action. I made the Town my Judges; and the greater part condemn'd it. After which I do not think it my Concernment to defend it, with the ordinary Zeal of a Poet for his decry'd Poem. Though *Corneille* is more resolute in his *Preface* before his *Pertharite*, which was condemn'd more Universally than this: for he avows boldly, That in spight of Censure his *Play* was well, and regularly written; which is more than I dare say for mine. Yet it was receiv'd at Court; and was more than once the Divertisement of His Majesty, by His own Command. But I have more modesty than to ascribe that to my Merit, which was His particular Act of Grace. It was the first attempt I made in *Dramatique Poetry;* and, I find since, a very bold one, to begin with *Comedy;* which is the most difficult part of it. The Plot was not Originally my own: but so alter'd, by me (whether for the better or worse, I know not) that, whoever the Author was, he could not have challeng'd a Scene of it. I doubt not but you will see in it, the uncorrectness of a young Writer: which is yet but a small excuse for him, who is so little amended since. The best Apology I can make for it, and the truest, is onely this; That you have since that time receiv'd with Applause, as bad, and as uncorrect *Playes* from other Men.

PROLOGUE to the WILD GALLANT, as it was first Acted.

IS *it not strange, to hear a Poet say,*
He comes to ask you, how you like the Play?
You have not seen it yet! alas 'tis true,
But now your Love and Hatred judge, not You.
And cruel Factions (brib'd by Interest) come,
Not to weigh Merit, but to give their Doome:
Our Poet therefore, jealous of th' Event,
And (though much boldness takes) not confident,
Has sent me, whither you, fair Ladies, too
Sometimes upon as small occasions goe,
And from this Scheme, drawn for the hour and day,
Bid me inquire the fortune of his Play.

The Curtain drawn discovers two Astrologers; The Prologue is presented to them.

First Astrol. reads. *A Figure of the heavenly Bodies in their several Apartments,* Feb. *the* 5th. *half an hour after three after Noon, from whence you are to judge the success of a new Play called the* Wild Gallant.

2. Astrol. *Who must Judge of it, we, or these Gentlemen? We'l not meddle with it, so tell your Poet. Here are in this House the ablest Mathematicians in* Europe *for his purpose.*
They will resolve the question e'r they part.

1. Ast. *Yet let us judge it by the rules of Art.*
First Jupiter, *the Ascendants Lord disgrac'd,*
In the twelfth House, and near grim Saturn *plac'd,*
Denote short life unto the Play:———

2. Ast. ———————————Jove *yet,*
In his Apartment Sagittary, *set*
Under his own Roof, cannot take much wrong;

1. Ast. *Why then the Lifes not very short, nor long;*

2. Ast. *The Luck not very good, nor very ill,*

Prolo. *That is to say, 'tis as 'tis taken still.*

1. Ast. *But, Brother,* Ptolomy *the Learned says,*
'Tis the fifth house from whence we judge of Plays.
Venus *the Lady of that House I find*
Is Peregrine, *your Play is ill design'd,*
It should have been but one continued Song,
Or at the least a Dance of 3 *hours long.*

2. Ast. *But yet the greatest Mischief does remain,*
The twelfth apartment bears the Lord of Spain;
Whence I conclude it is your Authors lot,
To be indanger'd by a Spanish Plot.

Prolo. *Our Poet yet protection hopes from you,*
But bribes you not with any thing that's new.
Nature is old, which Poets imitate,
And for Wit, those that boast their own estate,
Forget Fletcher *and* Ben *before them went,*
Their Elder Brothers, and that vastly spent:
So much 'twill hardly be repair'd again,
Not, though supply'd with all the wealth of Spain;
This play is English, *and the growth your own;*
As such it yields to English *Plays alone.*
He could have wish'd it better for your sakes;
But that in Plays he finds you love mistakes:
Besides he thought it was in vain to mend
What you are bound in honour to defend,
That English *Wit (how e'r despis'd by some)*
Like English *Valour still may overcome.*

PROLOGUE
to the WILD-GALLANT Reviv'd

AS *some raw Squire, by tender Mother bred,*
Till one and Twenty keeps his Maidenhead,
(Pleas'd with some Sport which he alone does find,
And thinks a secret to all Humane kind;)
Till mightily in Love, yet halfe afraid,
He first attempts the gentle Dairymaid:
Succeeding there, and led by the renown
Of Whetstones Park, *he comes at length to Town,*
Where enter'd, by some School-fellow, or Friend,
He grows to break Glass-Windows in the end:
His valour too, which with the Watch began,
Proceeds to duell, and he kills his Man.
By such degrees, while knowledge he did want,
Our unfletch'd Author, writ a Wild Gallant.
He thought him monstrous leud (I'l lay my Life)
Because suspected with his Landlords Wife:
But since his knowledge of the Town began,
He thinks him now a very civil man:
And, much asham'd of what he was before,
Has fairly play'd him at three Wenches more.
'Tis some amends his frailties to confess;
Pray pardon him his want of wickedness:
He's towardly, and will come on apace;
His frank confession shows he has some grace.
You balk'd him when he was a young beginner,
And almost spoyl'd a very hopeful sinner:
But, if once more you slight his weak indeavour;
For ought I know, he may turn taile for ever.

THE WILD GALLANT

The SCENE *LONDON*

NAMES of the PERSONS

LORD *Nonsuch*,	An old rich humorous Lord.
Justice *Trice*,	His Neighbour.
Mr. *Loveby*,	The Wild Gallant.
Sir *Timorous*,	A bashful Knight.
Failer, *Burr*,	Hangers on of Sir *Timorous*.
Bibber,	A Taylor.
Setstone,	A Jeweller.

WOMEN.

Lady *Constance*,	Lord *Nonsuch* his Daughter.
Madam *Isabelle*,	Her Cousin.
Mrs. *Bibber*,	The Taylers Wife.

Sergeants.
Boy to *Loveby*.
Servants.
A Bawd and Whores.
Watch and Constable.

THE
WILD GALLANT

SCENE LONDON

ACT I. SCENE I.

Failer *entering to* Burr; *who is putting on his Buff-coat.*

Fail. WHAT! Not ready yet, Man?

Burr. You do not consider my Voyage from *Holland* last Night.

Fail. Pish, a meer Ferry; get up, get up; my Cousins Maids will come and Blancket thee anon: Art thou not ashamed to lie a Bed so long?

Burr. I may be more ashamed to rise; and, so you'l say, dear Heart, if you look upon my Cloaths; the best is, my Buff-Coat will cover all.

Fail. I gad, there goes more cunning than one would think, to the putting thy Cloaths together: thy Doublet and Breeches are Guelphs and Ghibellins to one another; and the stitches of thy Doublet are so far asunder, that it seems to hang together by the teeth. No Man could ever guess to what part of the Body these fragments did belong, unless he had been acquainted with u'm as long as thou hast been. If they once lose their hold, they can never get together again, except by chance the Rags hit the Tallies of one another. He that gets into thy Doublet, must not think to do't by storme; no, he must win it inch by inch, as the *Turk* did *Rhodes.*

Burr. You are very merry with my Wardrobe: but, till I am provided of a better, I am resolv'd to receive all Visits in this Truckle-bed.

Fail. Then will I first scotch the Wheeles of it, that it may not run; thou hast Cattle enough in it, to carry it down stairs, and break thy Neck: 'tis got a yard nearer the door already.

Enter Boy.

Sir, Mr. *Bibber*, your Taylor's below, and desires to speak with you.

Fail. He's an honeſt Fellow, and a fashionable, he shall set thee forth I warrant thee.

Burr. I, but Where's the Money for this, dear Heart?

Fail.——Well, but what think you of being put into a Suit of Cloaths, without Money? [*Aside.*

Burr. You speak of Miracles.

Fail. Do you not know *Will. Bibbers* humor?

Burr. Prethee, What have I to do with his humor?

Fail. Break but a Jeſt, and he'll beg to truſt thee for a Suit; nay, he will contribute to his own deſtruction; and give thee occasions to make one: he has been my Artificer these three years; and all the while I have liv'd upon his favourable apprehension: Boy, conduct him up. [*Exit* Boy.

Burr. But, What am I the better for this? I ne'r made Jeaſt in all my life.

Fail. A bare clinch will serve the turne; a Carwhichet, a Quarter-quibble, or a Punn.

Burr. Wit from a Low-Countrey-Soldier? One that has convers'd with none but dull *Dutchmen* these ten yeares! What an unreasonable Rogue art thou? why, I tell thee, 'tis as difficult to me, as to pay him ready Money.

Fail. Come, you shall be rul'd for your own good: Lie down; I'll throw the Cloaths over you to help Meditation: and, upon the firſt opportunity, ſtart you up, and surprize him with a Jeaſt.

Burr. Well, I think this impossible to be done: but, however I'll attempt. [*Lies down*, Failer *covers him.*

Fail. Husht! he's coming up.

Enter Bibber.

Bib. Morrow Mr. *Failer:* What, I warrant you think I come a Dunning now?

Fail. No, I vow to Gad, *Will*, I have a better Opinion of thy Wit, than to think, thou would'ſt come to so little purpose.

Bib. Pretty well that: No, no; my business is to drink my mornings-Draught in Sack with you.

Fail. Will not Ale serve the turne, *Will?*

Bib. I had too much of that laſt night; I was a little disguis'd, as they say.

Fail. Why disguis'd? Hadst thou put on a clean Band, or wash'd thy Face lately? those are thy Disguises, *Bibber.*

Bib. Well, in short, I was drunk; damnably drunk with Ale: great Hogen Mogen bloody Ale: I was porterly drunk; and that I hate of all things in Nature.

Burr. Rising: And of all things in Nature I love it best.

Bib. Art thou there I'faith; and why, old Boy?

Burr. Because when I am porterly drunk, I can carry my self.

Bib. Ha, ha Boy.

Fail. This Porter brings sad Newes to you *Will:* You must trust him for a Suit of Cloaths, as bad as 'tis: come, he's an honest Fellow, and loves the King.

Bib. Why? it shall be my Suit to him, that I may trust him.

Burr. I grant your Suit, Sir.

Fail. Burr, make hast and dress you: Sir *Timorous* Dines here to day, you know him.

Burr. I, I, a good honest young Fellow; but, no Conjurer; he and I are very kind.

Fail. Igad we two have a constant Revenue out of him: he would now be admitted Suitor to my Lady *Constance Nonsuch,* my Lord *Nonsuch* his Daughter; our Neighbour here in *Fleet-street.*

Burr. Is the Match in any forwardness?

Fail. He never saw her before yesterday, and will not be brought to speak to her this Moneth yet.

Burr. That's strange.

Fail. Such a bashful Knight did I never see; but we must move for him.

Bib. They say here's a great Dinner to be made to day here, at your Cousin *Trices,* on purpose for the enterview.

Burr. What, he keeps up his old humour still?

Fail. Yes certain; he admires eating and drinking well, as much as ever, and measures every Man's wit by the goodness of his Pallat.

Burr. Who Dines here besides?

Fail. Jack Loveby.

Bib. O, my Ghest.

Burr. He has ever had the repute of a brave clear-spirited Fellow.

Fail. He's one of your Dear Hearts: a Debauche.

Burr. I love him the better for't: The best Heraldry of a Gentleman is a Clap deriv'd to him, from three Generations: What fortune has he?

Fail. Good Fortune at all Games; but no Estate: he had one; but he has made a Devil on't long ago: he's a bold Fellow, I vow to Gad: a person that keeps company with his betters; and commonly has Gold in's pockets: come *Bibber;* I see thou long'st to be at thy mornings watering: I'll try what credit I have with the Butler.

Burr. Come away my noble Festus, and new Customer.

Fail. Now will he drink till his Face be no bigger than a threepence. [*Exeunt.*

Enter Loveby *and* Boy; *follow'd by* Frances, Bibbers *Wife.*

Lov. Nay, the Devil take thee, sweet Landlady, hold thy tongue: Was't not enough thou hast scolded me from my Lodging, which, as long as I rent it, is my Castle; but to follow me here to Mr. *Trices*, where I am Invited; and to discredit me before strangers, for a lowsy, Paltry summ of Money?

Franc. I tell you truely, Mr. *Loveby*, my husband and I cannot live by Love, as they say; we must have wherewithal, as they say: and pay for what we take; and so shall you, or some shall smoak for't.

Lov. Smoak! Why a piece of hung Beefe in *Holland* is not more smoakt, than thou hast Smoak'd me already. Thou know'st I am now fasting; let me have but fair play; when I have lin'd my sides with a good dinner, I'll ingage upon reputation to come home again, and thou shalt scold at me all the afternoon.

Franc. I'll take the Law on you.

Lov. The Law allowes none to scold in their own causes: What do'st thou think the Lawyers take our money for?

Franc. I hope you intend to deale by my Husband like a Gentleman, as they say?

Lov. Then I should beat him most unmercifully, and not pay him neither.

Franc. Come, you think to fubb me off with your Jeasts as you do my Husband; but it wonn't be: yonder he comes, and company with him; Husband, husband; why, *William*, I say!

Enter Bibber, Burr, *and* Failer *at the other end.*

Lov. Speak softly, and I will satisfie thee.

Franc. You shall not satisfie me, Sir, pay me for what you owe me, for Chamber-rent, and Diet, and many a good thing besides, that shall be nameless.

Lov. What a Stygian woman's this to talk thus? hold thy tongue till they be gone, or I'll Cuckold thy husband:

Franc. You Cuckold him———would you durst Cuckold him; I will not hold my Tongue, Sir.

Bib. Yonders my Guest; What say you Gentlemen? Shall I call him to go down with us?

Lov. I must make a loose from her, there's no other way: Save ye Mr. *Failer;* Is your Cousin *Trice* ſtirring yet: Answer me quickly, Sir, Is your Cousin *Trice* yet ſtirring?

Fail. I'll go and see, Sir; sure the man has a mind to beat me; but I vow to Gad I have no mind to be beaten by him: Come away *Burr: Will*, you'll follow us. [*Exeunt* Burr, Failer.

Bib. I'll be with you immediately———

Lov. Who was that with *Failer*, *Will?*

Bib. A man at Armes, that's come from *Holland.*

Lov. A man out at Armes thou mean'ſt, *Will.*

Bib. Good I'faith.

Franc. I, I; you run queſting up and down after your Gambols, and your Jeaſts *William;* and never minde the main Chance, as they say: Pray get in your Debts, and think upon your Wife and Children.

Lov. Think upon the Sack at *Cary-House*, with the *Apricot* flavour *Will:* hang a Wife; What is she, but a lawful kind of Manslayer? every little hugg in bed, is a degree of murdering thee: And for thy Children fear u'm not: thy part of u'm shall be Taylors, and they shall truſt; and those thy Cuſtomers get for thee shall be Gentlemen, and they shall be truſted by their Brethren; and so thy children shall live by one another.

Bib. Did you mark that *Frances?* there was wit now; he call'd me Cuckold to my face, and yet for my heart I cannot be angry with him: I perceive you love *Frances*, Sir; and I love her the better for your sake; speak truely, Do you not like such a pretty brown kind of woman?

Lov. I do I'faith, *Will;* your fair Women have no subſtance in u'm; they shrink i'th' wetting.

Franc. Well, you may be undone if you will Husband: I hear there are 2 or 3 Actions already out againſt him: you may be the laſt, if you think good.

Bib. 'Tis true she tells me; I love your wit well, Sir; but I muſt cut my coat according to my cloath.

Franc. Sir, we'll come by our own as we can; if you put us off from week to week thus.

Lov. Nay, but good Landlady———

Franc. Will good Landlady set on the Pot, as they say; or make the Jack goe; then I'll hear you.

Bib. Now she's too much on t'other hand: hold your prating *Frances;* or I'll put you out of your Pater Noſters with a sorrow to you.

Franc. I did but lay the Law open to him, as they say,

whereby to get our money in: but if you knew how he has us'd me Husband.

Bib. Has he us'd you *Frances;* put so much more into his Bill for Lodging.

Lov. Honeﬆ *Will*, and so he dy'd; I thank thee little *Bibber*, being sober, and when I am drunk, I will kiss thee for't.

Bib. Thank me, and pay me my money, Sir; though I could not forbear my jeeﬆ, I do not intend to lose by you; if you pay me not the sooner, I muﬆ provide you another Lodging; say I gave you warning.

Lov. Againﬆ next quarter Landlord?

Bib. Of an hour, Sir.

Lov. That's short warning, *Will.*

Bib. By this hand you shall up into the Garret where the little bed is; I'll let my beﬆ roome to a better pay-maﬆer; you know the Garret, Sir.

Franc. I, he knows it by a good Token Husband.

Lov. I sweat to think of that Garret, *Will;* thou art not so unconscionable to put me there: why 'tis a kind of little ease, to cramp thy rebellious Prentices in; I have seen an Usurers Iron Cheﬆ would hold two on't: a penny Looking-glass cannot ﬆand upright in the Window; that and the Brush fills it: The Hat-case muﬆ be dispos'd under the Bed, and the Comb-case will hang down from the Seeling to the Floore. If I chance to Dine in my Chamber, I muﬆ ﬆay till I am empty before I can get out: and if I chance to spill the Chamber-pot, it will over-flow it from top to bottom.

Bib. Well, for the description of the Garret, I'll bate you something of the Bill.

Lov. All, all, good *Will;* or to ﬆay thy fury till my Rents come up; I will describe thy little Face.

Bib. No, rather describe your own little money; I am sure that's so little, it is not visible.

Lov. You are i'th' right, I have not a cross at present, as I am a sinner; and you will not believe me, I'll turn my Pockets inside outward.———Ha! What's the meaning of this, my Pockets heavy? Has my small Officer put in Counters to abuse me?——— How now, yellow Boyes, by this good light! Sirrah, Varlet, How came I by this Gold? Ha!

Boy. What Gold do you meane, Sir? the Devil-a-piece you had this morning: in these laﬆ three weeks I have almoﬆ forgot what my Teeth were made for: laﬆ night good Mrs. *Bibber* here took pitty on me, and crumm'd me a Mess of Gruel, with the Children, and I popt and popt my Spoon three or four times to my mouth, before I could find the way to't.

Lov. 'Tis strange, how I should come by so much Money! (*aside.*) Has there been no body about my Chamber this morning Landlady?

Boy. O yes, Sir; I forgot to tell you that: this Morning a strange Fellow, as ever eyes beheld, would needs come up to you when you were asleep; but when he came down again, he said, He had not wak'd you.

Lov. Sure this Fellow, who e'r he was, was sent by Fortune to mistake me into so much Money——Well, this is not the first time my necessities have been strangely supply'd: some *Cadua* or other has a kindness for me, that's certain: (*aside.*)———Well Monsieur *Bibber*, from henceforward I'l keep my wit for more refin'd spirits; you shall be paid with dirt;—there's Money for you.

Bib. Nay, Good Sir.———

Lov. What's your summ? Tell it out: Will the Money burn your fingers? Sirrah, Boy, fetch my Suit with the Gold Lace at Sleeves from Tribulation———[*Gives him Gold.* [*Exit* Boy. Mr. *Taylor*, I shall turn the better Bill-man, and knock that little Coxcomb of yours, if you do not answer me what I owe you.

Bib. Pray, Sir, trouble not your self; 'tis nothing; Ifeck now 'tis not.

Lov. How, nothing Sir?

Franc. And 't please your worship, it was seventeen pounds and a Noble, yesterday at noon, your worship knows: And then your worship came home ill last night, and complain'd of your worships head; and I sent for 3 Dishes of *Tea* for your good worship, and that was six pence more, and please your worship's honor.

Lov. Well: there's eighteen pieces; tell u'm.

Bib. I say, *Frances*, do not take u'm.

Lov. What, Is all your pleading of necessity come to this?

Bib. Now I see he will pay he shall not pay, *Frances;* go home, and fetch him the whole bag of forty pounds, I'll lend it him, and the Lease of the House too; he shall want for nothing.

Lov. Take the Money, or I'll leave your house.

Bib. Nay, rather than displease his Worship, take it. [*She takes it.*

Lov. So so; go home quietly, and Suckle my God-son, *Francis.* [*Exit* Frances.

Bib. If you are for the Cellar, Sir, you know the way. [*Exit* Bibber.

Lov. No, my first visit shall be to my Mistriss, the Lady *Constance Nonsuch:* She's discreet, and how the Devil she comes to love me, I know not; yet I am pretty confident she loves me: well, no woman can be wiser than, you know what will give her leave to be.

Enter Lady Constance, *and Madam* Isabelle.

Isa. Look, look; Is not that your Servant *Loveby*?

Lov. 'Tis she; there's no being seen, till I am better habited——
[*Exit* Loveby.

Const. Let him go, and take no notice of him: Poor Rogue! He little thinks I know his poverty.

Isa. And less, that you supply it by an unknown hand.

Const. I, and falsified my Fathers Keyes to do it.

Isa. How can you answer this to your discretion?

Const. Who could see him want she loves?

Enter Setstone.

Isa. Oh here's Mr. *Setstone* come, your Jeweller, Madam.

Const. Wellcome *Setstone;* Hast thou perform'd thy visit
Happily, and without discovery?

Set. As you would wish it, Madam: I went up to his
Chamber without interruption; and there found him
Drowning his cares, and pacifying his hunger with sleep;
Which advantage I took, and undiscovered by him left
The Gold divided in his Pockets.

Const. Well, this Money will furnish him I hope, that we may have his company again.

Set. Two hundred and fifty good pounds, Madam! Has your Father miss'd it yet?

Const. No; if he had, we should have all heard on't before now: but, pray God Monsieur *Loveby* has no other haunts to divert him now he's ransom'd: What a kind of a woman is his Landlady?

Set. Well enough to serve a Tailor; or to kiss when he comes home drunk, or wants Money; but, farr unlikely to create jealousie in your Ladyship.

Enter Servant.

Serv. Madam, Justice *Trice* desires your Ladiship's excuse, that he has not yet perform'd the Civilities of his hour to you: he is dispatching a little business, about which he is earnestly employed.

Const. He's Master of his own occasions. [*Exit* Servant.

Isa. We shall see him anon with his Face as red, as if it had been boyl'd in Pump-water: but, When comes this Mirror of Knighthood that is to be presented you for your Servant?

Const. Oh, 'tis well thought on; 'Faith thou know'st my affections are otherwise dispos'd; he's rich, and thou want'st a Fortune; atchieve him if thou canst; 'tis but trying, and thou hast as much wit as any Wench in *England*.

Isa. On condition you'l take it for a Courtesie to be ridd of an Ass, I care not if I marry him: the old foole, your Father, would be so importunate to match you with a young Foole, that partly for quietness sake I am content to take him.

Const. To take him! then you make sure on't.

Isa. As sure, as if the Sack Posset were already eaten.

Const. But, What meanes wilt thou use to get him?

Isa. I'll bribe *Failer*, he's the man.

Const. Why this Knight is his inheritance; he lives upon him: Do'st thou think he'll ever admit thee to govern him? no, he fears thy wit too much: besides, he has already received an hundred pound to make the Match between Sir *Timorous* and me.

Isa. 'Tis all one for that; I warrant you he sells me Fee-simple of him.

Set. Your Father, Madam.——

Enter Nonsuch.

Isa. The Tempest is risen; I see it in his face; he puffs and blowes yonder, as if two of the Winds were fighting upwards and downwards in his belly.

Set. Will he not find your false Keyes, Madam?

Isa. I hope he will have more Humanity then to search us.

Const. You are come after us betimes, Sir.

Non. Oh Child! I am undone; I am robb'd, I am robb'd; I have utterly lost all stomach to my dinner.

Const. Robb'd! good my Lord, how, or of what?

Non. Two hundred and fifty Pounds in fair Gold out of my Study: an hundred of it I was to have paid a Courtier this afternoon for a Bribe.

Set. I protest, my Lord, I had as much a do to get that parcel of Gold for your Lordship———

Non. You must get me as much more against to morrow; for then my Friend at Court is to pay his Mercer.

Isa. Nay, if that be all, there's no such hast: the Courtiers are not so forward to pay their Debts.

Const. Has not the *Monkey* been in the Study? he may have carried it away, and dropt it under the Garden-window: the grass is long enough to hide it.

Non. I'll go see immediately.

Enter Failer, Burr, Timorous.

Fail. This is the Gentleman, my Lord.

Non. He's wellcome———

Fail. And this the particular of his Estate.

Non. That's wellcome too.

Fail. But, besides the Land here mentioned, he has wealth in specie.

Non. A very fine young Gentleman.

Tim. Now, my Lord, I hope there's no great need of Wooing: I suppose my Estate will speak for me; yet, if you please to put in a word.

Non. That will I instantly.

Tim. I hope I shall have your good word too Madam, to your Cousin for me? [*To* Isabelle.

Isa. Any thing within my power, Sir *Timorous.*

Non. Daughter, here's a person of Quality, and one that loves and honours you exceedingly———

Tim. Nay, good my Lord! you discover all at first dash.

Non. Let me alone, Sir; Have not I the dominion over my own Daughter? *Constance*, here's a Knight in love with you, Childe.

Const. In love with me, my Lord, it is not possible.

Non. Here he stands that will make it good, Childe.

Tim. Who I, my Lord? I hope her Ladyship has a better opinion of me than so.

Non. What, Arc not you in love with my Daughter? I'll be Sworn you told me so but ev'n now: I'll eat Words for no man.

Tim. If your Ladyship will believe all reports that are raised on Men of Quality——

Non. He told it me with his own mouth, Child: I'll eat words for no man; that's more than ever I told him yet.

Fail. You told him so but just now; fye, Sir *Timorous.*

Non. He shall have no Daughter of mine and he were a thousand Knights; he told me, he hop'd I would speak for him: I'll eat no man's words; that's more than ever I told him yet.

Isa. You need not keep such a pudder about eating his words; you see he has eaten u'm already for you.

Non. I'll make him stand to his words, and he shall not marry my Daughter neither: by this good day, I will. [*Exit* Nonsuch.

Const. 'Tis an ill day to him; he has lost 250 *l.* in't. [*To* Isab.

Burr. He swears at the rate of two thousand pounds a year, if the *Rump* Act were still in being.

Fail. He's in passion man; and besides, he has been a great

Fanatick formerly, and now has got a habit of Swearing, that he may be thought a Cavalier.

Burr. What noise is that? I think I hear your Cousin *Trice*'s Voice.

Fail. I'll go see——— [*Exit* Fail.

Isa. Come, Sir *Timorous*, be not discourag'd: 'tis but an old man's frowardness; he's alwayes thus against raine.

Enter Failer.

Fail. O Madam follow me quickly; and if you do not see sport, Melancholy be upon my head—— *Exeunt omnes.*

The Scene changes, and Trice *is discovered playing at Tables by himself, with Spectacles on, a Bottle, and Parmezan by him; they return and see him, undiscovered by him.*

Trice. Cinque and Cater: My Cinque I play here Sir, my Cater here, Sir: Now for you, Sir: but first I'll drink to you Sir; upon my faith I'll do you reason, Sir: mine was thus full Sir: pray mind your play, Sir:——Size Ace I have thrown: I'll play em at length, Sir:——will you Sir? then you have made a blot, Sir; I'll try if I can enter: I have hit you, Sir.

———I think you can cog a Dye, Sir.

———I cog a Dye, Sir? I play as fair as you, or any man.

———You lye, Sir: how! lye, Sir; I'll teach you what 'tis to give a Gentleman the lye, Sir——— *throws down the Tables.*

They all laugh and discover themselves.

Isa. Is this your serious business?

Trice. O you rogue are you there? you are welcome huswife, and so are you *Constance, fa tol de re tol de re la.* *claps their backs.*

Isa. Prithee be not so rude *Trice.*

Trice. Huswife *Constance*, I'll have you into my Larder, and shew you my provision: I have Cocles, dainty fat Cocles that came in the night; if they had seen the day I would not have given a fart for u'm. I would the King had 'um.

Const. He has as good I warrant you.

Trice. Nay, that's a lye, I could sit and cry for him sometimes; he does not know what 'tis to eat a good meal in a whole year: his Cooks are Asses: I have a delicate dish of Ruffs to dinner Sirrah.

Const. To dinner!

Trice. To dinner! Why by supper they had been past their prime. I'll tell thee the story of 'um: I have a friend———

Enter Servant.

Sir, Dinner's upon the Table.

Trice. Well, well; I have a friend as I told you———

Serv. Dinner ſtayes, Sir; 'tis Dinner that ſtayes: sure he will hear now.

Trice. I have a friend as I told you———

Isa. I believe he's your friend, you are so loath to part with him———

Trice. Away; away; I'll tell the ſtory between the courses. Go you to the Cook immediately, sirrah; and bring me word what we have to supper, before we go to dinner; I love to have the satisfaction of the day before me. *Exeunt omnes.*

ACT II. SCENE I.

Enter as from Dinner, Trice, Timerous, Failer, Burr, Conſtance, Isabelle.

Trice. SPeak thy conscience; was it not well dress'd, sirrah?

Tim. What think you of the Park, after our plenteous entertainment Madam?

Isa. I defie the Park, and all its works.

Con. Come, Mr. *Trice*, we'll walk in your Garden.

[*Exeunt*, *preter* Failer *and* Burr.

Fail. O, one thing I had almoſt forgot to tell you: one of us two muſt ever be near, Sir *Timerous.*

Burr. Why ?

Fail. To guard our intereſt in him from the Enemy Madam *Isabelle;* who, I doubt, has designes upon him. I do not fear her wit, but her sex; she carries a prevailing argument about her.

Enter Bibber *with a Bottle.*

Bib. By this hand, I have light upon the beſt wine in your Cousins Cellar: drink but one glass to me, to shew I am welcome, and I am gone.

Fail. Here then, honeſt *Will*, 'tis a cup of forbearance to thee.

Bib. Thank you, Sir, I'll pledge you——now here's to you again.

Fail. Come away; what is't *Will*?

Bib. 'Tis what you chriſtned it, a cup of forbearance, Sir.

Fail. Why, I drank that to thee *Will*, that thou shouldſt forbear thy money.

Bib. And I drink this to you, Sir; hence forward I'll forbear working for you.

Fail. Then say I: take a little *Bibber*, and throw him in the river, and if he will truſt never, then there let him lie ever.

Bib. Then say I: take a little *Failer*, and throw him to the Jailour; and there let him lye, till he has paid his Tailor.

Burr. You are very smart upon one another Gentlemen.

Fail. This is nothing between us; I use to tell him of his Title, *Fiery facias;* and his setting dog, that runs into Ale-Houses before him, and comes queſting out again, if any of the Woots his cuſtomers be within.

Bib. I faith 'tis true; and I use to tell him of his two Capons tails about his hat, that are laid spread eagle wise to make a feather; I would go into the snow at any time, and in a quarter of an hour I would come in with a better feather upon my head; and so farewell Sir; I have had the better on you hitherto, and for this time I am resolved to keep it. *Exit* Bibber.

Fail. The rogue's too hard for me; but the beſt on't is, I have my revenge upon his purse.

Enter Isabelle.

Isa. Came not, Sir *Timerous*, this way, Gentlemen? He left us in the Garden, and said he would look out my Lord *Nonsuch*, to make his peace with him.

Fail. Madam, I like not your enquiring after Sir *Timerous:* I suspeɛt you have some design upon him: You would fain undermine your Cousin, and marry him your self.

Isa. Suppose I should design it; what are you the worse for my good fortune? Shall I make a proposition to you: I know you two carry a great ſtroke with him: make the match between us, and propound to your selves, what advantages you can reasonably hope: you shall chouse him of horses, cloaths, and money, and I'll wink at it.

Bur. And if he will not be chous'd, we shall beat him out ont?

Isa. For that, as you can agree.

Fail. Give us handsel of the bargain; let us enjoy you, and 'tis a match.

Isa. Gramarcy ifaith boyes; I love a good offer how e'r the world goes: but you would not be so base to wrong him that way.

Fail. I vow to gad but I would Madam: in a horse or a woman I may lawfully cheat my own Father: Besides, I know the Knights complexion; he would be sure to follow other women; and all that.

Isa. Nay, if he fought with the sword, he should give me leave to fight with the Scabbard.

Bur. What say you, Madam? is't a bargain.

Isa. 'Tis but a promise; and I have learnt a Court trick for performing any thing. (*Aside.*) Well Gentlemen when I am married I'll think upon you; you'll grant there's a necessity I should Cuckold him, if it were but to prove my self a Wit.

Fail. Nay, there's no doubt you'll Cuckold him; and all that; for look you, he's a person fit for nothing else; but I fear we shall not have the graffing of the horns: We must have Livery and Seisin before hand of you, or I protest to gad we believe you not.

Isa. I have past my word, is't not sufficient? what do you think I would tell a lie to save such a paltrie thing as a nights lodging? ——Hark you, Sir : [*To* Burr.

Fail. Now will she attempt *Burr;* igad she has found him out for the weaker vessel.

Isa. I have no kindness for that *Failer*, we'll strike him out, and manage Sir *Timerous* our selves.

Burr. Indeed we wonnot.

Isa. *Failer's* a Rook, and besides, he's such a debauch'd fellow.

Burr. I am ten times worse.

Isa. Leave it, and him that taught it you: you have virtuous inclinations, and I would not have you ruine your self. He that serves many Mistresses, surfeits on his diet, and grows dead to the whole sex: 'tis the folly in the world next long ears and braying.

Burr. Now I'm sure you have a mind to me; when a woman once falls to preaching, the next thing is ever use and application.

Isa. Forbear your rudeness.

Burr. Then I am sure you meant to jilt me: you decline *Failer* because he has wit; and you think me such an ass, that you may pack me off so soon as you are married; no, no, I'll not venture certainties for uncertainties.

Isa. I can hold no longer; Mr. *Failer*, what do you think this fellow was saying of you?

Fail. Of me, Madam.

Isa. That you were one of the errantest Cowards in Christendom, though you went for one of the Dear Hearts: that your name had been upon more posts than play-bills: and that he had been acquainted with you these seven years, drunk and sober, and yet could never fasten a quarrel upon you.

Burr. Do you believe this, Dear Heart?

Isa. If you deny it, I'll take his sword, and force you to confess it.

Fail. I vow to gad, this will not do, Madam: you shall not set us at variance so easily; neither shall you have, Sir *Timerous*.

Isa. No! then mark my words: I'll marry him in spight of you;

and which is worse you shall both work my ends; and I'll discard you for your pains.

Fail. You shall not touch a bit of him: I'll preserve his humbles from you igad; they shall be his Keepers Fees.

Burr. She shall cut an Atome sooner than divide us.

Exeunt Burr *and* Failer.

Enter Constance.

Con. I have give u'm the slip in the Garden, to come and overhear thee: no fat over-grown virgin of forty ever offer'd her self so dog cheap, or was more despis'd: me-thinks now this should mortifie thee exceedingly.

Isa. Not a whit the more for that: Cousin mine, our Sex is not so easily put out of conceit with our own beauties.

Con. Thou hast lost the opinion of thy honesty, and got nothing in recompence: now that's such an oversight in a Lady.

Isa. You are deceiv'd; they think me too virtuous for their purpose; but I have yet another way to try, and you shall help me.

Enter Loveby *new habited.*

Con. Mr. *Loveby,* welcome, welcome: where have you been this fortnight.

Lov. Faith, Madam, out of Town to see a little thing that's fallen to me upon the death of a Grandmother.

Con. You thank death for the windfall, Servant: But why are you not in mourning for her.

Lov. Troth Madam, it came upon me so suddenly I had not time: twas a fortune utterly unexpected by me.

Isa. Why, was your Grandmother so young you could not look for her decease?

Lov. Not for that neither; but I had many other kindred whom she might have left it to, only she heard I liv'd here in fashion, and spent my money in the eye of the world.

Con. You forge these things prettily; but I have heard you are as poor as a decimated Cavalier, and had not one foot of land in all the world.

Lov. Rivals tales, Rivals tales, Madam.

Con. Where lies your land, Sir?

Lov. I'll tell you, Madam, it has upon it a very fair Manor house; from one side you have in prospect an hanging Garden.

Isa. Who was hang'd there? not your Grandmother I hope?

Lov. In the midst of it you have a Fountain: you have seen that at *Hampton-Court;* it will serve to give you a slight image of it.

Beyond the Garden you look to a River through a Perspective of fruit-trees; and beyond the River you see a Mead so flowry: well I shall never be at quiet, till we two make hay there.

Const. But where lies this Paradice?

Lov. Pox on't; I am thinking to sell it, it has such a villanous unpleasant name; it would have sounded so harsh in a Ladies ear. But for the Fountain, Madam—

Con. The Fountain's a poor excuse, it will not hold water; come the name, the name.

Lov. Faith it is come so lately into my hands, that I have forgot the name on't.

Isa. That's much, now, you should forget the name, and yet could make such an exact description of the place.

Lov. If you will needs know, the name's *Bawdy;* sure this will give a stop to their curiosity. [*Aside.*

Isa. At least you'll tell us in what County it lies, that my Cousin may send to enquire about it; come, this shall not serve your turn, tell us any Town that's near it.

Lov. 'Twill be somewhat too far to send; it lies in the very North of *Scotland.*

Isa. In good time, a Paradice in the *Highlands;* is't not so, Sir?

Con. It seems you went Post, Servant: in troth you are a rank rider, to go to the North of *Scotland*, stay and take possession, and return again, in ten days time.

Isa. I never knew your Grandmother was a *Scotch* woman: is she not a *Tartar* too: pray whistle for her, and lets see her dance: Come————whist Grannee!

Con. Fie fie Servant; what no invention in you? all this while a studying for a name of your Manor? come, come, where lyes it? tell me.

Lov. No faith, I am wiser than so; I'll discover my Seat to no man; so I shall have some damn'd Lawyer keep a prying into my title to defeat me of it.

Con. How then shall I be satisfied there is such a thing in Nature?

Lov. Tell me what Jewel you would wear, and you shall have it: Enquire into my money, there's the triall.

Con. Since you are so flush, Sir, you shall give me a Locket of Diamonds of three hundred pounds.

Isa. That was too severe; you know he has but 250 *l.* to bestow. [*to her.*

Lov. Well you shall have it, Madam: but I cannot higgle: I know you'll say it did not cost above 200 pieces.

Isa. I'll be hang'd if he does not present you with a parcel of melted Flints set in gold, or *Norfolk* pebbles.

Lov. Little Gentlewoman you are so keen:——Madam, this night I have appointed business, to morrow I'll wait upon you with it. *Exit* Loveby.

Isa. By that time he has bought his Locket, and paid his Landlady, all his Money will be gone: but, Do you meane to prosecute your plot, to see him this evening?

Con. Yes, and that very privately, if my Father know it I am undone.

Enter Setstone.

Isa. I heard him say this night he had appointed business.

Set. Why that was it Madam; according to your order I put on a disguise, and found him in the *Temple*-Walkes: having drawn him aside, I told him, if he expected happiness, he must meet me in a blind Alley I nam'd to him, on the backside of Mr. *Trices* house, just at the close of evening; there he should be satisfied from whom he had his supplies of Money.

Con. And how did he receive the Summons?

Set. Like a bold Hector of *Troy*; without the least doubt or scruple: but, the jeest on't was, he would needs believe that I was the Devil.

Con. Sure he was afraid to come then?

Set. Quite contrary; he told me I need not be so shy, to acknowledge my self to him; he knew I was the Devil; but he had learnt so much civility, as not to press his Friend to a farther discovery than he was pleas'd: I should see I had to do with a Gentleman; and any Courtesie I should confer on him he would not be unthankful; for he hated ingratitude of all things.

Con. 'Twas well carried not to disabuse him: I laugh to think what sport I shall have anon, when I convince him of his lies, and let him know I was the Devil to whom he was beholding for his Money: Go *Setstone;* and in the same disguise be ready for him. [*Exit* Setstone.

Isa. How dare you trust this fellow?

Con. I must trust some body; gain has made him mine, and now fear will keep him faithful.

To them, Burr, Failer, Timorous, Trice, Nonsuch.

Fail. Pray, my Lord, take no picque at it: 'tis not given to all men to be confident: Igad you shall see Sir *Timorous* will redeem all upon the next occasion.

Non. A raw mieking Boy.

Isa. And what are you but an old Boy of five and fifty; I never knew any thing so humorsome——I warrant you, Sir *Timorous*, I'll speak for you.

Non. Would'st thou have me be friends with him! for thy sake he shall onely add five hundred a year to her Joynture, and I'll be satisfied: come you hither, Sir.

Here Trice, *and* Nonsuch, *and* Timorous, *talk privately;* Burr *with* Failer *apart;* Constance *with* Isabelle.

Con. You'l not find your account in this trick to get *Failer* beaten; 'tis too palpable and open.

Isa. I warrant you 'twill pass upon *Burr* for a time: so my revenge, and your interest will go on together.

Fail. *Burr*, there's mischief a brewing, I know it by their whispring, I Vow to Gad: Look to your self, their design's on you; for my part I am a person that am above u'm.

Tim. to *Trice.*] But then you must speak for me Mr. *Trice*; and you too my Lord.

Non. If you deny't again, I'll beat you; look to't Boy.

Trice. Come on; I'll make the bargain.

Isa. You were ever good in a Flesh Market.

Trice. Come you little Harlotry; What satisfaction can you give me for running away before the Ruffs came in?

Con. Why I left you to u'm, that ever invite your own belly to the greatest part of all your feasts.

Trice. I have brought you a Knight here Huswife, with a plentiful Fortune to furnish out a Table; and, What would you more? Would you be an *Angel* in Heaven?

Isa. Your minds ever upon your belly.

Trice. No; 'tis sometimes upon yours: but, What say'st thou to Sir *Timorous*, little *Constance?*

Const. Would you have me married to that King *Midas* Face?

Trice. *Midas* me no *Midas;* he's a Wit; he understands eating and drinking well: *Poeta coquus*, the heathen Philosopher, could tell you that.

Con. Come on, Sir; What's your will with me? [*Laughs.*

Tim. Why, Madam, I could onely wish we were a little better acquainted, that we might not Laugh at one another so.

Con. If the Fool puts forward I am undone.

Tim. Fool! Do you know me, Madam?

Con. You may see I know you, because I call you by your name.

Fail. You must endure these rebukes with patience, Sir *Timorous.*

Con. What, Are you Planet-ſtrook? Look you, my Lord, the Gentleman is Tongue-ty'd.

Non. This is paſt induring.

Fail. 'Tis nothing, my Lord; Courage, Sir *Timorous*.

Non. I say, 'tis paſt enduring; that's more than ever I told you yet: Do you come to make a Fool of my Daughter?

Isa. Why Lord———

Non. Why Lady——— [*Exit* Nonsuch.

Trice. Let's follow the old Man, and pacifie him.

Isa. Now Cousin——— [*Exeunt* Isabelle, Trice, Burr.

Con. Well, Mr. *Failer*, I did not think you of all the reſt would have endeavoured a thing so much againſt my inclination as this Marriage: if you had been acquainted with my heart, I am sure you would not.

Fail. What can the meaning of this be? you would not have me believe you love me; and yet how otherwise to underſtand you I vow to Gad I cannot comprehend.

Con. I did not say I lov'd you, but if I should take a fancy to your Person and Humour, I hope it is no Crime to tell it you: Women are ty'd to hard, unequal Laws: The passion is the same in us, and yet we are debarr'd the freedome to express it. You make Poor *Grecian* beggars of us Ladies; our desires muſt have no language; but onely be faſtned to our breaſts.

Fail. Come, come; I Gad I know the whole Sex of you: your Love's at beſt but a kind of blind-mans-buff, catching at him that's next in your way.

Con. Well, Sir, I can take nothing ill from you; when 'tis too late, you'll see how unjuſt you have been to me———I have said too much already.—— [*Is going*.

Fail. Nay, ſtay, sweet Madam: I vow to Gad my fortunes better than I could imagine.

Con. No, pray let me go, Sir; perhaps I was in jeaſt.

Fail. Really, Madam, I look upon you as a Person of such worth, and all that, that I Vow to Gad I honour you of all persons in the World; and though I am a person that am inconsiderable in the World, and all that, Madam, yet for a person of your worth and excellency, I would———

Con. What would you, Sir?

Fail. Sacrifice my Life and Fortunes, I Vow to Gad, Madam.

Enter Isabelle, Burr, *and* Timorous *at a diſtance from them*.

Isa. There's *Failer* close in Talk with my Cousin; he's solliciting your Suit, I warrant you, Sir *Timorous:* do but observe with what passion he courts for you.

Burr. I do not like that kneading of her hand though.

Isa. Come, you are such a jealous Coxcomb: I warrant you suspect there's some amour between u'm; there can be nothing in't it is so open: pray observe.

Burr. But, How come you so Officious, Madam; you, that e'n now had a design upon Sir *Timorous* for your self?

Isa. I thought you had a better opinion of my Wit, than to think I was in earnest. My Cousen may do what she pleases, but he shall never pin himself upon me assure him.

Con. to *Fail.*] Sir *Timorous* little knows how dangerous a person he has employed in making Love:—— [*aloud.*

Burr. How's this! Pray my Lady *Constance*, What's the meaning of that you say, to *Failer.*

Fail. What luck was this, that he should over-hear you! Pax on't!

Con. Mr. *Burr*, I owe you not that satisfaction; what you have heard you may interpret as you please.

Tim. The Rascal has betray'd me.

Isa. In earnest, Sir, I do not like it.

Fail. Dear Mr. *Burr* be pacify'd; you are a Person I have an honour for; and this change of Affaires shall not be the worse for you I gad, Sir.

Con. Bear up resolutely Mr. *Failer;* and maintain my Favours, as becomes my Servant.

Burr. He maintain u'm! go you *Judas!* I'll teach you what 'tis to play fast and loose with a Man of Warr. [*Kickes him.*

Tim. Lay it on *Burr.*

Isa. Spare him not, *Burr.*

Con. Fear him not, *Servant.*

Fail. Oh, oh; would no body were on my side; here I am prais'd I vow to Gad into all the Colours of the Rainbow.

Con. But, remember 'tis for me.

Burr. As you like this, proceed, Sir; but, come not near me to night, while I'm in wrath. [*Exeunt* Burr *and* Timorous.

Con. Come, Sir; How fare you after your sore trial: You bore it with a most heroick patience.

Isa. Brave man at Armes, but weak to *Balthazar!*

Fail. I hope to Gad, Madam, you'l consider the merit of my sufferings: I would not have been beaten thus, but to obey that person in the World———

Con. Heaven reward you for't: I never shall.

Fail. How Madam!

Isa. Art thou such an Ass as not to perceive thou art abus'd? this beating I contriv'd for you: you know upon what account; and have yet another or two at your service: yield up the Knight in time, 'tis your beſt course.

Fail. Then, Does not your Ladyship Love me, Madam?

Con. Yes, yes; I love to see you beaten.

Isa. Well; methinks now you have had a hard bargain on't: you have loſt your Cully, Sir *Timorous;* and your Friend *Burr*, and all to get a poor beating: but I'll see it mended againſt next time for you.

[*Exeunt* Conſtance, Isabelle *Laughing*.

Fail. I am so much amaz'd, I Vow to Gad I do not underſtand my own condition. [*Exit* Failer.

Enter Loveby, *solus, in the dark; his Sword drawn; groping out his way*———

Loveby. This is the time and place he 'pointed me; and 'tis certainly the Devil I am to meet; for no mortal creature could have that kindness for me, to supply my necessities as he has done, nor could have done it in so ſtrange a manner: he told me he was a Scholar, and had been a Parson in the Fanatick times; a shrewd suspition it was the Devil; or at leaſt a limb of him. If the Devil can send Churchmen on his Errands, Lord have mercy on the Layety! Well, let every man speak as he finds, and give the Devil his due; I think him a very honeſt and well-natur'd fellow; and if I hear any man speak ill of him, (except it be a Parson that gets his living by it) I wear a Sword at his Service: yet for all this I do not much care to see him. He does not meane to hook me in for my Soul, Does he? If he does, I shall desire to be excus'd. But, What a Rogue am I, to suspeċt a person that has dealt so like a Gentleman by me? he comes to bring me Money, and would do it handsomely, that it might not be perceiv'd: let it be as 'twill, I'll seem to truſt him, and then if he have any thing of a Gentleman in him, he will scorn to deceive me, as much as I would to cousin him, if I were the Devil, and he *Jack Loveby*.

Enter Failer *at t'other end of the Stage*.

Fail. What will become of me to night! I am juſt in the condition of an out-lying-Deere, that's beaten from his walk for offering to rutt: Enter I dare not for fear of *Burr*.

Lov. I hear a voice, but nothing do I see; speak what thou art.

Fail. There he is, watching for me: I muſt venture to run by him; and when I am in, I hope my Cousin *Trice* will defend me: the Devil would not lie abroad in such a night.

Lov. I thought it was the Devil before he nam'd himself.

[Failer *goes to run off, and falls into* Loveby's *armes*.

Lov. Honest Sathan! well encounter'd! I am sorry with all my heart it is so dark: 'Faith I should be very glad to see thee at my Lodging; prethee let's not be such strangers to one another for the time to come: and, What hast thou got under thy Cloak there little Sathan? I warrant thou hast brought me some more Money.

Fail. Help, Help; Thieves, Thieves. [Loveby *lets him go.*

Lov. This is *Failer's* voice: How the Devil was I mistaken! I must get off, e'r Company comes in. [*Exit* Loveby.

Fail. Thieves! Thieves!

Enter Trice, Burr, Timorous, *undress'd.*

All: Where! Where!

Fail. One was here just now; and it should be *Loveby* by his voice, but I have no Witness.

Trice. It cannot be he; he wants no Money.

Burr. Come, Sirrah; I'll take pitty on you to night; you shall lie in the Truckle-bed.

Trice. Pox o'this noise, it has disturb'd me from such a Dreame of Eating!

EXEUNT OMNES.

ACT III.

Constance, Isabelle.

Con. 'TWas ill luck to have the meeting broke last night, just as *Setstone* was coming towards him.

Isa. But in part of recompence you'll have the pleasure of putting him on farther streights: O, these little mischiefs are meat and drink to me.

Con. He shall tell me from whence he has his Money: I am resolv'd now to try him to the utmost.

Isa. I would devise something for him to do, which he could not possibly perform.

Con. As I live yonder he comes with the Jewel in his hand he promis'd me; prithee leave me alone with him.

Isa. Speed the Plough; if I can make no sport I'll hinder none: I'll to my Knight, Sir *Timorous;* shortly you shall hear newes from *Damætas.* [*Exit* Isabelle.

Enter Loveby.

Lov. Look you, Madam, here's the Jewel; do me the favour to accept it, and suppose a very good Complement deliver'd with it.

Con. Believe me a very fair Jewel: but, Why will you be at this needless charge? What acknowledgment do you expect? You know I will not Marry you.

Lov. How the Devil do I know that? I do not conceive my self, under correction, so inconsiderable a person.

Con. You'll alter your partial opinion, when I tell you 'tis not a flash of wit fires me; nor is it a gay out-side can seduce me to Matrimony.

Lov. I am neither Fool, nor deform'd so much as to be despicable. What do I want.

Con. A good Estate, that makes every thing handsome; nothing can look well without it.

Lov. Does this Jewel express poverty?

Con. I conjure you by your love to me, tell me one truth not minc'd by your invention: How came you by this Jewel?

Lov. 'Tis well I have a Voucher; pray ask your own Jeweller *Setstone*, if I did not buy it of him.

Con. How glad you are now, you can tell a truth so near a lie: but, Where had you the Money that purchas'd it? come,———without circumstances and preambles——

Lov. Umh,——perhaps that may be a secret.

Con. Say it be one; yet he that lov'd indeed, could not keep it from his Mistriss.

Lov. Why should you be thus importunate?

Con. Because I cannot think you love me, if you will not trust that to my knowledge, which you conceal from all the World beside.

Lov. You urge me deeply———

Con. Come, sweet Servant, you shall tell me; I am resolv'd to take no denial: Why do you sigh?

Lov. If I be blasted it must out.

Con. Either tell me, or resolve to take your leave for ever.

Lov. Then know I have my means; I know not how.

Con. This is a fine secret.

Love. Why then if you will needs know, 'tis from the Devil; I have Money from him, what, and when I please.

Con. Have you seal'd a Covenant, and given away your Soul for Money?

Lov. No such thing intended on my part.

Con. How then?

Lov. I know not yet what conditions he'll propose: I should have spoke with him last night, but that a cross chance hinder'd it.

Con. Well, my opinion is, some great Lady that is in love with you, supplies you still; and you tell me an incredible Tale of the Devil, meerly to shadow your infidelity.

Lov. Devise some meanes to try me.

Con. I take you at your word; you shall swear freely to beſtow on me, what ever you shall gain this unknown way; and for a proofe, because you tell me you can have Money, what and when you please; bring me an hundred pounds e'r night: [If I do marry him for a Wit, I'll see what he can do; he shall have none from me. [*aside*.

Lov. You overjoy me, Madam; you shall have it, and 'twere twice as much.

Con. How's this!

Lov. The Devil a cross that I have; or know where to get; but I muſt promise well to save my credit: now Devil, if thou do'ſt forsake me! [*aside*.

Con. I miſtruſt you; and therefore if you faile, I'll have your hand to show againſt you; here's inke and paper. Loveby *Writes*.

Enter Burr *and* Timorous.

Burr. What makes *Loveby* yonder? he's Writing somewhat.

Tim. I'll go see——— [*Lookes over him*.

Lov. Have you no more manners than to overlook a man when he's a Writing?———Oh, Is't you Sir *Timorous?* You may ſtand ſtill; now I think on't you cannot read Written hand.

Burr. You are very familiar with Sir *Timorous*.

Lov. So I am with his Companions, Sir.

Burr. Then there's hope you and I may be better acquainted: I am one of his Companions.

Lov. By what title, as you are an Ass Sir.

Con. No more *Loveby*———

Lov. I need not, Madam; alas this fellow is onely the Sollicitor of a quarrel, till he has brought it to an head; and will leave the fighting part to the Curteous pledger. Do not I know these fellowes? You shall as soon persuade a Maſtiff to faſten on a Lyon, as one of these to ingage with a courage above their own: they know well enough who they can beat, and who can beat them.

Enter Failer *at a diſtance*.

Fail. Yonder they are; now would I compound for a reasonable summ that I were Friends with *Burr:* If I am not, I shall lose Sir *Timorous*.

Con. O, Servant, have I spy'd you! let me run into your Armes.

Fail. I renounce my Lady *Conſtance:* I Vow to Gad I renounce her.

Tim. To your Task, *Burr*.

Enter Nonsuch *and* Isabelle.

Con. Hold, Gentlemen; no sign of quarrel!

Non. O Friends! I think I shall go mad with Griefe: I have loſt more Money.

Lov. Would I had it: that's all the harme I wish my self: your Servant, Madam; I go about the business.——— [*Exit* Loveby.

Non. What! Does he take no pity on me?

Con. Prithee moane him *Isabelle*.

Isa. Alass, alass poor Nuncle! could they find in their hearts to rob him!

Non. Five hundred pounds out of poor six thousand pounds a year! I and mine are undone for ever.

Fail. Your own House you think is clear, my Lord?

Con. I dare answer for all there, as much as for my self.

Burr. Oh that he would but think that *Loveby* had it!

Fail. If you'll be Friends with me, I'll try what I can perswade him to.

Burr. Here's my hand, I will Dear Heart.

Fail. Your own House being clear, my Lord; I am apt to suspect this *Loveby* for such a person: Did you mark how abruptly he went out?

Non. He did indeed, Mr. *Failer*: but, Why should I suspect him? his carriage is fair, and his meanes great: he could never live after this rate if it were not.

Fail. This ſtill renders him the more suspicious: he has no land to my knowledge.

Burr. Well said mischief—— [*aside*.

Con. My Father's credulous, and this Rogue has found the blind-side of him; would *Loveby* heard him!—— [*To* Isab.

Fail. He has no Meanes, and he loses at Play: So that for my part, I proteſt to Gad, I am resolv'd he picks Locks for his Living.

Burr. Nay, to my Knowledge, he picks Locks.

Tim. And to mine.

Fail. No longer ago than laſt night he met me in the dark, and offer'd to dive into my Pockets.

Non. That's a main argument for suspition.

Fail. I remember once when the Keyes of the *Exchequer* were loſt in the *Rump*-time, he was sent for upon an extremity, and I gad he opens me all the Locks with the Blade-bone of a Breaſt of Mutton.

Non. Who, this *Loveby*?

Fail. This very *Loveby*: Another time, when we had sate up very late at *Ombre* in the Country, and were hungry towards morning, he plucks me out, I Vow to Gad I tell you no lie, four ten-penny-Nailes from the Dairy-Lock with his teeth, fetches me out a Mess of Milk; and knocks me 'um in again with his Head, upon Reputation.

Isa. Thou Boy!

Non. What shall I do in this case? my comfort is, my Gold's all mark'd.

Con. Will you suspect a Gentleman of *Loveby's* worth, upon the bare report of such a Rascal as this *Failer*?

Non. Hold thy tongue, I charge thee; upon my blessing hold thy tongue, I'll have him apprehended before he sleeps; come along with me, Mr. *Failer*.

Fail. Burr. Look well to Sir *Timorous*; I'll be with you instantly.

Con. I'll watch you, by your favour. [*aside.*

[*Exeunt* Nonsuch, Failer, Constance *following them.*

Isa. A word, Sir *Timorous*.

Burr. She shall have a course at the Knight, and come [*Gets behind.*] up to him; but when she is ready to pinch he shall give such a loose from her, shall break her heart.

Isa. Burr there still, and watching us? there's certainly some Plot in this, but I'll turne it to my own advantage. [*aside.*

Tim. Did you mark *Burr*s retirement, Madam?

Isa. I; his guilt it seems makes him shun your company.

Tim. In what can he be guilty?

Isa. You must needs know it; he Courts your Mistriss.

Tim. Is he too, in Love with my Lady *Constance*?

Isa. No, no; but which is worse, he Courts me.

Tim. Why, What have I to do with you? you know I care not this for you.

Isa. Perhaps so; but he thought you did: and good reason he had for it.

Tim. What reason, Madam?

Isa. The most convincing in the World: he knew my Cousin *Constance* never lov'd you: he has heard her say, you were as invincibly ignorant as a Town-fop judging a new Play: as shame-fac'd as a great over-grown School-Boy: in fine, good for nothing but to be worm'd out of your estate, and Sacrific'd to the god of Laughter.

Tim. Was your Cousin so barbarous to say this?

Isa. In his hearing.

Tim. And would he let me proceed in my suit to her?

Isa. For that I must excuse him: he never thought you could love one of my Cousin's humour: but took your Court to her, only as a blind to your affection for me: and being possessed with that opinion, he thought himself as worthy as you to marry me.

Tim. He is not half so worthy; and so I'll tell him, in a fair way.

Burr to a *Boy* entring.] Sirrah Boy, deliver this Note to Madam *Isabelle;* but be not known I am so near.

Boy. I warrant you, Sir.

Burr. Now Fortune, all I desire of thee, is, that Sir *Timorous* may see it; if he once be brought to believe there is a kindness between her and me, it will ruine all her Projeϕts.

Isa. to the *Boy.* From whom!

Boy. From Mr. *Burr*, Madam.

Isabelle reads. These for Madam *Isabelle.*

Dear rogue,

Sir Timorous *knows nothing of our kindness, nor shall for me; seem ſtill to have designs upon him, it will hide thy affection the better to thy Servant* Burr.

Isa. Alas, poor Woodcock, doſt thou go a birding: thou haſt ee'n set a Sprindge to catch thy own neck: look you here Sir *Timorous*; here's something to confirm what I have told you.

Gives him the Letter.

Tim. D, e, a, r, e, dear, r, o, g, u, e, ro-gue. Pray Madam read it: this written hand is such a damn'd pedantique thing I could never away with it.

Isa. He would fain have robb'd you of me: Lord, Lord! to see the malice of a man.

Tim. She has perswaded me so damnably, that I begin to think she's my Miſtress indeed.

Isa. Your Miſtress? Why I hope you are not to doubt that at this time of day. I was your Miſtress from the firſt day you ever saw me.

Tim. Nay, like enough you were so; but I vow to gad now, I was wholly ignorant of my own affection.

Isa. And this Rogue pretends he has an intereſt in me meerly to defeat you: look you, look you where he ſtands in ambush, like a Jesuite behind a Quaker, to see how his design will take.

Tim. I see the Rogue: now could I find in my heart to marry you in spight to him; what think you on't in a fair way?

Isa. I have brought him about as I would wish; and now I'll make my own conditions (*Aside.*) Sir *Timorous*, I wish you well; but he I marry muſt promise me to live at *London:* I cannot abide to be in the Countrie, like a wild beaſt in the wilderness, with no Chriſtian Soul about me.

Tim. Why I'll bear you company.

Isa. I cannot endure your early hunting matches there; to have my sleep diſturb'd by break of day, with heigh *Jowler*, *Jowler*, there *Venus*, ah *Beauty*! And then a serenade of deep mouth'd curres, to answer the salutation of the Huntsman, as if hell were broke loose about me: and all this to meet a pack of gentlemen Salvages to ride all day like mad men, for the immortal fame of being first in at the Hares death: to come upon the spur after a trayl at four in the afternoon to destruction of cold meat and cheese, with your leud companie in boots; fall a drinking till Supper time, be carried to bed, top'd out of your Seller, and be good for nothing all the night after.

Tim. Well, Madam, what is it you would be at? You shall find me reasonable to all your propositions.

Isa. I have but one condition more to add; for I will be as reasonable as you, and that is a very poor request, to have all the money in my disposing.

Tim. How, all the money?

Isa. I, for I am sure I can huswife it better for your honour; not but that I shall be willing to encourage you with pocket money, or so sometimes.

Tim. This is somewhat hard.

Isa. Nay, if a woman cannot do that, I shall think you have an ill opinion of my virtue: not trust your own flesh and blood, Sir *Timorous.*

Tim. Well, is there any thing more behind?

Isa. Nothing more only the choise of my own companie, my own hours, and my own actions: these trifles granted me, in all things of moment, I am your most obedient Wife and Servant *Isabelle.*

Tim. Is't a match then?

Isa. For once I am content it shall; but 'tis to redeem you from those Rascals *Burr* and *Failer*——that way Sir *Timorous*, for fear of Spies; I'll meet you at the Garden Dore—— *Exit* Timorous.

Sola. I have led all women the way, if they dare but follow me; and now march off, if I can scape but spying, with my Drums beating, and my Colours flying. *Exit* Isabelle.

Burr. So their wooing's at an end; thanks to my wit.

Enter Failer.

Fail. Oh *Burr*! whither is it Sir *Timorous* and Madam *Isabelle* are gone together?

Burr. Adore my wit, boy; they are parted never to meet again.

Fail. I saw 'um meet just now at the Garden dore: so ho, ho, ho, who's within there: help here, quickly, quickly.

Enter Nonsuch *and two Servants.*

Non. What's the matter?

Fail. Your Niece *Isabelle* has stollen away Sir *Timerous.*

Non. Which way took they?

Fail. Follow me, I'll shew you.
Non. Break your necks after him, you idle Varlets. *Exeunt Omnes.*

Enter Loveby: Loveby's *Collar unbutton'd, Band carelesly on, Hat on the table, as new rising from sleep.*

Lov. Boy! How long have I slept Boy?

Enter Boy.

Boy. Two hours and a half, Sir.
Lov. What's't a clock Sirrah?
Boy. Near four Sir.
Lov. Why there's it: I have promis'd my Lady *Constance* an hundred pounds e'r night; I had four hours to perform it in when I engag'd to do it: and I have slept out more than two of them: all my hope to get this money lies within the compass of that hat there ———before I lay down I made bold a little to prick my finger, and write a note in the blood of it, to this same friend of mine in to'ther world, that uses to supply me: the Devil has now had above two hours to perform it in; all which time I have slept to give him the better opportunity: time enough for a Gentleman of his agility to fetch it from the *East-Indies*, out of one of his Temples where they worship him; or if he were lazy, and not minded to go so far; 'twere but stepping over sea, and borrowing so much money, out of his own Banck at *Amsterdam*! hang't, what's an hundred pounds between him and me———Now does my heart go pit a pat, for fear I should not find the money there: I would fain lift it up to see, and yet I am so fraid of missing: yet a plague, why should I fear he'll fail me; the name of friend's a sacred thing; sure he'll consider that: ———methinks this Hat looks as if it should have something under it: if one could see the yellow boyes peeping underneath the brims now: ha! (*looks under round about*) in my conscience I think I do: stand out oth'way, sirrah, and be ready to gather up the pieces that will flush out of the hat as I take it up.
Boy. What is my Master mad trow.

Loveby *Snatches up the hat, looks in it hastily, and sees nothing but the Paper.*

Lov. Now the Devil take the Devil: ah plague! was ever man serv'd so as I am: (*throws his hat upon the ground.*) to break the bonds of Amity for 100 pieces: well, it shall be more out of thy way than thou imagin'st, Devil: I'll turn Parson, and be at open defiance with thee; I'll lay the wickedness of all people upon thee though thou art never so innocent; I'll convert thy Bawds and Whores; I'll

Hector thy Gamesters, that they shall not dare to swear, curse or bubble; nay, I'll set thee out so, that thy very Usurers and Aldermen shall fear to have to do with thee.

[*a noise within of* Isabelle *and* Frances.

Enter Frances, *thrusting back* Isabelle *and* Timorous.

Fran. How now what's the matter?

Isa. Nay, sweet Mistress, be not so hard-hearted: all I desire of you is but harbour for a minute: you cannot in humanity deny that small succour to a Gentlewoman.

Franc. A Gentlewoman*!* I thought so, my house affords no harbour for Gentlewomen: you are a company of proud Hallotries; I'll teach you to take place of Tradesmen's Wives with a wannion to you.

Lov. How's this, Madam *Isabelle.*

Isa. Mr. *Loveby*! how happy am I to meet with you in my distress!

Lov. What's the matter Madam?

Isa. I'll tell you, if this Gentlewoman will give me leave.

Franc. No Gentlewoman, I will not give you leave; they are such as we maintain your pride, as they say. [Isabelle, Loveby *whispers.*] Our Husbands trust you, and you must go before their Wives. I am sure my Goodman never goes to any of your Lodgings but he comes home the worse for it, as they say.

Love. Is that all! prithee good Landlady, for my sake entertain my friends.

Franc. If the Gentlemans Worship had come alone, it may be I might have entertain'd him; but for you Minion!

Enter Nonsuch, Failer, Burr, *and Officers: cry within here, here,*

Fail. My Lord, arrest Sir *Timerous* upon a promise of marriage to your Daughter, and we'll witness it.

Tim. Why, what a strange thing of you's this, Madam *Isabelle*, to bring a man into trouble thus!

Fail. You are not yet married to her;

Tim. Not that I remember.

Isa. Well *Failer*, I shall find a time to reward your diligence.

Lov. If the Knight would have own'd his action, I should have taught some of you more manners, than to come with Officers into my Lodging.

Franc. I'm glad with all my heart this Minx is prevented of her design: the Gentleman had got a great catch of her, as they say. His old Father in the Country would have given him but little thanks for't, to see him bring down a fine-bred Woman, with a Lute, and a Dressing-box, and a handful of money to her Portion.

Isa. Good Mistress Whatdeelack! I know your quarrel to the Ladies, do they take up the Gallants from the Tradesmen's wives? Lord, what a grievous thing it is for a she-Citizen to be forc'd to have Children by her own Husband!

Franc. Come, come, you're a slanderful huswife, and I squorn your hallottry trick that I do, so I do.

Isa. Steeple-hat your Husband never gets a good look when he comes home, except he brings a Gentleman to dinner; who if he casts an amorous eye towards you; then, trust him good Husband, sweet Husband trust him for my sake: verily the Gentleman's an honest man, I read it in his countenance: and if you should not be at home to receive the mony, I know he will pay the debt to me, Is't not so Mistress?

Enter Bibber *in Slippers, with a skein of Silk about his neck.*

Franc. Will you see me wrong'd thus, under my own roof, as they say, *William*?

Isa. Nay, 'tis very true Mistress: you let the men with old complements take up new cloaths: I do not mean your Wives cloaths Mr. Merchant-Tailor.

Bib. Good ifaith! a notable smart Gentlewoman!

Isa. Look to your Wife. Sir, or in time she may undo your Trade: for she'll get all your men-Customers to her self.

Bib. And I should be hang'd, I can forbear no longer.

He plucks out his Measure, and runs to Isabelle *to take measure of her.*

Isa. How now! what means Prince *Pericles* by this?

Bibber *on his knees.* I must beg your Ladiship e'n to have the honour to trust you but for your Gown, for the sake of that last jeast. Flowr'd Satten, wrought Tabby, Silver upon any grounds: I shall run mad if I may not trust your Ladiship.

Franc. I think you are mad already, as they say, *William*: You shall not trust her—— *plucks him back.*

Bib. Let me alone *Frances*; I am a Lyon when I am anger'd.

Isa. Pray do not pull your Lyon by the tail so Mistress———In these Cloaths that he now takes measure of me for, will I marry Sir *Timorous*, mark that, and tremble, *Failer.*

Fail. Never threaten me, Madam, you'r a person I despise,

Isa. I vow to gad I'll be even with you, Sir. *Exit* Isabelle.

Nonsuch to the Bailiffs.]———And when you have arrested him, be sure you search him for my gold.

Bailiffs to Loveby.] We arrest you Sir at my Lord *Nonsuch* his Suit.

Lov. Me you Rascals!

Non. Search him for my gold; you know the marks on't.

Lov. If they can find any mark'd or unmark'd gold about me; they'll find more than I can. You expect I should resist now; no, no, I'll hamper you for this——————

Bail. There's nothing to be found about him.

Fail. 'Tis no matter, to prison with him; there all his debts will come upon him.

Lov. What hurried to durance like a Stinkard!

Bib. Now as I live a pleasant Gentleman; I could find in my heart to bail him; but I'll overcome my self, and steal away. *is going.*

Bail. Come, Sir, we must provide you of another Lodging; but I believe you'l scarce like it.

Lov. If I doe not I ask no favour; pray turn me out of dores.

Bib. Turn him out of door! What a jeast was there? Now and I should be hang'd I cannot forbear Bayling him: stay Officers! I Bayle him Body and Soul for that jeast.

Fail. Let us be gone in time, *Burr.*

[*Exeunt* Burr, Failer, Timorous.

Franc. You shall not Bayle him.

Bib. I know I am a Rogue to do it; but his Wit has prevail'd upon me, and a man must not go against his Conscience. There Officers ————

Lov. to *Non.*] Old Man, if it were not for thy Daughter——

Non. Well, well; take your course, Sir. [*Exit* Nonsuch *and* Bailiffs.

Lov. Come *Will*; I'll thank thee at the Tavern. *Frances*, remember this the next time you come up to make my Bed.

Franc. Do your worst, I fear you not, Sir. This is twice to day, *William*; to trust a Gentlewoman, and Bayle a Ragamuffin: I am sure he call'd you Cuckold but yesterday, and said he would make you one.

Lov. Look you *Frances*, I am a man of Honour, and if I said it, I'll not break my word with you.

Bib. There he was with you again, *Frances*: an excellent good jeast Ifaith la.

Franc. I'll not endure it, that I won't, so I won't: I'll go to the Justices Worship and fetch a Warrant for him.

Lov. But Landlady, the word Cuckold will bear no Action in the Law, except you could prove your Husband prejudic'd by it. Have any of his Customers forsook him for't? or, any Mercer refus'd to trust him the less, for my calling him so.

Franc. Nay, I know not for the Mercers; perhaps the Citizens may take it for no slander among one another, as they say; but for the Gentlemen——

Lov. *Will*, Have they forsaken thee upon it?

Bib. No, I assure you, Sir.

Lov. No, I warrant 'um: a Cuckold has the signification of an honeſt well-meaning Citizen; one that is not given to jealousies or suspitions; a juſt Person to his Wife, *&c.* one that, to speak the worſt of him, does but to her, what he would be content should be done to her by other men.

Franc. But that another man should be the Father of his Children, as they say; I don't think that a civil thing Husband.

Lov. Not civil, Landlady! Why all things are civil that are made so by Cuſtome.

Bib. Why may not he get as fine Children as I, or any man?

Franc. But if those Children, that are none of yours, should call you Father, *William*!

Bib. If they call me Father, and are none of mine; I am the more beholding to 'um.

Franc. Nay, if that be your humour, husband, I am glad to know it, that I may please you the better another time, as they say.

[*Exit* Frances.

Bib. Nay, but *Frances*, *Frances*; 'tis such another woman.

Exit Bibber.

Lov. 'Tis such another Man:———My Coate and Sword, *Boy*, I muſt go to Juſtice *Trice*s; bring the Women, and come after me.

[*Exit* Loveby.

ACT IV.

Table set with Cards *upon it.*

Trice *walking: Enter* Servant.

Serv. SIR, some Company is without upon Juſtice-business.

Trice. Sawcy Rascal, to diſturb my Meditations.

Exit Servant.

———I, it shall be he: *Jack Loveby*, What think'ſt thou of a Game of Picquet, we two, hand to fiſt! you and I will play one single Game for ten Pieces: 'tis deep ſtake *Jack*; but, 'tis all one between us two: You shall Deale *Jack*: Who, I, Mr. Juſtice, that's a good one, you muſt give me use for your hand then; that's six i'th'hundred? Come, lift, lift; mines a ten; Mr. Justice:——mines a King, oh ho, *Jack*, you Deale. I have the advantage of this Ifaith, if I can keep it.

He Deales 12 a Piece; 2 by 2.
And looks on his own Cards.

I take seven, and look on this——Now for you *Jack Loveby*.

Enter Loveby *behind*.

Lov. How's this? Am I the Man he fights with?

Trice. I'll do you right *Jack*; as I am an honest Man you must discard this, there's no other way: if you were my own Brother I could do no better for you——Zounds, the Rogue has a Quint-Major, and three Aces younger hand—— *Looks on t'other Cards*.

Stay; What am I for the Point? but bare Forty, and he Fifty one: Fifteen and Five for the Point: 20, and 3 by Aces, 23, well, I am to play first: 1. 23. 2. 23. 3. 23. 4. 23——Pox on't, now I must play into his hand: 5——now you take it *Jack*, 5. 24. 25. 26. 27. 28. 29. 30. and the Cards Forty.

Lov. Hitherto it goes well on my side——

Trice. Now I Deale: How many do you take *Jack*? All? then I am gone: What a rise is here! 14 by Aces, and a Sixieme Major: I am gone, without looking into my Cards——I, I (*Takes up an Ace and bites it*.) thought so: If ever Man Play'd with such curs'd Fortune, I'll be hang'd, and all for want of this damn'd Ace——there's your ten Pieces, with a Pox to you, for a Rooking beggarly Rascal as you are.

Loveby *Enters*.

Lov. What occasion have I given you for these words, Sir? Rook and Rascal! I am no more Rascal than your self, Sir.

Trice. How's this; how's this!

Lov. And though for this time I put it up, because I am a winner. [*Snatches the Gold*.

Trice. What a Devil do'st thou put up? not my Gold I hope *Jack*?

Lov. By your favour but I do; and 'twas won fairly; a Sixieme, and Fourteen by Aces by your own confession——What a Pox we don't make Childrens Play I hope?

Trice. Well, remember this, *Jack;* from this hour I forswear playing with you when I am alone; What, Will you bate me nothing on't?

Lov. Not a Farthing, *Justice*: I'll be Judged by you, if I had lost you would have taken every piece on't: what I win, I win——And there's an end.

Enter Servant.

Serv. Sir, these People ſtay without, and will not be answer'd.

Trice. Well, What's their business?

Serv. Nay, no great matter: onely a Fellow for getting a Wench with Childe.

Trice. No great matter saiſt thou; 'Faith but it is: Is he a poor Fellow, or a Gentleman?

Serv. A very poor Fellow, Sir.

Trice. Hang him, Rogue, make his Mittimus immediately; muſt such as he presume to get Children?

Lov. Well consider'd: a poor lowsie Rascal, to intrench upon the Game of Gentlemen! he might have pass'd his time at Nine-pins, or Shovel-board, that had been fit sport for such as he; Juſtice, have no Mercy on him.

Trice. No, by the Sword of Juſtice will I not.

Lov. Swear'ſt thou, ungracious Boy? that's too much on t'other hand for a Gentleman. I Swear not, I Drink not, I Curse not, I Cheat not; they are unnecessary Vices: I save so much out of those Sins, and take it out in that one necessary Vice of Wenching.

Enter Loveby'*s Boy.*

Boy. Sir, the Parties are without according to your order.

Lov. 'Tis well; bring u'm in *Boy.*

Enter Lady Du Lake, *and two or three Whores.*

Juſtice, I recommend this antient Gentlewoman, with these vertuous Ladies, to thy Patronage; for her part, she is a person of exemplary life and behaviour; of singular conduct to break through, and patience to bear the assaults of Fortune: a general Benefactress of Mankind, and in fine a promoter of that great Work of Nature, Love.

Trice. Or, as the Vulgar Translation hath it, a very sufficient, and singular good-Bawd: Is't not so *Boy?*

Lov. I Boy: Now for such a petty-fogging Fellow as thy Clerk to persecute this Lady; prithee think on't: 'tis a grievance of the Free-born-Subject.

L. *Dulake.* To see the ingratitude of this Generation! I that have spent my youth, set at nought my Fortune, and what is more dear to me, my honour, in the service of Gentlemen; should now in my old Age be left to want and Beggary, as if I were the vileſt, and moſt unworthy creature upon Gods Earth. [*Crying.*

Lov. Nay, good Mother, do not take it so bitterly.

L. *Dulake.* I confess the unkindness of it troubles me.

Lov. Thou shalt not want so long as I live: look, here's five

Pieces, of Cordial Gold to comfort thy Heart with, I won it ev'n now of Mr. Justice; and I dare say he thinks it well bestow'd.

Trice. My Money's gone to very pious uses.

L. *Dulake*, (Laying her hand on *Lovebyes* head.) Son *Loveby*, I knew thy Father well; and thy Grandfather before him; Fathers they were both to me; and I could weep for joy to see how thou tak'st after them. (*Weeping again.*) I wish it lay in my power too, to gratifie this worthy Justice in my Vocation.

Trice. 'Faith I doubt I am past that noble Sin.

Lov. Prithee good Magistrate drink to her, and wipe sorrow from her eyes.

Trice. Right Reverend, my Service to you in Canary.

[*She Drinks after him*) *and stayes at halfe-Glass.*

L. *Dulake*. 'Tis a great way to the bottom; but Heaven is All-sufficient to give me strength for it:———(*Drinks it up.*) Why God's blessing on your heart, Son *Trice*. I hope 'tis no offence to call you Son: Hem, hem! Son *Loveby*, I think my Son *Trice* and I are much of the same yeares: let me see Son if Nature be utterly extinct in you: are you ticklish, Son *Trice*? [*Tickles him.*

Trice. Are you Ticklish Mother *Dulake*. [*Tickles her sides.*

She falls off her Chair; he falls off his to her; they rowle one over the other.

Lov. I would have all *London* now show me such another sight of kindness in Old Age: [*They help each other up.*
Come, a Dance, a dance; call for your Clerk, Justice, he shall make one in sign of Amity: [*Strike up Fidlers.*

They Dance a round Dance, and Sing the Tune.

Enter Isabelle *and* Constance.

Isa. Are you at that Sport, I'faith? Have among you blind Harpers. *She falls into the Dance.*

At the Dances ending, Loveby *sees* Constance.

Trice. Is she come! A Pox of all honest Women at such a time!

Lov. If she knows who these are, by this Light I am undone.

Con. Oh Servant, I come to mind you of your Promise; come, produce my hundred pounds; the times out I set you.

Love. Not till dark night upon my Reputation: I have not yet spoke with the Gentleman in the black Pantaloons; you know he seldome walkes abroad by day-light: Dear Madam, let me waite you to your Coach, and if I bring it not within this hour, discard me utterly.

Con. You must give me leave to salute the Company: What are they?

Lov. Persons of Quality of my acquaintance: but, I'll make your excuse to u'm.

Con. Nay, if they are Persons of Quality, I shall be rude to part from 'um so abruptly.

Lov. Why so! The Devil ow'd me a shame; and now he has paid me. I must present 'um what e'r come on't. (*aside.*)——This, Madam, is my Lady *Du Lake*——the Lady *Spring-well*——the Lady *Hoyden.* (*She and* Isabelle *Salute 'um.*

Isa. What a Whiff was there came from my Lady *Hoyden*! And, what a Garlick breath my Lady *Spring-well* had?

Trice. Ha, ha, ha, ha.

Lov. Do not betray me, Justice; if you do——

Isa. Oh, Are you thereabouts, Sir; then I smell a Rat Ifaith; but I'll say nothing.

Con. Ladies, I am an humble Servant to you all: and account it my happiness to have met with so good Company, at my Cousin *Trices.*

Trice. Ha, ha, ha.

L. *Dulake.* Are these two Ladies of your acquaintance Son *Loveby?*

Lov. Son quoth a! a Pox of our Relation——— [*aside.*

L. *Dulake.* I shall be glad to be better known to your Ladiships.

Con. You too much honour your Servants, Madam.

Isa. How *Loveby* fidges up and down: in what pain he is! well, if these be not they they call Whores, I'll be hanged, though I never saw one before:—— [*aside.*

Lov. Will your Ladiship please to go, Madam?

Con. I must beg the favour of these Ladies first, that I may know their Lodgings, and waite of u'm.

L. *Dulake.* It will be our Duty to pay our Respects first to your Ladiship.

Con. I beg your Ladiship's pardon, Madam——

L. *Dulake.* Your Ladiship shall excuse us, Madam———

Isa. Trice. Ha, ha, ha!

Lov. Ah devil grin you—— *aside.*

Trice. I must go out, and laugh my belly-ful. *Exit* Trice.

Con. But in earnest, Madam, I must have no denyal; I beseech your Ladiship instruct me where I may tender my devoyres?

L. *Dulake.* Since your Ladiship commands me, Madam, I dare disobey no longer. My Lodgings are in St. *Luknors* Lane at the Cat and Fiddle.

Con. Whereabouts is that Lane, Servant?

Lov. Faith, Madam, I know not that part o'th' Town—Lord, how I sweat for fear—— *Aside.*

Con. And yours, Madam, where, I beseech your Ladyship.

2*d. Wh.* In *Dog and Bitch Yard*, and't please your Ladiship.

3*d. Wh.* And mine in *Sodom*, so like your Ladiship.

Con. How *Loveby*! I did not think you would have us'd me thus?

Lov. I beseech your Ladiship but hear my Justification as I lead you.

Con. By no means, Sir; that were such a rudeness to leave persons of quality, to wait upon me: unhand me, Sir.

Isa. Ha, ha, ha——— *Exeunt* Constance, Isabelle.

Lov. I am ruin'd! for ever ruin'd: plague had you no places in the Town to name but *Sodom*, and *Luknors-lane* for Lodgings!

L. *Dulake.* If any prejudice arise from it, upon my honour Son 'twas by mistake, and not intended you: I thought she desir'd to have been admitted of the quality.

Lov. I was curst when I had first to do with you—— *kicks u'm.*

L. *Dulake.* Well, I thank Heaven, that has indued me with such patience. *Exeunt all but* Loveby *and his* Boy.

Lov. I have made a fair hand ont to day——both lost my Mistress, and hear no news from my friend below: the World frowns upon me, and the Devil and my Mistress have forsaken me: My Godfathers and Godmothers have promised well for me: instead of renouncing them, they have renounc'd me.

Boy. Sir, I saw my Lady *Constance* smile as she went out: I am confident she's angry but from the teeth outwards; you might easily make fair weather with her, if you could get the money you promis'd her, but there's the devil———

Lov. Where is he boy? shew me him quickly.

Boy. Marry God bless us! I mean Sir, there's the difficulty.

Lov. Damn'd rogue to put me in hope so——

Enter Bibber *at the other end.*

Lov. Uds so, look where *Bibber* is: now I think on't, he offer'd me a bag of forty pounds, and the Lease of his house yesterday: but that's his pocky humour, when I have money and do not ask him, he will offer it; but when I ask him he will not lend a farthing——— turn this way, sirrah, and make as though we did not see him———

Bib. Our Gentleman I think a talking with his boy there———

Lov. You understand me———

Boy. I warrant you Sir.

Lov. No news yet! what an unlucky rascal 'tis! if the rogue should hereafter be reduc'd to the raiment of his own Shreds, I should not pity him——

Bib. How's this!

Lov. Now is this rascal hunting after jeests, to make himself the greatest to all that know him.

Bib. This must be me.

Boy. I can hear neither tale nor tydings of him: I have search'd him in his haunts; among his Creditors; and in all Companies where they are like to break the least jeast. I have visited the Coffee-houses for him; but among all the news there, I heard none of him.

[Bib. *Good ifaith.*

Lov. Where's the Warrant, I'll put in my own name, since I cannot find him.

Boy. Sir, I gave it a Scrivener at next dore because I could not write, to fill up the blank place with Mr. *Bibber's* name.

Lov. What an unlucky vermin 'tis; now for an 100 *l.* could I have gratified him with a Waiters Place at Custom-house, that had been worth to him an 100 *l.* a year upon the nail.

Bib. Could you so, could you so Sir? give me your hand, and I thank you heartily Mr. *Loveby.*

Lov. Art there, honest *Will*? faith 'tis not worth thy thanks till it be done: I wish I had had the money for thee.

Bib. How much is't, Sir?

Lov. An hundred pounds would do it.

Bib. Let me see, forty I have already by me; take that in part Sir; ———and that, and the Lease of my house would over-do it.

Lov. By all means thy Lease *Will*: near scruple at that; hang a piece of Parchment, and two bits of soft wax: thou shalt do't, thou shalt boy.

Bib. Why then I will, Sir:———but stay, stay; now I think on't, *Frances* has an 120 pieces of old Grandam and Aunt gold left her, that she would never let me touch: if we could get that Mr. *Loveby* ———but she'll never part with't.

Lov. 'Tis but saying the place is for her; a Waiting-woman's place in the Custom-house: Boy, go and tell her on't immediately.

Exit Boy.

Bib. Hold a little; she has been very desirous to get a place in Court, that she might take place as the Queens Servant.

Lov. She shall have a Dressers place, if thou'lt keep counsel. The worst on't is, I have never a Warrant ready.

Bib. 'Tis all one for that Sir; she can neither write nor read; 'tis but my telling her 'tis a Warrant and all's well. I can but laugh to think how she'll be chous'd.

Lov. And you too: *Mum.* She's here *Will.*

Enter Frances.

Franc. A Waiting-woman's place in the Custom-house! there's news for me! thank you kind Mr. *Loveby*; you have been instrumental I hear of my preferment.

Lov. No, 'tis a Dressers place at Court, Landlady.

Franc. O gemini! that's better news.

Bib. I, but you must make hast and fetch an hundred pieces: I can assure you 500 are bidden for it; and the Courtiers are such slippery youths, they are ever for the fairest Chapman.

Franc. I'll fetch it presently; oh how my heart quops now, as they say: I'll fetch it presently: sweet Mr. *Loveby*, if the business can be done, it shall be a good thing in your Worship's way I promise you: O the father! that it could be done: O sweet father!

Loveby *plucks out a Paper.*

Lov. Here Mrs. *Bibber*, pray put in Madam *Bibber's* name into the Warrant.

Bib. Madam *Bibber*, there's joy. I must call you Wife no more, 'tis Madam *Bibber* now.

Franc. Pray read it Mr. *Bibber*.

Bib. An Order for the admission of the Illustrious Lady Madam *Bibber* into her Majesties Service.

Franc. Pray give me the Paper, I'll have no body touch it but my self; I am sure my money pays for it as they say. These are the finest words; Madam *Bibber*; pray Chicken shew me where Madam is written that I may kiss it all over. I shall make bold now to bear up to these flirting Gentlewomen, that sweep it up and down with their long tails. I thought my self as good as they when I was, as I was; but now I am, as I am.

Lov. Good Landlady dispatch, and bring the Money——

Franc. Truely in the place of a Dresser, I dare be bold to say, as they say; I shall give their Majesties Worships good content: I'll go fetch it—— [*Exit* Frances.

Bib. We must keep the poor Soul in ignorance as long as we can, Sir; for, when she has once smoak'd it, I have no other way but to retreat into the body of my *Janizaries* my Journey-men; and never come out into her presence more: Where will you be at nine a Clock, Sir, that we may rejoyce over our good Fortune.

Lov. Call me at my Lord *Nonsuch* his House, and I'll go with you.

Bib. We'll have the Fiddles and triumph Ifaith. [*Exit* Bib.

Lov. Lord, how eager this Vermin was to cheat himself: well, I'll after, I long to finger these Jacobus's: perhaps they may make my Peace again with my Mistriss. [*Exit* Loveby.

Enter Failer, Nonsuch.

[Constance *and* Isabelle *listning*.

Fail. I Vow to Gad my Lord, Sir *Timorous* is the most dejected person in the World, and so full of regret for what is past. 'Twas his misfortune to be drawn in by such a Person as Madam *Isabelle*.

Non. 'Tis well his Estate pleads for him; he should ne'r set foot more within my doores else.

Fail. All be security for him for time to come: leave it to me to get the Licence: all I desire is your Daughter may be ready to morrow morning.

Non. Well, let me alone with her. [*Exeunt* Failer, Nonsuch.

Isa. You heard the dreadful sound to morrow Cousin.

Con. I would not throw my self away upon this Foole, if I could help it.

Isa. Better marry a Tertian Ague than a Foole, that's certain; there's one good day and night in that.

Con. And yet thou art mad of him thy self.

Isa. Nay, the Foole is a handsome Foole, that's somewhat; but 'tis not that; 'tis a kind of fancy I have taken to a Glass Coach, and six *Flanders* Mares; rich Liveries, and a good Fortune.

Con. Prithee do not mind me of u'm; for though I want u'm not, yet I find all Women are caught with Gayeties: one grain more would turn the ballance on his side; I am so vexed at the wilde courses of this *Loveby*.

Isa. Vex'd, Why vex'd? the worst you can say of him, is, he loves Women: and such make the kindest Husbands I am told. If you had a Summ of Money to put out; you would not look so much whether the Man were an honest Man, (for the Law would make him that) as if he were a good sufficient Pay-master.

Enter Setstone.

Con. As I live thou art a mad Girle.

Set. She must be us'd as Mad-folkes are then; had into the dark and cur'd.

Con. But, all this is no comfort to the word Tomorrow.

Isa. Well, What say you, if I put you to night into the Armes of *Loveby*?

Con. My condition's desparate, and past thy Physick.

Isa. When Physicks past, what remaines but to send for the Divine? here's little *Nicodemus* your Fathers Chaplain; I have spoke with him already; for a brace of Angels he shall make all sure betwixt you without a License. I, and prove ten at night a more Canonical hour than ten i'th' Morning.

Con. I see not which way thou canst perform it; but if thou do'st I have many Admirations in store for thee. [*Whispers*.

Isa. Step in, and get a Cushion underneath your apron.

Con. O, I must be with Childe it seems!

Isa. And *Loveby* shall bring you to Bed to night, if the Devil be not in the Dice: away, make hast— [*Exit* Constance.

Setstone Be not you far off; I shall have need of you too: I hear my Uncle coming—Me thinks I long to be reveng'd of this wicked Elder for hindering of my Marriage to day: Hark you *Setstone*——

Set. 'Tis impossible, Madam: 'twill never take.

Isa. I warrant you: Do not I know him? he has not Braines enough, if they were butter'd, to feed a Black-bird—Nay, no replies —Out of what I have said, you may instruct my Cousin too——

[*Exit* Setstone.

Enter Nonsuch.

Isa. Oh, Are you there, Sir? Faith it was kindly done of you to hinder me of a good Husband this afternoon: and but for one thing, I would resolve to leave your house.

Non. I'm glad there's any thing will stay thee.

Isa. If I stay 'tis for love of my Cousin *Constance*, not of you: I should be loath to leave her in this sad condition!

Non. What condition?

Isa. Nay, I know not; she has not worn her Busk this fortnight. I think she's grown fat o'th' sudden.

Non. O Devil, Devil! What a fright am I in?

Isa. She has qualmes too every morning: ravins mightily for green-fruit; and swoones at the sight of hot meat.

Non. She's with Childe! I am undone: I am undone!

Isa. I understand nothing of such matters: She's but in the next roome; best call her, and examine her about it.

Non. Why *Constance*, *Constance*?

Enter Constance, *as with Childe*.

Isa. Now for a broad-side; turn your prow to him Cousin.

[*to her*.

Non. Now Gentlewoman! Is this possible?

Con. I do not reach your meaning, Sir.

Non. Where have you been of late?

Con. I seldome stir without you, Sir: these Walls most commonly confine me.

Non. These Walls can get no Children; nor these Hangings; though there be Men wrought in u'm.

Isa. Yet, by your favour Nuncle, children may be wrought behind the Hangings.

Non. O *Constance, Constance*! How have my gray hairs deserv'd this of thee? Who got that Belly there?

Con. You, I hope, Sir.

Non. Tell me the truth; for I will know it; come, the Story.

Con. The Story's quickly told, Sir, I'm with Child.

Non. And whose the Father?

Con. I do not know, Sir.

Non. Not know! went there so many to't?

Con. So far from that, that there went none at all, to my best knowledge, Sir.

Non. Wast got by Miracle? Who was the Father?

Con. Who got your Money, Sir, that you have lost?

Non. Nay, Heaven knows who got that.

Con. And, Heaven knowes who got this; for, on my Conscience, he that had your Money, was the Father on't.

Non. The Devil it was as soon.

Con. That's all I fear, Sir.

Isa. 'Tis strange: and yet 'twere hard, Sir, to suspect my Cousin's Vertue, since we know the House is haunted.

Non. 'Tis true, that nothing can be laid, though under lock and key, but it miscarries.

Isa. 'Tis not to be believed what these villanous Spirits can do: they go invisible.

Con. First they stole away my Prayer-Book; and a little after that a small Treatise I had against Temptation; and when they were gone, you know Sir——

Isa. If there be such doings, pray Heaven we are not all with Childe: 'tis certain that none live within these Walls, but they have power of; I have fear'd *Toby* the Coachman any time this fortnight.

Non. Out impudence! a man with Childe! why 'tis unnatural.

Isa. I, so is he that got it.

Non. Thou art not in earnest.

Isa. I would I were not; hark, I hear him groan hither: come in poor *Toby*.

Enter Toby *Coachman, with an Urinal.*

Non. How now! What have you there, Sirrah?

Tob. And't please your Worship 'tis my Water: I had a spice oth' new Disease here i'th' house, and so carried it to Master Doctor.

Non. Well; And what did he say to you?

Tob. He told me very sad newes, and please you: I am somewhat bashful to speak on't.

Isa. Out with it Man.

Tob. Why truly he told me the party that ow'd the Water was with Child.

Isa. I told you so Uncle.

Non. To my beſt remembrance I never heard of such a thing before.

Tob. I never ſtretch out my self to snap my Whip, but it goes to th' heart of me.

Isa. Alas poor *Toby.*

Non. Be gone, and put off your Livery Sirrah: you shall not ſtay a minute in my Service.

Tob. I beseech your good Worship be good to me; 'twas the firſt fault I ever committed in this kind: I have three poor Children by my Wife, and if you leave me to the wide World, with a new charge upon my self.

Non. Be gone, I will not hear a word.

Tob. If I muſt go, I'll not go alone: *Ambrose Tinis* the Cook is as bad as I am.

Non. I think you'l make me mad: Call the Rascal hither: I muſt acount with him upon another score now I think on't.

Enter Ambrose Tinis.

Non. Sirrah, what made you send a Pheasant with one wing to the Table yeſterday?

Amb. I beseech your Worship to pardon me, I long'd for't.

Isa. I fear'd as much.

Amb. And I beseech your Worship let me have a boy to help me in the Kitchin; for I find my self unable to go through with the work: besides the Doctor has warn'd me of ſtooping to the fire, for fear of a mischance.

Non. Why, are you with child sirrah?

Amb. So he tels me: but if I were put to my oath, I know not that ever I deserv'd for't:

Non. Still worse and worse: and here comes *Setſtone* groaning.

Enter Setſtone.

Set. O, Sir, I have been so troubled with swooning fits; and have so long'd for cherries.

Non. He's poopt too.

Isa. Well, this is not the worſt yet: I suspect something more than I will speak on.

Non. What doſt thou suspect; ha!

Isa. Is not your Lordship with child too?

Non. Who, I with child, Marry Heaven forbid: what doſt thou see by me to ground it on?

Isa. You'r very round of late; that's all, Sir.

Non. Round, that's only fat I hope: I have had a very good stomach of late I'm sure.

Isa. Alas, and well you may: you eat for two, Sir.

Non. *Setſtone* look upon me, and tell me true: do you observe any alteration in me?

Set. I would not dishearten your Ladiship:———your Lordship I would say: but I have observ'd of late, your colour goes and comes extremely: methinks your Lordship looks very sharp, and bleak i'th'face, and mighty puff i'th' body.

Non. O the Devil! wretched men that we are all: nothing grieves me, but that in my old age, when others are paſt child-bearing, I should come to be a disgrace to my family.

Con. How do you, Sir? your eyes look wondrous dim: is not there a miſt before u'm?

Isa. Do you not feel a kicking in your belly? when do you look Nuncle?

Non. Uh, uh! me-thinks I am very sick o'th' sudden?

Isa. What ſtore of old shirts have you againſt the good time? shall I give you a shift Nuncle?

Non. Here's like to be a fine charge towards: we shall all be brought to bed together: well, if I be with Devil I will have such Gossips: An Usurer and his Scrivener shall be Godfathers.

Isa. I'l help you Nuncle: and *Saundyes* two Grannies shall be Godmothers: the Child shall be chriſtned by the Directory, and the Gossips Gift shall be the gude Scotch Kivenant.

Conſt. Set. Non. Toby. Ambr. Uh, uh, uh!

Isa. What rare musick's here!

Non. When e'r it comes from me 'twill kill me, that's certain:

Set. Beſt take a vomit.

Isa. And't comes upward the horns will choak him.

Non. Mass and so they will.

Isa. Your only way is to make sure o'th' Man-midwife.

Non. But my Childs dishonor troubles me the moſt: if I could but see her well married, before I underwent the labour and peril of Child-bearing! what would you advise Neece!

Isa. That which I am very loath to do: send for honeſt *Jack Loveby*, and let him know the truth on't: he's a fellow without a fortune and will be glad to leap at the occasion.

Non. But why *Loveby* of all the world? 'tis but ſtaying till to morrow, and then Sir *Timerous* will marry her.

Con. Uh! I swell so faſt, I cannot hide it till to morrow.

Isa. Why there's it now!

Non. I'll send for the old Alderman *Getwell* immediately: he'll father the Devils Baſtard I warrant you.

Isa. Fie Nuncle! my Cousins somewhat too good yet for an Alderman; if it were her third child she might hearken to you.

Non. Well, since it muſt be so, *Setſtone* go you to *Loveby*, make my excuse to him for the arreſt, and let him know what fortune may attend him.

Isa. Mr. *Setſtone*, pray acquaint him with my Cousins affection to him; and prepare him to father the Cushion underneath her Peticoat. [*aside to* Set.

Set. I'll bring him immediately. *Exit* Setſtone.

Isa. When he comes Nuncle, pray cover your great belly with your hat, that he may not see it.

Non. It goes againſt my heart to marry her to this *Loveby*; but what muſt be, muſt be.

Enter Loveby.

Con. O, Mr. *Loveby!* the welcomſt man alive: you met *Setſtone* I hope, that you came so opportunely.

Lov. No faith Madam, I came of my own accord.

Isa. 'Tis unlucky he's not prepar'd.

Lov. Look you, Madam, I have brought the 100 *l.* the Devil was as punctual as three a clock at a Play-house: here,'tis right I warrant it without telling; I took it upon his word——— *gives it.*

Con. Your kindness shall be requited Servant: but I sent for you upon another business: Pray Cousin tell't him, for I am asham'd to do't.

Lov. Ha! 'tis not that great belly I hope! is't come to that?

Isa. Hark you Mr. *Loveby*———a word with you.

Lov. A word with you, Madam: whither is your Cousin bound?

Isa. Bound, Sir?

Lov. I, bound; look you she's under sail, with a luſty forewind.

Non. I sent for you, Sir, but to be plain with you 'twas more out of necessity than Love.

Lov. I wonder my Lord at your invincible ill nature: you forget the arreſt that I passed by: but this 'tis to be civil to unthankful persons; 'tis feeding an ill-natur'd dog, that snarles while he takes the victuals from your hand.

Non. All friends, all friends; no ripping up old ſtories; you shall have my Daughter.

Lov. Faith I see your Lordship would let Lodgings ready furnish'd, but I am for an empty Tenement.

Non. I had almoſt forgot my own great belly; if he should discover that too! [*claps his hat before it.*

Isa. to *Loveby.*] You will not hear me, Sir: 'tis all roguery as I live.

Lov. Flat roguery I'll swear; if I had been father ont; nay, if I had but laid my breeches upon the bed, I would have married her: but I see we are not ordaind for one another—— *is going.*

Non. I beseech you, Sir.

Lov. Pray cover, my Lord.

Isa. He does his great belly, methinks——

Non. I'll make it up in money to you.

Lov. That cannot tempt me; I have a friend that shall be nameless, that will not see me want——and so your Servant.

Exit Loveby.

Isa. I'll after and bring him back——

Non. You shall not ſtir after him; does he scorn my daughter.

Isa. Lord how fretful you are: this breeding makes you so peevish Nuncle.

Non. 'Tis no matter, she shall ſtraight be married to Sir *Timerous.*

Con. I am ruin'd Cousin.

Isa. I warrant you:——My Lord I wish her well married to Sir *Timerous*; but *Loveby* will certainly infect him with the news of her great belly.

Non. I'll dispatch it e'r he can speak with him.

Isa. When e'r he come, he'll see what a *bona roba* she is grown.

Non. Therefore it shall be done i'th' evening.

Isa. It shall my Lord.

Con. Shall it?

Isa. Let me alone Cousin——and to this effect she shall write to him, that *to conform to your will, and his modeſty, she desires him to come hither alone this Evening.*

Non. Excellent Wench! I'll get my Chaplain ready. *Exit* Non.

Con. How can you hope to deceive my father?

Isa. If I do not I have hard luck.

Con. You go so ſtrange a way about, your bowl muſt be well byassed to come in.

Isa. So plain a ground there's not the leaſt rub in't, I'll meet Sir *Timorous* in the dark, and in your room marry him.

Con. You'll be sure to provide for one.

Isa. You miſtake me Cousin: oh! here's *Setſtone* again;

Enter Setſtone.

Mr. Jeweller, you muſt again into your Devils shape, and speak with *Loveby*: but pray be carefull not to be discover'd.

Set. I warrant you, Madam; I have cousned wiser men than he in my own shape; and if I cannot continue it in a worse, let the Devil I make bold with, e'n make as bold with me.

Isa. You muſt guide him by back wayes, to my Uncles House, and so to my Cousins Chamber, that he may not know where he is when he comes there: the reſt I'll tell you as we go along.

Exeunt Omnes.

Enter Timorous; *after him* Burr *and* Failer.

Tim. Here here, read this Note; there's news for us.

Fail. Let me see't. [*reads.*

Sir Timorous.

Be at the Garden dore at nine this Evening, there I'll receive you with my daughter, to gratifie your modeſty I design'd this way, after I had better consider'd on it: and pray leave your Caterpillars, Burr *and* Failer *behind you.* Yours *Nonsuch.*

There is some trick in this, what e'r it be: but this word Caterpillars: you see *Burr*, Sir *Timorous*, is like to be lur'd from us——

to him aside.

Burr. Is there no prevention?

Fail. One way there is: Sir *Timorous* pray walk a turn while *Burr* and I conferre a little upon this matter——Look you *Burr*, there is but one remedy in Nature I vow to gad: that is for you to have a new Sir *Timorous*, exceeding this person in bounty to you. Observe then, in Sir *Timorous* his place will I go, and igad I'll marry my Lady *Conſtance*: and then from the bowels of friendship bless thee with a thousand pounds, besides Lodging and Diet for thy life, boy——

Burr. Umh——very well thought on——No Sir, you shall truſt to my bounty; I'll go in his place, murmure or repine, speak the leaſt word, or give thy lips the leaſt motion; and I'll beat thee till thou art not in condition to go.

Fail. I vow to gad this is extreme injuſtice: was it not my invention?

Burr. Why doſt thou think thou art worthy to make use of thy own invention?——Speak another word dee see——come help me quickly to ſtrip Sir *Timorous*: his Coat may conduce to the deceipt ——Sir *Timorous* by your leave—— *falls on him.*

Tim. O Lord! What's the matter?——murder——murder.

Burr. Dee open; I have something in my pocket that will serve for a gag now I think on't. [*gags and binds him.* So lye there Knight. Come, Sir, and help to make me Sir *Timorous*; and when I am married, remember to increase your manners with my fortune—yet we'll alwayes drink together. *Exeunt.*

ACT V.

Constance, Isabelle, Nonsuch.

Con. THIS is just the Knights hour; and Lovers seldome come after their time.

Non. Good night Daughter, I'll to bed; and give you joy to morrow morning. [*Exit* Nonsuch.

Isa. I'm glad he's gone: what, your train takes?

Con. Yes, yes; *Loveby* will come: *Setstone* has been with him in disguise; and promis'd him golden Mountains if he will not be wanting to his own fortune.

Isa. Is your habit provided too?

Con. All is ready.

Isa. Away then; for this is the place where we must part like Knights Errant, that take several paths to their adventures.

Con. 'Tis time; for I hear some body come along the Alley; without question 'tis *Timorous*. Farewel, the Captains stayes for me in my Chamber.

Isa. And I'll post after you to Matrimony; I have laid a fresh Parson at the next Stage that shall carry me tantivy. *Exit* Constance.

Enter Burr *with* Timorous *his Coat on.*

Burr. My Lady *Constance*!

Isa. The same: Sir *Timorous*!

Burr. The same.

Isa. Sir *Timorous* takes me for my Cousin. [*aside.*

Burr. My Lady *Constance* mistakes me for the Knight. [*aside.*

Isa. Here, Sir; through the dark walk; 'tis but a little way about: ——he's my own beyond Redemption—— [*aside.*

Burr. The Indies are mine; and a handsome Lady into the bargain— [*Exeunt.*

Enter Failer, *dogging them as they go off.*

Fail. He shall be hang'd e'r he shall get her. Thus farr I have dogg'd 'um, and this way I am sure they must pass e'r they come to the house: the Rogue had got the old Dog-trick of a Statesman; to fish things out of wiser heads than his own, and never so much as take notice of him that gave the Counsel——

Enter Isabelle *and* Burr *again.*

Now if I can but give her the hint without his knowledge!——Madam——my Lady *Constance*——

Isa. Whose voice is that?

Fail. A word in private, or you are undone:——Pray step aside.

Burr. Where are you, Madam?

Isa. Immediately, Sir *Timorous.*

Fail. You are mistaken, Madam: 'tis not Sir *Timorous*; but *Burr* in his cloaths: he has stript the Knight; gag'd him, and lock'd him up.

Isa. Failer?

Fail. The same: I could not but prevent your unhappiness, though I hazard my Person in the discovery I Vow to Gad, Madam.

Burr. Whose that talkes to you my Lady *Constance.*

Isa. A Maid of my acquaintance that's come to take her leave of me before I marry; the poor soul does so pity me.

Burr. How will that Maid lie thinking of you and me to night !

Isa. Has he the Key about him? [*To* Failer.

Fail. I think so, Madam.

Isa. Could not you possibly pick his pocket, and give me the Key; then let me alone to release Sir *Timorous*; and you shall be witness of the Wedding.

Fail. Igad you want your Cousin *Isabells* wit to bring that to pass, Madam.

Isa. I warrant you my own wit will serve to fool *Burr*——and you too, or I am much deceiv'd—— [*aside.*

Fail. I am a little apprehensive of the Rascall's fingers since I felt 'um last; and yet my fear has not power to resist the sweet temptation of revenge; I Vow to Gad I'll try, Madam——

Isa. Never fear; let me alone to keep him busie——

Burr. Come, Madam, and let me take off those tastless Kisses the Maid gave you; May we not joyn lips before we are Married?

Isa. No, fye, Sir *Timorous.*

They struggle a little, and in that time Failer *picks his Pocket of the Key.*

Fail. I have it——here 'tis——now shift for your self as I'll do: Ill waite you in the Alley. [*Exit* Fail.

Isa. Sir *Timorous*, pray go into my Chamber; and make no noise till I return: I'll but fetch the little Man of God, and follow you in a twinckling.

Burr. There's no light I hope——

Isa. Not a spark

Burr. For to light me to the Mark—— [*Exit* Burr.

Isa. What a scowring have I scapt to night! fortune, 'tis thou haſt been ingenious for me! Allons *Isabelle!* courage! now to deliver my Knight from the Enchanted Caſtle. [*Exit* Isabelle.

Enter Loveby *led by* Setſtone *antickly habited*; *with a torch in one hand, and a wand in the other.*

Lov. What art thou that haſt led me this long houre
Through Lanes and Alleys, and blind passages?

Set. I am thy *Genius*; and conduct thee to
Wealth, Fame, and Honour; what thou com'ſt to do
Do boldly: fear not; with this rod I charme thee;
And neither Elf nor Goblin now can harm thee.

Lov. Well, march on; if thou art my *Genius*, thou art bound to be Answerable for me: I'll have thee hang'd if I miscarry.

Set. Fear not my Son.

Lov. Fear not quoth a! then prithee put on a more familiar shape: ——one of us two ſtinks extreamely: prithee do not come so near me: I do not love to have my face bleach'd like a Tiffany with thy Brimſtone———

Set. Fear not, but follow me———

Lov. 'Faith I have no great minde to't: I am somewhat godly at present; but ſtay a moneth longer and I'll be proud, and fitter for thee: in the mean time prithee ſtay thy ſtomach with some *Dutchman*: an *Hollander* with Butter will fry rarely in Hell.

Set. Mortal, 'tis now too late for a retreat: go on and live: ſtep back and thou art mine.

Lov. So I am however; firſt or laſt, but for once I'll truſt thee——

The Scene opens, and discovers Conſtance; *and a Parson by her, she habited like Fortune.*

Enter again.

Set. Take here the mighty Queen of good and ill;
Fortune: firſt Marry, then enjoy thy fill
Of lawful pleasures; but depart e'r morn:
Slip from her Bed, or else thou shalt be torn
Piece-meale by Fiends; thy bloud carows'd in Bowles,
And thy foure quarters blown to th' top of *Pouls*.

Lov. By your favour I'll never venture it: is marrying the business; I'll none I thank you—— [*Here* Conſtance *whispers* Setſtone.

Set. Fortune will turne her back if twice deny'd.

Lov. Why she may turn her Girdle too on t'other side.
This is the Devil; I will not venture on her.

Set. Fear not; she swears thou shalt receive no harm.

Lov. I, if a man durst trust her; but the Devil is got into such an ill name for lying.

Set. When e'r you are not pleas'd, it shall be lawful to sue out your Divorce.

Lov. I; but where shall I get a Lawyer? there you are aforehand with me: you have retain'd most of them already——for the favours I have receiv'd, I am very much her servant, but in the way of Matrimony, Mr. Parson there can tell you 'tis an Ordinance; and must not be enter'd into without mature deliberation: besides, Marriages you know are made in Heaven; and that I am sure this was not.

Set. She bids you then, at least, restore that Gold, which she, too lavishly, pour'd out on you unthankful Man————

Lov. 'Faith I have it not at present; 'tis all gone, as I am a sinner; but, 'tis gone wickedly; all spent in the Devil her Fathers service.

Set. Where is the grateful sence of all your favours? Come, Fiends, with Flesh-hooks tear the wretch in pieces, and bear his Soul upon your leathern wings, below the Fountain of the dark Abyss.

Lov. What, Are you a Conjuring? if your good at that sport, I can Conjure as well as you—— [*Draws his Sword.*

Con. Hold; for Heaven's sake hold, I am no Spirit: touch but my hand; Ghosts have no Flesh and Blood. [*Discovering.*

Lov. My Lady *Constance*! I began to suspect it might be a trick; but never could imagine you the Author: it seemes you are desirous I should Father this *Hans en Kelder heere.*

Con. I know not how without a blush to tell you it was a cheat I practis'd for your Love.

Set. A meere Tympany, Sir, rais'd by a Cushion; you see 'tis gone already.

Con. *Setstone* was sent to have acquainted you; but by the way unfortunately miss'd you.

Lov. 'Twas you then that supply'd me all this while with Money; pretty Familiar, I hope to make thee amends e'r I sleep to night: come Parson, prethee make hast and joyn us. I long to be out of her debt poor Rogue.

The Parson takes them to the side of the Stage: they turn their backs to the Audience, while he mumbles to them.

Set. I'll be the Clark; Amen, give you joy Mr. Bridegroom, and Mrs. Bride.

Lov. Const. Thanks honest *Setstone.*

Bib. Franc. And Musick without, they Play.

Musick. God give your worship a good even Mr. *Loveby.*

Con. Hark! What noise is that? Is this Musick of your providing, *Setstone.*

Set. Alas, Madam, I know nothing of it.

Lov. We are betray'd to your Father; but the best on't is, he comes too late to hinder us——fear not, Madam, I'll bear you through 'um all——

As they rush out; Bibber, Frances, *and Musick are entring in:* Bibber *and* Frances *are beaten down.*

[*Exeunt* Loveby, Constance, Setstone, Parson.

All cry out. Oh the Devil! The Devil: The Devil!

Bib. Lord bless us, Where are you *Frances?*

Franc. Here *William*! this is a Judgment, as they say, upon you *William*; for trusting Wits: and calling Gentlemen to the Tavern, *William.*

Bib. No; 'twas a Judgment upon you, for desiring Preferment at Court, *Frances.* Let's call up the Watch, and Justice *Trice*, to have the house search'd.

Franc. I, I; there's more Devils there I warrant you. [*Exeunt.*

Enter Loveby, Constance, Setstone, *again.*

Lov. It was certainly *Will Bibber* and his Wife with Musick: for now I remember my self I 'pointed him this hour at your Fathers house: but we frighted them worse than they frighted us.

Con. Our Parson run away too:—when they cry'd out the Devil!

Lov. He was the wiser: for if the Devil had come indeed, he has Preach'd so long against him it would have gone hard with him.

Set. Indeed I have alwayes observ'd Parsons to be more fearful of the Devil than other People.

Lov. Oh the Devil's the Spirit, and the Parson's the Flesh: And betwixt those two there must be Warr: yet to do u'm both right, I think in my conscience they quarrel onely like Lawyers, for their Fees; and meet good friends in private to laugh at their Clients.

Con. I saw him run in at my Cousin *Isabell*s chamber doore, which was wide open; I believe she's return'd: we'll fetch a light from the Gallery, and give her joy————

Lov. Why is she Married, Madam?

Con. I'll tell you as we go—— [*Exeunt.*

The Scene *Changes*; Burr *and the Parson Enter, meeting in the dark.*

Burr. My Lady *Constance* are you come again? that's well: I have waited sufficiently for you in the dark.

Par. Help, help, help good Chriſtian People! the Devil, the Devil's here.

Bur. 'Tis I, Madam; What do you meane?

Par. Avoid Sathan! avoid, avoid.

Bur. What have I here, the hairy Woman?

Enter Loveby, Conſtance *with the Light.*

Bur. Ha! yonder's my Lady *Conſtance!* Who have I got, a ſtone-Prieſt by this good Light. How's this, *Loveby* too!

Lov. *Burr*, a beating my Reverend Clergy: What make you here at this unseasonable hour! I'll know your business— [*Draws.*

Bur. Will you, Sir?—— [*They Fight.*

Con. *Set.* *Parson.* Help, Murder, murder.

Enter at one Door, Trice *Drunk: with the Watch:* Bibber *and* Frances *following. At the other* Nonsuch, *and* Servants, *and* Failer.

Non. Murder, murder! beat down their weapons: Will you murder Sir *Timorous*, Mr. *Loveby*— [*They disarme both.*

Sir *Timorous!* Ha, *Burr!* Thieves; thieves! Sit down good Mr. Juſtice, and take their Examinations: now I shall know how my Money went.

Trice. They shall have Juſtice I warrant u'm.

[*Goes to sit and misses the chaire.*

Bib. The Juſtice is almoſt dead drunk, my Lord.

Franc. But and't please your Worship my Lord this is not the worſt sight that we have seen here to night in your Worships house, we met three or four hugeous ugly Devils, with eyes like Sawcers, that threw down my Husband, that threw down me, that made my heart so panck ever since, as they say.

Non. The Devil again in my house!

Lov. Nay, here he was, that's certain; he brought me hither, I know not how my self, and Married me; Mr. *Setſtone* there can juſtifie it: but the beſt is, I have a Charme about me that will lay him yet e'r Midnight.

Fail. And I Vow to Gad, my Lord, I know as little how I came hither as any man.

Bur. Nor I.

Trice. Nor I.

Lov. No I dare swear do'ſt thou not Mr. Juſtice.

Tric. But I wonder how the Devil durſt come into our Ward, when he knows I have been at the Duties of—my Family———this evening.

Enter one of the Watch, with Timorous, *and* Isabelle.

Watch. And please your Worship I met this couple in the street late, and so seeing them to be man and woman, I brought u'm along with me, upon suspition of Felony together.

Franc. This is the proud minx that sought shelter in my house this afternoon, Mr. Justice.

Fail. Sir *Timorous* and Madam *Isabelle!* I Vow to Gad we are undone *Burr*———

Isa. Do not you know me, Mr. Justice?

Lov. Justice is blind, he knows no body.

Isa. My name is *Isabelle.*

Franc. No, thy name is *Jezabelle*: I warrant you there's none but Rogues and Papists would be abroad at this time of night.

Bib. Hold *Frances*——

Trice. She's drunk I warrant her as any beast: I wonder woman you do not consider what a crying sin Drunkenness is? Whom do you learn it from in our Parish? I'm sure you never see me worse.

Isa. Burr and *Failer*; acknowledge your selves a couple of recreant Knights: Sir *Timorous* is mine: I have won him in fair Field from you.

Con. Give you joy Cousin—give you joy!

Lov. Married!

Isa. And in *Diana*'s Grove boy.

Lov. Why 'tis fine by heaven: 'tis wondrous fine, as the Poet goes on sweetly.

Tim. I am sure they had gagg'd me, and bound me, and stript me almost stark naked, and lockt me up as fast as a Butterfly, till she came and made me a man again; and therefore I have reason to love her the longest day I have to live.

Isa. I, and the longest night too, or you are to blame. And you have one argument I love you, if the proverb be true, for I took you almost in your bare shirt.

Burr. So much for us *Failer*!

Con. Well my Lord, it had as good at first as at last: I must beg your Lordship's blessing for this Gentleman and my self. *both kneel.*

Non. Why you are not married to him I hope! he's married to the devil.

Lov. 'Twas a white Devil of your Lordship's getting then; Mr. *Setstone*, and the Reverend here can witness it.

Set. Par. We must speak truth my Lord.

Non. Would I had another Child for your sake, you should ne'r see peny of my money.

Lov. Thank you my Lord; but methinks 'tis much better as 'tis.

Isa. Come Nuncle 'tis in vain to hold out now 'tis past remedy: 'tis like the last Act of a Play when People must marry; and if fathers will not consent then, they should throw Oranges at u'm from the Galleries: why should you stand off to keep us from a dance?

Non. But there's one thing still that troubles me, that's her great belly, and my own too.

Con. Nay for mine my Lord, 'tis vanished already: 'twas but a trick to catch the old one.

Lov. But I'll do my best, she shall not be long without another.

Isa. But as for your great belly Nuncle, I know no way to rid you on't but by taking out your guts.

Lov. 'Tis such a pretty smart rascal; 'tis well I am pleas'd with my own choice; but I could have got such Hectors and Poets and Gamesters out of thee.

Con. No, no; two Wits could never have liv'd well together; want would have so sharpned you upon one another.

Isa. A Wit should naturally be joynd to a fortune; by the same reason your Vintners feed their hungry Wines.

Con. And if Sir *Timorous* and I had married; we two Fortunes must have built Hospitals with our money, we could never have spent it else.

Lov. Or what think you of paying Courtiers debts with it.

Isa. Well, to shew I am in charity with my Enemies, I'll make a motion: while we are in Town let us hire a large house, and live together: *Burr* and *Failer*——

Fail. Shall be utterly discarded; I knew 'twould come to that I vow to gad.

Isa. Shall be our Ghests.

Burr *and* Failer *throw up their Caps, and cry* Vivi, Madame Isabelle.

Lov. And *Bibber* shall make our Wedding Cloaths without trusting.

Bib. No, henceforward I'll trust none but landed men; and such as have houses and apple-trees in the Country: Now I have got a Place in the Custome house.

Franc. Nothing vexes me, but that this flirting Gentlewoman should go before me; but I'll to the Heralds Office, and see whether the Queens Majesties Dresser should not take place of any Knights Wife in Christendom.

Bib. Now all will out———no more good *Frances*.

Franc. I will speak, that I will, so I will: what! shall I be a Dresser to the Queens Majesty, and no body must know on't; I'll send Mr. Church-warden word on't; and Gentlemen, when you come to St. *Brides* Church (if ever you come to Church Gentlemen) you shall see me in the Pew that's next the Pulpit; thank Mr. *Loveby*'s Worship for't.

Lov. Spare your thanks good Landlady, for the truth is we came too late; the Place is gone; and so is yours *Will*; but you shall have 200 *l.* for One, if that will satisfie you.

Franc. This is better news as they say.

Lov. Chear up thy Wife *Will*: where are thy fiddles? a dance should do it:

Bib. I'll run and call u'm.

Isa. I have found out that will comfort her: henceforward I christen her by the name of *Madam Bibber*.

All. A Madam *Bibber*, A Madam *Bibber*.

Franc. Why, I thank you sweet Gentlemen and Ladies, this is a Cordial to my drooping spirits: I confess I was a little eclips'd; but I'll chear up with abundance of love, as they say. Strike up fiddles—

Lov. That's a good Wench.

Dance.

Trice. This Musick, and a little nod has recover'd me; I'll in and provide for the Sack-Posset.

Non. To bed, to bed; 'tis late: Son *Loveby* get me a boy to night, and I'll settle three thousand a year upon him the first day he calls me Grandsire.

Lov. I'll do my best.

To make the bargain sure before I sleep.
Where Love and money strike, the blow goes deep.

EPILOGUE to the *WILD GALLANT*, as it was first Acted.

THE Wild Gallant *has quite play'd out his game;*
He's marry'd now, and that will make him tame;
Or if you think Marriage will not reclaim him,
The Critiques swear they'll damn him, but they'll tame him.
Yet though our Poet's threatned most by these,
They are the only People he can please:
For he to humour them, has shown to day,
That which they only like, a wretched Play:
But though his Play be ill, here have been shown
The greatest Wits and Beauties of the Town.
And his Occasion having brought you here,
You are too grateful to become severe.
There is not any Person here so mean,
But he may freely judge each Act and Scene:
But if you bid him choose his Judges then,
He boldly names true English Gentlemen:
For he ne'r thought a handsome Garb or Dress,
So great a Crime to make their Judgement less:
And with these Gallants he these Ladies joyns,
To judge that Language their Converse refines.
But if their Censures should condemn his Play,
Far from Disputing, he does only pray,
He may Leanders *Destiny obtain:*
Now spare him, drown him when he comes again.

EPILOGUE to the *WILD GALLANT* Reviv'd.

OF all Dramatique Writing, Comick Wit,
As 'tis the best, so 'tis most hard to hit.
For it lies all in level to the eye,
Where all may judge, and each defect may spye.
Humour is that which every day we meet,
And therefore known as every publick street;
In which, if e'r the Poet go astray,
You all can point, 'twas there he lost his way.

But, What's so common, to make pleasant too,
Is more than any wit can alwayes do.
For 'tis, like Turkes, *with* Hen *and Rice, to treat;*
To make regallio's out of common meat.
But, in your Diet you grow Salvages:
Nothing but Humane flesh your taste can please:
And, as their Feasts with slaughter'd slaves began,
So you, at each new Play, must have a Man.
Hither you come, as to see Prizes fought;
If no Blood's drawn, you cry the Prize is naught.
But fooles grow wary now; and when they see
A Poet eyeing round the Company,
Straight each man for himself begins to doubt;
They shrink like Seamen when a Press comes out.
Few of 'em will be found for Publick use,
Except you charge an Oph upon each house,
Like the Train'd-Bands, and every man ingage
For a sufficient Foole to serve the Stage.
And, when with much adoe you get him there,
Where he in all his glory shou'd appear,
Your Poets make him such rare things to say,
That he's more wit than any Man i'th' Play.
But of so ill a mingle with the rest,
As when a Parrat's taught to break a jeast.
Thus aiming to be fine, they make a show
As tawdry Squires in Country Churches do.
Things well consider'd, 'tis so hard to make
A Comedy, which should the knowing take:
That our dull Poet, in despair to please,
Does humbly beg by me his writ of ease.
'Tis a Land-tax which he's too poor to pay;
You, therefore must some other impost lay.
Would you but change for serious Plot and Verse.
This mottley garniture of Fool and Farce,
Nor scorn a Mode, because 'tis taught at home,
Which does, like Vests, our Gravity become;
Our Poet yields you should this Play refuse,
As Tradesmen, by the change of fashions, lose
With some content their fripperies of France,
In hope it may their staple Trade advance.

FINIS

THE
RIVAL LADIES
A TRAGI-COMEDY

NOS HAEC NOVIMUS ESSE NIHIL

SOURCE

THE story of *The Rival Ladies* is to some extent suggested by a novella *Las Dos Doncellas* which Dryden read in the *Novelas Ejemplares* of Cervantes. Cleverly told and highly interesting as the original is, the poet has by no means assiduously followed every turn, but rather with fine art remodelled and vastly improved many of the adventures.

Las Dos Doncellas was extremely popular in England, having been translated as *The Two Damosels* in *Exemplarie Novels*, folio, 1640, done by Thomas Mabbe, who called himself Don Diego Puede-Ser. As *The Rival Ladies*, translated by Dr. Walter Pope, it appears in *Select Novels*, 8vo., 1694. Again, *The Rival Ladies* is given in volume IV of *A Select Collection of Novels*, 1729; and during the eighteenth century it was frequently reprinted.

Dryden no doubt knew, and I think he borrowed a hint or two from Jean Rotrou's tragi-comédie *Les Deux Pucelles*, produced with great success in 1636. This is very closely derived from *Las Dos Doncellas*, and it was itself amply utilized by Philippe Quinault in his first play *Les Rivales*. Some account of these two French pieces will be found in the Introduction.

It is remarkable how admirably Dryden has achieved his atmosphere in *The Rival Ladies*, for, setting on one side the locale, Alicant, the swift incidents, the bandits on land and picaroons at sea, the masques and disguises, the twilight street, the duels, the ornate gallantry and brocaded honour, the thrust and riposte of clinquant dialogue, are all extremely Spanish in character and taste.

To cite parallels to many of the incidents would be easy: such must, indeed, suggest themselves to every reader. To derive the two doncellas "in man's habit" from Euphrasia in Beaumont and Fletcher's *Philaster*, a maiden dressed in page's hose and called Bellario, love-lorn for Philaster, is impertinent and inept. As early as 1569–70 a Latin play, *Byrsa Basilica*, had incidentally presented a girl in boy's apparel. In Lyly's *Gallathea* (1585), Gallathea and Phillida have been disguised as boys in order to escape Neptune's demand for the sacrifice of a virgin. Martia, disguis'd as Ansaldo, in *The Widow* (*c.* 1615, ascribed to Middleton, Jonson, and Fletcher), is set upon by footpads and stripped to the shirt. Edward Sharpman's *The Fleire* (1606) presents us with two girls who assume male trunks to thwart their lovers' looser intrigues. In Fletcher's *Love's Pilgrimage* (acted as "renewed" in 1636), which is also founded upon *Las Dos Doncellas*, we have two maidens in boy's garb both in quest of the same faithless lover. In Spanish and Italian drama, indeed, such disguises abound:

> This poet is that poet's plagiary,
> And he a third's, till they all end in Homer.
> And Homer filched all from an Egyptian priestess,
> The world's a theatre of theft.

Love's Pilgrimage was familiar enough to Dryden, and inevitably between two plays derived from the same novella there must be resemblances.

It may be remarked that John Corye in his comedy *The Generous Enemies; or, The Ridiculous Lovers,* Theatre Royal, 1671; 4to, 1672; has some very considerable conveyances from Fletcher, and these even extend to a few verbal borrowings.

Langbaine, of course, does not fail to point out that in the Fifth Act of *The Rival Ladies*, a shipboard, Dryden has taken a hint ("pillage" grum Gerard calls it) from Petronius. When Encolpius and Giton with Eumolpus find themselves on the vessel of Lycas they form plans of escape much in the same way as Gonsalvo, Manuel, Hippolito, and Amideo, consult together how they may get ashore from the pirate carrack. Giton suggests they shall feign to be sea-sick, Encolpius advises slipping down by a rope into the boat, Eumolpus would sew the two runaways in skins and at the next port convey them on land as baggage. There is no further resemblance in the situations.

Dryden certainly knew Scarron's Spanish novel *Les deux Frères Rivaux*, which forms Chapter XIX of the Second Part of *Le Roman Comique* (Seconde partie, achevé d'imprimer pour la 1re fois du 20 Septembre, 1657; both Parts, 1658; Second Part, 1663, with Third Part, 1663. Two Parts, 1663). Here we have two characters, Dom-Sanche de Silva and Dom-Juan de Péralte, who are the rival brothers. The little, however, the poet has taken from the novel is not merely negligible, but extremely improved in the borrowing.

The scene where the disguised Amideo finds that the gallant whom she loves is her brother and that therefore her affection is all vain is a favourite turn with Dryden. He has used it comically in *The Spanish Fryar*, and with tragic doom in *Don Sebastian*.

THEATRICAL HISTORY

THE *Rival Ladies* was produced at the King's Theatre in the early summer of 1664, probably May. It met with considerable success, and for the first decade after the Restoration this poetical piece appears to have kept the boards, although it was soon to fall out of the regular repertory.

On Thursday, 4 August, 1664, Pepys writes: "Sir W. Pon . . . did carry me to a play and pay for me at the King's house, which is 'The Rivall Ladys,' a very innocent and most pretty witty play. I was much pleased with it."

Wednesday, 18 July, 1666, Pepys notes: "walked to Woolwich, reading 'The Rival Ladys' all the way, and find it a most pleasant and well writ play." A fortnight or so later, on 2 August, he went down to Woolwich again, "reading and making an end of the 'Rival Ladys,' and find it a very pretty play."

DEDICATION

To the Right Honourable

Roger Earl of *ORRERY*

MY LORD,

THIS *worthless Present was design'd you, long before it was a Play; when it was only a confus'd Mass of Thoughts, tumbling over one another in the Dark: When the Fancy was yet in its first Work, moving the Sleeping Images of things towards the Light, there to be Distinguish'd, and then either chosen or rejected by the Judgment: It was yours, my Lord, before I could call it mine. And, I confess, in that first Tumult of my Thoughts, there appear'd a disorderly kind of Beauty in some of them, which gave me hope, something worthy my Lord of* Orrery *might be drawn from them: But I was then in that eagerness of Imagination, which by over-pleasing Fancifull Men, flatters them into the Danger of Writing; so that when I had Moulded it to that Shape it now bears, I look'd with such Disgust upon it, that the Censures of our severest Critiques are Charitable to what I thought (and still think) of it my Self: 'Tis so far from me to believe this perfect, that I am apt to conclude our best Plays are scarcely so. For the Stage being the Representation of the World, and the Actions in it, how can it be imagin'd, that the Picture of Human Life can be more Exact than Life it Self is; He may be allowed sometimes to Err, who undertakes to move so many Characters and Humours as are requisite in a Play, in those narrow Channels which are proper to each of them: To conduct his imaginary Persons, through so many various Intrigues and Chances, as the Labouring Audience shall think them lost under every Billow; and then at length to work them so naturally out of their Distresses, that when the whole Plot is laid open, the Spectators may rest satisfied, that every cause was powerfull enough to produce the effect it had; and that the whole Chain of them was with such due order Linck'd together, that the first Accident would naturally beget the second, till they all render'd the conclusion necessary.*

These difficulties, my Lord, may reasonably excuse the Errors of my Undertaking; but for this confidence of my Dedication, I have an Argument which is too Advantagious for me, not to publish it to the World. 'Tis the kindness your Lordship has continually shown to all my Writings.

You have been pleas'd, my Lord, they should sometimes cross the Irish *Seas to Kiss your Hands; which passage (contrary to the Experience of others) I have found the least dangerous in the World. Your favour has shone upon me at a remote distance, without the least knowledge of my Person; and (like the Influence of the Heavenly Bodies) you have done good without knowing to whom you did it. 'Tis this Virtue in your Lordship, which imboldens me to this attempt: for did I not consider you as my Patron, I have little reason to desire you for my Judge; and should appear with as much awe before you in the Reading, as I had when the full Theater sat upon the Action. For who could so severely judge of Faults as he, who has given testimony he commits none? Your excellent Poems having afforded that knowledge of it to the World, that your Enemies are ready to upbraid you with it, as a Crime for a Man of business to Write so well. Neither durst I have justified your Lordship in it, if examples of it had not been in the World before you; if* Xenophon *had not written a Romance, and a certain* Roman, *call'd* Augustus Cæsar, *a Tragædy, and Epigrams. But their Writing was the entertainment of their Pleasure; Yours is only a Diversion of your Pain. The* Muses *have seldome employed your Thoughts, but when some violent fit of the Gout has snatch'd you from Affairs of State: And, like the Priestess of* Apollo, *you never come to deliver his Oracles but Unwillingly, and in Torment. So that we are oblig'd to your Lordships misery for our Delight: You treat us with the Cruel pleasure of a* Turkish *triumph, where those who Cut and Wound their Bodies, sing Songs of Victory as they pass, and divert others with their own Sufferings. Other men indure their Diseases, your Lordship only can enjoy them. Plotting and writing in this kind, are certainly more troublesome employments than many which signifie more, and are of greater moment in the World: The Fancy, Memory, and Judgment, are then extended (like so many Limbs) upon the Rack; all of them Reaching with their utmost stress at Nature; a thing so almost Infinite, and Boundless, as can never fully be Comprehended, but where the Images of all things are always present. Yet I wonder not, your Lordship succeeds so well in this attempt; the Knowledge of Men is your daily practice in the World; to work and bend their stubborn Minds, which go not all after the same Grain, but each of them so particular a way, that the same common Humours, in several Persons, must be wrought upon by several means. Thus, my Lord, your Sickness is but the imitation of your Health; the Poet but subordinate to the States-Man in you; you still govern Men with the same Address, and manage Business with the same Prudence; allowing it here (as in the World) the due Increase and Growth, till it come to the just highth; and then turning it when it is fully Ripe, and Nature calls out, as it, were to be deliver'd. With this only advantage of ease to you in your Poetry, that you have Fortune here at your command: with which,*

Wisdome, does often unsuccessfully struggle in the World. Here is no chance which you have not fore-seen; all your Heroes are more than your Subjects; they are your Creatures. And though they seem to move freely, in all the Sallies of their Passions, yet you make Destinies for them which they cannot shun. They are mov'd (if I may dare to say so) like the Rational Creatures of the Almighty Poet, who walk at Liberty, in their own Opinion, because their Fetters are Invicible; when indeed the Prison of their Will, is the more sure for being large: and instead of an absolute Power over their Actions, they have only a wretched Desire of doing that, which they cannot choose but do.

I have dwelt, my Lord, thus long upon your Writing, not because you deserve not greater and more noble Commendations, but because I am not equally able to express them in other Subjects. Like an ill Swimmer, I have willingly staid long in my own Depth: and though I am eager of performing more, yet am loath to Venture out beyond my Knowledge. For beyond your Poetry, my Lord, all is Ocean to me. To Speak of you as a Souldier, or a States-man, were only to betray my own ignorance: and I could hope no better success from it, than that miserable Rhetorician *had, who solemnly Declaim'd before* Hannibal, *of the Conduct of Armies, and the Art of War. I can only say in general, that the Souls of other Men shine out at little Cranies; they understand some one thing, perhaps, to Admiration, while they are Darkned on all the other Parts: But your Lordship's Soul is an intire Globe of Light, breaking out on every Side; and if I have only discover'd one Beam of it, 'tis not that the Light falls unequally, but because the Body which receives it, is of unequal Parts.*

The acknowledgment of which is a fair Occasion offer'd me, to retire from the consideration of your Lordship, to that of my Self: I here present you, my Lord, with that in Print which you had the Goodness not to Dislike upon the Stage; and account it happy to have met you here in England*: it being at best, like small Wines, to be Drunk out upon the place, and has not Body enough to endure the Sea. I know not whether I have been so carefull of the Plot and Language as I ought; but for the latter I have endeavour'd to write English, as near as I could distinguish it from the Tongue of* Pedants, *and that of affected Travellours. Only I am Sorry, that (Speaking so noble a Language as we do) we have not a more certain Measure of it, as they have in* France, *where they have an Academy erected for the purpose, and Indow'd with large Privileges by the present King. I wish we might at length leave to borrow Words from other Nations, which is now a Wantonness in us, not a Necessity; but so long as some affect to Speak them; there will not want others who will have the boldness to Write them.*

But I fear least defending the receiv'd words, I shall be accus'd for following the New way, I mean, of writing Scenes in Verse: though, to

Speak properly, 'tis not so much a New way amongst us, as an Old way new reviv'd; For many Years before Shakespears *Plays, was the Tragedy of Queen* Gorboduc *in* English *Verse, written by that famous Lord* Buckhurst, *afterwards Earl of* Dorset, *and Progenitor to that Excellent Person, who (as he Inherits his Soul and Title) I wish may Inherit his good Fortune. But supposing our Country-men had not receiv'd this Writing till of late; Shall we Oppose our selves to the most polish'd and civiliz'd Nations of* Europe? *Shall we with the same Singularity oppose the World in this, as most of us do in pronouncing* Latin; *Or do we desire that the Brand which* Barclay *has, (I hope) unjustly laid upon the* English *should still continue:* Angli suos ac sua omnia impense mirantur; cæteras nationes despectui habent. *All the* Spanish *and* Italian *Tragedies I have yet seen, are writ in Rhyme: For the* French, *I do not name them, because it is the Fate of our Country-men to admit little of theirs among us, but the Basest of their Men, the Extravagances of their Fashions, and the Frippery of their Merchandise.* Shakespear (*who with some Errors not to be avoided in that Age, had, undoubtedly a larger Soul of Pœsie, than ever any of our Nation) was the first, who to shun the pains of continual Rhyming, invented that kind of Writing, which we call Blanck Verse, but the* French *more properly,* Prose Mesureè: *into which the* English *Tongue so naturally Slides, that in Writing Prose 'tis hardly to be avoided. And therefore, I admire some Men should perpetually stumble in a way so easie. And inverting the order of their Words, constantly close their Lines with Verbs; which though commended sometimes in Writing Latin, yet we were Whipt at* Westminster *if we us'd it twice together. I know some, who if they were to Write in Blanck Verse, Sir,* I ask your Pardon, *would think it Sounded more Heroically to write, Sir,* I your Pardon ask. *I should judge him to have little command of* English, *whom the necessity of a Rhyme should force often upon this Rock; though sometimes it cannot easily be avoided: And indeed this is the only inconvenience with which Rhyme can be charged. This is that which makes them say, Rhyme is not natural, it being only so, when the Poet either makes a vicious choice of Words, or places them for Rhyme sake so unnaturally, as no Man would in ordinary Speaking: but when 'tis so iudiciously ordered, that the first Word in the Verse seems to beget the second, and that the next, till that becomes the last Word in the Line, which in the negligence of Prose would be so; it must then be granted, Rhyme has all the advantages of Prose, besides its own. But the Excellence and Dignity of it, were never fully known till Mr.* Waller *taught it; he first made Writing easily an Art: First shew'd us to conclude the Sense, most commonly, in Distichs; which in the Verse of those before him, runs on for so many Lines together, that the Reader is out of Breath to overtake it. This sweetness of Mr.* Wallers Lyrick *Poesie was afterwards follow'd in the*

Epick by Sir John Denham, *in his* Coopers-Hill: *A Poem which your Lordship knows for the Majesty of the Style, is, and ever will be the exact Standard of good Writing. But if we owe the Invention of it to Mr.* Waller, *we are acknowledging for the Noblest use of it to Sir* William D'avenant; *who at once brought it upon the Stage, and made it perfect, in the Siege of* Rhodes.

The advantages which Rhyme has over Blanck Verse, are so many, that it were lost time to name them: Sir Philip Sidney, *in his defence of Poesie gives us one, which, in my Opinion, is not the least considerable; I mean the help it brings to Memory: which Rhyme so Knits up by the Affinity of Sounds, that by remembring the last Word in one Line we often call to Mind both the Verses. Then in the quickness of Reparties, (which in Discoursive Scenes fall very often) it has so particular a Grace, and is so aptly Suited to them, that the suddain Smartness of the Answer, and the Sweetness of the Rhyme, set off the Beauty of each other. But that benefit which I consider most in it, because I have not seldome found it, is, that it Bounds and Circumscribes the Fancy. For Imagination in a Poet is a faculty so Wild and Lawless, that, like an High-ranging Spaniel it must have Cloggs tied to it, least it out-run the Judgment. The great easiness of Blanck Verse, renders the Poet too Luxuriant; He is tempted to say many things, which might better be Omitted, or at least shut up in fewer Words: But when the difficulty of Artfull Rhyming is interpos'd, where the Poet commonly confines his Sence to his Couplet, and must contrive that Sence into such Words, that the Rhyme shall naturally follow them, not they the Rhyme; the Fancy then gives leisure to the Judgment to come in; which seeing so heavy a Tax impos'd, is ready to cut off all unnecessary Expences. This last Consideration has already answer'd an Objection which some have made; that Rhyme is only an Embroidery of Sence, to make that which is ordinary in it self pass for excellent with less Examination. But certainly, that which most regulates the Fancy, and gives the Judgment its busiest Employment, is like to bring forth the richest and clearest Thoughts. The Poet examines that most which he produceth with the greatest Leisure, and which, he knows, must pass the severest Test of the Audience, because they are aptest to have it ever in their Memory: as the Stomach makes the best Concoction when it strictly embraces the Nourishment, and takes account of every little Particle as it passes through. But as the best Medicines may lose their Virtue by being ill applied, so it is with Verse, if a fit Subject be not chosen for it. Neither must the Argument alone, but the Characters, and Persons be great and noble; Otherwise, (as* Scaliger *says of* Claudian) *the Poet will be,* Ignobiliore materiâ depressus. *The Scenes, which, in my Opinion, most commend it, are those of Argumentation and Discourse, on the result of which the doing or not doing some considerable action should depend.*

But, my Lord, though I have more to say upon this Subject, yet I must remember 'tis your Lordship to whom I speak; who have much better commended this way by your Writing in it, than I can do by Writing for it. Where my Reasons cannot prevail, I am sure your Lordship's example must. Your Rhetorick has gain'd my cause; at least the greatest part of my Design has already succeeded to my Wish, which was to interest so noble a Person in the Quarrel, and withall to testifie to the World how happy I esteem my Self in the honour of being,

My Lord,
Your Lordship's most
Humble, and most
Obedient Servant,

John Driden.

PROLOGUE *to the* RIVAL–LADIES

'TIS *much Desir'd, you Judges of the Town*
Would pass a Vote to put all Prologues *down;*
For who can show me, since they first were Writ,
They e'r Converted one hard-hearted Wit;
Yet the World's mended well; in former Days
Good Prologues *were as scarce, as now good* Plays.
For the reforming Poets of our Age,
In this first Charge, spend their Poetique rage:
Expect no more when once the Prologue'*s done;*
The Wit is ended e'r Play'*s begun.*
You now have Habits, Dances, Scenes, and Rhymes;
High Language often; I, and Sense, sometimes:
As for a clear Contrivance doubt it not;
They blow out Candles to give Light to th' Plot.
And for Surprize, two Bloody-minded Men
Fight till they Dye, then rise and Dance agen:
Such deep Intrigues you'r welcome to this Day:
But blame your Selves, not him who Writ the Play;
Though his Plot's Dull, as can be well desir'd,
Wit stiff as any you have e'r admir'd:
He's bound to please, not to Write well; and knows
There is a Mode in Plays as well as Cloaths:
Therefore kind Judges———

A Second PROLOGUE

Enters.

2——HOld; *Would you admit*
For Judges all you see within the Pit.
1. *Whom would he then Except, or on what Score?*
2. *All, who (like him) have Writ ill Plays before;*
For they, like Thieves condemn'd, are Hang-men made,
To execute the Members of their Trade.
All that are Writing now he would disown:
But then he must Except, ev'n all the Town.
All Chol'rique, losing Gamesters, who in spight
Will Damn to Day, because they lost last Night:
All Servants whom their Mistress's scorn upbraids;
All Maudlin Lovers, and all Slighted Maids:
All who are out of Humour, or Severe;
All, that want Wit, or hope to find it here.

PERSONÆ DRAMATIS

DON *Gonsalvo de Peralta*, A young Gentleman, newly arriv'd from the *Indies;*	In love with *Julia.*
Don *Rhodorigo de Sylva*;	In love with the same Lady.
Don *Manuel de Torres.*	Brother to *Julia.*
Julia, Elder Sister to Don *Manuel*;	Promis'd to *Rhodorigo.*
Honoria, younger Sister to Don *Manuel*, disguis'd in the Habit of a Man, and going by the Name of *Hippolito*	In love with *Gonsalvo.*
Angellina, Sister to Don *Rhodorigo*, in Man's Habit	Likewise in Love with *Gonsalvo*, and going by the Name of *Amideo.*

Servants. Sea-men.
Robbers. Masquers.

The Scene Alicant.

THE
RIVAL-LADIES

ACT FIRST SCENE FIRST

Enter Gonsalvo, Servant.

The Scene A Wood.

Gons. NAY, 'twas a ſtrange as well as cruel Storm,
To take us almoſt in the Port of *Sevil*,
And drive us up as far as *Barcellona*;
The whole Plate-Fleet was scatter'd, some part wrack'd;
There one might see the Sailors diligent
To caſt o'r-board the Merchants envy'd Wealth,
While he, all Pale, and Dying, ſtood in doubt
Whether to ease the Burden of the Ship
By Drowning of his Ingots, or himself.
Serv. Fortune is a Woman every where,
But moſt upon the Sea.
Gons. Had that been all
I should not have Complain'd; but ere we could
Repair our ship, to drive us back again
Was such a Cruelty———
Serv. Yet that short time you ſtaid at *Barcellona*
You Husbanded so well, I think you left
A Miſtress there.
Gons. I made some small Essays
Of Love, what might have been I cannot tell:
But to leave that, upon what part of *Spain*
Are we now caſt?
Serv. Sir, I take that City to be *Alicante*.
Gons. Some days muſt of necessity be spent
In looking to our Ship; then back again
For *Sevil*.
Serv. There you'r sure you shall be welcome.
Gons. I, if my Brother *Rodorick* be return'd
From *Flanders*; but 'tis now three Years since I
Have heard from him, and since I saw him twelve.

Serv. Your growth, and your long absence in the *Indies*
Have alter'd you so much, he'l scarcely know you.
Gons. I'm sure I should not him, and less my Sister
Who, when I with my Uncle went this Voyage,
Was then one of those little prating Girls
Of whom fond Parents tell such tedious stories
Well, go you back.
Serv. I go, Sir.
Gons. And take care
None of the Sea-men slip ashore.
Serv. I shall, Sir; [*Exit* Servant.
Gons. Ile walk a little while among these Trees,
Now the fresh Evening air blows from the Hills,
And breaths the sweetness of the Orange flowers
Upon me, from the Gardens neer the City. *Robbers within.*
1. *Rob.* I say, make sure, and Kill him;
Hip. For Heaven's dear sake have pity on my Youth. [*Within.*
Gons. Some violence is offer'd in the Wood
By Robbers to a Traveller: Who ere
Thou art, humanity obliges me
To give thee succour.
Hip. Help! Ah cruel men! [*Within.*
Gons. This way I think the Voice came, 'tis not far. [*Exit.*

[*The Scene draws and discovers* Hippolito *bound to a Tree, and two Robbers by him with drawn Swords.*

2. *Rob.* Strip him, and let him go:
1. *Rob.* Dispatch him quite; off with his Doublet quickly.
Hip. Ah me unfortunate!

Enter Gonsalvo, *seizes the Sword of one of them, and runs him through; then after a little resistance Disarms the other.*

2. *Rob.* If you have mercy in you spare my Life;
I never was consenting to a Deed
So black as Murder, though my Fellow urg'd me:
I only meant to Rob, and I am punisht
Enough, in missing of my wicked aim.
Gons. Do they rob Angels there? This sweet Youth has
A Face so like one which I lately saw
It makes your Crime of Kin to Sacrilege:
But Live; and henceforth
Take noble Courses to maintain your Life:

Here's something that will rescue you from want,
Till you can find employment.
[*Gives him Gold, and unbinds* Hippolito.

Hip. What ſtrange adventure's this! How little hop'd I,
When thus Disguis'd I ſtole from *Barcellona*,
To be reliev'd by brave *Gonsalvo* here? [*Aside*.

2. *Rob*. That Life you have preserv'd shall ſtill be yours;
And that you may perceive how much my Nature
Is wrought upon by this your generous Act;
That goodness you have shown to me, Ile use
To others for your Sake, if you dare truſt me
A moment from your Sight.

Gons. Nay, take your Sword,
I will not so much crush a Budding virtue
As to suspect. [*Gives him his Sword. Exit* Robber.
———Sweet Youth, you shall not leave me
Till I have seen you safe.

Hip. You need not doubt it:
Alas! I find I cannot if I would;
I am but free to be a greater Slave: [*Aside*.
How much am I oblig'd, Sir, to your Valour?

Gons. Rather to your own Sweetness, pretty Youth;
You muſt have been some way preserv'd, though I
Had not been neer; my Aid did but prevent
Some Miracle more slowly setting out
To save such Excellence.

Hip. How much more gladly could I hear those words,
If he that Spoke them knew he Spoke to me; [*Aside*.

Enter the Robber *again with Don* Manuel, *and* Julia *bound*.

My Brother and my Siſter Pris'ners too!
They cannot sure discover me through this
Disguise; however Ile not Venture it. [*Steps behind the Trees*.

2. *Rob*. This Gentleman and Lady [*To* Gonsalvo *privately*.
My Fellows bound. [*Exit* Robber.

Man. We muſt prepare to Dye;
This is the Captain of the Picarons.

Jul. Me-thinks he looks like one; I have a ſtrange
Aversion to that Man; He's fatal to me.

Gons. I ne'r saw Excellence in Woman-kind [*Stares on her*.
Till now, and yet discern it at the firſt:
Perfection is discover'd in a moment.
He that ne'r saw the Sun before, yet knows him.

Jul. How the Villain ſtares upon me!

Gons. Wonder prepares my Soul, and then Love enters:
But wonder is so close pursu'd by Love,
That like a Fire, it warms as soon as born.

Man. If we muſt Dye, what need these Circumſtances?

Jul. Heav'n defend me from him.

Gons. Why Madam, can you doubt a Rudeness from me?
Your very Fears and Griefs create an awe.
Such Majeſty they bear; me-thinks I see
Your Soul retir'd within her inmoſt Chamber,
Like a fair Mourner sit in State, with all
The silence Pomp of Sorrow round about her.

Man. Your Language does express a Man bred up
To worthier ways than those you follow now.

Gons. What does he mean? [*Aside.*

Man. If (as it seems) you Love; Love is a passion
Which kindles honour into noble Acts:
Reſtore my Siſters liberty; oblige her,
And see what Gratitude will work.

Gons. All this is ſtranger yet.

Man. What ere a Brother's power
To morrow can do for you, claim it boldly.

Gons. I know not why you think your selves my Pris'ners;
This Ladies freedome is a thing too precious
To be dispos'd by any but her Self:
But value this small Service as you please,
Which you reward too Prodigally, by
Permitting me to Pay her more.

Jul. Love from an Out-law! from a Villain love!
If I have that pow'r on thee thou pretend'ſt,
Go and persue thy Mischiefs, but presume not
To follow me:——come Brother. [*Exeunt* Julia, Manuel.

Gons. Those foul names of Out-law, and of Villain,
I never did deserve: They raise my wonder. [*Walks.*
Dull that I was, not to find this before?
She took me for the Captain of the Robbers:
It muſt be so; Ile tell her her miſtake.

Goes out haſtily, and returns immediately.

She's gone, She's gone; and who or whence she is
I cannot tell; me-thinks she should have left
A Track so bright I might have follow'd her;
Like setting Suns that Vanish in a Glory.
O Villain that I am! O hated Villain!

Enter Hippolito *again.*

Hip. I cannot suffer you to wrong your self
So much; for though I do not know your Person,
Your Actions are too fair, too noble, Sir,
To merit that foul Name.

Gons. Prithee do not flatter me, I am a Villain;
That admirable Lady said I was.

Hip. I fear you Love her, Sir.

Gons. No, no; not Love her:
Love is the name of some more gentle passion;
Mine is a Fury grown up in a moment
To an extremity, and lasting in it:
An heap of Powder set on Fire, and burning
As long as any ordinary Fewel.

Hip. How could he Love so soon? and yet alas!
What cause have I to ask that question?
Who lov'd him the first Minute that I saw him:
I cannot leave him thus, though I perceive
His heart ingag'd another way. [*Aside.*
Sir, can you have such pity on my Youth, [*To him.*
On my forsaken, and my helpless Youth,
To take me to your Service?

Gons. Would'st thou serve
A Mad-man? how can he take care of thee
Whom Fortune and his Reason have abandon'd?
A Man that saw, and Lov'd and disoblig'd,
Is Banish'd, and is Mad, all in a moment.

Hip. Yet you alone have Title to my Service;
You make me Yours by your preserving me:
And that's the title Heav'n has to Mankind.

Gons. Prithee no more.

Hip. I know your Mistriss too:

Gons. Ha! dost thou know the person I adore?
Answer me quickly; Speak, and Ile receive thee:
Hast thou no Tongue?

Hip. Why, Did I say I knew her?
All I can hope for, If I have my wish
To Live with him, is but to be Unhappy. [*Aside.*

Gons. Thou false and lying Boy, to say thou knewst her;
Prethee say something, though thou Cosen'st me.

Hip. Since you will know, her name is *Julia*, Sir,
And that young Gentleman you saw, her Brother,
Don *Manuel de Torres.*

Gons. Say I should take thee, Boy, and should employ thee
To that fair Lady, wouldst thou serve me faithfully?
Hip. You ask me an hard question; I can Dye
For you, perhaps I cannot Woo so well.
Gons. I knew thou wouldst not do't.
Hip. I swear I would:
But, Sir, I grieve to be the Messenger
Of more unhappy News; She must be Married
This day to one Don *Rodorick de Sylva*,
Betwixt whom and her Brother there has been
A long, (and it was thought a mortal) Quarrel,
But now it must for ever end in Peace:
For hapning both to Love each others Sisters,
They have concluded it in a cross Marriage;
Which, in the Pallace of *Don Rodorick*,
They went to Celebrate from their Country-house,
When, taken by the Thieves, you rescu'd them.
Gons. Me-thinks I am grown patient on a suddain:
And all my Rage is gone: Like losing Gamesters
Who fret and storm, and swear at little Losses:
But, when they see, all hope of Fortune vanish'd,
Submit and gain a Temper by their Ruine.
Hip. Would you could cast this Love, which troubles you
Out of your mind.
Gons. I cannot Boy; but since
Her Brother, with intent to Cozen me,
Made me the promise of his best assistance;
Ile take some course to be reveng'd of him. *Is going out;*
But stay, I charge thee, Boy, discover not
To any who I am;
Hip. Alas I cannot, Sir, I know you not.
Gons. Why, there's it; I am Mad again; Oh Love!
Hip. Oh Love! [*Exeunt ambo.*

Scene the Second

Enter two Servants of Don Rodorick's, *placing Chairs, and Talking as they place them.*

1. *Serv.* Make ready quickly there; *Don Manuel*
And his fair Sister, that must be our Lady,
Are coming in.

2. They have been long expected;
'Tis Evening now, and the Canonique hours
For Marriage are past.
1. The nearer Bed-time
The better still; my Lord will not deferr it:
He swears the Clergy are no fit Judges
Of our Necessities.
2. Where is my Lord?
1. Gone out to meet his Bride.
2. I wonder that my Lady *Angellina*
Went not with him, She's to be Married too.
1. I do not think she Fancies much the Man;
Only, to make the Reconcilement perfect
Betwixt the Families, she's Passive in it;
The choice being but her Brother's, not her Own.
2. Troth, wer't my case, I care not who chose for me:
1. Nor I; 'twould save the Process of a tedious Passion,
A long Law-suit of Love, which quite consumes
An honest Lover ere he gets Possession:
I would come plump, and fresh, and all my Self,
Serv'd up to my Brides Bed like a fat Fowl,
Before the Frost of Love had nipt me through.
I look on Wives as on good dull Companions,
For elder Brothers to Sleep out their time with;
All we can hope for in the Marriage-bed,
Is but to take our Rest; and what care I
Who lays my Pillow for me.

Enter a Poet *with Verses.*

2. Now, what's your business Friend?
Poet. An *Epithalamium*, to the Noble Bridegrooms.
1. Let me see; what's here? as I live [*Takes it.*
Nothing but down-right Bawdry: Sirrah, Rascal,
Is this an Age for Ribaldry in Verse?
When every Gentleman in Town, speaks it
With so much better grace, than thou canst write it;
I'll beat thee with a staff of thy own Rhimes.
Poet. Nay, good Sir? [*Runs off, and Exit.*
2. Peace, They are here.

Enter Don Rodorick, *Don* Manuel, Julia, *and Company.*

1. My Lord looks sullenly, and fain would hide it.
2. Howe'r he weds Don *Manuels* Sister, yet
I fear he's hardly reconcil'd to him.

Jul. I tremble at it still.
Rod. I must confess
Your danger great: But, Madam, since 'tis past
To speak of it were to renew your Fears.
My noble Brother, welcome to my Breast.
Some call my Sister; say, *Don Manuel*
Her Bridegroom waits.
Man. Tell her, in both the Houses
There now remains no Enemy but she.
Rod. In the mean time lets Dance; Madam, I hope
You'l grace me with your Hand:——

Enter Leonora, *Woman to* Angellina; *Takes the two Men aside.*

Leon. O Sir, my Lady *Angellina!*
Rod. Why comes she not?
Leon. Is fall'n extreamly Sick.
Both. How.
Leon. Nay, trouble not your selves too much,
These Fits are usual with Her; and not Dangerous.
Rod. O rarely Counterfeited. [*Aside.*
Man. May not I see her?
Leon. She does by me, deny her Self that honour.
[*As she Speaks steals a Note into his hand.*
I shall return, I hope, with better News;
In the mean time she prays, you'l not disturb
The Company. [*Exit* Leonora.
Rod. This troubles me exceedingly.
Man. A Note put privately into my hand
By *Angellina's* Woman? She's my Creature:
There's something in't; I'l read it to my Self—— [*Aside.*
Rod. Brother, what Paper's that?
Man. Some begging Verses
Deliver'd me this Morning on my Wedding.
Rod. Pray let me see 'um:
Man. I have many Copies,
Please you to entertain your Self with these.
[*Gives him another Paper.*
Sir, [Manuel *Reads.*
My Lady feigns this Sickness to delude you:
Her Brother hates you still; and the Plot is,
That he shall Marry first your Sister,
And then deny you his—— *Yours* Leonora——

Poſtscript.

Since I writ this, I have so wrought upon her,
(Who of her Self, is Timorous enough)
That she believes her Brother will betray her,
Or else be forc'd to give her up to You;
Therefore, unknown to him, she means to Fly:
Come to the Garden door at seven this Evening,
And there you may Surprize her; mean time I
Will keep her ignorant of all things, that
Her fear may ſtill Increase.

Enter Leonora *again.*

Rod. How now? how does your Lady?
Leon. So ill, she cannot possibly wait on you.
Man. Kind Heav'n give me her Sickness.
Rod. Those are wishes:
What's to be done?
Man. We muſt deferr our Marriages.
Rod. Leonora, now! [*Aside to her.*
Leon. My Lady, Sir, has absolutely charged
Her Brother's should go forward.
Rod. Absolutely!
Leon. Expresly, Sir, because she says there are
So many honourable Persons here,
Whom to Defraud of their intended Mirth,
And of each others Company, were rude:
So hoping your Excuse. [*Exit* Leonora.
Rod. That privilege of Pow'r which Brothers have
In *Spain*, I never us'd: Therefore submit
My Will to hers, but with much sorrow, Sir;
My Happiness should go before, not wait
On yours: Lead on.
Man. Stay, Sir, though your fair Siſter in reſpect
To this Assembly seems to be content
Your Marriage should proceed, we muſt not want
So much good Manners as to suffer it.
Rod. So much good manners, Brother?
Man.———————— I have said it.
Should we to show our Sorrow for her Sickness,
Provoke our easie Souls to careless Mirth,
As if our drunken Revels were design'd
For joy of what she Suffers?

Rod. 'Twill be over
In a few Days.
Man. Your ſtay will be the less.
Rod. All things are now in Readiness, and muſt not
Be put off, for a peevish Humour thus.
Man. They muſt; or I shall think you mean not fairly:
Rod. Explain your Self.
Man. That you would Marry firſt,
And afterwards refuse me *Angellina.*
Rod.———Think so.
Man. You are
Rod. Speak softly.
Man. A foul Villain.
Rod. Then———
Man. Speak softly.
Rod. I'l find a time to tell you, you are one.
Man. 'Tis well.
Ladies, you wonder at our Whispers, [*To the company.*
But more will wonder when you know the cause;
The Beauteous *Angellina* is fall'n Ill;
And since she cannot with her presence grace
This days Solemnity, the Noble *Rodorick*
Thinks fit it be Deferr'd, till she recover;
Then, we both hope to have your Companies.
Lad. Wishing her Health, we take our Leaves. [*Exeunt company*
Rod. Your Siſter yet will Marry me.
Man. She will not: come hither *Julia.*
Jul. What ſtrange afflicting News is this you tell us?
Man. 'Twas all this false Man's Plot, that when he had
Poſseſt you, he might cheat me of his Siſter.
Jul. Is this true, *Rodorick?* Alas, his silence
Does but too much confess it: How I blush
To own that Love I cannot yet take from thee!
Yet for my Sake be Friends.
Man. 'Tis now too late:
I am by honour hinder'd.
Rod. I by hate.
Jul. What shall I do?
Man. Leave him, and come away;
Thy Virtue bids thee.
Jul. But Love bids me ſtay.
Man. Her Love's so like my own, that I should blame
The Brother's passion in the Siſter's flame.

Rodorick, we shall meet——He little thinks
I am as sure this Night of *Angellina*,
As he of *Julia*. [*Aside*. [*Exit Manuel*.

Rod. Madam, To what an Extasie of Joy
Your Goodness raises me! This was an act
Of kindness which no Service e'r can pay.

Jul. Yes, *Rodorick*, 'tis in your Pow'r to quit
The Debt you owe me.

Rod. Do but name the way.

Jul. Then briefly thus, 'tis to be just to me
As I have been to you.

Rod. You cannot doubt it.

Jul. You know I have adventur'd for your sake.
A Brothers anger, and the Worlds opinion:
I value neither; for a setled Virtue
Makes it self Judge, and satisfy'd within,
Smiles at that common Enemy, the World.
I am no more affraid of flying Censures,
Than Heav'n of being Fir'd with mounting Sparkles.

Rod. But wherein must my Gratitude consist?

Jul. Answer your Self, by thinking what is fit
For me to do.

Rod. By Marriage to confirm
Our mutual Love.

Jul. Ingratefull *Rodorick!*
Canst thou name Marriage, while thou entertain'st
A Hatred so unjust against my Brother?

Rod. But, unkind *Julia*, you know the causes
Of Love and Hate are hid deep in our Stars,
And none but Heav'n can give account of both.

Jul. Too well, I know it; for my Love to thee
Is Born by Inclination, not by Judgment:
And makes my Virtue shrink within my heart,
As loath to leave it, and as loath to mingle.

Rod. What would you have me do?

Jul. Since I must tell thee,
Lead me to some near Monastery: there,
(Till Heav'n find out some way to make us Happy)
I shall be kept in safety from my Brother:

Rod. But more from me; What hopes can *Rodorick* have,
That she who leaves him freely, and unforc'd,
Should ever of her own accord return?

Jul. Thou hast too great assurance of my Faith,

That in despight of my own Self I love thee;
Be Friends with *Manuel*, I am thine, till when
My Honour's;———Lead me. [*Exeunt.*

Scene the Third.

Enter Don Manuel, *Solus.*

The Scene is the Representation of a Street discover'd by Twilight.

Man. This is the time and place where I expect
My fugitive Mistress; if I meet with her
I may forget the wrongs her Brother did me:
If otherwise, his Blood shall expiate them.
I hope her Woman keeps her Ignorant
How all things pass'd, according to her promise.

A door opens———Enter Angellina *in Boy's Cloaths.* Leonora *behind at the Door.*

Leon. I had forgot to tell him of this Habit
She has put on; but sure hee'l know her in it. [*Aside.*
Man. Who goes there?
Ang. 'Tis *Don Manuel*'s Voice; I must run back:
The Door shut on me? *Leonora*, Where?
Does she not follow me?——I am betray'd.
Man. What are you?
Ang. A poor Boy.
Man. Do you belong to *Rodorick*?
Ang. Yes, I do.
Man. Here's Money for you, tell me where's his Sister:
Ang. Now I met her coming down the stairs,
Which lead into the Garden.
Man. 'Tis well, leave me
In silence.
Ang. With all my heart; Was ever such a scape! [*Exit running.*
Man. She cannot now be long; sure by the Moon-shine
I shall discover her:

Enter Rodorick, *and* Julia.

This must be she; Ile seize her.
Jul. Help me, *Rodorick*;

Rod. Unhand the Lady, Villain.
Man. *Rodorick*!
I'm glad we meet alone; now is the time
To end our Difference.
Rod. I cannot stay.
Man. You must.
Rod. I will not:
Man. 'Tis base to injure any Man; but yet
'Tis far more base, once done not to defend it.
Rod. Is this an hour for Valiant Men to Fight?
They love the Sun should witness what they do;
Cowards have Courage when they see not Death:
And fearfull Hares, that sculk in forms all Day,
Yet Fight their feeble Quarrels by the Moon-light.
Man. No, Light and Darkness are but poor distinctions,
Of such, whose Courage comes by fits and starts.
Rod. Thou urgest me above my patience:
This minute of my Life was not my own,
But hers I love beyond it: *They draw, and Fight.*
Jul. Help, help; none hear me!
Heav'n I think is Deaf too:
O *Rodorick*! O Brother!——

Enter Gonsalvo, *and* Hippolito.

Jul. Who ere you are, if you have honour part 'um——
[Manuel *stumbles and falls.*
Gons. Hold, Sir, you are too cruel; he that Kills
At such advantage fears to Fight again: [*Holds* Rodorick.
Man. Cavalier, I may Live to thank you for this favour.
[*Rises.*
Rod. I will not quit you so.
Man. Ile breath, and then——
Jul. Is there no way to save their Lives?
Hip. Run out of sight,
If 'tis concerning you they Quarrel. [Julia *retires to a Corner.*
Hip. Help, help, as you are Cavaliers; the Lady
From whom you thus contend, is seiz'd by some
Night-robbing Villains.
All. Which way took they?
Hip. 'Twas so dark I could not see distinctly.
Rod. Let us divide; I this way. [*Exit.*
Gons. Down yonder street Ile take.

Man. And I down that. [Exeunt *severally.*
Hip. Now, Madam, may we not lay by our fear?
They are all gone.
Jul. 'Tis true, but we are here,
Expos'd to Darkness without guide or aid,
But of our selves.
Hip. And of our selves affraid.
Jul. These dangers while 'twas Light I could despise,
Then I was bold; but watch'd by many Eyes:
Ah! could not Heav'n for Lovers find a way,
That prying People still might sleep by Day.

Enter Angellina.

Hip. Me-thinks I'm certain I discover some;
Jul. This was your speaking of 'um made 'um come.
Hip. There is but one, perhaps he may go by.
Ang. Where had I courage for this bold disguise,
Which more my Nature than my Sex belies?
Alas! I am betraid to darkness here;
Darkness which Virtue hates, and Maids most fear:
Silence and Solitude dwell every where:
Doggs cease to bark; the Waves more faintly roar,
And rowl themselves asleep upon the Shore:
No noise but what my Foot-steps make, and they
Sound dreadfully, and Louder than by Day:
They double too, and every step I take
Sounds thick me-thinks, and more than one could make.
Ha! Who are these?
I wish'd for Company, and now I fear.
Who are you gentle People that go there?
Jul. His Voice is soft as is the upper Air,
Or dying Lovers words: O pity us.
Ang. O pity me! Take freely as your own
My Gold, my Jewels; spare my Life alone.
Hip. Alas he fears as much as we.
Jul. What say you,
Sir, Will you joyn with us.
Amid. Yes Madam, but
If you would take my Sword, you'l use it better.
Hip. I, But you are a Man.
Amid. Why, so are you.
Hip. Truly my fear had made me quite forget it.

Enter Gonsalvo.

Gons. Hippolito! How barbarous was I
To leave my Boy! *Hippolito*!
Hip. Here, here.
Now Madam fear not, you are safe:
Jul. What is become, Sir, of those Gentlemen?
Gons. Madam, They all went several ways; not like
To meet.
Jul. What will become of me!
Gons. 'Tis late,
And I a stranger in the Town: yet all
Your dangers shall be mine.
Jul. You'r noble, Sir.
Gons. I'll pawn the hopes of all my Love, to see
You safe.
Jul. Who ere your Mistress be, she has
My curses if she prove not Kind.
Ang. And mine.
Hip. My Sister will repent her when she knows
For whom she makes that Wish; but I'l say nothing
Till Day discovers it: a Door opens, [*Aside.*
I hope it is some Inn. [*A door opens, at which a Servant appears.*
Ang. Friend, can you Lodge us here?
Serv. Yes, Friend, we can:
Jul. How shall we be dispos'd?
Serv. As Nature would;
The Gentleman and you: I have a rule,
That when a Man and Woman ask for Lodging
They are ever Husband and Wife.
Jul. Rude and Unmanner'd.
Gons. Sir, this Lady must be Lodged apart.
Serv. Then the two Boys that are good for nothing
But one another, they shall go together.
Ang. Lye with a Man? sweet Heav'n defend me!
Hip. Alas, friend, I ever lye alone.
Serv. Then to save trouble, Sir, because 'tis late
One of the Youths shall be dispos'd with you.
Ang. Who I! not for the World.
Hip. Neither of us; for though I would not lodge with you
My self; I never can indure he should.
Ang. Why then, to end the difference, if you please
I and that Lady will be Bed-fellows.

Hip. No, she and I will Lodge together rather.
Serv. You are sweet Youths indeed; not for the World
You would not Lodge with Men! none but the Lady
Would serve your turn.
Ang. Alas I had forgot I am a Boy;
I am so lately one. [*Aside.*
Serv. Well, well; all shall be Lodg'd apart.
Gons. to *Hip.* I did not think you Harbour'd wanton thoughts:
So young, so Bad!
Hip. I can make no defence
But must be sham'd by my own Innocence. *Exeunt omnes.*

Act the Second.

Enter Gonsalvo, Hippolito, Amideo, *at a distance.*

The Scene is a Chamber.

Gons. H*Ippolito*, what is this pretty Youth
That follows us?
Hip. I know not much of him
Handsome you see, and of a gracefull Fashion;
Of noble Blood, he says, and I believe him;
But in some distress; he'l tell no more,
And I cou'd cry for that which he has told,
So much I pity him.
Gons. My pretty Youth;
Would I could do thee any Service.
Ang. Sir,
The greatest you can do me, is accepting mine.
Hip. How's this? me-thinks already I begin
To hate this Boy, whom but ev'n now I moan'd.
You serve my Master? Do you think I cannot
Perform all Duties of a Servant better
And with more care than you?
Ang. Better you may,
But never with more care:
Heav'n which is serv'd with Angels, yet admits
Poor man to pay his Duty, and receives it.
Hip. Mark but, my Lord, how ill behav'd a Youth,
How very ugly, what a Dwarf he is.
Ang. My Lord, I yet am Young enough to grow,

And 'tis the commendation of a Boy
That he is little. [*Cries.*
Gons. Prithee do not Cry;
Hippolito, 'twas but juſt now you prais'd him,
And are you chang'd so soon?
Hip. On better View.
Gons. What is your Name, sweet-heart.
Hip. Sweet heart! since I
Have serv'd you, you ne'r call'd me so.
Ang. O, ever,
Ever call me by that kind name, I'l own
No other, because I would ſtill have that.
Hip. He told me, Sir, his name was *Amideo*,
Pray call him by't.
Gons. Come, I'l employ you both;
Reach me my Belt, and help to put it on.
Amid. I run my Lord.
Hip. You run? it is my Office.
[*They both take it up, and ſtrive for it;* Hippolito *gets it, and puts it on.*
Amid. Look you, my Lord, he puts it on so awkardly; [*Crying.*
The Sword does not sit right.
Hip. Why, where's the fault?
Amid. I know not that; but I am sure 'tis wrong.
Gons. The fault is plain, 'tis put on the wrong Shoulder.
Hip. That cannot be, I look'd on *Amideo*'s,
And hung it on that Shoulder his is on.
Amid. Then I doubt mine is so.
Gons. It is indeed:
You'r both good Boys, and both will learn in time:
Hippolito, go you and bring me word,
Whether that Lady we brought in laſt Night
Be willing to receive a Visit from me.
Hip. Now *Amideo*, since you are so forward
To do all Service, you shall to the Lady.
Amid. No, I'l ſtay with my Maſter, he bid you.
Hip. It Mads me to the Heart to leave him here:
But I will be reveng'd. [*Aside.*
My Lord, I beg
You would not truſt this Boy with any thing
Till my return; pray know him better firſt. [*Exit* Hippolito.
Gons. 'Twas my unhappiness to meet this Lady
Laſt night; because it ruin'd my design

Of walking by the House of *Rodorick*:
Who knows but through some Window I had spy'd
Fair *Julia*'s shaddow passing by the Glass;
Or if some others, I would think it hers;
Or if not any, yet to see the place
Where *Julia* Lives: O Heav'n, how small a blessing
Will serve to make despairing Lovers happy!
Amid. Unhappy *Angellina*, thou art lost:
Thy Lord loves *Julia*. [*Aside*.

Enter Hippolito, *and* Julia.

Jul.————Where is thy Master?
I long to give him my acknowledgements
For my own safety, and my Brothers both.
Ha! Is it he? [*Looks*.
Gons. Can it be *Julia?*
Could Night so far disguise her from my Knowledge!
Jul. I would not think thee him I see thou art:
Prithee disown thy Self in pity to me:
Why should I be oblig'd by one I hate?
Gons. I could say something in my own defence;
But it were half a Crime to plead my cause
When you would have me Guilty.
Amid. How I fear
The sweetness of those words will move her pity:
I'm sure they should do mine.
Gons. You took me for a Robber, but so farr
I am from that———
Jul. O prithee be one still,
That I may know some cause for my Aversion.
Gons. I freed you from them, and more gladly did it;—
Jul. Be what thou wilt, 'tis now too late to tell me:
The Blackness of that Image I first fancy'd,
Has so infected me, I still must hate thee.
Hip. Though (if she Loves him) all my hopes are ruin'd,
It makes me Mad to see her thus unkind. [*Aside*.
Madam, what see you in this Gentleman,
Deserves your scorn, or hatred; Love him, or
Expect just Heav'n should strangely punish you.
Gons. No more: what ere she does is best; and if
You would be mine, you must like me submit
Without dispute.
Hip. How can I love you, Sir, and suffer this?

She has forgot that which laſt Night you did
In her defence.

Jul. O call that Night again;
Pitch her with all her Darkness round; then set me
In some farr Desart, hemm'd with Mountain Wolves
To howl about me: This I would indure,
And more, to Cancel my Obligements to him.

Gons. You owe me nothing, Madam, if you do,
I make it Void; and only ask your leave
To love you ſtill; for to be Lov'd again
I never hope.

Jul. If that will clear my Debt, enjoy thy wish
Love me, and long, and Desperately love me.
I hope thou wilt, that I may Plague thee more:
Mean time take from me that Deteſted object;
Conveigh thy much loath'd Person from my Sight.

Gons. Madam, you are Obey'd.
Hippolito, and *Amideo*, wait
Upon fair *Julia*; Look upon her for me
With dying Eyes, but do not Speak one word
In my behalf; for to disquiet her,
Ev'n happiness it self were bought too dear.

[*Goes farther off, towards the end of the Stage.*

My passion swells too high:
And like a Vessel ſtrugling in a Storm,
Requires more hands than one to Steer her upright;
I'l find her Brother out. [*Exit* Gonsalvo.

Jul. That Boy, I see he truſts above the other:
He has a ſtrange resemblance with a Face.
That I have seen, but when, or where, I know not.
I'l watch till they are parted; then perhaps
I may corrupt that little one to free me. [*Aside.*] [*Exit* Julia.

Amid. Sweet *Hippolito*, let me speak with you;

Hip. What would you with me?

Amid. Nay, you are so fierce;
By all that's good I love and honour you,
And would you do but one poor thing I'l ask you,
In all things else you ever shall command me.
Look you, *Hippolito*, here's Gold, and Jewels,
These may be yours.

Hip. To what end doſt thou show
These trifles to me? or how cam'ſt thou by them?
Not honeſtly, I fear.

Amid. I swear I did:
And you shall have 'um; but you always press
Before me in my Maſter's service so:———
Hip. And always will.
Amid. But dear *Hippolito*,
Why will you not give way, that I may be
Firſt in his favour, and be ſtill imploy'd?
Why do you Frown? 'tis not for gain I ask it;
What ever he shall give me shall be yours,
Except it be some Toy, you would not care for,
Which I should keep for his dear sake that gave it.
Hip. If thou wouldſt offer both the *Indies* to me,
The *Eaſtern* Quarries, and the *Weſtern* Mines,
They should not Buy one look, one gentle smile
Of his from me: assure thy Soul they should not,
I hate thee so.
Amid. Henceforth I'i hate you worse.
But yet there is a Woman whom he Loves,
A certain *Julia*, who will ſteal his heart
From both of us; wee'l joyn at leaſt againſt
The common Enemy.
Hip. Why does he fear my Lord should love a Woman?
The passion of this Boy is so like mine
That it amazes me.

Enter a Servant.

Piet. Young Gentleman,
Your Maſter calls for you.
Hip. I'l think upon't——— [*Exit* Hippolito, *cum* Pietro.

Enter Julia *to* Amideo.

Jul. Now is the time, he is alone.
Amid. Here comes
The Saint my Lord adores; Love, pardon me
The fault I muſt commit.
Jul. Fair Youth, I am
A Suitor to you.
Amid. So am I to you.
Jul. You see me here a Pris'ner.
Amid. My requeſt
Is, I may set you free; make haſte sweet Madam:
Which way would you go?

Jul. To the next
Religious House.
Amid. Here through the Garden, Madam;
How I commend your holy Resolution! [*Exeunt ambo.*

Enter Don Manuel *in the Streets, and a* Servant *with him.*

Man. Angellina fled to a Monaſtery say you?
Serv. So 'tis giv'n out: I could not see her Woman:
But for your Siſter, what you heard is true:
I saw her at the Inn:
They told me she was brought in late laſt Night,
By a young Cavalier they show'd me there.
Man. This muſt be he that Rescu'd me:
What would I give to see him.
Serv. Fortune is
Obedient to your wishes; He was coming
To find out you; I waited on him to
The turning of the Street; and ſtept before
To tell you of it.
Man. You o'r-joy me.
Serv. This, Sir, is he.——

Enter Gonsalvo.

Don Manuel *is running to Embrace him, and ſtops.*
Man.——————The Captain of the Robbers!
Gons. As such indeed you promis'd me your Siſter.
Man. I promis'd all the int'reſt I should have,
Because I thought before you came to claim it,
A Husbands right would take my Title from me.
Gons. I come to see if any Manly virtue
Can dwell with falshood: Draw, thou'ſt injur'd me.
Man. You say already I have done you wrong,
And yet would have me right you by a greater.
Gons. Poor abjeƈt thing!
Man. Who doubts another's Courage
Wants it himself; but I who know my own,
Will not receive a Law from you to Fight,
Or to forbear: for then I grant your Courage
To maſter mine, when I am forc'd to do
What of my self I would not.
Gons. Your reason?
Man. You sav'd my Life.

Gons. I'l quit that Debt to be
In a capacity of forcing you
To keep your promise with me; for I come
To learn, your Sister is not yet dispos'd.
Man. I've lost all privilege to defend my Life;
And if you take it now, 'tis no new Conquest;
Like Fish, first taken in a River, then
Bestow'd in Ponds to catch a second time.
Gons. Mark but how partially you plead your cause,
Pretending breach of honour if you Fight;
Yet think it none to Violate your word.
Man. I cannot give my Sister to a Robber.
Gons. You shall not; I am none, but Born of Blood
As noble as your self; my Fortunes, equal
At least with Yours; my Reputation, yet
I think unstain'd.
Man. I wish, Sir, it may prove so;
I never had so strong an Inclination
To believe any Man as you:———but yet———
Gons. All things shall be so clear, there shall be left
No room for any scruple: I was Born
In *Sevil*, of the best House in that City;
My name *Gonsalvo de Peralta:* being
A younger Brother, 'twas my Uncles care
To take me with him in a Voyage to
The *Indies*, where since Dying, he has left me
A Fortune not Contemptible; returning
From thence all my Wealth in the Plate-fleet,
A furious Storm almost within the Port
Of *Sevil*, took us, scatter'd all the Navy:
My Ship, by the unruly Tempest born
Quite through the Streights, as far as *Barcellona*;
There first cast Anchor; there I stept Ashore:
Three Days I staid, in which small time I made
A little Love, which Vanish'd as it came.
Man. But were you not Ingag'd to her you Courted?
Gons. Upon my Honour, no; what might have been
I cannot tell: but ere I could repair
My beaten Ship, or take fresh Water in,
One night, when there by chance I lay Aboard,
A Wind tore up my Anchor from the bottom,
And with that Violence it brought me thither;
Has thrown me in this Port:——

Man. But yet our meeting in the Wood was ﬅrange.
Gons. For that I'l satisfie you as we walk.

Enter Hippolito.

Hip. O Sir, how glad am I to find you——— [*Whispers.*
Man. That Boy I have seen some where, or one like him,
But where, I cannot call to mind:———
Hip. I found it out, and got before 'um———
And here they are——

Enter Amideo, *and* Julia.

Man. My Siﬅer! As I could have wish'd it:
Amid. O! we are caught?
Jul. I did expeƈt as much:
Fortune has not forgot that I am *Julia.*
Man. Siﬅer, I'm glad you'r happily return'd;
'Twas kindly done of you thus to prevent
The trouble of my search.
Jul. I would not have you
Miﬅake my Love to *Rodorick* so much,
To think I meant to fall into your hands,
My purpose is for the next Nunnery;
There I'l pray for you: So farewell.
Man. Stay, *Julia* you muﬅ go with me.
Jul. Lead, lead;
You think I am your Pris'ner now:———
Gons. If you will needs to a Religious house,
Leave that fair Face behind; a worse will serve
To spoil with Watching, and with Faﬅing there.
Man. Prithee no more of this; the only way
To make her happy is to force it on her.
Julia, prepare your self ﬅrait to be Married.
Jul. To whom.
Man. You see your Bridegroom: and you know
My Fathers will, who with his Dying breath
Commanded, you should pay as ﬅriƈt Obedience
To me as formerly to him: if not,
Your Dowry is at my dispose.
Jul. O would
The loss of that dispense with Duty in me,
How gladly would I suffer it! and yet
If I durﬅ queﬅion it, me-thinks 'tis hard!

What right have Parents over Children, more
Than Birds have o'r their Young; yet they impose
No rich Plum'd Miſtriss on their Feather'd Sons;
But leave their Love, more open yet and free
Than all the Fields of Air, their spacious Birth-right.
[Gonsalvo *seems to beg* Manuel *not to be harsh.*

Man. Nay, good *Gonsalvo* trouble not your self,
There is no other way, when 'tis once done
She'l thank me for't.

Jul. I ne'r expected other usage from you;
A kind Brother you have been to me,
And to my Siſter: you have sent they say
To *Barcellona*, that my Aunt should force her
To marry the old *Don* you brought her.

Hip. Who could! that once had seen *Gonsalvo's* Face?
Alas she little thinks I am so neer!—— [*Aside.*

Man. Mind not what she says;——
A word with you—— [*To* Gonsalvo.

Amid. Don *Manuel* eyes me ſtrangely; the beſt is
He never saw me yet but at a diſtance:
My Brothers jealousie (who ne'r intended
I should be his) reſtrain'd our neer Converse. [*Aside.*

Jul. My pretty Youth, I am inforc'd to truſt thee [*To* Amid.
With my moſt neer concerns; Friend I have none,
If thou deny'ſt to help me.

Amid. Any thing
To break your Marriage with my Maſter.

Jul. Go to *Rodorick*, and tell him my condition:
But tell it as from thy self, not me.

Amid. That you are forc'd to Marry.

Jul. But do not ask him
To succour me; if of himself he will not:
I scorn a Love that muſt be taught its Duty.

Man. What Youth is that? I mean the little one?

Gons. I took him up laſt Night.

Man. A sweet fac'd Boy,
I like him ſtrangely: would you part with him?

Amid. Alas, Sir, I am good for no Body
But for my Maſter.

Hip. Sir, I'l do your Errand.
Another time for letting *Julia* go. [*To* Amideo.

Man. Come, Sir;

Gons. I beg your pardon for a moment,

I'l but dispatch some business in my Ship,
And wait upon you presently.
Man. Wee'l go before.
I'l make sure *Rodorick* shall never have her;
And 'tis at leaſt some Pleasure to deſtroy
His Happiness, who ruin'd firſt my Joy.
[*Exeunt all but* Gonsalvo; *who before he goes, whispers* Hippolito.
Gons. Againſt her will fair *Julia* to possess,
Is not t'enjoy but Ravish happiness:
Yet Women pardon force, because they find
The Violence of Love is ſtill moſt kind:
Juſt like the Plots of well built Comedies,
Which then please moſt, when moſt they do surprize.
But yet conſtraint Love's nobleſt end deſtroys,
Whose higheſt Joy is in anothers Joys:
Where Passion rules, how weak does Reason prove!
I yield my Cause, but cannot yield my Love. [*Exit.*

Act the Third.

The Scene a great Room in Don Manuel's *House.*

Hippolito, Solus.

MY Maſter bid me speak for him to *Julia*:
Hard fate that I am made a confident
Againſt my self;——
Yet though unwillingly I took the Office,
I would perform it well: But how can I
Prove lucky to his Love, who to my own
Am so unfortunate! He truſts his passion
Like him that Ventures all his Stock at once
On an unlucky hand:

Enter Amideo.

Amid. Where is the Lady *Julia*?
Hip. What new Treason
Againſt my Maſters Love have you contriv'd
With her?
Amid. I shall not render you account.

Enter Julia.

Jul. I sent for him; yet if he comes there's danger;
Yet if he does not, I for ever lose him.
What can I wish? and yet I wish him here!
Only to take the care of me from me.
Weary with sitting out a Losing hand,
'Twill be some ease to see another Play it.
Yeſterday I refus'd to Marry him,
To day I run into his Arms unask'd;
Like a mild Prince inchroach'd upon by Rebels,
Love yielded much, till Honour ask'd for all. [*Sees* Hippolito.
How now, where's *Rodorick*? (sees *Amideo*)———I mean *Gonsalvo*?

Hip. You would do well to meet him:———

Amid. Meet him! You shall not do't: I'l throw my self
Like a young fawning Spaniel in your way
So often, you shall never move a ſtep
But you shall tread on me.

Jul. You need not beg me:
I would as soon meet a Serene, as see him.

Hip. *His sweetness for those Frowns no subjeſt finds:*
Seas are the Field of Combat for the Winds:
But when they sweep along some flowry Coaſt,
Their wings move Mildly, and their Rage is loſt.

Jul. *'Tis that which makes me more unfortunate:*
Because his sweetness muſt upbraid my hate.
The wounds of Fortune touch me not so near;
I can my Fate, but not his Virtue bear.
For my disdain with my eſteem is rais'd;
He moſt is hated when he moſt is prais'd:
Such an eſteem, as like a Storm appears,
Which rises but to Ship-wrack what it bears.

Hip. *Infeſtion dwells upon my Kindness sure,*
Since it deſtroys ev'n those whom it would cure.
[*Cries, and Exit* Hippolito.

Amid. Still weep *Hippolito*; to me thy Tears
Are soveraign, as those drops the Balm-Tree sweats.———
———But, Madam, are you sure you shall not love him!
I ſtill fear———

Jul. Thy fear will never let thee be a Man.

Amid. Indeed I think it won't.

Jul. We are now
Alone; What news from *Rodorick?*

Amid. Madam, he beggs you not to fear; He has
A way, which when you think all desperate
Will set you free.
Jul. If not, I will not Live
A moment after it.
Amid. Why! There's some comfort.
Jul. I strongly wish, for what I faintly hope:
Like the Day-dreams of melancholy Men,
I think and think on things impossible,
Yet love to wander in that Golden maze.

Enter Don Manuel, Hippolito, *and Company*.

Amid. Madam, your Brother's here.
Man. Where is the Bridegroom?
Hip. Not yet return'd, Sir, from the Ship.
Man. Sister, all this good Company is met
To give you Joy.
Jul. While I am compass'd round
With mirth, my Soul lies hid in shades of Grief:
Whence, like the Bird of Night, with half shut Eyes
She peeps, and sickens at the sight of Day. [*Aside*.

Enter Servant.

Serv. Sir, some Gentlemen, and Ladies are without,
Who to do honour to this Wedding come
To present a Masque.
Man. 'Tis well; desire 'um
They would leave out the Words, and fall to Dancing;
The Poetry of the Foot takes most of late:
Serv. The Poet, Sir, will take that very ill,
He's at the Door, with th' Argument o'th' Masque
In Verse.
Man. Which of the Wits is it that made it?
Serv. None of the Wits, Sir; 'tis one of the Poets.
Man. What Subject has he chose.
Serv. The Rape of *Proserpine*.

Enter Gonsalvo.

Man. Welcome, welcome you have been long expected.
Gons. I staid to see th' Unlading of some Rarities
Which are within:——
Madam, your pardon that I was so long absent.
Jul. You need not ask it for your absence, Sir.

Gons. Still cruel, *Julia*:——
Jul. The danger's here, and *Rodorick* not here:
I am not griev'd to Dye; but I am griev'd
To think him false. [*Aside.*
Man. Bid 'um begin.

The Musique Plays.

A *Cupid* descends in swift Motion, and Speaks these Verses.

Cup. *Thy Conquests* Proserpine, *have stretch'd too far,*
Amidst Heav'n's peace thy Beauty makes a War:
For when, last Night, I to Joves *Pallace went,*
(The brightest part of all the Firmament)
Instead of all those Gods, whose thick resort
Fill'd up the presence of the Thund'rer's Court;
There Jove *and* Juno *all forsaken sate,*
Pensive, like Kings in their declining State:
Yet (wanting Pow'r) they would perserve the show,
By hearing Pray'rs from some few Men below:
Mortals to Jove *may their Devotions pay;*
The Gods themselves to Proserpine *do Pray.*
To Sicily *the Rival pow'rs resort;*
'Tis Heav'n where ever Ceres *keeps her Court.*
Phœbus *and* Mercury *are both at strife,*
The Courtliest of our Gods who want a Wife:
But Venus, *what ere Kindness she pretends.*
Yet, (like all Females, envious of their Friends,)
Has, by my Aid, contriv'd a black design,
The God of Hell should Ravish Proserpine:
Beauties, beware; Venus *will never bear*
Another Venus *shining in her Sphere.*

After *Cupid*'s Speech, *Venus* and *Ceres* descend in the slow Machines; *Ceres* drawn by Dragons, *Venus* by Swans.

After them *Phœbus* and *Mercury* descend in swift Motion. Then *Cupid* turns to *Julia*, and Speaks.

Cup. *The Rival Deities are come to wooe*
A Proserpine, *who must be found below:*
Would you (fair Nymph) become this happy hour,
In name a Goddess as you are in pow'r,
Then to this change the King of Shades will owe
A fairer Proserpine *than Heav'n can show.*

Julia, *first whisper'd by* Amideo, *goes into the Dance*, *perform'd by* Cupid, Phœbus, Mercury, Ceres, Venus, Julia.

Towards the end of the Dance, *Rodorick* in the Habit of *Pluto*, rises from below in a black Chariot all Flaming, and drawn by black Horses; he Ravishes *Julia*, who personated *Proserpine*, and as he is Carrying her away, his Vizard falls off: *Hippolito* first discovers him.

Hip. A Rape, A Rape; 'tis *Rodorick*, 'tis *Rodorick*.
Rod. Then I must have recourse to this:—— [*Draws*.
Jul. Oh Heavens.

[*Don* Manuel *and* Gonsalvo *draw*, *and a Servant*; *the two that Acted* Phœbus *and* Mercury *return to assist* Rodorick, *and are beat back by* Manuel *and a Servant*, *while* Gonsalvo *attacques* Rodorick.

Gons. Unloose thy hold, foul Villain;
Rod. No, I'l grasp her
Ev'n after Death.
Jul. Spare him, or I'l Dye with him:
Gons. Must Ravishers and Villains Live, while I
In Vain implore her Mercy?——
[*Thrusts at him*, *and hurts* Julia *in the Arm*.
Jul. Oh, I am Murther'd!
Gons. Wretched that I am
What have I done? To what strange Punishment
Will you condemn this guilty Hand? and yet
My Eyes were guilty first: for they could look
On nothing else but you; and my Unlucky hand
Too closely follow'd them!——

Enter Manuel again.

Man. The Pow'rs above are just that thou still Liv'st
For me to Kill.
Rod. You'l find no easie task on't
Alone; come both together, I defie you:
Curse on this Disguise, that has betray'd me
Thus cheaply to my Death——
Man. Under a Devils shape thou couldst not be
Disguis'd——
Jul. Then must he Dye?
Yet I'l not bid my *Rodorick* farewell;
For they take leave, who mean to be long absent.

Gons. Hold Sir; I have had Blood enough already,
And muſt not murder *Julia* again
In him she loves: Live, Sir, and thank this Lady.
Rod. Take my Life, and spare my Thanks.
Man. Though you
Forgive him, let me take my juſt Revenge.
Gons. Leave that Distinction to our dull Divines;
That ill I suffer to be done, I do.
Hip. My heart bleeds Tears for him; to see his Virtue
O'rcome so fatally againſt such Odds
Of Fortune and of Love!———
Man. Permit his Death, and *Julia* will be yours:
Jul. Permit it not, and *Julia* will thank you,
Gons. Who ere could think that one kind word from *Julia*
Should be prefer'd to *Julia* her self!
Could any Man think it a greater good
To save a Rival, than possess a Miſtress:
Yet this I do; these are thy riddles Love.
What Fortune gives me I my self Deſtroy;
And feed my Virtue, but to ſtarve my Joy.
Honour sits on me like some heavy Armour,
And with its ſtiff Defence incumbers me:
And yet when I would put it off, it ſticks.
Like *Hercules* his Shirt; heats me at once,
And Poysons me!——
Man. I find my self grow Calm by thy example;
My panting Heart heaves less and less each Pulse;
And all the boyling Spirits scatter from it.
Since thou desir'ſt he should not Dye, he shall not
Till I on Nobler terms can take his Life.
Rod. The next turn may be Yours: Remember *Julia*,
I ow'd this Danger to your Wilfulness;
Once you might easily have been mine, and would not.
[*Exit* Rodorick.
Man. Lead out my Siſter, Friend, her hurt's so small
'Twill scarce diſturb the Ceremony:
Ladies once more your Pardons. [*Leads out the Company*, Exeunt.
[*Manent* Julia, Gonsalvo, Amideo: Gonsalvo *offers his hand*, Julia *pulls back hers*.
Jul. This hand would rise in Bliſters should'ſt thou touch it:
My *Rodorick*'s displeas'd with me, and thou
Unlucky Man the cause; dare not so much
As once to follow me——— [*Exit* Julia.

Gons. Not follow her! Alas she need not bid me!
O how could I presume to take that hand
To which mine prov'd so Fatal!
Nay, if I might, Should I not fear to touch it?
A Murd'rers touch would make it bleed afresh.

Amid. I think, Sir, I could Kill her for your sake.

Gons. Repent that word, or I shall hate thee ſtrangely:
Harsh words from her, like blows from angry Kings,
Though they are meant Affronts, are conſtrued Favours

Hip. Her Inclinations and Aversions
Are both alike unjuſt; and both, I hope,
Too violent to laſt, chear up your Self;
For if I Live (I hope I shall not long) [*Aside*.
She shall be yours.

Amid. 'Twere much more Noble in him
To make a Conqueſt of himself than her.
She ne'r can merit him, and hadſt not thou
A mean low Soul, thou wouldſt not name her to him.

Hip. Poor child, who wouldſt be Wise above thy Years,
Why doſt thou talk like a Philosopher,
Of conquering Love, who art not yet Grown up
To try the force of any Manly passion?
The sweetness of thy Mothers milk is yet
Within thy Veins, not sowr'd and turn'd by Love.

Gons. Thou haſt not Field enough in thy Young breaſt,
To entertain such Storms to ſtruggle in.

Amid. Young as I am, I know the pow'r of Love,
Its less Disquiets, and its greater Cares,
And all that's in it, but the Happiness.
Truſt a Boys word, Sir, if you please, and take
My Innocence for Wisdome; Leave this Lady;
Cease to perswade your Self you are in Love,
And you will soon be freed: Not that I wish
A thing so noble as your Passion, loſt
To all the Sex; beſtow it on some other;
You'l find many as Fair, though none so Cruel.
Would I could be a Lady for your sake.

Hip. If I could be a Woman with a wish,
You should not be without a Rival long,

Amid. A Cedar of your Stature would not cause
Much Jealousie.

Hip. More than a Shrub of yours.

Gons. How eagerly these Boys fall out for nothing!

Tell me *Hippolito*, wert thou a Woman,
Who would'st thou be?
Hip. I would be *Julia*, Sir,
Because you Love her.
Amid. I would not be She,
Because she Loves not you.
Hip. True, *Amideo*:
And therefore I would wish my self a Lady,
Who I am sure does Infinitely love him.
Amid. I hope that Lady has a Name:———
Hip. She has;
And she is call'd *Honoria*, Sister to
This *Julia*, and bred up at *Barcellona*.
Who loves him with a Flame so pure and noble,
That did she know his Love to *Julia*,
She would beg *Julia* to make him happy.
Gons. This startles me!
Amid. Oh Sir, believe him not;
They Love not truly, who on any terms
Can part with what they Love.
Gons. I saw a Lady
At *Barcellona* of what Name I know not,
Who next to *Julia* was the fairest Creature
My Eyes did ere behold: but how cam'st thou
To know her?
Hip. Sir, some other time I'l tell you.
Amid. It could not be *Honoria* whom you saw,
For, Sir, she has a Face so very Ugly,
That if she were a Saint for Holiness,
Yet no Man would seek Virtue there.
Hip. This is the lying'st Boy, Sir; I am sure
He never saw *Honoria*; for her Face
'Tis not so bad to fright any Man;
None of the Wits have Libell'd it.
Amid. Don *Rodorick's* Sister, *Angellina*, does
So far exceed her in the Ornaments
Of Wit and Beauty, though now hid from sight,
That like the Sun (ev'n while Eclips'd) she casts
A Yellowness upon all other Faces.
Hip. I'll not say much of her; but only this,
Don *Manuel* saw not with my Eyes, if e'r
He Lov'd that *Flanders* shape, that Lump of Earth
And Flegm together.

Amid. You have often seen her
It seems by your Description of her Person:
But I'l maintain on any *Spanish* ground,
What ere she be, yet she is far more worthy
To have my Lord her Servant, than *Honoria.*
Hip. And I'l maintain *Honoria*'s right against her
In any part of all the World.
Gons. You go
Too far, to Quarrel on so slight a Ground.
Hip. O pardon me, my Lord, it is not slight:
I must confess I am so much concern'd
I shall not bear it long.
Amid. Nor I, assure you.
Gons. I will believe what both of you have said,
That *Honoria*, and *Angellina*
Both equally are Fair.
Amid. Why did you name
Honoria first?
Gons. And since you take their parts so eagerly,
Henceforth I'l call you by those Ladies Names:
You, my *Hippolito*, shall be *Honoria*;
And you my *Amideo*, *Angellina.*
Amid. Then all my Services, I wish may make
You kind to *Angellina*, for my sake.
Hip. Put all my Merits on *Honoria*'s score,
And think no Maid could ever love you more. *Exeunt.*

Act the Fourth.

Scene First.

Manuel, Solus.

THUS I provide for others Happiness,
And lose my Own: 'Tis true, I cannot blame
Thy hatred *Angellina*, but thy silence.
Thy Brother's hatred made thine just; but yet
'Twas cruel in thee not to tell me so.
Conquest is noble when an Heart stands out;
But mine which yielded, how could'st thou betray?
That heart of which thou could'st not be depriv'd,
By any force of pow'r beside thine own;

Like Empires to that Fatal height arriv'd,
They must be Ruin'd by themselves alone.
My guarded Freedome cannot be a prize
To any scornful Face a second time.
For thy Idea like a Ghost would rise,
And fright my Thoughts from such another Crime.

Enter a Servant *with a Letter.*

Man. From whom?
2. *Ser.* Sir, the Contents will soon resolve you. [*He reads.*
Man. Tell *Rodorick* he has prevented me
In my Design of sending to him first.
I'l meet him Single at the time and place;
But for my Friend tell him he must excuse me:
I'l hazard no Man in my Quarrel, but [*Exit* Mess.
My self alone:———Who's within there?

Enter a Servant.

Go call my Sister, and *Gonsalvo* hither. [*Exit* Servant.
'Twas push'd so far, that like two Armies, we
Were drawn so closely up we could not part
Without ingagement:——But they must not know it.

Enter Julia, Gonsalvo, Amideo.

I have some Business calls me hence, and know not
When I shall return: But e'r I go,
That pow'r I have by my Dead Fathers will
Over my Sister, I bequeath to you: [*To* Gonsalvo.
She and her Fortunes both be firmly Yours;
And this when I Revoke, let Cowardise
Blast all my Youth, and Treason taint my Age.
Gons. Sir,———
Man. Nay, good, no thanks, I cannot stay.—— [*Exit* Manuel.
Gons. There's something more than ordinary in this:
Go *Amideo*, quickly follow him,
And bring me word which way he takes.
Amid. I go, Sir. [*Exit* Amideo.
Gons. Madam, *When you implore the Pow'rs divine,* [*Julia* kneels.
You have no Pray'rs in which I will not joyn,
Though made against my Self. [Kneels with her.
Jul.———————————*In vain I sue,*
Unless my Vows may be Conveigh'd by you.
Gons. *Conveigh'd by me!*———*My ill success in Love*

Shews me too sure I have few Friends above.
How can you fear your just desires to want?
When the Gods pray, they both request and grant.
Jul. *Heav'n has resign'd my Fortune to your hand*
If you, like Heav'n, th' Afflicted understand.
Gons. *The Language of th' Afflicted is not new;*
Too well I learnt it when I first saw you.
Jul. *In spight of me, you now command my Fate;*
And yet the vanquish'd seeks the Victors hate:
Ev'n in this low Submission, I declare,
That had I Pow'r, I would renew the Warr.
I'm forc'd to stoop, and 'twere too great a blow
To bend my Pride, and to deny me too.
Gons. *You have my Heart; dispose it to your will;*
If not, you know the way to use it ill.
Jul. *Cruel to me, though Kind to your desert,*
My Brother gives my Person, not my Heart:
And I have left no other means to sue,
But to you only to be freed from you.
Gons. *From such a Sute how can you hope success,*
Which giv'n, destroys the Givers happiness?
Jul. *You think it equal you should not resign*
That pow'r you have; yet will not leave me mine:
Yet on my will I have the Pow'r alone,
And since you cannot move it, move your Own.
Your Worth and Virtue my esteem may win,
But Womens passions from themselves begin;
Merit may be, but Force still is in vain.
Gons. *I would but Love you, not your Love constrain;*
And though your Brother left me to command,
He plac'd his Thunder in a gentle hand.
Jul. *Your Favour from constraint has set me free*
But that secures not my Felicity;
Slaves, who, before, did cruel Masters serve,
May fly to Desarts, and in Freedome starve.
The noblest part of Liberty they loose,
Who can but shun, and want the Pow'r to choose.
Gons. *O whither would your Fatal reasons move!*
You court my Kindness to destroy my Love.
Jul. *You have the Pow'r to make my Happiness,*
By giving that which you can ne'r possess:
Gons. *Give you to* Rodorick*? there wanted yet*
That Curse to make my Miseries compleat.

Jul. *Departing Misers bear a Nobler mind;*
They, when they can enjoy no more, are Kind:
You, when your Love is Dying in despair,
Yet want the Charity to make an Heir.
Gons. *Though hope be Dying, yet it is not Dead;*
And Dying people with small Food are fed.
Jul. *The greatest kindness Dying friends can have,*
Is to dispatch them when we cannot save.
Gons. *Those Dying people, could they Speak at all;*
That pity of their Friends would Murder call.
For Men with Horrour dissolution meet;
The Minutes, ev'n of painfull Life are sweet.
Jul. *But I'm by Pow'rfull inclination led;*
And Streams turn seldome to their Fountain head.
Gons. *No, 'tis a Tide which carries you away;*
And Tides may turn though they can never stay.
Jul. *Can you pretend to Love, and see my Grief*
Caus'd by your Self, yet give me no relief?
Gons. *Where's my Reward?*
Jul. *The honour of the Flame.*
Gons. *I loose the Substance then, to gain the Name.*
Jul. *I do too much a Mistress's pow'r betray;*
Must Slaves be won by Courtship to Obey?
Thy Disobedience does to Treason rise,
Which thou, like Rebells, wouldst with Love disguise.
I'l Kill my Self, and if thou canst deny
To see me Happy, thou shalt see me Dye.
Gons. *O stay! I can with less Regret bequeath*
My love to Rodorick, *than you to Death:*
And yet——————
Jul. *What new Objections can you find?*
Gons. *But are you sure you never shall be Kind?*
Jul. *Never.*
Gons. *What never!*
Jul. *Never to remove.*
Gons. *Oh fatal Never to Souls damn'd in Love!*
Jul. *Lead me to* Rodorick.
Gons. *If it must be so!*
Jul. *Here, take my Hand, swear on it thou wilt go.*
[He kisses her Hand.
Gons. *Oh balmy Sweetness! but 'tis lost to me,*
Like Food upon a Wretch condemn'd to Dye:
Another, and I Vow to go:——*one more;*

If I Swear often I shall be forswore.
Others against their Wills may haste their Fate;
I only Toyl to be unfortunate:
More my own Foe than all my Stars could prove;
They give her Person, but I give her Love.
I must not trust my Self.————*Hippolito.*

Enter Hippolito.

Hip. My Lord!
Gons. Quickly go find Don *Rodorick* out:
Tell him the Lady *Julia* will be Walking
On the broad Rock that lies beside the Port,
And there expects to see him instantly.
In the mean time I'l call for *Amideo.*
Jul. You'l keep your promise to *Don Rodorick.*
Gons. Madam, *Since you bring Death I welcome it;*
But to his Fortune not his Love submit——— [*Exit* Gonsalvo.
Hip. *I dare not ask what I too fain would hear:*
But, like a tender Mother, Hope and Fear;
My equal Twins, my equal care I make; [*Aside.*
And keep Hope quiet least that Fear should wake. [*Exit* Hippolito.
Jul. So, now I'm firmly at my own Dispose;
And all the Lets, my Virtue caus'd, remov'd:
Now *Rodorick* I come——

Enter Gonsalvo *again.*

Gons. Madam, My Boy's not yet return'd.
Jul. No matter, wee'l not stay for him.
Gons. Pray make not too much haste. [*Exeunt* Julia, Gonsalvo.

Scene the Second.

Enter Don Rodorick, *and* Servant.

Rod. Have you bespoke a Vessel as I bid you?
Serv. I have done better; for I have employ'd
Some, whom I know this Day to seize a Ship;
Which they have done; Clapping the Men within her
All under Hatches, with such speed and silence,
That though she Rides at Anchor in the Port
Among the rest, the Change is not discover'd.

Rod. Let my beſt Goods and Jewels be Embarqued
With secrecy: wee'l put to Sea this Night.
Have you yet found my Siſter, or her Woman?
Serv. Neither Sir; but in all probability
She is with *Manuel.*
Rod. Would God the meaneſt Man in *Alicante*
Had *Angellina* rather than Don *Manuel.*
I never can forgive, much less forget
How he (the younger Souldier) was preferr'd
To that Command of Horse which was my due;
Serv. And after that, by force Disseiz'd you of
Your Quarters———
Rod. Should I meet him sev'n Years hence
At th' Altar, I would Kill him there:———I had
Forgot to tell you the Design we had;
To carry *Julia* by force away
Will now be needless; Shee'l come to the Rock
To see me, you unseen shall ſtand behind,
And carry her into the Vessel.
Serv. Shall I not help you to dispatch Don *Manuel?*
Rod. I neither doubt my Valour, nor my Fortune:
But if I Dye, revenge me: presently
About your business; I muſt to the Rock
For fear I come too late. [*Exeunt severally.*

Scene the Third.

Through a Rock is discover'd a Navy of Ships Riding at a diſtance.

Enter Amideo.

Amid. Thus far unseen by *Manuel,* I have trac'd him:
He can be gone no farther than the Walk
Behind the Rock; I'l back and tell my Maſter.

Enter Hippolito *at the other end.*

Hip. This is the place where *Rod'rick* muſt expect
His *Julia*: ——How! *Amideo* here!
Amid. Hippolito!
Hip. This were so fit a time
For my Revenge; had I the Courage, now:
My Heart swells at him, and my Breath grows short,

But whether Fear or Anger choaks it up,
I cannot tell.
Amid. He looks so Ghaſtfully,
Would I were paſt him; yet I fear to try it,
Because my mind mis-gives me he will ſtop me.
B' your leave *Hippolito*.
Hip. Whether so faſt?
Amid. You'l not presume to hinder my Lord's business?
He shall know it.
Hip. I'l make you sure, before,
For telling any Tales: Do you remember
Since you defended *Angellina*'s Beauty
Againſt *Honoria*'s; nay, and would maintain it.
Amid. And so I will do ſtill; (I muſt feign Courage [*Aside.*
There is no other way.)
Hip. I'l so revenge
That Injury, (if my Heart fails me not.)
Amid. Come, confess truly, for I know it fails you.
What would you give to avoid Fighting now?
Hip. No, 'tis your Heart that fails.
Amid. I scorn the Danger;
Yet, what Compassion on your Youth might do
I cannot tell; and therefore do not work
Upon my Pity; for I feel already
My ſtout Heart melts.
Hip. Oh! Are you thereabout?
Now I am sure you fear; and you shall Fight.
Amid. I will not Fight.
Hip. Confess then *Angellina*
Is not so Fair as is *Honoria*.
Amid. I do confess; now are you satisfied?
Hip. There's more behind; confess her not so worthy
To be belov'd; nor to possess *Gonsalvo*
As Fair *Honoria* is.
Amid. That's somewhat hard:
Hip. But you muſt do't or Dye.
Amid. Well, Life is sweet;
She's not so worthy: now let me be gone.
Hip. No, never to my Maſter; Swear to quit
His service, and no more to see his Face.
Amid. I fain would save my Life, but that which you
Propose, is but another Name to Dye.
I cannot Live without my Maſter's sight.

Hip. Then you must Fight with me for him.
Amid. I would
Do any thing with you, but Fighting for him.
Hip. Nothing but that will serve.
Amid. Lay by our Swords
And I'l scratch with you for him.
Hip. That's not Manly.
Amid. Well, since it be so, I'l Fight:—Unbutton.
[Hippolito *unbuttons slowly*.
How many Buttons has he? I'l be one
Behind him still. [*Aside*.
[*unbuttons one by one after him*.] Hippolito *makes more haste*.
You are so Prodigal; if you Lov'd my Master
You would not tear his Doublet so:——How's this!
Two swelling Breasts! a Woman, and my Rival!
The Stings of Jealousie have giv'n me Courage
Which Nature never gave me:
Come on thou vile Dissembler of thy Sex;
Expect no mercy; either thou or I
Must dye upon this spot: Now for *Gonsalvo*——
Sa———Sa——
Hip. This courage is not counterfeit; Ah me!
What shall I do? for pity, gentle Boy——
Amid. No pity; such a Cause as ours
Can neither give nor take it: If thou yield'st
I will not spare thee; therefore fight it out. [*Tears open his Doublet*.
Hip. Death to my Hopes! a Woman! and so rare
A Beauty that my Lord must needs Doat on her.
I should my Self if I had been a Man:
But as I am, her Eyes shoot Death at me.
Amid. Come, have you said your Pray'rs?
Hip. For thy Confusion
Thou Ravenous Harpy, with an Angel's face;
Thou art Discover'd, thou too Charming Rival;
I'l be reveng'd upon those fatal Eyes.
Amid. I'l tear out thine.
Hip. I'l bite out hungry morsels
From those plump Cheeks, but I will make 'um thinner.
Amid. I'd beat thee to the Blackness of a Moor,
But that the Features of thy Face are such;
Such Damnable, invincible good Features,
That as an *Ethiop* thou would'st still be Lov'd.
Hip. I'l quite unbend that black Bow o'r thine Eyes;

I'l Murther thee, and *Julia* shall have him.
Rather than thou.
Amid. I'l Kill both thee and her
Rather than any one but I shall have him.
Hip. Come on, thou Witch,
Amid. Have at thy Heart thou Syren.
[*They draw, and Fight awkardly, not coming near one another.*
Amid. I think I paid you there.
Hip. O ſtay a little
And tell me in what Corner of thy Heart
Gonsalvo lies, that I may spare that place:
Amid. He lies in the laſt drop of all my Blood,
And never will come out, but with my Soul.
Hip. Come, come, we Dally;
Would one of us were Dead, no matter which. [*They Fight nearer.*

Enter Don Manuel.

Man. The pretty Boys that serv'd *Gonsalvo*, Fighting!
I come in time to save the Life of one.
[Hippolito *gets* Amideo *down in Closing*: Manuel *takes away the Swords.*
Hip. For goodness sake hinder not my Revenge.
Amid. The Noble *Manuel* has sav'd my Life:
Heav'ns, how unjustly have I hated him! [*Aside.*
Man. What is it, gentle Youths that moves you thus?
I cannot tell what Causes you may find;
But truſt me, all the World, in so much sweetness,
Would be to seek where to begin a Quarrel:
You seem the little *Cupids* in the Song,
Contending for the Honey-bagg.
Hip. 'Tis well
You'r come; you may prevent a greater mischief:
Here 'tis *Gonsalvo* has appointed *Rodorick*———
Man. To Fight?
Hip. What's worse; to give your Siſter to him.
Won by her Tears, he means to leave her free,
And to redeem her Misery with his:
At leaſt I so Conjecture.
Man. 'Tis a doubtfull
Problem; either he Loves her Violently,
Or not at all.
Amid. You have betray'd my Maſter:—— [*To* Hippolito, *Aside.*

Hip. If I have Injur'd you, I mean to give you
The satisfaction of a Gentlewoman—

Enter Gonsalvo, *and* Julia.

Man. Oh they are here; now I shall be resolv'd.
Jul. My Brother *Manuel*! what Fortune's this!
Man. I'm glad I have prevented you.
Gons. With what
Variety my Fate torments me still!
Never was Man so Dragg'd along by Virtue;
But I must follow her.
Jul. Noble *Gonsalvo*,
Protect me from my Brother.
Gons. Tell me, Sir,
When you bestow'd your Sister on me, did not
You give her freely up to my dispose?
Man. 'Tis true, I did; but never with intent
You should restore her to my Enemy.
Gons. 'Tis past; 'tis done: She undermin'd my Soul
With tears; as Banks are Sapp'd away by streams.
Man. I wonder what strange Blessing she expects
From the harsh Nature of this *Rodorick;*
A Man made up of Malice and Revenge.
Jul. If I possess him I may be unhappy;
But if I lose him I am surely so.
Had you a Friend so desperately Sick,
That all Physitians had forsook his Cure;
All Scorch'd without, and all Parch'd up within,
The Moisture that maintain'd consuming Nature
Lick'd up, and in a Feaver fry'd away;
Could you behold him Beg, with Dying eyes
A glass of Water, and refuse it him
Because you knew it Ill for his Disease?
When he would Dye without it, how could you
Deny to make his Death more easie to him?
Man. Talk not to me of Love, when Honour suffers;
The Boys will Hiss at me.
Gons. I suffer most:
Had there been choice, what would I not have chose?
To save my Honour I my Love must lose:
But promises once made are past debate,
And Truth's of more necessity than Fate.
Man. I scarce can think your promise absolute;

There might some way be thought on, if you would
To keep both her, and it.
Gons. No, no, my promise was no trick of State:
I meant to be made truly Wretched first.
And then to Dye; and I'l perform them both.
Man. Then that Revenge I meant on *Rodorick*
I'l take on you. [*Draws*.
Gons———I draw with such Regret
As Merchants throw their Wealth into the Sea,
To save their sinking Vessels from a Wrack.
Man. I find I cannot lift my Hand against thee:
Do what thou wilt; but let not me behold it, *Goes off a little way*.
I'l cut this Gordian Knot I cannot loose:
To keep his promise, *Rodorick* shall have her,
But I'l return and rescue her by force;
Then giving back what he so Franckly gave,
At once my Honour and his Love I'l save. [*Exit* Manuel.

Enter Rodorick.

Rod. How! *Julia* brought by him?—Who sent for me?
Gons. 'Twas I
Rod. I know your business then; 'tis Fighting.
Gons. You'r mistaken; 'tis something that I fear:
Rod. What is't?
Gons. Why,——'twill not out: Here take her
And deserve her; but no thanks;
For fear I should consider what I give,
And call it back———
Jul. O my dear *Rodorick*!
Gons. O cruel *Julia*!
For pity shew not all your Joy before me;
Stifle some part of it one Minute longer
Till I am Dead.
Jul. My *Rodorick* shall know
He ows his *Julia* to you; thank him, Love;
In faith I take it Ill you are so slow.
Rod. You know he has forbid me; and beside
Hee'l take it better from your Mouth than mine;
All that you do must needs be pleasing to him:
Jul. Still sullen and unkind!
Rod. Why then in short,
I do not understand the benefit:

Gons. Not, to have *Julia* in thy free Possession?
Rod. Not brought by you; not of another's leaving:
Jul. Speak softly *Rodorick:* let not these hear thee;
But spare my Shame for the ill Choice I made
In loving thee.
Rod. I will speak Loud, and tell thee,
Thou com'st, all Cloy'd and tyr'd with his Embraces,
To proffer thy pall'd Love to me: his Kisses
Do yet bedew thy Lips; the very Print
His Arms made round thy Body, yet remains.
Gons. O Barb'rous Jealousie!
Jul. 'Tis an harsh word,
I am too Pure for thee; but yet I love thee:
Offers to take his Hand.
Rod. Away, foul Impudence.
Gons. Madam, you wrong
Your Virtue thus to clear it by Submission.
Jul. Whence grows this boldness, Sir? did I ask you
To be my Champion?
Rod. He chose to be your Friend, and not your Husband:
Left that Dull part of Dignity to me;
As often the worst Actors play the Kings.
Jul. This Jealousie is but excess of Passion,
Which grows up, Wild, in every Lovers breast;
But changes Kind when Planted in an Husband.
Rod. Well, what I am, I am; and what I will be,
When you are mine, my Pleasure shall determine.
I will receive no Law from any Man.
Jul. This strange unkindness of my *Rodorick*,
I owe to thee, and thy unlucky Love;
Henceforth go lock it up within thy Breast;
'Tis only harmless while it is conceal'd,
But opened spreads Infection like a Vault,
Go, and my Curse go with thee:——
Gons. I cannot go till I behold you Happy:——
———Here, *Rodorick*, receive her on thy Knees;
Use her with that respect which thou would'st pay
Thy Guardian Angel if he could be seen.
———Do not provoke my Anger by refusing——
I'l watch thy least Offence to her; each Word,
Nay, every sullen Look:——
And as the Devils who are Damn'd to Torments,
Yet have the Guilty Souls their Slaves to punish:

So under me, while I am Wretched, thou
Shalt be Tormented———
Rod. Would'st thou make me the Tenant of thy Lust;
To Toyl, and for my Labour take the Dreggs,
The Juicy Vintage being left for thee?
No; She's an Infamous, leud Prostitute;
I loath her at my Soul;
Gons. I can forbear
No longer; Swallow down thy Lye, foul Villain.
[*They fight, off the Stage,* Exeunt.
Jul. Help, Help!
Amid. Here is that Witch whose fatal Beauty
Began the Mischief; She shall pay for all. [*Goes to Kill* Julia.
Hip. I hate her for it more than thou canst do;
But cannot see her Dye my Master loves.
[*Goes between with her Sword.*

Enter Gonsalvo, *following* Rodorick; *who Falls.*

Rod. So, now I am at rest:——
I feel Death rising higher still, and higher,
Within my Bosom; every Breath I fetch
Shuts up my Life within a shorter compass:
And like the Vanishing sound of Bells grows less
And less each Pulse, till it be lost in Air. [*Swoons away.*
Gons. Down at your Feet, much injur'd Innocence,
I lay that Sword, which——
Jul. Take it up again,
It has not done its work till I am Kill'd:
For ever, ever, thou hast Robb'd me of
That Man, that only Man whom I could Love:
Dost thou thus Court thy Mistress? thus Oblige her?
All thy Obligements have been Fatal yet,
Yet the most Fatal now would most Oblige me.
Kill me:———yet I am Kill'd before in him.
I lie there on the Ground; Cold, cold, and Pale:
That Death I Dye in *Rodorick* is far
More pleasant than that Life I live in *Julia*——
——See how he stands———when he is bid dispatch me!
How Dull! how Spiritless! that Sloath possest
Thee not, when thou didst kill my *Rodorick.*
Gons. I'm too Unlucky to Converse with Men:
I'l pack together all my Mischiefs up,
Gather with care each little remnant of 'um,

That none of 'um be left behind: Thus loaded,
Fly to some Desart, and there let them loose,
Where they may never prey upon Mankind.
But you may make my Journey shorter:———Take
This Sword; 'twill show you how:——

Jul. I'l gladly set you on your way: [*Takes his Sword.*

Enter three of Rodorick's *Servants.*

1. Make haste; He's now Unarm'd; we may with ease
Revenge my Masters Death.

Jul. Now these shall do it.

Gons. I'l Dye by none but you———

Hip. O here, take my Sword, Sir.

Amid. He shall have mine. [*Both give their Swords to* Gonsalvo.

Enter Manuel.

Man. Think not of Death,
Wee'l Live and Conquer. [*They beat them off.*

Man. These Fellows, though beat off, will strait return
With more; we must make haste to save our selves.

Hip. 'Tis far to th' Town,
And ere you reach it you will be Discover'd.

Gons. My Life's a burden to me, were not *Julia*'s
Concern'd; but as it is, she being present
Will be found accessary to his Death.

Man. See where a Vessel lies, not far from Shore;
And near at hand a Boat belonging to her;
Let's haste Aboard, and what with Pray'rs and Gifts
Buy our Concealment there:——Come *Julia.*

Gons. Alas, She Swoons away upon the Body.

Man. The Night grows on apace; Wee'l take her in
Our Arms and bear her hence.

[*Exeunt* Gonsalvo, *and the Boys with* Manuel, *carrying* Julia.

The Servants *enter again.*

1. They are all gone, we may return with Safety:
Help me to bear the Body to the Town.

2. He Stirs, and Breaths a little; there may be
Some hope.

3. The Town's far off, and th' Evening cold,
Let's carry him to th' Ship.

1. Hast then away.
Things once resolv'd are ruin'd by Delay. [*Exeunt.*

Act the Fifth.

Enter a Pyrat, *and the* Captain.

The Scene lying in a Carrack.

Pyr. WElcome a Ship-board, *Captain*, you ſtaid long:
Capt. No longer than was necessary for shifting Trades;
To change me from a *Robber* to a *Pyrat*.
Pyr. There's a fair Change wrought in you since Yeſter-day
Morning; then you Talk 't of nothing but Repentance, and
Amendment of Life.
Capt. 'Faith I have consider'd better on't:
For conversing a whole Day together with honeſt Men,
I found 'um all so Poor and Beggarly, that a civil
Person would be asham'd to be seen with 'um.
But you come from *Don Rodorick*'s Cabin; what
Hopes have you of his Life?
Pyr. No danger of it, only loss of Blood
Had made him Faint away; he call'd for you:
Capt. Well, are his Jewels and his Plate brought in?
Pyr. They are; when Hoyſt we Sails?
Capt. At the firſt break
Of Day: When we are got out clear, wee'l seize
On *Rod'rick* and his Men: They are not many,
But fear may make 'um Desp'rate.
Pyr. We may take 'um,
When they are laid to Sleep.
Capt. 'Tis well advis'd.
Pyr. I forgot to tell you, Sir, that a little before *Don Rod'rick*
Was brought in, a company of Gentlemen (pursu'd
It seems by Juſtice) procur'd our Boat to Row 'um
Hither: Two of 'um carried a very fair Lady betwixt 'um,
Who was either Dead, or Swoonded.
Capt. Wee'l Sell 'um altogether to the *Turk*,
(At leaſt I'l tell him so.) [*Aside.*
Pyr. Pray, Sir, let us reserve the Lady to our own uses;
It were a shame to good Catholiques to give her up
To Infidells.
Capt. Don *Rod'rick's* Door opens, I'l speak to him.
[*The Scene draws and discovers the* Captains *Cabin*; Rodorick *on a Bed, and two* Servants *by him.*]
Capt. How is it with the brave *Don Rodorick?*
Do you want any thing?

Rod. I have too much
Of that I would not, Love;
And what I would have, that I want, Revenge.
I must be set Ashore.
Capt. That you may, Sir;
But our own Safety must be thought on first.
[*One enters and Whispers the* Captain.
Capt. I come:——Sennor, think you are Lord here, and command
All freely. [*Exit* Captain *and* Pyrat.
Rod. He does well to bid me think so: I am of opinion
We are fall'n into Hucksters hands.
1. *Serv.* Indeed he talk'd Suspitiously enough;
He half denied to Land us.
Rod. These, *Pedro*,
Are your Confiding men.———
2. *Serv.* I think 'um still so.
Rod. Would I were from 'um.
2. 'Tis impossible
T' attempt it now; you have not Strength enough
To Walk.
Rod. That Venture must be mine; wee'r lost
If we stay here to morrow.
2. I hope better.
1. One whom I saw among 'um, to my knowledge
Is a notorious Robber.
2. He look'd so like a Gentleman, I could not know him then.
Rod. What became of *Julia* when I fell?
2. We left her Weeping over you, till we
Were beaten off; but She, and those with her
Were gone when we return'd.
Rod. Too late I find
I wrong'd her in my Thoughts; I'm every way
A wretched Man:——
Something we must resolve on e'r we Sleep;
Draw in the Bed, I feel the Cold. [*Bed drawn in*, Exeunt.

Scene the Second.

Enter Gonsalvo, Manuel, Hippolito, Amideo.

Hip. Nay, 'tis true; for Peeping through a Chink
I saw *Don Rod'rick* lying on a Bed,

Not Dead, as we suppos'd, but only Hurt;
So waited on as spoke him Master here.
Man. Was there ever so Fatal an adventure?
To fly into that very Ship for refuge
Where th' only Person we would shun, Commands!
This Mischief is so strange it could not happen,
But was the Plot and Juggle of our Fate
To free it Self, and cast the Blame on us.
Gons. This is not yet our Fortune's utmost Malice;
The Gall remains behind: This Ship was that
Which Yester-day was mine; I can see nothing
Round me, but what's familiar to my Eyes,
Only the Persons new; which makes me think
'Twas seiz'd upon by *Rod'rick*, to revenge
Himself on me.
Man. 'Tis wonderfull indeed.
Amid. The only comfort is, we are not known,
For when we Enter'd it was Dark.
Hip. That comfort
Is of as short continuance as the Night,
The Day will soon discover us.
Man. Some way must be invented to get out.
Hip. Fair *Julia*, sadly pining by her Self,
Sits on her Bed; Tears falling from her Eyes
As silently as Dews in dead of Night.
All we consult of must be kept from her:
That moment that she knows of *Rodorick*'s Life
Dooms us to certain Death.
Man. 'Tis well consider'd.
Gons. For my part, were not you and she concern'd,
I look on my Life, like an Estate
So charg'd with Debts, it is not worth the keeping.
We cannot long be undiscover'd by them;
Let us then Rush upon them on the suddain,
(All hope of Safety plac'd in our despair)
And gain quick Victory, or speedy Death.
Man. Consider first th' impossibility
Of the attempt; four Men, and two poor Boys
(Which added to our Number make us Weaker)
Against ten Villains, more resolv'd for Death
Than any ten among our Holiest Priests.
Stay but a little longer, till they all
Disperse to rest within their several Cabins,

Then more securely we may Set upon them,
And Kill them half before the rest can Wake:
By this means too, the Boys are usefull for us;
For they can cut the Throats of Sleeping men.
Hip. Now have I the greatest Temptation in the World to reveal
Thou art a Woman. [*To* Amideo.
Amid. If 'twere not for thy Beauty, my Master should know
What a Man he keeps. [*To her.*
Hip. Why should we have Recourse to desp'rate ways,
When safer may be thought on?
'Tis like giving the extream Unction
In the begining of a Sickness:
Can you imagine to find all Asleep?
The wicked Joy of having such a Booty
In their Possession, will keep some Awake:
And some, no doubt, will watch with Wounded *Rod'rick.*
Amid. What would your Wisdome now propose?
Hip. To say
That some of us are Sea-sick; (your Complexion
Will make th' excuse for us who are less Fair:)
So by good words and promises procure
We may be set Ashore, e'er Morning come.
Amid. O the deep Reasons of the grave *Hippolito!*
As if 'twere likely in so Calm a Season
We should be Sick so soon; or if we were,
Whom should we choose among us to go tell it?
For who ere Ventures out must needs be known;
Or if none knew us, can you think that Pyrats
Will let us go upon such easie terms
As promising Rewards?——Let me advise you.
Hip. Now we expect an Oracle.
Amid. Here are Bundles
Of Canvas and of Cloath you see lye by us,
In which one of us shall Sow up the rest,
Only some Breathing place, for Air, and Food;
Then call the Pyrats in, and tell them, we
For fear had Drown'd our selves: And when we come
To the next Port, find means to bring us out.
Hip. Pithily spoken!
As if you were to bind up Marble Statues,
Which only bore the shapes of Men without,
And had no need of ever easing Nature.
Gons. There's but one way left, that's this:

You know the Rope by which the Cock-boat's ty'd,
Goes down by th' Stern, and now we are at Anchor,
There sits no Pylot to discover us;
My Counsel is, to go down by the Ladder,
And being once there, unloose, and Row to Shore.
Man. This, without doubt, were beſt; but there lies ever
Some one or more within the Boat to watch it.
Gons. I'l slide down firſt, and run the Venture of it;
You shall come after me, if there be need,
To give me Succour.
Man. 'Tis the only way.
Gons. Go in to *Julia* then, and firſt prepare her
With knowledge of the Pyrats, and the danger
Her Honour's in among such Barb'rous people.
Man. Leave it to me.
Amid. *Hippolito* and *Julia*,
My Rivals like two pointed Rocks appear;
And I through both muſt to *Gonsalvo* ſteer. [*Aside*.
[*Exeunt all but* Hippolito.
Hip. As from some ſteep and dreadfull Precipice,
The frighted Travellour caſts down his Eyes,
And sees the Ocean at so great a diſtance,
It looks as if the Skies were sunk below him;
Yet if some Neighb'ring shrub (how weak soe'r)
Peeps up, his willing Eyes ſtop gladly there,
And seem to ease themselves, and reſt upon it:
So in my Desp'rate ſtate, each little comfort
Peserves me from despair; *Gonsalvo* ſtrove not
With greater care to give away his *Julia*,
Than I have done to part with my *Gonsalvo*,
Yet neither brought to pass our hatefull wish:
Then we may meet, since different ways we move,
Chasing each other in the Maze of Love. [*Exit* Hippolito.

Scene the Third.

Enter Don Rodorick, *carried by two* Servants.

1. *Serv*. It was the only way that could be thought on,
To get down by the Ladder to the Boat.
2. You may thank me for that Invention,

Rod. What a noise is here! when the least Breath's
As Dang'rous as a Tempest.
2. If any of those Rogues should hear him talk,
In what a case were we?
Rod. O Patience, patience!
This Ass brays out for Silence.

Enter at the other end, Manuel, *leading* Julia; Gonsalvo, Hippolito, Amideo.

Gons. Hark! what Noise is that? Go softly.
They meet on the middle of the Stage.
Rod. Who's here! I am betray'd; and nothing grieves me
But I want strength to Dye with honour.
Jul. Rod'rick!
Is it thy Voice my Love? Speak and resolve me
Whether thou Liv'st, or I am Dead with thee?
Man. Kill him, and force our way.
Rod. Is *Manuel* there?
Hold up my Arm that I may make one thrust
At him before I Dye.
Gons. Since we must fall,
Wee'l Sell our Lives as dearly as we can.
1. *Serv.* And wee'l defend our Master to the last. [*Fight.*

Enter Pyrats, *without their* Captain.

1. *Pyr.* What's the meaning of this Uproar? Quarrelling
Amongst your selves at Midnight?
2. *Pyr.* We are come in a fit time to decide the difference.
Man. Hold Gentlemen, wee'r equally concern'd,
[*To* Rodorick's Servants.
We for our own, you for your Masters safety;
If we joyn forces we may then resist 'um,
If not, both Sides are ruin'd.
1. *Serv.* We agree;
Gons. Come o'r on our Side then. [*They joyn.*
1. *Pyr.* A mischief on our Captain's Drowsiness;
Wee'r lost for want of him. [*They Fight.*
Gons. Dear Madam, get behind, while you are safe [*To* Julia.
We cannot be o'rcome.
[*They drive off the* Pyrats, *and follow them off.* Rodorick *remains on the Ground.*
Rod I had much rather my own Life were lost
Than *Manuel*'s were preserv'd.———

Enter the Pyrats *retreating before* Gonsalvo, *&c.*

1. *Pyr.* All's lost; they Fight like Devils, and our Captain
Yet Sleeping in his Bed.
2. Here lies Don *Rod'rick*;
If we must Dye, wee'l not leave him behind. [*Goes to Kill him.*
Jul. O spare my *Rod'rick*'s Life, and in exchange
Take mine; I put my Self within your Pow'r,
To Save or Kill.
1. *Pyr.* So, here's another Pawn
For all our Safeties.
Man. Heav'n! What has she done?
Gons. Let go the Lady, or expect no mercy:
The least drop of her Blood is worth all yours
And mine together.
1. *Pyr.* I am glad you think so:
Either deliver up your Sword, or mine
Shall pierce her Heart this moment.
Gons. Here, here, take it.
Man. You are not Mad to give away all hopes [Manuel *holds him.*
Of safety and defence, from us, from her,
And from your self at once!
Gons. When she is Dead
What is there worth Defending
Man. Will you trust
A *Pyrat*'s promise sooner than your Valour?
Gons. Any thing, rather than see her in Danger.
1. *Pyr.* Nay, if you dispute the matter!
[*Holds his Sword to her Breast.*
Gons. I yield, I yield; Reason to Love must bow:
Love, that gives Courage, can make Cowards too.
[*Gives his Sword.*
Jul. O strange effect of a most Generous Passion!
Rod. His Enemies themselves must needs admire it.
Man. Nay, if *Gonsalvo* makes a Fashion of it,
'Twill be Valour to Dye tamely. [*Gives his.*
Hip. I am for Dying too with my dear Master.
Amid. My life will go as eas'ly as a Flies;
The least Fillip does it in this Fright.
1. *Pyr.* One call our Captain up: Tell him, he deserves little of the Booty.
Jul. It has so much prevail'd upon my Soul,
I ever must acknowledge it. [*To* Gonsalvo.

Rod. *Julia* has reason, if she Love him; yet
I find I cannot bear it. [*Aside.*
Gons. Say but you Love me; I am more than Paid.
Jul. You ask that only thing I cannot give;
Were I not *Rod'ricks* first, I should be yours;
My violent Love for him, I know is faulty,
Yet Passion never can be plac'd so ill,
But that to change it is the greater Crime:
Inconstancy is such a Guilt, as makes
That very Love suspected which it brings;
It brings a Gift, but 'tis of ill-got Wealth,
The spoils of some forsaken Lovers heart:
Love alter'd once, like Blood let out before,
Will lose its Virtue, and can Cure no more.
Gons. In those few Minutes which I have to live
To be call'd yours is all I can enjoy;
Rodorick receives no Prejudice by that;
I would but make some small Acquaintance here,
For fear I never should enquire you out
In that new World which we are going to.
Amid. Then I can hold no longer;———you desire
In death to be call'd Hers; and all I wish
Is Dying to be Yours.
Hip. You'l not discover? [*Aside.*
Amid. See here the most unfortunate of Women,
That *Angellina* whom you all thought lost;
And lost she was indeed; when she beheld
Gonsalvo first.
All. How *Angellina*!
Rod. Ha!
My Sister?
Amid. I thought to have fled Love in flying *Manuel*,
But Love pursu'd me in *Gonsalvo's* Shape;
For him I Ventur'd all that Maids hold dear,
Th' opinion of my Modesty, and Virtue,
My loss of Fortune, and my Brothers Love.
For him I have expos'd my Self to Dangers,
Which, (great themselves, yet) greater would appear,
If you could see them through a Womans fear:
But why do I my Right by Dangers prove?
The greatest argument for Love, is Love:
That Passion, *Julia*, while he Lives, denies,
He should refuse to give her when he Dyes:

Yet grant he did his Life to her bequeath,
May I not claim my share of him in Death?
I only begg, when all the Glory's gone,
The heatless Beams of a departing Sun.
Gons. Never was Passion hid so modeſtly,
So generously reveal'd.
Man. Wee'r now a chain of Lovers linck'd in Death;
Julia goes firſt, *Gonsalvo* hangs on her,
And *Angellina* holds upon *Gonsalvo*,
As I on *Angellina*.
Hip. Nay, here's *Honoria* too:———
You look on me with wonder in your Eyes,
To see me here, and in this ſtrange disguise.
Jul. What new Miracle is this? *Honoria*!
Man. I left you with my Aunt at *Barcellona*,
And thought ere this you had been Married to
The old Rich man, Don *Estevan de Gama*:
Hip. I ever had a ſtrange Aversion for him;
But when *Gonsalvo* Landed there, and made
A kind of Courtship, (though it seems in Jeaſt)
It serv'd to Conquer me, which *Estevan*
Perceiving, preſt my Aunt to haſte the Marriage.
What should I do? my Aunt importun'd me
For the next Day: *Gonsalvo*, though I Lov'd him,
Knew not my Love; nor was I sure his Courtship
Was not th' effect of a bare Gallantry.
Gons. Alas! how griev'd I am, that slight address
Should make so deep impressions on your Mind
In three Days time.
Hip. That accident in which
You sav'd my Life, when firſt you saw me, caus'd it.
Though now the Story be too long to tell;
Howe'r it was, hearing that Night you lay
Aboard your Ship, thus as you see Disguis'd,
In Cloaths belonging to my Youngeſt Nephew,
I rose e'r Day, resolv'd to find you out,
And, if I could, procure to wait on you
Without discovery of my Self; but Fortune
Croſt all my Hopes.
Gons. It was that dismal Night
Which tore my Anchor up, and toſt my Ship
Paſt hope of Safety, many Days together,
Untill at length it threw me on this Port.

Hip. I will not tell you what my Sorrows were
To find you gone; but there was now no help.
Go back again I durst not: But, in fine,
Thought best, as fast as my weak Leggs would bear me
To come to *Alicant*, and find my Sister,
Unknown to any else: But being neer
The City, I was seiz'd upon by Thieves,
From whom you Rescu'd me; the rest you know.
Gons. I know too much indeed for my Repose.

Enter Captain.

Capt. Do you know me?
Gons. Now I look better on thee,
Thou seem'st a greater Villain than I thought thee.
Jul. 'Tis he.
Hip. That Bloody wretch who Robb'd us in
The Woods.
Gons. Slave! Dar'st thou lift thy Hand against me?
Dar'st thou touch any one whom he protects;
Who gave thee Life? But I accuse my self,
Not thee: The Death of all these Guiltless persons
Became my Crime that Minute when I spar'd thee.
Capt. It is not all your Threats can alter me
From what I have resolv'd.
Gons. Begin then first
With me.
Capt. I will, by laying here my Sword.
[*Lays his Sword at* Gonsalvo'*s feet.*
All. What means this suddain Change?
Capt. 'Tis neither new, nor suddain: from that time
You gave me Life, I watch'd how to Repay it;
And *Rod'rick*'s Servant gave me speedy means
T' effect my Wish: For telling me, his Master
Meant a Revenge on you, and on Don *Manuel*,
And then to seize on *Julia*, and depart:
I proffer'd him my Aid to seize a Vessel;
And having by Enquiry found out Yours,
Acquainted first the Captain with my purpose,
To make a seeming Mast'ry of the Ship.
Man. How durst he take your Word?
Capt. That I secur'd
By letting him give notice to the Ships

That lay about: This done, knowing the place
You were to Fight on was behind the Rock;
Not far from thence, I, and some chosen Men,
Lay out of Sight, that if foul Play were offer'd,
We might prevent it.
But came not in; because when there was need,
Don *Manuel*, who was nearer, ﬅept before me.

Gons. Then the Boat which seem'd
To lye by chance, Hulling not far from Shore,
Was plac'd by your Direction there?

Capt. It was.

Gons. You'r truly Noble; and I owe much more
Than my own Life and Fortunes to your worth.

Capt. 'Tis time I should reﬅore their Liberty
To such of Yours as yet are seeming Pris'ners.
I'l wait on you again. [*Exit* Captain.

Rod. My Enemies are happy, and the Storm
Prepar'd for them, muﬅ break upon my Head.

Gons. So far am I from Happiness, Heav'n knows
My Griefs are Doubled:———
I ﬅand Ingag'd in hopeless Love to *Julia*;
In Gratitude to these:
Here I have giv'n my Heart, and here I owe it.

Hip. Dear Maﬅer, trouble not your Self for me;
I ever made your Happiness my own;
Let *Julia* witness with what Faith I serv'd you,
When you employ'd me in your Love to her.
I gave your Noble heart away, as if
It had been some light Gallant's, little worth:
Not that I Lov'd you less than *Angellina*,
But my Self less than You.

Gons. Wonder of Honour,
Of which my Own was but a fainter Shadow,
When I gave *Julia*, whom I could not keep.
You fed a Fire within, with too rich Fuel,
In giving it your Heart to Prey upon;
The sweeteﬅ Off'ring that was ever Burnt
Since laﬅ the *Phœnix* Dy'd.

Hip. If *Angellina* knew, like me, the Pride
Of Noble minds, which is to give, not take;
Like me she would be Satisfy'd, her Heart
Was well beﬅow'd, and ask for no return.

Amid. Pray let my Heart alone; you'l use it as

The Gipsies do our Money;
If they once Touch it, they have Pow'r upon't.

Enter the Servant, *who appear'd in the first Act with* Gonsalvo.

Serv. O my dear Lord, *Gonsalvo de Peralta*!
Rod. De Peralta, said you? You amaze me
Gons. Why, do you know that Family in *Sevil?*
Rod. I am my self the elder Brother of it.
Gons. Don Rod'rick de Peralta!
Rod. I was so,
Untill my Mother Dy'd, whose Name *de Sylva*
I chose, (our Custom not forbidding it)
Three years ago, when I return'd from *Flanders*:
I came here to possess a fair Estate
Left by an Aunt; her Sister, for whose sake,
I take that Name, and lik'd the place so well,
That never since I have return'd to *Sevil*.
Go. 'Twas then that change of Name which caus'd my Letters.
All to miscarry: What an happy Tempest
Was this, which would not let me rest at *Sevil*,
But Blew me farther on to see you here.
Amid. Brother, I come to claim a Sisters share;
But you'r too near me, to be nearer now.
Gons. In my room let me beg you to receive
Don Manuel.
Amid. I take it half unkindly,
You give me from your Self so soon; *Don Manuel*
I know is Worthy, and but Yester-day
Preserv'd my Life; but it will take some time
To change my Heart:
Man. I'l watch it patiently, as *Chymists* do
Their golden Birth; and when 'tis Chang'd, receive it
With greater care than they the rich Elyxir.
Just passing from one Vial to another.
Rod. Julia is still my Brother's, though I loose her.
Gons. You shall not loose her; *Julia* was born
For none but you;
And I for none but my *Honoria*:
Julia is Yours by Inclination;
And I by Conquest am *Honoria*'s.
Hon. 'Tis the most glorious one that e'r was made:
And I no longer will dispute my Happiness.
Rod. Julia, you know my peevish Jealousies;

I cannot promise you a better Husband
Than you have had a Servant.
Jul. I receive you
With all your Faults.
Rod. And think, when I am Froward,
My sullen Humour punishes it self;
I'm like a Day in *March*, sometimes o'r-cast
With Storms, but then the after Clearness is
The greater: The worst is, where I Love most,
The Tempest falls most heavy.
Jul. Ah, Ah! What a little time to Love is Lent?
Yet half that time is in Unkindness spent.
Rod. That you may see some hope of my Amendment,
I give my Friendship to *Don Manuel*, ere
My Brother asks, or he himself desires it.
Man. I'l ever Cherish it.
Gons. Since for my Sake you become Friends, my care
Shall be to keep you so: You, Captain, shall
Command this Carrack, and with her my Fortunes:
You, my *Honoria*, though you have an Heart
Which *Julia* left, yet think it not the worse;
'Tis not worn out, but Polish'd by the wearing.
Your merit shall her Beauties pow'r remove;
Beauty but gains, Obligement keeps our Love.

[*Exeunt.*

THE INDIAN QUEEN

A TRAGEDY

THE INDIAN QUEEN

SOURCE

SINCE it has already been shown in the Introduction that the romantic scenario and some episodes which Dryden and Howard have utilized to form the ground-work of *The Indian-Queen* were suggested by "*The History of* Zelmatida, *heire to the Empire of the* Incas, *and of the Princesse* Isatida," which is related at ample length by Garruca, the servant of Zelmatida, in *Polexandre*, the most celebrated romance of Marin de Roy, seigneur de Gomberville (1600-1674), it were superfluous to traverse the same ground again here, and it will suffice to remind ourselves that *Polexandre* was first published at Paris, 1632-1638; and translated into English by William Browne, folio, 1647.

It should be noted that there are few attempts at local colour, and scant reference to Indian customs. Sir Robert Howard, following the romance, obviously recked nothing of the vast distance between Peru and Mexico, and it must not be forgotten that so far from those two countries having engaged in war there was no communication of any kind between them. Yet indeed he was right, for these things are of no account at all in a heroic play or mediaeval romance. They are not to be deemed absurd, or even incongruities. We accept them, and sometimes such dreamland vision will lend a touch of fantasy, ay, even beauty to the poet's theme.

THEATRICAL HISTORY

T*HE Indian-Queen* was produced at the Theatre Royal in January, 1663–4. The performance was arranged on a scale of the greatest possible magnificence; special scenery was painted; original and elaborate effects were devised; all costumes were new made of the richest material; and in fine no expense was grudged to display the golden splendours of a legendary Peru and a fabled Mexico. The title-rôle was played by Ann Marshall, the leading tragedienne of the day. The result proved an overwhelming success that for many a long year remained a tradition in the theatre.

On Monday, 25 January, a command performance was given, and there is extant "A Warrant to the Master of the Great Wardrobe to prouide and deliuer to Thomas Killigrew Esqr to the value of forty pounds in silkes for to cloath the Musick for the play called the Indian Queene to bee acted before their Maties Jan. 25th 1663."

In her famous novel *Oroonoko, the Royal Slave*, 12mo., 1688, Mrs. Behn writes of Surinam: "We trade for Feathers, which they order into all Shapes, make themselves little short Habits of 'em, and glorious Wreaths for their Heads, Necks, Arms and Legs, whose Tinctures are unconceivable. I had a Set of these presented to me, and I gave 'em to the *King's Theatre;* it was the Dress of the *Indian Queen*, infinitely admir'd by Persons of Quality; and was inimitable."

Since J. Smith's rare and beautiful mezzotint "The Indian-Queen," usually printed as a portrait of Mrs. Bracegirdle, has more than once been taken by writers, who are insufficiently equipped, to be a representation of Zempoalla in the Howard-Dryden tragedy, it is worth remarking that this picture shows us Mrs. Bracegirdle as the "*Indian Queen*, call'd *Semernia*, belov'd by *Bacon*," the heroine of Mrs. Behn's drama *The Widdow Ranted; or, The History of Bacon in Virginia*, produced at Drury Lane in the winter of 1689, when Mrs. Bracegirdle created this effective rôle.

On Wednesday, 27 January, 1663–4, Pepys on his way to Covent Garden observed "the streete full of coaches at the new play, 'The Indian Queene'; which for show, they say, exceeds 'Henry the Eighth,'" which had been produced at Lincoln's Inn Fields with a world of pomp and display. On being told by Mr. Pierce that the King had visited the theatre to see *The Indian-Queen*, and upon his friend's further commending the play "for a very fine thing," Pepys, on Monday, 1 February, immediately after dinner took his wife to the Theatre Royal, "and there saw 'The Indian Queene' acted; which indeed is a most pleasant show, and beyond my expectation; the play good, but spoiled with the ryme, which breaks the sense. But above my expectation most, the eldest Marshall did do her part most excellently well as I ever heard woman in my life; but her voice not so sweet as Ianthe's [Mrs. Betterton]; but, however, we came home mightily contented."

On the following Friday, 5 February, Evelyn notes: "I saw *The Indian Queen* acted, a tragedy well written, so beautiful with rich scenes as the like had never been seen here, or haply (except rarely) elsewhere on a mercenary theatre."

The Indian-Queen continued to be a great attraction for wellnigh twenty years until such time as the members of the original cast had already left or were on the point of retiring from the stage. Ann Marshall was acclaimed by the Town as unapproachable in Zempoalla. Pepys, it is true, on Saturday, 27 June, 1668, records that he went with his wife and Deb "to the King's playhouse, and saw 'The Indian Queene,' but do not doat upon Nan Marshall's acting therein, as the world talks of her excellence therein." This criticism, however, may be discounted, inasmuch as he was vexed and weary, with failing sight, ever haunted by the dread of blindness.

In 1689–90 there was a revival of *The Indian-Queen*, which probably had not been given since the Union of the two Companies. This met with such success that plans were formed for a production upon an elaborate scale, and Betterton who had invented the machinery and decorations for *Albion and Albanius*, Dorset Garden, June, 1685, was entrusted therewith. However, it appears that this did not come to pass, since in the reply of the Patentees, 10 December, 1694, to the actors' petition, it is stated that Betterton "has had 50^{ls} for his care and trouble to gett up ye Indian Queen tho he hath not yet done itt."

Attention, none the less, had been called to this drama, and taking advantage of the fashion which turned plays into so-called "Operas", whereof *Dioclesian*, produced at Dorset Garden in 1690, and the magnifical *The Fairy Queen*, produced at the same theatre in 1692, are such notable examples, an adapter presently set to work upon *The Indian-Queen*. In 1695 there was published "The Songs in the Indian Queen: As it is now Compos'd into an Opera. By Mr. *Henry Purcell*. Composer in Ordinary to his Majesty." The exact date of the issue of the book, which was not advertised in either the *London Gazette* or *The Post-Boy*, is not known. However, a very important manuscript, now in the British Museum (*E Libris Juliani Marshall*, 1880–1, AD. MS. 31,449), not only gives the words of the operatic version, but also the whole of the music, partly in Purcell's autograph, together with the names of the principal players. This cast, by the absence of any of the actors who seceded with Betterton to Lincoln's Inn Fields in April, 1695, points conclusively to the production having taken place after that event. In this case the music must have been one of Purcell's very latest compositions. It is remarkable, too, that the music to the Masque of Hymen with which the work ends is by Daniel Purcell, and as Henry Purcell died in November, 1695, it is probable that he was prevented by illness from finishing the opera, which was accordingly completed by his brother. The cast is as follows: Ynca of Peru, Mills; Montezuma, Powell; Acacis, Harland; Garrucca, Disney; The God of Dreams, Bowen; Ismeron, Leveridge; Zempoalla, Mrs. Knight; Orazia, Mrs. Rogers. To Amexia no name is given, and Traxalla, although of great importance, is strangely enough omitted from the list of characters. The main change is that the dialogue is considerably curtailed to allow of the ample musical divertissements. From the printed songs we know that in the Prologue the Indian Boy was sung by Freeman, and Quevira (the Indian Girl) by "the Boy," young Jemmy Bowen, the son of the actor. Fame in Act II was sung by Freeman; in Act III the duet "Ah, how happy are we" by Freeman and Church; the song "I attempt from love's sickness to fly" by Mrs. Letitia Cross, who also sang "They tell us that your mighty powers" in Act IV. The conjurer's song, sung by Leveridge, "You twice ten hundred deities," appears in Book IV of *Deliciae Musicae*, 1696, and with several of the other songs was included in *Orpheus Britannicus*. The songs from the Masque of Hymen (Daniel Purcell) are printed in the scarce "First Book of the Second Volume" of *Deliciae Musicae*, the title-page of which states that it contains "The Additional Musick to the *Indian Queen*, by Mr. *Daniel Purcell*, as it is now Acted at *His Majesties Theatre*." This book appeared early in 1695–6: its publication is advertized in the *Post-Boy*, Feb. 29 –March 3 of that year. The opera became exceedingly popular, and Giles Jacob in his notice of *The Indian-Queen* says: "This Play is writ in Heroick Verse, and was acted with very great Applause. It has since been converted to an Opera, and been represented with the like Success."

At Drury Lane, 19 July, 1715, *The Indian-Queen* was announced as "not acted 10 years". This is certainly a loose and inaccurate assertion, and in any case it refers to the original tragedy, not the opera. The piece was given three times during the summer season. George Powell probably played Montezuma.

2 April, 1706, at Drury Lane, *The Indian-Queen* was given for the benefit of Mills.

THE INDIAN QUEEN

A tragedy, *The Indian Empress, or, The Conquest of Peru,* produced at the Little Theatre in the Haymarket on Wednesday, 17 February, 1731, would from its title certainly seem to be founded upon *The Indian-Queen,* but as the later drama was never printed this must remain a matter of mere conjecture.

PROLOGUE

As the Musick plays a soft Air, the Curtain rises softly, and discovers an *Indian* Boy and Girl sleeping under two Plantain-Trees; and when the Curtain is almost up, the Musick turns into a Tune expressing an Alarm, at which the Boy wakes and speaks.

Boy. *WAke, wake,* Quevira; *our soft Rest must cease,*
And fly together with our Country's Peace;
No more must we sleep under Plantain shade,
Which neither Heat could pierce, nor Cold invade;
Where bounteous Nature never feels decay,
And op'ning Buds drive falling Fruits away.
Que. *Why should men quarrel here, where all possess*
As much as they can hope for by success?
None can have most, where Nature is so kind
As to exceed Man's Use, though not his Mind.
Boy. *By ancient Prophesies we have been told*
Our World shall be subdu'd by one more old;
And see that World already's hither come.
Que. *If these be they, we welcom then our Doom.*
Their Looks are such, that Mercy flows from thence,
More gentle than our Native Innocence.
Boy. *Why should we then fear these are Enemies,*
That rather seem to us like Deities?
Que. *By their protection let us beg to live;*
They came not here to Conquer, but Forgive.
If so, your Goodness may your Pow'r express;
And we shall judg both best by our success.

DRAMATIS PERSONÆ

T*HE* Ynca *of* Peru.
Montezuma *his General.*
Acacis *Son to* Zempoalla.
Traxalla *General to* Zempoalla.
Garrucca, *a faithful Subject to* Amexia.
The God of Dreams.
Ismeron, *one of their Prophets, a Conjurer.*
Officers and Souldiers.
Peruvians *and* Mexicans.
Priests.

Amexia, *the lawful Queen of* Mexico.
Zempoalla, *the Usurping* Indian *Queen.*
Orazia, *Daughter to the* Ynca.
Attendants, of Ladies.

THE

INDIAN-QUEEN

ACT I. SCENE I.

Enter Ynca, Orazia, Montezuma, Acasis, *Prisoners, with* Peruvians.

Ynca. THrice have the *Mexicans* before us fled,
Their Armies broke, their Prince in Triumph led;
Both to thy valour, brave young man, we owe;
Ask thy Reward, but such as it may show
It is a King thou hast oblig'd, whose Mind
Is large, and like his Fortune unconfin'd.
Mont. Young and a Stranger to your Court I came,
There by your Favour rais'd to what I am:
I Conquer, but in right of your great fate,
And so your Arms, not mine, are fortunate.
Ynca. I am impatient, till this debt be paid,
Which still encreases on me while delay'd;
A Bounteous Monarch to himself is kind;
Ask such a Guift as may for ever bind
Thy service to my Empire, and to me.
Mont. What can this Guift he bids me ask him be!
Perhaps he has perceiv'd our mutual fires,
And now with ours, wou'd crown his own Desires;
'Tis so, he sees my Service is above
All other payments but his Daughters Love. [*Aside.*
Ynca. So quick to merit, and to take so slow?
I first prevent small wishes, and bestow
This Prince, his Sword and Fortunes to thy hand;
He's thine unask'd; Now make thy free demand.
Mont. Here, Prince, receive this Sword, as only due
[*Gives* Acacis *his Sword.*
To that excess of Courage shown in you.
When you without demand, a Prince bestow,
Less than a Prince to ask of you, were low.
Ynca. Then ask a Kingdom; say where thou wilt Reign.
Mont. I beg not Empires, those my Sword can gain;
But for my past and future Service too,
What I have done, and what I mean to do;

For this of *Mexico* which I have won,
And Kingdoms I will Conquer yet unknown;
I only ask from fair *Orazia*'s Eyes
To reap the Fruits of all my Victories.
1. *Peru*. Our *Ynca*'s Colour mounts into his Face.
2. *Peru*. His Looks speak Death.
Ynca. Young Man of unknown Race,
Ask once again, so well thy merits plead;
Thou shalt not die for that which thou hast said:
The price of what thou ask'st, thou dost not know;
That Gift's too high.
Mont. And all besides too low.
Ynca. Once more I bid thee ask.
Mont. Once more I make
The same demand.
Ynca. The *Ynca* bids thee take
Thy choice, what Towns, what Kingdoms thou wouldst have.
Mont. Thou giv'st me only what before I gave.
Give me thy Daughter.
Ynca. Thou deserv'st to die.
O thou great Author of our Progeny,
Thou glorious Sun, dost thou not blush to shine,
While such base Blood attempts to mix with thine!
Mont. That Sun thou speakst of did not hide his face,
When he behold me Conquering for his Race.
Ynca. My Fortunes gave thee thy success in Fight;
Convey thy boasted Valour from my sight;
I can o'recome without thy feeble aid.
[*Exit* Ynca, Orazia, Peruvians.
Mont. And is it thus, my Services are paid!
Not all his Guards—— [*Offers to go*, Acaces *holds him*.
Aca. Hold, Sir.
Mont. Unhand me.
Aca. No, I must your Rage prevent,
From doing what your Reason wou'd repent;
Like the vast Seas, your Mind no limits knows,
Like them lies upon to each Wind that blows.
Mont. Can a Revenge that is so just, be ill?
Aca. It is *Orazia*'s Father you wou'd kill.
Mont. *Orazia*, how that name has charm'd my Sword?
Aca. Compose these wilde Distempers in your breast;
Anger, like madness, is appeas'd by rest.
Mont. Bid children sleep, my spirits boil too high;

But since *Orazia*'s Father must not dye,
A nobler vengeance shall my actions guide,
I'le bear the conquest, to the conquered side,
Until this *Ynca* for my friendship sues,
And proffers that his pride does now refuse.

Aca. Your honor is oblig'd to keep your trust.

Mont. He broke that Bond in ceasing to be just.

Aca. Subjects to Kings shou'd more obedience pay.

Mont. Subjects are bound, not strangers to obey.

Aca. Can you so little your *Orazia* prize,
To give the conquest to her Enemies?
Can you so easily forego her sight?
I that hold liberty more dear then light:
Yet to my freedom, shou'd my chains prefer,
And think it were well lost to stay with her.

Mont. How unsuccessfully I still o'recome,
I brought a Rival, not a Captive home;
Yet I may be deceiv'd; but 'tis too late
To clear those doubts, my stay brings certain fate. [*aside*.
Come, Prince, you shall to *Mexico* return,
Where your sad Armies do your absence mourn;
And in one Battle I will gain you more
Than I have made you lose in three before.

Aca. No, *Montezuma*, though you change your side,
I as a Prisoner am by Honor ty'd.

Mont. You are my Prisoner, and I set you free.

Aca. 'Twere baseness to accept such liberty.

Mont. From him that conquer'd you, it shou'd be sought.

Aca. No, but from him, for whom my Conqueror fought.

Mont. Still you are mine, his gift has made you so.

Aca. He gave me to his General, not his Foe.

Mont. How poorly have you pleaded Honors Laws?
Yet shun the greatest in your Countreyes Cause.

Aca. What succour can the Captive give the Free?

Mont. A needless Captive is an enemy,
In painted Honor you wou'd seem to shine;
But 'twou'd be clouded, were your wrongs like mine.

Aca. When choller such unbridled power can have,
Thy vertue seems but thy revenges slave:
If such injustice shou'd my Honor stain,
My aid wou'd prove my Nations loss, not gain.

Mont. Be cousen'd by thy guilty honesty,
To make thy self thy Countreyes enemy.

Aca. I do not mean in the next fight to ſtain
My Sword in blood of any Mexican,
But will be present in the fatal ſtrife
To guard *Orazia*'s, and the *Yncas* Life.
Mont. *Orazia*'s life fond man: firſt guard thy own,
Her safety she muſt owe to me alone.
Aca. Your Sword that does such wonders cannot be,
In an ill cause, secure of victory.
Mont. Hark, hark. [*noise of trampling*.
Aca. What noise is this invades my ears?
Fly, *Montezuma*, fly; the guards are near
To favour your retreat: I'le freely pay
That life, which you so frankly gave this day.
Mont. I muſt retire, but those that follow me,
Pursue their deaths, and not their victory. [*Ex*. Mont.
Aca. Our quarrels kinder, then our friendships prove:
You for my Countrey Fight, I for your Love.

Enter Ynca *and Guards*.

Ynca. I was to blame, to leave this mad man free,
Perhaps he may revolt to th' Enemy,
Or ſtay, and raise some fatal mutiny.
Aca. Stop your pursuits, for they muſt pass through me.
Ynca. Where is the slave?
Aca. Gon.——
Ynca. Whither?
Aca. O're the plain.——
Where he may soon the Camp, or City gain.
Ynca. Curse on my dull neglect—
And yet I do less cause of wonder find,
That he is gone, then that thou ſtayeſt behinde.
Aca. My treatment since you took me was so free,
It wanted but the name of liberty.
I with less shame can ſtill your Captive live,
Then take that freedom which you did not give.
Ynca. Thou brave young man, that haſt thy years out-done,
And losing Liberty haſt Honor won:
I muſt my self thy Honors Rival make,
And give that freedom which thou wo'dſt not take.
Go and be safe.——
Aca. But that you may be so—
Your dangers muſt be paſt before I go.
Fierce *Montezuma* will for fight prepare,

And bend on you the fury of the War,
Which by my presence I will turn away,
If Fortune gives my *Mexicans* the Day.
Ynca. Come then, we are alike to honor juſt,
Thou to be truſted thus, and I to truſt.— [*Ex. all.*

Enter Zempoalla, Traxalla, *and Attendants.*

Zemp. O my *Acacis!*
Does not my grief, *Traxalla*, seem too rude,
Thus to press out before my Gratitude
Has paid my debts to you?——yet it does move
My Rage and Grief, to see those Powers above
Punish such men, as if they be Divine,
They know will moſt Adore, and leaſt Repine.
Trax. Those that can only mourn when they are croſt,
May lose themselves with grieving for the loſt.
Rather to your retreated Troops appear,
And let them see a Woman void of fear:
The shame of that may call their Spirits home.
Were the Prince safe, we were not overcom,
Though we retir'd: O his too youthful heat,
That thruſt him where the dangers were so great!
Heaven wanted power his Person to protect,
From that which he had Courage to neglect:
But since he's loſt, let us draw forth, and pay
His Fun'ral Rites in Blood; that we ere they
May in our Fates perform his Obsequies,
And make Death Triumph when *Acacis* dies.
Zemp. That Courage thou haſt shown in Fight seems less
Than this, amidſt Despair to have Excess:
Let thy great deeds force Fate to change her mind;
He that Courts Fortune boldly makes her kind.
Trax. If ere *Traxalla* so successful proves,
May he then say he hopes as well as Loves;
And that aspiring Passion boldly own,
Which gave my Prince his Fate, and you his Throne?
I did not feel Remorse to see his Blood
Flow from the spring of life into a flood;
Nor did it look like Treason, since to me
You were a Sovereign much more great than he.
Zemp. He was my Brother, yet I scorn'd to pay
Nature's mean debts, but threw those bonds away;
When his own Issue did my hopes remove,

Not only from his Empire, but his Love.
You that in all my wrongs then bore a part,
Now need not doubt a place within my heart:
I cou'd not offer you my Crown and Bed,
Till Fame and Envy with long time were dead;
But Fortune now does happily present
Occasions fit to second my intent.
Your Valour may regain the Publick Love,
And make the Peoples Choice their Queens approve. [*Shout.*
Hark, hark, what noise is this that strikes my ear!
Trax. 'Tis not a sound that should beget a fear;
Such Shouts as these have I heard often fly
From Conquering Armies crown'd with Victory.
Zemp. Great God of Vengeance, here I firmly vow,
Make but my *Mexicans* successful now,
And with a thousand Feasts thy flames I'le feed;
All that I take shall on thy Altars bleed;
Princes themselves shall fall, and make thy Shrine,
Dy'd with their blood, in glorious blushes shine.

Enter Messenger.

Trax. How now!——
What News is this that makes thy haste a flight?
Mess. Such as brings Victory without a Fight;
The Prince *Acaces* lives.——
Zemp. Oh, I am blest.——
Mess. Reserve some joy till I have told the rest.
He's safe, and only wants his liberty;
But that great Man that carries Victory
Where ere he goes; that mighty Man by whom
In three set Battels we were overcome;
Ill us'd (it seems) by his ungrateful King,
Does to our Camp his Fate and Valour bring.
The Troops gaze on him, as if some bright Star
Shot to their Aids, call him the God of War:
Whilst he, as if all Conquest did of right
Belong to him, bids them prepare to fight;
Which if they shou'd delay one hour, he swears
He'l leave them to their Dangers or their Fears,
And Shame (which is th' ignoble Cowards choice.)
At this the Army seem'd to have one voice,
United in a shout, and call'd upon
The God-like Stranger, *Lead us, lead us on.*

Make haste, Great Sir, lest you should come too late,
To share with them in Victory or Fate.
Zemp. My Gen'ral go; the Gods be on our side;
Let Valour act, but let Discretion guide. [*Exit* Traxalla.
Great God of Vengeance—
I see thou dost begin to hear me now;
Make me thy Off'ring if I break my Vow. [*Exeunt*.

ACT II. SCENE I.

Enter Ynca, Orazia, *as persued in a Battle*.

Orazia. O Fly, Sir, fly, like torrents your swift Foes
Come rowling on.——
Ynca. The Gods can but destroy.
The noblest way to fly, is that death shows;
I'le court her now, since victory's grown coy.
Oraz. Death's wing'd to your pursuit, and yet you wait
To meet her——
Ynca. Poor *Orazia*, time and fate
Must once o're take me, though I now shou'd fly.
Oraz. Do not meet death; but when it comes then dye.

Enter three Souldiers.

3. *Sould*. Stand, Sir, and yield your self, and that fair prey.
Ynca. You speak to one unpractis'd to obey.

Enter Montezuma.

Mont. Hold, villains, hold, or your rude lives shall be
Lost in the midst of your own victory:
These I have hunted for; nay do not stare,
Be gone, and in the common plunder share. [*Ex. Sould*.
How different is my Fate, from theirs, whose Fame
From Conquest grows! from Conquest grows my shame.
Ynca. Why do'st thou pause? thou canst not give me back
With fruitless grief, what I enjoyed before,
No more than Seas repenting of a wrack,
Can with a calm our buried wealth restore.
Mont. 'Twere vain to own repentance, since I know
Thy scorn, which did my passions once despise,
Once more would make my swelling anger flow;

Which now ebbs lower than your miseries:
The Gods that in my fortunes were unkinde,
Gave me not Scepters, nor such gilded things;
But whilst I wanted Crowns, inlarg'd my minde
To despise Scepters, and dispose of Kings.

Ynca. Thou art but grown a Rebel by success,
And I that scorn'd *Orazia* shou'd be ty'd
To thee my slave, must now esteem thee less:
Rebellion is a greater guilt then Pride.

Mont. Princes see others faults but not their own;
'Twas you that broke that bond, and set me free:
Yet I attempted not to climb your Throne,
And raise my self; but level you to me.

Oraz. O *Montezuma*, cou'd thy love engage
Thy soul so little, or make banks so low
About thy heart, that thy revenge and rage,
Like suddain floods, so soon shou'd over-flow!
Ye Gods, how much was I mistaken here!
I thought you gentle as the gaulless Dove;
But you as humorsome as windes appear,
And subject to more passions then your Love.

Mont. How have I been betray'd by guilty rage,
Which like a flame rose to so vast a height
That nothing cou'd resist, nor yet asswage,
Till it wrapt all things in one cruel fate,
But I'le redeem my self, and act such things,
That you shall blush *Orazia* was deny'd;
And yet make Conquest, though with wearied wings,
Take a new flight to your now fainting side.

Ynca. Vain man, what foolish thoughts fill thy swell'd mind?
It is too late our ruine to recal;
Those that have once great Buildings undermin'd
Will prove too weak to prop them in their fall.

Enter Traxalla *with the former Souldiers*.

1 *Sould*. See, mighty Sir, where the bold stranger stands,
Who snatch'd these glorious Prisoners from our hands.

Trax. 'Tis the great *Ynca*, seize him as my prey,
To crown the triumphs of this glorious day.

Mont. Stay your bold hands from reaching at what's mine,
If any title springs from victory;
You safer may attempt to rob a shrine,
And hope forgiveness from the Deity.

Enter Acacis.

Trax. O my dear Prince, my joys to see you live
Are more then all that victory can give.
Aca. How are my best endeavors crost by fate!
Else you had ne'er been lost, or found so late.
Hurried by the wilde fury of the fight,
Far from your presence, and *Orazia*'s sight,
I could not all that care and duty show,
Which as your Captive (mighty Prince) I owe.
Ynca. You often have preserv'd our lives this day,
And one small debt with many bounties pay.
But humane actions hang on springs that be
Too small, or too remote for us to see.
My glories freely I to yours resign,
And am your prisoner now, that once were mine.
Mont. These Prisoners Sir are mine by right of War;
And I'le maintain that right, if any dare.
Trax. Yes, I wou'd snatch them from thy weak defence;
But that due reverence which I owe my Prince,
Permits me not to quarrel in his sight,
To him I shall refer his Generals right.
Mont. I knew too well what justice I shou'd finde
From an arm'd Plaintiff, and a Judge so kinde.
Aca. Unkindly urg'd, that I shou'd use thee so;
Thy vertue is my Rival, not my foe;
The Prisoners fortune gave thee shall be thine.
Trax. Would you so great a prize to him resign?
Aca. Shou'd he who boldly for his Prey design'd
To dive the deepest under swelling tides,
Have the less title if he chance to finde
The richest Jewel that the Ocean hides?
They are his due——
But in his vertue I repose that trust,
That he will be as kinde as I am just:
Dispute not my commands, but go with haste,
Rally our men, they may pursue too fast,
And the disorders of the inviting Prey
May turn again the fortune of the day. [*Ex.* Trax.
Mont. How gentle all this Prince's actions be!
Vertue is calm in him, but rough in me.
Aca. Can *Montezuma* place me in his breast?
Mont. My heart's not large enough for such a guest.

Aca. See, *Montezuma*, see, *Orazia* weeps. [Orazia *weeps.*
Mont. Acacis, is he deaf, or waking, sleeps?
He does not hear me, sees me not, nor moves;
How firm his eyes are on *Orazia* fixt!
Gods that take care of men, let not our loves
Become divided by their being mixt.
Aca. Weep not fair Princess, nor believe you are
A Prisoner subject to the chance of War;
Why shou'd you waste the stock of those fair Eyes
That from mankinde can take their liberties?
And you, great Sir, think not a generous mind
To vertuous Princes, dares appear unkind,
Because those Princes are unfortunate,
Since over all men hangs a doubtful fate:
One gains by what another is bereft;
The frugal Deities have only left
A common bank of happiness below,
Maintain'd like nature, by an ebb and flow. [*Ex. omnes.*

Zempoalla *appears seated upon a Throne, frowning upon her Attendants; then comes down and speaks.*

Zemp. No more, you that above your Princes dare proclaim
With your rebellious breath a strangers name.
1. *Peru.* Dread Empress——
Zemp. Slaves, perhaps you grieve to see
Your young Prince glorious, 'cause he sprang from me;
Had he been one of base *Amexia*'s brood,
Your Tongues, though silent now, had then been loud.

Enter Traxalla.

Traxalla, welcome, welcomer to me,
Then what thou bring'st, a Crown and Victory.
Trax. All I have done is nothing, fluttering fame
Now tells no news, but of the Stranger's name,
And his great deeds; 'tis he they cry by whom
Not men, but War it-self is overcome;
Who bold with his success, dares think to have
A Prince to wear his Chains, and be his slave.
Zemp. What Prince——
Trax. The great Peruvian *Ynca*, that of late
In three set Battles was so fortunate,
Till this strange man had power to turn the tide,
And carry conquest unto any side.

Zemp. Wou'd you permit a private man to have
The great Peruvian *Ynca* for his slave!
Shame to all Princes! was it not just now
I made a sacred, and a solemn vow
To offer up (if blest with Victory)
The Prisoners that were took, and they shall dye.
Trax. I soon had snatched from this proud strangers hand
That too great object for his bold demand;
Had not the Prince your Son, to whom I owe
A kinde obedience, judg'd it shou'd be so.
Zemp. I'le hear no more; go quickly take my Guards,
And from that man force those usurpt rewards;
That Prince upon whose ruines I must rise,
Shall be the Gods, but more my sacrifice:
They with my slaves in Triumph shall be tyed,
While my devotion justifies my pride.
Those Deities in whom I place my trust,
Shall see when they are kinde, that I am just. [*Ex*. Zemp.
Trax. How gladly I obey——
There's something shoots through my enliven'd frame,
Like a new soul, but yet without a name:
Nor can I tell what the bold guest will prove,
It must be Envy, or it must be love;
Let it be either, 'tis the greatest bliss
For man to grant himself, all he dares wish;
For he that to himself, himself denies,
Proves meanly wretched, to be counted wise. [*Ex*. Traxal.

Enter Montezuma, Acacis.

Aca. You wrong me, my best friend, not to believe
Your kindeness gives me joy, and when I grieve,
Unwillingly my sorrows I obey,
Showres sometimes fall upon a shining day.
Mont. Let me then share your griefs, that in your fate
Wou'd have took Part——
Aca. Why shou'd you ask me that?
Those must be mine, though I have such excess;
Divided griefs increase, and not grow less.
Mont. It does not lessen Fate, nor satisfie
The Grave, 'tis true, when friends together dye;
And yet they are unwilling to divide.
Aca. To such a friend nothing can be deny'd
You, when you hear my story will forgive

My grief, and rather wonder that I live.
Unhappy in my Title to a Throne,
Since blood made way for my succession:
Blood of an Uncle too, a Prince so free
From being cruel, it taught cruelty.
His Queen *Amexia* then was big with childe;
Nor was he gentler then his Queen was milde:
Th' impatient people long'd for what shou'd come
From such a Father, bred in such a Womb——
When false *Traxalla*, weary to obey,
Took with his life their joyes and hopes away.
Amexia by th' assistance of the night,
When this dark deed was acted, took her flight;
Only with true *Garrucca* for her aid;
Since when, for all the searches that were made,
The Queen was never heard of more: yet still
This Traytor lives, and prospers by the ill:
Nor does my Mother seem to reign alone,
But with this Monster shares the guilt and Throne:
Horror choaks up my words; now you'l believe
Tis just I shou'd do nothing else but grieve.
Mont. Excellent Prince.——
How great a proof of vertue have you shown,
To be concern'd for griefs, though not your own!
Aca. Pray say no more.——

Enter a Messenger hastily.

Mont. How now, whither so fast?
Mess. O Sir, I come too slow with all my haste!
The fair *Orazia*——
Mont. Ha, what do'st thou say?
Mess. *Orazia* with the *Ynca*'s forc'd away
Out of your Tent; *Traxalla* in the head
Of the rude Souldiers, forc'd the door, and led
Those glorious Captives, who on Thrones once shin'd,
To grace the Triumph that is now design'd. [*Ex. Mess.*
Mont. *Orazia* forc'd away! what tempests roul
About my thoughts, and toss my troubled soul?
Can there be Gods to see, and suffer this?
Or does mankinde make his own fate or bliss;
While every good and bad happens by chance,
Not from their orders, but their ignorance—

But I will pull a ruine on them all,
And turn their Triumph to a Funeral.
Aca. Be temperate friend.
Mont. You may as well advise
That I shou'd have less love, as grow more wise.
Aca. Yet ſtay—I did not think to have revealed
A secret which my heart has ſtill concealed;
But in this cause since I muſt share with you,
'Tis fit you know—I love *Orazia* too:
Delay not then, nor waſt the time in words,
Orazia's cause calls only for our Swords.
Mont. That tyes my hand, and turns from thee that rage
Another way; thy blood shou'd else asswage:
The ſtorm on our proud foes shall higher rise,
And changing, gather blackness as it flies:
So when windes turn, the wandering waves obey,
And all the Tempeſt rouls another way.
Aca. Draw then a Rivals Sword, as I draw mine,
And like friends suddenly to part, let's joyn
In this one act, to seek one deſtiny;
Rivals with honor may together die. [*Exeunt.*

ACT III. SCENE I.

Zempoalla *appears seated upon her Slaves in Triumph, and the Indians as to celebrate the Victory, advance in a warlike Dance; in the midſt of which Triumph,* Acacis *and* Montezuma *fall in upon them.*

Zempoalla *descends from her triumphant Throne, and* Acacis *and* Montezuma *are brought in before her.*

Zemp. SHame of my blood, and traytor to thy own,
Born to dishonor, not command a Throne;
Haſt thou with envious eyes my Triumph seen?
Or cou'dſt not see thy Mother in the Queen?
Cou'dſt thou a ſtranger above me prefer?
Aca. It was my Honor made my Duty erre;
I cou'd not see his Prisoners forc'd away,
To whom I ow'd my life, and you the day.
Zemp. Is that young man the Warrior so renown'd?
Mont. Yes, he that made thy men thrice quit their ground.

Do, smile at *Montezuma's* chains; but know,
His valour gave thee power to use him so.
Trax. Grant that it did, what can his merits be,
That sought his vengeance, not our victory?
What has thy bruitish fury gain'd us more,
Than only heal'd the wounds it gave before?
Dye then, for whilst thou liv'st, Wars cannot cease;
Thou may'st bring Victory, but never Peace.
Like a black storm thou roul'st about us all,
E'ne to thy self unquiet till thy fall. [*Draws to kill him.*
Aca. Unthankful villain, hold.
Trax. You must not give
Him succour, Sir.
Aca. Why then I must not live.
Posterity shall ne're report they had
Such thankless fathers, or a Prince so bad.
Zemp. You'r both too bold to will or to deny,
On me alone depends his destiny.
Tell me, audacious stranger, whence cou'd rise
The confidence of this rash enterprize?
Mont. First tell me how you dar'd to force from me
The fairest spoils of my own victory?
Zemp. Kill him—hold, must he dye?—why let him dye;
Whence shou'd proceed this strange diversity
In my resolves?—
Does he command in chains? what wou'd he do
Proud slave, if he were free, and I were so?
But is he bound ye Gods, or am I free?
'Tis love, 'tis love, that thus disorders me:
How pride and love tear my divided soul!
For each too narrow, yet both claim it whole:
Love as the younger must be forc'd away;
Hence with the Captives (General) and convey
To several Prisons that—young man, and this——
——Peruvian woman—
Trax. How concern'd she is!
I must know more.
Mont. Fair Princess, why shou'd I
Involve that sweetness in my destiny?
I cou'd out-brave my death, were I alone
To suffer, but my fate must pull yours on.
My breast is armed against all sence of fear,
But where your image lies, 'tis tender there.

Ynca. Forbear thy saucy love, she cannot be
So low, but ſtill she is too high for thee.
Zemp. Be gone, and do as I command, away.
Mont. I ne're was truly wretched 'till this day.
Orazia. Think half your sorrows on *Orazia* fall,
And be not so unkinde to suffer all:
Patience in cowards is tame hopeless fear,
But in brave mindes a scorn of what they bear.
[*Exit* Ynca, Montezuma, Orazia, Traxalla.
Zemp. What grief is this which in your face appears?
Aca. The badge of sorrow, which my soul ſtill wears.
Zemp. Though thy late actions did my anger move,
It cannot rob thee of a mothers love:
Why shou'dſt thou grieve?—
Grief seldom joyn'd with blooming youth is seen,
Can sorrow be where knowledge scarce has been;
Fortune does well for heedless youth provide,
But wisdom does unlucky age misguide;
Cares are the train of present power and ſtate,
But hope lives beſt that on himself does wait:
O happieſt fortune if well underſtood,
The certain prospect of a future good!
Aca. What joy can Empire bring me, when I know
That all my greatness to your crimes I owe?
Zemp. Yours be the joy, be mine the punishment.
Aca. In vain alas that wish to heaven is sent
For me, if fair *Orazia* muſt not live.
Zemp. Why shou'd you ask me what I cannot give?
She muſt be sacrific'd: Can I beſtow
What to the Gods by former vows I owe?
Aca. O plead not vows; I wish you had not shown
You slighted all things sacred for a Throne.
Zemp. I love thee so, that though fear follow ſtill,
And horrour urges, all that have been ill
I cou'd for thee——
Act o're my crimes agen,—and not repent,
Even when I bore the shame and punishment.
Aca. Cou'd you so many ill acts undertake,
And not perform one good one for my sake?
Zemp. Prudence permits not pity shou'd be shown
To those that rais'd the War to shake my Throne.
Aca. As you are wise, permit me to be juſt;
What Prudence will not venture, Honor muſt;

We owe our Conquest to the strangers Sword,
'Tis just his Prisoners be to him restor'd.
I love *Orazia*, but a nobler way——
Then for my love my Honor to betray.
Zemp. Honor is but an itch in youthful blood,
Of doing acts extravagantly good;
We call that Vertue, which is only heat
That reigns in Youth, till age findes out the cheat.
Aca. Great actions first did her affections move,
And I by greater, wou'd regain her love.
Zemp. Urge not a suit which I must still deny;
Orazia and her Father both shall dye:
Be gone, I'le hear no more——
Aca. You stop your ears——
But though a Mother will not, Heaven will hear;
Like you I vow, when to the Pow'rs divine
You pay her guiltless Blood, I'le offer mine. [*Ex*. Acacis.
Zemp. She dyes, this happy Rival that enjoys
The strangers love, and all my hopes destroyes;
Had she triumph'd, what cou'd she more have done,
Then robb'd the Mother, and enslav'd the Son?
Nor will I at the name of cruel stay,
Let dull successive Monarchs mildly sway:
Their conquering Fathers did the Laws forsake,
And broke the old e're they the new cou'd make.
I must pursue my love—yet love enjoy'd,
Will with esteem that caus'd it first grow less;
But thirst and hunger fear not to be cloy'd,
And when they be, are cur'd by their excess.

Enter Traxalla.

Trax. Now I shall see, what thoughts her heart conceals;
For that which Wisdom covers, Love reveals.
Madam, the Prisoners are dispos'd.
Zemp. They are——
And how fares our young blustering Man of War?
Does he support his chains with patience yet?
Trax. He, and the Princess, Madam.
Zemp. Are they met?—
Trax. No, but from whence is all this passion grown?
Zemp. 'Twas a mistake.
Trax. I finde this rash Unknown

Is dangerous; and if not timely slain,
May plunge your Empire in new Wars again.
Zemp. Thank ye, I shall consider.
Trax. Is that all?—
The Army doat on him, already call
You cruel; and for ought I know, they may
By force unchain, and crown him in a day.
Zemp. You say, I have already had their curse
For his bad usage; shou'd I use him worse?
Trax. Yet once you fear'd his reputation might
Obscure the Princes in the peoples sight.
Zemp. Time will inform us beſt what course to ſteer,
But let us not our sacred vows defer:
The *Ynca*, and his daughter both shall dye.
Trax. He suffers juſtly for the War; but why
Shou'd she share his sad fate? a poor pretence,
That birth shou'd make a crime of innocence.
Zemp. Yet we deſtroy the poisonous Vipers young,
Not for themselves, but those from whom they sprung.
Trax. O no, they die not for their Parents sake,
But for the poisonous seed which they partake;
Once more behold her, and then let her dye,
If in that face or person you can see
But any place to fix a cruelty:
The heavens have clouds, and spots are in the Moon;
But faultless beauty shines in her alone.
Zemp. Beauty has wrought compassion in your minde.
Trax. And you to valour are become as kinde.
To former services there's something due.
Yet be advised—
Zemp. Yes by my self, not you—
Trax. Princes are sacred.
Zemp. True, whilſt they are free;
But power once loſt, farewell their sanctity:
'Tis power to which the Gods their worship owe,
Which, uncontroul'd, makes all things juſt below:
Thou do'ſt the plea of saucy rebels use,
They will be judge of what their Prince muſt chuse:
Hard fate of Monarchs, not allow'd to know
When safe, but as their Subjects tell them so.
Then Princes but like publick pageants move,
And seem to sway because they sit above. [*Ex.* Zemp.
Trax. She loves him; in one moment this new gueſt

Has drove me out from this false womans breast;
They that wou'd fetter Love with constancy,
Make bonds to chain themselves, but leave him free.
With what impatience I her falshood bear!
Yet do my self that which I blame in her;
But Interest in my own Cause makes me see
That Act unjust in her, but just in me. [*Exit* Traxalla.

Ismeron *asleep in the Scene.*

Enter Zempoalla.

Zemp. Ho, *Ismeron*, *Ismeron*.
He stirs not; ha, in such a dismal Cell
Can gentle Sleep with his soft blessings dwell?
Must I feel tortures in a humane brest,
While Beasts and Monsters can enjoy their Rest?
What quiet they possess in sleeps calm bliss!
The Lions cease to roar, the Snakes to hiss,
While I am kept awake—
Only to entertain my Miseries.
Or if a slumber steal upon my Eyes,
Some horrid Dream my lab'ring Soul benums,
And brings Fate to me sooner then it comes.
Fears most oppress when sleep has seiz'd upon
The outward parts, and left the Soul alone.
What envy'd blessing's these curs'd things enjoy!
Next to possess, 'tis pleasure to destroy.
Ismeron; ho *Ismeron*, *Ismeron*. [*Stamps.*
Ism. Who's that with so loud and fierce a call
Disturbs my rest?
Zemp. She that has none at all,
Nor ever must, unless thy powerful Art
Can charm the passions of a troubled heart.
Ism. How can you have a discontented mind,
To whom the Gods have lately been so kind?
Zemp. Their envious kindness how can I enjoy,
When they give Blessings, and the use destroy?
Ism. Dread Empress, tell the cause of all your grief;
If Art can help, be sure of quick Relief.
Zemp. I dream'd before the Altar that I led
A mighty Lion in a twisted thred;
I shook to hold him in so slight a tie,
Yet had not power to seek a remedy:

When in the midst of all my fears a Dove,
With hovering wings, descended from above,
Flew to the Lion, and Embraces spread,
With Wings, like clasping Arms, about his head,
Making that murm'ring noise that cooing Doves
Use in the soft expression of their Loves.
While I, fix'd by my wonder, gaz'd to see
So mild a Creature with so fierce agree,
At last the gentle Dove turn'd from his head,
And pecking try'd to break the slender thred,
Which instantly she sever'd, and releas'd
From that small bond the fierce and mighty Beast,
Who presently turn'd all his rage on me,
And with his Freedom brought my Destiny.
Ism. Dread Empress, this strange Vision you relate
Is big with wonder, and too full of fate
Without the Gods assistance to expound.
In those low Regions where sad Night hangs round
The drowsie Vaults, and where moist Vapors steep
The God's dull brows that sways the Realm of Sleep;
There all th' informing Elements repair,
Swift Messengers of Water, Fire, and Air,
To give account of Actions whence they came,
And how they govern every mortal frame;
How from their various mixture, or their strife,
Are known the Calms and Tempests of our Life:
Thence Souls, when Sleep their Bodys overcom,
Have some imperfect knowledg of their doom.
From those dark Caves those Powers shall strait appear;
Be not afraid whatever shapes they wear.
Zemp. There's nothing thou canst raise can make me start;
A living form can only shake my heart.
Ism. *You twice Ten Hundred Deities,*
To whom we daily Sacrifice;
You Powers that dwell with Fate below,
And see what men are doom'd to do;
Where Elements in discord dwell;
Thou God of Sleep, arise and tell
Great Zempoalla *what strange Fate*
Must on her dismal Vision wait.
Zemp. How slow these Spirits are! Call, make them rise,
Or they shall fast from Flame and Sacrifice.
Ism. Great Empress——

Let not your rage offend what we adore,
And vainly threaten, when we muſt implore.
Sit and silently attend,—
While my powerful Charms I end.

By the croaking of the Toad,
In their Caves that make aboad,
Earthy Dun *that pants for breath,*
With her swell'd sides full of death;
By the Creſted Adders Pride
That along the Clifts do glide;
By thy visage fierce and black;
By the Deaths-head on thy back;
By the twiſted Serpents plac'd
For a Girdle round thy Waſte.
By the Hearts of Gold that deck
Thy Breſt, thy Shoulders, and thy Neck:
From thy sleepy Mansion rise,
And open thy unwilling Eyes,
While bubling Springs their Musick keep,
That use to lull thee in thy sleep.

[*God of Dreams rises.*

God. Seek not to know what muſt not be reveal'd;
Joys only flow where Fate is moſt conceal'd:
Too-buisie Man wou'd find his Sorrows more,
If future Fortunes he shou'd know before;
For by that knowledg of his Deſtiny
He wou'd not live at all, but always die.
Enquire not then who shall from bonds be freed,
Who 'tis shall wear a Crown, and who shall bleed:
All muſt submit to their appointed doom;
Fate and Misfortune will too quickly come:
Let me no more with powerful Charms be preſt,
I am forbid by Fate to tell the reſt. [*The God descends.*

Zemp. Stay Couz'ner, thou that hat'ſt clear truth like light,
And useſt words dark as thy own dull night.
You Tirants Gods do you refuse to free
The Soul you gave from its perplexity?
Why shou'd we in your mercies ſtill believe,
When you can never pity though we grieve?
For you have bound your selves by harsh decrees;
And those, not you, are now the Deities. [*Sits down sad.*

Ism. She droops under the weight of Rage and Care:
You Spirits that inhabit in the Air,

With all your powerful Charms of Musick try
To bring her Soul back to its Harmony.

SONG is suppos'd sung by Aerial-Spirits.

POor Mortals that are clog'd with Earth below
Sink under Love and Care,
While we that dwell in Air
Such heavy Passions never know.
Why then shou'd Mortals be
Unwilling to be free
From Blood, that sullen Cloud,
Which shining Souls does shroud?
Then they'l shew bright,
And like us light,
When leaving Bodies with their Care,
They slide to us and Air.

Zemp. Death on these Trifles: Cannot your Art find
Some means to ease the Passions of the Mind?
Or if you cannot give a Lover reſt,
Can you force Love into a Scornful Breſt?
Ism. 'Tis Reason only can make Passions less; —
Art gives not new, but may the old encrease;
Nor can it alter Love in any Breſt
That is with other flames before possess'd.
Zemp. If this be all your slighted Art can do,
I'le be a Fate both to your Gods and you;
I'le kindle other Flames, since I muſt burn,
And all their Temples into ashes turn.
Ism. Great Queen.
Zemp. If you wou'd have this Sentence ſtaid,
Summon their Godheads quickly to your aid,
And presently compose a Charm that may
Loves flames into the Strangers breſt convey,
The Captive Stranger, he whose Sword and Eyes
Where ere they ſtrike meet ready Victories:
Make him but burn for me in flames like mine,
Victims shall bleed, and feaſted Altars shine:
If not—
Down go your Temples, and your Gods shall see
They have small use of their Divinity. [*Exeunt.*

ACT IV. SCENE I.

The Scene opens and discovers Montezuma *sleeping in Prison.*

Enter Traxalla *leading in* Orazia.

Trax. NOW take your choice, and bid him live or die;
To both shew Pity, or shew Cruelty:
'Tis you that must condemn, I'le only act;
Your Sentence is more cruel than my Fact.
Oraz. You are most cruel to disturb a mind
Which to approaching Fate was so resign'd.
Trax. Reward my Passions, and you'l quickly prove
There's none dare sacrifice what I dare love
Next to thee, Stranger, wake, and now resign
The bold pretences of thy Love to mine,
Or in this fatal minute thou shalt finde—
Mont. Death, fool; in that thou maist be just and kind:
'Twas I that lov'd *Orazia*, yet did raise
The storm in which she sinks: why dost thou gaze,
Or stay thy hand from giving that just stroke,
Which rather than prevent, I wou'd provoke?
When I am dead, *Orazia* may forgive;
She never must, if I dare wish to live.
Oraz. Hold, hold——O *Montezuma*, can you be
So careless of your self, but more of me?
Though you have brought me to this misery,
I blush to say I cannot see you die.
Mont. Can my approaching Fate such pity move?
The Gods and you at once forgive and love.
Trax. Fond fool, thus to mispend that little breath
I lent thee to prevent, not hasten Death:
Let her thank you she was unfortunate,
And you thank her for pulling on your fate;
Prove to each other your own Destinies. [*Draws.*

Enter Zempoalla *hastily, and sets a Dagger to* Orazia'*s breast.*

Zemp. Hold, hold, *Traxalla*, or *Orazia* dies.
O, is't *Orazia*'s Name that makes you stay?
'Tis her great Power, not mine, that you obey.
Inhumane wretch, dar'st thou the murtherer be
Of him that is not yet condemn'd by me?

Trax. The wretch that gave you all the pow'r you have,
May venture sure to execute a Slave;
And quench a flame your fondness would have burn,
Which may this City into ashes turn.
The Nation in your guilty passion loſt,
To me ungrateful, to your Country moſt:
But this shall be their Offering, I their Prieſt.

Zemp. The wounds thou giv'ſt I'le copy on her breſt.
Strike, and I'le open here a spring of blood,
Shall add new Rivers to the crimson flood.
How his pale looks are fix'd on her!——'tis so.
Oh, does amazement on your spirit grow?
What, is your publick Love *Orazia*'s grown?
Cou'dſt thou see mine, and yet not hide thy own?
Suppose I shou'd ſtrike firſt, wou'd it not breed
Grief in your publick Heart to see her bleed?

Trax. She mocks my passions, in her sparkling eyes
Death and a close dissembled fury lies:
I dare not truſt her thus.——If she muſt die,
The way to her lov'd Life through mine shall lie.

[*He puts her by and ſteps before* Orazia,
and she runs before Montezuma.

Zemp. And he that does this Strangers fate design,
Muſt to his heart a passage force through mine.

Trax. Can fair *Orazia* yet no pity have?
'Tis juſt she shou'd her own Preserver save.

Zemp. Can *Montezuma* so ungrateful prove
To her that gave him Life, and offers Love?

Oraz. Can *Montezuma* live, and live to be
Juſt to another, and unjuſt to me?
You need not be ungrateful; can she give
A Life to you, if you refuse to live?
Forgive me Passion, I had rather see
You dead, than kind to any thing but me.

Mont. O my *Orazia!*
To what new joys and knowledg am I brought!
Are deaths hard lessons by a Woman taught?
How to despise my Fate I always knew;
But ne're durſt think at once of death and you:
Yet since you teach this generous jealousie,
I dare not wish your life, if I muſt die.
How much your Love my Courage does exceed!
Courage alone would shrink to see you bleed.

Zemp. Ungrateful Stranger, thou shalt please thy eyes,
And gaze upon *Orazia* while she dies.
I'le keep my Vow:——It is some joy to see
That my Revenge will prove my Piety.
Trax. Then both shall die; we have too long withstood,
By private Passions urg'd, the Publick good.
Zemp. Sure he dissembles, and perhaps may prove
My ruine with his new ambitious Love:
Were but this Stranger kind, I'de cross his Art,
And give my Empire where I gave my heart. [*Aside*.
Yet thou ungrateful Man,
Let thy approaching ruine make thee wise.
Mont. Thee and thy Love and Mischief I despise.
Zemp. What shall I do?——some way must yet be try'd.
What Reasons can she use whom Passions guide?
Trax. Some black designs are hatching now; false Eyes
Are quick to see anothers Treacheries.
Zemp. Rash Stranger, thus to pull down thy own fate.
Mont. You, and that life you offer me, I hate.

Enter Jaylor.

Zemp. Here Jaylor,——take——what title must he have?
Slave——Slave——Am I then Captive to a Slave!
Why art thou thus unwilling to be free?
Mont. Death will release me from these Chains and thee.
Zemp. Here, Jaylor, take this Monster from my sight,
And keep him where it may be always night;
Let none come near him; if thou dost, expect
To pay thy life the price of the Neglect.
Mont. I scorn thy Pity and thy Cruelty,
And shou'd despise a Blessing sent from thee.
Zemp. Oh horror to my Soul! take him away;
My Rage like damb'd up Streams swell'd by some stay
Shall from this opposition get new force,
And leave the bound of its old easie course.
Come, my *Traxalla*, let us both forgive,
And in these Wretches Fates begin to live.
The Altars shall be crown'd with Fun'ral Boughs,
Peace-offrings pay'd,—but with unquiet Vows. [*Ex*. Zem. Tr.
Oraz. How are things ordered, that the wicked shou'd
Appear more kind and gentle than the good!
Her Passion seems to make her kinder prove,
And I seem cruel through excess of Love:

She loves, and wou'd prevent his death; but I
That love him better, fear he shou'd not die.
My Jealousie, immortal as my Love,
Wou'd rob my Grave below, and me above,
Of Reſt.—Ye Gods, if I repine, forgive;
You neither let me die in Peace, nor live.

Enter Acacis, *Jaylor, and Indians.*

Jaylor. They are juſt gone, Sir.
Aca. 'Tis well: be faithful to my juſt design,
And all thy Princes Fortune shall be thine. [*Exit* Acacis.
Indian. This shall to the Empress. [*Exit Indian.*
Oraz. What can this mean!—
'Twas Prince *Acacis*, if I durſt believe
My sight; but Sorrow may like Joy deceive:
Each object different from it self appears,
That comes not to the Eyes but through their Tears.

Enter Acacis *bringing in* Montezuma.

Ha!—
Aca. Here, Sir, wear this again;
Now follow me.
Mont. So, very good;—
I dare not think, for I may guess amiss;
None can deceive me while I truſt to this. [*Exeunt Omnes.*

Enter Orazia, *conducted by two Indians with their Swords drawn:* Montezuma, Acacis, *whispering another Indian.*

Aca. Think what a weight upon thy faith I lay.
Ind. I ne're did more unwillingly obey.
Aca. Firſt, *Montezuma*, take thy liberty;
Thou gav'ſt me freedom, here I set thee free;
We're equal now. Madam, the danger's great
Of close pursuit; to favour your Retreat
Permit we two a little while remain
Behind, while you go softly o're the Plain.
Oraz. Why shou'd I go before? what's your intent?
Where is my Father? whither am I sent?
Aca. Your doubts shall soon be clear'd. Conduct her on.
So, *Montezuma*, we are now alone: [*Exit* Orazia.
That which my Honour ow'd thee I have paid;
As Honour was, so Love muſt be obey'd.

I set *Orazia* as thy Captive free,
But as my Miſtress ask her back from thee.
Mont. Thou haſt perform'd what Honour bid thee do;
But Friendship bars what Honor prompts me to.
Friends shou'd not fight.
Aca. If Friendship we profess,
Let us secure each others happiness;
One needs muſt die, and he shall happy prove
In her Remembrance, t'other in her Love.
My Guards wait neer, and if I fail they muſt
Give up *Orazia*, or betray their truſt,
Mont. Suppose thou conquerſt, wou'dſt thou wander o're
The South-Sea Sands, or the rough Northern Shore,
That parts thy spacious Kingdom from *Peru*;
And leaving Empire, hopeless Love pursue?
Aca. By which of all my actions cou'd you guess,
Though more your merit, that my Love was less?
What prize can *Empire* with *Orazia* bear?
Or where Love fills the breſt, what room for Fear?
Mont. Let fair *Orazia* then the Sentence give,
Else he may die whom she desires to live.
Aca. Your greater merits bribe her to your side;
My weaker Title muſt by Arms be try'd.
Mont. Oh Tyrant Love, how cruel are thy Laws!
I forfeit Friendship, or betray thy Cause.
That Person whom I wou'd defend from all
The World, that Person by my hand muſt fall.
Aca. Our Lives we to each others Friendships owe;
But Love calls back what Friendship did beſtow:
Love has its Cruelties, but Friendship none;
And we now fight in Quarrels not our own. [*Fight.*

Enter Orazia.

Oraz. What noise is this?—
Hold, hold; what cause cou'd be so great to move
This furious hatred?——
Mont. 'Twas our furious Love.——
Aca. Love which I hid till I had set you free,
And bought your pardon with my liberty:
That done, I thought I less unjuſtly might
With *Montezuma* for *Orazia* fight;
He has prevail'd, and I muſt now confess

His fortune greater, not my passion less;
Yet cannot yield ye till his Sword remove,
A dying Rival that holds faſt his Love.
Orazia. Who ever falls, 'tis my Protector ſtill,
And then the crime's as great to dye as kill.
Acacis, do not hopeless love pursue,
But live, and this soft malady subdue.
Aca. You bid me live, and yet command me dye,
I am not worth your care, fly Madam, fly,
While I fall here unpittied, o're this Plain,
Free from pursuit, the faithless Mountains gain;
And these I charge as they wou'd have me think their friendship true.
Leave me alone to serve and follow you:
Make haſte fair Princess to avoid that fate,
Which does for your unhappy Father wait.
Orazia Is he then left to dye, and shall he see
Himself forsaken, e're his death, by me?
Mont. What wou'd you do.——
Orazia. To Prison I'le return,
And there in fetters with my father mourn.
Mont. That saves not his, but throws your life away.
Orazia. Duty shall give what nature once muſt pay.
Aca. Life is the gift, which Heaven and Parents give,
And duty beſt preserves it, if you live.
Orazia. I shou'd but further from my fountain fly,
And like an unfed stream run on and dye:
Urge me no more, and do not grieve to see
Your Honor rival'd by my Piety. [*Exit. She goes softly off, and often looks back.*
Mont. If Honor wou'd not, shame wou'd lead the way.
I'le back with her.
Aca. Stay, *Montezuma*, ſtay——
Thy Rival cannot let thee go alone,
My love will bear me, though my blood is gone. [*As they are going off.*

Enter Zempoalla, Traxalla, *the Indian that went to tell her, and the reſt, and seizes them.*

Zemp. Seize them——
Aca. Oh, *Montezuma*, thou art loſt. [Orazia *comes back.*
Mont. No more, proud heart, thy useless courage boaſt.
Courage thou curse of the unfortunate,
That canſt encounter, not resiſt ill fate.

Zemp. *Acacis* bleeds.——
What barbarous hand has wounded thus my Son?
Mont. 'Twas I, by my unhappy Sword 'twas done.
Thou bleedst, poor Prince, and I am left to grieve
My Rivals fall.
Trax. He bleeds, but yet may live.
Aca. Friendship and love my failing strength renew,
I dare not dye when I shou'd live for you;
My death were now my crime, as it wou'd be
My guilt to live when I have set you free:
Thus I must still remain unfortunate,
Your life and death are equally my fate.

Orazia *comes back.*

Orazia. A noise again, alas what do I see!
Love thou didst once give place to Piety:
Now Piety, let Love triumph a while;
Here binde my hands: come *Montezuma* smile
At Fortune, since thou sufferest for my sake,
Orazia will her Captives chains partake.
Mont. Now fate thy worst.
Zemp. Lead to the Temple straight,
A Priest, and Altar for these Lovers wait:
They shall be joyn'd, they shall.
Trax. And I will prove—
Those joyes in vengeance, which I want in love.
Aca. I'le quench your thirst with Blood, and will destroy
My self, and with my self, your cruel joy.
Now *Montezuma* since *Orazia* dyes,
I'le fall before thee, the first Sacrifice;
My title in her death shall exceed thine,
As much as in her life, thy hopes did mine:
And when with our mixt blood the Altar's dy'd,
Then our new Title let the Gods decide. [*Exeunt.*

ACT V. SCENE I.

The Scene opens, and discovers the Temple of the Sun all of Gold, and four Priests in habits of white, and red Feathers, attending by a bloody Altar, as ready for Sacrifice.

Then Enter the Guards, and Zempoalla, *and* Traxalla; Ynca, Orazia, *and* Montezuma *bound; as soon as they are plac'd, the Priest sings.*

SONG.

YOU to whom Victory we owe,
Whose glories rise
By sacrifice,
And from our fates below;
Never did yet your Altars shine
Feasted with Blood so nere divine;
Princes to whom we bow,
As they to you,
Thus you can ravish from a throne,
And by their loss of power declare your own.

Zemp. NOW to inflict those punishments that are
Due to the Authors of invasive War;
Who to deceive the oppressed world, like you,
Invent false quarrels to conceal the true.
Ynca. My quarrel was the same that all the Gods
Must have to thee, if there be any oddes
Betwixt those Tytles that are bad or good,
To Crowns descended or usurpt by Blood:
Swell not with this success 'twas not to thee,
But to this man the Gods gave Victory.
Mont. Since I must perish by my own success,
Think my misfortunes more, my Crimes the less;
And so forgiving make me pleas'd to dye,
Thus punish'd for this guilty victory.
Ynca. Death can make vertue easie; I forgive:
That word wou'd prove too hard were I to live;
The Honor of a Prince wou'd then deny,
But in the Grave all our distinctions dye.
Mont. Forgive me one thing yet; to say I love,

Let it no more your scorn or anger move,
Since dying in one flame, my ashes must
Embrace and mingle with *Orazia*'s dust.
Ynca. Name thy bold love no more, lest that last breath
Which shou'd forgive, I stifle with my death.
Orazia. Oh my dear Father! Oh, why may not I,
Since you gave life to me, for you now dye?
Mont. 'Tis I that wrought this mischief ought to fall;
A just and willing sacrifice for all.
Now, *Zempoalla*, be both just and kinde,
And in my fate let me thy mercy finde:
Be grateful then, and grant me that esteem,
That as I live, so dead I may redeem.
Oraz. O do not for her cruel mercy move;
None shou'd ask pitty but from those they love. [*Weeps*.
Ynca. Fond Girl, to let thy disobedient eyes
Show a concern for him whom I despise.
Orazia. How love and nature may divide a breast,
At once by both their Pow'rs severely prest!
Yet Sir, since love seems less, you may forgive,
I wou'd not have you dye, nor have him live;
Yet if he dyes, alas what shall I do?
I cannot dye with him, and live with you.
Mont. How vainly we pursue this generous strife,
Parting in death more cruel then in life!
Weep not, we both shall have one destiny,
As in one flame we liv'd, in one we'l dye.
Trax. Why do we waste in vain these precious hours?
Each minute of his life may hazzard ours:
The Nation does not live whilst he enjoyes
His life, it is his safety that destroyes.
He shall fall first, and teach the rest to dye.
Zemp. Hold——
Who is it that commands—ha, you or I?
Your zeal grows saucy; sure you may allow
Your Empress freedom first to pay her vow.
Trax. She may allow—a justice to be done
By him that rais'd his Empress to her Throne.
Zemp. You are too bold——
Trax. And you too passionate.
Zemp. Take heed with his, you urge not your own fate.
For all this pitty is now due to mee.
Mont. I hate thy offer'd mercy more then thee.

Trax. Why will not then the fair *Orazia* give
Life to her self, and let *Traxalla* live?
Mont. Orazia will not live, and let me dye;
She taught me first this cruel jealousie.
Orazia. I joy that you have learn'd it——
That flame not like immortal love appears
Where death can cool its warmth, or kill its fears.
Zemp. What shall I do? am I so quite forlorn,
No help from my own pride, nor from his scorn!
My Rivals death may more effectual prove,
He that is robb'd of hope, may cease to love:
Here, lead these Offerings to their deaths.
Trax. Let none——
Obey, but he that will pull on his own.
Zemp. Tempt me not thus, false and ingrateful too.
Trax. Just as ungrateful, and as false as you.
Zemp. 'Tis thy false loue that fears her destiny.
Trax. And your false love that fears to have him dye.
Zemp. Seize the bold Traytor.
Trax. What a slighted frown
Troubles your brow? feared nor obeyed by none;
Come prepare for sacrifice.

Enter Acacis *weakly.*

Aca. Hold, hold, such sacrifices cannot be,
Devotion's but a solemn cruelty:
How can the Gods delight in humane blood?
Think 'um not cruel; if you think 'um good.
In vain we ask that mercy, which they want,
And hope that pitty, which they hate to grant.
Zemp. Retire, *Acacis*——
Preserve thy self, for 'tis in vain to waste
Thy breath for them: the fatal vow is past.
Aca. To break that vow is juster then commit
A greater crime, by your preserving it.
Zemp. The Gods themselves their own will best express
To like the vow by giving the success.
Aca. If all things by success, are understood,
Men that make War, grow wicked to be good:
But did you vow those that were overcome,
And he that conquer'd both shou'd share one doom.
There's no excuse; for one of these must be
Not your devotion, but your cruelty.

Trax. To that rash ſtranger Sir we nothing owe,
What he had rais'd he ſtrove to overthrow:
That duty loſt which shou'd our actions guide,
Courage proves guilt, when merits swell to pride.
Aca. Dar'ſt thou, who didſt thy Princes life betray,
Once name that duty thou haſt thrown away:
Like thy injuſtice to this ſtranger shown,
To tax him with a guilt, that is thy own?——
Can you brave Souldiers suffer him to dye,
That gave you life in giving victory?
Look but upon this ſtranger, see those hands,
That brought you freedom fetter'd up in bands.
Not one looks up——
Leſt suddain pitty shou'd their hearts surprize,
And ſteal into their bosoms through their eyes.
Zemp. Why thus in vain are thy weak spirits preſt?
Reſtore thy self to thy more needful reſt.
Aca. And leave *Orazia*——
Zemp. Go, you muſt resign—
For, she muſt be the Gods, not yours nor mine.
Aca. You are my Mother, and my tongue is ti'd
So much by duty that I dare not chide.
Divine *Orazia*——
Can you have so much mercy to forgive?
I do not ask it, with design to live,
But in my death to have my torments cease:
Death is not death when it can bring no peace.
Orazia. I both forgive and pitty——
Aca. O say no more, leſt words less kinde deſtroy,
What these have rais'd in me of peace and joy;
You said you did both pitty and forgive;
You wou'd do neither shou'd *Acacis* live.
By death alone the certain way appears,
Thus to hope mercy and deserve your tears. [*Stabs himself*.
Zemp. O my *Acacis!*——
What cruel cause cou'd urge this fatal deed! [*Weeps*.
He faints, help, help, some help, or he will bleed,
His life and mine away:
Some water there—Not one ſtirs from his place;
I'le use my tears to sprinkle on his face.
Aca. *Orazia*.—
Zemp. Fond childe, why do'ſt thou call upon her name?
I am thy Mother.

Aca. No, you are my shame,
That blood is shed that you had title in,
And with your title may it end your sin:
Unhappy Prince, you may forgive me now,
Thus bleeding for my mothers cruel vow.
Ynca. Be not concern'd for me—
Death's easier then the changes I have seen,
I wou'd not live to truſt the world again.
Mont. Into my eyes sorrow begins to creep,
When hands are ty'd it is no shame to weep.
Aca. Dear *Montezuma.*
I may be ſtill your Friend, though I muſt dye
Your Rival in her love; Eternity
Has room enough for both, there's no desire,
Where to enjoy is only to admire:
There we'l meet friends, when this short ſtorm is paſt.
Mont. Why muſt I tamely wait to perish laſt?
Aca. Orazia weeps, and my parch't soul appears
Refresh'd by that kinde shower of pittying tears;
Forgive those faults my passion did commit,
'Tis punish'd with the life that nourish'd it:
I had no power in this extremity
To save your life, and less to see you dye.
My Eyes wou'd ever on this object ſtay,
But sinking Nature takes the props away.
——Kinde death——
To end with pleasures all my miseries
Shuts up your image in my closing eyes. [*Dyes.*

Enter a Messenger.

1 *Mess.* To Armes, to Armes.
Trax. From when this suddain fear?
1 *Mess.* Stand to your guard my Lord, the danger's near:
From every quarter crowds of people meet,
And leaving houses empty, fill the ſtreet. [*Ex. Mess.*
Trax. Fond Queen, thy fruitless tears a while defer.
Rise, we muſt joyn again——Not speak nor ſtir!
I hear the peoples voice like windes that roar,
When they pursue the flying waves to shore.

Enter second Messenger.

2 *Mess.* Prepare to fight my Lord; the Banisht Queen,
With old *Garrucca*, in the ſtreets are seen.

Trax. We muſt go meet them ere it be too late;
Yet, Madam rise, have you no sence of fate.

Enter third Messenger.

3 *Mess.* King *Montezuma* their Lord shouts proclaim,
The City rings with their new Sovereigns name;
The banish'd Queen declares he is her Son,
And to his succor all the people run. [Zempoalla *rises.*
Zemp. Can this be true? O Love! O Fate! have I
Thus doated on my mortal enemy.
Trax. To my new Prince I thus my homage pay;
Your Reign is short young King.
Zemp. *Traxalla* ſtay——
'Tis to my hand that he muſt owe his fate,
I will revenge at once my love and hate.
[*She sets a Dagger to* Montezuma'*s breaſt.*
Trax. Strike, ſtrike, the conquering enemy is near,
My guards are press'd while you detain me here.
Zemp. Dye then ungrateful, dye; *Amexia's* Son
Shall never triumph on *Acacis* Throne:
Thy death muſt my unhappy flames remove;
Now where is thy defence—againſt my love?
[*She cuts the cords, and gives him the Dagger.*
Trax. Am I betrayed?
[*He draws and thruſts at* Montezuma, *he puts it by and kills him.*
Mont. So may all Rebels dye:
This end has treason joyn'd with cruelty.
Zemp. Live thou whom I muſt love, and yet muſt hate;
She gave thee life, who knows it brings her fate.
Mont. Life is a trifle which I wou'd not take,
But for *Orazias* and her father's sake:
Now *Ynca* hate me, if thou canſt; for he
Whom thou haſt scorn'd will dye or rescue thee.

As he goes to attaque the Guards with Traxalla'*s Sword, Enter* Amexia, Garrucca, *Indians, driving some of the other Party before them.*

Gar. He lives, ye Gods, he lives great Queen, see here
Your coming joys, and your departing fear.
Amex. Wonder and joy so faſt together flow,
Their haſte to pass has made their passage slow;
Like ſtruggling waters in a Vessel pent,

Whose crowding drops choak up the narrow Vent.
My Son.—— [*She imbraces him.*

Mont. I am amaz'd, it cannot be
That fate has such a joy in store for me.

Amex. Can I not gain belief, that this is true?

Mont. It is my fortune I suspect, not you.

Gar. First ask him if he old *Garrucca* know.

Mont. My honored Father, let me fall thus low.

Gar. Forbear great Prince, 'tis I must pay to you
That adoration, as my Sovereigns due:
For from my humble Race you did not spring,
You are the issue of our murthered King,
Sent by that Traytor to his blest abode,
Whom to be made a King, he made a God:
The story is too full of fate to tell,
Or what strange fortune our lost Queen befel.

Amex. That sad relation longer time will crave;
I liv'd obscure, he bred you in a Cave,
But kept the mighty secret from your ear,
Lest heat of blood to some strange course shou'd steer
Your youth—

Mont. I owe him all that now I am,
He taught me first the noble thirst of fame,
Shew'd me the baseness of unmanly fear,
Till th' unlick'd whelp I pluck'd from the rough Bear,
And made the Ounce and Tyger give me way,
While from their hungry jaws I snatch'd the Prey:
'Twas he that charg'd my young armes first with toils,
And drest me glorious in my salvage spoils.——

Gar. You spent in shady Forest all the day,
And joy'd returning to shew me the Prey.
To tell the story, to describe the place,
With all the pleasures of the boasted chase;
Till fit for armes, I reav'd you from your sport,
To train your Youth in the Peruvian Court:
I left you there, and ever since have been,
The sad attendant of my exil'd Queen.

Zemp. My fatal Dream comes to my memory;
That Lion whom I held in bonds was he,
Amexia was the Dove that broke his chains;
What now but *Zempoalla*'s death remains?

Mont. Pardon fair Princess if I must delay
My love a while, my gratitude to pay.

Live, *Zempoalla*—free from dangers live,
For present merits I paſt crimes forgive:
Oh might she hope *Orazia*'s pardon too.——
Orazia. I wou'd have none condemn'd for loving you;
In me her merit much her fault o're powers,
She sought my life, but she preserv'd me yours.
Amex. Taught by my own I pitty her eſtate,
And wish her penitence, but not her fate.
Ynca. I wou'd not be the laſt to bid her live;
Kings beſt revenge their wrongs when they forgive.
Zemp. I cannot yet forget what I have been,
Wou'd you give life to her that was a Queen:
Muſt you then give, and muſt I take; there's yet
One way, that's by refusing to be great:
You bid me live——bid me be wretched too,
Think, think, what pride unthron'd muſt undergo:
Look on this youth *Amexia*, look, and then
Suppose him yours, and bid me live again;
A greater sweetness on these lips there grows,
Then breath shut out from a new folded Rose:
What lovely charms on these cold cheeks appear,
Cou'd any one hate death and see it here?
But thou art gone——
Mont. O that you wou'd believe,
Acacis lives in me, and cease to grieve.
Zemp. Yes, I will cease to grieve, and cease to be,
His soul ſtayes watching in his wound for me;
All that cou'd render life desir'd is gone,
Orazia has my love, and you my Throne:
And death *Acacis*——yet I need not dye,
You leave me Miſtriss of my deſtiny;
In spight of dreams how am I pleas'd to see,
Heavens truth or falshood shou'd depend on me;
But I will help the Gods;
The greateſt proof of courage we can give,
Is then to dye when we have power to live. [*Kills her self.*
Mont. How fatally that inſtrument of death
Was hid——
Amex. She has expir'd her lateſt breath.
Mont. But there lies one to whom all griefs is due.
Orazia. None e're was so unhappy and so true.
Mont. Your pardon royal Sir.
Ynca. You have my Love. [*Gives him* Oraz.

Amex. The Gods my Son your happy choice approve.
Mont. Come my *Orazia* then, and pay with me, [*Leads her to* Acacis.
Some tears to poor *Acacis* memory;
So ſtrange a fate for men the Gods ordain
Our cleareſt Sun shine shou'd be mixt with rain;
How equally our joyes and sorrows move!
Death's fatal triumphs joyn'd with those of love.
Love crowns the dead, and death Crowns him that lives,
Each gains the Conqueſt which the other gives. [*Ex. omnes*.

FINIS.

EPILOGUE to the *INDIAN-QUEEN*, Spoken by *Montezuma*.

YOU see what Shifts we are inforc'd to try
To help out Wit with some Variety;
Shows may be found that never yet were seen,
'Tis hard to finde such Wit as ne're has been:
You have seen all that this old World cou'd do,
We therefore try the fortune of the new,
And hope it is below your aim to hit
At untaught Nature with your practis'd Wit:
Our naked Indians then, when Wits appear,
Wou'd as soon chuse to have the Spaniards here:
'Tis true, y'have marks enough, the Plot, the Show,
The Poet's Scenes, nay, more, the Painters too;
If all this fail, considering the cost,
'Tis a true Voyage to the Indies lost:
But if you smile on all, then these designs,
Like the imperfect Treasure of our Mindes,
'Twill pass for currant wheresoe're they go,
When to your bounteous hands their stamps they owe.

FINIS.

THE INDIAN EMPEROUR

OR THE CONQUEST OF MEXICO BY THE SPANIARDS

BEING THE SEQUEL OF THE INDIAN QUEEN

Dum relego scripsisse pudet, quia plurima cerno
Me quoque, qui feci, judice, digna lini. Ovid.

SOURCE

IN his Epistle Dedicatory to the Duchess of Monmouth Dryden himself says: "I have neither wholly follow'd the truth of the History, nor altogether left it: but have taken all the liberty of a Poet, to adde, alter, or diminish, as I thought might best conduce to the beautifying of my work. It not being the business of a Poet to represent [Historical] truth, but probability." It may be remembered that in the first edition Dryden wrote "to represent truth," but finding this was an ambiguous phrase, he added the qualification "Historical." The question how far a dramatist is bound to history certainly has wide and difficult issues. A few remarks upon this interesting point will be found in the Introduction.

The Indian-Queen, as already noticed, was founded upon, or at least suggested by episodes in De Gomberville's *Polexandre*, but for *The Indian-Emperour* Dryden has in the main outlines of his drama adhered to facts, romance is subsidiary, and it is clear from various telling touches and minute details in the conduct of the plot that Dryden had read the historians of the Conquest of Mexico with some attention. I have accordingly once or twice in the notes explanatory quoted parallel passages from the old chroniclers. Amongst the authors whom Dryden consulted were no doubt the following: Francisco Lopez de Gómara (1510–*c.* 1565) who in 1552 published at Saragossa his "Hispania Victrix; First and Second Parts of the General History of the Indies, with the whole discovery and notable things that have happened since they were acquired until the year 1551, with the conquest of Mexico and New Spain." This was translated into French by Martin Fumée, Paris, 1578; and into Italian by Augustin Gravaliz, Venice, 1560. Gómara who, after the return of Cortes, served as his private and domestic chaplain, relied upon the information he thus acquired. He also sought details from others of the expedition, particularly Gonzalo de Tapia and Gonzalo de Umbria. Since he never was in America, Gómara seems to have fallen into error, and his book was answered by a companion of the Conqueror, Bernal Diaz del Castillo, whose *Verdadera historia de la Conquista de Nueva España* was undoubtedly known to Dryden.

The letters of Cortes, *Segunda Carta de Relacion*, 30 October, 1520, published at Seville, 1522; *Carta tercera*, 15 May, 1522, Seville, 1523; and the fourth letter, 20 October, 1524, printed at Toledo in 1525; all appear to have been read by the poet. The first letter is missing.

The learned work on the history of Spain by Juan Mariana, S.J. (1536–1624), *De Rebus Hispaniae*, was familiar in the later edition (libri XXX) published at Mainz, 1605.

Langbaine says: "For the Plot of this Play 'tis founded chiefly on History." He then cites one or two general works, amongst which he very absurdly writes: "*De Bry Americae*, Pars 9, l. 7. *Ogleby's America*, Chap. 3, Sect. 10." The immense work of Theodore de Bry or Brie (1528–1598), commonly known as *Grands et Petits Voyages*, is comprised in twenty-four volumes. De Bry was a famous engraver, and his books are ornamented with the finest plates. His *Historia Americae siue Noui Orbis*, in thirteen sections, was published at Frankfort, "Sumptibus Matth. Meriani," 1634. Book VII contains: Uera & iucunda descriptio præcipuarum quarundam Indiae occidentalis regionum & insularum, ab Vlrico Fabro Straubingensi perlustratarum an. 1534." Pars 9 has the following rubric: *Perueniunt ad Carios. Describitur regio & indigenarum nores &c.* I cannot find that Dryden was at all indebted to this.

The *America* of John Ogilby, "His Majesty's *Cosmographer*," is a splendid folio, 1671. Chapter III, Section 10, is "Ferdinando Cortez *his Voyage*." The narrative is spirited if concise, but the publication of the book was, of course, later than *The Indian Emperour*, and so Dryden could not well have been beholding to Ogilby.

THEATRICAL HISTORY

THE *Indian Emperour, or, The Conquest of Mexico by the Spaniards*, being the Sequel of the *Indian Queen*, was produced at the Theatre Royal in the spring of 1665, probably early April. The play was cast (Downes) as follows: Montezuma, Michael Mohun; Odmar, William Wintershal; Guyomar, Edward Kynaston; High Priest, William Cartwright; Cortez, Charles Hart; Vasquez, Nicholas Burt; Almeria, Mrs. Marshall; Cydaria, Nell Gwyn. Alibech, originally played by Mrs. Elizabeth Weaver, was shortly afterwards taken by Mrs. Mary Knepp (Pepys, 15 January, 1666–7). Mrs. Weaver, one of the earliest actresses in Killigrew's company, became a mistress of Charles II, when she seems to have retired from the stage. (Pepys, 11 January, 1667–8: "Knepp . . . says that the King first spoiled Mrs. Weaver, which is very mean, methinks, in a prince.")

On 30 June, 1666, Mrs. Weaver is mentioned in a warrant as among the actresses of the Royal company, but on 8 February, 1667–8 her name is cancelled. There is also extant a petition (1662) of one Henry Dobson asserting that Elizabeth Farley hath "gone by the name of Eliz: Weaver," pretending to be the wife of a gentleman in Gray's Inn, the father of her child. She proved not to be married, and she is further accused of enrolling herself as one of the King's Servants to escape her creditors.

At its first production the success of *The Indian Emperour* rivalled, if it did not actually surpass, the triumph of *The Indian Queen*, and Dryden's tragedy, perhaps the most popular of his plays, was continually given during the next forty years, never failing to draw a crowded house.

Pepys appears to have seen this favourite drama for the first time on Thursday, 22 August, 1667, when, "after dinner with my Lord Bruncker and his mistress to the King's playhouse, and there saw 'The Indian Emperour,' where I find Nell come again, which I am glad of; but was most infinitely displeased with her being put to act the Emperour's daughter; which is a great and serious part, which she do most basely. The rest of the play, though pretty good, was not well acted by most of them, methought; so that I took no great content in it." On this occasion Mrs. Mary Knepp was the Alibech, and she caused the worthy diarist some confusion by desiring to see him after the show, an appointment he avoided, being in fear his wife might reach home before his own return. Which amply accounts for his petulant mood and terse words. On Monday, 11 November, 1667, he was with Mrs. Pepys at the Theatre Royal, "and there saw 'The Indian Emperour,' a good play, but not so good as people cry it up, I think, though above all things Nell's ill speaking of a great part made me mad." On Saturday, 28 March, 1668, upon another visit he judged it "a very good play indeed." Tuesday, 21 April, 1668, was memorable for him, since after escorting Mrs. Turner to see *The Indian Emperour*, he took Mrs. Knepp to supper at Kensington, where they remained until dark, "and had a dear reckoning, but merry."

King Charles was frequently present at *The Indian Emperour*, and on Monday, 14 January, 1667–8, an amateur performance in which the Duke and Duchess of Monmouth, Captain Charles O'Bryan, Mrs. Cornwallis, and other persons of quality took part was given at Court. Pepys was told that the Duchess of Monmouth and Mrs. Cornwallis "did do most extraordinary well," but that the other ladies were "like fools and stocks," and that "not any man did any thing well but Captain O'Bryan, who spoke and did well, but, above all things, did dance most incomparably."

In Thomas Duffett's *New Songs*, 1676, we have a Prologue and Epilogue written for *The Indian Emperour*, as "Acted by the Duchess of *Portsmouth's* Servants," a touring company.

There is an interesting allusion to *The Indian Emperour* in Samuel Chappuzeau's *Le Théâtre François* (1674) when speaking of the large number of supers employed upon the English stage he says: "Toutes les fois qu'vn Roy sort, & vient à parêtre sur le Théâtre, plusiers Officiers marchent devant luy, & crient en leur langue: *Place! place!* comme lorsque le Roy passe a Vvit-thal d'un quartier à l'autre, parce qu'ils veulent, disent ils, representer les choses naturellement. Ils en vsent de méme à proportion en d'autres rencontres, & introduisent quantité de personnages muets que nous nommons *Assistans*, pour bien remplir le Théâtre; et qui satisfait la veüe, & cause aussi quelquefois de l'embarras. Estant à Londres il y a six ans, j'y vis deux fort belles Troupes de Comediens, l'vne du Roy, & l'autre du duc d'Yorc, & ie fus a deux representations, à *la Mort de Montezume, Roy de Mexique* [*The Indian Emperour*], & à celle de *Mustapha*, qui se defendoit vigoureusement sur le Théâtre contre les muets qui le vouloient étrangler; ce qui faisoit rire & ce que les François n'auroient representé que dans vn recit."

Concerning the original music to *The Indian Emperour* nothing is known. The song "Ah, fading joy," sung by an Indian woman in Act IV, was set (as a song with a three-part chorus) by Pelham Humphrey, and published for the first time in the 1678 edition of Playford's *Choice Ayres, Songs, and Dialogues*. It may be mentioned that no music for the Saraband with castagnets has been traced.

After the Union of the two Companies in 1682, when Hart and Mohun had retired, and their great parts fell to other actors, *The Indian Emperour* was revived with Betterton as Montezuma. This was a favourite rôle with the great tragedian, and during his lifetime he enjoyed to the full the ample opportunities afforded by such effective scenes and situations.

In *The Gentleman's Journal* for January, 1691–2, Motteux writes: "The *Indian* Emperor hath been reviv'd and play'd many times." It was probably for this revival that Henry Purcell wrote his setting to the Song sung by the spirit Kalib in Act II, "I look'd and saw within the book of Fate."

Even until the end of his stage career Betterton loved continually to appear as Montezuma, and the rôle indeed was not altogether unsuitable to the veteran of threescore years and ten.

It is interesting to note that in a bright little novel, *The Adventures of Covent Garden, in imitation of Scarron's City Romance*, 16mo, 1699, Peregrine sits in a box with Lady Selinda at a performance of *The Indian Emperour*, and during the play they discuss critical and dramatic questions with no little acumen.

At the Haymarket, 14 April, 1705, George Powell made a vigorous, but it is hardly to be doubted, a vehement Cortez.

At the Haymarket again 25 January, 1707, Betterton is Montezuma; Mills, Cortez; Booth, Guyomar; Theophilus Keen, Odmar; Mrs. Barry, Almeria; Mrs. Porter, Cydaria; Mrs. Bowman, Alibech. It was perhaps at this revival that the amusing incident occurred which Chetwood in his *History of the Stage* relates concerning Griffith the well-known comedian, whose "Person was well made, tho' low in stature," a history, says the writer, "I had from his own mouth." "After his commencing Actor, he contracted a Friendship with Mr. *Wilks;* which chain remained unbroke till the Death of that excellent Comedian. Tho' Mr. *Griffith* was very young, Mr. *Wilks* took him with him to *London*, and had him enter'd for that Season at a small Salary. The *Indian Emperor* being on a sudden to be play'd, the Part of *Pizarro*, a *Spaniard*, was wanting, which Mr. *Griffith* procur'd, with some Difficulty. Mr. *Betterton* being a little indisposed, would not venture out to Rehearsal, for Fear of increasing his Indisposition, to the Disappointment of the audience, who had not seen our young Stripling rehearse. But, when he came ready, at the Entrance, his Ears were pierc'd with a Voice not familiar to him: He cast his Eyes upon the Stage, when he beheld the diminutive *Pizarro*, with a Truncheon as long as himself (his own Words). He steps up to *Downs* the Prompter, and cry'd, *Zounds*, Downs! *what sucking Scaramouch have you sent on there? Sir*, reply'd *Downs, He's good enough for a* Spaniard; *the Part is small. Betterton* return'd, *If he had made his Eye-brows his Whiskers, and each Whisker a Line, the Part would have been two Lines too much for such a Monkey in Buskins.* Poor *Griffith* stood on the Stage, near the Door, and heard every Syllable of the short Dialogue, and by his Fears, knew who was meant by it; but, happy for him, he had no more to speak that Scene. When the first Act was over (by the Advice of *Downs*) he went to make his Excuse, with—*Indeed, Sir, I had not taken the Part, but there was only I alone out of the Play.* I! I! (reply'd *Betterton*, with a Smile) *Thou art but the Tittle of an I. Griffith* seeing him in no ill Humour, told him, *Indians* ought to be the best figures on the Stage, as Nature had made them. *Very like*, reply'd *Betterton; but it would be a double Death to an* Indian *Cobler to be* conquer'd by such a Weazle of a Spaniard as thou art! *And, after this Night, let me never see a Truncheon in thy Hand again, unless to Stir the Fire.* This Story, as I said before, was of his own telling."

In the winter of 1708 at the Haymarket, on 8 November, Wilks appears as Cortez; Mrs. Bradshaw, Cydaria; Mrs. Rogers, Alibech.

At Drury Lane, 7 January, 1709, Powell is Cortez and Mills Odmar. The play was acted several times that season with great applause.

At the Haymarket, 13 March, 1710, *The Indian Emperour* was performed for Mrs. Barry's benefit.

Even after the death of Betterton the popularity of Dryden's tragedy was maintained. We find Keen as Montezuma, with Wilks as Cortez; Booth, Guyomar; Mills, Odmar; Mrs. Knight, Almeria; Mrs. Santlow, Cydaria; Mrs. Porter, Alibech. The same cast played at Drury Lane, 27 January, 1711.

On Tuesday, 17 April, 1711, *The Indian Emperour* was given at the Haymarket for Powell's benefit, and Addison in an Advertisement to *The Spectator*, No. 40, Monday, 16 April, 1711, says: "*Having spoken of Mr.* Powell, *as sometimes raising himself Applause from the ill Taste of an Audience; I must do him the Justice to own, that he is excellently formed for a Tragædian, and when he pleases, deserves the Admiration of the best Judges, as I doubt not but he will in the* Conquest of Mexico, *which is acted for his Benefit To-morrow Night.*"

8 January, 1717, at Lincoln's Inn Fields, Keen again plays Montezuma; with Elrington as Cortez; Bullock junior, Guyomar; Mrs. Knight, Almeria; Mrs. Rogers, Alibech; Mrs. Cross, Cydaria. *The Country Wake*, a broad comedy by Doggett with Jemmy Spiller, a great farceur, "blithe as a bird when mellow," as Hob, the rustic lout, followed the tragedy.

Season after season, wellnigh for the next decade, with few interruptions, this heroic drama is played, though perhaps as the years went by it became less frequent and less familiar.

At Drury Lane, 27 January, 1731, *The Indian Emperour* was revived with Mills as Montezuma; Wilks, Cortez; Bridgewater, Odmar; Mrs. Porter, Almeria; Mrs. Cibber, Cydaria; and the lovely Mrs. Horton, Alibech.

On 14 January, 1734, Dryden's tragedy won a great success at Goodman's Fields. It was played four consecutive nights to packed houses. Hulett acted Montezuma; Gifford, Cortez; Delane, Guyomar; Mrs. Thurmond, who, says Chetwood, was excelled by few of her contemporaries, and who was very great as Roxana in *The Rival Queens*, Almeria; Mrs. Giffard, Cydaria.

Before the middle of the century, however, *The Indian Emperour* may be said to have disappeared from the theatre.

There is one amateur performance which from its singularity certainly deserves to be recorded. In 1731 *The Indian Emperour* was performed by children at Mr. Conduit's, Master of the Mint, before a most distinguished audience. Hogarth has painted the prison scene in Act IV, 4, where we have Lord Lempster as Cortez; Lady Caroline Lenox, Cydaria; Lady Sophia Fermor, Almeria; and Miss Conduit (afterwards Lady Lymington), Alibech. The prompter, Dr. Desaguliers, is seen intent on the book. Among the audience are the Duke of Cumberland, Princess Mary, Princess Louisa, Lady Deloraine and her two daughters, the Duke and Duchess of Richmond, the Earl of Pomfret, the Earl of Montague, and Mr. Tom Hill. The performance appears to be very spirited, and done in true heroic style, and Mlle de Scudéry herself might have led the loud applause. Hogarth's picture was engraved by Robert Dodd, and published by Boydell.

Chetwood in his *General History of the Stage* tells us that Farquhar the dramatist "began very early to apply himself to the Stage [at Dublin] as an *Actor*. . . . Mr. *Farquhar*, having the advantage of a very good Person tho' with a weak Voice, was never repulsed by the Audience; but the following Accident made him determine to leave off the Occupation: Playing the Part of *Guyomar* in the *Indian Emperor*, who is supposed to kill *Vasquez*, one of the *Spanish* Generals; not remembering to change his Sword for a *Foil*, in the Mock Engagement, he wounded the Person that represented *Vasquez*, tho' (as it fell out) not dangerously; nevertheless, it put an End to his appearing on the Stage as an Actor." The representative of Vasquez was an actor named Price.

A DEFENCE

of an Essay of Dramatique Poesie, being an Answer to the Preface of *The Great Favourite, or the Duke of Lerma.*

THE former Edition of *The Indian Emperour* being full of faults which had escaped the Printer, I have been willing to overlook this second with more care; and though I could not allow my self so much time as was necessary yet by that little I have done, the Press is freed from some gross errors which it had to answer for before. As for the more material faults of writing, which are properly mine, though I see many of them, I want leisure to amend them. 'Tis enough for those who make one Poem the business of their lives, to leave that correct: yet, excepting *Virgil*, I never met with any which was so in any Language.

But while I was thus employed about this Impression, there came to my hands a new printed Play, called, *The Great Favourite, or The Duke of Lerma.* The Author of which, a noble and most ingenious Person, has done me the favour to make some Observations and Animadversions upon my *Dramatique Essay.* I must confess he might have better consulted his Reputation, than by matching himself with so weak an Adversary. But if his Honour be diminished in the choice of his Antagonist, it is sufficiently recompens'd in the election of his Cause: which being the weaker, in all appearance, as combating the received Opinions of the best Ancient and Modern Authors, will add to his glory, if he overcome; and to the opinion of his generosity, if he be vanquished, since he ingages at so great odds, and, so like a Cavalier, undertakes the protection of the weaker party. I have only to fear on my own behalf, that so good a cause as mine may not suffer by my ill management, or weak defence; yet I cannot in Honour but take the Glove, when 'tis offered me: though I am only a Champion by succession; and no more able to defend the right of *Aristotle* and *Horace*, than an Infant *Dimock* to maintain the Title of a King.

For my own concernment in the Controversie, it is so small, that I can easily be contented to be driven from a few Notions of Dramatique Poesie; especially by one, who has the reputation of understanding all things: and I might justly make that excuse for my yielding to him, which the Philosopher made to the Emperour; why should I offer to contend with him, who is Master of more than twenty Legions of Arts and Sciences? But I am forced to fight, and therefore it will be no shame to be overcome.

Yet I am so much his Servant, as not to meddle with any thing which does not concern me in his Preface: therefore, I leave the good sense and other excellencies of the first twenty lines to be considered by the Critiques. As for the play of the Duke of *Lerma*, having so much alter'd and beautifi'd it, as he has done, it can justly belong to none but him. Indeed, they must be extream ignorant as well as envious, who would rob him of that Honour; for you see him putting in his claim to it, even in the first two lines:

Repulse upon repulse like waves thrown back,
That slide to hang upon obdurate rocks.

After this let detraction do its worst; for if this be not his, it deserves to be. For my part, I declare for distributive Justice; and from this and what follows, he certainly deserves *those advantages, which he acknowledges to have received from the opinion of sober men.*

In the next place, I must beg leave to observe his great Address in courting the Reader to his party. For intending to assault all Poets, both Ancient and Modern, he discovers not his whole design at once, but seems only to aim at me, and attacques me on my weakest side, my defence of Verse.

To begin with me, he gives me the Compellation of *The Author of a Dramatique Essay*, which is a little Discourse in Dialogue, for the most part borrowed from the observations of others: therefore, that I may not be wanting to him in civility, I return his Complement by calling him *The Author of The Duke of Lerma.*

But (that I may pass over his salute) he takes notice of my great pains to prove Rhyme as natural in a serious play, and more effectual than blanck Verse. Thus indeed I did state the question; but he tells me, *I pursue that which I call Natural in a wrong application: for 'tis not the question whether Rhyme or not Rhyme be best or most natural for a serious subject, but what is nearest the nature of that it represents.*

If I have formerly mistaken the Question, I must confess my ignorance so far, as to say I continue still in my mistake: But he ought to have proved that I mistook it; for it is yet but *gratis dictum:* I still shall think I have gained my point, if I can prove that Rhyme is best or most natural for a serious subject. As for the question as he states it, whether Rhyme be nearest the nature of what it represents, I wonder he should think me so ridiculous as to dispute whether Prose or Verse be nearest to ordinary Conversation?

It still remains for him to prove his inference, that, since Verse is granted to be more remote than Prose from ordinary Conversation, therefore no serious Plays ought to be writ in Verse: and when he clearly makes that good, I will acknowledge his Victory as absolute as he can desire it.

The question now is, which of us two has mistaken it; and if it appear I have not, the world will suspect *what Gentleman that was, who was allowed to speak twice in Parliament, because he had not yet spoken to the Question*; and perhaps conclude it to be the same, who, 'tis reported, maintained a contradiction *in terminis*, in the face of three hundred persons.

But to return to Verse; whether it be natural or not in Plays, is a problem which is not demonstrable of either side: 'tis enough for me that he acknowledges he had rather read good Verse than Prose: for if all the Enemies of Verse will confess as much, I shall not need to prove that it is natural. I am satisfied, if it cause delight: for delight is the chief, if not the only, end of Poesie: instruction can be admitted but in the second place; for Poesie only instructs as it delights. 'Tis true, that to imitate well is a Poet's work; but to affect the Soul, and excite the Passions, and above all to move admiration, (which is the delight of serious Plays,) a bare imitation will not serve. The converse therefore which a Poet is to imitate, must be heighten'd with all the Arts and Ornaments of Poesie; and must be such, as, strictly considered, could never be supposed spoken by any without premeditation.

As for what he urges, that *a Play will still be supposed to be a composition of several Persons speaking* ex tempore; *and that good Verses are the hardest things which can be imagined to be so spoken*: I must crave leave to dissent from his opinion, as to the former part of it: for, if I am not deceived, a Play is supposed to be the work of the Poet, imitating or representing the conversation of several persons; and this I think to be as clear, as he thinks the contrary.

But I will be bolder, and do not doubt to make it good, though a Paradox, that one great reason why Prose is not to be used in serious Plays, is because it is too near the nature of converse: there may be too great a likeness; as the most skilful Painters affirm, that there may be too near a resemblance in a Picture: to take every lineament and feature, is not to make an excellent piece; but to take so much only as will make a beautiful Resemblance of the whole; and, with an ingenious flattery of Nature, to heighten the beauties of some parts, and hide the deformities of the reſt. For so says *Horace:*

> *Ut pictura Poesis erit &c. . . . . .*
> *Hæc amat obscurum, vult hæc sub luce videri,*
> *Judicis argutum quæ non formidat acumen*
> ——————————*Et quæ*
> *Desperat, tractata nitescere posse, relinquit.*

In *Bartholomew-Fair*, or the Loweſt kind of Comedy, that degree of heightning is used, which is proper to set off that Subject: 'tis true the Author was not there to go out of Prose, as he does in his higher Arguments of Comedy, *The Fox and Alchymiſt;* yet he does so raise his matter in that Prose, as to render it delightful; which he could never have performed, had he only said or done those very things that are daily spoken or practised in the Fair: for then the Fair itself would be as full of pleasure to an ingenious person as the Play; which we manifeſtly see it is not. But he hath made an excellent Lazar of it: the Copy is of price, though the Original be vile. You see in *Catiline* and *Sejanus*, where the Argument is great, he sometimes ascends to Verse, which shews he thought it not unnatural in serious Plays: and had his Genius been as proper for Rhyme, as it was for Humour, or had the Age in which he liv'd, attain'd to as much knowledge in Verse as ours, 'tis probable he would have adorned those Subjects with that kind of Writing.

Thus Prose, though the rightful Prince, yet is by common consent depos'd, as too weak for the government of serious Plays; and he failing, there now ſtart up two Competitors; one the nearer in blood, which is blanck Verse; the other more fit for the ends of government, which is Rhyme. Blanck Verse is, indeed, the nearer Prose, but he is blemish'd with the weakness of his Predecessor. Rhyme (for I will deal clearly) has somewhat of the Usurper in him; but he is brave and generous, and his Dominion pleasing. For this reason of delight, the Ancients (whom I will ſtill believe as wise as those who so confidently correct them) wrote all their Tragedies in Verse, though they knew it moſt remote from Conversation.

But I perceive I am falling into the danger of another rebuke from my Opponent; for when I plead that the Ancients used Verse, I prove not that they would have admitted Rhyme, had it then been written: all I can say is only this; that it seems to have suceeded Verse by the general consent of poets in all Modern Languages: for almoſt all their serious Plays are written in it: which, though it be no demonſtration that therefore they ought to be so, yet at leaſt the practice firſt, and then the continuation of it, shews that it attain'd the end, which was to please; and if that cannot be compass'd here, I will be the first who shall lay it down. For I confess my chief endeavours are to delight the Age in which I live. If the humour of this, be for low Comedy, small Accidents, and Raillery, I will force my Genius to obey it, though with more reputation I could write in Verse. I know I am not so fitted by Nature to write Comedy: I want that gayety of humour which is required to it. My conversation is slow and dull, my humour Saturnine and reserv'd: In short, I am none of those who endeavour to break Jests in Company, or make reparties. So that those who decry my Comedies do me no injury, except it be in point of profit: reputation in them is the last thing to which I shall pretend. I beg pardon for entertaining the Reader with so ill a Subject; but before I quit that Argument, which was the cause of this digression, I cannot but take notice how I am corrected for my quotation of *Seneca*, in my Defence of Plays in Verse. My words are these. Our Language is Noble, Full, and Significant, and I know not why he who is Master of it, may not cloath ordinary things in it as decently as the Latine, if he use the same diligence in his *choice of Words*. One would think, *Unlock a door*, was a thing as vulgar as could be spoken; yet *Seneca* could make it sound high and lofty in his Latine:

Reserate Clusos Regii postes Laris.

But he says of me, *That being fill'd with the Precedents of the Ancients, who writ their Plays in Verse, I commend the thing; declaring our Language to be Full, Noble, and Significant, and charging all defects upon the* ill placing of words, *which I prove by quoting* Seneca *loftily expressing such an ordinary thing as* shutting a door.

Here he manifestly mistakes; for I spoke not of the placing, but of the choice of words; for which I quoted that aphorism of *Julius Cæsar*: *Delectus verborum est origo Eloquentiæ:* but *delectus verborum* is no more Latine for the placing of words, than *Reserate* is Latine for *shut the door*, as he interprets it, which I ignorantly construed unlock or open it.

He supposes I was highly affected with the sound of those words; and I suppose I may more justly imagine it of him; for if he had not been extreamly satisfied with the sound, he would have minded the sense a little better.

But these are now to be no faults; for ten days after his Book is published, and that his mistakes are grown so famous, that they are come back to him, he sends his *Errata* to be printed, and annexed to his Play; and desires, that instead of *shutting* you would read *opening*; which, it seems, was the Printers fault. I wonder at his modesty, that he did not rather say it was *Seneca's*, or mine; and that in some

Authors, *Reserare* was to *shut* as well as to *open*, as the word *Barach*, say the Learned, is both to *bless* and *curse*.

Well, since it was the Printer, he was a naughty man to commit the same mistake twice in six lines: I warrant you *delectus verborum* for *placing of words* was his mistake too, though the Author forgot to tell him of it: if it were my Book, I assure you I should. For those Rascals ought to be the Proxies of every Gentleman Author, and to be chastis'd for him, when he is not pleased to own an Errour. Yet since he has given the *Errata*, I wish he would have inlarged them only a few sheets more, and then he would have spared me the labour of an Answer: for this cursed Printer is so given to mistakes, that there is scarce a sentence in the Preface without some false Grammar or hard sence in it; which will all be charg'd upon the Poet, because he is so good natur'd as to lay but three Errours to the Printers account, and to take the rest upon himself, who is better able to support them. But he needs not apprehend that I should strictly examine those little faults, except I am call'd upon to do it: I shall return therefore to that quotation of *Seneca*, and answer, not to what he writes, but to what he means. I never intended it as an Argument, but only as an illustration of what I had said before concerning the election of words: and all he can charge me with is only this, that if *Seneca* could make an ordinary thing sound well in Latine by the choice of words, the same, with the like care, might be performed in English: if it cannot, I have committed an Errour on the right hand, by commending too much the copiousness and well-sounding of our Language; which I hope my Countrymen will pardon me. At least the words which follow in my Dramatique Essay will plead somewhat in my behalf; for I say there, that this Objection happens but seldom in a Play; and then too either the meanness of the expression may be avoided, or shut out from the Verse by breaking it in the midst.

But I have said too much in the defence of Verse; for after all, it is a very indifferent thing to me, whether it obtain or not. I am content hereafter to be ordered by his rule, that is, to write it sometimes, because it pleases me; and so much the rather, because he has declared that it pleases him. But he has taken his last farewell of the Muses, and he has done it civilly, by honouring them with the name of *his long acquaintances*; which is a Complement they have scarce deserved from him. For my own part, I bear a share in the publick loss; and how emulous soever I may be of his fame and reputation, I cannot but give this testimony of his Style, that it is extream poetical, even in Oratory; his Thoughts elevated, sometimes above common apprehension; his Notions politick and grave, and tending to the instruction of Princes, and reformation of States; that they are abundantly interlaced with variety of Fancies, Tropes, and Figures, which the Criticks have enviously branded with the name of obscurity and false Grammar.

Well he is now fettered in business of more unpleasant nature: the Muses have lost him, but the Commonwealth gains by it; the corruption of a Poet is the Generation of a Statesman.

He will not venture again into the civil wars of Censure; ubi . . . nullos habitura triumphos: if he had not told us he had left the Muses, we might have half suspected it by that word, *ubi*, which does not any way belong to them in that place; the rest of the Verse is indeed *Lucan's*: but that *ubi*, I will answer for it, is his own. Yet he has another reason for this disgust of Poesie; for he says immediately after, that *the manner of Plays which are now in most esteem, is beyond his power to perform*: to perform the manner of a thing, I confess is new English to me. *However, he condemns not the satisfaction of others; but rather their unnecessary understanding, who, like* Sancho Pança's *Doctor, prescribe too strictly to our appetites; for, says he, in the difference of* Tragedy *and* Comedy, *and of* Farce *itself, there can be no determination but by the taste, nor in the manner of their composure.*

We shall see him now as great a Critick as he was a Poet; and the reason why he excell'd so much in Poetry will be evident, for it will appear to have proceeded from the exactness of his judgment. *In the difference of* Tragedy, Comedy, *and* Farce *itself, there can be no determination but by the taste.* I will not quarrel with the obscurity of his Phrase, though I justly might; but beg his pardon if I do not rightly understand him: if he means, that there is no essential difference betwixt *Comedy*, *Tragedy*, and *Farce*, but what is only made by the peoples taste, which distinguishes one of them from the other, that is so manifest an Errour, that I need not lose time to contradict it. Were there neither Judge, Taste, nor Opinion in the world, yet they would differ in their natures; for the action, character, and language of *Tragedy*, would still be great and high; that of *Comedy* lower and more familiar; Admiration would be the Delight of one, and Satyr of the other.

I have but briefly touch'd upon these things, because, whatever his words are, I can scarce imagine, that *he who is always concern'd for the true honour of reason, and would have no spurious issue fathered upon her*, should mean any thing so absurd as to affirm, *that there is no difference betwixt* Comedy *and* Tragedy, *but what is made by the taste only*: Unless he would have us understand the Comedies of my Lord *L*, where the first act should be pottages, the second Fricassees, &c. and the fifth a *Chère Entière* of Women.

I rather guess he means, that betwixt one *Comedy* or *Tragedy* and another, there is no other difference but what is made by the liking or disliking of the Audience. This is indeed a less errour than the former, but yet it is a great one. The liking or disliking of the people gives the Play the denomination of good or bad; but does not really make or constitute it such. To please the people ought to be the Poets aim, because Plays are made for their delight; but it does not follow that they are always pleased with good Plays, or that the Plays which please them are always good. The humour of the people is now for *Comedy*; therefore, in hope to please them, I write *Comedies* rather than serious Plays; and so far their taste prescribes to me: but it does not follow from that reason, that *Comedy* is to be preferred before *Tragedy* in its own nature; for that which is so in its own nature cannot be otherwise; as a man cannot but be a rational creature: but the opinion of the people may alter, and in another Age, or perhaps in this, serious Plays may be set up above Comedies.

This I think a sufficient Answer: if it be not, he has provided me of an Excuse; it seems, in his wisdom, he foresaw my weakness, and has found out this expedient for me, *That it is not necessary for Poets to study strict reason; since they are so used to a greater latitude than is allowed by that severe inquisition; that they must infringe their own jurisdiction, to profess themselves oblig'd to argue well.*

I am obliged to him for discovering to me this back door; but I am not yet resolv'd on my retreat: For I am of opinion that they cannot be good Poets, who are not accustomed to argue well. False Reasonings and colours of Speech are the certain marks of one who does not understand the Stage; For Moral Truth is the Mistress of the Poet, as much as of the Philosopher. Poesie must resemble Natural truth, but it must *be* Ethical. Indeed the Poet dresses Truth, and adorns Nature, but does not alter them:

Ficta voluptatis causa sint proxima veris.

Therefore, that is not the best Poesie, which resembles notions of things that are not to things that are: though the fancy may be great, and the words flowing, yet the Soul is but half satisfied when there is not Truth in the foundation. This is that which makes *Virgil* be preferred before the rest of Poets: in variety of fancy and sweetness of expression, you see *Ovid* far above him; for *Virgil* rejected many of those things which *Ovid* wrote. *A great wits great Work is to refuse*, as my worthy Friend, Sir *John Berkenhead*, has ingeniously expressed it: you rarely meet with any thing in *Virgil* but Truth, which therefore leaves the strongest impression of pleasure in the Soul. This I thought myself obliged to say in behalf of Poesie; and to declare, though it be against myself, that when Poets do not argue well, the defect is in the Work-men, not in the Art.

And now I come to the boldest part of his Discourse, wherein he attacques not me, but all the Ancients and Moderns; and undermines, as he thinks, the very foundations on which Dramatique Poesie is built. I could wish he would have declin'd that envy which must of necessity follow such an undertaking, and contented himself with triumphing over me in my opinions of Verse, which I will never hereafter dispute with him; but he must pardon me, if I have that veneration for *Aristotle*, *Horace*, *Ben. Johnson*, and *Corneille*, that I dare not serve him in such a Cause, and against such Heroes, but rather fight under their protection, as *Homer* reports of little *Teucer*, who shot the Trojans from under the large buckler of *Ajax Telamon*:

Στῆ δ' ἄ̓ρ' ὑπ' Αἴαντος σάκεϊ Τελαμωνιάδαο, &c.

He stood beneath his Brothers ample shield,
And cover'd there, shot death through all the field,

The words of my noble Adversary are these:

But if we examine the general Rules laid down for Plays by strict reason, we shall find the errours equally gross; for the great foundation which is laid to build upon, is nothing, as it is generally stated, as will appear upon the examination of the Particulars.

These Particulars, in due time, shall be examin'd: in the mean while, let us consider what this great foundation is, which he says is nothing, as it is generally stated. I never heard of any other foundation of Dramatique Poesie than the imitation of Nature; neither was there ever pretended any other by the Ancients, or Moderns, or me, who endeavour to follow them in that Rule. This I have plainly said in my definition of a Play; that it is a just and lively image of humane Nature, &c. Thus the Foundation, as it is generally stated, will stand sure, if this definition of a Play be true; if it be not, he ought to have made his exception against it, by proving that a Play is not an imitation of Nature, but somewhat else which he is pleased to think it.

But it is very plain, that he has mistaken the foundation for that which is built upon it, though not immediately: for the direct and immediate consequence is this; if Nature be to be imitated, then there is a Rule for imitating Nature rightly; otherwise there may be an end, and no means conducing to it. Hitherto I have proceeded by demonstration; but as our Divines, when they have prov'd a Deity, because there is order, and have inferred that this Deity ought to be worshipped, differ afterwards in the manner of the Worship; so, having laid down that Nature is to be imitated, and that Proposition proving the next, that then there are means which conduce to the imitating of Nature, I dare proceed no farther positively; but have only laid down some opinions of the Ancients and Moderns, and of my own, as means which they used, and which I thought probable for the attaining of that end. Those means are the same which my Antagonist calls the Foundations, how properly, the world may judge; and to prove that this is his meaning, he clears it immediately to you, by enumerating those Rules or Propositions against which he makes his particular exceptions, as namely, those of time, and place, in these words: *First, we are told the plot should not be so ridiculously contrived, as to crowd two several Countries into one stage; secondly, to cramp the Accidents of many years or days into the representation of two hours and an half; and lastly, a Conclusion drawn, that the only remaining Dispute is, concerning time, whether it should be contained in* 12 *or* 24 *hours; and the place to be limited to that spot of ground where the Play is supposed to begin: and this is called nearest Nature; for that is concluded most natural which is most probable, and nearest to that which it presents.*

Thus he has only made a small mistake of the means conducing to the end, for the end itself; and of the superstructure for the foundation: but he proceeds. *To shew, therefore, upon what ill grounds they dictate laws for Dramatique Poesie,* &c. He is here pleased to charge me with being Magisterial, as he has done in many other places of his Preface. Therefore in vindication of myself, I must crave leave to say, that my whole Discourse was Sceptical, according to that way of reasoning which was used by *Socrates*, *Plato*, and all the Academiques of old, which *Tully* and the best of the Ancients followed, and which is imitated by the modest Inquisitions of the Royal Society. That it is so, not only the name will shew, which is, *an Essay*, but the frame and Composition of the Work. You see it is a Dialogue sustained by persons of several opinions, all of them left doubtful, to be determined by the Readers in general; and more particularly defer'd to the accurate Judgment of my Lord *Buckhurst*, to whom I made a Dedication of my Book. These are my words in my Epistle, speaking of the persons whom I introduced in my Dialogue. 'Tis true, they differed in their opinions, as 'tis probable they would; neither do I take upon me to reconcile, but to relate them, leaving your Lordship to decide it in favour of that part which you shall judge most reasonable. And after that, in my Advertisement to the Reader I said this: The drift of the ensuing discourse is chiefly to vindicate the honour of our English Writers from the Censure of those who unjuﬆly prefer the French before them. This I intimate, leﬆ any should think me so exceeding vain, as to teach others an Art which they underﬆand much better than myself. But this is more than necessary to clear my modeﬆy in that point; & I am very confident that there is scarce any man who has loﬆ so much time as to read that trifle, but will be my Compurgator as to that arrogance whereof I am accused. The truth is, if I had been naturally guilty of so much vanity as to dictate my opinions, yet I do not find that the Character of a positive or self-conceited person is of such advantage to any in this Age, that I should labour to be publickly admitted of that Order.

But I am not now to defend my own Cause, when that of all the Ancients and Moderns is in queﬆion: for this Gentleman, who accuses me of arrogance, has taken a course not to be taxed with the other extream of modeﬆy. Those propositions which are laid down in my Discourse, as helps to the better imitation of Nature, are not mine, (as I have said,) nor were ever pretended so to be, but derived from the authority of *Ariﬆotle* and *Horace*, and from the rules and examples of *Ben. Johnson* and *Corneille*. These are the men with whom properly he contends, and againﬆ *whom he will endeavour to make it evident, that there is no such thing as what they All pretend.*

His Argument againﬆ the Unities of place and time, is this; *That 'tis as impossible for one Stage to present two Rooms or Houses truly, as two Countries or Kingdoms; & as impossible that five hours or twenty four hours should be two hours, as that a thousand hours or years should be less than what they are, or the greateﬆ part of time to be comprehended in the less: for all of them being impossible, they are none of them neareﬆ the Truth or Nature of what they present; for impossibilities are all equal, and admit of no degree.*

This Argument is so scattered into parts, that it can scarce be united into a Syllogism; yet, in obedience to him, *I will abbreviate* and comprehend as much of it as I can in few words, that my Answer to it may be more perspicuous. I conceive his meaning to be what follows, as to the unity of place: (if I miﬆake, I beg his pardon, professing it is not out of any design to play the *Argumentative Poet.*) If one Stage cannot properly present two Rooms or Houses, much less two Countries or Kingdoms, then there can be no Unity of place; but one Stage cannot properly perform this: therefore there can be no Unity of place.

I plainly deny his minor Proposition; the force of which, if I miﬆake not, depends on this; that the Stage being one place cannot be two. This, indeed, is as great a Secret, as that we are all mortal; but to requite it with another, I must crave leave to tell him, that though the Stage cannot be two places, yet it may properly represent them, successively, or at several times. His Argument is indeed no more than a meer fallacy, which will evidently appear, when we distinguish place, as it relates to Plays, into real and imaginary. The real place is that Theater, or piece of ground, on which the Play is acted. The imaginary, that House, Town, or Country, where the action of the *Drama* is supposed to be; or more plainly, where the Scene of the Play is laid. Let us now apply this to that Herculean Argument, *which if strictly and duely weighed, is to make it evident, that there is no such thing as what they all pretend.* 'Tis impossible, he says, for one Stage to present two Rooms or Houses: I answer, 'tis neither impossible, nor improper, for one real place to represent two or more imaginary places, so it be done successively; which in other words is no more than this; That the imagination of the Audience, aided by the words of the Poet, and painted Scenes, may suppose the Stage to be sometimes one place, sometimes another; now a Garden, or Wood, and immediately a Camp: which, I appeal to every mans imagination, if it be not true. Neither the Ancients nor Moderns, as much Fools as he is pleased to think them, ever asserted that they could make one place two; but they might hope, by the good leave of this Author, that the change of a Scene might lead the imagination to suppose the place alter'd: So that he cannot fasten those absurdities upon this Scene of a Play, or imaginary place of Action, that it is one place, and yet two. And this being so clearly proved, that it is past any shew of a reasonable denial, it will not be hard to destroy that other part of his Argument which depends upon it; namely that it is as impossible for a Stage to represent two Rooms or Houses, as two Countries or Kingdoms; for his reason is already overthrown, which was, because both were alike impossible. This is manifestly otherwise; for it is prov'd that a Stage may properly represent two Rooms or Houses; for the imagination being Judge of what is represented, will in reason be less chocqu'd with the appearance of two rooms in the same house, or two houses in the same City, than with two distant Cities in the same Country, or two remote Countries in the same Universe. Imagination in a man, or reasonable Creature, is supposed to participate of reason; and when that governs, as it does in the belief of fiction, reason is not destroyed, but misled, or blinded: that can prescribe to the reason, during the time of the representation, somewhat like a weak belief of what it sees and hears; and reason suffers itself to be so hood-wink'd, that it may better enjoy the pleasures of the fiction: but it is never so wholly made a captive, as to be drawn headlong into a perswasion of those things which are most remote from probability: 'tis in that case a free-born Subject, not a Slave; it will contribute willingly its assent, as far as it sees convenient, but will not be forc'd. Now there is a greater vicinity in Nature betwixt two Rooms than betwixt two Houses, betwixt two Houses than betwixt two Cities, and so of the rest; reason therefore can sooner be led by imagination to step from one room into another, than to walk to two distant houses, and yet rather to go thither, than to flye like a Witch through the air, and be hurried from one Region to another. Fancy and Reason go hand in hand; the first cannot leave the last behind; and though Fancy, when it sees the wide Gulph, would venture over as the nimbler, yet it is with-held by Reason, which will refuse to take the leap, when the distance over it appears too large. If *Ben. Johnson* himself will remove the Scene from *Rome* into *Tuscany* in the same Act, and from thence return to *Rome*, in the Scene which immediately follows, reason will consider there is no proportionable allowance of time to perform the journey, and therefore will chuse to stay at home. So then the less change of place there is, the less time is taken up in transporting the persons of the *Drama*, with Analogy to reason; and in that Analogy, or resemblance of Fiction to Truth, consists the excellency of the Play.

For what else concerns the Unity of place, I have already given my opinion of it in my *Essay*; that there is a latitude to be allowed to it, as several places in the same Town or City, or places adjacent to each other in the same Country, which may all be comprehended under the larger denomination of one place; yet with this restriction, that the nearer and fewer those imaginary places are, the greater resemblance they will have to Truth; and Reason, which cannot make them one, will be more easily led to suppose them so.

What has been said of the Unity of place, may easily be applied to that of time: I grant it to be impossible, that the greater part of time should be comprehended in the less, that twenty-four hours should be crowded into three: but there is no necessity of that Supposition. For as *Place*, so *Time* relating to a Play, is either imaginary or real: The real is comprehended in those three hours, more or less, in the space of which the Play is represented; The imaginary is that which is supposed to be taken up in the Representation, as twenty four hours more or less. Now no man ever could suppose that twenty four real hours could be included in the space of three: but where is the absurdity of affirming that the feigned business of twenty four imagin'd hours may not more naturally be represented in the compass of three real hours, than the like feigned business of twenty four years in the same proportion of real time? For the proportions are always real, and much nearer, by his permission, of twenty four to three, than of four thousand to it.

I am almoſt fearful of illuſtrating any thing by similitude, leſt he should confute it for an Argument; yet I think the comparison of a Glass will discover very aptly the fallacy of his Argument, both concerning time and place. The ſtrength of his Reason depends on this, That the less cannot comprehend the greater. I have already answered, that we need not suppose it does: I say not that the less can comprehend the greater, but only that it may represent it: As in a Glass or Mirrour of half a yard Diameter, a whole room and many persons in it may be seen at once; not that it can comprehend that room or those persons, but that it represents them to the sight.

But the Author of *The Duke of Lerma* is to be excus'd for his declaring againſt the Unity of time; for, if I be not much miſtaken, he is an intereſted person; the time of that Play taking up so many years as the favour of the Duke of *Lerma* continued; nay, the second and third Aċt including all the time of his Prosperity, which was a great part of the Reign of *Philip* the Third: for in the beginning of the second aċt he was not yet a Favourite, and before the end of the third, was in disgrace. I say not this with the leaſt design of limiting the Stage too servilely to 24 hours, however he be pleased to tax me with dogmatizing in that point. In my Dialogue, as I before hinted, several persons maintained their several opinions: one of them, indeed, who supported the Cause of the French Poesie, said, how ſtriċt they were in that Particular; but he who answered in behalf of our Nation, was willing to give more latitude to the Rule; and cites the words of *Corneille* himself, complaining againſt the severity of it, and observing what Beauties it banished from the Stage, *pag*. 44. of my *Essay*. In few words, my own opinion is this, (and I willingly submit it to my Adversary, when he will please impartially to consider it,) that the imaginary time of every Play ought to be contrived into as narrow a compass as the nature of the Plot, the quality of the Persons, and variety of Accidents will allow. In comedy I would not exceed 24 or 30 hours: for the Plot, Accidents, and Persons of Comedy are small, and may be naturally turned in a little compass: But in Tragedy the Design is weighty, and the Persons great; therefore there will naturally be required a greater space of time in which to move them. And this, though *Ben. Johnson* has not told us, yet 'tis manifeſtly his opinion: for you see that to his Comedies he allows generally but 24 hours; to his two Tragedies, *Sejanus* and *Catiline*, a much larger time: though he draws both of them into as narrow a compass as he can: For he shews you only the latter end of *Sejanus* his Favour, and the Conspiracy of *Catiline* already ripe, and just breaking out into action.

But as it is an errour on the one side, to make too great a disproportion betwixt the imaginary time of the Play, and the real time of its representation; so on the other side, it is an over-sight to compress the accidents of a Play into a narrower compass than that in which they could naturally be produc'd. Of this last errour the French are seldom guilty, because the thinness of their Plots prevents them from it; but few Englishmen, except *Ben. Johnson*, have ever made a Plot with variety of design in it, included in 24 hours, which was altogether natural. For this reason, I prefer the *Silent Woman* before all other Plays, I think justly; as I do its Author in Judgment, above all other Poets. Yet of the two, I think that errour the most pardonable, which in too straight a compass crowds together many accidents, since it produces more variety, and consequently more pleasure to the Audience; and because the nearness of proportion betwixt the imaginary and real time, does speciously cover the compression of the Accidents.

Thus I have endavoured to answer the meaning of his Argument; for as he drew it, I humbly conceive that it was none; as will appear by his Proposition, and the proof of it. His Proposition was this.

If strictly and duely weighed, 'tis as impossible for one Stage to present two Rooms or Houses, as two Countries or Kingdoms, &c. And his Proof this: *For all being impossible, they are none of them nearest the Truth or Nature of what they present.*

Here you see, instead of Proof or Reason, there is only *Petitio principii*: for in plain words, his sense is this; Two things are as impossible as one another, because they are both equally impossible: but he takes those two things to be granted as impossible which he ought to have prov'd such, before he had proceeded to prove them equally impossible: he should have made out first, that it was impossible for one Stage to represent two Houses, & then have gone forward to prove that it was as equally impossible for a Stage to present two Houses, as two Countries.

After all this, the very absurdity to which he would reduce me is none at all: for he only drives at this, That if his Argument be true, I must then acknowledge that there are degrees in impossibilities, which I easily grant him without dispute: and if I mistake not, *Aristotle* and the *School* are of my opinion. For there are some things which are absolutely impossible, and others which are only so *ex parte*; as 'tis absolutely impossible for a thing *to be*, and *not be*, at the same time; but for a Stone to move naturally upward, is only impossible *ex parte materiæ*; but it is not impossible for the first Mover to alter the Nature of it.

His last Assault, like that of a French man, is most feeble: for whereas I have observed, that none have been violent against Verse, but such only as have not attempted it, or have succeeded ill in their attempt, he will needs, according to his usual custom, improve my Observation to an Argument, that he might have the glory to confute it. But I lay my Observation at his feet, as I do my Pen, which I have often employ'd willingly in his deserved commendations, and now most unwillingly against his Judgment. For his person and parts, I honour them as much as any man living, and have had so many particular Obligations to him, that I should be very ungrateful, if I did not acknowledge them to the World. But I gave not the first occasion of this difference in opinions. In my Epistle Dedicatory, before my *Rival Ladies*, I had said somewhat in behalf of Verse, which he was pleased to answer in his Preface to his Plays: that occasioned my Reply in my Essay; and that Reply begot this rejoynder of his in his Preface to the Duke of *Lerma*. But as I was the last who took up Arms, I will be the first to lay them down. For what I have here written, I submit it wholly to him; and if I do not hereafter answer what may be objected against this Paper, I hope the World will not impute it to any other reason, than only the due respect which I have for so noble an Opponent.

THE INDIAN EMPEROUR

TO THE
Most Excellent and Most Illustrious Princess

ANNE,

Dutchess of *Monmouth* and *Bucclugh*, Wife to the
Most Illustrious and High-born Prince
JAMES DUKE of *Monmouth*.

May it please your Grace,

THE favour which Heroick Plays have lately found upon our Theaters, has been wholly deriv'd to them from the countenance and approbation they have receiv'd at Court. The most eminent persons for Wit and Honour in the Royal Circle having so far ownd them, that they have judg'd no way so fit as Verse to entertain a Noble Audience, or to express a noble passion. And amongst the rest which have been written in this kind, they have been so indulgent to this Poem, as to allow it no inconsiderable place. Since, therefore, to the Court I owe its fortune on the Stage, so, being now more publickly expos'd in Print, I humbly recommend it to your Graces Protection, who by all knowing persons are esteem'd a principal Ornament of the Court. But though the rank which you hold in the Royal Family, might direct the Eyes of a Poet to you, yet your beauty and goodness detain and fix them. High Objects, 'tis true, attract the sight; but it looks up with pain on Craggy Rocks and Barren Mountains, and continues not intent on any object, which is wanting in shades and greens to entertain it. Beauty, in Courts, *is so necessary to the young, that those who are without it, seem to be there to no other purpose than to wait on the triumphs of the fair; to attend their motions in obscurity, as the Moon and Stars do the Sun by day; or, at best, to be the refuge of those hearts which others have despis'd; and, by the unworthiness of both, to give and take a miserable comfort. But, as needful as beauty is, Virtue and Honour are yet more: the reign of it without their support is unsafe and short, like that of Tyrants. Every Sun which looks on Beauty wasts it; and, when it is once decaying, the repairs of Art are of as short continuance, as the after Spring when the Sun is going farther off. This,* Madam, *is its ordinary Fate; but yours, which is accompanied by Virtue, is not subject to that common destiny. Your Grace has not only a long time of Youth to flourish in, but you have likewise found the way, by an untainted preservation of your Honour, to* make that perishable good more lasting. And if Beauty, like Wines could be preserv'd by being mix'd and embodied with others of their own natures, then your Graces would be immortal, since no part of Europe can afford a parallel to your Noble Lord, in masculine Beauty, and in goodliness of shape. To receive the blessings and prayers of mankind, you need only to be seen together; we are ready to conclude that you are a pair of Angels sent below to make Virtue amiable in your persons, or to sit to Poets when they would pleasantly instruct the Age, by drawing goodness in the most perfect and alluring shape of Nature. But though Beauty be the Theme, on which Poets love to dwell, I must be forced to quit it as a private praise, since you have deserv'd those which are more publick. For Goodness and Humanity, which shine in you, are Virtues which concern Mankind: and by a certain kind of interest all people agree in their commendation, because the profit of them may extend to many. 'Tis so much your inclination to do good, that you stay not to be ask'd; which is an approach so nigh the Deity, that Humane Nature is not capable of a nearer. 'Tis my Happiness that I can testifie this Virtue of your Graces by my own experience; since I have so great an aversion from sollliciting Court Favours, that I am ready to look on those as very bold, who dare grow rich there without desert. But I beg your Graces pardon for assuming this Virtue of Modesty to my self, which the sequel of this Discourse will no way justifie. For in this address I have already quitted the character of a modest Man, by presenting you this Poem as an acknowledgment, which stands in need of your protection; and which ought no more to be esteem'd a Present, then it is accounted Bounty in the Poor, when they bestow a Child on some wealthy Friend, who will better breed it up. Off-springs of this Nature are like to be so numerous with me, that I must be forc'd to send some of them abroad; only this is like to be more fortunate then his Brothers, because I have landed him on an Hospitable shore. Under your Patronage Montezuma hopes he is more safe than in his Native Indies: and therefore comes to throw himself at your Graces feet, paying that homage to your Beauty, which he refus'd to the violence of his Conquerours. He begs only, that when he shall relate his sufferings, you will consider him as an Indian Prince, and not expect any other Eloquence from his simplicity, than what his griefs have furnish'd him withal. His story is, perhaps, the greatest which was ever represented in a Poem of this nature; (the action of it including the Discovery and Conquest of a New World.) In it I have neither wholly follow'd the truth of the History, nor altogether left it: but have taken all the liberty of a Poet, to adde, alter, or diminish, as I thought might best conduce to the beautifying of my work. It being not the business of a Poet to represent truth, but probability. But I am not to make the justification of this Poem, which I wholly leave to your Graces mercy. 'Tis an irregular piece, if compar'd with many of

Corneilles, *and, if I may make a judgment of it, written with more Flame then Art; in which it represents the mind and intention of the Author, who is with much more Zeal and Integrity, then Design and Artifice,*

MADAM,
Your Graces most Obedient,
and most Obliged Servant.
John Dryden.

October the 12th
1667.

Connexion of the Indian Emperour, *to the* Indian Queen.

THE Conclusion of the *Indian Queen*, (part of which Poem was writ by me) left little matter for another Story to be built on, there remaining but two of the considerable Characters alive, (*viz.*) *Montezuma* and *Orazia:* thereupon the Author of this, thought it necessary to produce new persons from the old ones; and considering the late *Indian Queen*, before she lov'd *Montezuma*, liv'd in clandestine Marriage with her General *Traxalla*; from those two he has rais'd a Son and two Daughters, suppos'd to be left young Orphans at their Death: On the other side, he has given to *Montezuma* and *Orazia*, two Sons and a Daughter: all now supposed to be grown up to Men and Womens Estate; and their Mother *Orazia* (for whom there was no further use in the story) lately dead.

So that you are to imagine about Twenty years elaps'd since the Coronation of *Montezuma*; who, in the Truth of the History, was a great and glorious Prince; and in whose time hapned the Discovery and Invasion of *Mexico* by the *Spaniards*, under the conduct of *Hernando Cortez*, who joyned with the *Taxallan-Indians*, the inveterate Enemies of *Montezuma*, wholly Subverted that flourishing Empire; the Conquest of which is the subject of this *Dramatique* Poem.

I have neither wholly followed the story, nor varied from it; and, as near as I could, have traced the Native simplicity and ignorance of the *Indians*, in relation to *European* Customes: The Shipping, Armour, Horses, Swords, and Guns of the *Spaniards*, being as new to them, as their Habits and their Language.

The difference of their Religion from ours, I have taken from the Story it self; and that which you find of it in the first and fifth Acts touching the sufferings and constancy of *Montezuma* in his Opinions, I have only illustrated, not alter'd from those who have written of it.

THE INDIAN EMPEROUR

The Names of the Persons represented.

Indians Men,
- *Montezuma*, Emperour of *Mexico.*
- *Odmar*, his Eldest Son.
- *Guyomar*, his Younger Son.
- *Orbellan*, Son to the late *Indian Queen* by *Traxalla.*
- *High Priest of the Sun.*

Women,
- *Cydaria*, *Montezuma*'s Daughter.
- *Almeria*, *Alibech*, — Sisters; and Daughters to the late *Indian Queen.*

Spaniards,
- *Cortez*, the *Spanish* General.
- *Vasquez*, *Pizarro*, — Commanders under him.

The Scene *MEXICO*, and two Leagues about it.

PROLOGUE.

A*Lmighty Critiques! Whom our* Indians *here*
Worship, just as they do the Devil, for fear.
In reverence to your pow'r I come this day
To give you timely warning of our Play.
The Scenes are old, the Habits are the same
We wore last year, before the Spaniards *came.*
Our Prologue, th' old-cast too——
For to observe the new it should at least
Be spoke, by some ingenious Bird or Beast.
Now, if you stay, the blood that shall be shed
From this poor Play, be all upon your head.
We neither promise you one Dance, or Show,
Then Plot and Language they are wanting too:
But you kind Wits, will those light faults excuse:
Those are the common frailties of the Muse;
Which who observes he buyes his place too dear:
For 'tis your business to be couzen'd here.
These wretched spies of Wit must then confess
They take more pains to please themselves the less.

Grant us such Judges, Phœbus, *we request,*
As still mistake themselves into a jest;
Such easie Judges, that our Poet may
Himself admire the fortune of his Play;
And arrogantly, as his fellows do,
Think he writes well, because he pleases you.
This he conceives not hard to bring about,
If all of you would join to help him out.
Would each man take but what he understands,
And leave the rest upon the Poet's hands.

THE
Indian Emperour:
OR, THE
CONQUEST of *MEXICO*

ACT I. SCENE I.

The Scene a pleasant Indian *Country.*

Enter Cortez, Vasquez, Pizarro, *with* Spaniards *and* Indians *of their party.*

Cort. ON what new happy Climate are we thrown,
So long kept secret, and so lately known?
As if our old world modestly withdrew,
And here, in private, had brought forth a new!
Vasq. Corn, Wine and Oyl are wanting to this Ground,
In which our Countries fruitfully abound:
As if this Infant world, yet un-array'd,
Naked and bare, in Nature's Lap were laid.
No useful Arts have yet found footing here;
But all untaught and salvage does appear.
Cort. Wild and untaught are Terms which we alone
Invent, for fashions differing from our own:
For all their Customs are by Nature wrought,
But we, by Art, unteach what Nature taught.
Piz. In *Spain* our Springs, like Old Mens Children, be
Decay'd and wither'd from their Infancy:
No kindly Showers fall on our barren earth,
To hatch the seasons in a timely birth.
Our Summer such a Russet Livery wears,
As in a Garment often dy'd appears.
Cort. Here nature spreads her fruitful sweetness round,
Breathes on the Air, and broods upon the ground.
Here days and nights the only seasons be,
The Sun no Climat does so gladly see:
When forc'd from hence, to view our parts, he mourns;
Takes little journies, and makes quick returns.

Vasq. Methinks we walk in dreams on fairy Land,
Where golden Ore lies mixt with common sand;
Each downfal of a flood the Mountains pour
From their rich bowels rolls a silver shower.
Cort. Heaven from all ages wisely did provide
This wealth, and for the braveſt Nation hide,
Who with four hundred foot, and forty horse,
Dare boldly go a New found World to force.
Piz. Our men, though Valiant, we should find too few,
But *Indians* joyn the *Indians* to subdue;
Taxallan, shook by *Montezumas* powers,
Has to reſiſt his forces, call'd in ours.
Vasq. Rashly to arm againſt so great a King,
I hold not safe, nor is it juſt to bring
A War, without a fair defiance made.
Piz. Declare we firſt our quarrel: then Invade.
Cort. My self, my Kings Embassadour, will go;
Speak, *Indian* Guide, how far to *Mexico*?
Indi. Your eyes can scarce so far a proſpect make,
As to discern the City on the Lake.
But that broad Caus-way will direct your way,
And you may reach the Town by noon of day.
Cort. Command a party of our *Indians* out,
With a ſtrict charge not to engage, but scout;
By noble ways we Conqueſt will prepare,
Firſt offer peace, and that refus'd, make war. [*Exeunt.*

SCENE II.

A Temple, and the high Prieſt with other Prieſts.

To them an Indian.

Ind. Haſte Holy Prieſt it is the King's command.
High Pr. When sets he forward?
Ind. ——He is near at hand.
High Pr. The Incense is upon the Altar plac'd,
The bloody Sacrifice already paſt.
Five hundred Captives saw the rising Sun,
Who loſt their light e're half his race was run.
That which remains we here muſt celebrate;

Where far from noise, without the City Gate,
The peaceful power that governs love repairs,
To feaſt upon soft vows and silent pray'rs.
We for his Royal presence only ſtay,
To end the rites of this so solemn day. *Exit* Indian.

Enter Montezuma; *his eldeſt Son* Odmar; *his Daughter* Cydaria, Almeria, Alibech, Orbellan, *and Train.*

They place themselves.

High Pr. On your birth day, while we sing
To our Gods and to our King,
Her, among this beauteous quire,
Whose perfections you admire,
Her, who faireſt does appear,
Crown her Queen of all the year.
Of the year and of the day,
And at her Feet your Garland lay.

Odm. My Father this way does his looks direct,
Heaven grant he give it not where I suspect.

Montezuma *rises, goes about the Ladies, and at length ſtays at* Almeria, *and bows.*

Mont. Since my *Orazia*'s Death I have not seen
A beauty so deserving to be Queen
As fair *Almeria.*

Alm.———Sure he will not know [*To her Brother and Siſter aside.*
My birth I to that injur'd Princess owe,
Whom his hard heart not only love deny'd,
But in her sufferings took unmanly Pride.

Alib. Since *Montezuma* will his choice renew,
In dead *Orazia*'s room electing you,
'Twill please our Mothers Ghoſt that you succeed
To all the glories of her Rivals Bed.

Alm. If news be carried to the shades below,
The *Indian* Queen will be more pleas'd, to know
That I his scorns on him, that scorn'd her, pay.

Orb. Would you could right her some more noble way.

She turns to him who is kneeling all this while.

Mont. Madam, this poſture is for Heaven design'd, [*Kneeling.*
And what moves Heaven I hope may make you kind.

Alm. Heaven may be kind, the Gods uninjur'd live,
And crimes below coſt little to forgive.

By thee, Inhumane, both my Parents dy'd;
One by thy sword, the other by thy pride.
Mont. My haughty mind no fate could ever bow,
Yet I must stoop to one who scorns me now:
Is there no pity to my sufferings due?
Alm. As much as what my mother found from you.
Mont. Your mother's wrongs a recompence shall meet,
I lay my Scepter at her Daughter's feet.
Alm. He, who does now my least commands obey,
Would call me Queen, and take my pow'r away.
Odm. Can he hear this, and not his Fetters break?
Is love so pow'rful, or his soul so weak?
I'le fright her from it, Madam, though you see
The King is kind, I hope your modesty
Will know, what distance to the Crown is due.
Alm. Distance and modesty prescrib'd by you?
Odm. *Almeria* dares not think such thoughts as these.
Alm. She dares both think an act what thoughts she please.
'Tis much below me on his Throne to sit;
But when I do, you shall petition it.
Odm. If, Sir, *Almeria* does your bed partake,
I'll mourn for my forgotten mother's sake.
Mont. When Parents loves are order'd by a Son,
Let streams prescribe their fountains where to run.
Odm. In all I urge I keep my duty still,
Not rule your reason but instruct your will.
Mont. Small use of reason in that Prince is shown,
Who follows others, and neglects his own.

Almeria *to* Orbellan *and* Alibech, *who are this while whispering to her.*

Alm. No, he shall ever love, and always be
The subject of my scorn and cruelty.
Orb. To prove the lasting torment of his Life,
You must not be his Mistress, but his Wife,
Few know what care, an Husbands Peace destroys,
His real griefs, and his dissembled joys.
Alm. What mark of pleasing vengeance could be shown,
If I to break his quiet lose my own?
Orb. A brother's life upon your love relies,
Since I do homage to *Cydarias* eyes:
How can her Father to my hopes be kind,
If in your heart, he no example find?
Alm. To save your life I'le suffer any thing,

Yet I'le not flatter this tempestuous King;
But work his stubborn soul a nobler way,
And, if he love, I'le force him to obey.
I take this Garland, not as given by you,
But as my merit, and my beauties due. *to* Montez.
As for the Crown that you, my slave, possess,
To share it with you would but make me less.

Enter Guyomar *hastily.*

Odm. My brother *Guyomar*! methinks I spye
Hast in his steps, and wonder in his eye.
Mont. I sent thee to the frontiers, quickly tell
The cause of thy return, are all things well?
Guy. I went, in order, Sir, to your command,
To view the utmost limits of the land:
To that Sea shore where no more world is found,
But foaming billows breaking on the ground,
Where, for a while, my eyes no object met
But distant skies that in the Ocean set:
And low hung clouds that dipt themselves in rain.
To shake their fleeces on the earth again.
At last, as far as I could cast my eyes
Upon the Sea, somewhat, methought did rise
Like blewish mists, which still appearing more,
Took dreadful shapes, and mov'd towards the shore.
Mont. What forms did these new wonders represent?
Guy. More strange than what your wonder can invent.
The object I could first distinctly view
Was tall streight trees which on the waters flew,
Wings on their sides instead of leaves did grow,
Which gather'd all the breath the winds could blow:
And at their roots grew floating Palaces,
Whose out-blow'd bellies cut the yielding Seas.
Mont. What Divine Monsters, O ye gods, were these
That float in air and flye upon the Seas!
Came they alive or dead upon the shore?
Guy. Alas, they liv'd too sure, I heard them roar:
All turn'd their sides, and to each other spoke,
I saw their words break out in fire and smoke.
Sure 'tis their voice that Thunders from on high,
Or these the younger brothers of the Skie.
Deaf with the noyse I took my hasty flight,
No mortal courage can support the fright.

High Pr. Old Prophecies foretel our fall at hand,
When bearded men in floating Caſtles Land,
I fear it is of dire Portent.
Mont. ———Go see
What it fore-shows, and what the gods decree.
Mean time proceed we to what rites remain.
Odmar, of all this presence does contain,
Give her your wreath whom you esteem moſt fair.
Odm. Above the reſt I judge one beauty rare,
And may that beauty prove as kind to me,
He gives Alibech *the wreath.*
As I am sure fair *Alibech* is she.
Mont. You *Guyomar*, muſt next perform your part.
Guy. I want a Garland, but I'le give a heart:
My brothers pardon I muſt firſt implore,
Since I with him fair *Alibech* adore.
Odm. That all should *Alibech* adore 'tis true,
But some reſpect is to my birth-right due.
My claim to her by Eldership I prove.
Guy. Age is a plea in Empire, not in Love.
Odm. I long have ſtaid for this solemnity
To make my passion publick.
Guy.——So have I.
Odm. But from her birth my soul has been her slave,
My heart receiv'd the firſt wounds that she gave:
I watch'd the early glories of her Eyes,
As men for day break watch the eaſtern Skies.
Guy. It seems my soul then mov'd the quicker pace,
Yours firſt set out, mine reach'd her in the race.
Mont. *Odmar*, your choice I cannot disapprove;
Nor juſtly, *Guyomar*, can blame your love.
To *Alibech* alone refer your Suit,
And let her sentence finish your dispute.
Alib. You think me Sir a Miſtress quickly won,
So soon to finish what is scarce begun:
In this surprise should I a Judgment make,
'Tis answering Riddles e're I'm well awake:
If you oblige me suddenly to chuse,
The choice is made, for I muſt both refuse.
For to my self I owe this due regard,
Not to make love my gift, but my reward:
Time beſt will show whose services will laſt.
Odm. Then judge my future service by my paſt.

What I shall be by what I was, you know,
That love took deepeſt root which firſt did grow.
Guy. That love which firſt was set will firſt decay,
Mine of a fresher date will longer ſtay.
Odm. Still you forget my birth.
Guy.——But you, I see,
Take care ſtill to refresh my memory.
Mont. My Sons, let your unseemly discord cease,
If not in friendship, live at leaſt in peace.
Orbellan, where you love beſtow your wreath.
Orb. My Love I dare not, ev'n in whispers breathe.
Mont. A vertuous Love may venture any thing.
Orb. Not to attempt the Daughter of my King?
Mont. Whither is all my former fury gone?
Once more I have *Traxalla*'s chains put on,
And by his Children am in triumph led,
Too well the living have reveng'd the dead!
Alm. You think my brother born your enemy,
He's of *Traxalla*'s blood, and so am I.
Mont. In vain I ſtrive,
My Lyon-heart is with Loves toyls beset,
Strugling I fall ſtill deeper in the net.
Cydaria your new lovers Garland take,
And use him kindly for your Fathers sake.
Cyd. So ſtrong an hatred does my nature sway,
That spight of duty I muſt disobey.
Besides you warn'd me ſtill of loving two,
Can I love him, already loving you?

Enter a Guard *haſtily*.

Mont. How now.——
You look amaz'd, as if some sudden fear
Had seiz'd your hearts, is any danger near?
1. *Guard*. Behind the covert where this Temple ſtands,
Thick as the shades, there issue swarming bands
Of ambush'd men, whom, by their arms and dress,
To be *Taxcallan* Enemies I guess. *Another Enters*.
2. *Guard*. The Temple, Sir, is almoſt compaſt round.
Mont. Some speedy way for passage muſt be found.
Make to the City by the Poſtern Gate,
I'le either force my Victory, or Fate:
A glorious death in arms I'le rather prove,
Than ſtay to perish tamely by my Love.

An Alarm within. Enter Montezuma, Odmar, Guyomar, Alibech, Orbellan, Cydaria, Almeria, *as pursued by* Taxallans.

Mont. No succour from the Town?
Odm. ——None, none is nigh.
Guy. We are inclos'd, and must resolve to dye.
Mont. Fight for revenge now hope of life is past,
But one stroke more and that will be my last.

Enter Cortez, Vasquez, Pizarro, *to the* Taxallans, Cortez *stays them, just falling on.*

Cort. Contemn'd? my orders broke even in my sight!
[*To his* Indians.
Did I not strictly charge you should not fight?
Ind. Your choler, General, does unjustly rise,
To see your Friends pursue your Enemies;
The greatest and most cruel foes we have
Are these whom you would ignorantly save,
By ambush'd men, behind their Temple laid,
We have the King of *Mexico* betray'd.
Cort. Where, banish'd Vertue, wilt thou shew thy face,
If treachery infects thy *Indian* race?
Dismiss your rage, and lay your weapons by;
Know I protect them and they shall not dye.
Ind. O wond'rous mercy shown to foes distrest!
Cort. Call them not so, when once with odds opprest,
Nor are they Foes my clemency defends,
Until they have refus'd the name of Friends:
Draw up our *Spaniards* by themselves, then Fire
Our Guns on all who do not straight retire. *To* Vasq.
Ind. O mercy, mercy, at thy feet we fall, Ind. *kneeling.*
Before thy roaring gods destroy us all:
See we retreat without the least reply, *The* Taxallans *retire.*
Keep thy gods silent, if they speak we dye.
Mont. The fierce *Taxallans* lay their weapons down,
Some miracle in our relief is shown.
Guy. These bearded men, in shape and colour be
Like those I saw come floating on the Sea. [Mont. *kneels to* Cort.
Mont. Patron of *Mexico* and god of Wars,
Son of the Sun, and brother of the Stars.
Cort. Great Monarch, your devotion you misplace.
Mont. Thy actions shown thee born of Heavenly Race,
If then thou art that cruel god whose eyes
Delight in Blood, and Humane Sacrifice,

Thy dreadful Altars I with Slaves will store,
And feed thy nostrils with hot reeking gore;
Or if that mild and gentle god thou be,
Who dost mankind below with pity see,
With breath of incense we will glad thy heart:
But if, like us, of mortal seed thou art,
Presents of choicest Fowls, and Fruits I'le bring,
And in my Realms thou shalt be more then King.
Cort. Monarch of Empires, and deserving more
Than the Sun sees upon your Western shore;
Like you a Man, and hither lead by fame,
Not by constraint but by my choice I came;
Ambassadour of Peace, if Peace you chuse,
Or Herauld of a War if you refuse.
Mont. Whence or from whom dost thou these offers bring?
Cort. From *Charles* the Fifth, the Worlds most Potent King.
Mont. Some petty Prince, and one of little fame,
For to this hour I never heard his name:
The two great Empires of the World I know,
That of *Peru*, and this of *Mexico*;
And since the earth none larger does afford,
This *Charles* is some poor Tributary Lord.
Cort. You speak of that small part of earth you know.
But betwixt us and you wide Oceans flow,
And watry desarts of so vast extent,
That passing hither, four Full Moons we spent.
Mont. But say, what news, what offers dost thou bring
From so remote, and so unknown a King?
Vasq. *Spain*'s mighty Monarch, to whom Heaven thinks fit
That all the Nations of the Earth submit,

While Vasquez *speaks,* Cortez *spies the Ladies, and goes to them, entertaining* Cydaria *with Courtship in dumb show.*

In gracious clemency, does condescend
On these conditions to become your Friend.
First, that of him you shall your Scepter hold,
Next, you present him with your useless Gold:
Last, that you leave those Idols you implore,
And one true Deity with him adore.
Mont. You speak your Prince a mighty Emperour,
But his demands have spoke him Proud, and Poor;
He proudly at my free-born Scepter flies,
Yet poorly begs a mettal I despise.

Gold thou may'st take, what-ever thou canst find,
Save what for sacred uses is design'd:
But, by what right pretends your King to be
The Soveraign Lord of all the World, and me?
Piz. The Soveraign Priest,———
Who represents on Earth the pow'r of Heaven,
Has this your Empire to our Monarch given.
Mont. Ill does he represent the Powers above,
Who nourishes debate, not Preaches love;
Besides, what greater folly can be shown?
He gives another what is not his own.
Vasq. His pow'r must needs unquestion'd be below,
For he in Heaven an Empire can bestow.
Mont. Empires in Heaven he with more ease may give,
And you perhaps would with less thanks receive;
But Heaven has need of no such Vice-roy here,
It self bestows the Crowns that Monarchs wear.
Piz. You wrong his power as you mistake our end,
Who came thus far Religion to extend.
Mont. He who Religion truely understands,
Knows its extent must be in Men, not Lands.
Odm. But who are those that truth must propagate
Within the confines of my Fathers state?
Vasq. Religious Men, who hither must be sent
As awful Guides of Heavenly Government;
To teach you Penance, Fasts, and Abstinence,
To punish Bodies for the Souls offence.
Mont. Cheaply you sin, and punish crimes with ease,
Not as th' offended, but th' offenders please.
First injure Heaven, and when its wrath is due,
Your selves prescribe it how to punish you.
Odm. What numbers of these Holy Men must come?
Piz. You shall not want, each Village shall have some
Who, though the Royal Dignity they own,
Are equal to it and depend on none.
Guy. Depend on none! you treat them sure in state,
For 'tis their plenty does their pride create.
Mont. Those ghostly Kings would parcel out my pow'r,
And all the fatness of my Land devour;
That Monarch sits not safely on his Throne,
Who bears, within, a power that shocks his own.
They teach obedience to Imperial sway,
But think it sin if they themselves obey.

Vasq. It seems then our Religion you accuse.
And peaceful homage to our King refuse.
Mont. Your gods I slight not, but will keep my own.
My Crown is absolute, and holds of none;
I cannot in a base subjection live,
Nor suffer you to take, though I would give.
Cort. Is this your answer, Sir?
Mont.———This as a Prince,
Bound to my Peoples and my Crowns defence,
I must return, but, as a man by you
Redeem'd from death, all gratitude is due.
Cort. It was an act my Honour bound me to,
But what I did were I again to do,
I could not do it on my Honours score,
For Love would now oblige me to do more.
Is no way left that we may yet agree?
Must I have War, yet have no Enemy?
Vasq. He has refus'd all terms of Peace to take.
Mont. Since we must fight, hear Heavens, what Prayers I make,
First, to preserve this Antient State and me,
But if your doom the fall of both decree,
Grant only he who has such Honour shown,
When I am dust, may fill my empty Throne.
Cort. To make me happier than that wish can do,
Lies not in all your gods to grant, but you;
Let this fair Princess but one minute stay,
A look from her will your obligements pay.
Exeunt Montezuma, Odmar, Guyomar, Orbellan,
Almeria, *and* Alibech.
Mont. to *Cyd.* Your duty in your quick return be shown.
Stay you, and wait my Daughter to the Town. *To his Guards.*
Cydaria *is going, but turns and looks back upon* Cortez,
who is looking on her all this while.
Cyd. My Father's gone, and yet I cannot go, *Aside.*
Sure I have something lost or left behind!
Cort. Like Travellers who wander in the Snow,
I on her beauty gaze till I am blind, *Aside.*
Cyd. Thick breath, quick pulse, and heaving of my heart,
All signs of some unwonted change appear:
I find my self unwilling to depart,
And yet I know not why I would be here.
Stranger you raise such torments in my breast,
That when I go, if I must go again,

I'le tell my Father you have rob'd my reſt,
And to him of your injuries complain.
Cort. Unknown, I swear, those wrongs were which I wrought,
But my complaints will much more juſt appear,
Who from another world my freedom brought,
And to your conquering Eyes have loſt it here.
Cyd. Where is that other world from whence you came?
Cort. Beyond the Ocean, far from hence it lies.
Cyd. Your other world, I fear, is then the same
That souls muſt go to when the body dies.
But what's the cause that keeps you here with me?
That I may know what keeps me here with you?
Cort. Mine is a love which muſt perpetual be,
If you can be so juſt as I am true.

Enter Orbellan.

Orb. Your Father wonders much at your delay.
Cyd. So great a wonder for so small a ſtay!
Orb. He has commanded you with me to go.
Cyd. Has he not sent to bring the ſtranger too?
Orb. If he to morrow dares in fight appear,
His high plac'd Love, perhaps may coſt him dear.
Cort. Dares——that word was never spoke to *Spaniard* yet
But forfeited his Life who gave him it;
Haſt quickly with thy pledge of safety hence,
Thy guilt's protected by her innocence.
Cyd. Sure in some fatal hour my Love was born,
So soon o'rcaſt with absence in the morn!
Cort. Turn hence those pointed glories of your Eyes,
For if more charms beneath those Circles rise,
So weak my Vertue, they so ſtrong appear,
I shall turn ravisher to keep you here. *Exeunt omnes.*

ACT II.

SCENE, *The Magitians Cave.*

Enter Montezuma, *High Prieſt.*

Mont. NOT that I fear the utmoſt Fate can do,
Come I th' event of doubtful War to know,
For Life and Death are things indifferent,
Each to be chose as either brings content;

My motive from a Nobler cause does spring,
Love rules my heart, and is your Monarchs King;
I more desire to know *Almeria*'s mind,
Than all that Heaven has for my ﬅate design'd.

High Pr. By powerful Charms which nothing can withﬅand,
I'le force the Gods to tell what you demand.

Charm,

Thou Moon, that aid'ﬅ us with thy Magick might,
And ye small Starrs, the scattered seeds of light,
Dart your pale beams into this gloomy place,
That the sad powers of the Infernal race
May read above what's hid from Humane Eyes,
And in your walks, see Empires fall and rise.
And ye Immortal Souls, that once were Men,
And now resolv'd to Elements agen,
Who wait for Mortal frames in depths below,
And did before what we are doom'd to do;
Once, twice, and thrice, I wave my Sacred wand,
Ascend, ascend, ascend at my command. *An Earthy Spirit rises.*

Spir. In vain, O mortal men, your Prayers implore
The aid of powers below, that want it more:
A God more ﬅrong, who all the gods commands,
Drives us to exile from our Native Lands;
The Air swarms thick with wandring Deities,
Which drowsily like humming Beetles rise
From our lov'd Earth, where peacefully we slept,
And far from Heaven a long possession kept.
The frighted *Satyrs* that in Woods delight,
Now into Plains with prick'd up Ears take flight;
And scudding thence, while they their horn-feet ply
About their Syres the little *Silvans* cry:
A Nation loving Gold muﬅ rule this place,
Our Temples ruine, and our Rites Deface:
To them, O King, is thy loﬅ Scepter given,
Now mourn thy fatal search, for since wise Heaven
More ill than good to Mortals does dispense,
It is not safe to have too quick a sense. *Descends.*

Mont. Mourn they who think repining can remove
The firm decrees of those that rule above;
The brave are safe within, who ﬅill dare dye,
When e're I fall I'le scorn my deﬅiny.
Doom as they please with my Empire not to ﬅand.
I'le grasp my Scepter with my dying hand.

High Pr. Those Earthy Spirits black and envious are:
I'le call up other gods, of form more fair:
Who Visions dress in pleasing Colour still,
Set all the good to show, and hid the ill:
Kalib ascend, my fair-spoke servant rise,
And sooth my Heart with pleasing Prophecies.

Kalib *ascends all in White in the shape of a Woman, and Sings.*

Kalib. I look'd and saw within the Book of Fate,
Where many days did lower,
Where lo one happy hour
Leapt up, and smil'd to save thy sinking State;
A day shall come when in thy power
Thy cruel Foes shall be;
Then shall thy Land be free,
And thou in Peace shalt reign.
But take, O take that opportunity,
Which once refus'd will never come again. *Descends.*

Mont. I shall deserve my Fate if I refuse
That happy hour which Heaven allots to use;
But of my Crown thou too much care do'st take,
That which I value more, my Love's at stake.
High Pr. Arise ye subtle Spirits that can spy,
When Love is enter'd in a Females eye;
You that can read it in the midst of doubt,
And in the midst of frowns can find it out;
You that can search those many corner'd minds,
Where Womans crooked fancie, turns, and winds,
You that can Love explore, and truth impart,
Where both lye deepest hid in Womans heart.
Arise——

The Ghosts of Traxalla *and* Acacis *arise, they stand stil. and point at* Montez.

High Pr. I did not for these Ghastly Visions send,
Their sudden coming does some ill portend,
Begon———begon———they will not dis-appear,
My Soul is seiz'd with an unusual fear.
Mont. Point on, point on, and see whom you can fright,
Shame and Confusion seize these shades of night.
Ye thin and empty forms am I your sport? *They smile.*
If you were flesh——
You know you durst not use me in this sort.

The Ghost of the Indian Queen *rises betwixt the Ghosts with a Dagger in her Breast.*

Mont. Ha!
I feel my Hair grow stiff, my Eye-Balls rowl,
This is the only form could shake my Soul.
Ghost. The hopes of thy succesless Love resign,
Know *Montezuma*, thou art only mine;
For those that here on Earth their passion shew
By death for Love, receive their right below.
Why dost thou then delay my longing Arms?
Have Cares, and Age, and Mortal life such Charms!
The Moon grows sickly at the sight of day,
And early Cocks have summon'd me away:
Yet I'le appoint a meeting place below.
For there fierce winds o're dusky Vallies blow:
Whose every puff bears empty shades away,
Which guideless in those dark Dominions stray.
Just at the entrance of the Field below,
Thou shalt behold a tall black Poplar grow,
Safe in its hollow trunk I will attend,
And seize thy Spirit when thou dost descend. *Descends.*
Mont. I'le seize thee there, thou Messenger of Fate:
Would my short Life had yet a shorter date!
I'm weary of this flesh which holds us here,
And dastards manly Souls with hope and fear:
These heats and colds still in our breasts make War,
Agues and Feavers all our passions are. *Exeunt.*

SCENE II.

Cydaria, Alibech, *betwixt the two Armies.*

Alib. Blessings will Crown your Name if you prevent
That Blood, which in this Battel will be spent;
Nor need you fear so just a sute to move,
Which both becomes your duty and your Love.
Cyd. But think you he will come? their Camp is near,
And he already knows I wait him here.
Alib. You are too young your power to understand,
Lovers take wing upon the least command;
Already he is here.

Enter Cortez *and* Vasquez *to them.*

Cort. Methinks like two black storms on either hand,
Our *Spanish* Army and your *Indians* stands;
This only space betwixt the Cloud, is clear,
Where you, like day, broke loose from both, appear.
Cyd. Those closing Skies might still continue bright,
But who can help it if you'l make it night?
The Gods have given you power of Life and Death,
Like them to save or scatter with a breath.
Cort. That power they to your Father did dispose,
'Twas in his choice to make us Friends or Foes.
Alib. Injurious strength would rapine still excuse,
By off'ring terms the weaker must refuse:
And such as these your hard conditions are,
You threaten Peace, and you invite a War.
Cort. If for my self to Conquer here I came,
You might perhaps my actions justly blame:
Now I am sent, and am not to dispute
My Princes orders, but to execute.
Alib. He who his Prince so blindly does obey,
To keep his Faith his Vertue throws away.
Cort. Monarchs may err, but should each private breast
Judge their ill Acts, they would dispute their best.
Cyd. Then all your care is for your Prince I see,
Your truth to him out-weighs your love to me;
You may so cruel to deny me prove,
But never after that, pretend to love.
Cort. Command my Life, and I will soon obey,
To save my Honour I my Blood will pay.
Cyd. What is this Honour which does Love controul.
Cort. A raging Fit of Vertue in the Soul;
A painful burden, which great minds must bear,
Obtain'd with danger, and possess'd with fear.
Cyd. Lay down that burden, if it painful grow,
You'l find, without it, Love will lighter go.
Cort. Honour once lost is never to be found.
Alib. Perhaps he looks to have both passions Crown'd:
First dye his Honour in a Purple Flood.
Then Court the Daughter in the Fathers Blood.
Cort. The edge of War I'le from the Battel take,
And spare her Father's Subjects for her sake.
Cyd. I cannot love you less when I'm refus'd,

But I can dye to be unkindly us'd;
Where shall a Maids diſtracted heart find reſt,
If she can miss it in her Lovers breaſt?
Cort. I till to morrow will the fight delay:
Remember you have conquer'd me to day.
Alib. This grant deſtroys all you have urg'd before,
Honour could not give this, or can give more;
Our Women in the foremoſt ranks appear,
March to the Fight, and meet your Miſtress there:
Into the thickeſt Squadrons she muſt run,
Kill her, and see what Honour will be won.
Cyd. I muſt be in the Battel; but I'le go
With empty Quiver, and unbended Bow;
Not draw an Arrow in this fatal ſtrife,
For fear its point should reach your Noble Life.

[*Enter* Pizarro.

Cort. No more, your kindness wounds me to the death,
Honour, be gone, what art thou but a breath?
I'le live, proud of my infamy and shame,
Grac'd with no Triumph but a Lovers name;
Men can but say Love did his reason blind,
And Love's the nobleſt frailty of the mind.
Draw off my Men, the War's already done.
Piz. Your Orders come too late, the Fight's begun,
The Enemy drives on with fury led,
And fierce *Orbellan* combats in their head.
Cort. He juſtly fears a Peace with me would prove
Of ill concernment to his haughty Love;
Retire, fair Excellence, I'le go to meet
New Honour, but to lay it at your Feet.
Exeunt Cortez, Vasquez, Pizarro.

Enter Odmar *and* Guyomar *to* Alibech *and* Cydaria.

Odm. Now, Madam, since a danger does appear
Worthy my Courage, though below my Fear,
Give leave to him who may in Battel dye,
Before his Death to ask his deſtiny.
Guy. He cannot Dye whom you command to Live,
Before the Fight you can the Conqueſt give;
Speak where you'l place it?
Alib. ———Briefly then, to both,

One I in secret Love, the other Loath;
But where I hate, my hate I will not show,
And he I love, my Love shall never know;
True worth shall gain me, that it may be said,
Desert, not fancy, once a Woman led.
He who in fight his courage shall oppose
With most success against his Countries Foes,
From me shall all that recompence receive
That Valour Merits, or that Love can give:
'Tis true my hopes and fears are all for one;
But hopes and fears are to my self alone.
Let him not shun the danger of the strife,
I but his Love, his Country claims his Life.

Odm. All Obstacles my Courage shall remove.
Guy. Fall on, fall on.
Odm. ———For Liberty.
Guy. ———For Love. *Exeunt, the Women following.*

SCENE *changes to the* Indian *Country.*

Enter Montezuma *attended by his* Indians.

Mont. Charge, charge, their ground the faint *Taxallans* yield,
Bold in close Ambush, base in open Field:
The envious Devil did my Fortune wrong:
Thus Fought, thus Conquer'd I, when I was young. *Exit.*

Alarm. Enter Cortez *Bloudy.*

Cort. Furies pursue these false *Taxallans* Flight,
Dare they be Friends to us, and dare not Fight?
What Friends can Cowards be, what hopes appear
Of help from such, who where they hate show fear!

Enter Pizarro, Vasquez.

Piz. The Field grows thin, and those that now remain
Appear but like the shadows of the Slain.
Vasq. The fierce old King is vanish'd from the place,
And in a cloud of dust pursues the Chase.
Cort. Their eager Chase disorder'd does appear,
Command our Horse to charge them in the Rear; [*To* Pizarro.
You to our old *Castillian* Foot retire, [*To* Vasquez.
Who yet stand firm, and at their backs give Fire. *Exeunt severally.*

Enter Odmar *and* Guyomar, *meeting each other in the Battel.*

Odm. Where haſt thou been since firſt the Fight began,
Thou less then Woman in the shape of Man?
Guy. Where I have done what may thy Envy move,
Things worthy of my Birth, and of my Love.
Odm. Two bold *Taxallans* with one Dart I slew,
And left it ſticking ere my Sword I drew.
Guy. I sought not Honour on so base a Train,
Such Cowards by our Women may be Slain;
I fell'd along a Man of Bearded face,
His Limbs all cover'd with a Shining case:
So wondrous hard, and so secure of wound,
It made my Sword, though edg'd with Flint, rebound.
Odm. I kill'd a double Man, the one half lay
Upon the ground, the other ran away. *Guns go off within.*

Enter Montezuma *out of breath, with him* Alibech *and an* Indian.

Mont. All's loſt———
Our Foes with Lightning and with Thunder Fight,
My Men in vain shun death by shameful Flight;
For Death's invisible come wing'd with Fire,
They hear a dreadful noise and ſtraight expire.
Take, gods, that Soul ye did in spight create,
And made it great to be unfortunate:
Ill Fate for me unjuſtly you provide,
Great Souls are Sparks of your own Heavenly Pride:
That luſt of power we from your god-heads have,
You're bound to please those Appetites you gave.

Enter Vasquez *and* Pizarro *with* Spaniards.

Vasq. Pizarro, I have hunted hard to day
Into our toyls the nobleſt of the prey;
Seize on the King, and him your Prisoner make,
While I in kind revenge my taker take.

Pizarro *with two goes to Attaque the King*, Vasquez *with another to seize* Alibech.

Guy. Their danger is alike, whom shall I free?
Odm. I'le follow Love.
Guy.———I'le follow Piety.

Odmar *retreats from* Vasquez *with* Alibech *off the Stage*, Guyomar *Fights for his Father.*

Guy. Fly, Sir, while I give back that life you gave,
Mine is well loſt, if I your life can save.

Montezuma *Fights off*, Guyomar *making his retreat*, *ſtays*.

Guy. 'Tis more than Man can do to 'scape them all,
Stay, let me see where nobleſt I may fall.

He runs at Vasquez, *is seized behind and taken*.

Vasq. Conduct him off,
And give command he ſtrictly guarded be.

Guy. In vain are guards, Death sets the Valiant free.

Exit Guyomar *with Guards*.

Vasq. A Glorious Day! and bravely was it Fought,
Great Fame our General in great Danger sought;
From his ſtrong Arm I saw his Rival run,
And in a crowd, th' unequal Combat shun.

Enter Cortez, *leading* Cydaria, *who seems crying, and begging of him*.

Cort. Man's force is fruitless, and your gods would fail
To save the City, but your Tears prevail:
I'le of my Fortune no advantage make,
Those Terms they had once given, they ſtill may take.

Cyd. Heaven has of right all Victory design'd,
Where boundless power dwells in a will confin'd;
Your *Spanish* Honour does the World excel.

Cort. Our greateſt Honour is in loving well.

Cyd. Strange ways you practise there to win a Heart,
Here Love is Nature, but with you 'tis Art.

Cort. Love is with us, as Natural as here,
But fetter'd up with cuſtom more severe.
In tedious Courtship we declare our pain,
And ere we kindness find, firſt meet disdain.

Cyd. If Women love they needless pains endure,
Their Pride and Folly but delay their Cure.

Cort. What you mis-call their Folly, is their care,
They know how fickle common Lovers are:
Their Oaths and Vows are cautiously believ'd,
For few there are but have been once deceiv'd.

Cyd. But if they are not truſted when they vow,
What other marks of passion can they show?

Cort. With Feaſts and Musick, all that brings delight,
Men treat their Ears, their Pallats, and their Sight.

Cyd. Your Gallants sure have little Eloquence,

Failing to move the Soul, they court the Sence:
With Pomp, and Trains, and in a crowd they Woe,
When true Felicity is but in two;
But can such Toys your Womens Passion move?
This is but noise and tumult, 'tis not Love.
Cort. I have no reason, Madam, to excuse
Those ways of Gallantry I did not use;
My Love was true, and on a Nobler score.
Cyd. Your Love! Alas! then have you Lov'd before!
Cort. 'Tis true I lov'd, but she is Dead, she's Dead,
And I should think with her all Beauty fled,
Did not her fair resemblance live in you,
And by that Image my first Flames renew.
Cyd. Ah happy Beauty, whosoe're thou art!
Though dead, thou keep'st possession of his Heart;
Thou mak'st me jealous to the last degree,
And art my Rival in his Memory;
Within his Memory, ah, more then so,
Thou liv'st and triumph'st ore *Cydaria* too.
Cort. What strange disquiet has uncalm'd your breast,
Inhumane fair, to rob the dead of rest!
Poor Heart!
She slumbers deep, deep in her silent Tomb,
Let her possess in Peace that narrow Room.
Cyd. Poor heart, he pities and bewails her death,
Some god, much hated soul, restore thy breath,
That I may kill thee, but some ease 'twill be,
I'le kill my self for but resembling thee.
Cort. I dread your anger, your disquiet fear,
But blows from hands so soft who would not bear?
So kind a passion why should I remove?
Since jealousie but shows how well we love;
Yet jealousie so strange I never knew,
Can she who Loves me not disquiet you?
For in the Grave no Passions fill the Breast,
'Tis all we gain by Death to be at rest.
Cyd. That she no longer Loves brings no relief,
Your Love to her still lives, and that's my grief.
Cort. The object of desire once tane away,
'Tis then not Love but pitty which we pay.
Cyd. 'Tis such a pitty I should never have,
When I must lye forgotten in the Grave;
I meant to have oblig'd you when I dy'd,

That after me you should love none beside,
But you are false already.
Cort. ——If untrue,
By Heaven, my falshood is to her, not you.
Cyd. Observe, sweet Heaven, how falsly he does swear,
You said you Lov'd me for resembling her.
Cort. That Love was in me by resemblance bred,
But shows you chear'd my sorrows for the Dead.
Cyd. You still repeat the greatness of your grief.
Cort. If that was great, how great was the relief?
Cyd. The first Love still the strongest we account.
Cort. That seems more strong which could the first surmount:
But if you still continue thus unkind,
Whom I Love best, you by my Death shall find.
Cyd. If you should dye my death should yours pursue,
But yet I am not satisfi'd you'r true.
Cort. Hear me, ye gods, and punish him you hear,
If ought within the World, I hold so dear.
Cyd. You would deceive the gods and me, she's dead,
And is not in the World whose Love I dread.
Name not the world, say nothing is so dear.
Cort. Then nothing is, let that secure your fear.
Cyd. 'Tis Time must wear it off, but I must go,
Can you your constancy in absence show.
Cort. Mis-doubt my constancy and do not try,
But stay and keep me ever in your eye.
Cyd. If as a Prisoner I were here, you might
Have been insisted on a Conqu'rours right,
And stay'd me here; but now my Love would be
Th' effect of force, and I would give it free.
Cort. To doubt your Vertue or your Love were sin;
Call for the Captive Prince and bring him in.

Enter Guyomar *bound and sad.*

You look, Sir, as your Fate you could not bear. [*To* Guyomar.
Are *Spanish* Fetters then so hard to wear?
Fortune's unjust, she ruines oft the Brave,
And him who should be Victor, makes the Slave.
Guy. Son of the Sun, my Fetters cannot be
But Glorious for me, since put on by thee;
The ills of Love, not those of Fate I fear,
These I can brave, but those I cannot bear;

My Rival Brother, while I'm held in Chains,
In freedom reaps the fruit of all my Pains.
Cort. Let it be never said, that he whose breaſt
Is fill'd with Love, should break a Lovers reſt;
Haſte, lose no time, your Siſter sets you Free,
And tell the King, my Generous Enemy,
I offer ſtill those terms he had before,
Only ask leave his Daughter to adore.
Guy. Brother, that Name my breaſt shall ever own,
[*He embraces him.*
The name of Foe be but in Battels known;
For some few days all Hoſtile Acts forbear,
That if the King consents, it seems not fear:
His Heart is Noble, and great Souls muſt be
Moſt sought and Courted in Adversity.
Three days I hope the wisht success will tell.
Cyd. Till that long time——
Cort. ——Till that long time, farewel. *Exeunt severally.*

ACT III.

SCENE, *Chamber Royal.*

Enter Odmar *and* Alibech.

Odm. THE gods fair *Alibech* had so decreed,
Nor could my Valour againſt fate succeed;
Yet though our Army brought not Conqueſt home,
I did not from the Fight inglorious come:
If as a Victor you the brave regard,
Succesless Courage then may hope reward:
And I returning safe, may juſtly boaſt
To win the prize which my dead Brother loſt.

Enter Guyomar *behind him.*

Guy. No, no thy Brother lives, and lives to be
A Witness, both againſt himself and thee:
Though both in safety are return'd agen,
I blush to ask her Love for vanquisht Men.
Odm. Brother, I'le not dispute, but you are brave,
Yet I was free, and you it seems a Slave.

Guy. *Odmar*, 'tis true, that I was Captive led
As publickly is known, as that you fled;
But of two shames if she must one partake,
I think the choice will not be hard to make.
Odm. Freedom and Bondage in her choice remain,
Dar'st thou expect she will put on thy Chain?
Guy. No, no, fair *Alibech*, give him the Crown,
My Brother is return'd with high Renown.
He thinks by Flight his Mistress must be won,
And claims the prize because he best did run.
Alib. Your Chains were glorious, and your Flight was wise,
But neither have o'recome your Enemies:
My secret wishes would my choice decide,
But open Justice bends to neither side.
Odm. Justice already does my right approve,
If him who Loves you most, you most should Love.
My Brother poorly from your aid withdrew,
But I my Father left to succour you.
Guy. Her Country she did to her self prefer
Him who Fought best, not who Defended her;
Since she her interest for the Nations wav'd,
Then I who sav'd the King, the Nation sav'd;
You aiding her, your Country did betray,
I aiding him, did her commands obey.
Odm. Name it no more, in Love, there is a time
When dull Obedience is the greatest Crime;
She to her Countries use, resign'd your Sword,
And you, kind Lover, took her at her word;
You did your Duty to your Love prefer,
Seek your reward from Duty, not from her.
Guy. In acting what my Duty did require,
'Twas hard for me to quit my own desire,
That Fought for her which when I did subdue,
'Twas much the easier task I left for you.
Alib. *Odmar* a more then common Love has shown,
And *Guyomar*'s was greater, or was none;
Which I should chuse some god direct my breast.
The certain good, or the uncertain best:
I cannot chuse, you both dispute in vain,
Time and your future Acts must make it plain;
First raise the Siege, and set your Country free,
I not the Judge, but the reward will be.

Enter Montezuma *talking with* Almeria *and* Orbellan.

Mont. Madam, I think with reason I extol
The Vertue of the *Spanish* General;
When all the Gods our Ruine have fore-told,
Yet generously he does his Arms with-hold,
And offering Peace, the first conditions make.
Alm. When Peace, is offer'd, 'tis too late to take;
For one poor loss to stoop to terms like those,
Were we o'recome what could they worse impose?
Go, go, with homage your proud Victors meet,
Go lie like Dogs, beneath your Masters Feet.
Go and beget them Slaves to dig their Mines,
And groan for Gold which now in Temples shines;
Your shameful story shall record of me,
The Men all crouch'd, and left a Woman free.
Guy. Had I not Fought, or durst not Fight again,
I my suspected Counsel should refrain:
For I wish Peace, and any terms prefer
Before the last extremities of War.
We but exasperate those we cannot harm,
And Fighting gains us but to dye more warm:
If that be Cowardise, which dares not see
The insolent effects of Victory,
The rape of Matrons, and their Childrens cries;
Then I am fearful, let the Brave advise.
Odm. Keen cutting Swords, and Engines killing far,
Have prosperously begun a doubtful War:
But now our Foes with less advantage Fight,
Their strength decreases with our *Indians* Fright.
Mont. This Noble Vote does with my wish comply,
I am for War.
Alm. ——And So am I.
Orb. ——And I.
Mont. Then send to break the truce, and I'le take care
To chear the Souldiers, and for fight prepare.
Exeunt Montezuma, Odmar, Guyomar, Alibech.
Alm. to Orb. 'Tis now the hour which all to rest allow.
[Almeria *stays* Orbellan.
And sleep sits heavy upon every brow;
[Guyomar *returns and hears them.*
In this dark silence softly leave the Town,
And to the Generals Tent, 'tis quickly known,

Direct your steps: you may dispatch him strait,
Drown'd in his sleep, and easie for his fate:
Besides, the truce will make the Guards more slack.
Orb. Courage which leads me on will bring me back:
But I more fear the baseness of the thing:
Remorse, you know, bears a perpetual sting.
Alm. For mean remorse no room the valiant finds,
Repentance is the Vertue of weak minds,
For want of judgement, keeps them doubtful still,
They may repent of good who can of ill;
But daring Courage makes ill actions good,
'Tis foolish pity spares a Rivals blood;
You shall about it streight—— *Exeunt* Almeria, Orbellan.
Guy. ——Would they betray
His sleeping Vertue, by so mean a way!
And yet this *Spaniard* is our Nations Foe,
I wish him dead——but cannot wish it so;
Either my Country never must be freed,
Or I consenting to so black a deed.
Would Chance had never led my steps this way,
Now if he dies I Murther him, not they;
Something must be resolv'd e're 'tis too late;
He gave me freedom, I'le prevent his fate. *Exit* Guyomar.

SCENE II. *A Camp.*

Enter Cortez *alone in a Night-gown.*

Cort. All things are hush'd, as Natures self lay dead,
The Mountains seem to nod their drowsie head;
The little Birds in dreams their Songs repeat,
And sleeping Flowers, beneath the night-dew sweat;
Ev'n Lust and Envy sleep, yet Love denies
Rest to my Soul, and slumber to my Eyes.
Three days I promis'd to attend my Doom,
And two long days and nights are yet to come:
'Tis sure the noyse of some Tumultuous Fight, *Noyse within.*
They break the truce, and sally out by Night.

Enter Orbellan *flying in the dark, his Sword drawn.*

Orb. Betray'd! pursu'd! Oh whither shall I flye?
See, see, the just reward of Treachery;

I'm sure among the Tents, but know not where,
Eevn night wants darkness to secure my fear.

Comes near Cortez *who hears him.*

Cort. Stand, who goes there?
Orb. ——Alas, what shall I say! *Aside.*
A poor *Taxallan* that miſtook his way, *To him.*
And wanders in the terrours of the night.
Cort. Souldier thou seem'ſt afraid, whence comes thy fright?
Orb. The insolence of *Spaniards* caus'd my fear,
Who in the dark pursu'd me entring here.
Cort. Their Crimes shall meet immediate punishment,
But ſtay thou safe within the Generals Tent.
Orb. Still worse and worse.
Cort. ——Fear not, but follow me,
Upon my Life I'le set thee safe and free.

Cortez *Leads him in, and returns.*
To him Vasquez, Pizarro *and* Spaniards *with Torches.*

Vasq. O Sir, thank Heaven, and your brave *Indian* Friend,
That you are safe, *Orbellan* did intend
This night to kill you sleeping in your Tent:
But *Guyomar*, his truſty Slave has sent,
Who following close his silent ſteps by night,
Till in our Camp they both approach'd the light,
Cryed seize the Traytor, seize the Murtherer:
The cruel Villain fled I know not where,
But far he is not, for he this way bent.
Piz. Th' inraged Souldiers seek, from Tent to Tent,
With lighted Torches, and in Love to you,
With bloody Vows his hated Life persue.
Vasq. This Messenger does since he came relate,
That the old King, after a long debate,
By his imperious Miſtress blindly led,
Has given *Cydaria* to *Orbellan*'s Bed.
Cort. *Vasquez*, the truſty Slave with you retain,
Retire a while, I'le call you back again. *Exeunt* Vasquez, Pizarro.

Cortez *at his Tent Door.*

Cort. *Indian*, come forth, your Enemies are gone.
And I who sav'd you from them here alone;
You hide your Face, as you were ſtill afraid,
Dare you not look on him who gave you aid?

Enter Orbellan *holding his Face aside.*

Orb. Moon, slip behind some Cloud, some Tempest rise,
And blow out all the Stars that light the Skies,
To shrowd my Shame.
Cort. ——In vain you turn aside,
And hide your Face, your Name you cannot hide;
I know my Rival, and his black design.
Orb. Forgive it as my passions fault not mine.
Cort. In your excuse your Love does little say,
You might howere have took a fairer way.
Orb. 'Tis true, my passion small defence can make,
Yet you must spare me for your Honours sake;
That was engag'd to set me safe and free.
Cort. 'Twas to a Stranger, not an Enemy:
Nor is it prudence to prolong thy breath,
When all my hopes depend upon thy death——
——Yet none shall tax me with base perjury,
Something I'le do, both for my self and thee?
With vow'd revenge my Souldiers search each Tent,
If thou art seen none can thy death prevent.
Follow my steps with silence and with haste.

They go out, the Scene changes to the Indian *Countrey, they return.*

Cort. Now you are safe, you have my out-guards past.
Orb. Then here I take my leave.
Cort. ——*Orbellan*, no;
When you return you to *Cydaria* go,
I'le send a Message.
Orb. ——Let it be exprest,
I am in haste.
Cort. ——I'le write it in your Brest. *Draws.*
Orb. What means my Rival?
Cort. ——Either Fight or Dye,
I'le not strain Honour to a point too high;
I sav'd your Life, now keep it if you can,
Cydaria shall be for the bravest Man.
On equal terms you shall your Fortune try,
Take this and lay your flint-edg'd weapon by;
[*Gives him a Sword.*
I'le arm you for my Glory, and pursue
No Palm, but what's to manly vertue due.

Fame with my Conqueſt shall my Courage tell,
This you shall gain by placing Love so well.
Orb. Fighting with you ungrateful I appear.
Cort. Under that shadow thou wouldſt hide thy fear:
Thou wouldſt possess thy Love at thy return,
And in her Arms my easie Vertue scorn.
Orb. Since we muſt Fight, no longer let's delay:
The Moon shines clear, and makes a paler Day.
They Fight, Orbellan *is wounded in the Hand, his Sword falls out of it.*
Cort. To Courage, even of Foes, there's Pity due;
It was not I, but Fortune vanquish'd you:
[*Throws his Sword again.*
Thank me with that, and so dispute the prize,
As if you fought before *Cydarias* eyes.
Orb. I would not poorly such a gift requite,
You gave me not this Sword to yield, but Fight:
But see where yours has forc'd its bloody way,
My wounded Hand my Heart does ill obey.
[*He ſtrives to hold it, but cannot.*
Cort. Unlucky Honour that controul'ſt my will!
Why have I vanquish'd, since I muſt not Kill?
Fate sees thy Life lodg'd in a brittle Glass,
And looks it through, but to it cannot pass.
Orb. All I can do is frankly to confess,
I wish I could, but cannot love her less.
To swear I would resign her were but vain,
Love would recal that perjur'd breath again;
And in my wretched case 'twill be more juſt,
Not to have promis'd, then deceive your truſt.
Know, if I Live once more to see the Town,
In bright *Cydaria*'s Arms my Love i'le crown.
Cort. In spight of that I give thee Liberty,
And with thy person leave thy Honour free;
But to thy wishes move a speedy pace,
Or Death will soon o'retake thee in the Chace.
To Arms, to Arms, Fate shows my Love the way,
I'le force the City on thy Nuptial day. *Exeunt severally.*

SCENE III. *Mexico.*

Enter *Montezuma*, *Odmar*, *Guyomar*, *Almeria*.

Mont. It moves my wonder that in two days space,
This early Famine spreads so swift a pace.
Odm. 'Tis, Sir, the general cry, nor seems it ſtrange,
The face of plenty should so swiftly change;
This City never felt a Siege before,
But from the Lake receiv'd its daily ſtore,
Which now shut up, and Millions crowded here,
Famine will soon in multitudes appear.
Mont. The more the number, ſtill the greater shame.
Alm. What if some one should seek immortal Fame,
By ending of the Siege at one brave blow?
Mont. That were too happy.
Alm. ——Yet it may be so.
What if the *Spanish* General should be slain?
Guy. Juſt Heaven I hope does other-ways ordain. [*Aside.*
Mont. If slain by Treason I lament his Death.

Enter Orbellan *and whispers his Siſter.*

Odm. *Orbellan* seems in haſt, and out of breath.
Mont. *Orbellan* welcome, you are early here,
A Bridegrooms haſt, does in your looks appear.
Almeria *Aside to her Brother.*
Alm. Betray'd! no, 'twas thy Cowardise and Fear,
He had not scap'd with Life had I been there;
But since so ill you aƈt a brave design,
Keep close your shame, Fate makes the next turn mine.

Enter Alibech, Cydaria.

Alib. O Sir! if ever pity touch'd your breaſt,
Let it be now to your own blood expreſt:
In teares your beauteous Daughter drowns her sight,
Silent as dews that fall in dead of night.
Cyd. To your commands I ſtriƈt obedience owe,
And my laſt aƈt of it I come to show;
I want the Heart to dye before your Eyes.
But Grief will finish that which Fear denies.
Alm. Your will should by your Fathers precept move.
Cyd. When he was young he taught me truth in Love.
Alm. He found more love then he deserv'd, 'tis true,

And that it seems, is lucky too to you.
Your Father's Folly took a head-strong course,
But I'le rule yours, and teach you Love by force.

Enter Messenger.

Arm, Arm, O King! the Enemy comes on,
A sharp assault already is begun:
Their Murdering Guns play fiercely on the Walls.
Odm. Now Rival, let us run where Honour calls.
Guy. I have discharg'd what gratitude did owe,
And the brave *Spaniard* is again my Foe. [*Ex.* Odmar *and* Guyomar.
Mont. Our walls are high, and multitudes defend:
Their vain attempt must in their ruine end.
The Nuptials with my presence shall be grac'd.
Alib. At least but stay till the assault be past.
Alm. Sister, in vain you urge him to delay,
The King has promis'd, and he shall obey.

Enter Second Messenger.

From several parts the Enemy's repel'd,
One only quarter, to th' assault does yield.

Enter Third Messenger.

Some Foes are enter'd, but they are so few,
They only Death, not Victory pursue.
Orb. Hark, hark, they shout!——
From Vertues rules I do, too meanly swerve,
I by my Courage will your Love deserve.
Mont. Here in the heart of all the Town I'le stay,
And timely succour where it wants, convey.

A Noise within. Enter Orbellan, Indians *driven in,* Cortez *after them, and one or two* Spaniards.

Cort. He's found, he's found, degenerate Coward, stay:
Night sav'd thee once thou shalt not scape by day. [*Kills* Orbellan.
Orb. O I am kill'd——*Dyes.*

Enter Guyomar *and* Odmar.

Guy. Yield Generous Stranger and preserve your life,
[*He is beset.*
Why chuse you death in this unequal strife?
Almeria *and* Alibech *fall on* Orbellans *body.*
Cort. What nobler Fate could any Lover meet,
I fall reveng'd, and at my Mistress feet?
They fall on him and bear him down, Guyomar *takes his Sword.*

Alib. He's paſt recovery; my Dear Brother's slain;
Fate's hand was in it, and my care was vain.
Alm. In weak complaints you vainly waſt your breath:
They are not Tears that can revenge his Death,
Dispatch the Villain ſtrait.
Cort. ———The Villains Dead.
Alm. Give me a Sword and let me take his Head.
Mont. Though, Madam, for your Brothers loss I grieve,
Yet let me beg
Alm. ——His Murderer may Live?
Cyd. 'Twas his Misfortune, and the Chance of War.
Cort. It was my purpose, and I kill'd him fair;
How could you so unjuſt and cruel prove,
To call that Chance which was the aƈt of Love?
Cyd. I call'd it any thing to save your Life:
Would he were living ſtill, and I his Wife;
That wish was once my greateſt misery:
But 'tis a greater to behold you dye.
Alm. Either command his Death upon the place,
Or never more behold *Almeria*'s Face.
Guy. You by his Valour, once from Death were freed:
Can you forget so Generous a Deed? [*To* Montezuma.
Mont. How Gratitude and Love divide my breaſt!
Both ways alike my Soul is robb'd of reſt.
But——let him Dye——can I his Sentence give?
Ungrateful muſt he Dye by whom I Live?
But can I then *Almeria*'s Tears deny?
Should any Live whom she commands to Dye?
Guy. Approach who dares: he yielded on my word;
And as my Pris'ner, I reſtore his Sword; [*Gives his Sword.*
His Life concerns the safety of the State,
And I'le preserve it for a calm debate.
Mont. Dar'ſt thou Rebel false and degenerate Boy?
That being which I gave, I thus deſtroy.
Offers to kill him, Odmar *ſteps between.*
Odm. My Brother's blood I cannot see you spill,
Since he prevents you but from doing ill:
He is my Rival, but his Death would be
For him too glorious, and too base for me.
Guy. Thou shalt not Conquer in this noble ſtrife:
Alas, I meant not to defend my Life:
Strike, Sir, you never pierc'd a Breaſt more true;
'Tis the laſt Wound I e're can take for you.

You see I live but to dispute your will;
Kill me, and then you may my Pris'ner kill.
Cort. You shall not, Generous Youths, contend for me,
It is enough that I your Honour see;
But that your Duty may no blemish take,
I will my self your Father's Captive make;
When he dares strike, I am prepar'd to fall:
[*Gives his Sword to* Montezuma.
The *Spaniards* will revenge their General.
Cyd. Ah you too hastily your Life resign.
You more would Love it if you valued mine!
Cort. Dispatch me quickly, I my Death forgive,
I shall grow tender else, and wish to Live;
Such an infectious Face her sorrow wears,
I can bear Death, but not *Cydaria*'s Tears.
Alm. Make haste, make haste, they merit Death all three:
They for Rebellion, and for Murder he.
See, see, my Brother's Ghost hangs hovering there,
O're his warm Blood that steems into the Air,
Revenge, Revenge, it cries.
Mont.——And it shall have;
But two days respite for his Life I crave:
If in that space you not more gentle prove,
I'le give a fatal proof how well I Love.
Till when you *Guyomar*, your Pris'ner take;
Bestow him in the Castle on the Lake:
In that small time, I shall the Conquest gain
Of these few Sparks of Vertue which remain;
Then all who shall my head-long passion see,
Shall curse my Crimes, and yet shall pity me [*Exeunt Omnes.*

ACT IV.

SCENE, *A Prison.*

Enter Almeria *and an* Indian *they speak entring.*

Ind. A Dangerous proof of my respect I show.
Alm. Fear not, Prince *Guyomar* shall never know:
While he is absent, let us not delay,
Remember 'tis the King thou doest obey.
Ind. See where he sleeps. [Cortez *appears Chain'd and laid asleep.*

Alm. ———Without my coming wait:
And on thy Life secure the Prison Gate.——— [*Exit* Indian.
[*She plucks out a Dagger and approaches him.*
Spaniard, awake: thy Fatal hour is come:
Thou shall not at such ease receive thy Doom.
Revenge is sure, though sometimes slowly pac'd,
Awake, awake, or sleeping sleep thy laſt.
Cort. Who names Revenge?
Alm. ——Look up and thou shalt see.
Cort. I cannot fear so fair an Enemy.
Alm. No aid is nigh, nor canſt thou make defence:
Whence can thy Courage come?
Cort. ——From Innocence.
Alm. From Innocence? let that then take thy part,
Still are thy looks assur'd,——have at thy Heart.
[*Holds up the Dagger.*
I cannot kill thee, sure thou bear'ſt some Charm, [*Goes back.*
Or some Divinity holds back my Arm.
Why do I thus delay to make him Bleed, [*Aside.*
Can I want Courage for so brave a deed?
I've shook it off, my Soul is free from fear, [*Comes again.*
And I can now ſtrike any where,——but here
His scorn of Death how ſtrangely does it move!
A mind so haughty who could chuse but love! [*Goes off.*
Plead not a Charm, or any gods command,
Alas, it is thy heart that holds thy hand:
In spight of me I love, and see too late
My Mothers Pride muſt find my Mothers Fate.
——Thy Country's Foe, thy Brother's Murtherer,
For shame, *Almeria*, such mad thoughts forbear:
It w'onnot be if I once more come on, [*coming on again.*
I shall miſtake the Breaſt, and pierce my own.
[*Comes with her Dagger down.*
Cort. Does your revenge maliciously forbear
To give me Death, till 'tis prepar'd by fear?
If you delay for that, forbear or ſtrike,
Fore-seen and sudden death are both alike.
Alm. To show my love would but increase his Pride:
They have moſt Power who moſt their passions hide. [*Aside.*
Spaniard, I muſt confess I did expect
You could not meet your Death with such neglect;
I will defer it now, and give you time,
You may Repent, and I forget your Crime.

Cort. Those who repent acknowledge they did ill:
I did not unprovok'd your Brother Kill.
Alm. Petition me, perhaps I may forgive.
Cort. Who begs his Life does not deserve to live.
Alm. But if 'tis given you'l not refuse to take?
Cort. I can Live gladly for *Cydaria*'s sake,
Alm. Does she so wholly then possess your mind?
What if you should another Lady find,
Equal to her in birth, and far above
In all that can attract, or keep your Love,
Would you so doat upon your first desire,
As not to entertain a Nobler Fire?
Cort. I think that person hardly will be found,
With Gracious form and equal Vertue crown'd:
Yet if another could precedence claim,
My fixt desires could find no fairer Aim.
Alm. Dull Ignorance, he cannot yet conceive:
To speak more plain shame will not give me leave. [*Aside.*
——Suppose one lov'd you whom even Kings adore: [*To him.*
Who with your Life, your Freedom would restore,
And adde to that the Crown of *Mexico:*
Would you for her, *Cydaria*'s Love forego?
Cort. Though she could offer all you can invent,
I could not of my Faith, once vow'd repent.
Alm. A burning blush hath covered all my face,
Why am I forc'd to publish my disgrace?
What if I Love, you know it cannot be,
And yet I blush to put the case 'twere me.
If I could Love you with a flame so true,
I could forget what hand my Brother slew?——
——Make out the rest——I am disorder'd so,
I know not farther what to say or do:
———But answer me to what you think I meant.
Cort. Reason or Wit no answer can invent:
Of words confus'd who can the meaning find?
Alm. Disorder'd words show a distemper'd mind.
Cort. She has oblig'd me so, that could I chuse,
I would not answer what I must refuse. [*Aside.*
Alm. ——His mind is shook;——suppose I lov'd you, speak,
Would you for me *Cydaria*'s Fetters break?
Cort. Things meant in Jest, no serious answer need.
Alm. But put the case that it were so indeed.
Cort. If it were so, which but to think were Pride,

My constant Love would dangerously be try'd:
For since you could a Brothers death forgive,
He whom you save for you alone should live:
But I the most unhappy of mankind,
E're I knew yours, have all my Love resign'd:
'Tis my own loss I grieve, who have no more;
You go a begging to a Bankrupts door.
Yet could I change, as sure I never can,
How could you Love so Infamous a Man?
For Love once given from her, and plac'd in you,
Would leave no ground I ever could be true.
Alm. You construed me aright,——I was in Jest:
And by that offer meant to sound your breast;
Which since I find so constant to your Love,
Will much my value of your worth improve.
Spaniard, assure your self you shall not be
Oblig'd to quit *Cydaria* for me:
'Tis dangerous though, to treat me in this sort,
And to refuse my offers, though in sport. *Exit* Almeria.
Cort. In what a strange Condition am I left, Cortez *solus*.
More then I wish I have, of all I wish bereft!
In wishing nothing we enjoy still most;
For even our wish is in possession lost:
Restless we wander to a new desire,
And burn our selves by blowing of the fire:
We toss and turn about our Feaverish will,
When all our ease must come by lying still:
For all the happiness Mankind can gain
Is not in pleasure, but in rest from pain.
Goes in, and the Scene closes upon him.

SCENE II. *Chamber Royal.*

Enter Montezuma, Odmar, Guyomar, Alibech.

Mont. My Ears are deaf with this impatient crowd.
Odm. Their wants are now grown Mutinous and loud:
The Gen'rals taken, but the Siege remains;
And their last Food our dying Men sustains.
Guy. One means is only left, I to this hour,
Have kept the Captive from *Almeria*'s Power,
And though by your command she often sent
To urge his doom, do still his death prevent.

Mont. That hope is past: him I have oft assayl'd,
But neither threats nor kindness have prevail'd;
Hiding our wants, I offer'd to release
His Chains, and equally conclude a Peace:
He fiercely answer'd I had now no way
But to submit, and without terms obey:
I told him, he in Chains demanded more
Than he impos'd in Victory before:
He sullenly reply'd, he could not make
These offers now; Honour must give, not take.
Odm. Twice have I sallyed, and was twice beat back:
What desp'rate course remains for us to take!
Mont. If either Death or Bondage I must chuse,
I'll keep my Freedom, though my Life I lose.
Guy. I'll not upbraid you that you once refus'd
Those means, you might have then with Honour us'd:
I'll lead your Men, perhaps bring Victory:
They know to Conquer best, who know to Dye.
[*Exeunt* Montezuma, Odmar.
Alib. Ah me, what have I heard! stay, *Guyomar*,
What hope you from this Sally you prepare?
Guy. A Death, with Honour for my Countries good:
A death, to which your self design'd my blood.
Alib. You heard, and I well know the Town's distress,
Which Sword and Famine both at once oppress:
Famine so fierce, that what's deny'd Mans use,
Even deadly Plants, and Herbs of pois'nous juice
Wild hunger seeks; and to prolong our breath,
We greedily devour our certain death:
The Souldier in th' assault of Famine falls:
And Ghosts not Men, are watching on the walls.
As Callow Birds———
Whose Mother's kill'd in seeking of their prey,
Cry in their Nest, and think her long away:
And at each leaf that stirs, each blast of wind,
Gape for the Food which they must never find:
So cry the people in their misery.
Guy. And what relief can they expect from me?
Alib. While *Montezuma* sleeps, call in the Foe:
The Captive General your design may know:
His Noble heart, to Honour ever true,
Knows how to spare as well as to subdue.
Guy. What I have heard I blush to hear: and grieve

Those words you spoke, I must your words believe;
I to do this! I, whom you once thought brave,
To sell my Countrey, and my King Enslave?
All I have done by one foul act deface,
And yield my right to you by turning base?
What more could *Odmar* wish that I should do
To lose your Love, then you perswade me to?
No, Madam, no, I never can commit
A deed so ill, nor can you suffer it:
'Tis but to try what Vertue you can find
Lodg'd in my Soul.
Alib. I plainly speak my Mind;
Dear as my Life my Vertue I'll preserve:
But Vertue you too scrupulously serve:
I lov'd not more then now my Countries good,
When for it's service I employ'd your Blood:
But things are alter'd, I am still the same,
By different ways still moving to one fame;
And by dis-arming you, I now do more
To save the Town, then arming you before.
Guy. Things good or ill by circumstances be;
In you 'tis Vertue, what is Vice in me.
Alib. That ill is pardon'd which does good procure.
Guy. The good's uncertain, but the ill is sure.
Alib. When Kings grow stubborn, slothful, or unwise,
Each private man for publick good should rise.
As when the Head distempers does endure,
Each several part must join t' effect the cure.
Guy. Take heed, Fair Maid, how Monarchs you accuse:
Such reasons none but impious Rebels use:
Those who to Empire by dark paths aspire,
Still plead a call to what they most desire;
But Kings by free consent their Kingdoms take,
Strict as those Sacred Ties which Nuptials make;
And what e're faults in Princes time reveal,
None can be Judge where can be no Appeal.
Alib. In all debates you plainly let me see
You love your Vertue best, but *Odmar* me:
Go, your mistaken Piety pursue:
I'll have from him what is deny'd by you;
With my Commands you shall no more be grac'd,
Remember, Sir, this trial was your last.
Guy. The gods inspire you with a better mind;

Make you more juſt, and make you then more kind:
But though from Vertues rules I cannot part,
Think I deny you with a Bleeding Heart:
'Tis hard with me whatever choice I make;
I muſt not merit you, or muſt forsake:
But in this ſtreight, to Honour I'le be true,
And leave my Fortune to the gods and you.

Enter a Messenger *Privately.*

Mess. Now is the time; be aiding to your Fate:
From the Watch-Tower, above the Weſtern Gate,
I have discern'd the Foe securely lye,
Too proud to fear a beaten Enemy:
Their careless Chiefs to the cool Grottoes run,
The Bowers of Kings, to shade them from the Sun.
Guy. Upon thy life disclose thy news to none;
I'le make the Conqueſt or the shame my own.

[*Exit* Guyomar *and* Messenger.

Enter Odmar.

Alib. I read some welcome Message in his Eye:
Prince *Odmar* comes: I'le see if he'l deny.
Odmar I come to tell you pleasing News,
I beg a thing your Brother did refuse.
Odm. The News both pleases me, and grieves me too;
For nothing, sure, should be deny'd to you:
But he was bleſt who might commanded be;
You never meant that happiness to me.
Alib. What he refus'd your kindness might beſtow,
But my Commands, perhaps, your burden grow.
Odm. Could I but live till burdensome they prove,
My Life would be immortal as my Love.
Your wish, e're it receive a name I grant.
Alib. 'Tis to relieve your dying Countries want;
All hopes of succour from your Arms is paſt,
To save us now you muſt our Ruine haſte;
Give up the Town, and to oblige him more,
The Captive General's liberty reſtore.
Odm. You speak to try my Love, can you forgive
So soon, to let your Brother's Murderer live?
Alib. *Orbellan*, though my Brother, did disgrace
With treacherous Deeds our Mighty Mothers Race;
And to revenge his Blood, so juſtly spilt,

What is it less then to partake his guilt?
Though my Proud Sister to revenge incline,
I to my Country's good my own resign.
Odm. To save our Lives our Freedom I betray——
——Yet since I promis'd it, I will obey;
I'le not my Shame nor your Commands dispute:
You shall behold your Empire's Absolute. [*Exit* Odmar.
Alib. I should have thank'd him for his speedy grant:
And yet I know not how, fit words I want:
Sure I am grown distracted in my mind,
That joy this grant should bring I cannot find:
The one, denying, vex'd my Soul before;
And this, obeying, has disturb'd me more:
The one, with grief, and slowly did refuse,
The other, in his grant, much haste did use:
———He us'd too much—and granting me so soon,
He has the merit of the gift undone:
Methought with wondrous ease, he swallow'd down
His forfeit Honour, to betray the Town:
My inward choice was *Guyomar* before,
But now his Vertue has confirm'd me more——
——I rave, I rave, for *Odmar* will obey,
And then my promise must my choice betray.
Fantastick Honour, thou hast fram'd a Toyl
Thy self, to make thy Love thy Vertues Spoyl. [*Exit* Alibech.

SCENE III.

A pleasant Grotto discover'd: in it a Fountain spouting; round about it Vasquez, Pizarro, *and other* Spaniards *lying carelesly un-arm'd, and by them many* Indian *Women, one of which Sings the following Song.*

SONG.

Ah! fading joy, how quickly art thou past?
Yet we thy ruine haste:
As if the cares of Humane Life were few,
We seek out new:
And follow Fate that does too fast pursue.

See how on every bough the Birds express
In their sweet notes their happiness.

They all enjoy, and nothing spare;
But on their Mother Nature lay their care:
Why then should Man, the Lord of all below,
Such troubles chuse to know,
As none of all his Subjects undergo?

Hark, hark, the Waters fall, fall, fall:
And with a Murmuring sound
Dash, dash, upon the ground,
To gentle slumbers call.

After the Song two Spaniards *arise and dance a* Saraband *with* Castanieta'*s: at the end of which,* Guyomar *and his* Indians *enter, and e're the* Spaniards *can recover their Swords, seize them.*

Guy. Those whom you took without in Triumph bring,
But see these ſtreight conducted to the King.
Piz. Vasquez, what now remains in these extreams?
Vasq. Only to wake us from our Golden Dreams.
Piz. Since by our shameful conduct, we have loſt
Freedom, Wealth, Honour, which we value moſt,
I wish they would our Lives a Period give:
They live too long who Happiness out-live. [Spaniards *are led out.*
1. *Ind.* See, Sir, how quickly your success is spread:
The King comes Marching in the Armies head.

Enter Montezuma, Alibech, Odmar, *Discontented.*

Mont. Now all the gods reward and bless my Son: [*Embracing.*
Thou haſt this day, thy Fathers Youth out-done.
Alib. Juſt Heaven such Happiness upon him shower,
Till it confess it's will beyond it's power.
Guy. The heavens are kind, the gods propitious be,
I only doubt a Mortal Deity:
I neither Fought for Conqueſt, nor for Fame,
Your Love alone can recompence my Flame.
Alib. I gave my Love to the moſt brave in War;
But that the King muſt Judge.
Mont. ———'Tis *Guyomar.* [*Souldiers shout, A* Guyomar, *&c.*
Mont. This day your Nuptials we will Celebrate;
But guard these haughty Captives till their Fate:
Odmar, this night to keep them be your care,
To morrow for their Sacrifice prepare.
Alib. Blot not your Conqueſt with your Cruelty.
Mont. Fate says we are not safe unless they Dye:

The Spirit that fore-told this happy day,
Bid me use Caution, and avoid delay:
Posterity be juster to my Fame:
Nor call it Murder, when each private Man
In his defence may justly do the same:
But private persons more then Monarchs can:
All weigh our Acts, and whatere seems unjust,
Impute not to Necessity, but Lust.

[*Ex.* Montezuma, Guyomar, *and* Alibech.

Odm. Lost and undone! he had my Fathers voice,
And *Alibech* seem'd pleas'd with her new choice:
Alas, it was not new! too late I see,
Since one she hated, that it must be me.
——I feel a strange Temptation in my will
To do an action, great at once and ill:
Vertue ill treated, from my Soul is fled;
I by Revenge and Love am wholly led:
Yet Conscience would against my rage Rebel——
——Conscience, the foolish pride of doing well!
Sink Empire, Father Perish, Brother Fall,
Revenge does more then recompence you all.
——Conduct the Pris'ners in——
Spaniards, you see your own deplor'd Estate:

Enter Vasquez, Pizarro.

What dare you do to reconcile your Fate?
Vasq. All that despair, with Courage joyn'd can do.
Odm. An easie way to Victory I'le show:
When all are buried in their Sleep or Joy,
I'le give you Arms, Burn, Ravish, and Destroy;
For my own share one Beauty I design,
Engage your Honours that she shall be mine.
Piz. I gladly Swear.
Vasq. ——And I; but I request
That, in return, one who has touch'd my breast,
Whose name I know not, may be given to me.
Odm. *Spaniard*, 'tis just; she's yours who e're she be.
Vasq. The night comes on: if Fortune bless the bold,
I shall possess the Beauty.
Piz. I the Gold. [*Exeunt Omnes.*

SCENE IV. *A Prison.*

Cortez *discover'd, bound by one Foot,* Almeria *talking with him.*

Alm. I come not now your constancy to prove,
You may believe me when I say I Love.
Cort. You have too well instructed me before,
In your intentions to believe you more.
Alm. I'm justly plagu'd by this your unbelief,
And am my self the cause of my own grief:
But to beg Love, I cannot stoop so low;
It is enough that you my passion know:
'Tis in your choice; Love me, or Love me not,
[*Lays hold on the Dagger.*
I have not yet my Brother's Death forgot.
Cort. You Menace me and Court me in a breath:
Your *Cupid* looks as dreadfully as Death.
Alm. Your hopes, without, are vanish'd into smoak:
Your Captains taken, and your Armies broke.
Cort. In vain you urge me with my miseries:
When Fortune falls high Courages can rise.
Now should I change my Love, it would appear
Not the effect of gratitude, but fear.
Alm. I'le to the King and make it my Request,
Or my Command that you may be releast;
And make you Judge, when I have set you free,
Who best deserves your passion, I, or she.
Cort. You tempt my Faith so generous a way,
As without guilt might constancy betray:
But I'm so far from meriting esteem,
That if I Judge I must my self Condemn;
Yet having given my worthless heart before,
What I must not possess I'le still adore;
Take my devotion then this humbler way;
Devotion is the Love which Heaven we pay. [*Kisses her hand.*

Enter Cydaria.

Cyd. May I believe my Eyes! what do I see!
Is this her Hate to him, his Love to me!
'Tis in my Breast she sheaths her Dagger now.
False Man, is this the Faith? Is this the Vow? [*To him*
Cort. What words, dear Saint, are these I hear you use?
What Faith, what Vows are those which you accuse?

Cyd. More cruel than the Tyger o'er his spoyl;
And falser than the Weeping Crocodile:
Can you adde Vanity to Guilt, and take
A Pride to hear the Conquests which you make?
Go publish your Renown, let it be said
You have a Woman, and that Lov'd, betray'd.
Cort. With what injustice is my Faith accus'd?
Life, Freedom, Empire, I at once refus'd;
And would again ten thousand times for you.
Alm. She'l have too great content to find him true;
And therefore since his Love is not for me,
I'le help to make my Rivals misery. [*Aside.*
Spaniard, I never thought you false before: [*To him.*
Can you at once two Mistresses adore?
Keep the poor Soul no longer in suspence,
Your change is such as does not need defence.
Cort. Riddles like these I cannot understand!
Alm. Why should you blush? she saw you kiss my hand.
Cyd. Fear not, I will, while your first Love's deny'd,
Favour your shame, and turn my Eyes aside;
My feeble hopes in her deserts are lost:
I neither can such power nor beauty boast:
I have no tye upon you to be true,
But that which loosned yours, my Love to you.
Cort. Could you have heard my words!
Cyd. ———Alas, what needs
To hear your words, when I beheld your deeds?
Cort. What shall I say! the Fate of Love is such,
That still it sees too little or too much.
That act of mine which does your passion move,
Was but a mark of my Respect, not Love.
Alm. Vex not your self excuses to prepare:
For one you love not is not worth your care.
Cort. Cruel *Almeria* take that life you gave;
Since you but worse destroy me, while you save.
Cyd. No, let me dye, and I'le my claim resign;
For while I live, methinks you should be mine.
Cort. The bloodiest Vengeance which she could pursue,
Would be a triffle to my loss of you.
Cyd. Your change was wise: for had she been deny'd,
A swift Revenge had follow'd from her Pride:
You from my gentle Nature had no Fears,
All my Revenge is only in my Tears.

Cort. Can you imagine I so mean could prove,
To save my Life by changing of my Love?
Cyd. Since Death is that which Nat'rally we shun,
You did no more then I, perhaps, had done.
Cort. Make me not doubt, Fair Soul, your constancy;
You would have dy'd for Love, and so would I.
Alm. You may believe him; you have seen it prov'd.
Cort. Can I not gain belief how I have Lov'd?
What can thy ends, Inhumane Creature, be?
Can he who kill'd thy Brother live for thee?

[*A noyse of Clashing of Swords.*
[Vasquez *within*, Indians *against him.*

Vasq. Yield Slaves or dye; our Swords shall force our way. [*within.*
Ind. We cannot, though o're-power'd, our trust betray. [*within.*
Cort. 'Tis *Vasquez* voice, he brings me Liberty.
Vasq. In spight of Fate I'le set my General Free: [*within.*
Now Victory for us, the Town's our own.
Alm. All hopes of safety and of love are gone:
As when some dreadful Thunder-clap is nigh,
The winged Fire shoots swiftly through the Skie,
Strikes and consumes e're scarce it does appear,
And by the sudden ill, prevents the fear:
Such is my state in this amazing wo;
It leaves no pow'r to think, much less to do:
——But shall my Rival Live, shall she enjoy
That Love in Peace I labour'd to destroy? [*Aside.*
Cort. Her looks grow black as a Tempestuous wind;
Some raging Thoughts are rowling in her mind
Alm. Rival, I must your jealous Thoughts remove,
You shall, hereafter, be at rest for Love.
Cyd. Now you are kind.
Alm. ——He whom you love is true:
But he shall never be possest by you.

[*Draws her Dagger, and runs toward her.*

Cort. Hold, hold, Ah, Barb'rous Woman! flye, oh flye!
Cyd. Ah, pity, pity! is no succour nigh?
Cort. Run, run behind me, there you may be sure,
While I have Life I will your Life secure. [Cydaria *gets behind him.*
Alm. On him or thee light Vengeance any where:

[*She stabs and hurts him.*

——What have I done? I see his blood appear!

Cyd. It ﬅreams, it ﬅreams from every Vital part:
Was there no way but this to find his Heart?
Alm. Ah! Cursed Woman, what was my Design?
At leaﬅ this Weapon both our Blood shall joyn.
[*Goes to ﬅab her self, and being within his reach, he snatches the Dagger.*
Cort. Now neither Life nor Death are in your Power.
Alm. Then sullenly I'le wait my Fatal hour.

Enter Vasquez *and* Pizarro *with drawn Swords.*

Vasq. He Lives, he Lives.
Cort. ——Unfetter me with speed,
Vasquez, I see you troubled that I bleed:
But 'tis not deep, our Army I can head.
Vasq. You to a certain Victory are led:
Your Men all Arm'd, ﬅand silently within:
I with your Freedom, did the Work begin.
Piz. What Friends we have, and how we came so ﬅrong,
We'l softly tell you as we March along.
Cort. In this safe place let me secure your fear: [*To* Cydaria.
No Clashing Swords, no Noyse can enter here.
Amidﬅ our Arms as quiet you shall be
As Halcyons Brooding on a Winter Sea.
Cyd. Leave me not here alone, and full of fright,
Amidﬅ the Terrors of a Dreadful night:
You judge, alas, my Courage by your own,
I never durﬅ in Darkness be alone:
I beg, I throw me humbly at your Feet———
Cort. You muﬅ not go where you may dangers meet.
Th' unruly Sword will no diﬅinction make:
And Beauty will not there give Wounds but take.
Alm. Then ﬅay and take me with you; though to be
A Slave to wait upon your Victory.
My Heart unmov'd, can Noyse and Horrour bear:
Parting from you is all the Death I fear.
Cort. *Almeria*, 'tis enough I leave you free:
You neither muﬅ ﬅay here, nor go with me.
Alm. Then take my Life, that will my reﬅ reﬅore:
'Tis all I ask for saving yours before.
Cort. That were a Barbarous return of Love.
Alm. Yet leaving it you more inhumane prove:
In both extreams I some relief should find:
Oh either hate me more, or be more kind.

Cort. Life of my Soul, do not my absence Mourn:
But chear thy Heart in hopes of my Return. [*To* Cydaria.
Thy Noble Father's Life shall be my care;
And both thy Brothers I'm oblig'd to spare.
Cyd. Fate makes you Deaf while I in vain implore,
My Heart forebodes I ne'r shall see you more:
I have but one request, when I am Dead,
Let not my Rival to your Love succeed.
Cort. Fate will be kinder than your Fears foretel;
Farewel my Dear.
Cyd. ———A long and last farewel:
——So eager to imploy the cruel Sword;
Can you not one, not one last look afford!
Cort. I melt to Womanish Tears, and if I stay,
I find my Love my Courage will betray:
Yon Tower will keep you safe, but be so kind
To your own Life that none may Entrance find.
Cyd. Then lead me there—— [*He leads her.*
For this one Minute of your Company,
I go methinks, with some content to Dye.
[*Exeunt* Cortez, Vasquez, Pizarro, Cydaria.
Alm. Farewel, O too much Lov'd, since Lov'd in vain! [*Sola.*
What Dismal Fortune does for me remain!
Night and Despair my Fatal Foot-steps guide;
That Chance may give the Death which he deny'd. [*Exit.*

Cortez, Vasquez, Pizarro, *and* Spaniards, *return again.*

Cort. All I hold dear, I trust to your defence, [*To* Pizarro.
Guard her, and on your Life, remove not hence.
[*Exeunt* Cortez, *and* Vasquez.
Piz. I'le venture that——
The gods are good; I'le leave her to their care,
Steal from my Post, and in the Plunder share. [*Exit.*

ACT V. SCENE I.

The Chamber Royal, an Indian Hamock *discover'd in it.*

Enter Odmar *with Souldiers,* Guyomar, Alibech, *bound.*

Odm. FAte is more just then you to my desert,
And in this Act you blame, Heaven takes my part.
Guy. Can there be Gods, and no Revenge provide?
Odm. The Gods are ever of the Conquering side:

She's now my Queen, the *Spaniards* have agreed
I to my Fathers Empire shall succeed.
Alib. How much I Crowns contemn I let thee see,
Chusing the younger, and refusing thee.
Guy. Were she Ambitious, she'd disdain to own
The Pageant Pomp of such a Servile Throne:
A Throne which thou by Parricide do'st gain,
And by a base submission must retain.
Alib. I lov'd thee not before, but, *Odmar*, know
That now I hate thee and despise thee too.
Odm. With too much Violence you Crimes pursue,
Which if I Acted 'twas for Love of you:
This, if it teach not Love, may teach you Fear:
I brought not Sin so far, to stop it here.
Death in a Lovers Mouth would sound but ill:
But know, I either must enjoy, or Kill.
Alib. Bestow, base Man, thy idle Threats elsewhere,
My Mothers Daughter knows not how to fear.
Since, *Guyomar*, I must not be thy Bride,
Death shall enjoy what is to thee deny'd.
Odm. Then take thy wish—
Guy. Hold, *Odmar*, hold——
My Right in *Alibech* I will resign;
Rather than see her Dye, I'le see her thine.
Alib. In vain thou wouldst resign, for I will be,
Ev'n when thou leav'st me, Constant still to thee:
That shall not save my Life: wilt thou appear
Fearful for her who for her self wants Fear?
Odm. Her Love to him shows me a surer way:
I by her Love, her Vertue must betray: [*Aside.*
Since, *Alibech*, you are so true a Wife: [*To her.*
'Tis in your power to save your Husbands Life:
The gods, by me, your Love and Vertue try:
For both will suffer if you let him Dye.
Alib. I never can believe you will proceed
To such a Black and Execrable Deed.
Odm. I only threatn'd you; but could not prove
So much a Fool to Murder what I love:
But in his Death, I some advantage see:
Worse then it is I'm sure it cannot be.
If you consent, you with that gentle Breath
Preserve his Life: if not, behold his Death.
[*Holds his Sword to his breast.*

Alib. What shall I do!
Guy. ——What, are your thoughts at ſtrife
About a ransom to preserve my Life?
Though to save yours I did my Int'reſt give,
Think not when you were his I meant to live.
Alib. O let him be preserv'd by any way:
But name not the foul price which I muſt pay. [*To* Odm.
Odm. You would and would not; I'le no longer ſtay.
[*Offers again to Kill him.*
Alib. I yield, I yield; but yet e're I am ill,
An innocent desire I would fulfil:
With *Guyomar* I one Chaſt Kiss would leave,
The firſt and laſt he ever can receive.
Odm. Have what you ask: that Minute you agree
To my desires, your Husband shall be free.
[*They unbind her, she goes to her Husband.*
Guy. No, *Alibech*, we never muſt embrace: [*He turns from her.*
Your guilty kindness why do you mis-place?
'Tis meant to him, he is your private Choice:
I was made yours but by the publick Voice.
And now you leave me with a poor pretence,
That your ill Aƈt is for my life's defence.
Alib. Since there remains no other means to try,
Think I am false; I cannot see you Dye.
Guy. To give for me both Life and Honour too,
Is more, perhaps, then I could give for you.
You have done much to cure my Jealousie,
But cannot perfeƈt it unless both Dye:
For since both cannot Live, who ſtays behind
Muſt think the other fearful, or unkind.
Alib. I never could propose that Death you chuse;
But am like you, too jealous to refuse. [*Embracing him.*
Together dying, we together show
That both did pay that Faith which both did owe.
Odm. It then remains I aƈt my own design:
Have you your wills, but I will firſt have mine.
Assiſt me Souldiers—— [*They go to bind her, she cries out.*

Enter Vasquez, *two* Spaniards.

Vasq. Hold, *Odmar*, hold, I come in happy time
To hinder my Misfortune, and your Crime.
Odm. You ill return the kindness I have shown.
Vasq. *Indian*, I say, desiſt.

Odm. ———*Spaniard*, be gone.
Vasq. This Lady I did for my self design:
Dare you attempt her Honour who is mine?
Odm. You're much miſtaken; this is she whom I
Did with my Father's loss, and Countries buy:
She whom your promise did to me convey,
When all things else were made your common prey.
Vasq. That promise made excepted one for me;
One whom I ſtill reserv'd, and this is she.
Odm. This is not she, you cannot be so base.
Vasq. I Love too deeply to miſtake the Face:
The Vanquish'd muſt receive the Victors Laws.
Odm. If I am Vanquish'd I my self am cause.
Vasq. Then thank your self for what you undergo.
Odm. Thus Lawless Might does Juſtice overthrow.
Vasq. Traytors, like you, should never Juſtice name.
Odm. You owe your Triumphs to that Traytors shame.
But to your General I'le my Right refer.
Vasq. He never will protect a Ravisher:
His Generous Heart will soon decide our ſtrife;
He to your Brother will reſtore his Wife.
It reſts we two our claim in Combat try,
And that with this fair prize, the Victor flye.
Odm. Make haſte,
I cannot suffer to be long perplext:
Conqueſt is my firſt wish, and Death my next.
[*They Fight, the* Spaniards *and* Indians *Fight.*
Alib. The gods the Wicked by themselves o'rethrow:
All Fight againſt us now and for us too! [*Unbinds her Husband.*
[*The two* Spaniards *and three* Indians *kill each other*, Vasquez *kills* Odmar, Guyomar *runs to his Brothers Sword.*
Vasq. Now you are mine; my greateſt Foe is slain.
[*To* Alibech.
Guy. A greater ſtill to Vanquish does remain.
Vasq. Another yet!
The Wounds I make but sow new Enemies:
Which from their Blood, like Earth-born Brethren rise.
Guy. *Spaniard* take breath; some respit I'le afford,
My Cause is more advantage then your Sword.
Vasq. Thou art so brave——could it with Honour be,
I'd seek thy Friendship more then Victory.
Guy. Friendship with him whose hand did *Odmar* kill!
Base as he was, he was my Brother ſtill:

And since his Blood has wash'd away his guilt,
Nature asks thine for that which thou has spilt.

[*They Fight a little and breath*, Alibech *takes up a Sword, and comes on.*

Alib. My Weakness may help something in the strife.

Guy. Kill not my Honour to preserve my Life: [*Staying her.*
Rather then by thy Aid I'le Conquest gain,
Without defence I poorly will be slain.

[*She goes back, they Fight again*, Vasquez *falls.*

Guy. Now, *Spaniard*, beg thy Life and thou shalt live.

Vasq. 'Twere vain to ask thee what thou canst not give:
My breath goes out, and I am now no more;
Yet her I Lov'd, in Death I will adore. [*Dyes.*

Guy. Come, *Alibech*, let us from hence remove:
This is a Night of Horror, not of Love.
From every Part I hear a dreadful noyse:
The Vanquish'd Crying, and the Victor's Joys.
I'le to my Father's Aid and Countries flye,
And succour both, or in their Ruine Dye. [*Exeunt.*

SCENE II. *A Prison.*

Montezuma, Indian High Priest *bound*, Pizarro, Spaniards *with Swords drawn, a* Christian Priest.

Piz. Thou hast not yet discover'd all thy store.

Mont. I neither can nor will discover more:
The gods will Punish you, if they be Just;
The gods will Plague your Sacrilegious Lust.

Chr. Priest. Mark how this impious Heathen justifies
His own false gods, and our true God denies:
How wickedly he has refus'd his wealth,
And hid his Gold, from Christian hands, by stealth:
Down with him, Kill him, merit Heaven thereby.

Ind. High Pr. Can Heaven be Author of such Cruelty?

Piz. Since neither threats nor kindness will prevail,
We must by other means your minds assail;
Fasten the Engines; stretch 'um at their length,
And pull the streightned Cords with all your strength.

[*They fasten them to the rack, and then pull them.*

Mont. The gods, who made me once a King, shall know
I still am worthy to continue so:
Though now the subject of your Tyranny,

I'le Plague you worse then you can punish me.
Know I have Gold, which you shall never find,
No Pains, no Tortures shall unlock my Mind.
Chr. Pr. Pull harder yet; he does not feel the rack.
Mont. Pull till my Veins break, and my Sinews crack.
Ind. High Pr. When will you end your Barb'rous Cruelty?
I beg not to escape, I beg to Dye.
Mont. Shame on thy Prie\ſt-hood, that such pray'rs can bring
Is it not brave to suffer with thy King?
When Monarchs suffer, gods themselves bear part;
Then well may'ſt thou, who but my Vassal art:
I charge thee dare not groan, nor shew one sign,
Thou at thy Torments doeſt the leaſt repine.
Ind. High Pr. You took an Oath when you receiv'd your Crown,
The Heavens should pour their usual Blessings down;
The Sun should shine, the Earth it's fruits produce,
And nought be wanting to your Subjects use:
Yet we with Famine were oppreſt, and now
Muſt to the Yoke of Cruel Maſters bow.
Mont. If those above, who made the World, could be
Forgetful of it, why then blam'ſt thou me?
Chr. Pr. Those Pains, O Prince, thou suffereſt now, are light,
Compar'd to those, which when thy Soul takes flight,
Immortal, endless, thou muſt then endure,
Which Death begins, and Time can never cure.
Mont. Thou art deceiv'd: for whensoe're I Dye,
The Sun my Father bears my Soul on high:
He lets me down a Beam, and mounted there,
He draws it back, and pulls me through the Air:
I in the Eaſtern Parts, and rising Sky,
You in Heaven's downfal, and the Weſt muſt lye.
Chr. Pr. Fond Man, by Heathen Ignorance misled,
Thy Soul deſtroying when thy Body's Dead:
Change yet thy Faith, and buy Eternal Reſt.
Ind. High Pr. Dye in your own, for our Belief is beſt.
Mont. In seeking happiness you both agree,
But in the search, the paths so different be,
That all Religions with each other Fight,
While only one can lead us in the Right,
But till that one hath some more certain Mark ,
Poor humane kind muſt wander in the dark;
And suffer pains, eternally below,
For that, which here, we cannot come to know.

Chr. Pr. That which we worship, and which you believe,
From Natures common hand we both receive:
All under various names, Adore and Love
One power Immense, which ever rules above.
Vice to abhor, and Virtue to pursue,
Is both believ'd and taught by us and you:
But here our Worship takes another way.
Mont. Where both agree 'tis there most safe to stay:
For what's more vain then Publick Light to shun,
And set up Tapers while we see the Sun?
Chr. Pr. Though Nature teaches whom we should Adore,
By Heavenly Beams we still discover more.
Mont. Or this must be enough, or to Mankind
One equal way to Bliss is not design'd.
For though some more may know, and some know less,
Yet all must know enough for happiness.
Chr. Pr. If in this middle way you still pretend
To stay, your Journey never will have end.
Mont. Howe're 'tis better in the midst to stay,
Then wander farther in uncertain way.
Chr. Pr. But we by Martyrdom our Faith avow.
Mont. You do no more then I for ours do now,
To prove Religion true——
If either Wit or Suff'rings would suffice,
All Faiths afford the Constant and the Wise:
And yet ev'n they, by Education sway'd
In Age defend what Infancy obey'd.
Chr. Pr. Since Age by erring Child-hood is misled,
Refer your self to our Un-erring Head.
Mont. Man and not erre? What reason can you give?
Chr. Pr. Renounce that carnal reason, and believe.
Mont. The Light of Nature should I thus betray,
'Twere to wink hard that I might see the day.
Chr. Pr. Condemn not yet the way you do not know;
I'le make your reason judge what way to go.
Mont. 'Tis much too late for me new ways to take,
Who have but one short step of life to make.
Piz. Increase their Pains, the Cords are yet too slack.
Chr. Pr. I must by force, convert him on the Rack.
Ind. High Pr. I faint away, and find I can no more:
Give leave, O King, I may reveal thy store,
And free my self from pains I cannot bear.
Mont. Think'st thou I lye on Beds of Roses, here,

Or in a Wanton Bath ﬅretch'd at my ease?
Dye, Slave, and with thee dye such thoughts as these.
[High Prieﬅ *turns aside and dyes.*

Enter Cortez *attended by* Spaniards, *he speaks entring.*

Cort. On pain of death kill none but those who fight;
I much repent me of this bloody night:
Slaughter grows murder when it goes too far,
And makes a Massacre what was a War:
Sheath all your weapons, and in silence move,
'Tis sacred here to Beauty and to Love. [*Sees* Montezuma.
Ha——
What dismal sight is this which takes from me
All the delight that waits on Victory! [*Runs to take him off the Rack.*
Make haﬅe: how now, Religion, do you Frown?
Haﬅe holy Avarice, and help him down!
Ah, Father, Father, what do I endure, [*Embracing* Montezuma.
To see these Wounds my pity cannot Cure!
Mont. Am I so low, that you should pity bring,
And give an Infants Comfort to a King?
Ask these if I have once unmanly groan'd;
Or ought have done deserving to be moan'd.
Cort. Did I not charge thou should'ﬅ not ﬅir from hence?
[*To* Pizarro.
But Martial Law shall punish thy Offence.
And you, [*To the* Chr. Prieﬅ.
Who sawcily, teach Monarchs to obey,
And the wide World in narrow Cloyﬅers sway;
Set up by Kings as humble aids of Power,
You that which bred you, Viper-like, devour,
You Enemies of Crowns.
Chr. Pr. ——Come, let's away,
We but provoke his fury by our ﬅay.
Cort. If this go free, farewel that Discipline,
Which did in Spanish Camps severely shine:
Accursed Gold, 'tis thou haﬅ caus'd these crimes;
Thou turn'ﬅ our Steel againﬅ thy Parent Climes!
And into *Spain* wilt fatally be brought,
Since with the price of Blood thou here art bought.
[*Exeunt* Prieﬅ *and* Pizarro.
[Cortez *kneels by* Montezuma, *and weeps.*
Cort. Can you forget those Crimes they did commit?
Mont. I'le do what for my dignity is fit:

Rise, Sir, I'm satisfied the fault was theirs:
Trust me you make me weep to see your Tears:
Must I chear you?
Cort. Ah Heavens!
Mont. ——You're much to blame;
Your grief is cruel, for it shews my shame,
Does my lost Crown to my remembrance bring:
But weep not you, and I'le be still a King.
You have forgot that I your Death design'd,
To satisfie the Proud *Almeria*'s Mind;
You, who preserv'd my Life, I doom'd to Dye.
Cort. Your Love did that, and not your Cruelty.

Enter a Spaniard.

Span. Prince *Guyomar* the Combat still maintains,
Our Men retreat, and he their ground regains:
But once incourag'd by our Generals sight,
We boldly should renew the doubtful Fight.
Cort. Remove not hence, you shall not long attend:
[*To* Montezuma.
I'le aid my Souldiers, yet preserve my Friend.
Mont. Excellent Man! [*Exit* Cortez, *&c.*
But I, by living, poorly take the way
To injure Goodness, which I cannot pay.

Enter Almeria.

Alm. Ruine and Death run Arm'd through every Street;
And yet that Fate I seek I cannot meet:
What guards Misfortunes are!
Such is th' infectious strength of Misery,
Death that strikes all, yet seems afraid of me.
Mont. *Almeria*'s here: o turn away your Face!
Must you be witness too of my disgrace?
Alm. I am not that *Almeria* whom you knew,
But want that pity I deny'd to you:
Your Conquerour, alas! has Vanquish'd me;
But he refuses his own Victory:
While all are Captives, in your Conquer'd State,
I find a wretched freedom in his hate.
Mont. Couldst thou thy Love on one who scorn'd thee lose?
He saw not with my Eyes who could refuse:
Him who could prove so much unkind to thee,
I ne're will suffer to be kind to me.

Alm. I am content in Death to share your Fate;
And dye for him I love with him I hate.
Mont. What shall I do in this perplexing ſtreight!
My tortur'd Limbs refuse to bear my weight:
[*Endeavouring to walk, and not being able.*
I cannot go to Death to set me free:
Death muſt be kind, and come himself to me.
Alm. I've thought upon't: I have Affairs below, [Alm. *musing.*
Which I muſt needs dispatch before I go:
Sir, I have found a place where you may be, [*To him.*
(Though not preserv'd) yet like a King dye free:
The General left your Daughter in the Tower,
We may a while resiſt the *Spaniards* power.
If *Guyomar* prevail——
Mont. ———Haſte then, and call;
She'l hear your Voice, and answer from the Wall.
Alm. My voice she knows and fears, but use your own,
And to gain entrance, feign you are alone.
[Almeria *ſteps behind.*
Mont. Cydaria!
Alm. ——Lowder.
Mont. ——Daughter!
Alm. ——Lowder yet.
Mont. Thou canſt not, sure, thy Father's voice forget.
[*He knocks at the door, at laſt* Cydaria *looks over the* Zoty.
Cyd. Since my Love went, I have been frighted so,
With Dismal Groans and Noyses from below:
I durſt not send my Eyes abroad, for fear
Of seeing dangers, which I yet but hear.
Mont. Cydaria!
Cyd. ——Sure 'tis my Father calls.
Mont. ——Dear Child make haſte;
All hope of succour, but from thee is paſt:
As on the sand the frighted Traveller
Sees the high Sea come rolling from a far,
The Land grow short, he mends his weary pace,
While Death behind him covers all the place:
So I swift mis-fortunes am pursu'd,
Which on each other, are like Waves renew'd.
Cyd. Are you alone?
Mont. ——I am.
Cyd. ——I'le ſtreight descend;
Heaven did you here for both our safeties send.

[Cydaria *descends and opens the Door*, Almeria *rushes betwixt with* Montezuma.

Cyd. *Almeria* here! then I am loſt again. [*Both thruſt*.

Alm. Yield to my ſtrength; you ſtruggle but in vain.
Make haſte and shut, our Enemies appear.

[Cortez *and* Spaniards *appear at the other end*.

Cyd. Then do you enter and let me ſtay here.

[*As she speaks*, Almeria *over-powers her*, *thruſts her in*, *and shuts*.

Cort. Sure, I both heard her voice, and saw her face,
She's like a Vision vanish'd from the place.
Too late I find my absence was too long;
My hopes grow sickly, and my fears grow ſtrong.

[*He knocks a little*, *then* Montezuma, Cydaria, Almeria *appear above*:

Alm. Look up, look up, and see if you can know
Those whom, in vain, you think to find below.

Cyd. Look up and see *Cydaria*'s loſt eſtate.

Mont. And caſt one look on *Montezuma*'s Fate.

Cort. Speak not such dismal words as wound my Ear:
Nor name Death to me when *Cydaria*'s there.
Despair not, Sir, who knows but Conquering *Spain*
May part of what you loſt reſtore again?

Mont. No, *Spaniard*, know, he who to Empire born,
Lives to be less, deserves the Victors scorn:
Kings and their Crowns have but one Deſtiny:
Power is their Life, when that expires they dye.

Cyd. What Dreadful Words are these!

Mont. ———Name Life no more;
'Tis now a Torture worse then all I bore:
I'le not be brib'd to suffer Life, but dye
In spight of your miſtaken Clemency.
I was your Slave, and I was us'd like one;
The Shame continues when the Pain is gone:
But I'm a King while this is in my Hand—— [*His Sword*.
He wants no Subjects who can Death Command:
You should have ty'd him up, t' have Conquer'd me,
But he's ſtill mine, and thus he sets me free. [*Stabs himself*.

Cyd. Oh my dear Father!

Cort. Haſte, break ope the Door.

Alm. When that is forc'd there yet remain two more.

[*The Souldiers break open the firſt door*, *and go in*.

We shall have time enough to take our way,
'Ere any can our Fatal Journey ſtay.

Mont. Already mine is paſt: O powers divine;
Take my laſt thanks; no longer I repine:
I might have liv'd my own mishaps to Mourn,
While some would Pity me, but more would Scorn!
For Pity only on fresh Objects ſtays;
But with the tedious sight of Woes decays.
Still less and less my boyling Spirits flow;
And I grow ſtiff as cooling Mettals do:
Farewel *Almeria*——— [*Dyes.*

Cyd. —He's gone, he's gone,
And leaves poor me defenceless here alone.

Alm. You shall not long be so: prepare to Dye,
That you may bear your Father Company.

Cyd. Oh! name not Death to me, you fright me so,
That with the Fear I shall prevent the Blow:
I know your Mercy's more, then to deſtroy
A thing so young, so Innocent, as I.

Cort. Whence can proceed thy cruel thirſt of Blood?
Ah Barb'rous Woman! Woman! that's too good,
Too mild for thee; there's pity in that name,
But thou haſt loſt thy pity with thy shame.

Alm. Your cruel words have pierc'd me to the Heart;
But on my Rival, I'le revenge my smart.

Cort. Oh, ſtay your hand! and to redeem my fault,
I'le speak the kindeſt words——
That Tongue e're utter'd, or that Heart e're thought.
Dear——Lovely——Sweet——

Alm. These words offend me more;
You act your kindness on *Cydaria*'s score.

Cyd. For his dear sake let me my Life receive.

Alm. Fool, for his sake alone you muſt not Live:
Revenge is now my Joy; he's not for me,
And I'le make sure he ne're shall be for thee.

Cyd. But what's my Crime?

Alm.—'Tis Loving where I Love.

Cyd. Your own example does my act approve.

Alm. 'Tis such a Fault I never can forgive.

Cyd. How can I mend, unless you let me live?
I yet am Tender, Young, and full of Fear,
And dare not Dye, but fain would tarry here.

Cort. If Blood you seek, I will my own resign:
O spare her Life, and in exchange take mine.

Alm. The Love you shew but haſtes her Death the more.

Cort. I'le run, and help to force the inner door. [*Is going in haste.*
Alm. Stay, *Spaniard*, stay, depart not from my Eyes:
That moment that I lose your sight, she dyes.
To look on you I'le grant a short Reprieve.
Cort. O make your gift more full, and let her live:
I dare not go; and yet how dare I stay?
Her I would save, I murder either way.
Cyd. Can you be so hard-hearted, to destroy
My ripening hopes, that are so near to joy?
I just approach to all I would possess:
Death only stands 'twixt me and happiness.
Alm. Your Father, with his Life has lost his Throne:
Your Countries Freedom and Renown is gone.
Honour requires your Death: you must obey.
Cyd. Do you dye first; and shew me then the way.
Alm. Should you not follow, my Revenge were lost.
Cyd. Then rise again, and Fright me with your Ghost.
Alm. I will not trust to that, since Death I chuse,
I'le not leave you that Life which I refuse:
If Death's a pain 'twill not be less to me;
And if 'tis nothing, 'tis no more to thee.
But hark! the noyse increases from behind,
They're near, and my prevent what I design'd:
Take, there's a Rival's Gift— [*Stabs her.*
Cort. Perdition seize thee for so Black a Deed,
Alm. Blame not an Act which did from Love proceed:
I'le thus revenge thee with this Fatal blow; [*Stabs her self.*
Stand fair, and let my Heart-blood on thee flow.
Cyd. Stay Life, and keep me in the chearful Light;
Death is too black, and dwells in too much Night.
Thou leav'st me, Life, but Love supplies thy part,
And keeps me warm by lingring in my Heart:
Yet dying for him, I thy Claim remove;
How dear it costs to Conquer in my Love;
Now strike; that thought, I hope, will arm my Breast.
Alm. Ah, with what differing passions am I prest!
Cyd. Death, when far off, did terrible appear;
But looks less dreadful as he comes more near.
Alm. O Rival, I have lost the power to kill;
Strength hath forsook my Arm, and Rage my will:
I must surmount that Love which thou hast shown:
Dying for him is due to me alone.
Thy weakness shall not boast the Victory,

Now thou shalt live, and dead I'le Conquer thee:
Souldiers assist me down.
[*Exeunt from above led by* Souldiers, *and enter, both led by* Cortez.
Cort. Is there no danger then? [*To* Cydaria.
Cyd. You need not fear
My Wound, I cannot dye when you are near.
Cort. You, for my sake, Life to *Cydaria* give; [*To* Almeria.
And I could dye for you, if you might Live.
Alm. Enough, I dye content, now you are kind;
Kill'd in my Limbs, reviving in my Mind:
Come near, *Cydaria*, and forgive my Crime. [Cydaria *starts back.*
You need not fear my Rage a second time:
I'le bathe your Wounds in Tears for my Offence:
That Hand which made it makes this Recompence.
[*Ready to join their hands.*
I would have joyn'd you, but my Heart's too high:
You will, too soon, possess him when I dye.
Cort. She Faints, O softly set her down.
Alm. 'Tis past!
In thy Lov'd Bosom let me breathe my last.
Here in this one short Moment that I Live,
I have what e're the longest Life could give—— [*Dyes.*
Cort. Farewel, thou Generous Maid: ev'n Victory
Glad as it is, must lend some Tears to thee:
Many I dare not shed, lest you believe [*To* Cydaria.
I joy in you less then for her I grieve.
Cyd. But are you sure she's dead?
I must embrace you fast, before I know
Whether my Life be yet secure or no:
Some other hour I will to Tears allow;
But having you, can shew no sorrow now.

Enter Guyomar *and* Alibech *bound with Souldiers.*

Cort. Prince *Guyomar* in bonds! O Friendship's shame!
It makes me blush to owne a Victors name.
[*Unbinds him*, Cydaria, Alibech.
Cyd. See, *Alibech*, *Almeria* lies there:
But do not think 'twas I that murther'd her.
Alibech *kneels and kisses her Dead Sister.*
Cort. Live and enjoy more than your Conquerour: [*To* Guyomar.
Take all my Love, and share in all my power.
Guy. Think me not proudly rude, if I forsake
Those Gifts I cannot with my Honour take:

I for my Country Fought, and would again,
Had I yet left a Country to maintain:
But since the Gods decreed it otherwise,
I never will on its dear Ruines rise.

Alib. Of all your Goodness leaves to our dispose,
Our Liberty's the only gift we chuse:
Absence alone can make our Sorrows less;
And not to see what we can ne're redress.

Guy. Northward, beyond the Mountains we will go,
Where Rocks lye cover'd with Eternal Snow:
Thin Herbage in the Plains and Fruitless Fields,
The Sand no Gold, the Mine no Silver yields:
There Love and Freedom we'l in Peace enjoy;
No *Spaniards* will that Colony destroy.
We to our selves will all our wishes grant;
And nothing coveting can nothing want.

Cort. First your Great Father's Funeral Pomp provide:
That done, in Peace your Generous Exiles guide.
While I loud thanks pay to the powers above,
Thus doubly Blest with Conquest and with Love.

[*Exeunt.*

FINIS

EPILOGUE,

By a Mercury.

TO *all and singular in this full meeting,*
Ladies and Gallants, Phœbus *sends me greeting.*
To all his Sons by what e're Title known,
Whether of Court, of Coffee-House, or Town:
From his most mighty Sons, whose confidence
Is plac'd in lofty sound, and humble sence,
Ev'n to his little Infants of the Time
That Write new Songs, and trust in Tune and Rhyme.
Be't known that Phœbus *(being daily griev'd*
To see good Plays condemn'd, and bad receiv'd,)
Ordains your judgement upon every Cause,
Henceforth be limited by wholsome Laws.
He first thinks fit no Sonnettier advance
His censure, further then the Song or Dance.
Your Wit Burlesque may one step higher climb,
And in his sphere may judge all Doggrel Rhyme:
All proves, and moves, and Loves, and Honours too:
All that appears high sence, and scarce is low.
As for the Coffee-wits he says not much,
Their proper bus'ness is to Damn the Dutch.
For the great Dons *of Wit*———
Phœbus *gives them full priviledge alone*
To Damn all others, and cry up their own.
Last, for the Ladies, 'tis Apollo's *will,*
They should have pow'r to save, but not to kill:
For Love and He long since have thought it fit,
Wit live by Beauty, Beauty raign by Wit.

TEXTUAL NOTES

TEXTUAL NOTES

OF DRAMATICK POESIE

OF *Dramatick Poesie, An Essay* was entered in the Stationers' Register by H. Herringman, 7 August, 1667, and appeared quarto, the title-page carrying the date 1668. The second edition was issued in 1684, and the third in 1693.

The second edition was very carefully revised by Dryden, who made some important changes in the text of the *Essay* from a stylistic point of view. He very deliberately set to work to get rid of all detached or pendent prepositions, even when these formed an integral part of the verbal phrase. This had the effect of knitting his periods more closely, and in some instances of adding weight and sonority to his sentences, not without, however, a considerable sacrifice of that easy elegance and sweetness of diction which so informs the earlier edition of the *Essay*, and which we cannot even for a more stringent correctness afford to lose. These variations have been carefully recorded in the Textual Notes.

It may be noted that the title-page of 4to 1684 adds: Servant to His Majesty; but 4to 1693 omits this as Dryden was no longer laureat.

The third edition is a reprint of the second, but it has introduced a few modernizations of spelling, which are to be regretted.

The text here given is that of 4to, 1668. The Greek and Latin quotations have been emended where they are at fault owing to the printer. Several variants will be found to have been dealt with in the Explanatory Notes. The name *Corneille* is given consistently throughout; 4to, 1668, has *Corneil* and *Corneile*; 1684 has *Corneille*, and I have felt justified in following this authority since we know it had the benefit of a very careful revision at Dryden's hands.

p. 3, l. 2. *Charles Lord Buckhurst.* 1693, Charles, Earl of *Dorset* and *Middlesex, Lord Chamberlain of Their Majesties Houshold; Knight of the most Noble Order of the Garter, &c.*

p. 3, l. 11. *being a little alter'd.* 1684, being not a little alter'd.

p. 3, l. 22. *will furnish me with.* 1684, as those with which the fourth Act of *Pompey* will furnish me.

p. 3, l. 31. *lookers on.* 1684, the sight.

p. 3, l. 32. *Writers.* 1684, Poets.

p. 4, l. 6. *part of it.* 1684, part of them.

p. 4, l. 11. *Le jeune homme.* 1668, La jeunesse.

p. 4, l. 11. *a.* 1684, à. 1693, à.

p. 4, l. 14. *ce n'est pas vray.* 1668, ce nest son vray.

p. 4, l. 15. *C'est.* 1668, Ce'st.

p. 5, l. 6. *ciuility.* 1684, Civility.

p. 5, l. 15. *upon this subject.* 1684, on the same subject.

p. 5, l. 26. *John Dryden.* 1684, John Dreyden.

p. 5, l. 37. *will be more fully.* 1684, wherein I shall more fully treat of the Virtues and Faults of the *English* Poets who have written either in this, the Epique, or the Lyrick way.
p. 7, l. 14. *all men.* 1668, al men.
p. 7, l. 15. *we knew.* 1684, they knew.
p. 7, l. 33. *Air break.* 1684, air to break.
p. 7, l. 35. *seeming.* 1668, seemng.
p. 8, l. 4. *we had.* 1684, that we had.
p. 8, l. 11. *he must.* 1668, must.
p. 8, l. 13. *upon it.* 1684, on that subject.
p. 8, l. 18. *call'd for.* 1684, desired.
p. 8, l. 18. *There.* 1668, there.
p. 8, l. 19. *you speak of.* 1684, of whom you speak.
p. 8, l. 22. *and after.* 1684, wherein.
p. 8, l. 23. *at last.* 1684, they will at last.
p. 8, l. 33. *the Dictator.* 1684, than one of their brethren was by *Sylla* the Dictator.
p. 9, l. 5. *one that.* 1684, who.
p. 9, l. 6. *he spares.* 1684, intends at least to spare.
p. 9, l. 7. *yet ought.* 1684, he ought.
p. 9, l. 9. *so.* 1684, to be such.
p. 10, l. 5. *the great Ones.* 1684, great Persons.
p. 10, l. 5. *of a great person.* 1684, of one.
p. 10, l. 10. *hardly dealt with.* 1684, think he had hard measure.
p. 10, l. 23. *I live in.* 1684, in which I live.
p. 10, l. 27. *themselves.* 1684, themselves were.
p. 11, l. 3. *told Eugenius . . . pleased.* 1684, told Eugenius that if he pleased.
p. 11, l. 17. *were so: they can.* 1684, were: they can.
p. 11, l. 32. *Rime.* 1693, Rhyme.
p. 11, l. 36. *it was.* 1684, that it was.
p. 11, l. 38. *who writ.* 1684, who had writ.
p. 12, l. 19. *foundation.* 1684, foundations.
p. 12, l. 23. *to a great.* 1684, to great.
p. 13, l. 12. *wishing they had it, is.* 1684, wishing they had it, that desire is.
p. 13, l. 17. *through with it.* 1684, through the work.
p. 13, l. 29. *Poets, which.* 1684, poets, who.
p. 13, l. 36. *have been.* 1668, has been.
p. 13, l. 38. *as namely.* 1684, namely.
p. 14, l. 23. *you behold him not.* 1684, they suffer you not to behold him.
p. 15, l. 1. *enters the second.* 1684, who enters second.
p. 15, l. 4. *Corneille.* 1668, Corneil.
p. 15, l. 13. *are to be.* 1684, are (as near as may be) to be.
p. 15, l. 24. *Corneille.* 1668, Corneile.
p. 15, l. 37. *to have writ.* 1684, to have written.
p. 15, l. 41. *of his.* 1684, of them.
p. 15, l. 42. *and of Varius.* 1684, and may judge of Varius.

TEXTUAL NOTES

p. 15, l. 43. *Horace, Martial,* 1668, Horace Martial,
p. 16, l. 1. *Aristophanes . . . extant.* 1684, Aristophanes and Plautus are extant.
p. 16, l. 2. *are to be had.* 1684, are in our hands.
p. 16, l. 7. *whose wit.* 1684, the wit of which.
p. 16, l. 10. *know it perfectly.* 1684, understand perfectly.
p. 16, l. 27. *Father Ben. to you.* 1684, before you Father Ben.
p. 16, l. 30. *good ones.* 1684, good Plays.
p. 16, l. 31. *esteem.* 1684, admire.
p. 16, l. 33. *who waited.* 1684, who had waited.
p. 17, l. 34. *Counterturn.* 1684, Thirdly, the *Catastasis*, called by the Romans *Status*, the height and full growth of the play: we may call it properly the Counterturn.
p. 17, l. 36. *distant.* 1668, dsstant.
p. 17, l. 40. λύσις. 1668, δέσις.
p. 18, l. 32. *or two of Verses.* 1684, or more verses.
p. 18, l. 42. *the same City.* 1684, the City.
p. 19, l. 5. *take.* 1684, taking.
p. 19, l. 8. *Wench.* 1684, Mistres. 1693, Mistress.
p. 19, l. 12. *built upon.* 1684, on whom the Story is built.
p. 19, l. 15. *way.* 1684, way, which was.
p. 19, l. 32. *two dayes.* 1684, two days, says *Scaliger*, the two first Acts concluding the first day, the three last the day ensuing.
p. 19, l. 40. *that is not.* 1684, which is not.
p. 19, l. 43. *in a mistake the house.* 1684, by mistake into the house.
p. 20, l. 1. *to give an ample.* 1684, to give ample.
p. 20, l. 2. *Garboyles.* 1684, disorders.
p. 20, l. 3. *employer.* 1668, employé.
p. 20, l. 13. *not every.* 1684, not only every.
p. 20, l. 28. *Phaedria.* All quartos read (incorrectly): *Phœdria.*
p. 20, l. 31. *enter after.* All quartos: Enter; after.
p. 20, l. 35. *and managing.* 1684, in the management.
p. 21, l. 22. *Phaedria.* 1668 and 1684, *Phœdria.*
p. 22, l. 6. *Æneid.* 1668, *Æeneid.*
p. 23, l. 6. *liv'd.* 1668, live'd.
p. 23, l. 9. *sententiousness.* 1668, sentiousness.
p. 23, l. 15. *Seneca.* 1668, Sencca.
p. 23, l. 19. *their Tragedies.* 1684, in the Tragedies of the Ancients.
p. 23, l. 33. *then indeed . . . offence.* Both 1684 and 1693 omit this.
p. 23, l. 43. *of the Historian.* 1684, from the Historian.
p. 24, l. 21. *not as natural.* 1684, not natural.
p. 24, l. 22. *he liv'd in.* 1684, in which he liv'd.
p. 25, l. 8. *Beaumont, Fletcher.* 1668, *Beaumont Fletcher.*
p. 25, l. 14. *Corneille.* 1668, Corneil.
p. 25, l. 18. *touching upon.* 1684, observing.
p. 26, l. 4. *a third.* 1684, and a third.
p. 26, l. 5. *and fourth a Duel.* 1684, and a Duel.

p. 26, l. 17. *forced in.* 1684, forced in to it.
p. 26, l. 19. *restringents upon it?* 1684, restringents?
p. 26, l. 37. *example, the death.* 1684, example, in the death.
p. 27, l. 24. *close.* 1684, closely.
p. 27, l. 30. *Spanish Plotts.* 1684, Spanish Plots.
p. 27, l. 34. *Herodian;* 1668, Herodian,
p. 28, l. 1. *Golia's.* 1693, *Goliah's.*
p. 29, l. 8. *we are subject to.* 1684, to which we are subject.
p. 29, l. 24. *but naturally do it.* 1684, but do it.
p. 29, l. 27. *perswade us to.* 1684, insinuate into us.
p. 30, l. 15. *till they come.* 1684, till the Players come.
p. 30, l. 29. *impossibility.* 1668, impossiblity.
p. 31, l. 3. *remarkable.* 1668, remakable.
p. 31, l. 12. *managing.* 1684, management.
p. 31, l. 20. *them off.* 1684, them off their design.
p. 31, l. 30. *to get it up again.* 1684, to get up again what he had lost.
p. 31, l. 32. *hear of in a Sermon.* 1684, hear in a Sermon.
p. 31, l. 36. *which.* 1684, which rule.
p. 31, l. 41. *exits of the Actors.* 1684, exit of the Actor.
p. 31, l. 41. *their purpose.* 1684, his purpose.
p. 32, l. 23. *observe.* 1684 misprints, and obseve.
p. 32, l. 38. *He that.* 1684, He who.
p. 33, l. 1. *by Mr. Hart.* 1684 and 1693 omit "by Mr. *Hart.*"
p. 33, l. 3. *put in.* 1684, put it in.
p. 33, l. 7. *clear it up.* 1684, clear it, and reconcile them.
p. 33, l. 8. *de Moliere.* 1684, Moliere.
p. 33, l. 9. *imitating of afar.* 1684, imitating afear.
p. 33, l. 16. *after.* 1668, afer.
p. 33, l. 40. *that we find.* 1684, which we find.
p. 34, l. 9. *Ours, besides.* 1684, Our Plays besides.
p. 34, l. 12. *Plot: just as they say.* 1684, Plot: as they say.
p. 34, l. 37. *in the tedious.* 1684, in tedious.
p. 35, l. 2. *as our Parsons.* 1684, like our Parsons.
p. 35, l. 5. *Speech . . . lines.* 1684, Speech of an hundred lines.
p. 35, l. 9. *Comedy is.* 1684, Comedy's are. 1693, Comedies are.
p. 35, l. 16. *powr'd.* 1684, pour'd.
p. 35, l. 23. *can arrive at.* 1684, can, reasonably, hope to reach.
p. 36, l. 1. *appear.* 1668, appears.
p. 36, l. 6. *he aym'd at.* 1684, at which he aym'd. 1693, at which he aim'd.
p. 36, l. 7. *Virtue, which.* 1684, Virtue, both which.
p. 36, l. 12. *when they hide.* 1684, to hide.
p. 36, l. 13. *and choose.* 1684, and to choose.
p. 36, l. 23. *which are struck.* 1684 and 1693 omit.
p. 36, l. 29. *writ.* 1668, has 'writ?'
p. 36, l. 33. *Ballette.* 1693, Balette.
p. 37, l. 14. *ti'd up.* 1684, bounded.
p. 37, l. 21. *bound up.* 1684, limited.

p. 38, l. 11. *in through a door.* 1684, into a place of safety.
p. 38, l. 16. *goes on.* 1684, goes forward.
p. 38, l. 21. *Shakespeare*? 1668, *Shakespeare?*
p. 38, l. 31. *writing, ours.* 1668, writing ours.
p. 38, l. 38. *Presidents.* 1693, Precedents.
p. 39, l. 2. *look* 1684, read.
p. 39, l. 2. *upon his Sad.* 1684, on the subject of his said.
p. 39, l. 9. *return from whence.* 1684, return whence.
p. 39, l. 27. *looking . . . him.* 1684, earnestly regarding him.
p. 39, l. 33. *a little envy.* 1684, some envy.
p. 40, l. 11. *treated of.* 1684, done.
p. 40, l. 31. *can ever paint.* 1684, before them can paint.
p. 40, l. 32. *Humour.* 1668, This Humour of.
p. 40, l. 36. *necessary.* 1684, ornamental.
p. 40, l. 40. *serious Playes.* 1684, Comedies especially.
p. 41, l. 26. *too much.* 1668, to much.
p. 41, l. 29. *followed the Idiom of their.* 1684, followed their.
p. 42, l. 11. *once apiece.* 1684, once.
p. 42, l. 22. *and this . . . Morose.* 1684, and to this the Poet seems to allude . . . Morose.
p. 42, l. 24. *diverse.* 1684, divers.
p. 42, l. 37. *is his wit.* 1668, in his wit.
p. 43, l. 28. *from common customes.* 1684, from customs.
p. 44, l. 2. λύσις. 1668, δέσις.
p. 44, l. 18. *had prevail'd himself.* 1684, has made use.
p. 44, l. 28. *True-wit.* 1668, *Truwit.*
p. 44, l. 37. *Collegiate.* 1668, *Cellegiate.*
p. 45, l. 8. *while.* 1668, whille.
p. 46, l. 9. *This, my Lord, was.* 1684, This was.
p. 46, l. 23. *the great Plague.* 1684, the late Plague.
p. 47, l. 26. *not onely light upon the Wit.* 1684, not only imagine the Wit.
p. 48, l. 6. *tend to, and seek after Truth.* 1684, tend to truth.
p. 48, l. 11. *And yet . . . forc'd upon.* 1684, And yet you are often forc'd on this miserable necessity.
p. 48, l. 32. *being these.* 1684, since these.
p. 49, l. 27. *disposing.* 1684, disposition.
p. 49, l. 39. *concludes upon.* 1684, establishes.
p. 49, l. 42. *farther off.* All quartos read: father of.
p. 50, l. 1. *Latine,* 1668, Latiñe.
p. 50, l. 9. *improper to.* 1684, unnatural in.
p. 50, l. 27. *brought in.* 1684, introduced.
p. 51, l. 2. *in a Hemistick.* 1684, in an Hemystick.
p. 51, l. 14. *of all Nations.* 1684, of Nations.
p. 51, l 15. *it: All the French.* 1684, it, the French.
p. 51, l. 18. *to include.* 1668, include.
p. 52, l. 5. *blown upon.* 1684, used.
p. 52, l. 6. *not make.* 1684, not now make.

p. 52, l. 9. *Tentanda.* 1693, *Tentandia.*
p. 52, l. 33. *said the Dialogue.* 1684, said that the Dialogue.
p. 53, l. 17. *Dramatick, . . . alledges, ranck'd.* 1668 punctuates: Dramatick; . . . alledges ranck'd.
p. 54, l. 1. *I have said, to be.* 1668, I have said to be.
p. 54, l. 9. *say) yet makes.* All quartos: say, yet) makes.
p. 54, l. 12. *ones.* 1684, mans.
p. 55, l. 13. *you pass to the most mean ones: those which are common.* 1684, you pass to those which are most mean and which are common.
p. 55, l. 37. *Laris.* 1684 and 1693 add: *Set wide the Palace gates.*
p. 55, l. 41. *excuse them. Besides.* 1684, excuse them. For if they are little and mean in Rhyme, they are of consequence such in Blank Verse. Besides.
p. 56, l. 11. *fancy, the.* 1668, fancy, The. 1684 and 1693, fancy. The.
p. 56, l. 25. *to prove: But you add.* 1684, to prove on that supposition. But you add.
p. 56, l. 33. *so strong, so infallible.* 1684, so strong, or rather so infallible.
p. 56, l. 42. *who was.* 1684, who is.
p. 56, l. 43. *had.* 1684, has.
p. 57, ll. 25–6. *which the Moon-beams play'd upon.* 1684, upon which the Moon-beams play'd.

THE WILD GALLANT

In 1694, A2, (recto) there is a misprint two lines from bottom, "to begin. The." The next line begins with "Comedy," so "The" must be deleted. A note at the end of the Preface calls attention to this.

The Wild Gallant was entered at Stationers' Hall, 7 August, 1667. The first quarto (two separate issues) is 1669, and there are quartos 1684, 1686, 1694.

The two separate issues of the First Edition, 4to, 1669, can be easily distinguished by the spelling of the words "Theatre" and "Theater," "Heringman" and "Herringman" on the title-pages, and by the headlines. Without wishing to deliver any opinion as to the priority of either of these two issues I have marked the quarto which gives "Theatre" on the title-page, A; and the quarto which gives " Theater," B. This, I would emphasize, is merely done for convenience and clarity sake. The text here reprinted is that of A, which only differs from B in the spelling of several words. The headlines of A are *The Wilde Gallant* throughout upon both sides of the page. B has *The VVilde* [sometimes *Wilde*] *Gallant* as headline. In both issues an error occurs in the pagination; a gap of eight numbers 49 to 56. This is the more curious as the type was certainly reset.

Mr. T. J. Wise in *A Dryden Library*, 1930, when describing the issue I have differentiated as B says: "This I consider to be the *Editio Princeps* of *The Wild*

Gallant." He also adds: "There is no certainty whatever that the two editions of *The Wild Gallant* were issued in the order in which I have ranged them, though I am strongly of opinion that the one I have placed first was the first to appear." It is true that A presents a more archaic form of spelling than B, but Mr. Wise writes: "This matter of spelling is merely the result, I think, of the personal taste or habit of the compositor employed on the job."

p. 65, l. 2. *Prologue . . . as it was first Acted.* 1684, 1694 omit.
p. 65, l. 21. *We'l.* 1669 B, We'll.
p. 65, l. 32. *Lifes.* 1669 B, Lif's.
p. 67, l. 26. *frank.* 1669 B, franck.
p. 68, l. 4. *humorous.* 1669 B, humerous. 1684, 1694, humorous.
p. 69, l. 10. *Blancket.* 1669 B, Blanket. So 1684, 1694.
p. 69, l. 28. *Wheeles.* 1669 B, 1684, 1694, Wheels.
p. 70, l. 19. *turne.* 1669 B, 1684, 1694, turn.
p. 71, l. 32. *Pallat.* 1669 B, 1684, 1694, Palate.
p. 72, l. 5. *than.* 1669 B, 1684, then. 1694, than.
p. 72, l. 18. *lin'd.* 1669 B, 1684, 1694, lined.
p. 72, l. 22. *allowes.* 1669 B, 1684, 1694, allows.
p. 72, l. 24. *deale.* 1669 B, 1684, 1694, deal.
p. 72, l. 28. *fubb.* 1669 B, 1684, 1694, fobb.
p. 72, l. 28. *Jeasts.* 1669 B, 1684, 1694, Jests.
p. 73, l. 13. *Jeasts.* 1669 B, 1684, 1694, Jests.
p. 73, l. 13. *minde.* 1669 B, 1684, 1694, mind.
p. 73, l. 26. *truely.* 1669 B, 1684, 1694, truly.
p. 74, l. 1. *has.* 1669 B, 1684, 1694, had.
p. 74, l. 15. *roome.* 1669 B, 1684, 1694, room.
p. 74, l. 15. *pay-master.* 1669 B, 1684, 1694, paymaster.
p. 74, l. 40. *meane, Sir.* 1669 B, 1684, 1694, mean, Sir.
p. 75, l. 19. *Gives him Gold.* So all 4tos. But this surely a stage-direction.
p. 75, l. 38. *God-son, Francis.* 1684, 1694, *Frances.*
p. 76, l. 29. *Tailor.* 1669 B, 1684, 1694, Taylor.
p. 76, l. 30. *farr unlikely.* 1669 B, 1684, 1694, far.
p. 76, l. 38. *Mirror.* 1669 B, Miror. 1684, 1694, Mirror.
p. 77, l. 24. *then to search.* 1694, than.
p. 79, l. 9. *Melancholy.* So 1684. 1669 B, 1694, Melancholly.
p. 79, l. 22. *throws down.* 1669 B, 1684, 1694, *Throws down.*
p. 79, l. 26. *claps their backs.* 1669 B, 1684, 1694, Claps.
p. 80, l. 10. *Act II. Scene* I. All 4tos and folio 1701 misprint ACT II. SCENE II.
p. 80, l. 23. *designes.* 1684, 1694, designs.
p. 80, l. 26. *have light.* 1669 B, 1684, 1694, have a light. Folio 1701, have lit.
p. 81, l. 1. *little Bibber.* Folio 1701 misprints, litter.
p. 81, l. 31. *chous'd.* 1669 B, chous'd.
p. 81, l. 34. *handsel.* 1669 B, 1684, 1694, a handsel.
p. 83, l. 10. *despis'd.* 1669 B, 1684, 1694, despis'd.

p. 84, l. 8. *hold water.* Folio 1701 misprints, it will not water.
p. 85, l. 40. *picque.* Folio 1701, pick.
p. 86, l. 15. *I Vow to Gad.* 1669 B, 1684, 1694, I Vow to gad.
p. 88, l. 14. *Pax.* 1689 B, 1684, pax.
p. 89, l. 19. *Layety.* 1694, Laiety.
p. 93, l. 6. *pity.* 1684, 1694, pitty.
p. 93, l. 17. *Dear Heart.* 1669 B, 1684, 1694, dear heart.
p. 94, l. 11. *Burr. Look.* 1669 A, B, *Bur.* Look.
p. 94, l. 35. *Sacrific'd.* 1669 A, Sacrifis'd. 1669 B, 1684, 1694, Sacrificed.
p. 96, l. 5. *Supper time.* 1669 A, 1669 B, Supper, time,.
p. 96, l. 6. *top'd.* 1669 A, 1669 B, 1684, 1694, rop'd. Folio 1701, top'd.
p. 97, l. 33. *Loveby Snatches.* All 4tos print this stage-direction as though it were the spoken script.
p. 98, l. 11. *Hallotrics.* So all 4tos. Folio 1701, "Harlotrics," but the word is evidently a malapropism of Frances.
p. 98, l. 27. *you Minion.* 1669 B, 1684, 1694, your Minion.
p. 98, l. 33. *Fail. You.* 1669 A, *Fail.* you.
p. 99, l. 7. *squorn.* Folio 1701, *skorn.*
p. 99, l. 8. *hallottry.* Folio 1701, harlotry.
p. 104, l. 4. *Lovebyes.* 1684, 1694, *Lovebys.*
p. 104, l. 30. *She falls.* 1669 B, She fals.
p. 105, l. 8. *Salute 'um.* 1669 A, *Salute u*'m.
p. 105, l. 23. *well, if these.* 1669 A, *we'l.*
p. 107, l. 24. *near.* 1684, ner'e. 1694, ne'er. Folio 1701, Near.
p. 107, l. 40. *chous'd.* 1669 B, chous'd.
p. 110, l. 26. *ravins.* Folio 1701, raving.
p. 110, l. 33. *prow.* Folio 1701, Plough.
p. 112, l. 30. *tels.* 1684, 1694, tells.
p. 113, l. 33. *Isa. And't.* 1669 A, *Isa.* and't.
p. 113, l. 38. *advise Neece!* 1669 B, advice Niece! 1694, advise, Niece.
p. 118, l. 31. *revenge; I Vow.* 1669 B, 1684, 1694, revenge; I vow.
p. 119, l. 14. *Well, march.* 1669 B, VVell.
p. 119, l. 22. *minde to't.* 1669 B, mind.
p. 121, l. 17. *Watch.* 1669 B, VVatch.
p. 121, l. 24. *run.* Folio 1701, turn.
p. 122, l. 21. *chaire.* 1669 B, *Chair.*
p. 125, l. 9. *This is better.* 1669 A, this.

THE RIVAL LADIES

The Rival Ladies was entered at Stationers' Hall, 27 June, 1664. The first quarto is 1664, "A Tragi-Comedy. As it was Acted at the Theater-Royal . . . *London*, Printed by *W.W.* for *Henry Heringman*," and this is the authoritative text. The book was issued without a half-title. There are also quartos of 1669, 1675, 1693.

Mr. T. J. Wise, *A Dryden Library*, notes: "There is said to be an edition of *The Rival Ladies*, bearing the same date [1664], the imprint upon the title-page reading '*Printed by T.N. for Henry Heringman*,' &c. I have never been able to trace a copy of it, and very much doubt if such an edition ever existed."

p. 133, l. 4. *My Lord.* 1693 and folio 1701 have headlines *The Epistle Dedicatory.*
p. 133, l. 14. *Fancifull.* 1675, 1693, Fanciful.
p. 133, l. 15. *Moulded.* 1669, 1675, 1693, molded; folio 1701, Molded.
p. 133, l. 16. *Critiques.* 1675, 1693, and folio 1701, Criticks.
p. 133, l. 20. *Human.* 1669, 1675, 1693, and folio 1701, humane.
p. 133, l. 21. *than.* 1669, then.
p. 133, l. 23. *requisite.* 1669, folio 1701, requisit.
p. 133, l. 28. *powerfull.* 1675, 1693, powerful.
p. 133, l. 29. *Linck'd.* 1669, 1675, 1693, folio 1701, link'd.
p. 134, l. 10. *Theater.* 1675, 1693, Theatre.
p. 134, l. 23. *triumph.* 1675, 1693, folio 1701, Triumph.
p. 134, l. 41. *highth.* 1675, 1693, folio 1701, heightt.
p. 135, l. 7. *Invincible.* 1675, 1693, invincible.
p. 135, l. 17. *Souldier.* 1693, folio 1701, Soldier.
p. 135, l. 19. *Armies.* 1669, armes; 1675, 1693, folio 1701, Arms.
p. 135, l. 26. *acknowledgment.* 1669, acknowledgement.
p. 135, l. 32. *carefull.* 1675, 1693, careful.
p. 135, l. 33. *endeavour'd.* 1669, folio 1701, indeavor'd.
p. 136, l. 20. *Blanck.* 1669, blanck; 1693, Blank; folio 1701, blank.
p. 137, l. 16. *seldome.* 1693, seldom.
p. 137, l. 22. *Artfull.* 1675, 1693, folio 1701, Artful.
p. 138, l. 13. *Driden.* Folio 1701, Dryden.
p. 141, l. 3. *Act First. Scene First.* 1669, 1675, 1693, Act I. Scene I.
p. 141, l. 6. *Storm.* And so 1693; 1669, 1675, folio 1701, storm.
p. 141, l. 11. *Merchants.* 1669, Masters; 1675, 1693, Master's.
p. 141, l. 13. *Burden.* 1669, burden; 1675, 1693, burthen.
p. 143, l. 22. *Sweetness.* 1669, 1675, sweetness.
p. 143, l. 24. *neer.* 1669 and later, near.
p. 143, l. 35. *Dye.* 1669 and later, die.
p. 144, l. 24. *freedome.* 1669, 1675, freedom; 1693, Freedom.
p. 144, l. 31. *persue.* 1669 and later, pursue.
p. 145, l. 14. *Fewel.* 1669, 1693, Fuel; 1675, fuel.
p. 145, l. 32. *Mistriss.* 1693, Mistress.
p. 146, l. 15. *Pallace.* 1675, 1693, Palace.
p. 146, l. 22. *Ruine.* 1675, 1693, ruine.
p. 147, l. 2. *Canonique.* 1693, folio 1701, Canonick.
p. 148, l. 15. *extreamly.* 1675, 1693, extremely.
p. 148, l. 33. *'um.* 1675, 1693, 'em.

p. 151, l. 25. *Ingratefull.* 1669, 1675, 1693, Ingrateful.
p. 154, l. 7. *affraid.* 1669 and all later, afraid.
p. 154, l. 18. *betraid.* 1669, 1675, 1693, betray'd.
p. 154, l. 21. *Doggs.* 1669 and later, Dogs.
p. 154, l. 36. *joyn.* 1693, join.
p. 155, l. 34. *Lye.* 1675, 1693, *Lie.*
p. 158, l. 3. *shaddow.* 1669 and later, shadow.
p. 158, l. 39. *ere.* 1669, 1675, e'r; 1693, folio 1701, e'er.
p. 159, l. 5. *farr.* 1675, 1693, far.
p. 159, l. 5. *Mountain.* 1701 folio misprints, Mountatin.
p. 159, l. 6. *howl.* 1675, houl.
p. 159, l. 9. *only ask.* 1675, onely.
p. 160, l. 2. *have 'um.* 1693 and folio 1701, 'em.
p. 160, l. 20. *wee'l.* 1669, we'l; 1675, 1693, we'll.
p. 160, l. 20. *joyn.* 1693, join.
p. 161, l. 10. *late laſt Night.* The subsequent 4tos and folio 1701 omit "late." This hampers the metre.
p. 161, l. 19. *o'r-joy.* 1693, oe'r-joy.
p. 163, l. 21. *farewell.* 1669, farewel.
p. 164, l. 16. *neer.* Subsequent editions, near.
p. 165, l. 18. *Act the Third.* Subsequent editions, Act III.
p. 166, l. 19. *Serene.* Subsequent editions, Siren.
p. 166, l. 37. *shall not.* Subsequent editions, should.
p. 172, l. 14. *pure and noble.* 1669, 1675, so noble; 1693, folio 1701, so Noble.
p. 172, l. 24. *My eyes.* Folio 1701 misprints his eyes.
p. 173, l. 20. *I'l call.* Folio 1701 misprints can.
p. 173, l. 27. *Act the Fourth. Scene Firſt.* Subsequent editions, Act IV. Scene I.
p. 174, l. 39. *Conveigh'd.* 1675, 1693, *convey'd.*
p. 175, l. 11. *Warr.* Subsequent editions, *War.*
p. 177, l. 28. *Scene the Second.* Subsequent editions, Scene II.
p. 178, l. 9. *Souldier.* 1669, soldier; 1675, 1693, Soldier.
p. 178, l. 25. *Scene the Third.* Subsequent editions, Scene III.
p. 179, l. 7. *Whether so faſt.* Subsequent editions, whither.
p. 179, l. 33. *nor to possess.* Subsequent editions, Not.
p. 180, l. 5. *our Swords.* Subsequent editions, your.
p. 182, l. 26. *Physitians.* 1675, 1693, Physicians.
p. 183, l. 8. *such Regret.* Subsequent editions misprint, much.
p. 187, l. 1. *Act the Fifth.* Subsequent editions, Act V.
p. 187, l. 31. *Swoonded.* 1669 and subsequent 4tos, swooned.
p. 187, l. 35. *Catholiques.* 1693, *Catholicks.*
p. 188, l. 37. *Scene the Second.* Subsequent 4tos, Scene II.
p. 189, l. 17. *only comfort.* 1675, onely.
p. 190, l. 11. *extream.* 1675, 1693, Extreme; folio 1701, extreme.
p. 191, l. 3. *Pylot.* 1669 and all later 4tos, Pilot.
p. 191, l. 20. *dreadfull.* 1669 and all later 4tos, dreadful.

p. 191, l. 21. *Travellour.* 1669, folio 1701, Travellor; 1675, 1693, Traveller.
p. 191, l. 31. *hatefull.* 1669 and all later 4tos, hateful.
p. 191, l. 34. *Scene the Third.* 1669 and all later 4tos, Scene III.
p. 191, l. 36. *only way.* 1675, onely.
p. 192, l. 16. *our way.* 1669 and all subsequent 4tos, your way.
p. 192, l. 19. *before I Dye.* 1669, dy; 1675, 1693, folio 1701, die.
p. 192, l. 24. *Quarrelling.* 1669, folio 1701, Quarelling; 1675, quarrelling; 1693 ends line at Uproar? and begins a new line with Quarrelling.
p. 192, l. 35. *want of him.* [*They Fight.* Folio 1701 omits the stage direction.
p. 192, l. 37. *o'rcome.* 1693 and folio 1701, o'ercome.
p. 194, l. 4. *only thing.* 1675, onely.
p. 195, l. 3. *begg.* 1669 and subsequent 4tos, beg.
p. 195, l. 7. *linck'd.* 1669 and subsequent 4tos, link'd.
p. 195, l. 20. *Jeast.* 1669 and subsequent 4tos, jest.
p. 195, l. 43. *Untill.* 1669 and subsequent 4tos, Until.
p. 196, l. 4. *Leggs.* 1669, 1675, legs; 1693, Legs.
p. 196, l. 6. *neer.* 1669 and subsequent 4tos, near.
p. 196, l. 16. *The Woods.* 1693 and folio 1701 make this separate line a part of the preceding line.
p. 196, l. 25. *With me.* 1693 and folio 1701 add this line to the preceding line.
p. 197, l. 7. *Don Manuel.* 1693 and folio 1701 add this line to the preceding line.
p. 199, l. 4. *With all your Faults.* 1693 and folio 1701 add this line to the preceding line.
p. 199, l. 25. [*Exeunt.* No Epilogue is printed.

THE INDIAN-QUEEN

THE *Indian-Queen* was first printed in *Four New Plays*, folio, 1665. It was reprinted 1692 in *Five New Plays* . . . "Written by the Honourable Sir Robert Howard", folio, general title-page 1692; and the same edition, folio, with the separate title 1692, was re-issued in *Five New Plays* . . . "The Second Edition Corrected", general title-page 1700.

The texts of the eighteenth-century editions of *The Indian-Queen*, in Sir Robert Howard's Plays, 12mo, 1722 (The Third Edition), and in the various collected editions of Dryden's theatre, 12mo., 1717, 1735, 1762, are of no several value, as they follow the text of 1692. *The Indian-Queen* was not included among Dryden's works until 1717, when it appears as "Written by the Honourable Sir Robert Howard and Mr. Dryden." Thus it has no place in the folio, 1701.

p. 207, l. 19. *welcom*. 1692, welcome.
p. 207, l. 27. *judg*. 1692, judge.
p. 209, l. 7. *valour*. 1692, Valour.
p. 209, l. 15. *debt*. 1692, Debt.
p. 209, l. 18. *Guift*. 1692, Gift.
p. 210, l. 9. *die*. 1692, dye.
p. 210, l. 41. *wilde*. 1692, wild.
p. 211, l. 5. *that his pride*. 1692, what.
p. 211, l. 6. *honor*. 1692, Honour.
p. 211, l. 13. *then light*. 1692, than Light.
p. 211, l. 21. *sad Armies do*. 1665, sad Arms does.
p. 211, l. 24. *No, Montezuma*. 1665 misprints, *No, Montzuma*.
p. 211, l. 33. *Countreyes*. 1692, Country's.
p. 211, l. 38. *choller*. 1692, Choler.
p. 211, l. 42. *cousen'd*. 1692, cousend.
p. 211, l. 43. *Countreyes*. 1692, Countrey's.
p. 212, l. 17. *Countrey*. 1692, Country. 1665 misprints, Couutrey.
p. 212, l. 30. *then*. 1692, than.
p. 212, l. 30. *behinde*. 1692, behind.
p. 212, l. 38. *wo'dst*. 1692, wou'dst.
p. 213, l. 19. *overcom*. 1692, overcome.
p. 213, l. 25. *ere*. 1692, e'r.
p. 214, l. 16. *I'le*. 1692, I'll.
p. 214, l. 29. *ere*. 1692, e'er.
p. 214, l. 38. *He'l*. 1692, He'll.
p. 215, l. 8. *Act II. Scene I*. 1665, Act II. Scen. I.
p. 215, l. 9. *persued*. 1692, pursued.
p. 215, l. 18. *o're take*. 1692, o'ertake.
p. 216, l. 2. *unkinde*. 1692, unkind.
p. 216, l. 4. *minde*. 1692, mind.
p. 216, l. 20. *windes*. 1692, Winds.
p. 217, l. 6. *wilde fury*. 1692, wild fury.
p. 217, l. 21. *Generals*. 1692, General's.
p. 217, l. 22. *finde*. 1692, find.
p. 217, l. 23. *Judge so kinde*. 1692, judge so kind.
p. 218, l. 10. *mankinde*. 1692, Mankind.
p. 218, l. 30. *Then what*. 1692, Than what.
p. 219, l. 10. *kinde*. 1692, kind.
p. 219, l. 11. *I'le*. 1692, I'll.
p. 219, l. 30. *Your kindeness*. 1692, Your kindness.
p. 220, l. 6. *childe*. 1692, Child.
p. 220, l. 7. *milde*. 1692, mild.
p. 220, l. 31. *Mess. Orazia*. 1665, 3 *Mess. Orazia*. But there is only one Messenger.
p. 220, l. 39. *mankinde*. 1692, Mankind.
p. 221, l. 16. *windes*. 1692, Winds.
p. 221, l. 19. *let's joyn*. 1692, let's join.

p. 221, l. 21. *honor.* 1692, honour.
p. 221, l. 22. *Act III. Scene* 1. 1665, Act III. Seen. I.
p. 221, l. 25. *fall in upon them.* 1665, *falls in upon them.*
p. 221, l. 26. *triumphant.* 1692, *Triumphant.*
p. 221, l. 29. *dishonor.* 1692, *dishonour.*
p. 221, l. 33. *erre.* 1692, err.
p. 222, l. 15. *ne're report.* 1692, ne'er report.
p. 223, l. 6. *so unkinde.* 1692, so unkind.
p. 223, l. 8. *mindes.* 1692, minds.
p. 223, l. 36. *o're.* 1692, o'r.
p. 224, l. 12. *her Father both.* 1692, her Father, both.
p. 224, l. 19. *destroyes.* 1692, destroys.
p. 224, l. 41. *I finde.* 1692, I find.
p. 225, l. 27. *minde.* 1692, mind.
p. 225, l. 28. *kinde.* 1692, kind.
p. 226, l. 5. *I blame.* 1665, I blam.
p. 226, l. 13. *I feel.* 1665, I feell.
p. 226, l. 40. *thred.* 1692, thread.
p. 227, l. 24. *frame.* 1665, fram.
p. 227, l. 27. *Bodys overcom.* 1692, Bodies overcome.
p. 227, l. 28. *knowledg.* 1692, knowledge.
p. 227, l. 42. *from Flame.* 1665 misprints, fram Flame.
p. 228, l. 7. *Earthy Dun.* Saintsbury has a mighty pother here in a note on the incantation, which he unnecessarily tinkers at and alters, reading "*In the caves*" for "*In their Caves*"; and "*makes abode*" for "*make aboad.*" "*Earthy* Dun" he changes to "*Earthy, dun,*" explaining this nonsense as a "conjectural emendation . . . of 'dun' in its usual sense, for 'Dun' an unintelligible substantive." A dun, of course, is a toad, a word that is common enough and nowise unintelligible. Of such editorial efforts we can only say: "Qui autem fatuus est, aperit stultitiam."
p. 228, l. 24. *Too-buisie.* 1692, Too busie.
p. 228, l. 36. *Tirants.* 1692, Tyrants.
p. 229, l. 19. *Brest.* 1692, Breast.
p. 230, l. 1. *Act IV. Scene* 1. 1665, Act IV, Seen. 1.
p. 230, l. 6. *I'le only.* 1692, I'll only.
p. 230, l. 10. *you'l quickly.* 1692, you'll quickly.
p. 230, l. 14. *finde.* 1692, find.
p. 231, l. 8. *I'le copy.* 1692, I'll copy.
p. 231, l. 8. *brest.* 1692, Breast.
p. 231, l. 39. *ne're durst.* 1692, ne'er durst.
p. 232, l. 9. *I'de cross.* 1692, I'd cross.
p. 232, l. 32. *damb'd.* 1692, dam'd.
p. 234, l. 10. *wait neer.* 1692, wait near.
p. 236, l. 17. *binde my hands.* 1692, bind my hands.
p. 236, l. 23. *joyn'd.* 1692, join'd.

p. 236, l. 25. *joyes.* 1692, joys.
p. 237, l. 1. *Act V. Scene* 1. 1665, Act V. Seen. 1.
p. 237, l. 13. *nere divine.* 1692, *near divine.*
p. 237, l. 23. *oddes.* 1692, odds.
p. 238, l. 10. *kinde.* 1692, kind.
p. 238, l. 11. *finde.* 1692, find.
p. 238, l. 18. *breast.* 1692, Breast.
p. 238, l. 22. *dyes.* 1692, dies.
p. 238, l. 30. *enjoyes.* 1692, enjoys.
p. 238, l. 31. *destroyes.* 1692, destroys.
p. 238, l. 41. *pitty . . . mee.* 1692, pity . . . me.
p. 239, l. 17. *false loue.* 1692, false love.
p. 240, l. 1. *stranger Sir we.* 1692, Stranger, Sir, we.
p. 240, l. 9. *Souldiers.* 1692, Soldiers.
p. 240, l. 21. *ti'd.* 1692, ty'd.
p. 240, l. 28. *pitty.* 1692, Pity.
p. 240, l. 42. *Fond childe.* 1692, Fond Child.
p. 241, l. 18. *parch't.* 1692, parch'd.
p. 241, l. 19. *pittying.* 1692, pitying.
p. 241, l. 26. *Kinde.* 1692, Kind.
p. 241, l. 31. *suddain.* 1692, sudden.
p. 241, l. 37. *windes.* 1692, Winds.
p. 242, l. 7. *succor.* 1692, succour.
p. 242, l. 26. *joyn'd.* 1692, join'd.
p. 242, l. 33. *Enter Amexia.* 1665, *Enter* Amexica.
p. 243, l. 8. *honored.* 1692, honoured.
p. 243, l. 28. *armes.* 1692, arms.
p. 243, l. 42. *Pardon fair Princess if I must.* 1692, Pardon, fair Princess, if I must.
p. 244, l 27. *stayes.* 1692, stays.
p. 244, l. 36. *have power.* 1692 misprints, have to power.
p. 244, l. 40. *griefs.* 1692, grief.
p. 245, l. 1. *The Gods my Son your happy.* 1692, The Gods, my Son, your happy.
p. 245, l. 7. *joyes.* 1692, joys.
p. 246, l. 6. *finde.* 1692, *find.*
p. 246, l. 14. *Painters.* 1692, Painter's.
p. 246, l. 18. *Mindes.* 1692, Minds.
p. 246, l. 19. *wheresoe're.* 1692, *wheresoe'er.*

TEXTUAL NOTES

THE INDIAN EMPEROUR

The Indian Emperour, Or, The Conquest Of Mexico By The Spaniards. Being the sequel of the Indian Queen, was entered at Stationers Hall, 26 May, 1665. The first quarto is 1667; and there are quartos 1668, 1670, 1681, 1686, 1692, 1694, 1696, 1703.

There is preserved in the Library of Trinity College, Cambridge, an important MS. of *The Indian Emperour* (R. 3. 10), written in 1665, two years before the publication of the play. This was formerly the property of Elizabeth Pickering Newton, and after her decease (1689) was presented to Trinity College with many other books and MSS. by her husband, Sir Henry Pickering Newton, in 1693.

The variants in spelling are very considerable throughout, and the same word is found to be spelled in two or even three ways in the course of the MS. To record these, which are in themselves unimportant, would require a facsimile. The copy, which is written in a neat hand—there are only four erasures—between red rules, consists of 42 folio sheets, of which both recto and verso have been used. There is neither Prologue nor Epilogue; no Dedication, nor Prefatory matter (*Connexion of* the Indian Emperour), no list of Persons Represented; whilst stage directions and exits are often omitted. None the less the MS. presents features of great interest. It was obviously made for purposes of reading, not for the theatre, and indeed since there was delay in the publication of *The Indian Emperour* this copy was done in 1665 to be sent into the country to Elizabeth Pickering, who was anxious to obtain the script of the great London success.

The important variants are recorded below. As I have just said, it is not possible to record every alteration and alternation in spelling. The MS. commences:

Act: 1st Sc: 1st

Enter Cortez, Vasquez, Pizarro with Spaniards & Indians.

Cortez. In what new happy Climate are wee throwne,
Soe long kept secret, & so lately knowne

p. 255, l. 1. *A Defence of an Essay.* This Defence is only found in 4to, 1668, "The Second Edition," where it occupies pp. 3–21.

p. 271, l. 4. *Monmouth and Bucclugh.* 4to, 1, 1667 reads, Dutchess of *Monmouth*, Countess of *Bucclugh*, &c.

p. 271, l. 8. *The favour.* In 4tos 1694 and 1703 and folio 1701 the Dedication is printed in roman letter.

p. 271, l. 11. *ownd.* 1668 and subsequent 4tos, owned.

p. 271, l. 34. *to flourish in.* 1668 and subsequent 4tos, "in which to flourish.'

p. 272, l. 25. *then it is.* 1668, *than it is.*

p. 272, l. 28. *then his Brothers.* 1668, 1670, 1686, and subsequent 4tos, *than his Brothers.*

p. 272, l. 30. *Indies.* Folio 1701, *India.*

p. 272, l. 32. *Conquerours.* 1686, *Conquerors.* 1694, Conquerors.

p. 272, l. 41. *to represent truth.* 1668 and later 4tos, "*to represent Historical Truth.*"

p. 273, l. 2. *Flame then Art.* 1668 and later, "*Flame than Art.*"

p. 273, l. 29. *joyned.* 1668 and later, joyning. But 4to, 1694 reverts to joyned.

p. 273, l. 29. *Taxallan-Indians.* 1668, 1670, 1686, *Tlaxcallan-Indians.* 1694, 1703, folio 1701, *Traxallan-Indians.*

p. 273, l. 36. *Language.* 1668 adds, "were to the Christians."

p. 274, l. 21. *Our Prologue, th' old-cast too.* This line and the following couplet are only found in 4to 1, 1667.

p. 277, l. 18. *untaught and salvage.* MS., untaught, and Salvage,.

p. 277, l. 21. *by Nature wrought.* 1667 misprints by Nature taught.

p. 277, l. 23. *Old Mens Children, be.* So 1667, 1670, 1686, 1694. 1668 has no punctuation from "Springs," . . . to . . . "infancy." Folio 1701, like Old Mens Children be,

p. 277, l. 31. *seasons be.* 1668 and later 4tos, Seasons be.

p. 277, l. 34. *journies.* MS., Journeys.

p. 278, l. 1. *fairy.* MS., fayry.

p. 278, l. 2. *Ore.* MS., Oare.

p. 278, l. 16. *quarrel.* MS., Quarrell.

p. 278, l. 17. *Cort. My self.* 4to 1, 1667 obviously mistakes in giving this couplet to Pizarro. 4to 2, 1668 makes the correction.

p. 278, l. 28. *A Temple.* MS., A Temple, and Caliban the high Preist and other Preists appearing in it.

p. 278, l. 28. *High Priest* MS. has speech-prefix Calib. throughout for High Priest. Dryden, before his MS. went to press, deleted the name Caliban and substituted "High Priest." As remarked in the Textual Notes, by a slip, speech-prefix "*Calib.*" was retained in the First Quarto, 1667, in one place.

p. 278, l. 31 *High Pr.* When sets he. So 4to 2, 1668 correcting "When gets he" of 4to 1, 1667.

p. 278, l. 33. *Incense.* MS., Incence.

p. 279, l. 9. *High Pr. On your birth day.* 4to 1, 1667, gives speech-prefix *Callib.* The High Priest was originally called Caliban. See the note on the MS. (1665) reading of this passage. 4to 2 as text.

p. 279, l. 9. *On your birth day, while.* MS., On your birth while.

p. 279, l. 14. *of all the year.* MS.,

> Chorus. Of the yeare, and of the day
> Crowne her Queen whom you obey
> Crowne her Queene Crowne her Queene
> And at her feet your Garlands lay,

p. 279, l. 18. *grant.* MS., graunt.

p. 279, l. 20. *and bows.* MS., he kneels.
p. 279, l. 25. [*To her Brother . . . aside.* MS. omits.
p. 279, l. 35. *scorns on him, that scorn'd.* 1668 and later, who scorn'd. An improvement.
p. 279, l. 37. *She turns.* MS. omits.
p. 279, l. 38. *Madam.* MS., Madame.
p. 280, l. 29. *Almeria to Orbellan.* MS. omits.
p. 281, l. 23. *blewish.* 1686, 1694, folio 1701 and later editions, bluish.
p. 281, l. 32. *out-blow'd.* 4to 1, 1667, out-bow'd, corrected in 4to 2.
p. 281, l. 41. *noyse.* 4to 2, 1668, and later, noise.
p. 282, l. 12. *As I am sure.* MS. omits "sure."
p. 282, l. 25. *wounds that.* 4to 2, 1668, and later, which.
p. 282, l. 36. *surprise.* 1668, surprize.
p. 283, l. 24. *And use him kindly.* MS., And—use him—kindly.
p. 283, l. 30. *Mont. How now*—— 4to 2, 1668, and later omit.
p. 283, l. 36. *Taxcallan Enemies.* 1686, 1694, folio 1701 misprint "*Traxallan.*" MS., Taxallan.
p. 283, l. 42. *my Love.* MS. adds "Exeunt omnes" which is clearly needed as the stage is empty whilst there is *An Alarm within.*
p. 284, l. 1. *Enter Montezuma.* 4to 1, 1667, abbreviates "*Enter* Montez. Odm. Guy. Alib. Orb. Cyd. Alm. as pursued . . ." 4to 2, 1668, spells the names in full as text.
p. 284, l. 2. *Orbellan, Cydaria.* MS., Orbellan, behind them Cydaria.
p. 284, l. 11. [*To his* Indians. MS. omits.
p. 284, l. 29. *To Vasq. Ind. kneeling.* MS. omits.
p. 284, l. 42. *Blood.* 1686, 1693, folio 1701, Bloud.
p. 285, l. 1. *I with Slaves will store.* MS., I'll with captives store.
p. 285, l. 2. *hot reeking.* MS., that reeking.
p. 285, l. 5. *we will glad.* 1668 and later, I will glad.
p. 285, l. 8. *then King.* 1686 and later, than King.
p. 285, l. 14. *Herauld.* MS., Herrald. 1686 and later, Herald.
p. 285, ll. 31–2. *while Vasquez . . . dumbshow.* MS. omits.
p. 285, l. 42. *mettal.* 1686 and later, metal.
p. 286, l. 1. *what-ever.* 1668 and later 4tos, whatever.
p. 286, l. 3. *your King.* MS., thy King.
p. 286, l. 16. *Vice-roy.* 1686 and later, Viceroy.
p. 286, l. 20. *truely.* 1668 and subsequently, truly.
p. 286, l. 26. *Fasts.* 1694, folio 1701, 4to 1703, Fast.
p. 287, l. 13. *But what I did.* MS., but I what I did.
p. 287, l. 18. *Vasq. He has refus'd.* MS. omits speech-prefix.
p. 287, l. 20. *Antient.* 1668 and subsequently, Ancient.
p. 287, l. 28. *Exeunt Montezuma.* Thus 1668. 1667 abbreviates, "*Exeunt* Mont. Odm. Guy. Orbel. Alm. *and* Alib." So in following stage direction "Cyd. is going . . ."
p. 287, ll. 30–31. *Your duty . . . Town.* MS. omits this couplet.
p. 287, l. 37. *blind. Aside.* MS. omits Aside.
p. 288, l. 1. *I'le tell.* 1686 and later, I'll.

p. 288, l. 1. *rob'd.* 1686 and later, robb'd.
p. 288, l. 14. *so just.* MS., as kind.
p. 288, l. 15. *Enter Orbellan.* 1667, *Enter* Orb.
p. 288, l. 31. *Exeunt omnes.* MS., Exeunt severally.
p. 288, l. 33. *Magitians.* 1686 and subsequently, Magicians.
p. 288, l. 34. *Montezuma, High Priest.* MS., Montezuma, Caliban.
p. 289, l. 9. *ye small.* 1667 misprints yea. Folio 1701, yee.
p. 289, l. 14. *that once.* 1668 and subsequently, who once.
p. 289, l. 19. *Earthy.* Folio 1701, *earthly.*
p. 289, l. 21. *that want.* 1668 and subsequently, which want.
p. 289, ll. 28–31. *The frighted . . . Silvans cry.* MS. omits these four lines.
p. 289, l. 31. *Silvans.* 1686 and later, *Sylvans.*
p. 289, l. 39. *that rule.* 1668 and subsequently, who rule.
p. 290, l. 7. *Kalib ascends.* MS., Kalib ascends to a light ayrie tune.
p. 290, l. 22. *Love's.* 1667 misprints, Lov's.
p. 290, l. 23. *High Pr. Arise ye subtle.* MS.,

Calib. Arise,
Arise ye subtill Spiritts that can spie . . .

p. 290, l. 28. *Womans.* MS., Womens.
p. 290, l. 32. *The Ghosts.* 1686 and later 4tos and folio 1701 misprint, *The Ghost of* Traxalla.
p. 290, l. 36. *dis-appear.* 1686 and later, disappear.
p. 290, l. 40. *They smile.* MS. omits.
p. 291, l. 6. *The hopes.* 1686, later 4tos, and folio 1701 print this speech in italics.
p. 291, l. 8. *that here on Earth.* 1668 and subsequently, who here.
p. 291, l. 18. *Field.* MS., Fields.
p. 291, l. 29. *betwixt the two Armies.* MS. omits.
p. 291, l. 31. *Battel.* MS., Battaill.
p. 292, l. 1. *Enter Cortez.* 1667, Enter Cort. and Vasq.
p. 292, l. 9. *scatter.* 1668 and later 4tos, ruine. Folio 1701, 4to 1703, ruin.
p. 292, l. 32. *burden.* Folio 1701, Burthen.
p. 293, l. 3. *her Lovers.* Folio 1701, a Lover's.
p. 293, l. 3. *breast.* 1668, 1670, brest. 1686, 1694, Brest. Folio 1701, 4to 1703, Breast.
p. 293, l. 16. [*Enter Pizarro.* MS. omits. 4to 1, 1667 omits.
p. 293, l. 29. *I'le go.* 1668 and subsequently, I go.
p. 294, l. 4. *said.* 1667 misprints, sed.
p. 294, l. 9. *That Valour.* 1667, that.
p. 294, l. 19. *Montezuma attended.* MS., Scene changes to ye Indian Countrey. Montezuma enters at the doore behind.
p. 294, l. 19. *his Indians.* 1668 and subsequently, *the* Indians.
p. 294, l. 24. *Bloudy.* 1668 and subsequently, *Bloody.*
p. 295, l. 1. *each. . . . Battel.* MS. omits.
p. 295, l. 1. *in the Battel.* 1667 omits.

p. 295, l. 21. *come wing'd.* 1686 and subsequently, comes.
p. 295, l. 31. *of the prey.* MS. originally read "of our play," corrected to "of the prey."
p. 295, l. 32. *Seize on.* MS., Seize your.
p. 295, l. 34. *Attaque.* 1668, 1670, *attaque.* 1686, 1694, folio 1701, *attacque.* 4to 1703, *attack.*
p. 296, l. 6. *runs at Vasquez.* MS., runs at Pizarro.
p. 296, l. 15. *leading Cydaria.* 1667, *leading* Cidaria.
p. 296, l. 31. *endure.* 1686 and subsequently, indure.
p. 297, l. 2. *Woe.* 1686, 1694, 1703, wooe. Folio 1701, woe.
p. 297, l. 21. *Inhumane Fair.* MS., Too Cruell faire.
p. 297, l. 22. *Poor Heart!* 1668 and all later editions omit "deep, deep" from the following line which is joined to "Poor Heart." The rearrangement is by no means an improvement.
p. 297, l. 43. *oblig'd.* MS., obleidg'd.
p. 298, l. 34. [*To Guyomar.* MS. omits.
p. 299, l. 10. [*He embraces him.* MS. omits.
p. 299, l. 21. *Enter Odmar and Alibech.* MS., Odmar, Alibech.
p. 299, l. 30. *Enter Guyomar.* MS. omits.
p. 300, l. 2. *publickly.* MS., publiquely.
p. 300, l. 5. *Odm. Freedom.* 1667 continues this couplet as part of Guyomar's speech, but 1668 is obviously correct in assigning it to Odmar. 1667 prints "remains" . . . "Chains." 1668 again corrects.
p. 301, l. 1. *Enter Montezuma.* 1668 and subsequently prefix *To them.*
p. 301, l. 38. *Alm. to Orb.* Not in 4to 1, 1667.
p. 301, l. 38. [*Almeria stays Orbellan.* MS. omits. Not in 4to 1, 1667. 1668 introduces this necessary stage-direction.
p. 301, l. 40. *Guyomar returns and hears them.* MS. omits.
p. 302, l. 1. *strait.* 1668 and subsequently, straight.
p. 302, l. 3. *the Guards.* MS., his Guards.
p. 302, l. 34. *Noyse within.* MS. omits.
p. 303, l. 7. *And wanders . . . night.* MS., "wanders in this blinde, and moonelesse night." This line was altered because later it is said "The Moon shines clear, and makes a paler Day."
p. 303, l. 8. *fright.* 1667 misprints, flight.
p. 303, l. 9. *The insolence.* 1667 wrongly adds this couplet to the line spoken by Cortez. 1668 corrects.
p. 303, l. 15. *I'le.* 1668, i'le.
p. 304, l. 1. *Enter Orbellan.* MS. omits.
p. 304, l. 37. *On equal terms . . . so well.* MS. omits these six lines.
p. 305, l. 13. [*Throws . . . again.* MS. omits.
p. 306, l. 17. *ordain.* [*Aside.* MS. omits [Aside.
p. 306, l. 21. *early here.* 1667, hear.
p. 307, l. 10. *Ex. Odmar.* MS. omits.
p. 307, l. 22. *They only Death.* MS., that they but death.
p. 307, l. 25. *deserve.* MS. adds "Exit."

p. 307, l. 28. *Orbellan, Indians.* MS., Orbellan & Indian.
p. 307, l. 30. *He's found . . . by day.* MS.,

> hee's found, hees found
> that loue thou didst usurp thy life shall pay
> thus thy night Treason I reward by day.

p. 307, l. 32. *Dyes.* 1667 gives this as part of the text.
p. 307, l. 36. [*He is beset.* MS. omits.
p. 307, l. 38. *Almeria . . . body.* MS. omits.
p. 308, l. 2. *was vain.* MS., is vain.
p. 308, l. 21. *were freed.* Folio 1701, was freed.
p. 308, l. 22. [*To Montezuma.* MS. omits.
p. 308, l. 30. [*Gives his Sword.* MS. omits.
p. 308, l. 35. *Offers to kill.* MS. omits.
p. 309, l. 3. *Youths.* MS., youth.
p. 309, l. 8. [*Gives . . . Montezuma.* MS. omits.
p. 309, l. 28. *which remain.* MS., that remain.
p. 309, l. 37. *doest.* 1668, dost.
p. 309, l. 38. [*Cortez . . . asleep.* MS. omits.
p. 310, l. 2. [*Exit Indian.* MS. omits. 1667 omits; supplied by 1668.
p. 310, l. 3. [*She plucks . . . him.* MS. omits.
p. 310, l. 12. *Whence can.* MS., whence then can.
p. 310, l. 31. *w'onnot.* MS., cannot.
p. 311, l. 7. *wholly.* 1667, wholy.
p. 311, l. 16. *could find.* MS., would find.
p. 311, l. 21. *adde.* 1686 and later, add.
p. 311, l. 38. *what I must.* MS., that I must.
p. 312, l. 6. *grieve, who have.* MS., grieve that have.
p. 312, l. 19. *Exit Almeria.* MS. omits.
p. 312, l. 25. *blowing of.* 1668 and later, blowing up.
p. 312, l. 31. *SCENE II. Chamber Royal.* MS., 2d Scene Mexico.
p. 313, l. 1. *assayl'd.* 1670 and later, assail'd.
p. 313, l. 10. *These offers.* Folio 1701, 4to 1703, Those.
p. 313, l. 10. *Honour must give.* MS., Honour would give.
p. 313, l. 13. *chuse.* 1668 and later, choose.
p. 313, l. 33. *their prey.* 1668 and later, the prey.
p. 314, l. 3. *Countrey.* 1668 and later, Country.
p. 314, l. 25. *stubborn, slothful.* MS., slothfull, stubborn.
p. 314, l. 26. *Each private man . . . the cure.* MS.,

> for publique good each private man should rise
> Virtue though straight doth of loose folds consist
> Which larger Soules can can [*sic*] widen as they list.

p. 314, ll. 27–8. *As when the Head.* This couplet is only in 4to 1, 1667.
p. 315, l. 8. *Enter a Messenger.* 1668 and later, *Enter* Messenger.
p. 315, l. 17. [*Exit Guyomar.* MS. omits.
p. 315, l. 18. *Enter Odmar.* MS. omits.

p. 315, l. 22. *I beg.* 1668 and later, I beg'd. This is not such a good reading.
p. 316, l. 7. [*Exit Odmar.* MS. adds, Alibech sola.
p. 316, l. 26. *SCENE III.* MS. omits the Song, reading, "3d Scene, a pleasant Grotto discovered a Fountaine spouting in it Indian rarities round about. Vasquez Pizarro and other Spaniards lying carelessly disarm'd, two Spaniards dancing a Saraband at the end of which Guyomar enters and ere they can recurr their swords seizes them."
Guy. Those whom you took . . .
p. 316, l. 35. *that does.* 1668 and later, *which would.*
p. 317, l. 20. [*Spaniards are led out.* MS. omits.
p. 317, l. 26. *such Happiness.* 1668 and later, all Happiness.
p. 318, l. 31. *Honours.* 1686 and later, Honour.
p. 319, l. 2. *by one Foot.* MS., by the Foot.
p. 319, l. 2. *bound by one Foot,* 1668 and subsequently, *bound:*
p. 319, l. 4. *Love.* 1668 and later, love. Folio 1701, Love.
p. 319, l. 12. [*Lays . . . Dagger.* MS. omits.
p. 319, l. 16. *smoak.* 1668 and later, smoke.
p. 319, l. 31. *not possess I'le ſtill.* 1668 and later, ne're possess I will.
p. 319, l. 34. *Enter Cydaria.* MS. adds, "and sees it."
p. 320, l. 39. *triffle.* So 1667, 1668, 1670. Later, trifle.
p. 321, l. 9. *Inhumane Creature, be.* 1668 and later, malicious Beauty, be.
p. 321, l. 25. *wo.* 1694, 1703, folio 1701, Woe.
p. 321, l. 31. *jealous Thoughts.* 1668 and later, jealousie.
p. 321, l. 36. [*Draws her Dagger.* MS. omits.
p. 321, l. 37. *Hold, hold . . . nigh?* MS. omits this couplet.
p. 322, l. 4. *At leaſt.* 1668 and later, This Weapons point shall mix that blood with mine!
p. 322, l. 5. [*Goes to ſtab . . . Dagger.* MS. omits.
p. 322, l. 9. *Enter Vasquez . . . Swords.* MS. omits.
p. 322, l. 41. *some relief.* 1686 and later, soft relief.
p. 323, l. 2. *thy Heart.* 1668 and later, your Heart.
p. 323, l. 3. *Thy Noble.* 1668 and later, Your Noble.
p. 323, l. 4. *thy Brothers.* 1668 and later, your Brothers.
p. 323, l. 18. [*He leads her.* MS. omits.
p. 323, l. 32. *share.* [*Exit.* MS., ſteales of and Exit.
p. 323, l. 36. *Odm. Fate.* MS., Odm. to Alibech. Fate . . .
p. 324, l. 8. *a base.* MS., moſt base.
p. 324, l. 37. *I only . . . prove.* MS., I threatn'd you, but thinke not I could prove.
p. 324, l. 42. *if not,* 1667, I'le not. 1668 gives the better reading, if not.
p. 324, l. 43. [*Holds . . . breaſt.* MS. omits.
p. 325, l. 16. [*They unbind . . . Husband.* MS. omits.
p. 325, l. 30. *Muſt think.* 1668 and subsequently, Muſt be thought fearful, or, whats worse, unkind.
p. 325, l. 37. [*They go . . . cries out.* MS. omits.

p. 325, l. 38. *Enter Vasquez, two Spaniards.* MS. omits.
p. 326, l. 4. *You're.* 1667, Your'e.
p. 326, l. 23. *with this fair prize.* MS., with his faire prize.
p. 326, l. 29. [*Unbinds her Husband.* MS. omits.
p. 326, l. 39. *My Cause is more advantage.* MS., I have enough Advantage.
p. 327, l. 13. [*Dyes.* MS. omits.
p. 327, l. 21. *Montezuma . . . Christian Priest.* MS., "Montezuma Caliban bound. Pizarro Spanniards with swords drawn, a Jesuitt." Where the printed copies have speech-prefix "Chr. Priest" MS. gives "Jes." Several priests accompanied Cortes, but actually the Franciscans and Mercedarians were the first missionaries of Mexico.
p. 327, l. 37. *and then pull.* MS., and pull.
p. 328, l. 14. *Ind. High Pr. You took.* 1667, *Ind. High. P.* You took.
p. 329, ll. 3–4. *All under . . . rules above.* MS. omits this couplet.
p. 329, l. 10. *see the Sun?* MS. omits the following ten lines.
p. 329, l. 33. *see the day.* MS. omits the following four lines.
p. 330, l. 4. *by Spaniards . . . entring.* MS. omits all after "attended" in the stage direction, and all from "On pain of death" to "Ha——" commencing at once, "What dismall sight . . ."
p. 330, l. 7. *murder.* 4to 1694, murther. Folio 1701 and 4to 1703, Murther.
p. 330, l. 12. *what dismal sight.* 1667, 1668, 1670, repeat speech-prefix *Cort.* before this line. It is not necessary as the same speech is continued, but the repetition is due to the fact that in the MS. the preceding lines are omitted and this line commences Cortez' speech.
p. 330, l. 32. *by our stay.* MS. adds, Ex. Jes. [Exit the Jesuit Priest. The next six lines are omitted as also stage-direction "[Cortez . . . weeps," and after the exit of the Jesuit, Cortez at once begins: "Can you forget . . ."
p. 331, l. 8. *weep not you, and I'le.* 1667, weep not, you and I'le.
p. 331, l. 16. *incourag'd.* 1686 and later, encourag'd.
p. 331, ll. 27–8. *What guards Misfortunes are!* 1668 and subsequent editions have a variation here:

> What guards Misfortunes are and misery!
> Death that strikes all, yet seems afraid of me.

p. 332, l. 5. [*Endeavouring . . . able.* MS. omits.
p. 332, l. 15. *Haste then,* 1668 and later, Make haste.
p. 332, l. 19. [*Almeria steps behind.* MS., Almeria absconds.
p. 332, l. 25. *Zoty.* MS., "Balcone;" which is also the reading of the Second Quarto, 1668. 1670, Balcone. 1686, Balcony. 1694, 1703, and folio 1701, *Balcony.*
p. 332, l. 34. *As on the sand.* 1668 and subsequent editions vary, "As when upon the sands the Traveller."
p. 332, l. 36. *The Land.* MS., And Land.

p. 332, l. 40. *Cyd. Are you alone?* MS. adds, "Almeria beckons earneﬅly to him."

p. 333, l. 7. *ﬅay here.* MS. adds, Oh Heav'ns. [*As she speaks . . . shutts.* Cyd. within. Oh Heav'ns!

p. 333, l. 13. *Montezuma, Cydaria, Almeria.* MS., Montezuma, Almeria, Cydaria.

p. 333, l. 40. *Alm. When that.* This line has dropped out in 4to 1, 1667.

p. 333, l. 41. [*The Souldiers . . . go in.* MS. omits.

p. 334, l. 23. *smart.* MS. adds, going to kill her.

p. 334, l. 28. *These words offend.* 1668 and later, This but offends.

p. 335, l. 19. *leave you.* MS., leave thee.

p. 335, l. 20. *'twill not be less.* 1668 and subsequently, it is not less.

p. 335, l. 24. *Take, there's.* MS., Take there. 1668 and 1670; Take, these a Rival's gift. 1681, subsequent 4tos, and 12mo 1717, Take these a Rival's gift.

p. 335, l. 28. *on thee flow.* MS. adds, Cortez here gooes in as to her. 1667 misprints, on the flow.

p. 336, l. 1. *Conquer thee.* MS. adds, "Enter Souldiers" (obviously in the Zoty).

p. 336, l. 8. *if you might.* MS., so you might.

p. 336, l. 15. *their hands.* MS. adds, shoves her back.

p. 336, l. 31. *But having you.* MS., But having you I cannot shedd one now. both kissing.

p. 336, l. 35. [*Unbinds him*, Cydaria, Alibech. Saintsbury here has the following ineptitude, of a piece truly with his usual "annotations", "It has not been said that Cydaria was bound. If it be not a miﬅaken direction the binding muﬅ have been implied in Almeria's 'overpowering' her." It muﬅ surely be obvious even to the crasseﬅ that Cortez unbinds Guyomar, whilﬅ Cydaria releases Alibech. The 1665 MS. has: "Vnbinds him & Cydaria Alibech."

p. 336, l. 35. [*Unbinds him.* MS., vnbinds him & Cydaria Alibech.

p. 337, l. 8. *not to see what.* MS., not to be what.

p. 338, l. 4. *me greeting.* 1694, 1703, folio 1701, *you Greeting*, an error favoured in moﬅ reprints.

p. 338, l. 10. *That Write.* 1668 and later, *Who Write.*

p. 338, l. 29. *Beauty raign.* 1694, 1703, folio 1701, *Beauty reign.*

EXPLANATORY NOTES

EXPLANATORY NOTES

OF DRAMATICK POESIE

p. 2. *Fungar vice cotis.* Horace, *Ars Poetica*, 304–305.

p. 3. *Charles Lord Buckhurst.* Charles Sackville, Lord Buckhurst (1638–1706), was made Earl of Middlesex in 1675, and succeeded his father as sixth Earl of Dorset in 1677.

p. 3. *the last Plague.* The Great Plague of 1665. The Court left London on Thursday, 29 June of that year, under which date Pepys noted: "This end of the towne every day grows very bad because of the plague."

On June 5, 1665, the King ordered that no more plays should be acted owing to the infection of the plague, and the theatres remained closed for a considerable time. The first performances seem to have been recommenced towards the end of 1666. On October 18, 1666, Evelyn saw *Mustapha* performed at the Royal Cockpit. On Thursday, October 25, 1666, Mrs. Knepp told Pepys "they begin at both houses to act on Monday next." On Saturday, October 27, he heard, "the playhouses begin to play next week." This, however, seems to have been a premature expectation, and on Friday, December 7, when he, Pepys, crept into the Theatre Royal "in might pain lest I should be seen by any body to be at a play," he notes that the theatres have "acted now about fourteen days publickly." So we may safely say that they did not open until the end of November, 1666, although performances at Court and probably private performances had been given.

Dryden himself withdrew to Charlton, near Malmesbury, in Wiltshire, a seat of his father-in-law, the Earl of Berkshire, and it was probably in this retreat that he wrote the *Of Dramatick Poesie* as well as the *Annus Mirabilis*.

p. 3. *the way of writing Playes in verse.* After the reopening of the theatres Dryden produced four plays which are not in heroic couplets, and did not return to rhyme until he composed *Tyrannick Love; or, The Royal Martyr*, given in June, 1669. *Secret Love; or, The Maiden Queen*, is a romantic play in blank verse with lighter scenes in prose; *The Tempest; or, The Enchanted Island*, in which he collaborated with Davenant, is again in blank verse with comic episodes in prose; *Sr Martin Mar-all; or, The Feigned Innocence*, and *An Evening's Love; or, The Mock-Astrologer*, are comedies in prose, although the latter opens with a short passage of some twenty lines in blank verse.

p. 3. *none are very violent.* This is a reference to Sir Robert Howard, who notices the allusion in his address to The Reader which prefaces *The Great Favourite; or, The Duke of Lerma*, 4to, 1668, where he remarks: "But, writing this Epistle in so much haste, I had almost forgot one Argument, or Observation, which that Author has most good fortune in; It is in his *Epistle Dedicatory*, before his *Essay of Dramaticke Poesie*, where, speaking of Rhyme in Playes, he desires it may be observ'd, That none are violent against it, but such as have not attempted it, or who have succeeded ill in the attempt; which as to my self and him I easily acknowledge; for I confess none has written in that way better then himself, nor few worse than I: Yet, I hope, he is so ingenuous, that he would not wish this Argument should extend further then to him and me; for if it should be received as a good one, all *Divines* and *Philosophers*, would find a readier way of Confutation then they yet have done, of any that should oppose the least Thesis or Definition, by saying, they were denied by none but such as never attempted to write, or succeeded ill in the attempt."

Dryden's bob at Howard is scarcely just, since of Howard's half a dozen plays (one of which, *The Blind Lady*, was unacted) *The Indian-Queen*, wholly in rhyme, was a triumphant success. Moreover, there are rhyming passages in *The Vestal-Virgin; or, The Roman Ladies*, a tragedy (afterwards altered and '*Acted the Comical Way*') that was very well received by the Town. Moreover, Dryden collaborated with Howard in *The Indian-Queen*, a typical heroic drama.

p. 3. *fourth Act of Pompey*. In 1664 was published "Pompey the Great A Tragedy. As it was Acted by the Servants of His Royal Highness the Duke of York. *Translated out of French by Certain* Persons of Honour." This is a translation in rhyming verse of Pierre Corneille's *La Mort de Pompée*, produced in 1641, and printed 4to, 1644. The matchless Orinda, otherwise Katherine Phillips, who had herself produced a version of the same French play, was a little perturbed when she learned that another Pompey was in the field. She writes: "I long to hear what becomes of the other Translation of *Pompey* and what Opinion the Town and Court have of it; I have laid out several ways to get a Copy, but cannot yet procure one except only of the first Act that was done by Mr. *Waller*. Sir *Edward Filmer* did one, Sir *Charles Sedley* another, and my Lord *Buckhurst* another; but who the fifth I cannot learn." *Letters of Orinda to Poliarchus*, 1705 (p. 112). This is dated 10 January, 1662–3. The "confederate translator" whose name Orinda could not immediately learn was Sidney Godolphin (1645–1712), who afterwards became a well-known statesman, and who is not to be confused with his relative the poet Sidney Godolphin (1610–1643).

Pompey was given at Lincoln's Inn Fields, and Mrs. Phillips describes the piece in a letter dated 22 January, 1663–4. It had probably been first acted some three weeks or more earlier, but it met with a cold, one might say, a harsh reception.

p. 3. *Spurina*. Valerius Maximus, *De Verecundia:* "Excellentis in ea regione [Etruria] pulchritudinis adulescens nomine Spurinna, cum mira specie conplurium feminarum inlustrium sollicitaret oculos ideoque viris ac parentibus earum se suspectum esse sentiret, oris decorem vulneribus confudit deformitatemque sanctitatis suae fidem quam formam inritamentum alienae libidinis esse maluit."

p. 3. *Pars, indocili.* Horace, *Epodes*, XVI, 37–38.

p. 4. *Prætorian Bands.* In A.D. 41 the Praetorian Guard created Claudius Caesar. In January, 69, they raised Otho, their commander, to the throne. There are many examples of the soldiers setting the imperial diadem upon their leader; such were the elections of Septimius Severus (193), Maximinus (235), Diocletian (284), Julian the Apostate (360), Jovian (363), and many more.

p. 4. *allow'd.* Approved. "To *allow* in the last age signified to *approve.*" Malone. *Allow* is from the old French *alouer*, which represents both *allaudare* to praise, and *allocare* to bestow, assign. These two were identified and viewed as senses of one word, which earlier than 1300 had been adopted with both significations into English. A variety of uses arose which combined the two primary meanings into a general idea of *granting* with *approval.* The use of *allow* for *approve* was beginning to get a little old-fashioned, although by no means obsolete, after the Restoration.

p. 4. *you have yet youth.* Lord Buckhurst was at this time just thirty years old.

p. 4. *Le jeune homme.* The author of these lines has not been traced. Mr. W. T. Arnold in the third edition, 1926, of the *Of Dramatick Poesie* (first edition, 1889, by Thomas Arnold) has an interesting note in which he tells us that the lines were submitted to M. Beljame, who, as it appeared, had already tried to identify the source but without success. Several authorities, famous for their knowledge of French seventeenth-century poetry, to whom M. Beljame had sent these lines, also failed to recognize them, and it remains a question whether they were not merely *vers de société* handed about from salon to salon but never printed.

p. 4. *Poem to the King.* From Sir William Davenant's *Poem to the King's Most Sacred Majesty*, 4to, 1663; and included in the folio Davenant, 1673 (pp. 260–271). The lines run:

> So *Nature*, when she Fruit designs, thinks fit
> With Beautious Blossoms to proceed to it:
> And whilst she does accomplish all the Spring,
> Birds to her secret operations sing.

p. 4. *Homer tells us.* *Iliad*, XVI.

p. 4. *first made publick.* In the Epistle Dedicatory addressed to the Earl of Orrery, before *The Rival Ladies*, 4to, 1664, Dryden had argued that "*The advantages which Rhyme has over Blanck Verse, are so many, that it were lost time to name them.*" Sir Robert Howard controverted this in the Preface to his *Four New Plays*, folio, 1665.

p. 5. *Tully.* The reference is to the *De Finibus*, V, 2: "Tum Pomponius: At ego quem vos ut deditum Epicuro insectari soletis."

p. 5. *Caesar.* Of whom Suetonius, *Julius Caesar*, LVI, says: "Reliquit et *De analogia* libros duos, et *Anticatones* totidem." Cicero had written a treatise entitled *Cato* praising the virtues of Cato of Utica. Caesar replied with an *Anticato* in two books, wherein, whilst condemning Cato, he took occasion to speak very highly of Cicero. See Cicero, Letters to Atticus, XII, 40; also Plutarch's *Life of Caesar*, LIV. Also Juvenal, VI, 335–337:

> sed omnes
> Noverunt Mauri, atque Indi quae psaltria penem
> Maiorem, quam sunt duo Caesaris Anticatones . . .

p. 5. *Sine studio.* Dryden, as is frequently the case, quotes from memory. The exact words are: "Sine ira et studio quorum causas procul habeo." *Annales*, I, 1.

p. 5. *more fully treated.* The Second Part was never written, although in his *Dedication of the Æneis*, folio, 1697, addressed to the Earl of Mulgrave, Dryden considers "the Epique" at some length. This fine piece of criticism was sometimes known as *A Discourse on Epique Poetry.*

p. 7. *memorable day.* 3 June, 1665. The engagement between the English and Dutch fleets took place some eight miles off Lowestoft in Suffolk. The English naval force was commanded by the Duke of York, afterwards James II. Opdam, the Dutch admiral, who engaged his Royal Highness's ship, was blown up, when he and all his crew perished. Eighteen large Dutch ships were taken and fourteen others destroyed.

p. 7. *noise of the Cannon.* Thus Dryden says again in his *Verses to Her Highness the* Dutches *on the Memorable Victory gained by the* Duke *against the* Hollanders, June *the* 3[d], 1665, which usher in *Annus Mirabilis:*

> While, from afar, we heard the Cannon play,
> Like distant Thunder on a shiny day.

p. 7. *the Park.* S. James Park.

p. 7. *Eugenius.* Lord Buckhurst. Thus Matthew Prior in the Dedication of his Poems to Buckhurst's son, Lionel, Earl of Dorset and Middlesex, definitely states that "Dryden determines by him, under the character of Eugenius, as to the Laws of Dramatic Poesy." It has been argued that as Lord Buckhurst actually took part in the engagement of 3 June, 1665, it is not possible without bilocation that he should that afternoon have been discussing poetry with Howard, Sedley and Dryden in a boat on the lower reaches of the Thames. (Prior's statement that Buckhurst composed his famous song *To all you Ladies now at land* on the night before the battle with the Dutch fleet will not be forgotten.) It must, however, be borne in mind that this particular meeting of the four literary friends however well told is purely imaginative, as also are all the circumstances of the river excursion. No doubt the views expressed are those of the several interlocutors, but obviously they could not have been elaborated in the very words and under the very conditions Dryden presents.

p. 7. *Crites.* Sir Robert Howard (1626–1698), Dryden's brother-in-law.

p. 7. *Lisideius.* Sir Charles Sedley (1639–1701). It will be noticed that *Lisideius* is an anagram of the Latin form "Sidleius" for Sidley, as this name was very frequently spelled and pronounced.

p. 7. *Neander.* Dryden himself. He probably used this name (*novus homo*) to differentiate his own social position from that of the three persons of "witt and Quality."

p. 8. *congratulated to the rest.* This construction became obsolete towards the beginning of the eighteenth century. Cf. The Epistle Dedicatory to *Aureng-Zebe*, 4to, 1676; "*the Subjects of* England *may justly congratulate to themselves, that both the Nature of our Government, and the Clemency of our King, secure us from any such Complaint.*"

p. 8. *birds of Prey.* Cf. Steele's *The Tender Husband; or, The Accomplish'd Fools*, produced at Drury Lane, April, 1705; 4to, 1705; II, 1:

Clerimont. Oh, *Blenheim, Blenheim!*
Niece. You mention the Place of Battle. . . . Were there not a great many Flights of Vultures before the Battle began?
Clerimont. Oh, Madam, they have eaten up half my Acquaintance.
Niece. Certainly never Birds of Prey were so feasted.—By report, they might have lived half a Year on the very Legs and Arms our Troops left behind 'em.

p. 8. *seditious Preachers.* In allusion to the Act of Uniformity (1662), the Conventicle Act (1664), and the Five Mile Act (1665), all of which regarded the suppression of fanatics and seditious Preachers.

p. 8. *Quem in concione.* Cicero, *Pro Archia*, X, 25.

p. 8. *two Poets.* Robert Wild, D.D., and Richard Flecknoe. It will be noticed that Dryden contrasts the flowery verbiage and fanfares of Wild with Flecknoe's "gentle numbers" that "feebly creep." Robert Wild (1609–1679) was a dissenting minister. The "famous Poem" which men were reading even "in the midst of Change-time" is "Iter Boreale. Attempting something upon the Successful and Matchless March of the Lord General George Monck, from Scotland to London, The Last Winter, &c. *Veni, Vidi, Vici.* By a Rural Pen. London, Printed on St. George's Day, Being the 23[d] of April, 1660." 4to, 1660. *Iter Boreale* was extremely popular and ran into several editions. Wild's Works were collected and published in 1668.

There can be little doubt that Dryden saw the poem in which Wild celebrated the defeat of the Dutch, *An Essay upon the late Victory obtained by the Duke of York upon June* 3, 1665 (licensed

16 June). The opening lines will sufficiently show the justice of Dryden's censure:

> Gout! I conjure thee by the powerful names
> Of *Charles* and *James*, and their Victorious fames,
> On this great day set all thy Prisoners free
> Triumph demands a gaol Delivery.
> Set them all free, leave not a limping toe
> From my Lord Chancellor's to mine below.
> Unless thou giv'st us leave this day to dance,
> Thou art not the old loyal gout, but com'st from *France.*

Richard Flecknoe, who died in 1678, was notoriously long the particular butt of Dryden's ridicule. His *Discourse of the English Stage* is valuable, and there is much that is pleasing, even if it be not distinguished, in other of his work. He also celebrated the victory over the Dutch in:

> "To His Royal Highness The Duke of York, Returning from our Naval Victory over the Hollanders, June 3, Ann. 1665. Under His Royal Highnesses happy conduct." (*A Farrago of several Pieces*, 1666, pp. 4, 5.)

p. 9. *clenches.* Quibbles and puns. Butler in his *Characters*, "A Small Poet" (ed. Thyer, 1759), writes: "He has all Sorts of *Echoes*, *Rebus's*, *Chronograms*, &c. besides *Carwitchets*, *Clenches*, and *Quibbles.*" Dryden in the Prologue to *Troilus and Cressida*, 4to, 1679, girds at

> *The fulsome clench that nauseates the Town.*

p. 9. *Catacresis.* Quintilian, VIII, 6, 34, has: "En magis necessaria κατάχρησις, quam recte dicimus abusionem, quae non habentibus nomen suum accommodat quod in proximo est: sic *Equum divina Palladis arte Aedificant;* et apud tragicos, *Et iam leo pariet*, at pater est.

John Smith, in his *Mysterie of Rhetorique Unvail'd*, 1657 (pp. 48, 49), of Catachresis says: " It is an improper kinde of speech, somewhat more desperate than a Metaphor, and is the expressing of one matter by the name of another, which is incompatible with, and sometimes clean contrary to it; and is when the change of speech is hard, strange and unwonted: or, It is the abuse of a Trope . . . They build a horse by *Pallas* art divine: here the Poet traduceth that to a beast, which is proper to the making of a house."

p. 9. *Clevelandism.* John Cleveland (1613–1638) is prominent among the "metaphysical" school of poets; and although fantastic, perhaps, in certain of his conceits, his work must be allowed great beauties. As a loyal satirist he ranks high. Dryden is a little severe, and it will be remarked that he also takes occasion to mention Cleveland later. In *The Late Converts Exposed*, Part the Second, 4to, 1690, a venomed railing pasquil by Tom Brown, Bays mentions Cleveland

and is made to say (p. 55): "You know Gentlemen how I have treated him in my Essay upon Dramatic Poetry, a thousand times worse I gad than any of his Presbyterian friends. I lash him there for his tall Hyperbole's, his affected obscurity, his unworthy expressions, and (wou'd you think it) for his ill Husbandry in tacking together too much wit. . . . In short, a *Clevelandism* and a *Catachresis* were with me, terms full as conversible as——

Crites. Nay never pump for't man, as Beef and Mustard, Pork and Pease, Hand and Glove, or Brawn and *Christmas.*
Bays. No, no, as *Protestantism* and opiniarete.

A famous example of Clevelandism is the Poem *On the Memory of Mr.* Edward King, *drown'd in the* Irish *Seas*, which appeared in the "Obsequies to the memorie of *Mr.* Edward King, *Anno Dom.* 1638." Cambridge, 1638.

p. 9. *Witches.* In England the last execution for witchcraft appears to have been that of Alice Molland, who was tried at the Exeter Lent Assizes in 1 Jas. II [20 March, 1684] before Sir Francis North, chief justice of Common Pleas, and Sir Thomas Raymond, justice of the King's Bench, found guilty and sentenced.

p. 9. *ten little words.* Pope, *Essay on Criticism*, 346–347:

While expletives their feeble aid do join,
And ten low words oft creep in one dull line.

p. 9. *Pauper videri.* Martial, VIII, 19.

p. 9. *Withers.* George Wither (1588–1667) finished his best work early, for he has little of value after his *Philarete*, published in 1622. However, he continued to write most industriously, and whilst his lyrics were forgotten the doggerel he poured forth was jeered by the wits of a later day. Butler apostrophizes the Puritan Muse (*Hudibras*, I, 1) as:

Thou that with Ale or viler Liquors,
Didst inspire *Withers*, *Prior*, and *Vickars*,
And force them, though it were in spight
Of Nature, and their Stars, to write; . . .

p. 10. *Candles ends.* Chambers' Dictionary explains: "Auction by inch of Candle, is when, a piece of candle being lighted, people are allowed to bid while it burns, but as soon as extinct, the commodity is adjudged to the last bidder."

In some country districts of France, whence indeed the method was adopted, this practice still prevails. The *Reading Mercury*, 16 December, 1899, records such a sale at Aldermaston, in Berkshire; cf. also *Notes and Queries*, 4th Series, Vol. XI, pp. 276 and 371.

p. 10. *great Ones.* In his *Defence of the Epilogue, Or, An Essay on the Dramatique Poetry of the last Age*, subjoined to the Second Part of *The*

Conquest of Granada, 4to, 1672, Dryden criticizes Ben Jonson for using "*Ones* in the plural Number; but that is frequent with him."

p. 10. *qui Bavium*. Vergil, *Eclogue*, III, 90.

p. 10. *Pace vestra. Satyricon*, 2. Tertium edidit Buecheler; Berolini, 1895; p. 7, ll. 16, 17.

p. 10. *Indignor quidquam*. Horace, *Epistularum*, II, 76–77.

p. 10. *Si meliora. Ibid.*, 34–35.

p. 11. *Sir John Suckling*. (1609–1642). Suckling may in a very real sense be considered the predecessor of Buckhurst and Sedley with the rest, "The Mob of Gentlemen who wrote with Ease," as Pope says: (*Imitations of Horace*, II, Ep. 1, 108).

p. 11. *Waller*. (1606–1687). Both Edmund Waller and Sir John Denham (1615–1660) are again mentioned with very similar praise in the Epistle Dedicatory before *The Rival-Ladies*.

p. 11. *Cowley*. (1618–1667). The more particular reference is probably to Cowley's *Pindarique Odes*, which gained him an immense reputation and set a fashion in Pindariques. It may be remembered that the name was applied to almost any irregular set of stanzas, and that it was Congreve who first drew attention to the careful structure of the real Odes of Pindar. See *The Works of Congreve*, by the present editor, Vol. I, pp. 62–63. Nonesuch Press, 1923.

p. 11. *the Drama is wholly ours*. This takes over a phrase of Quintilian, X, 93: "Satira quidem tota nostra est." Dryden quotes the words in his *Discourse concerning the Original and Progress of Satire* prefixed to the *Juvenal*, folio, 1693.

p. 11. *never mis-lead the sence*. Thus Butler in his *Characters* (ed. Thyer, 1759), "A Small Poet": "When he writes, he commonly steers the Sense of his Lines by the Rhime that is at the End of them, as Butchers do Calves by the Tail."

p. 11. *the definition of a Play*. This follows the favourite method of Socrates, who was very justly wont to insist that before a discussion was entered upon the subjects of the discussion should be defined as exactly as possible. This method was practised and followed almost as a law by the schoolmen.

p. 12. *a genere & fine*. Logically this definition is imperfect, because although it gives the general class (*genere*) to which a play belongs, as also the end (*fine*) a play serves, there is no *differentia* or specific difference included. Hence the definition might be applied to a narrative poem, as for example an epic; to a romance; or even indeed to a novella.

p. 12. *Thespis*. Thespis was a native of Icaria in Attica who lived about 536 B.C., in the later years of Peisistratus. He introduced notable improvements in the mode of performances, since hitherto the leader, who recited some adventure of Dionysus, had addressed the Chorus and had been answered by them. Thespis set apart one individual to reply to the leader, and hence regular dialogue ensued, and the one who answered or replied was called ὑποκρίτης, which afterwards came to mean "an actor." The ancients generally regarded Thespis as πρῶτος τραγικός. (But see Suidas.)

Actually Susarion, a native of Tripodiscus in Megara, is considered to have made some first attempts at comedy at Icaria even earlier than Thespis. In the third year of the 50th Olympiad, 578 B.C., Susarion seems to have substituted for the old improvisations of the chorus and its leader regular compositions, although it is quite uncertain in what these consisted, and it is very doubtful whether there was an actor separate from the chorus with its leader. (Schol. *ad* Dionys. Thrac. *ap*. Bekker, *Anecd. Gr.*, p. 748; and Meineke, *Hist. Crit. Comic. Graec.*, p. 559). In any case comedy was not received as a literary form until after tragedy.

Aristophanes is generally considered to have been born about 444 B.C., and to have died not later than 380 B.C.

p. 12. *It has been observed.* Velleius Paterculus, *Historia Romana*, I, 16, 17. The passage commences: "Una, neque multorum annorum spatio divisa, aetas, per divini spiritus viros, Aeschylum, Sophoclem, Euripidem, illustravit tragoedias: una priscam illam et veterem sub Cratino Aristophane et Eupolide comoediam, ac novam comicam Menandrus, aequalesque eius aetatis magis quam operis, Philemon ac Diphilus. . . ."

p. 12. *The Study of Philosophy.* To-day we should probably say "science" or "natural philosophy." Dryden has in mind the Royal Society, which is usually considered to have been founded in 1660. It has been believed that Dryden was long a prominent and active member of the Royal Society, but such in fact was not the case. The poet was proposed for membership of the Society by Dr. Walter Carleton on 12 November, 1662; he was elected 19 November, and formally admitted on the 26th of that month. But Sprat's *History of the Royal Society of London*, which appeared towards the end of 1667, gives a list of the members and in this Dryden's name is not included. Precisely his name was on the roll for three years and twenty-seven days. He was much occupied with other pursuits, and accordingly allowed his membership to lapse.

p. 12. *Lycophron.* This famous grammarian and poet lived at Alexandria under Ptolemy Philadelphus (285–247 B.C.). He wrote a number of tragedies, of which the tale is variously stated to be forty-six or sixty-four, and was one of the famous Pleiad of seven. Of his plays only four lines survive, and he is now better remembered by his *Cassandra* or *Alexandra*, a poem whose obscure allusions and involved periods gained him the title of ὁ Σκοτεινός.

p. 13. *Paterculus. Historia Romana*, I, 17.

p. 13. *that Second Book of his.* Aristotle in the *Poetics* designed to treat of comedy and epic poetry as well as of tragedy. He writes (c. VI) περὶ κωμῳδιας ὕστερον ἐροῦμεν; but this latter part of his dissertation has not been preserved to us.

p. 13. *The Three Unities.* It will be noticed that Dryden writes *Des Trois Unitez*, not, as we might expect, *Les Trois Unitez*. He had been glancing at Corneille's *Discours des Trois Unitez.*

It will suffice to emphasize briefly here how entirely false and confused are the assumptions of sixteenth and seventeenth-century critics with regard to the law of the Unities, which they conceived might be found, not in set phrase indeed but in substance, at any rate, in Aristotle's *Poetics* and in Horace's *Ars Poetica*, and how baseless the further supposition that these laws were observed by the classical tragedians, particularly by Sophocles and Euripides, from a due observance and criticism of whom Aristotle drew his rules. The full theory of the Unities, that there must be only one *action* in a play, that the *time* of this action should not exceed one day, that the scene is not to be changed but the action confined to one *place*, was not formulated until towards the end of the sixteenth century, and it proceeded to develop on French rather than on Italian lines.

According to Ebner, *Beitrag zu einer Geschichte der dramatischen Einheiten in Italien*, the first Italian tragedy to observe all three unities is the *Tullia* of Martelli in 1527, but it cannot be decided whether this was an intentional obedience to rule. The critics were first occupied with the unity of time, and some rejected 24 hours for 12, or even demanded a length of time exactly corresponding to the performance. Castelvetro in his *Poetica d'Aristotele vulgarizzata e sposta*, 1570, laid down a hard-and-fast regulation for place, which must be limited "non solamente ad vna citta, o villa, e campagna, o simile sito, ma anchora a quella vista, che sola puo apparere a gli occhi d'vna persona." It was about 1629 that the Comte de Cramail and the Cardinal de la Vallette persuaded Mairet to write a pastoral *Silvanire* "auec toutes les rigueurs que les Italiens ont accoustumé de pratiquer en cet agreable genre d'escrire." *Silvanire* was acted in 1630, and published 4to. on 31 March, 1631, with a Preface which advocates the observance of the three unities, yet not in their most pedantic interpretation, since although the time must not exceed twenty-four hours, the place may extend to the limits of a city, a forest, or some similar place; whilst episodes closely connected with the main theme are admissible if they do not affect the course of the action and the natural result. It must be remembered that the introduction of the rule of the Unities was gradual, and that (at first at any rate) it was only intended to apply to tragedy and to pastoral.

p. 14. *variation of painted Scenes.* The elaborate decorations of the Jacobean and Carolan masques had a marked influence upon the English stage, since Aubrey tells us that when Suckling's tragi-comedy *Aglaura* was produced at Blackfriars, a private house, at Christmas, 1637, and shortly afterwards was acted at Court, "he had some scenes to it which in those days were only used at Masques." It was not owing to the actors that scenery was introduced into the private theatres even before the Great Rebellion, but owing to the courtier dramatists who, well acquainted with the staging of a masque, gave money that their plays might be presented on somewhat similar lines. Thus in the Prologue to the Duke of Newcastle's *The Country Captaine*, produced at the Blackfriars in the spring of 1640 (4to, 1649), the speaker commences:

> Gallants, I'le tell you what we do not meane
> To shew you here, a glorious painted Scene,
> With various doores, to stand instead of wit,
> Or richer cloathes with lace for lines well writ;
> Taylors and Painters thus, your deare delight,
> May prove your Poets only for your sight.

The allusion is to Habington's *The Queen of Arragon*, given by amateurs at Whitehall before the King and Queen on 9 April, 1640, and after a second performance transferred to Blackfriars with professional actors. According to Sir Henry Herbert "the cloathes and sceanes . . . were very riche and curious." These were paid for by the author.

In the autumn of 1656, probably in September, Davenant in a hall at the back of his mansion, Rutland House, gave the first performance of his opera *The Siege of Rhodes*. Owing to the narrowness of the room elaborate effects could not be attempted, but the scenery was "design'd and order'd" by John Webb, the pupil of Inigo Jones. Fortunately there have been preserved six drawings by Webb for *The Siege of Rhodes*, and although Davenant writes that these scenes were "confin'd to eleven foot in height" they must have been extremely striking, and he has described them for us in some detail. "The Scene before the First Entry: The Curtain being drawn up, a lightsom Skie appear'd, discov'ring a Maritime Coast, full of craggy Rocks, and high Cliffs, with several Verdures naturally growing upon such situations; and afar off, the true Prospect of the City of RHODES when it was in prosperous estate; with so much view of the Gardens and Hills about it, as the narrowness of the Room could allow the Scene. In that part of the Horizon, terminated by the Sea, was represented the Turkish Fleet, making towards a Promontory, some few miles distant from the Town."

In January, 1663–4, *The Indian-Queen* by Dryden and Howard had been produced at the Theatre Royal with especial magnificence and splendid scenery, which was used the following year for *The Indian Emperour* at the same house.

p. 15. *la Liaison des Scenes.* Corneille in his *Examen* (1660) of *La Suivante*, 1637, has much to say of "la liaison de scene," which in his opinion may be either "de présence" or "de vûe," although the latter is far inferior to the former. In his *Troisieme Discours des Trois Unites*, 1660 (ed. Amsterdam, 1740), he says: "La liaison des Scènes qui unit toutes les actions particulières de chaque Acte l'une avec l'autre, & dont j'ai parlé en l'Examen de la Suivante, est un grand ornement dans un pöeme & qui fert beaucoup à former une continüité d'action par la continüité de la répresentation, mais enfin ce n'est qu'un ornement, & non pas un régle." And later he adds: "Un Acteur occupant une fois le Théâtre, aucun n'y doit entrer qui n'aye sujet de parler à lui ou de moins qui n'aye lieu de prendre l'occasion quand elle s'offre. Sur-tout lorsqu'un Acteur entre deux fois dans un Acte, soit dans la Comédie, soit dans la Tragédie, il doit absolument, ou faire juger qu'il reviendra bien-tôt quand il sort la prémière fois, comme Horace dans le second Acte, & Julie dans le troisiéme de la même piéce; ou donner raison en rentrant pourquoi il revient si-tôt." Corneille largely draws upon Aristotle: *ταῦτα δὲ δεῖ γίνεσθαι ἐξ αὐτῆς τῆς συστάσεως τοῦ μύθου, ὥστε ἐκ τῶν προγεγενημένων συμβαίνειν ἢ ἐξ ἀνάγκης ἢ κατὰ τὸ εἶκος γίγνεσθαι ταῦτα. Poetics*, x. 3.

p. 15. *Discoveries. Timber, or, Discoveries, (Explorata; Sylva)*, 4to, 1641; in which Jonson lays down: "*Now*, that it should be one, and intire. One is considerable two waies; either, as it is only separate, and by it self; or as being compos'd of many parts, it beginnes to be one as those parts grow, or are wrought together. That it should be one the first way alone, and by it self, no man that hath tasted letters ever would say, especially having required before a just Magnitude, and equall Proportion of the parts in themselves. Neither of which can possibly bee, if the Action be single and separate, not compos'd of parts, which laid together in themselves, with an equall and fitting proportion, tend to the same end; which thing out of Antiquitie it selfe, hath deceived many; and more this Day it doth deceive."

p. 15. *There ought to be.* This is translated from Corneille's *Troisieme Discours sur les Unites:* "Il n'y doit avoir qu'une action complètte qui laisse l'esprit de l'auditeur dans le calme; mais elle ne peut le devenir que par plusieurs autres imparfaites, qui lui servent d'acheminemens, et tiennent cet auditeur dans une agréable suspension."

p. 15. *Caecilius.* Aulus Gellius, *Noctes Atticae*, II, 23, discusses the *Plocius* of Menander and Caecilius. IV, 20, he has: "Caecilius quoque ille comoediarum poeta inclytus servus fuit, et propterea nomen habuit *Statius.*" Also, XV, 24, where he speaks of Vulcatius: "Sedigitus in libro, quem scripsit De Poetis, quid dicis sentiat, . . . his versibus suis demonstrat . . .

Caecilio palmam statuo dandam comico,
Plautus secundus facile exsuperat omnes. . . ."

Dryden probably had in mind Velleius Paterculus, *Historia Romana*, I, 17: "dulcesque Latini leporis facetiae per Caecilium, Terentiumque et Afranium sub pari aetate nituerunt."

p. 15. *the Half-Menander.* In his *Terentii Vita*, Suetonius, after quoting Cicero's praises of the dramatist, continues:

Item C. Caesar:

Tu quoque, tu in summis, o dimidiate Menander,
Poneris, et merito, puri sermonis amator.
Lenibus atque utinam scriptis adiuncta foret vis
Comica, ut aequato virtus polleret honore
Cum Graecis, neve in hac despectus parte iaceres.
Unum hoc maceror ac doleo tibi deesse, Terenti.

The phrase "o dimidiate Menander" has been often discussed. Meineke suggests that Caesar misses τὸ παθητικόν in Terence, a quality which Menander mingled with τῷ ἠθικῷ. It was this which is the point of the famous saying of Aristophanes the grammarian: Ὦ Μένανδρε, καὶ βίε, πότερος ἄρ' ὑμῶν πρότερον ἐμιμήσατο; (or as Scaliger read, πότερον ἀπεμιμήσατο;).

p. 15. *Varius.* Horace, *Carminum*, I, vi:

Scriberis Vario fortis et hostium
Victor Maeonii carminis alite. . . .

Also *Sermonum*, I, ix, 22–25:

si bene me novi non Viscum pluris amicum,
non Varium facies: nam quis me scribere pluris
aut citius possit versus? quis membra movere
mollius?

Also *Sermonum*, I, x, 43–44:

forte epos acer
ut nemo Varius ducit.

And *Ars Poetica*, 53–55:

quid autem
Caecilio Plautoque dabit Romanus ademptum
Vergilio Varioque?

Martial, VIII, 18, 5–8:

Si Maro nec Calabri tentavit carmina Flacci
Pindaricos posset cum superare modos,
Et Vario cessit Romani laude cothurni
Cum posset tragico fortius ore loqui.

Velleius Paterculus does not mention Varius.

p. 16. *Macrobius.* Ambrosius Aurelius Theodosius Macrobius lived in the reigns of Theodosius I (378–395) and Honorius (395–423). His *Saturnaliorum Conviviorum Libri VII* is a volume consisting of a number of dissertations on history, mythology, criticism, and various points of antiquarian interest. These are supposed to have been delivered *colloquio liberali* during the holidays of the Saturnalia at the house of Vettius Praetextatus, who held the highest honours of state under Valentinian I and Valens. Books III–VI are concerned with Vergil, whose religious learning, devotion, and command of pathos, as well as his debt to Homer and earlier Latin poets, are discussed and apprised at considerable length.

p. 16. *a professed Imitator.* In his "Comicall Satyre" *Poetaster, Or His Arraignment*, acted in 1601, Ben Jonson depicted himself as Horace, and as Horace he appears in Dekker's *Satiro-mastix, or, The untrussing of the Humorous Poet*, 4to, 1602. He himself translated the *Ars Poetica*, and in his *Discoveries* he says that the poet "must read many, but ever the best and choicest; those that can teach him anything he must ever account his masters, and reverence: among whom Horace and he that taught him, Aristotle, deserved to be the first in estimation."

p. 16. *you, Eugenius, prefer him.* Buckhurst was a prominent and zealous Jonsonian. After the Restoration he wrote an "Epilogue *upon the Reviving of* Ben Johnson's *Play call'd* Every Man in his Humour." The concluding seventeen lines of this address are spoken by Jonson's Ghost. Although Jonson's comedies were frequently given with the greatest applause, a party of enthusiasts urged that the Roman tragedies should be revived, and in spite of the fact that very practical considerations of expense stood in the way of any adequate production of these great and magnificent poems, the Jonsonians were so far influential that *Catiline* was revived at the Theatre Royal with Hart in the title-rôle. Davies, *Dramatic Miscellanies*, London, 1783, Vol. II, pp. 88–89, says: "The Duke of Buckingham and Lord Dorset were admirers of Jonson to a degree of idolatry; it is very probable that, by liberal promises, they encouraged the actors to bring forward this forgotten tragedy. Certain it is that the play was acted several times during the reign of Charles II. The action of Hart in *Catiline* was universally applauded."

p. 17. *Nature.* Since it is often supposed that the heroic romances of the school of Scudéry with which Dryden was so familiar were strained and artificial to the last degree, it is interesting to note that in the preface to *Ibrahim ou l'Illustre Bassa*, 1641, Scudéry himself remarks: "Pour moy je tiens que plus les avantures sont naturelles, plus elles donnent de satisfaction: et le cours ordinaire du soleil me semble plus merveilleux, que les estranges et funestes rayons des comettes."

p. 17. *Audita visis.* Velleius Paterculus, *Historia Romana*, XCII. In the original it is "laudamus libentius"; and "veneratione prosequimur."

p. 17. *Aristotle indeed divides.* Dryden is here mistaken as this division is not found in Aristotle, nor indeed in any extant Greek writer. He doubtless derived it from the *Poetices libri septem*: "Partes legitimae sunt, sine quibus nequit fabula constare, quibusque contentam esse oportet. Protasis est, in qua proponitur et narratur summa rei sine declaratione exitus; ita enim argutior est, animum semper auditoris suspensum habens ad expectationem. Si enim praedicitur exitus, frigidiuscula fit. Tametsi ex argumento omnem rem tenes: tamen adeo expedita ac brevis est indicatio, ut non tam saturet animum quam incendat. Epitasis, in qua turbae aut excitantur, aut intenduntur. Catastasis est vigor ac status fabulae, in qua res miscetur in ea fortunae tempestate, in quam subducta est. Hanc partem multi non animadvertere; necessaria tamen est. Catastrophe, conversio negotii exagitati in tranquillitatem non expectatam. His partibus additus, uti dicebamus, Prologus, quem Latinis solis attribuunt quidam." Liber I, caput ix, *Comoediae et Tragoediae partes* (folio, 1561, p. 15).

This division, however, is by no means originally due to Scaliger, who has taken it from an Essay, *Fragmentum de Comoedia et Tragoedia* by Aelius Donatus (A.D. 350), the celebrated Commentator on Terence. Donatus says: "Comoedia autem dividitur in quatuor partes, Prologum, Protasin, Epitasin, Catastrophen. . . . Protasis est primus actus initiumque dramatis, quo pars argumenti explicatur, pars reticetur ad populi expectationem tenendam. Epitasis est incrementum processusque turbarum, ac totius ut ita dixerim nodus erroris. Catastrophe est conversio rerum ad iocundos exitus patefacta cunctis cognitione gestarum." *Terentii Comœdiæ Sex*, Lugduni Batavorum, apud Franciscum Hackium, 1662. Apparently Scaliger evolved the Catastasis. In Jonson's *The Magnetick Lady*, 1632, Act I, the boy says: "Doe you looke Mr. *Damplay* for conclusions in a *Protesis*? I thought the Law of *Comedy* had reserv'd them to the *Catastrophe;* and that the *Epitasis*, (as wee are taught) and the *Catastasis*, had beene intervening parts, to have beene expected. But you would have all come together it seemes: the Clock should strike five, at once, with the Acts."

p. 17. *the Catastasis, or Counterturn.* Davenant in his address "To the Reader," prefixed to *The Siege of Rhodes*, 4to, 1656, apologizes for the narrow allowance of the stage, and points out how "these limits have hinder'd the splendor of our scene. . . . Therefore you cannot expect the chief ornaments belonging to a History dramatically digested into Turns and Counter-turns, to double walks, and interweavings of design."

Dryden made various MS. glosses in a copy of Rymer's *Remarks on the Tragedies of the Last Age*, 1678, a book once belonging to Garrick, by whom it was handed to Dr. Johnson that he might reproduce these annotations in his life of the great poet. Among these marginalia Dryden wrote: "For the fable itself, 'tis in the English more adorned with episodes, and larger then in the Greek poets; consequently more diverting. For if the action be but one, and that plain, without any counterturn of design or episode, *i.e.* under-plot, how can it be so pleasing as the English, which have both under-plot and a turned design, which keeps the audiences in expectation of the catastrophe? whereas in the Greek poets we see through the whole design at first?" Johnson's *Lives of the Poets*, ed. Hill, 1905, Vol. I, p. 474.

p. 17. λύσις. The first edition has in error δέσις, the tying. Corneille translates δέσις by *nœud*. Boileau, *L'Art Poetique*, III, 405–408, has:

> Il faut que ses acteurs badinent noblement;
> Que son noeud bien formé se dénoue aisément;
> Que l'action, marchant où la raison la guide,
> Ne se perde jamais dans une scène vide.

Thus translated in *The Art of Poetry*, 1683:

> With well-bred Conversation you must please,
> And your Intrigue unravel'd be with ease:
> Your Action still should Reason'd Rules obey,
> Nor in an empty Scene may lose its way.

p. 18. *Neu brevior*. Horace, *Ars Poetica*, 189: Neve minor neu sit quinto productior actu.

p. 18. *Jornadas*. *Jornada* literally means a day's work; the business of a day. This term is derived from the *journée* of the old French *Mystère*, miracle-play. *Journée* was still used in France by Alexandre Hardy (1595?–1631?), but it signifies a "part" of a play. Thus *Théagène et Cariclée* (*c.* 1612) is in 40 acts, grouped in 8 *journées*. The lost *Pandoste* was in 2 *journées*, as also was *Parténie*. In 1517, when he published his *Propaladia*, a collection of nine comedies, Torres Naharro introduced the word *jornada* into Spain and divided his *comedias* into a *prologo* and five *jornadas*. His best plays are *La Calamita*, *La Serafina*, *La Soldadesca*, *La Himenca*, and *La Aquilina*. Francisco de Avendaño preferred three *jornadas* for his comedy *Florisea* (1551). This was the number that Lope de Vega Carpîo (1562–1635) established as the recognized divisions for a Spanish play. It was thus fixed for very definite reasons, since in his *Arte Nuevo de Hacer Comedias*, an epistle written in verse to a friend who requested him to defend his works against the more pedantic critics tied to pseudo-classical rules, de Vega explains that the first act must be expository, introducing the characters and beginning to weave the business of the play; the second act must cleverly develop the intrigue; while the third act is chiefly concerned with the *dénouement* (λύσις) which is to be evolved on natural and simple lines.

p. 18. *τό μῦθος*. Rather, *ὁ μῦθος*.

p. 18. *τῶν πραγμάτων συνθεσις*. The arrangement of the incidents.

p. 18. *a late Writer*. In his *Osservationi sopra l'Aminta*, Paris, 1655 (pp. 101–104, *Osservationi del Prologo*), Ménage had already drawn attention to the point made here. Castelvetro remarked that no Prologue was necessary in a tragedy since the plot would already be known to the audience. In a comedy such was not the case. Ménage quotes (with an Italian translation) a passage from Antiphanes *comicus* which is preserved by Athenaeus, *Deipnosophistae*, VI, 1:

μακάριόν ἐστιν ἡ τραγῳδία
ποίημα κατὰ πάντ' εἴγε πρῶτον οἱ λόγοι
ὑπὸ τῶν θεατῶν εἰσιν ἐγνωρισμένοι,
πρὶν καί τιν' εἰπεῖν· ὥσθ' ὑπομνῆσαι μόνον
δεῖ τὸν ποιητήν. Οἰδίπουν γὰρ φῶ. . . .
τὰ δ'ἄλλα πάντ' ἴσασιν· ὁ πατὴρ Λαίος,
μήτηρ 'Ιοκάστη, θυγατέρες, παῖδες τίνες,
τί πείσεθ' οὗτος, τί πεποίηκεν.

The reference, however, is more particularly to Sir Robert Howard' who in his address "To the Reader" prefixed to *Four New Plays*' folio, 1665, after reviewing "*the general manner of Plays among the Ancients*," remarks that these dramas were made up "*with almost entire and discursive Scenes*," hence "*It is first necessary to consider why probably the Compositions of the Ancients, especially in their serious Plays, were after this manner; and it will be found, that the Subjects they commonly chose drove them upon the necessity, which were more usually the most known Stories and Fables.*"

p. 18. *Talkative Greeklings*. "Which of the *Greekelings* durst ever give precepts to *Demosthenes*, or to *Pericles*?" Jonson's *Discoveries*, 1641 (p. 128). Cf. Cicero, *De Oratore*, I, xxii, 102: "Quid? mihi nunc vos, inquit Crassus, tanquam alicui Graeculo otioso loquaci, et fortasse docto atque erudito quaestiunculam dc qua mco arbitratu loquar ponitis?"

p. 18. *one Oedipus*. These subjects were treated again and again. Thus Aeschylus wrote an *Œdipodeia*, composed of *Laius*, the *Sphinx*, and *Œdipus*.

Meletus the tragedian (who may or may not be Meletus the accuser of Socrates) also produced an *Œdipodeia*.

Neophron of Sikyon composed a *Medea*, from which a speech has been preserved for us by Stobaeus.

A certain Diogenes, concerning whose plays later grammarians exhaust their vocabulary to express disgust at their obscenities (ἀῤῥήτων ἀῤῥητότερα καὶ κακῶν πέρα), is the author of a *Medea*.

Very many such examples might be cited.

p. 18. *good cheap*. On advantageous terms (now abbreviated to 'cheap'), and therefore 'easily.' " Better cheap" and "best cheap" were in use. Thus L'Estrange, *Works of Flavius Josephus; Antiquities* (1702), XVII, xii: "The *Romans* . . . came off better Cheap."

p. 19. *Juno Lucina*. In the *Andria*, III, i, 15, of Terence, Glycerium within the house having fallen in labour calls out:

Iuno Lucina fer opem; serva me obsecro.

In the *Adelphi*, III, 4, 40–41, Pamphila is heard crying from the house of Sostrata:

Miseram me, differor doloribus
Iuno Lucina, fer opem; serva me obsecro.

"Puella enim cum parit, non prodit, sed intus clamat

Iuno Lucina fer opem, serva me obsecro."

Scaliger, *Poetices*, I, xiii (1561, p. 22); and VI, 3: "Introducitur enim Glycerium parturiens cum hisce verbis, *Iuno Lucina fer opem*" (p. 297).

p. 19. *in a Machine.* Euanthius in his *De Tragoedia et Comoedia* particularly praises Terence because he does not exhibit θεοὺς ἀπὸ μηκανῆς, "Deos argumentis narrandis machinatos." "Ceteri Latinorum instar Graecorum habent. Terentius non habet." Corneille, *Second Discours sur la Tragedie*, writes: "Les apparitions de Vénus et d'Æole ont eu bonne grace dans Andromède: mais si j'avois fait descendre Jupiter pour reconcilier Nicomède avec son père, ou Mercure pour révéler à Auguste la conspiration de Cinna, j'aurois fait révolter tout mon auditoire, et cette merveille auroit détruit toute la croyance que le reste de l'action auroit obtenue. Ces dénouemens par des Dieux de machine sont fort fréquens chez les Grecs dans des Tragédies qui paroissent historiques, et qui sont vraisemblables à cela pres." Also in his *Discours des Trois Unites:* "Dans le dénouement je trouve deux choses à éviter, le simple changement de volonté, et la machine. . . . La machine n'a pas plus d'adresse, quand elle ne sert qu' à faire descendre un Dieu pour accomoder toutes choses, sur le point que les Acteurs ne savent plus comment les terminer. C'est ainsi qu' Apollon agit dans l'Oreste." Dryden himself has other references, particularly in his Dedication of the *Æneid*, to the machine and "machining work."

p. 19. *Old Elizabeth way.* Thus in *Sr Martin Mar-all; or, The Feign'd Innocence*, 4to, 1668, I, 1, Lady Dupe describes Mr. Moody:

> He loves none of the fine Town-tricks of breeding,
> But stands up for the old *Elizabeth* way in all things.

In D'Urfey's *The Old Mode & the New; or, Country Miss with her Furbeloe*, 1709, one of the principal characters is "*Sir Fumbler Oldmode*, a rich covetous Knight, a Lover of former ancient Methods and Fashions of Queen *Elizabeth's* Days," acted by Johnson. Lady Oldmode enters "*drest in the old Garb of Queen* Elizabeth." She bids a servant answer her not with "Madam" but "with anon forsooth, or, and please ye,—that was the laudable way in the Court of the renowned Queen *Elizabeth*."

p. 19. *The Unity of Place.* Corneille, *Troisieme Discours des Unites:* "Quant à l'unité de lieu, je n'en trouve aucun précepte ni dans Aristote, ni dans Horace." It was Castelvetro, *Poetica d'Aristotele vulgarizzata*, Bâle, 1576 (p. 535), who first emphasized the unity of place, as quoted in a previous note. In the *De l'art de la Tragédie*, published with his *Saül le furieux* in 1572, Jean de la Taille lays down the rule for "vn mesme lieu."

In the Prologue to *Euery Man in his Humour*, acted in 1598 (ed. 1616), Ben Jonson promises the audience:

> One such, to day, as other playes should be.
> Where neither *Chorus* wafts you ore the seas;
> Nor creaking throne comes downe, the boyes to please . . .

In the Induction to *Every Man out of his Humour* Jonson marvels at the "admirable dexteritie" with which the playwrights whew it away over land and sea.

p. 19. *sayes Scaliger*. This is from Scaliger's *Poetices*, VI, *Hypercriticus*, caput iii, which deals with Plautus and Terence. "Hoc primum obiiciebant: alterum hoc. Vasta, inquiunt et hians atque inanis Comoedia est: tota namque intercedit nox. Nam per initia cenam curant; postea Chremes ait, *lucescit*. Sane igitur abiit nox. Haec est illorum obiectio: quam sic diluimus—Datam actamque fabulam ludis Megalensibus. Itaque dimidium fabulae actum vesperi; noctem transactam ludis: alterum dimidium reliquum sub lucem: unam igitur quasi duas."

Sidney in his *An Apologie for Poetrie*, written in the autumn of 1581, although not published before 1595, echoes this explanation, but in error he applies it to the *Eunuchus* rather than to the *Heautontimorumenos:* "Yet will some bring in an example of *Eunuchus* in Terence, that containeth matter of two dayes, yet far short of twenty yeeres. True it is, and so it was to be played in two daies, and so fitted to the time it set forth." Many scholars hotly debated the question concerning the time of the *Heautontimorumenos*, and particularly Hédelin and Ménage. Hédelin wrote: "Beaucoup de Sçavans ont dit que la troisième Comedie de Terence contenoit deux jours: Scaliger, Muret, Vossius, le P. Membrun, et d'autres l'ont ainsi pensé; mais elle n'est pas seulement de dix heures, comme je l'ay montré dans la première dissertation du *Terence justifié*": *Pratique du Théâtre*, II, 2 (p. 90). Madame Dacier considers it a fact beyond all doubt that after the Second Act the Roman audience went away, and returned at daybreak the next morning for the representation of the third, since this commences with these words of Chremes: "Luciscit hoc iam." This is sad nonsense. The strained ingenuities of Scaliger, Sidney, and the rest have betrayed them into some precious bulls and blunders.

p. 19. *Eurypides*. The tragedy in question is the *Supplices*. Dryden translates this from Corneille, *Discours des Trois Unités:* "Euripide dans les *Suppliantes*, fait partir Thésée d'Athènes avec une Armée, donner une bataille devant les murs de Thèbes, qui en étoient éloignés de douze ou quinze lieues, et revenir victorieux en l'Acte suivant; et depuis qu'il est parti jusqu'à l'arrivée du messager qui vient faire le récit de sa victoire, Æthra et le chœur n'ont que trente-six vers à dire. C'est assez bien employer un temps si court."

Scaliger has much the same in the *Poetices*, III, *Idea*, xcvii. But as is pointed out in the Introduction, it is just nonsense, founded upon a misapprehension. One is relieved that Dryden did not originate this absurdity.

p. 20. *Antipho.* This one example is from Corneille, *Troisieme Discours des Trois Unités:* "Antiphon seul n'a aucune communication avec Chrémés et Pythias qui sortent du Théatre quand il y entre."

p. 21. *shaddow.* Prefigure. Thus Dryden in the Dedication to his *Æneid*, 1697, but in a slightly varying sense, writes: "Augustus is still shadow'd in the Person of Æneas."

p. 21. *Eurypides.* It should be observed, however, that Euripides has at least one Satyr play, *The Cyclops;* the *Autolycus* was also a Satyr play; and possibly the lost *Polyîdus* was some kind of folklore piece. The *Lycurgus* of Æschylus was a Satyr play concluding a trilogy, the *Edonians*, the *Bassarids*, and the *Young Men.* It seems probable that the *Lovers of Achilles*, 'Αχιλλέως ἔρασται, by Sophocles was Satyric.

p. 21. *Tandem ego.* Terence, *Eunuchus*, II, i, 17–18. *Si opus sit* should be *Si sit opus.*

p. 21. *Sed Proavi.* Horace, *Ars Poetica*, 270–272. The lines should commence: *at vestri proavi;* and conclude *ne dicam stulte.*

p. 21. *Multa renascentur. Ars Poetica*, 70–72. *quae iam cecidere* is the correct reading.

p. 22. *Mistaque ridenti.* Vergil, *Eclogue*, IV, 20.

p. 22. *Mirantur & undae. Æneid*, VIII (not VII), 91–93.

p. 22. *Si verbo. Metamorphoseon*, I, 175–176; more correctly:

si verbis audacia detur,
Haud timeam magni dixisse Palatia coeli.

Dryden has translated this (*Examen Poeticum*, 1691) as:

This Place, as far as Earth with Heav'n may vie,
I dare to call the *Loovre* of the Skie.

p. 22. *Et longas. Metamorphoseon*, I, 561. Malone prefers the reading *pompae*, which is given by Burmann. But *longae . . . pompae* has the better authority.

p. 22. *Doctor Donns.* Ben Jonson in his *Conversations with Drummond* said that Donne was "the first Poet in the world for some things," but again that he "for not keeping of accent deserved hanging."

p. 22. *Rebel Scot.* Cleveland's *Rebel Scot*, ll. 63–64. Nichols says that this couplet is one of the most quoted in the language.

p. 22. *Si sic omnia.* Juvenal, *Saturae*, X, 123–124: the allusion in the original is to Cicero:

Antoni gladios potuit contemnere, si sic
Omnia dixisset.

p. 22. *For Beauty.* Cleveland, *Rupertismus*, ll. 33–40:

Strange! That the Muses cannot wound your Mail;
If not their Art, yet let their Sex prevail.

At that known Leaguer, where the *Bonny Besses*
Supply'd the Bowstrings with their twisted tresses,
Your spells could ne'er have fenc'd you; ev'ry Arrow
Had lanc'd your noble Breast, and drunk the Marrow:
For Beauty, like white Powder, makes no Noise,
And yet the silent Hypocrite destroys.

For "*White-powder*" see Sir Thomas Browne's *Pseudodoxia Epidemica* (ed. Sayle, 1904, Vol. I, p. 274), Book I, c. 5: "He that would destroy the report of the Powder, must work upon the Petre: he that would exchange the colour, must think how to alter the Small-coal. For the one, that is to make white Powder, it is surely many ways feasible. . . . As for the other, that is, to destroy the Report, it is reasonably attempted but two ways: either by quite leaving out, or else by silencing the Salt-petre. How to abate the vigour thereof, or silence its bombulation, a way is promised by *Porta* . . . which saith he will so go off as scarce to be heard by the discharger; . . . That therefore white Powder there may be, there is no absurdity; that also such a one may give no report, we will not deny a possibility."

p. 23. *Medea.* Only one line of Ovid's *Medea* has been preserved. This is quoted by Quintilian, VIII, v, 6: "vehementius apud Ovidium Medea dicit;

Servare potui: perdere an possim, rogas?

The same author, X, i, 98, writes: "Ovidii *Medea* videtur mihi ostendere quantum ille vir praestare potuerit, si ingenio suo imperare quam indulgere maluisset."

Dr. Johnson has some just remarks upon the English passage in his *Life of Dryden:* "In his Dialogue on the Drama, he pronounces with great confidence that the *Latin* tragedy of *Medea* is not *Ovid's*, because it is not sufficiently interesting and pathetic. He might have determined the question upon surer evidence; for it is quoted by *Quintilian* as the work of *Seneca;* and the only line which remains of *Ovid's* play, for one line is left us, is not there to be found. There was therefore no need of the gravity of conjecture, or the discussion of plot or sentiment, to find what was already known upon higher authority than such discussions can ever reach."

p. 23. *Omne genus.* Ovid, *Tristia*, II, 381.

p. 23. *Myrrha. Metamorphoseon*, X, 297–502. This was translated by Dryden, and it will be found in the folio, 1700.

p. 23. *Caunus and Biblis. Metamorphoseon*, IX, 417–664.

p. 23. *Troades.* This scene commences at l. 533.

p. 23. *anima mea.* Juvenal, *Saturae*, VI, 190–196:

Concumbunt Graece. dones tamen ista puellis:
Tunc etiam; quam sextus et octogesimus annus
Pulsat, adhuc Graece? non est hic sermo pudicus

In vetula, quoties lascivum intervenit illud,
Ζωὴ και ψυχὴ, modo sub lodice relictis
Uteris in turba, quod enim non excitet inguen,
Vox blanda et nequam?

p. 24. *Heroes neither eat.* This circumstance of the romances of La Calprenède and Scudéry is very agreeably satirized by Mrs. Lennox in her novel *The Female Quixote; or, The Adventures of Arabella*, 2 vols., 12mo. London, 1752.

p. 24. *Sum pius. Æneid*, I, 378–379:

Sum pius Aeneas raptos qui ex hoste Penates
Classe veho mecum fama super aethera notus.

p. 24. *a Fanfaron or Hector.* A fanfaron is a braggart. The word is familiar from Mabbe in his translation of *Guzman d'Alfarache*, 1622, II (62): "They should not play the Fanfarrones." The word *Hector*, as a blustering bully, was coming into popular parlance. In literary use it does not occur before the middle of the seventeenth century.

p. 24. *Si foret.* Horace, *Sermonum*, I, x, 68.

p. 24. *Quos libitina.* Horace, *Epistularum*, II, i, 49: Miraturque nihil nisi quod Libitina sacravit.

p. 25. *bad Englishmen.* An allusion to the Great Rebellion.

p. 25. *the great Cardinal of Richlieu.* In 1628–1629 Cardinal Richelieu began to display some interest in the drama, of which he was to constitute himself so particular a patron. However, it must be emphasized that the introduction of the Unities, duly formulated by Chapelain, was not in the first place owing to Richelieu, since these rules were first shown in practice at the château of Chantilly, the home of the Duke of Montmorency and his Italian wife, Maria Felicia Orsini, when they persuaded Jean Mairet to write a pastoral *Silvanire* in strict accordance with the law of the Three Unities, as it was understood. Mairet composed a "Preface, en forme de discours poetique" which was printed before his pastoral in 1631. He was opposed, however, by Mareschale in the preface to his *Généreuse Allemande*, printed 18 November, 1630. Mairet's rules none the less began to win acceptation, and they were inculcated by Richelieu. Accordingly when *Le Cid* was given at the close of 1636 the Cardinal referred it to the supreme judgement of the Academie. The result was that after the *Sentiments sur le Cid*, a work largely from the pen of Chapelain, the law of the three unities shackled the French theatre until the romantic revival early in the nineteenth century.

p. 25. *it yet remains a dispute.* "La règle de l'unité de jour a son fondement sur ce mot d'Aristote, que la Tragédie doit renfermer la durée de son action dans un tour du Soleil, ou tâcher de ne le passer pas de beaucoup." Corneille, *Discours des Trois Unités:* "Ces paroles donnent lieu à cette dispute fameuse, si elles doivent être entendues d'un jour naturel de vingt-quatre heures, ou d'un jour artificiel de douze. Ce sont deux opinions dont chacune a des partisans considérables: et, pour moi, je trouve qu'il y a des sujets si mal aisés à renfermer en si peu de temps, que non-seulement je leur accorderois les vingt-quatre heures entières, mais je me servirois même de la licence que donne ce Philosophe de les excéder un peu, et les pousserois sans scrupule jusqu'à trente."

The exact phrase of Aristotle is: Ἡ μὲν γὰρ ὅτι μάλιστα πειρᾶται ὑπὸ μίαν περίοδον ἡλίου εἶναι ἢ μικρὸν ἐξαλλάττειν. *Poetics*, V, 4.

p. 26. *a Drama of our own invention.* In the Prologue to the *Amphitryon* of Plautus Mercury says:

faciam ut commixta sit: sit tragicomoedia.

Throughout the sixteenth century there was evident a general feeling that the two broad classes of tragedy and comedy by no means exhausted the matter, and in course of time the term tragi-comedy was revived. At first it was generally applied to a drama with a romantic plot of a serious nature which ended happily. It had been debated at length by Italian critics whether such a kind was permissible. In France, however, Alexandre Hardy made serious plays of this kind popular, and it has been said that between 1628 and 1641 there was no more favourite form. The Spanish theatre, also, is extremely rich in these tragi-comedies. But this was hardly the kind of play Dryden intended. By tragi-comedy he understands a piece that is indeed "commixta," where lighter episodes alternate and commingle with deeply emotional scenes. This is manifest from the following passage which occurs in his *A Parallel betwixt Painting and Poetry*, prefixed to *The Art of Painting*, 4to, 1695, an English translation of the Latin poem *De Arte Graphica* by Charles Alphonse Du Fresnoy (1611–1665): "The *Gothique* manner, and the barbarous Ornaments, which are to be avoided in a *Picture*, are just the same with those in an ill ordered *Play*. For example, our *English Tragi comedy* must be confessed to be wholly *Gothique*, notwithstanding the Success which it has found upon our *Theatre*, and in the *Pastor Fido* of Guarini; even though *Corisca* and the Satyr contribute somewhat to the main Action. Neither can I defend my *Spanish Fryar*, as fond as otherwise I am of it, from this Imputation: for though the comical parts are diverting, and the serious moving, yet they are of an unnatural mingle: for Mirth and Gravity destroy each other, and are no more to be allow'd for decent than a gay Widow laughing in a mourning Habit."

Addison, *The Spectator*, XL, Monday, 16 April, 1711, writes: "The Tragi-Comedy, which is the Product of the *English* Theatre, is one of the most monstrous Inventions that ever entered into a Poet's thought." His criticism, however, is no more than what Dryden has already said.

p. 26. *the Red-Bull.* The Red Bull was situated at the upper end of S. John Street in the parish of S. James, Clerkenwell. It was built not later, and possibly not much earlier, than 1606. The first recorded mention of this house seems to be that in *The Knight of the Burning Pestle*, which is to be assigned to the winter of 1607. There are very frequent references to this popular playhouse, which before 1633 (and probably even before 1625) had been to a certain extent reconstructed and much enlarged. (See Prynne's *Epistle to Histriomastix.*) It might boast "curtains of *Naples Silk*," but the audiences were rough and unruly. They loved to be regaled with drumming dramas and broadest comedy, "scenicall strutting, and furious vociferation," so that the house became as well-known for sensational display as for its rowdy spectators. The Fortune and the Red Bull, says Wright, *Historia Histrionica*, 8vo, 1699, "were mostly frequented by Citizens, and the meaner sort of People." They "were large Houses, and lay partly open to the Weather, and there they alwaies acted by Daylight." Surreptitious performances were attempted at the Red Bull under the Commonwealth, and after the Restoration until 1663 plays were still given here. On Saturday, 23 March, 1661, Pepys saw Rowley's *All Lost by Lust* at the Red Bull, but the play was "poorly done; and with so much disorder, among others, that in the musique-room the boy that was to sing a song not singing it right, his master fell about his ears and beat him so, that it put the whole house in an uproar."

p. 26. *Atque ursum.* Horace, *Epistularum*, II, i, 185–186.

p. 26. *admiration.* The famous words of Aristotle are: "*δι' ἐλέου καὶ φόβου περαίνουσα τὴν τῶν τοιούτων παθημάτων κάθαρσιν.*"
"Admiration" was added by the critics of the sixteenth and seventeenth centuries. Thus Sidney in his *Apologie for Poetry* speaks of "high and excellent tragedy . . . that with stirring the affects of admiration and commiseration, teacheth the uncertainety of the world."

p. 26. *Ex noto.* Horace, *Ars Poetica*, 240.

p. 26. *Atque ita mentitur. Ibid.*, 151–152.

p. 26. *success.* The upshot; outcome; issue. Thus Milton, *Paradise Lost*, II, 8–9 (Second Edition, 1674):

> insatiate to pursue
> Vain Warr with Heav'n, and by success untaught.

p. 26. *Justin.* This writer who lived in the age of the Antonines abridged the *History* of Pompeius Trogus, a contemporary of Livy, *Epitoma Historiarum Philippicarum Pompei Trogi.* The reference is to Liber I, viii, where the slaughter of Cyrus and his army by the Scythians is related. Also, XXXVII, iii: Scythae "qui Cyrum, Persarum regem, cum CC milibus trucidaverant." The "some others" who say that Cyrus fell in battle include Herodotus and Ctesias.

The *Cyropaedia* of Xenophon, which Sidney calls "the feigned Cyrus of Xenophon," is a romance founded upon history and nothing more. Nor did Xenophon himself pretend any other. In this narrative Cyrus on his death-bed addresses his sons at some length, and bids farewell to all: "*καὶ πάντες δε οἱ παρόντες καὶ οἱ ἀπόντες φίλοι χαίρετε. ταῦτ' εἰπὼν καὶ πάντας δεξιωσάμενος ἐνεκαλύψατο καὶ οὕτως ἐτελεύτησεν.*" VIII, vii, 28.

p. 27. *Perspective.* A telescope.

p. 27. *Quodcunque ostendis. Ars Poetica*, 188.

p. 27. *ἐτύμοισιν ὁμοῖα.* Homer, *Odyssey*, XIX, 203:

Ἴσκε ψεύδεα πολλὰ λέγων, ἐτύμοισιν ὁμοῖα.

And Hesiod, *Theogonia*, 27–28; the Muses are addressing the poet:

ἴδμεν ψεύδεα πολλὰ λέγειν ἐτύμοισιν ὁμοῖα
ἴδμεν δ' εὖτ' ἐθέλωμεν, ἀληθέα γηρύσασθαι.

p. 27. *Spanish Plotts.* Downes tells us that among other comedies acted at Lincoln's Inn Fields between 1662 and 1665 were "'*Tis better than it was: Worse and Worse:* These two Comedies were made out of *Spanish*, by the Earl of *Bristol.*" These two plays by George Digby, Earl of Bristol, do not appear to have been printed, but there can be no doubt that they were translations from Calderon, *'Tis Better Than It Was* being adapted from *Mejor Esta que Estaba*, and *Worse and Worse* from *Peor Esta que Estaba.* They seem to have been successful, and on Wednesday, July 20, 1664, Pepys writes:"I left the lottery, and went to a play, only a piece of it, which was at the Duke's house, 'Worse and Worse'; just the same manner of play, and writ, I believe, by the same man as 'The Adventures of Five Hours'; very pleasant it was, and I begin to admire Harris more than ever." It is not surprising that the diarist should have taken these two Spanish plays to be adaptations by the same hand, although actually such was not the case. *Worse and Worse* was performed at Court on Monday, November 26, 1666.

Tuke's *The Adventures of Five Hours* was produced at Lincoln's Inn Fields on Thursday, January 8, 1662–3. It is taken from *Los Empeños de Seis Horas*, a comedy long ascribed to Calderon, and even believed to be his by Tuke. It is almost certain, however, that the original play is the work of Don Antonio Coello y Ochoa. It does not appear that the Earl of Bristol had any hand in this adaptation.

In 1667 was printed quarto, as "written by a Person of Quality" who may be identified as the Earl of Bristol, *Elvira; or, The Worst not always True.* This comedy which was produced at Lincoln's Inn Fields, probably in 1663, is from Calderon's *No Siempre lo Peor es Cierto.*

In later years dramatists were to convey almost wholesale from Calderon and the Spanish theatre. Thus the original of Dryden's own *An Evening's Love; or, The Mock Astrologer*, is Calderon's *El*

Astrólogo Fingido. The main incidents of Wycherley's *The Gentleman Dancing-Master* are from Calderon's *El Maestro de Danzar*.

p. 27. *Rollo. The Bloody Brother, or, Rollo, Duke of Normandy*, was printed in 1639 as "By B. J. F.," but in 1640 at Oxford as by John Fletcher, and there seems no reason why the attribution to Jonson and Fletcher should not be correct. This excellent tragedy was very sharply criticized by Rymer, but Langbaine remarks that in spite of these strictures it still remained "much in request . . . being frequently acted by the present Company of Actors, at the Queen's Play-House in *Dorset Garden*." However, it has not, I think, been revived since the first decade of the eighteenth century.

The plot is taken from the Fourth Book of Herodian's History of the Roman Empire, a chronicle written in Greek in eight books from the death of Marcus Aurelius to the beginning of the reign of Gordianus III, A.D. 180–238. The characters have been transferred by the dramatists to Norman times and places. Thus Caracalla becomes Rollo, and Geta Otto.

p. 27. *Oleo*. A mixture or medley, from the Spanish *olla* in *olla podrida*, a mixed dish of meat and vegetables. Latin, *olla*, a pot. Cf. "A Discourse concerning the Original and Progress of Satire" prefixed to the *Juvenal*, folio, 1693, where Dryden speaks of "that *olla*, or hotch-potch, which is properly a satyr."

p. 28. *protatick persons*. These are characters who appear at the beginning of a play to convey certain information to the audience, but who are not themselves really necessary to the plot. Dryden borrowed the name from Corneille, *Discours du Poème Dramatique:* "Térence . . . a introduit une nouvelle sorte de personnages, qu'on a appellés protatiques, parce qu'ils ne parvissent que dans la protase, où se doit faire la proposition et l'ouverture du sujet. Ils en écoutoient l'histoire, qui leur étoit racontée par un autre acteur; & par ce récit qu'on leur en faisoit, l'auditeur demeuroit instruit de ce qu'il devoit savoir touchant les intérêts des prémiers acteurs avant qu'ils parussent sur le Théatre." This is from Donatus in his Preface to the *Andria*. He speaks of *προτατικὸν πρόσωπον*; "Persona autem protatica ea intelligitur, quae semel inducta in principio fabulae, in nullis deinceps fabulae partibus adhibetur." Scaliger echoes this, *Poetices*, I, *Historicus*, xiii.

p. 29. *ten or twenty years ago*. Corneille, *Discours des Trois Unités:* "J'ajoûte un conseil, de s'embarrasser le moins qu'il lui est possible de choses arrivées avant l'action qui se représente. Ces narrations importunent d'ordinaire, parce qu'elles ne sont pas attendues, et qu'elles gènent l'esprit de l'Auditeur, qui est obligé de charger sa mémoire de ce qui s'est fait dix ou douze ans auparavant, pour comprendre ce qu'il voit représenter; mais celles qui se font des choses qui arrivent et se passent derrière le Théâtre, depuis l'action commencée, font toujours un meilleur effet, parce qu'elles sont attendues avec quelque curiosité, et font partie de cette action qui se représente."

p. 29. *Duells, Battells.* Compare Shakespeare's *Henry V*, Act iv:

Chorus. When (O for pity!) we shall much disgrace,
With four or five most vile and ragged foils,
Right ill-disposed in brawl ridiculous,
The name of Agincourt.

Also Sidney in his *Apologie for Poetrie* writes: "in the meantime two armies flye in, represented with foure swords and bucklers, and then what harde heart will not receive it for a pitched fielde?"

p. 29. *fight Prizes.* To fight or to play "Prizes" is to fight as gladiators or fencers use. Thus Arbuthnot, *John Bull*, 1712, I, iv: "He . . . went about through all the country fairs, challenging the people to fight prizes, wrestling, and cudgel play."

p. 29. *cannot forbear laughing.* Jean Chappuzeau, *Europe Vivante*, Paris, 1674: "Estant à Londres il y a six ans, j'y vis deux fort belles troupes des Comediens, l'vne du Roy, & l'autre du Duc D'Yorc, & ie fus à deux representations, à la mort de *Montezume* Roy de Mexique, & à celle de *Mustapha*, qui se defendoit vigoureusement sur le Theatre contre les muets qui le vouloient étrangler; ce qui faisoit rire, & ce que les François n'auroient representé que dans vn recit." The Death of Montezuma is Dryden's *The Indian Emperour*, whilst *Mustapha* is Lord Orrery's *The Tragedy of Mustapha, Son of Solyman the Magnificent*, which was produced at Lincoln's Inn Fields in April, 1665. Betterton played Solyman, and Harris Mustapha, whom the Mutes are about to execute with the bow-string, when he draws his scimitar and resists, killing two of them (Act V).

When Saurin in 1786 adapted Edward Moore's tragedy *The Gamester*, first produced at Drury Lane, 7 February, 1753, for the Parisian stage as *Beverley, ou le Joueur*, although in French the play had a remarkable success, he was obliged to provide two fifth acts, in one of which Beverley poisons himself as Moore wrote it, but in the other the situation was salved and the sad hero is prevented in the nick from draining the fatal draught. The original conclusion was deemed too horrible for representation, and one poet wrote on the occasion:

Laissons à nos voisins ces excès sanguinaires,
Malheur aux nations que le sang divertie,
Ces exemples outrés, ces farces mortuaires,
Ne satisfont ni l'âme ni l'esprit,
Les Français ne sont point des tigres des feroces
Qu'on ne peut amouvoir que par des traits atroces.

This is certainly far from Sardou's *Théodora* and *La Tosca!*

p. 30. *may be related.* This was also advanced by Sir Robert Howard in his preface to *Four New Plays*. Horace, he says, "*directly declares his Judgment, That every thing makes more impression Presented than Related: Nor indeed can any one rationally assert the contrary; for if they affirm otherwise, they do by consequence maintain, That a whole Play might be as well Related as Acted.*

p. 30. *Corneille says. Discours des Trois Unités:* "C'est ce qui me donne lieu de remarquer, que le Poète n'est pas tenu d'exposer à la vûe toutes les actions particulières qui amènent à la principale. Il doit choisir celles qui lui sont les plus avantageuses à faire voir, soit par la beauté du spectacle, soit par l'éclat et la véhémence des passions qu'elles produisent, soit par quelque autre agrément qui leur soit attaché, et cacher les autres derrière la Scène, pour les faire connoître au spectateur, ou par une narration, ou par quelque autre adresse de l'art. Sur tout il doit se souvenir que les unes et les autres doivent avoir une telle liaison ensemble, que les dernières soient produites par celles qui les précèdent, et que toutes ayent leur source dans la protase qui doit fermer le premier Acte."

p. 30. *Segnius irritant. Ars Poetica*, 180–187:

> segnius irritant animos demissa per aurem,
> quam quae sunt oculis subiecta fidelibus et quae
> ipsi sibi tradit spectator: nec tamen intus
> digna geri promes in scaenam, multaque tolles
> ex oculis quae mox narret facundia praesens,
> ne pueros coram populo Medea trucidet,
> aut humana palam coquat exta nefarius Atreus,
> aut in avem Procne vertatur, Cadmus in anguem.

p. 30. *Magnetick Lady.* Folio, 1640. Act III, Scene 2. Towards the end of Act I we hear "*A noise within*," and then enter Compasse and Ironside. Compasse expostulates with Ironside who has brawled at table:

> *Com.* Were you a mad man to doe this at table?
> And trouble all the Guests, to affright the Ladies,
> And Gentle women?

p. 31. *the King And No King.* This excellent play was extremely popular in the Restoration theatre. The plot is certainly unravelled in Act V by Gobrias, the Lord-Protector, whose narrative sets all in kelter after much confusion, difficulty, and almost despair.

p. 31. *Scornful Lady.* This comedy was a great favourite in the days of Charles II. Theobald, Vol. I, p. 364 of his edition of Beaumont and Fletcher (10 vols.), 1750, likewise objects to Morecraft's change from niggard usury to lavish gallantry as improbable. The character is said to have been suggested by Demea in the *Adelphi* of Terence.

One may compare Voltaire's note when Corneille in his second *Discours* refers to the conversion of Felix at the end of *Polyeucte:* "La conversion miraculeuse de Félix le reconcilie sans doute avec le ciel, mais point du tout avec le parterre."

p. 32. *Corneille.* In the *Discours des Trois Unités*, Corneille emphasizes: "Il faut, s'il se peut, y rendre raison de l'entrée et de la sortie de chaque

Acteur. Sur tout pour la sortie, je tiens cette règle indispensable, et il n'y a rien de si mauvaise grâce qu'un Acteur qui se retire du Théâtre seulement parce qu'il n'a plus de vers à dire." He writes to the same effect in his *Discours du Poème Dramatique*.

p. 32. *an ancient Authour*. Velleius Paterculus, *Historia Romana*, I, 17. The original reads: *Et, ut primo ad consequendos, quos priores . . ., et quod assequi . . .* (Dryden, *quod, scilicet, assequi*) . . . *eminere non possimus* (Dryden, *eminere non possumus*). Dryden has marked the omission of "*et velut occupatam relinquens materiam quaerit novam.*"

p. 32. *The Lier*. Corneille's *Le Menteur*, which was produced in 1642; 4to, 1644; and of which the author himself wrote "Ce n'est ici qu'une copie d'un excellent original," is founded on *La Verdad Sospechosa*, published in 1630 under the name of Lope de Vega, but afterwards claimed by Juan Ruiz de Alarcón, and printed among his works. *Le Menteur* was translated into English as *The Lyar* and printed 4to, 1661. It was reprinted 4to, 1685, as *The Mistaken Beauty, or, The Lyar*. This poor version from the French was given at the Theatre Royal, Vere Street, in 1661 with Hart as Dorant.

Le Menteur has been used not infrequently on the English stage, notably by Steele in *The Lying Lover, or, The Ladies Friendship*, first given at Drury Lane in December, 1703; and by Foote in *The Lyar*, produced at Covent Garden, 12 January, 1762.

p. 33. *in good intelligence*. Corneille, *Premier Discours Du Poëme Dramatique:* "Ainsi dans les Comédies de ce prémier volume, j'ai presque toujours établi deux amans en bonne intelligence, je les ai brouillés ensemble par quelque fourbe, & les ai réunis par l'éclaircissement de cette même fourbe qui les séparoit."

p. 33. *Cardinal Richelieu*. Cardinal Richelieu died at Paris, 4 December, 1642.

p. 33. *Spanish Novells*. The Spanish novelists had been freely drawn upon by English dramatists, whilst the French playwrights preferred to adapt Spanish plays more directly. A very long list of such conveyances might be made, but it will suffice to indicate a few examples. Fletcher, in particular, depended very largely for his plots upon the *Novelas Ejemplares* of Cervantes, and among the plays of the Beaumont and Fletcher folio *The Chances* is from *La Señora Cornelia; Rule a Wife and Have A Wife* from *El Casamiento Engañoso; The Fair Maid of the Inn* from the *Ilustre Fregona; The Queen of Corinth* from *La Fuerza de la Sangre. Love's Pilgrimage* is a dramatization of *Las dos Doncellas; The Spanish Curate* is from a novel (called a *poema tragico*) of Gonzalo de Cespedes; *The Little French Lawyer* from *Guzman d'Alfarache. The Island Princess* seems to borrow something from a story appended to the first French translation of the *Novelas Ejemplares;* and the main episodes of *The Coxcomb* are from the famous *Curioso Impertinente* in *Don Quixote. A Very Woman* by Fletcher and Massinger is from

El Amante Liberal; and Middleton and Rowley's *The Spanish Gipsy* is *La Gitanilla* of Cervantes made into a charming play. Shirley used the Spanish dramatists. *The Young Admirall* takes the complications and climax of its principal plot from Lope de Vega's *Don Lope de Cardona*, whilst *The Opportunitie* is generously conveyed from *El Castigo del Penseque.*

With regard to French dramatists, Pierre Corneille's *Le Cid* seems at least to have been suggested by Guillen de Castro's *Las Macedades del Cid.* He had certainly read *El Honrado Hermano* before he wrote *Horace*, although the Spanish play must be ranked among the most mediocre productions of Lope de Vega. *Don Sanche d'Aragon* utilizes the first *jornada* of *El Palacio confuso* of Lope, and perhaps echoes once or twice *El Perro del Hortelano.*

Rotrou's *Laure persécutée* is slightly varied from Lope's *Laura perseguida;* his *Bélissaire* is from *El Exemplo mayor de la Desdicha y Capitan Belisario*, which may be by Lope or by Montalvan.

For *Les Engagements du hasard* Thomas Corneille drew upon *Casa con dos puertas mala es de guardar* and *Los Empeños de un acaso. La Charme de la Voix* is hardly an improvement upon *Lo que puede la aprehension. Le Geôlier de soi-même* is from Calderon's *El Alcaide de si mismo. Les Illustres Ennemis* has at least two sources, *Ofendidos y obligados y gorron de Salamanca* by de Rojas and *Amar despues de la muerte.*

Scarron translated Calderon's *No siempre lo peor es cierto* as *La Fausse apparence*, and *Jodelet ou le Maitre Valet* recalls *Donde hay agravios no hay celos, y amo criado. L'Héritier ridicule ou la Dame Intéressée* has been traced to *El mayorazzo figura* of Don Alonzo Castillo Solorzano.

p. 33. *a vail, and a trusty Diego.* Diego is the "Servant to *Octavio*, bred a Scholar. *A great Coward and a pleasant Droll*" in Tuke's *The Adventures of Five Hours.*

The mantilla to disguise and conceal a lady's features played a great part in Spanish comedies. In Restoration comedies the mask served much the same use. Both were pretty hard worked by the dramatists. Longfellow's lines aptly sum up favourite themes in a Spanish play, *The Spanish Student*, I:

> There were three duels fought in the first act,
> Three gentlemen receiving deadly wounds,
> Laying their hands upon their hearts, and saying,
> "O, I am dead!" a lover in a closet,
> An old hidalgo, and a gay Don Juan,
> A Doña Inez with a black mantilla,
> Followed at twilight by an unknown lover,
> Who looks intently where he knows she is not!

p. 33. *Adventures.* Tuke's *The Adventures of Five Hours*, produced at Lincoln's Inn Fields on Thursday, 8 January, 1662–3. It was "Acted so justly well" that "It took Successively 13 Days together, no other Play intervening." Diego was played by Cave Underhill.

p. 33. *contraries.* Thus in his *Parallel betwixt Painting and Poetry* prefixed to *The Art of Painting*, 4to, 1695, Dryden writes: "Thus in a *Play*, some characters must be rais'd to oppose others; and to set them off the better, according to the old Maxim, *Contraria juxta se posita, magis elucescunt.* Thus in the *Scornfull Lady*, the Usurer is set to confront the Prodigal. Thus in my *Tyrannique Love*, the Atheist *Maximin* is oppos'd to the character of St. *Catharine.*"

p. 34. *primum mobile.* This refers to a mediaeval addition to the laws of the Ptolemaic astronomy, according to which system the sun and stars revolve around the earth. The *primum mobile* is the imaginary outermost sphere (at first reckoned the ninth, afterwards the tenth) which was supposed to revolve round the fixed earth from east to west in twenty-four hours, carrying with it the eight (or nine) contained spheres. Thus Alexander Crawford, Lord Lindsay, *Sketches of the History of Christian Art*, 3 vols., 1847, I, p. xxxii, "Beyond the region of fire . . . succeeded the spheres of the seven planets: . . . the firmament, or eighth heaven; . . . the crystalline or ninth heaven; . . . and the *primum mobile*, a void;—the whole continually revolving round the earth, and encompassed in their turn by the empyrean."

p. 34. *Cinna. Cinna, ou La Clemence d'Auguste* was produced in 1640, and printed 4to, 1643. *La Mort de Pompée* was performed in 1641 and printed 4to, 1644. *Polyeucte, Martyr, Tragédie Chrétienne,* was first given in the winter of 1640, and printed 4to, 1643.

p. 35. *the Hour-glass.* The hour-glass was an indispensable and indeed prominent piece of pulpit furniture which retained its position until a comparatively recent date. In Hogarth's *The Sleeping Congregation* the hour-glass may be seen well in view whilst the old divine (said to be Dr. Desaguliers) drones his opiate periods. Upon this picture Thomas Clerk remarks: "As it was formerly the custom to place an hour-glass by the preacher's side by way of admonition, our pulpit orator is accordingly equipped with that memento of departing hours." Cf. Butler's *Hudibras*, I, 3, 1061–1065:

> As *gifted Brethren* preaching by
> A *Carnal Hour-glass*, do imply
> *Illuminator* can convey
> Into them what they have to say,
> But not how much; . . .

There is an hour-glass in Maisemore Church (two miles north-west of Gloucester) which is placed on a window sill (on the west-side) close to the pulpit. See a letter signed W. M. Meyrick-Jones, *Country Life*, vol. lxix; no. 1789; 2 May, 1931.

p. 35. *chase of wit.* Chase is a technical term in tennis, "Applied to the second impact on the floor (or in a gallery) of a ball which the opponent has failed or declined to return; the value of which is determined by the nearness of the spot of impact to the end wall. If the opponent on both sides being changed can 'better' this stroke (*i.e.* cause his ball to rebound nearer the wall) he wins and scores it; if not, it is scored by the first player; until it is so decided the 'chase' is a strike in abeyance."

p. 36. *objects of horrour*. Addison, *Spectator*, No. 44, Friday, 20 April, 1711, writes: "Among all our Methods of moving Pity or Terror, there is none so absurd and barbarous, and what more exposes us to the Contempt and Ridicule of our Neighbours, than that dreadful butchering of one another, which is so very frequent upon the *English* stage. To delight in seeing Men stabbed, poisoned, racked, or impaled, is certainly the sign of a cruel Temper; And as this is often practised before the *British* Audience, several *French* Criticks, who think these are grateful Spectacles to us, take Occasion from them to represent us as a People that delight in Blood. . . . Murders and Executions are always transacted behind the Scenes in the *French* Theatre. . . . But as there are no exceptions to this Rule on the *French* Stage, it leads them into Absurdities almost as ridiculous as that which falls under our present censure. . . . The *French* have refined too much upon *Horace's* Rule, who never designed to banish all kinds of death from the stage, but only such as had too much Horror in them."

p. 36. *our imagination*. Dr. Johnson in his *Preface to Shakespeare* writes: "It is false that any representation is mistaken for Reality; that any dramatick Fable, in its Materiality, was ever credible, or for a single moment was ever credited." This judgement may certainly be disputed, and there are indeed actual examples which might be adduced to the contrary. Thus when Calderon's *La Niña de Gomez Arias* was being acted at the theatre in Madrid, and Dorotea, betrayed by foulest treachery and about to be carried off by the Moors, cried sorrowfully:

doleos de mi;
Que me llevan presa
A Benamegi

extending hands in vain, a Spanish soldier who was on guard at the door of the house rushed forward, sword in hand, on to the stage to rescue the noble Spanish lady from the infidel.

p. 36. *Andromede*. Corneille's *Andromède* was produced with the utmost magnificence in January, 1650, at the Théâtre Royal de Bourbon, Rue des Poulies, and the King who had been present at the first performance was frequently present to enjoy the spectacle. Thus Dubuisson Aubenay notes in his *Journal*, Saturday, 26 February, 1650: "Le soir, Leurs Majestés vont voir la comédie d'*Andromède*, jouée avec machines très-belles dans la salle du Petit-Bourbon." It has been well said: "Dans une pièce de ce genre, le véritable auteur n'eſt ni le poëte, ni le musicien; c'eſt le machiniſte." The machines were devised by Torelli, and their ingenuity won the loudeſt applause. This "pompeux théâtre" was thronged, and a regular furore ensued. In the third scene of Act III we have "*Andromède*, attachée au rocher; *Persée*, en l'air sur le cheval *Pégase*." There is a "Choeur de Musique, cependant que Persée combat le Monſtre." It is to this that Dryden makes particular reference.

p. 37. *the incomparable Shakespeare.* In his *Discoveries*, 1641, Jonson criticizes Shakespeare, but he is hardly severe. The remark is merely "hee flow'd with that facility, that sometimes it was necessary he should be ſtop'd: *Sufflaminandus erat;* as *Auguſtus* said of *Haterius*. . . . But hee redeemed his vices, with his vertues. There was ever more in him to be praysed, then to be pardoned." And juſt before the famous reply to the players who boaſted that Shakespeare "never blotted out a line"; "Would he had blotted a thousand. Which they thought a malevolent Speech."

Dryden, however, more particularly alludes to the Prologue of *Euery Man in His Humour*, firſt acted in 1598:

> To make a child, now swadled, to proceede
> Man, and then shoote vp, in one beard, and weede,
> Paſt threescore yeeres; or, with three ruſtie swords,
> And help of some few foot-and-halfe-foot words,
> Fight ouer *York* and *Lancaſters* long iarres,
> And in the tyring-house bring wounds, to scarres.
> He rather prayes, you will be pleas'd to see
> One such, to-day, as other playes should be,
> Where neither *Chorus* wafts you ore the seas;
> Nor creaking throne comes downe, the boyes to please.

This is, of course, a dry bob for the whole group of plays on the Wars of the Roses.

p. 37. *Corneille's words.* "Il eſt facile aux spéculatifs d'être sévères, mais s'ils vouloient donner dix ou douze poëmes de cette nature au public, ils élargiroient peut-être les règles encore plus que je ne fais, si-tôt qu'ils auroient reconnu par l'expérience quelle contrainte apporte leur exactitude, et combien de belles choses elle bannit de notre Théâtre."

p. 38. *one of their neweſt Playes.* Thomas Corneille's *L'Amour à la Mode*, an adaptation of *El Amor al uso* by Antonio de Solis y Rivadeneira (1610–1686). *L'Amour à la Mode* was produced at Paris in 1651 with Floridor as Oronte and Jodelet as Cliton, and is doubtless thus referred to by Dryden on account of John Bulteel's translation in heroic verse *Amorous Orontes, Or The Love in Fashion*, acted at the Theatre Royal in 1664; 4to, 1665; and reprinted 4to, 1675 as *The Amorous Gallant: Or, Love in Fashion.* The scene of the comedia of Antonio de Solis is at Madrid; *L'Amour à la Mode* is transported to the Tuilleries; *Amorous Orontes* lives in London and

> Last night a certain Brown-Lass took my Eye,
> And was the object of my Gallantry
> For a long space, whilst we walk'd in the cool
> Shade of St. *James's*, . . .

The scene of Corneille's comedy which Dryden has in mind commences Act III. Oronte, gentilhomme Parisien, and Cliton, son valet, are talking in the street before the house of Lucie, who appears at a window and converses with him. (As Bulteel has it he speaks *Calling up to* Lucia *at the Windore.*) The lady retires (*She shuts the Windore*) and Florame appears. The scene then changes to the interior of the house of Argante, father of Dorotée, who has an appointment with Oronte. She and her maid Lysette are in their room. Eraste, a lover of Dorotée, joins them but is persuaded to leave, not before Oronte who comes in suspects his presence and inquires who has been there. Lysette declares it is a lover of hers which is overheard by Cliton who rushes in full of jealousy. Argante at the noise imagines that thieves are breaking in and is heard behind the scenes calling his servants. Presently he appears brandishing a great sword. Oronte escapes by pretending he has been attacked by Eraste, whereupon Argante allows him to depart and shields him from his supposed enemy. (Argante *speaking to* Eraste *whom he findes in his house, and shutting the door upon him to prevent his seeing of* Orontus . . .) Dryden seems to have confused this imbroglio with a scene in Quinault's *L'Amant Indiscret*, a play which we know he read carefully as he borrowed thence for *Sr Martin Mar-all.* Here the servant is Philipin and he drolls within thus, Act II, 4:

> Lisipe. Ha que ne tiens-je ici ce maudit Philipin!
> Philipin. Je ne me vis jamais si proche de ma fin.
> Lisipe. Qu'avez vous repondu, belle et chere Lucresse?
> Lucresse. J'ai trompé ce valet.
> Philipin. Ha la bonne traiteresse. . . .

It should perhaps be remarked that *Love a la Mode*, 4to, 1663, which is probably the work of T. Southland, has nothing to do with Corneille's *L'Amour a la Mode.*

p. 38. *been less in vogue. Pertharite, Roi des Lombards*, produced at the hôtel de Bourgogne in the spring of 1652, was a complete failure, and Corneille when the play was printed, 12mo, 1653, commenced his address "Au Lecteur " with "La mauvaise réception que le public a faite à cet ouvrage m'avertit qu'il est temps que je sonne la retraite . . . il est juste qu' après vingt années de travail je commence à m'apercevoir que je deviens trop vieux pour être encore à la mode."

p. 38. *Alexandrin's.* This is hardly correct. Many of the older comedies are written in rough "eight and sixes," and in any case the French

Alexandrines have practically nothing in common with the metre of such a piece as *Gammer Gurton's Needle*. They are not comparable. It will be noted that Dryden takes no account of Lyly.

p. 39. *Merry Wives of Windsor*. With regard to unity of time it has been calculated that *The Merry Wives of Windsor* commences shortly before noon, since the Elizabethans dined at 11.30 or midday. This is the First Day. A second day is required by the action; and the play ends in Windsor Park with the fairy revels at midnight on the third day. The business of the comedy covers two and a half days. The scene is one town Windsor, but it shifts from a street to the interior of Master Page's house; from a room in Doctor Caius' house to a room in the Garter Inn; and again to Windsor Park. How far the unities of time and place, as the stricter critics understood them, are preserved may well be questioned.

p. 39. *Shakespeare*. Dr. Johnson in his *Life of Dryden* writes with most admirable judgement: "The account of *Shakespeare* may stand as a perpetual model of encomiastic criticism; exact without minuteness, and lofty without exaggeration. The praise lavished by *Longinus* on the attestation of the heroes of *Marathon* by *Demosthenes* fades away before it. In a few lines is exhibited a character so extensive in its comprehension, and so curious in its limitations, that nothing can be added, diminished, or reformed; nor can the editors and admirers of *Shakespeare*, in all their emulation of reverence, boast of much more than of having diffused and paraphrased this epitome of excellence, of having changed *Dryden's* gold for baser metal, of lower value though of greater bulk."

p. 40. *Quantum lenta*. Vergil, *Eclogues*, I, 25.

p. 40. *Mr. Hales*. John Hales (1584–1656), Fellow of Eton, and a close friend of Sir Henry Wotton. He was dispossessed in 1640. Wood refers to him as "a walking library." The *Golden Remains of the Ever Memorable Mr. John Hales* was published in 1659.

This anecdote of his admiration for Shakespeare is often repeated, as by Charles Gildon in his *Reflections on Rymer's Short View*, 1694, and by Nicholas Rowe in the Life prefixed to his edition of Shakespeare, 9 vols, 8vo, 1709.

p. 40. *the Verses*. Ben Jonson's Epigram:

How I do love thee, *Beaumont*, and thy *Muse*,
That unto mee dost such Religion use!
How do I feare myself, that am not worth
The least indulgent Thought thy Pen drops forth!
At once thou mak'st mee happy, and unmak'st,
And giving largely to mee, more thou tak'st!
What Fate is mine, that soe itself bereaves?
What Art is thine, that so thy Friend deceives?
When even there, where most thou praisest me,
For Writing better, I must envy thee.

p. 40. *Philaster*. Malone was of opinion that *Phylaster; or, Love Lies A-Bleeding* was first represented in 1608–9, and this date is now very generally accepted. Much of the success of this play is said to have been due to the romantic figure of Eufrasia, "disguised like a Page, and called *Bellario*" who follows Phylaster for love's dear sake. Before *Phylaster*, among other plays Beaumont had written *The Woman Hater* (1606?); Fletcher, *The Faithful Shepherdess* (1608?) and the two dramatists together *The Knight of the Burning Pestle* (1607–8?), all three of which, however admired by the judicious, were disapproved by the public audiences and had been given very unsuccessfully in the theatre.

p. 40. *Ben Johnson*. Dryden probably alludes to plays written by Jonson for Henslowe which are not extant. Among these were *Page of Plymouth; Robert II King of Scots; Richard Crookback. The Case is Altered*, probably written in 1597, and acted by the Children of the Chapel in 1598, was scarcely owned by Jonson as his work.

p. 41. *dotages*. In spite of the fact that they are fine dramas, *The Staple of News*, folio, 1631; *The New Inn*, 8vo, 1631; *The Magnetick Lady*, folio, 1640; as also *A Tale of a Tub*, which although written long before Jonson did not bring on the stage until 1633, and which was published in the Second Folio, 1631–40, are the plays intended by Dryden in this censure.

p. 41. *Discoveries*. These "many and profitable rules for perfecting the stage" are in the main borrowed by Jonson from Heinsius, *De Tragoediaè Constitutione Liber* and *Ad Horatii de Plauto et Terentio iudicium Dissertatio*. Dryden does not seem to be aware of this.

Timber: or Discoveries is merely a selection from Jonson's notebooks which he revised with some care and published in the 1640 Folio (separate title-page, 1641). The text is headed "Explorata; or Discoveries."

p. 41. *Natural day*. Twenty-four hours. The "Artificial" day was twelve hours.

p. 42. *five hours*. Tuke's *The Adventures of Five Hours* which is translated from Antonio Coello y Ochoa's *Los Empeños de Seis Horas* (*The Complications of Six Hours*). It will not escape remark that the Spanish play allows one hour more than the English.

p. 42. *The Cid*. In his *Examen du Cid* Corneille writes: "Tout s'y passe donc dans Seville, et garde ainsi quelque espéce d'unité de lieu en général; mais le lieu particulier change de scéne en scéne, et tantôt c'est le palais du Roi, tantôt l'apartement de l'Infante, tantôt la maison de Chimène, et tantôt une rue, ou place publique. On le détermine aisément pour les scénes détachées, mais pour celles qui ont leur liaison ensemble, comme les quatre derniéres du premier acte, il est mal aisé d'en choisir un qui convienne à toutes." Voltaire sadly lamented this. Thus in reference to Act IV, scene 3, he complains: "Toujours la scène vide, et nulle liaison; c'était encore un des défauts du siècle. Cette négligence rend la tragédie bien plus facile à faire, mais bien plus défectueuse."

In his *Examen de Cinna* Corneille acknowledges: "Il est vrai qu'il s'y rencontre une duplicité de lieu particulier. La moitié de la pièce se passe chez Emilie, et l'autre dans le cabinet d'Auguste. J'aurois été ridicule si j'avois prétendu que cet empereur délibérât avec Maxime et Cinna, s'il quitteroit l'empire ou non, précisément dans la même place où ce dernier vient de rendre compte à Emilie de la conspiration qu'il a formée contre lui. C'est ce qui m'a fait rompre la liaison des scènes au quatrième acte."

p. 42. *instance in*. To instance in is to adduce as an example, to cite as a proof. Although now rare the term was very frequent. Thus Butler, *Analogy*, 1736, I, vi, 153: "Which is the Fallacy instanced in by the Ancients."

p. 42. *humour*. Asper in the Induction to *Euery Man out of his Humor* (ed. folio 1616) thus delivers himself:

> Why, Humour (as 'tis *ens*) we thus define it
> To be a quality of aire or water,
> And in it self holds these two properties,
> Moisture, and fluxure: As, for demonstration,
> Powre water on this floore, 'twill wet and runne:
> Likewise the aire (forc't through a horne, or trumpet)
> Flowes instantly away, and leaues behind
> A kind of dew; and hence we doe conclude
> That what so e're hath fluxure, and humitidie
> As wanting power to containe it selfe,
> Is Humour: So in euery humane bodie
> The choller, melancholy, flegme, and bloud,
> By reason that they flow continually
> In some one part, and are not continent,
> Receiue the name of Humors. Now thus farre
> It may by *Metaphore* apply it selfe
> Vnto the generale disposition,
> As when some one peculiar quality
> Doth so possesse a man, that it doth draw
> All his affects, his spirits, and his powers
> In their confluctions all to runne one way,
> This may be truly said to be a Humor.

p. 43. *τὸ γελοῖον*. The ludicrous. Aristotle, *Poetics*, V.

p. 43. *the old Comedy*. Jonson, *Discoveries* (p. 130): "all insolent, and obscene speaches, jest upon the best men; injuries to particular persons; perverse Sayings (and the rather unexpected) in the old Comedy did move laughter; especially when it did imitate any dishonesty; and scurrility came forth in the place of wit . . . of which *Aristophanes* affords an ample harvest."

p. 43. *Socrates.* Jonson, *Ibid.:* "What could have made them laugh, like to see *Socrates* presented, that Example of all good life, honeﬆy, and vertue, to have him hoiﬆed up with a Pullie, and then play the Philosopher, in a basquet. Measure, how many foote a Flea could skip *Geometrically*, by a juﬆ Scale, and edifie the people from the ingine. This was *Theatricall* wit, right Stage-jeﬆing, and relishing a Play-house, invented for scorne, and laughter." Socrates is thus caricatured in the *Clouds* of Ariﬆophanes.

p. 43. *ἦθος.* The character. *πάθος*, emotion. *ἦθος* implied "the characteriﬆic moral qualities, the permanant dispositions of the mind, which reveal a certain condition of the will"; *πάθος*, "the more transient emotions, the passing moods of feeling." (Butcher's *Ariﬆotle's Theory*, 1898, p. 123.)

p. 43. *Ex homine.* Terence, *Eunuchus*, III, ii, 7.

p. 43. *True-Wit.* In *The Defence of the Epilogue* appended to *The Conqueﬆ of Granada*, Part II, 4to, 1672, Dryden writes of Jonson: "*True-Wit* in the *Silent Woman*, was his Maﬆer-piece."

p. 44. *Creditur. Epiﬆularum*, II, i, 168–170.

p. 44. *Corneille has laid down. Discours des Trois Unités:* "Je ne puis oublier que c'eﬆ un grand ornement pour un poëme que le choix d'un jour illuﬆre, et attendu depuis quelque tems. Il ne s'en présente pas toujours des occasions; et dans tout ce que j'ai fait jusqu'ici, vous n'en trouverez de cette nature que quatre: celui d'Horace, où deux peuples devaient décider de leur Empire par une bataille, celui de Rodogune, d'Andromède, et de D. Sanche . . . les occasions ne s'en offrent pas souvent, dans le reﬆe de mes ouvrages je n'ai pû choisir des jours remarquables que par ce que le hasard y fait arriver, et non pas par l'emploi, où l'ordre public les aye deﬆinés de longue main."

p. 44. *another artifice.* Dryden himself employs this, as in *The Spanish Fryar*, where in Act I a friar is described and obviously intended for Dominic, who does not appear before the Second Act.

p. 45. *translated into French.* Ben Jonson's *Epicœne, or, The Silent Woman*, has since Dryden's day been translated into French and played with great success in Paris.

p. 45. *Playes out of Verse. Don Juan, ou le Feﬆin de Pierre*, produced 15 February, 1665, was the firﬆ five-act play Molière wrote in prose. He had used prose in plays of one act: *Les Precieuses Ridicules*, produced 18 November, 1659; *La Critique de l'Ecole des Femmes*, 1 June, 1663; *L'Impromptu de Versailles*, October, 1663; *Le Mariage Forcé*, 29 January, 1664; and in some scenes of *La Princesse d'Elide*, 7 May, 1664. The early farces *La Jalousie de Barbouillé* and *Le Médecin volant* are prose.

p. 45. *these seven years.* The supposed date is 3 June, 1665; but Dryden was thinking of the date at which he was actually writing, the year 1667.

p. 45. *Ubi plura.* Horace, *Ars Poetica*, 351–352.

p. 46. *Vivorum.* Velleius Paterculus, II, 36.

p. 46. *midst of the great Plague.* The Pestilence raged at its height in August and September, 1665, some two months after the day on which this imaginary dialogue took place.

p. 46. *Macrobius. Saturnalia*, II. 7. The "another Poet" was Publilius Syrus. For a Roman Knight to appear in a mime was degradation, but Caesar's request was a command.

"Laberium asperae libertatis equitem Romanum Caesar quingentis millibus invitavit, ut prodiret in scaenam et ipse ageret mimos quos scriptitabat. Sed potestas non solum si invitet, sed etiam si supplicet cogit, unde se et Laberius a Caesare coactum in prologo testatur his vocibus:

Ego bis tricenis annis actis sine nota
Eques Romanus e Lare egressus meo
Domum revertar mimus."

At such lines also as

Porro Quirites! libertatem perdimus,

and

Necesse est multos timeat quem multi timent,

which were spoken in the character of Syrus the whole audience turned their eyes to Caesar. He accordingly set up a rival to Laberius, Publilius Syrus. "Nec ullo recusante superavit omnes, in queis et Laberium. Unde Caesar adridens hoc modo pronuntiavit:

Favente tibi me victus es, Laberi, a Syro."

From the summary of the Eighth Book of Aulus Gellius, which is not extant, we see that he described this incident in his fifteenth chapter. See also his reference to Laberius, X, 17.

The Prologue of Laberius was translated by Goldsmith in the *Enquiry into the Present State of Polite Learning*, 1759: "What! no way left to shun th' inglorious stage."

Dryden's reference to the anecdote is perhaps not entirely apposite here.

p. 47. *Rhyme is unnatural.* It will be remembered that Crites is Sir Robert Howard, and these arguments may well be compared with those advanced in the Preface to *Four New Plays*, folio, 1665: "*Another way of the Ancients which the* French *follow, and our Stage has now lately practised, is to write in Rhime; and this is the dispute betwixt many Ingenious Persons, Whether Verse in Rhime, or Verse without the sound, which may be called Blank Verse, (though a hard Expression) is to be preferred? But take the Question largely, and it is never to be decided, but by right application I suppose it may: for in the general they are both proper, that is, one for a Play, the other for a Poem or Copy of Verses, a Blank Verse being as much too low for one, as Rhime is unnatural for the other: A Poem, being a premeditated form of Thoughts upon designed Occasions, ought not to be unfurnish'd of any harmony in Words or Sound: The other is presented as the present Effect of Accidents not thought of; so that 'tis impossible it should be equally proper to both these, unless it were possible that all Persons were born so much more than Poets, that Verses were not to be compos'd by them, but already made in them. Some may object, That this Argument is trivial, because, whatever is shew'd, 'tis known still to be but a Play; but such may as well excuse an ill Scene, that is not naturally painted, because they know 'tis only a Scene, and not really a City or Country.*

"*But there is yet another thing which makes Verse upon the Stage appear more unnatural; that is, when a Piece of a Verse is made up by one that knew not what the other meant to say, and the former Verse answered as perfectly in Sound as the last is supplied in Measure; so that the smartness of a Reply, which has its Beauty by coming from sudden Thoughts, seems lost by that which rather looks like a Design of two, than the Answer of one. It may be said that Rhime is such a confinement to a quick and luxuriant Phancy, that it gives a stop to its speed, till slow Judgment comes in to assist it; but this is no Argument for the Question in hand, for the dispute is not which way a Man may write best in, but which is most proper for the Subject he writes upon; and if this were let pass, the Argument is yet unresolv'd in it self; for he that wants Judgment in the liberty of his Phancy, may as well show the defect of it in its Confinement; and to say truth, he that has Judgment will avoid the errors, and he that wants it will commit them both. It may be objected, 'Tis improbable that any should speak* ex tempore *as well as* Beaumont *and* Fletcher *makes them, though in Blank Verse; I do not only acknowledg that, but that 'tis also improbable any will write so well that way; but if that may be allowed improbable, I believe it may be concluded impossible that any should speak as good Verses in Rhime as the best Poets have writ; and therefore that which seems nearest to what it intends, is ever to be preferr'd: Nor are great Thoughts more adorned by Verse, than Verse unbeautified by mean ones; so that Verse seems not only unfit in the best use of it, but much more in the worse, when a Servant is call'd, or a Door bid to be shut in Rhime. Verses (I mean good ones) do in their height of Phancy declare the labour that brought them forth, like Majesty that grows with care; and Nature that makes the Poet capably seems to retire and leave its offers to be made perfect by Pains and Judgment.*"

p. 47 *says Aristotle. Poetics,* IV: *λέξεως δὲ γενομένης αὐτὴ ἡ φύσις τὸ οἰκεῖον μέτρον εὗρε, μάλιστα γὰρ λεκτικὸν τῶν μέτρων τὸ ἰαμβεῖόν ἐστιν.* "Once dialogue had come in, Nature herself discovered the appropriate measure. For the iambic is, of all measures, the most colloquial." (Butcher.)

p. 47. *This nicking.* To nick off is to come in at exactly the right moment and to hit precisely. Thus Dr. Matthew Robinson (1628–1694) in his *Autobiography* (ed. Mayor, 1856) has: "His father . . . did admire to see how the boy would nick off the very sense of difficult passages."

p. 47. *Arcades omnes*. Rather: *Arcades ambo*. Vergil, Eclogue VII, 4–5.

p. 47. *quicquid conabar*. Ovid, *Tristia*, IV, x, 25–26:

> Sponte sua carmen numeros veniebat ad aptos
> Et quod temptabam dicere versus erat.

Cf. Pope's *Epistle to Dr. Arbuthnot*, l. 128 (*Prologue to the Satires*), 1735:

> I lisp'd in Numbers, for the Numbers came.

p. 47. *Ars est celare artem*. Erasmus, *Adagia*, folio, 1599, p. 572, we have: "Summi artificis, artem dissimulare. . . . Hinc illud vulgo iactatum, saepe apud Fabium iteratur: Summi artificis est, artem posse dissimulare. . . . Galli: Ouvrier gaillard, cele son art. Bartholomaeus Maranta Venus. Lucullianarum quaestionum lib: Maxime enim animadvertandum est in oratione soluta, ne ficte, et ex arte dicere videamur: sed latere oportet artificium, ut innata appareat elocutio, &c. Erasmus noster in Lingua: Qui docent esse caput artis, artem dissimulare, simulant contationem, quo magis attentos, magisque credulos habeant auditores."

Erasmus in his *Dialogus Ciceronianus* writes: "An non hoc ipse docuit Cicero, caput artis esse dissimulare artem?"

Ovid, *Ars Amatoria*, II, 313, writes: "Si latet ars, prodest . . ."

p. 48. *Ovid saying too much*. Chapelain in his "Lettre ov Discours . . . sur le Poëme d'*Adonis* du Cheualier *Marino*," *L'Adone*, Paris, folio, 1623, speaks of "l'intemperance" of Claudian, and "Ouide, (quoy qu'en ayt dit Quintilien) qui est estendu iusqu'à l'excez."

p. 48. *sayes Seneca*. The two Senecas, the rhetorician M. Annaeus Seneca and the philosopher Lucius Annaeus Seneca have been confused. M. Seneca may be called Marcus for convenience sake, although actually M. does not seem to be found before the fifteenth century. Marcus Seneca, rhetor, has left us *Controversiarum Libri decem*, and in IX, 5, 17 he writes: "Habet hoc Montanus vitium: sententias suas repetendo corrumpit; dum non est contentus unam rem semel bene dicere efficit ne bene dixerit. Et propter hoc et propter alia quibus orator potest poetae similis videri solebat Scaurus Montanum inter oratores Ovidium vocare; nam et Ovidius nescit quod bene cessit relinquere. Ne multa referam quae Montaniana Scaurus vocabat, uno hoc contentus ero: cum Polyxene esset abducta, ut ad tumulum Achillis immolaretur, Hecuba dicit:

> cinis ipse sepulti
> In genus hoc pugnat.

poterat hoc contentus esse; adiecit:

> tumulo quoque sensimus hostem.

nec hoc contentus est; adiecit:

Aeacidae fecunda fui.

Aiebat autem Scaurus rem veram: non minus magnam virtutem esse scire dicere quam scire desinere."

Lucius Annaeus Seneca the philosopher, in a discourse upon the Deluge (*Nat. Quaest.* iii, 27, 12), refers to Ovid's verses on the subject, and, after quoting his *montes et sparsas Cycladas augent*, goes on: "Ut ait ille poetarum ingeniosissimus egregie, sicut illud pro magnitudine rei dixit:

Omnia pontus erant, deerant quoque litora ponto,

nisi tantum impetum ingenii et materiae ad pueriles ineptias reduxisset:

Nat lupus inter oves, fulvos vehit unda leones.

Non est res satis sobria lascivire devorato orbe terrarum. Dixit ingentia et tantae confusionis imaginem cepit, cum dixit:

Exspatiata ruunt per apertos flumina campos
. . . pressaeque labant sub gurgite turres.

Magnifice haec, si non curaverit, quid oves et lupi faciant. Natari autem in deluvio et in illa rapina potest? Aut non eodem impetu pecus, quo raptum erat, mersum erat? Concepisti imaginem quantam debebas, obrutis terris omnibus, coelo ipso in terram ruente: perfer."

Dryden himself has said of Ovid, *Preface to the Translation of Ovid's Epistles*, 1680: "*But take him uncorrected as he is transmitted to us, and it must be acknowledged, in spite of his* Dutch *Friends, the Commentators, even of* Julius Scaliger *himself, that Seneca's Censure will stand good against him;* Nescivit quod bene cessit relinquere: *he never knew how to give over when he had done well; but, continually varying the same Sense an hundred Ways, and taking up in another Place, what he had more than enough inculcated before, he sometimes cloys his Readers instead of satisfying them.*"

The quotation

cinis ipse sepulti
In genus hoc saevit; tumulo quoque sensimus hostem
Aeacidae fecunda fui

is from the *Metamorphoseon*, XIII, 503–505. "Montes . . . augent," *Ibid.*, II, 264. "Omnia pontus . . . ponto," *Ibid.*, I, 292. "Nat lupus . . . leones," *Ibid.*, I, 304. "Exspatiata . . . campos," *Ibid.*, I, 285. "pressaeque . . . turres," *Ibid.*, I, 290.

p. 49. *prevail himself.* A Gallicism: *se prévaloir de* . . . M. Beljame in his valuable thesis *Quae e Gallicis Verbis in Anglicam Linguam Iohannes*

Dryden Introduxerit, 1881, does not appear to have remarked this interesting example.

p. 50. *perpetuo tenore fluere.* Cicero, *De Oratore,* VI, 21: "isque [stilus medius] uno tenore, ut aiunt, in dicendo fluit nihil afferens praeter facilitatem et aequalitatem."

p. 50. *in their own Nations.* The Second Edition, 4to, 1684, adds: "at least we are able to prove, that the Eastern people have us'd it from all Antiquity, *Vid. Dan. his Defence of Rhyme.*" Daniel's *Defence of Rhyme*, 1603, was written in reply to Campion's *Observations in the Art of English Poesie*, 1602. The passage to which Dryden refers runs as follows: "The universalitie argues the generall power of it: for if the Barbarian vse it, then it shewes that it swaies the affection of the Barbarian: if ciuill Nations practise it, it proves that it workes vpon the hearts of ciuill Nations: if all, then that it hath a power in nature on all. *Georgienez de Turcarum moribus*, hath an example of the Turkish Rymes iust of the measure of our verse of eleuen syllables, in feminine Ryme: never begotten I am persuaded by any example in *Europe;* but borne no doubt in *Scythia*, and brought over *Caucasus* and Mount Taurus. The Sclauonian and Arabian tongues acquaint a great part of Asia and Afrique with it. The Muscovite, Polacke, Hungarian, Germane, Italian, French, and Spaniard use no other harmonie of words. The Irish, Briton, Scot, Dane, Saxon, English, and all the Inhabiters of this Iland, either have hither brought, or heere found the same in use."

In contrast to this one may remember Milton's roughly uncouth note on "The Verse" prefixed to *Paradise Lost:* "Rime being no necessary Adjunct or true Ornament of Poem or good Verse, in longer Works especially, but the Invention of a barbarous Age, to set off wretched matter and lame Meeter." This was added in 1668 to the copies then remaining of the first edition.

p. 50. *Sermo pedestris.* Horace, *Ars Poetica*, 95–96:

> et tragicus plerumque dolet sermone pedestri
> Telephus et Peleus, . . .

p. 51. *the Siege of Rhodes.* Davenant wrote much of *The Siege of Rhodes* in lyric metres, and in measure adapted for *recitativo.* With the extremely loose connotation the word had then obtained it would be no exaggeration to say that many of the speeches were actually penned in "the Pindarique way."

p. 51. *Italian and Spanish.* Dryden has ignored the Italian tragedies composed in *versi sciolti*, as for example Trissino's famous *Sofonisba*, completed in 1515 and printed six times before it was first performed at Venice in 1562. This drama is written in blank verse mingled with lyric metres at moments of great emotion. Nor does he take into account the pastoral dream-world of Tasso's *Aminta* produced in the winter of 1572–3. These exceptions, and there are many more, should have modified his judgement. It may also be remarked that Spanish tragedies are generally in assonance, rather than in perfect rhyme.

p. 52. *Tentanda.* Vergil, Georgics, III, 8–9.

p. 52. *Faithful Shepherdess.* Fletcher's verse in *The Faithfull Shepheardesse* reaches heights of great loveliness. The first quarto is undated, but may be assigned to 1609–10. The second quarto was not issued until 1629.

The Sad Shepherd, or, A Tale of Robin Hood, unfinished, was published in the Jonson folio of 1640. The fact that it is not complete (Waldron essayed to continue it) must be a matter of deepest regret.

p. 52. *Hopkins and Sternholds Psalmes.* The doggerel into which Thomas Sternhold (*d.* 1549) and John Hopkins (*d.* 1570) hashed the *Psalms* was so popular with the vulgar that it is said no less than six hundred editions were printed between 1549 and 1828. This may well be the case as these jolting lurries were bawled full lustily Sunday by Sunday in every village kirk from Berwick to Land's End.

p. 52. *Sandys.* George Sandys (1578–1644) was the seventh and youngest son of Edwin Sandys, Archbishop of York. His "Paraphrase upon the Psalmes and upon the Hymnes dispersed throughout the Old and New Testaments" was licensed for the Press on 28 November, 1635. It was published in a small octavo, 1636. Certain portions were re-issued in 1648 as "Choice Psalmes put into Musick for Three Voices," a volume to which Henry Lawes and his brother William were the chief musical contributors. Sandys' *Psalmes* was a favourite with cultured readers, and was one of the three books King Charles I studied at Carisbrooke. However, the lilting doggerel of Sternhold and Hopkins still held among the vulgar. The most famous of his works, "Ovid's Metamorphoses Englished" by Sandys, was first published at Oxford, folio, 1632.

p. 52. *Est ubi.* Horace, *Epistolarum*, II, i, 63: Interdum vulgus rectum videt, est ubi peccat.

p. 52. *Mustapha.* Downes tells us of Orrery's tragedy that "All the Parts being new Cloath'd with new Scenes, Sir *William's* great Care of having it perfect and exactly perform'd, it produc'd to himself and Company vast profit." Of *The Siege of Rhodes* he says: "All Parts being Justly and Excellently Perform'd; it continu'd Acting 12 Days without Interruption with great Applause."

The Indian Queen and *The Indian Emperour* were the two great successes of the Theatre Royal. On Wednesday, 27 January, 1663–64, Pepys observed "the streete full of coaches at the new play, 'The Indian Queene,' which for show, they say, exceeds 'Henry the Eighth.'" On Monday, 1 February following, he saw the piece and found it "a most pleasant show, and beyond my expectation." *The Indian Emperour* was one of Dryden's most popular tragedies. No less than eleven quarto editions were printed between 1667 and 1709.

p. 53. *Indignatur.* Horace, *Ars Poetica*, 90–91.

EXPLANATORY NOTES

p. 53. *Effutire. Ars Poetica*, 231.

p. 53. *an ordinary Sonnet*. A sonnet was a general (if incorrect) name for any short poem. Thus George Gascoigne in his *Posies*, 1575, remarks: "Some thinke that all Poemes (being short) may be called Sonets." In Mrs. Radcliffe's *The Castles of Athlin and Dunbayne*, 1789, a lover indites sonnets of sixteen and twenty lines apiece.

p. 53. *by Aristotle. Poetics*, XXVI: *πότερον δε βελτίων ἡ ἐποποικὴ μίμησις ἢ ἡ τραγική, δια πορήσειεν ἄν τις . . . . . εἰ οὖν τούτοις τε διαφέρει πᾶσιν καὶ ἔτι τῷ τῆς τέχνης ἔργῳ (δεῖ γὰρ οὐ τὴν τυχοῦσαν ἡδονὴν ποιεῖν αὐτὰς ἀλλὰ τὴν ειρημένην), φανερὸν ὅτι κρείττων ἂν εἴη μᾶλλον τοῦ τέλους τυγχάνουσα τῆς ἐποποιίας. περὶ μὲν οὖν τραγῳδίας καὶ ἐποποιίας . . . ειρήσθω τοσαῦτα.*

p. 54. *quidlibet audendi*. Horace, *Ars Poetica*, 9–10:

> pictoribus atque poetis
> quidlibet audendi semper fuit aequa potestas.

p. 54. *Musas colere severiores*. Martial, IX, xii, "De Earino Domitiani," 16–17:

> nobis non licet esse tam disertis,
> qui Musas colimus severiores.

In other of his works Dryden more than once quotes these phrases. Thus in the Dedication to his *Examen Poeticum*, "Being the Third Part of Miscellany Poems," 8vo, 1693, he has, when discussing the *Synalepha*, "which is the cutting off one Vowel, immediately before another": "The *French* and the *Italians* have made it an inviolable Precept in their versification; therein following the severe Example of the *Latin* Poets. Our Countrymen have not yet Reform'd their Poetry so far, but content themselves with following the Licentious Practice of the *Greeks;* who though they sometimes use *Synalepha's*, yet make no difficulty, very often, to sound one Vowel upon another; as *Homer* does in the very first line of *Alpha*. *Μῆνιν ἄειδε, θεά, Πηληιάδεω 'Αχιλῆος*. 'Tis true, indeed, that in the second line, in those words *μυρί' 'Αχαιοῖς*, and *ἄλγε' ἔθηκεν*, the *Synalepha* in revenge is twice observ'd. But it becomes us, for the sake of *Euphony*, rather *Musas colere severiores*, with the *Romans*, than to give into the looseness of the *Grecians*."

In his *Dedication of the Æneis* (ii. 217) Dryden once more recurs to this favourite quotation:

"*Virgil* thinks it sometimes a Beauty to imitate the Licence of the *Greeks*, and leave two Vowels opening on each other, as in that verse of the third *Pastoral:*

> *Et succus pecori, et lac subducitur agnis.*

But *nobis non licet esse tam disertis*, at least if we study to refine our Numbers."

Rapin, whom Dryden much admired, in his *Comparaison d'Homère et de Virgile*, chap. X (ed. 1684) writes as follows: "Les transitions, qui doivent par leur caractère estre fort variées, pour desennuyer le Lecteur, sont toutes semblables dans la plus grande partie de son ouvrage. On n'en peut compter tout au plus que de vingt ou trente sortes dans toute l'étendue de près de trente mille Vers; & ainsi une même liaison se présentant d'ordinaire, est fort sujette à donner du dégoust par une si frequente répétition; ce qui a donné même sujet à Martial de railler un peu du τὸν δ' ἀπαμειβόμενος, & de dire que les Muses Latines ne sont pas tout-à-fait si relâchées, ny si libres que les Grecques: *Qui Musas colimus severiores.*"

p. 54. *repartee.* The stichomythia which forms so prominent a feature in Dryden's heroic tragedies, and which he has managed with such effective skill.

p. 55. *the Water Poet's Rhymes.* John Taylor (1580–1653) who complacently dubbed himself "the Water Poet," from his having been long a waterman on the Thames. He was tirelessly productive, his writings number some 170 items, but much, very much of his output is merest doggerel. Yet none the less this work has its value, since it mirrors intimate details of his own times, and thus it is full of interest for the historian and the antiquary. He has, however, been well called a literary bargee. Ben Jonson, who knew him personally, has the following reference in *Discoveries*, folio, 1641 (p. 97), a passage which Dryden here had in mind: "The Puppets are seene now in despight of the Players: *Heath's Epigrams*, and the *Skullers Poems* [marginal note: *Taylor*] have their applause. There are never wanting, that dare prefer the worst *Preachers*, the worst *Pleaders*, the worst *Poets:* not that the better have left to write, or speake better, but that they that heare them judge worse; *Non illi pejus dicunt, sed hi corruptius judicant.* Nay, if it were put to the question of the Water-rimers workes, against *Spencers;* I doubt not, but they would find more *Suffrages;* because the most favour common vices, out of a Prerogative the vulgar have, to lose their judgements and like that which is naught."

p. 55. *Julius Caesar.* "Qui etiam in magnis occupationibus quum . . . de ratione Latine loquendi accuratissime scripserit primoque in libro dixerit verborum delectum originem esse eloquentiae." Cicero, *Brutus*, LXXII.

p. 55. *Reserate clusos.* Seneca, *Hippolytus*, 863.

p. 56. *It had formerly been said.* By Dryden himself in the Epistle Dedicatory addressed to the Earl of Orrery before *The Rival Ladies*, 4to, 1664: "*The great easiness of Blanck Verse, renders the Poet too Luxuriant.*"

p. 56. *a most acute person.* Sir Robert Howard himself.

p. 57. *slow and painfull.* Thus Boileau, *L'Art Poëtique*, III, 309–312:

> Un poème excellent, où tout marche et se suit,
> N'est pas de ces travaux qu'un caprice produit:

Il veut du temps, des soins; et ce pénible ouvrage
Jamais d'un écolier ne fut l'apprentissage.

p. 57. *Somerset Stairs.* These lay to the west of old Somerset House. They were done away with when the present Georgian building was erected. Strype in his edition of Stow's *Survey of London*, 1720, vol. IV, p. 112, has: "More westwards is a large yard . . . at the bottom of which is a pair of stairs much used by watermen, this being a noted place for landing and taking water at."

p. 57. *Piazze.* An open arcade on the north and east sides of Covent Garden Market Place. It was built by Inigo Jones *circa* 1633–4, and for wellnigh a century remained a fashionable promenade. There are very frequent contemporary references. Wycherley lays Scene 3, Act V, of *The Country Wife*, 4to, 1675, in Covent Garden Piazza after dark, and Scene 2, Act IV of Otway's *The Souldiers Fortune*, 4to, 1681, is the Piazza at midnight. Cf. Brome, *The Covent Garden Weeded*, 8vo, 1658, I, 1, when Cochbrayne says: "Yond magnificent Peece, the *Piazzo*, will excell that at *Venice* by hearsay (I ne're travell'd)."

THE WILD GALLANT

p. 64. *indifferent success in the action.* See the Theatrical History.

p. 64. *Pertharite. Pertharite, Roy des Lombards*, a tragedy by Pierre Corneille, was produced at the hotel de Bourgogne early in 1652. It was badly received, soon withdrawn, and in the *Examen de Pertharite* the poet says: "Le succès de cette Tragédie a été si malheureux, que pour m'epargner le chagrin de m'en souvenir, je n'en dirai presque rien. . . . J'ajoûte icy, malgré sa disgrace, que les sentiments en sont assez vifs & nobles, les Vers assez bien tournez, & que la façon dont le Sujet s'explique dans la première Scene ne manque pas d'artifice."

p. 64. *The Plot was not Originally my own.* There is much in the fantastic incidents and tangled intrigue of *The Wild Gallant* that bears all the marks of a Spanish invention, the masquerade and facile machinery of the *comedias palaciegas*. In the face of Dryden's express assertion, however, it were superfluous to attempt to track the plot through the immense dramatic libraries of stage-struck Spain, more especially as such vast quantities of plays have perished.

p. 65. *two Astrologers.* Dryden was himself a profound astrologer, and there are continual references in his works to this science. With this Prologue one may compare the "Prologue to the last new Play A Duke and No Duke. Spoken by Mr. Jevon," a broadside. (Tate's

A Duke and No Duke was produced at Drury Lane in November, 1684.)

> But first let me Consult old *Erra Pater*
> And see what he advises in the Matter.
> Lets see———
> *Venus* and *Mars*, I find in *Aries* are
> In the Ninth *House*, a Damn'd dry Bobbing Year.
> The price of *Mutton*, will run high 'tis thought
> And Vizard *Masks* will fall to ten a Groat.
> The *Moon's* in *Scorpio's* House or *Capricorns*,
> Friends of the City govern well your *Hornes*.

Mutton here means venery. In Vanbrugh's *The Provok'd Wife*, Lincoln's Inn Fields, May, 1697, IV, Sir John Brute bawls to Constant and Heartfree: "I hope your Punks will give you sauce to your Mutton."

p. 65. *several Apartments*. Apartments=houses, for an explanation of which astrological term *vide infra*.

p. 65. *half an hour after three*. Davenant's *The Cruelty of the Spaniards in Peru*, given in 1658, was "Represented daily at the Cockpit in Drury-Lane, At Three afternoone punctually." At the end of the piece also the time is particularly indicated: "And it shall begin certainly at 3 after noon." For a decade or more after the Restoration the theatres actually opened about twelve o'clock. So on Monday, 18 May, 1668, being the first day of Sir Charles Sedley's "new play, so long expected, 'The Mulberry Guarden,'" Pepys took Mercer with Mrs. Horsfield and Gayet, "it being almost twelve o'clock, or a little more, and carried them to the King's playhouse, when the doors were not then open; but presently they did open; and we in, and find many people already come in, by private ways, into the pit." Pepys got a boy to keep his place, slipped out to the Rose Tavern and dined alone. Some time after he had returned to his seat, the King and Queen entered their box, and presently the play began. On Thursday, 25 February, 1669, he went to the Duke's Theatre to see Shadwell's *The Royal Shepherdess* "and there before one, but the house infinite full." When Mr. Bayes in *The Rehearsal*, produced 7 December, 1671, at the Theatre Royal, carries off the script of his tragedy the Stage-keeper cries: "Nay, good Sir, don't take a way the Book; you'l disappoint the company that comes to see it acted here, this after noon."

The hour of beginning the play gradually became later. The epilogue to Lansdowne's *The She-Gallants*, produced at Lincoln's Inn Fields in the late winter of 1695, mentions four o'clock, and on 18 May, 1703, "At the Theatre Royal . . . The Last Reviv'd Comedy call'd The Relapse, Or, Virtue in Danger" is "To begin exactly at half an hour after Five." The Play bill of *The*

Confederacy "the sixth day of November, 1705" has "beginning exactly at Five of the Clock," whilst in the Epilogue to Farquhar's *The Recruiting Officer*, produced in April, 1706, all who wish to see this comedy are bidden "repair To-morrow Night, by six o'Clock to the Sign of the *Theatre-Royal*, in *Drury-Lane*." Six o'clock seems to have remained the general hour for upwards of half a century.

p. 65. *Mathematicians.* Astrologers; fortune-tellers. In post-Augustan Latin *Mathematicus*=an astrologer. So in Fletcher's *Rollo, Duke of Normandy*, 4to, 1640, IV:

> *Latorch.* Sir, one suit . . .
> *Rollo.* About your mathematicians?
> *Latorch.* Yes, to have
> The scheme of your nativity judg'd by them
> I have 't already created. . . .
> My doubts for you are such as cannot hope
> Any security but from the stars.

p. 65. *The Ascendants Lord disgrac'd.* The house of the ascendant is from five degrees of Zodiac above this point to twenty-five below it, and the Lord of the Ascendant is any planet within this.
disgrac'd is a technical term in astrology.

p. 65. *twelfth House.* Cf. *Rollo*, IV, 2, where Norbret says: "Then Jupiter in the *twelfth*, the *Cacodemon*." A House is a twelfth part of the heavens as divided by great circles through the North and South part of the horizon: the whole sky, excluding those parts that never rise and that never set, being thus divided into Twelve houses, numbered eastwards beginning with the house of the Ascendant, and each having some special signification attached to it. The Twelfth House is malign, and signifies Enmity, κακοδαίμων. Jupiter, Saturn, Mars, are the three superior planets; Venus and Mercury the inferior planets. For "Grim Saturn" cf. Horace, *Carminum*, II, xvii:

> te Jovis impio
> tutela Saturno refulgens
> eripuit volucrisque fati
> tardavit alas.

Cicero *De Divinatione*, I, 85, has: "Cur stella Iovis, aut Veneris coniuncta cum luna ad ortus puerorum salutaris sit; Saturni Martisve contraria?"

p. 65. *Sagittary.* The Archer, the ninth Zodiacal constellation.

p. 65. *Ptolomy.* Ptolemaeus Alexandrinus, the eminent astrologer of the second century. His "Great Syntaxis," more generally known in the Middle Ages under the Arabic title *Almagest*, was for centuries the standard work upon astronomy. The seventh and eighth books, which are especially famous, give a lengthy catalogue of stars.

p. 65. *fifth house.* A favourable house; the house of children and long life.

p. 65. *Peregrine.* Peregrine is the term applied to a Planet situate in a part of the Zodiac where it has none of its essential dignities. *Vide* Philips (1706) *sub voce:* "Among Astrologers a Planet is said to be Peregrine when found in a Sign or Place of Heaven, where it has none of its five essential Dignities; viz. House, Exaltation, Triplicity, Term, or Face."

p. 65. *one continued Song.* Cf. Mr. Bayes in *The Rehearsal*, III, 1, who lays down "you must ever interlard your Playes with Songs, Ghosts, and Dances." In the first prologue to *The Womens Conquest*, produced at Lincoln's Inn Fields in the winter of 1670, Edward Howard makes Angel say: "We are to act a Farce to day that has sixteen Mimics in it . . . with two and thirty Dances and Jiggs à la mode."

p. 66. *Lord of Spain.* Saturn. The Spanish were regarded as "Saturnine," no doubt from their gravity and solemn dignity of demeanour. Afterwards the application took a darker shade. "All evil comes from Spain: all good from the north," according to Sir T. Challoner, writing from Florence, 1597, was then "a common proverb in every man's mouth." So the French were regarded as "Mercurial" and the Lord of France was Mercury, from their traditional gaiety and liveliness.

p. 67. *Whetstones Park.* "A Lane betwixt *Holborn* and *Lincoln's-Inn-Fields*, fam'd for a Nest of Wenches, now (*c.* 1696) de-park'd." Whetstone Park, constructed by one Whetstone, a tobacconist and a vestryman of S. Giles, is a narrow roadway, of which the name still remains, between the north side of Lincoln's Inn Fields and the south side of Holborn. In the reign of Charles II this district was infamous. There are innumerable references, *e.g.* Shadwell's *The Miser*, Theatre Royal, January, 1671–2, Act I, a "*Whetstone* Whore"; Crowne's *The Countrey Wit*, Dorset Garden, January, 1675–6, Act III. In Wycherley's *Love in a Wood*, Theatre Royal, autumn of 1671, Act I, 2, Dapperwit cries as the last insult to Lady Flippant: "If I had met you in *Wheatstone's*-Park, with a drunken Foot-Soldier, I should not have been jealous of you . . . now I call her Whore in plain English." Lee in the Dedication to *The Princess of Cleve* (4to, 1689) writes: "When they expected the most polish'd Hero in *Nemours*, I gave 'em a Ruffian reeking from *Whetstone's-Park*."

p. 67. *He grows to break Glass-Windows.* So Rochester's *Maim'd Debauchee* boasts of past exploits:

> I'll tell of Whores attack'd their Lords at home,
> Bawds Quarters beaten up, and Fortress won;
> Windows demolish'd, Watches overcome,
> And hansom Ills by my contrivance done.

Thus Betty Goodfield in *The Woman Turn'd Bully*, produced at Dorset Garden in the summer of 1675, 4to, 1675, on coming up to London disguis'd as a "town-gallant," is advised never to return home at night before one o'clock, and to break all windows that dare "oppose" her.

p. 67. *Has fairly play'd him at three Wenches more.* Whence it would appear that the episode of Lady Du Lake and the two or three Whores, Act IV, is an addition to spice the fare more palatably to the taste of the audience, and indeed it bears every sign of interpolation.

p. 68. *Burr.* Cf. *Dictionary of the Canting Crew* which defines: "*Burre*, a Hanger-on, or Dependant."

p. 69. *Blancket thee.* Toss you in a blanket for being lazy. So in *The Silent Woman* (1609), V, 4, Mistress Mavis threatens the disguised divine and pseudo-canonist: "Wee'll haue our men blanket 'hem i' the hall."

p. 69. *Guelphs and Ghibellins.* The names adopted by the two factions that kept Italy divided and devastated during the greater part of the Middle Ages. The terms seem to have originated in Germany, in the rivalry between the house of Welf (Dukes of Bavaria), and the House of Hohenstaufen (Dukes of Swabia), whose ancestral castle was Waiblingen in Franconia. "Guelfo" and "Ghibellino" were the Italian forms of "Welf" and "Waiblingen." As party catchwords the names may even be said to have survived until the coming to Italy of Charles V (1529), when a new epoch opened in the relations between Pope and Emperor.

p. 69. *Rhodes.* After a most heroic resistance on 24 October, 1522, Villiers de l'Isle Adam was compelled to make an honourable capitulation to Solyman II and deliver Rhodes definitely to the Turks. Davenant's famous opera *The Siege of Rhodes*, which had won great popularity, would give extra point to this allusion.

p. 69. *Cattle.* The word is sometimes used meaning "vermin." R. Burton (Nathaniel Crouch), *English Empire in America*, 1685, IV, 86, writes: "Tame Cattel they have none except lice." William Carr, *Primitive Christianity*, 1672, II, VII, 169, speaks of "Flies, Wasps, and such little Cattel."

p. 70. *a Carwichet.* A contraction of *carriwichet.* A jest; a pun. Cf. *Bartholomew Fair*, V, where Lanthorn says: "All the fowle i' the Fayre, I meane all the dirt in Smithfield (that's one of Master Littlewit's Carwitchets now) will be thrown at our Banner to day, if the matter do's not please the People."

A quarter-quibble is some weak puling quibble. Thus Thomas Cooke (Hesiod Cooke), in his *Tales, Epistles, Odes, Fables*, 1729 (p. 96), has:

"Quarter-quibbles made his Heart right glad."

A clinch is a sharp repartee involving some word-play. Cf. Killigrew's *The Parson's Wedding*, folio 1663 [1664], I, 3:

"the old Knight of the Shire . . . vies clinches with a silenc'd Minister."

In the satire, *To Poet Bavius*, 4to, 1688, occur these lines:

> O Luckey hit! what strange Prodigious skill
> Thou hast in Clinching, Quibling, *Doggeril.*
> The Colonels next; but by unhappy Chance
> No *Puns* the value of these Lines Advance:
> But *Dids*, and *Does*, and a quaint *Simely*,
> Which must the Place of smarter Clinch supply.

p. 70. *dull Dutchmen.* "Dull as a Dutchman," probably from the jingle, was proverbial. Cf. the Prologue to *Amboyna:*

> *And least hope Wit, in* Dutchmen *that would be*
> *As much improper as would Honesty.*

p. 70. *disguis'd.* A very common slang term for "drunk." Cf. Massinger and Dekker, *The Virgin Martyr;* 4to, 1622, III: "*Harpax.* I am a Prince disguis'd. *Hircius.* Disguised! how? drunk?"

p. 71. *great Hogen Mogen bloody Ale.* Hogan-mogan is a popular corruption, or rather perversion, of the Dutch *Hoogmogend-heiden*, "High Mightinesses," the title of the States-General. In a transferred manner it is used as a humorous or contemptuous adjective of those affecting grandeur and show; "high and mighty." And also of things, "topping"; "humming." The phrase is very common.

bloody. A very early, perhaps the earliest, use of this intensive. The O.E.D. gives no example before Etherege's *The Man of Mode*, 4to, 1676, I, where Medley says: "Not without he will promise to be bloody drunk." It should be noticed that the word is in its first employ connected with drinking.

For the phrase *hogan-mogan ale* one may compare Shadwell's rhyming letter to Wycherley, which commences: "Inspir'd with high and mighty Ale." *Vide Wycherley's Works*, 1924, by the present editor, II, p. 243.

p. 71. *porterly drunk.* i.e. vilely drunk. Porterly=characteristic of a street-porter. Torriano, 1659, has: *Facchinéso*, basely or porterly. A critic writing in the *Moderator*, Thursday 23 June, 1692, rebukes Langbaine for his "porterly language to Mr. *Dryden*," with reference to the abusive passages in the *English Dramatick Poets*, Oxford, 1691.

p. 71. *Art thou there I'faith; and why, old Boy?* A reminiscence of *Hamlet*, I, v. 150: "Ah, ha boy! say'st thou so? Art thou there, truepenny?"

p. 71. *he and I are very kind.* Kind in the somewhat unusual sense of "on intimate terms." Now rare except in dialect. J. T. Brockett, *Glossary of North Country Words in Use* (1825), gives: "Kind, intimate."

p. 71. *Dear Hearts.* In Shadwell's *The Sullen Lovers*, produced at the Duke's House, Saturday, 2 May, 1668; 4to, 1668; the expression "Dear Heart" is continually in the mouth of Woodcock, "A familiar loving Coxcomb, that embraces and kisses all Men; So used to his familiar endearing Expressions, that he cannot forbear them in the midst of his Anger." Here the term Dear Heart= a rakehell.

p. 71. *made a Devil on't.* As we say, "played the devil with it." So Lyndesay, *Complaynt* (1529), 236, has:

> Sum maid the fule, and sum did flatter.

We say "played the fool."

p. 72. *my noble Festus.* There is a reference here to *Acts* xxvi, 25: "I am not mad, most noble Festus; but speak forth the words of truth and soberness." (A.V.) " Noble Festus" would appear to be a catch-phrase of the day.

p. 72. *smoak for't.* Smoke in the rare sense "suffer" or "smart." In early use it is found with actual allusion to burning at the stake. The word is a favourite with Dryden. Cf. *Sr. Martin Mar-all*, V, where old Moody, discovering he is tricked, cries: "'Tis so, I discern it now, but some shall smoak for't." Also *The Kind Keeper; or, Mr. Limberham*, V, 1: "I am resolv'd I will go see 'em, or some-body shall smoak for't."

p. 73. *A man out at Armes thou mean'st, Will.* This scene of repartee between Loveby and Bibber is closely parodied in *The Rehearsal*, produced at the Theatre Royal, 7 December, 1671, III, 1, where Prince Pretty-man and Tom Thimble enact what is in the opinion of Mr. Bayes "a Scene of sheer Wit, without any mixture in the whole World."

p. 73. *Cary-House, i.e.* the Canary House, a much-frequented hostelry situated "between the Feathers Tavern and Long's Coffee house on the east side of Exeter Change." There is a Token of the Canary House dated 1665. See *Boyne's Tokens*, ed. Williamson, vol. I, p. 760. Cf. Pepys, 30 November, 1667: "then to Cary House, a house now of entertainment, next my Lord Ashly's . . . we after two hours stay, sitting at the table with our napkins open, had our dinners brought, but badly done. But here was good company."

p. 74. *and so he dy'd.* A slang expression of little meaning introduced saucily into a sentence, *e.g.* Duffett's farce *The Mock-Tempest: or the Enchanted Castle*, 4to, 1675, II, 2:

> *Lo here, here is Pride, that first left them aside.*
> *An honest true* Trojan, *and then she dy'd.*

p. 74. *little ease.* The name of a dungeon in the Tower of London; and also of an ancient place of punishment for unruly apprentices at the Guildhall, London. It is this second to which allusion is here made. The Little Ease in the Tower is first mentioned in the reign of Henry VIII. Hall in his *Chronicles* speaks of an officer of one of the Sheriffs of London who was thrust there. It is thus characteristically described by Harrison Ainsworth in his romance *The Tower of London* (1840): "The walls of this cell, which was called the Little Ease, were so low, and so contrived, that the wretched inmate could neither stand, walk, sit, nor lie at full length within them." (Chapter XIII.)

For the Guildhall Little Ease *vide Curiosity* (1739):

> Here ev'ry Creditor has Right to teize
> And make his Home a real Little-Ease.

A note says: "A Place of Punishment in Guildhall, London, for unruly 'Prentices."

p. 74. *the Comb-case.* The comb was used to adjust the periwig. There are continual references to this practice. So in *The Old Batchelour*, IV, where Belinda laughs at the shopping exploits of a country squire "with the Equipage of a Wife and two Daughters," she tells Araminta how "the Father bought a Powder-Horn, and an Almanack, and a Comb-Case."

p. 75. *Cadua.* This rare word, which is aptly defined by *The Stanford Dictionary* as a "representative name for an elderly woman desirous of admiration or courtship," I have only traced in two other passages. In *The Mistaken Husband*, 4to, 1675, IV, 3, Underwit says to Hazard: "Hast thou never a little Cadua that follows thee!"

In *Love for Love*, III, Sir Sampson says of Valentine: "You shall see the Rogue shew himself, and make Love to some desponding *Cadua* of Fourscore for Sustenance. Odd, I love to see a young Spendthrift forc'd to cling to an Old Woman for Support, like Ivy round a dead Oak." The derivation of Cadua is obscure.

p. 75. *Tribulation.* Obsolete slang for "in pawn." Cf. *Low Life* (3rd ed.), 1764: "Pawnbrokers . . . busy in altering the Dates of Cloaths under Tribulation." Cf. Limbo; hell. In Shadwell's *The Miser*, produced at the Theatre Royal, Drury Lane, in January, 1672; 4to, 1672; I. Goldingham enumerates a number of unredeemed articles pawned with him, and cries, "They are forfeited; to Hell with them, *ab inferis nulla redemptio.*" Cf. Mrs. Behn's *The Luckey Chance*, produced at Drury Lane in the winter of 1686, I, 1, where Gayman says, "I have been in Tribulation, that is to say, Moneyless."

I have ventured to give the obvious stage-direction *Gives him Gold* in italics. The 4tos, 1669, print it as part of Loveby's speech.

p. 75. *Bill-man.* Soldiers or watchmen armed with bills, weapons similar to halberds. So in Dekker's *The Honest Whore*, Part II (printed 1630, but acted much earlier), we have: "Enter Constable and Bilmen." The word is very common, and gave occasion for endless punning as here.

p. 75. *Ifeck.* Ifeck=in earnest. As an asseveration ifeck is a form of "i' faith." This mild expression, which was used even by Puritans, is laughed at by Jonson, *The Alchemist* (1610), I, 2: "I-fac's no oath." Even Fondlewife in *The Old Batchelour*, IV, 1, can cry: "I was but in Jest, I was ifeck.... Ifeck you'l break my Heart—Ifeck you will."

p. 75. *Noble.* A gold coin first minted by Edward III and worth 6/8 (or 10/–). *London Gazette*, No. 5207/3, 1714, has: "John Meercs of Gosport . . . was . . . Fined Twenty Nobles." The proverb "to bring one's noble to ninepence" or "one's noble is not worth ninepence" survived until the end of the nineteenth century.

p. 75. *eighteen pieces.* The piece is an English gold coin, originally applied to the *unite* of James I, and afterwards to a sovereign or a guinea, as each was the current coin. The *Dictionary of the Canting Crew*, *circa* 1700, explains the slang *Job* as "a Guinea, Twenty Shillings, or a Piece." Chambers, 1727–41, has "*Coin*, Guinea or Piece."

p. 76. *Mirror of Knighthood. Espejo de Caballerias*, a romance, or rather a vast collection of all manner of chivalrous stories of the Amadis family, was issued in four parts by several authors. The main theme is the adventuring of Don Febo, Knight of the Sun, and his brother Rosiclair. The first part appeared in 1562, and was dedicated by its author, Diego Ordonez de Calahorra, to Martin Cortes, son of the famous Hernan Cortes. Translated into English by Margaret Tyler and others between 1578 and 1601, it became exceedingly popular, and there are numberless allusions to characters and incidents. The book (Part I) was to be found in Don Quixote's library.

p. 77. *Sack Posset.* A draught of hot milk with sugar and spices curdled by an infusion of white wine (sack), which was considered highly invigorating and customarily taken on a wedding-night. So in Mrs. Behn's *The Luckey Chance* (Drury Lane, winter of 1686), II, 2, on his wedding-night Sir Feeble Fainwou'd, sharp-set, after the final dance bawls for the posset, "now the Posset; and then—ods bobs, another—— . . . away, Girls, away, and steal the Bride to Bed." The posset was eaten with spoons. See *The Scornful Lady*, II, 1, where Welford, Sir Roger, Martha, and Abigail share a mighty posset, "the full bowl of plenty."

p. 77. *Fee-simple*, *i.e.* Absolute and entire possession. Fee simple is literally an estate in land belonging to the owner and his heirs without let or limitation.

p. 77. *The Courtiers are not so forward to pay their Debts.* Parodied in *The Rehearsal*, III, 1: *Thimble.* I'm sure, Sir, I made your Cloaths, in the Court-fashion, for you never paid me yet. *Bayes.* There's a bob for the Court!

p. 78. *pudder.* A form of pother generally only found in dialect. Cf. Crowne's *Juliana: or, The Princess of Poland*, produced at Lincoln's Inn Fields, 1671; 4to, 1671; I, where the Host says: "Here's a pudder, ho! see if none of my cups, or silver spoons be missing."

p. 78. *Rump Act.* On 10 May, 1650, a very severe and stringent Act was passed against swearing, mulcting the offender in heavy penalties. 30 June, 1654, amongst the Day's Proceedings in Council was

"An Ordinance to empower the Customs' Commissioners and others for the better suppression of drunkenness and profane swearing." 8 January, 1655–6, Major-General Desborow gave further instructions to enforce the laws against swearing, blasphemy, drunkenness. 26 June, 1656, one Martin Holman of Bideford appealed against a conviction under the Act of 10 May, 1650, "made against profane swearing and cursing, being treble costs, he having been sued for goods distrained by force of a warrant upon that Act." See *Domestic State Papers, sub die*.

p. 79. *Fanatick*. A Puritan. This was the usual contemporary meaning of the word. So in the Epilogue to Tatham's Aristophanic comedy *The Rump*, 4to, 1660, we have:

> Let me survey your brows;—they are serene . . .
> So that we do conclude the Author's fear
> Is now remov'd; there's no phanatick here.

p. 79. *against raine*. When it is going to rain the old man's temper is uncertain, as he feels the coming wet-weather in his bones. Thus in Massinger's *The Guardian*, licensed 31 October, 1633, but not printed until 1655, I, 1, Durazzo says:

> I would have you know
> Though I write fifty odd, I do not carry
> An Almanack in my bones to predeclare
> What weather we shall have.

p. 79. *Tables*. Backgammon. Cf. Pepys, Thursday, 21 September, 1665, "after losing a crowne betting at Tables, we walked home."

p. 79. *Cinque and Cater*. Cinque, five; cater (quatre), four, at dice or cards.

p. 79. *Size Ace*. A throw with two dice turning up six and one.

p. 79. *made a blot*. A blot in backgammon (tables) is an exposed piece or man liable to be taken or forfeited. *To hit a blot* or *to make a blot* is to take such a piece. Cf. Wycherley's *Love in a Wood, or St. James Park*, 4to, 1672, V, the penultimate scene where Lydia says: "Yet, if I wou'd be rigorous, though I made the blot, your over-sight has lost the game."

p. 79. *cog a Dye*. A very frequent phrase meaning to direct the fall of the dice fraudulently. To cog the dice is not to load the dice as it has been wrongly explained, but to direct their fall by some sleight of hand. Dr. Johnson (1755) has: "*To cog a die*, to secure it so as to direct its fall; to falsify."

p. 79. *Cocles*. Molluscs, especially *Cardium edule*, common on sandy coasts and much used for food.

p. 79. *Ruffs*. The ruff is the male of a bird of the sandpiper family, his female being the reeve. Ruffs were accounted a great delicacy. So in Shadwell's *The Miser*, produced at the Theatre Royal, January, 1671–2; 4to, 1672; III, James Cook suggests among the dishes for a good supper, "Snipes, Ruffs, Woodcocks." In Wycherley's

The Gentleman Dancing-Master, Dorset Garden, March, 1672; 4to, 1672; I, Mrs. Flirt bespeaks "Some Ruffes" for her supper.

p. 79. *Sirrah.* A term of endearment as applied to a woman. The use is rare. Cf. Fletcher's *The Loyal Subject* (1618), II, where Alinda addresses Petesca as "Sirrah Petesca." Also *The Honest Whore*, I, 1604, the bordel scene where Matheo salutes the punk as "Sirrah Bellafront."

p. 81. *take a little Bibber.* Briscoe's *Key to the Rehearsal* (1704) calls particular attention to this passage as parodied by Buckingham. But the whole scene between Prince Pretty-man and Tom Thimble, the tailor, III, 1, burlesques Failer and Bibber.

p. 81. *questing.* Generally of a hunting dog, to break out into a peculiar bark at the sight of game, to give tongue, to yelp. So also of the noise made by dogs when fawning in pleasurable excitement. Now only in provincial use. Malory, *Morte d'Arthur* (1470–85), IX, xxi: "This lytel brachet . . . lepte upon him and . . . whyned and quested." Cf. also Otway's *The Souldier's Fortune*, produced at Dorset Garden early in 1680, Act IV, where *The Scene opens the middle of the House, and discovers Sir* Jolly Jumble, *and the Lady putting* Beaugard *in order as if he were dead.* Sir Jolly cries: "Ly still, ly still, you Knave, close, close, when I bid you: You had best quest and spoil the sport, you had!"

p. 81. *Woots.* A mincing malapropism for "Wits." Failer, it should be noted, is mightily given to affectations in his speech.

p. 81. *chouse.* The common word for "to cheat," "to swindle." It is said to be derived from *chiaus*, an envoy or special agent of the Sultan. Such an agent had, in 1609, bumfiddled the Turkish and Persian merchants of London out of some £4000.

p. 81. *handsel.* A gift or present (expressive of good wishes) bestowed upon a body who enters some new condition or state; *e.g.* a present given at the New Year. Both substantive and verb are in common use.

p. 81. *Scabbard.* An obscene jest. Scabbard is an indecent slang term, as in Fletcher's *The Chances*, folio, 1647, III, where Don John jeers his old landlady with:

> Worshipful lady,
> How does thy velvet scabbard? . . . now could I willingly . . .
> Venture my body with thee.

Cf. Latin, *Vagina*. In obscænis. Plautus, *Pseudolus*, IV, vii, 84 *sqq.*

> Noctu in vigiliam quando ibat miles, tum tu ibas simul?
> Conveniebatne in vaginam tuam machæra militis?

p. 82. *Livery and Seisin.* "Livery of seisin simply means the delivery of the feudal possession." *Williams on Seisin*, p. 99. Very often used in jesting metaphor. Cf. *The Plain-Dealer*, I, where Jerry says: "Ay, ay, Mother, he wou'd be taking Livery and Seizen of your Jointure." In Mrs. Behn's *The Luckey Chance* (Drury Lane, winter of 1686), III, 2, Sir Feeble Fainwou'd, when asked "And do you think this Marriage lawful, Sir?" replies: "Lawful! it shall be when I have had Livery and Seisin of her Body."

p. 82. *your name had been upon more posts than play-bills.* Dr. W. J. Lawrence, whose chapter *The Origin of the Theatre Programme* should be read (*The Elizabethan Playhouse*, Second Series, 1913, pp. 55–91), is of opinion that the origin of the regular play-bill as poster may be dated about 1560. At first the announcement would be of the briefest, and the Book-holder copied out the few bills required by hand. Yet to be stuck on a street post the bill must be bold if small. Dr. Lawrence cites a long catena of allusions to this custom. In Restoration days, on Tuesday, 24 March, 1662, Pepys writes: "I went to see if any play was acted, and I found none upon the post, being Passion week." Again, Thursday, 28 July, 1664, he notes: "At the office all the morning, dined, after 'Change, at home, and then abroad, and seeing 'The Bondman' upon the posts . . . I went thither. . . . Then I saw it acted."

Apparently there has survived only one complete specimen of a play-bill such as was set upon posts. This was described by Miss Eleanore Boswell, with a facsimile, in *The Library*, March, 1931. It was found among the State Papers Domestic, folio 215, volume III, part 2, and measures 9¼ × 14¼ inches. The Royal Arms and J.R. are on the top. It runs: "At the THEATRE ROYALL this present Tuesday, being the Twenty Second day of February, will be presented, A Play called: A King, and No King Beginning Exact[ly a]t Four of the Clock. [By the]ir MAJESTIES SERVANTS. VIVAT REX." The date must be Tuesday, 22 February, 1687.

The following anecdote of Field, the Elizabethan actor, is well known. "Master Field, the player, riding up Fleet Street a great pace, a gentleman called him and asked him what play was played that day? He (being angry to be stayed upon so frivolous a demand) answered that he might see what play was to be played upon every *post*. I cry you mercy (said the gentleman), I took you for a *post* you rode so fast."

p. 83. *humbles.* Better, Umbles, itself a later form of Numbles. The inwards of a deer or other animal. Cf. Greene, *Friar Bacon and Friar Bungay* (*c.* 1590): "*Lacy.* What have you fit for breakfast? *Margret.* Butter and cheese, and humbles of a deere." But there is also a bawdy bob here, and Failer with a double entendre means the dowsets too.

p. 83. *opinion of thy honesty.* Thy reputation for virtue. So in Shakespeare's *The Merchant of Venice*, I, 1, 91–2, we have "opinion" used in the same sense:

> With purpose to be dress'd in an opinion
> Of wisdom, gravity, profound conceit.

p. 83. *decimated.* In 1655, Cromwell instituted special taxes known as "decimations," being ten per cent of the income of the royalist gentry. The assessment and collections of these taxes were entrusted to the despotic major-generals assisted by gangs of local commissioners. Royalist squires were harried, fined, and dragooned until the gentry fell into direst penury.

In Shadwell's posthumous comedy *The Volunteers; or, The Stock Jobbers*, produced at Drury Lane in the spring of 1693, I, 1, Major-General Blunt, an old Cavalier officer, says: "I have a pretty good Estate, and might have had a Thousand Pound a year more, but that I must . . . run a Cavaliering, and so . . . be Sequestered and Decimated."

p. 84. *rank rider*. Rank=headlong; reckless. Cf. Florio's *Montaigne* (1603), II, xxii (ed. 1632, p. 382): "Sure he was a rancke-runner: for when any river hindred his way he swam it over."

p. 85. *Norfolk pebbles*. Stones of the same kind as rock-crystal, moss-agates, pyreneites, onyx, cornelians and other chalcedonics used in less expensive jewelry. One may compare the Bristol diamonds, which are particles of the quartz in the mountain limestone rocks bordering the Avon below Clifton.

> Hairs curl'd, ears pearl'd with Bristows brave and bryte
> Bought for true diamonds in his false sight.

F. Lenton, *Young Gent^n's Whirligig*, 1629.

p. 85. *Temple-Walkes*. There are innumerable references to the Temple walks, extremely popular as a public promenade and place of general resort. Cf. Pepys, Thursday, 28 May, 1663: "Thence by water home, after we had walked to and fro, backwards and forwards six or seven times in the Temple walks, disputing whether to go by land or water." Otway, *The Souldiers Fortune*, Dorset Garden, 1680, speaks of: "Your Peripatetick Philosophers of the Temple-walks, Rogues in Rags, and yet not honest."

p. 86. *micking*. Oftener "miching." Here, skulking; pettish; sullen. The word which has various shades of meaning is remembered from the Shakespearean "miching mallecho." Cf. *The Noble Gentleman* (licensed 3 February, 1625–6, as by John Fletcher), I, 1, where Longueville says: "O my miching varlet—I'll fit ye as I live."

p. 86. *King Midas Face*. Fool's face. Since King Midas, when Apollo and Pan contended before him on the lyre and the pipe, decided in favour of Pan, and for his stupidity his ears were changed by Apollo into a donkey's great souses. *Auriculas asini Mida rex habet*, wrote Persius in the original draft of his first Satire, l. 121. Midas is often used as meaning a nincompoop. Cf. Pope, *Dunciad* (1728), III, 324:

> Our Midas sits Lord Chancellor of Plays!

p. 86. *Poeta coquus*. The "heathen Philosopher" is Athenæus, and in his vast work Δειπνοσοφισταί we have the ultimate source of this phrase:

> Οὐδὲν ὁ μάγειρος τοῦ ποιητοῦ διαφέρει.

This is line 15 of a 16 line quotation which Athenæus makes from Euphron, one of the New Comedy writers about the beginning of the third century B.C. The reference in Athenæus is Book I, 7 *sq.* The Latin translations extant in Dryden's day hardly set *poeta* and *coquus* in actual juxtaposition, but Dryden was, we know, not very careful in his quotations. The Latin version of Natalis de Comitibus (Natalis Comes), Venice, 1536, p. 3, col. 1, has ". . . nihil differt pœta nam coquus." That of Jacques Dalechamp (or Dalechamps or d'Alechamp), Jacobus Dalechampius, reprinted in Casaubon's edition, 1597, is "A poëta nihil sane differt coquus." Dalechamp's Latin translation appeared first in 1583, and Casaubon's edition containing it was reprinted in 1612 and 1657. Hugo Grotius translates the Greek passage in his "Excerpta ex Tragœdiis et Comœdiis Græcis, tum quæ exstant tum quæ perierunt: Emendata et Latinis versibus reddita" (Paris, 1626) on p. 686:

Nihil à Poëta scilicet differt coquus.

The story in the extract from Euphron is how Nicomedes, King of Bithynia, when twelve days' journey from the sea and in the middle of winter was seized with a longing for an anchovy (or sardine—or whatever fish an ἀφύη is), and how his cook Soterides made an artificial anchovy out of chopped turnip boiled and seasoned which the king ate with high commendations. The account ends:

οὐδὲν ὁ μάγειρος τοῦ ποιητοῦ διαφέρει
ὁ νοῦς γὰρ ἐστιν ἑκατέρῳ τούτων τέχνη.

The actual combination *Pœta coquus* does not seem to appear. Schweighäuser in his elaborate edition in 14 vols. of Athenæus refers to no such place, and J. E. Sandys in his *History of Classical Scholarship*, II, 396, says of Schweighäuser's notes to Athenæus that they "invariably give proof of extensive reading, and are characterised by the minutest accuracy."

For the poetry of the cuisine one may remember the French cook in *Pendennis*.

p. 87. *Planet-strook.* Blasted by the malign influence of an adverse star; utterly bewildered. "They being affrighted (as it were Planet-struck) and confounded with shame." Bromhall, *Treatise of Specters*, 1658. Cf. Charles Cotton's *Burlesque upon Burlesque (the Scoffer Scoff'd)*, Sixth Edition, 1741, *Venus and Cupid*, p. 243:

But, like *an Aspen-leaf I shook*,
And star'd, as I'd been Planet-struck.

p. 87. *a Person of such worth, and all that.* Failer's expressions are constantly burlesqued in *The Rehearsal* by Bayes, who continually repeats "Persons"; "Igad"; "I vow to Gad"; "—and all that." Briscoe's *Key to the Rehearsal* (1704) draws particular attention to this passage in *The Wild Gallant*.

p. 88. *Pax on't.* Failer's mincing pronunciation should be noticed. Cf. Duffett's *Psyche Debauch'd* (4to, 1678), I: "a pax take ye." Later this affectation became one of the marks of the full-blown exquisite, as Vanbrugh's Lord Foppington.

p. 88. *weak to Balthazar. The Spanish Tragedy*, I, II, 162–3.

> And in that conflict was Andrea slain:
> Brave man at arms, but weak to Balthazar.

The Spanish Tragedy, reprinted as late as 1633, was seen by Pepys at the Nursery on Monday, 24 February, 1667–8. It seems from Dryden's quip that an audience in the earlier years after the Restoration would still take an allusion to this evergreen melodrame.

p. 88. *Heaven reward you.* A parody of the famous words which tradition tells were spoken by Queen Elizabeth to Catherine, Countess of Nottingham, who had withheld the ring entrusted to her by Essex. All modern authorities agree in rejecting the story.

p. 89. *Fanatick times.* During the Commonwealth. Fanatic was a very general word in the latter half of the seventeenth century. It was invariably applied to the Puritans and Nonconformists, and always in a hostile or derisive sense. It is thus used by Archbishop Maxwell as early as 1644, and Fuller in his *Mixt Contemplations* (1660) has: "A new word coined, within few months, called fanatics . . . seemeth well . . . proportioned to signify . . . the sectaries of our age."

p. 90. *O, these little mischiefs.* Cf. *As You Like It*, V, I: "It is meat and drink to me to see a clown."

p. 90. *Damætas.* A well-known character in Sidney's *Arcadia*, which, begun in 1580, appeared after the author's death, *The Countesse of Pembrokes Arcadia, written by Sir Philippe Sidnei*, London, 4to, 1590. No less than fourteen editions were issued by 1674, and the demand for this romance continued unabated. Sidney found numberless imitators, abbreviators, and continuators. In 1725 was published folio, London, *Sir Philip Sidney's Arcadia*, modernized by Mrs. [D.] Stanley. Abstracts and chap-books were popular as late as 1788. Damoetas is described as "one *Dametas*, the most arrant doltish clowne" (I, 3). This "loutish clowne" had "the voice of one that plaieth *Hercules* in a play" and he looked "like an Ape that had newly taken a purgation" (I, 13). Hence the name became proverbial for a rustic lob.

p. 92. *The Devil a cross that I have.* A cross was so frequently stamped upon coins that the word came to mean a piece of money. So in Heywood's *The Wise Woman of Hogsdon*, 4to, 1638 (but much earlier), I, I, Sencer the gamester says: "I will not leave myself one cross to bless me." So Charles Cotton, *Vergil Travestie*, IV:

> A wand'ring Beggar hither driven;
> Who had, when weak as he could crawl,
> No Cross to bless himself withal.

The landlady in *The Vicar of Wakefield*, 1766, c.XXI, was driving the penniless Olivia out of doors and abusing her roundly with: "You trumpery, to come and take up an honest house without cross or coin to bless yourself with; come along, I say."

p. 93. *Ombre*. The word is derived from the Spanish *hombre* =man. This card game, introduced into England by Queen Catherine of Braganza, long remained immensely fashionable, and in some circles has not been forgotten even to-day. There are numberless allusions, but the *locus classicus* is Pope's *Rape of the Lock*, Canto III, where

> *Belinda* now, whom Thirst of Fame invites,
> Burns to encounter two adventrous Knights,
> At *Ombre* singly to decide their Doom.

p. 94. *Sacrific'd to the god of Laughter*. See the account of the hoax played on Lucius to celebrate the festival of "deus Risus," Apuleius, *Metamorphoses*, Bk. III, ch. 1–11. But the words in Dryden seem to point to a secondary source, namely the section in Burton's *Anatomy of Melancholy* headed *Lectori malè feriato*, which comes after his introductory "Democritus to the Reader." In *Lectori malè feriato* (which is written in Latin) comes the phrase ". . . addo etiam, et *Deo Risui* te sacrificabit."

p. 95. *Woodcock*. The woodcock was proverbial for stupidity. Perhaps there is a reminiscence here of Polonius in *Hamlet*, I, 3: "Ay, springes to catch woodcocks."

p. 98. *wannion*. A mischief; a vengeance. A vulgar term. Cf. *Pericles*, II, where the First Fisherman bawls out to his man: "Come away, or I'll fetch thee with a wannion!"

p. 99. *squorn*. A dialect form of "scorn." Folio, 1701, reads "skorn."

p. 99. *Steeple-hat*. The high-crowned hat came into use early in the reign of Queen Elizabeth, and after having been fashionable for a while fell out of favour, but was still worn by citizens' wives and Puritans. In Hollar's *Ornatus Muliebris Anglicanus*, 1643, there are several plates showing the steeple-hat, a distinctive feature of the Puritan wife and city dame's costume. The court lady wears a snood. The steeple-hat persisted even after the Restoration, but the term as employed here is one of double reproach, implying that Frances is a mere citizen's wife and a Puritan to boot.

p. 99. *Prince Pericles*. *Pericles, Prince of Tyre*, was one of the dramas exclusively allotted to Sir William D'Avenant, and not allowed to be acted by Killigrew's company. Betterton appeared as Pericles at the Cockpit in earliest Restoration days, and apparently the play was a popular favourite for some three or four years, after which it fell out of the theatrical repertory.

p. 99. *wrought Tabby*. Tabby is silk taffeta, originally a striped taffeta, but afterwards any watered silk came under this designation. Cf. J. Davies' translation of Adamus Olearius, *Voyages and travells of the Ambassadors*, folio, 1669: "One piece of silver'd taby with flowers of Gold."

p. 100. *turn me out of dores*. This was a jest of the Blessed Thomas More, who when committed to the Tower on 18 April, 1534, said merrily to Sir Thomas Walsingham, the Lieutenant, upon receiving his apology for so strait a lodging, "If I complain of your cheer, good Master Lieutenant, all I ask is that you presently turn me out of doors."

p. 101. *Table set*. Dr. W. J. Lawrence, *The Origin of the English Picture-Stage*, *The Elizabethan Playhouse*, Second Series, 1913, pp. 140–1, quotes this scene as an example "of the nature of the stage on which [*The Wild Gallant*] was originally acted," *i.e.* the Vere Street "platform" stage, adorned with tapestries and not yet with scenery.

p. 102. *lift, lift*. Cut for deal.

p. 102. *Quint-Major*. In piquet, the ace, king, queen, knave, and ten of a suit.

p. 102. *Sixieme Major*. In piquet a sequence of six cards, the ace, king, queen, knave, ten, and nine of a suit. Cf. Cotton, *Compleat Gamester* (1674): "You must reckon for a Sixiesm."

p. 103. *Mittimus*. A warrant of commitment to prison. Cf. Duffett's *The Mock-Tempest;* 4to, 1675; III, where Stephania bawls out: "Make his *Mittimus*, before he answers, and send him to *Tyburn*."

p. 103. *Nine-pins, or Shovel-board*. In *The Country-Wife*, III, 1, Margery Pinchwife, longing for town pleasures, envies the London Ladies who "I warrant you, play at nine Pins every day of the week, so they do."

Shovel-board was a game in which a coin, a counter, or some other disk was driven by a smart blow with the hand along a highly polished board or table marked with transverse lines. Cf. Shadwell's *The Miser* (1672), III, 1: "He has already lost his *Edward* Shillings that he kept for Shovel-board." Among the Herbert documents is a License for the "use of one Shovelbord." (*Dramatic Records*, edited by T. Q. Adams, 1917, p. 131.)

p. 103. *Swear'st thou, ungracious Boy?* I *Henry IV*, II, iv.

p. 103. *Lady Du Lake*. The title "Lady" was humorously given to notorious bawds. Cf. Pepys, Saturday, 22 September, 1660: "He told me how the pretty woman that I always loved at the beginning of Cheapside that sells child's coats was served by the Lady Bennett (a famous strumpet)." Also Saturday, 30 May, 1668: "Here I first understood by their talk the meaning of the company that lately were called Ballers; Harris telling me how it was by a meeting of some young blades, where he was among them, and my Lady Bennett and her ladies; and their there dancing naked, and all the roguish things in the world." Wycherley with completest irony dedicates *The Plain-Dealer*, 4to, 1676, to this procuress, "To my Lady B——." *The Tatler*, 84, speaks of her as "the celebrated Madam Bennett."

p. 105. *St. Luknors Lane . . . Dog and Bitch Yard . . . Sodom.* All these were localities of the lowest description, infamous for their stews and kips. Lewknor's Lane afterwards became Charles Street, now rechristened Macklin Street, running out of Drury Lane on the east side, nearly opposite Short's Gardens. It was so named after Sir Lewis Lewknor, one of the Masters of Ceremonies of James I. This knight resided hard by in Drury Lane, and the street became known after him before the end of the reign of Charles I, by which time the estate had begun to be covered with small houses and tenements, all of which soon acquired a most evil reputation. Butler speaks of:

> The nymphs of chaste *Diana's* train
> The same with those of *Lewknor's Lane.*

As late as *The Beggar's Opera*, produced 29 January, 1728, at Lincoln's Inn Fields, the Drawer in reply to Macheath, who has dispatched the porter for his trulls, makes answer: "I expect him back every minute. But you know, sir, you sent him as far as Hockley-in-the-Hole for three of the ladies, for one in Vinegar Yard, and for the rest of them somewhere about Lewknor's Lane." It was in Lewknor's Lane that Jonathan Wild, amongst his other activities, kept a bagnio which was presided over by one Jane Sprackley.

William Boghurst in his "*Loimographia:* Or an Experimentall Relation of the Plague," 1666, writes: "Of all the common hackney prostitutes of Lutener's Lane, Dog Yard, Cross Lane, Baldwin's Gardens, Hatton Garden, and other places; the common criers of oranges, oysters, fruit, etc.; all the impudent, drunken, drabbing bayles and fellows, and many others of the Rouge Route, there are few missing."

The Poor Whores Petition, a "libertine libel" addressed to Lady Castlemaine and printed in 1668, upon the occasion of a 'prentice riot when many brothels were pulled down and sacked, concludes: "Signed by Us, *Madam Cresswell* and *Damaris Page*, in the behalf of our Sisters and Fellow-Sufferers (in this day of our Calamity) in *Dog and Bitch Yard, Lukeners Lane, Saffron-Hill, Moor-fields, Chiswell-Street, Rosemary-Lane, Nightingale-Lane, Ratcliffe-Highway, Well-close, Church-lane, East-Smithfield,* &c., this present 25th day of March, 1668."

In *The Kind Keeper; or, Mr. Limberham*, produced at Dorset Garden, March, 1677–8, Mrs. Tricksy's mother is said to have been "a Semstress in *Dog* and *Bitch-Yard.*"

Mol Medlar in *The Cheaters Cheated* (*Royal Arbour of Loyal Poesie*, T. Jordan, 1664) sings:

> Farewell *Bloomsberry* and *Sodom,*
> *Lukeners-Lane* and *Turnbull-street,*
> Woe was me when first I trod 'em
> With my wilde unwary feet.

Turnbull-street, Clerkenwell, from Elizabethan days was one of the lowest quarters of the town.

p. 107. *Grandam and Aunt gold.* Old hoarded wealth. *The Dictionary of the Canting Crew* gives: "*Grannam-gold*, old Hoarded Coin." Cf. *Juvenalis Redivivus*, 4to, 1683, p. 17: "*Grannums* old Gold from *Satin* Purse is brought." So in *Skialetheia*, 1598, we have grandam =obsolete. "Some blame deep *Spencer* for his grandam words," *Satire* VI. Dryden in the Preface to the *Fables*, 1700, writes of those scholars, "who, because they understand *Chaucer* would . . . hoord him up, as Misers do their Grandam Gold." One may compare Shadwell's *The Miser*, acted at the Theatre Royal, January 1671–2, III, 1, where Timothy Squeeze has fallen among sharpers, and Cheatly reports: "Mrs. *Joyce* . . . perswaded him to play with *Hazard* at Backgammon, and he has already lost his *Edward* Shillings that he kept for Shovel-board, and was pulling out Broad-pieces (that have not seen the Sun these many Years) when I came away." With "Grandam" one may also compare the transferred adjectival use of *anus*. Catullus has *carta anus*, LXVIII, 46; and LXXVIII, 10, *fama anus*. Martial, I, 106, has *testa anus*. Ciris, 41, *Nostra tuum senibus loqueretur pagina sæclis*, imitates Catullus. Martial often uses *senex* in this way, *senes mulli* (X, xxx, 24); *senibus dulcior cygnis* (V, xxxvii, 1); *fragrat testa senibus autumnis* (III, lviii, 7). Æschylus, fr. 323, Nauck, has γέρον γράμμα; Theocritus, VII, 17, γέρων πέπλος; *Odyssey*, XXII, 184, γέρον σάκος; Sophocles, *Oedipus Coloneus*, 1259, γέρων πίνος.

p. 108. *gemini.* Often corrupted to *Leminy* or *Lemine*, a mild expression or petty oath childishly used by the innocent and vulgar. Cf. Otway's *The Souldier's Fortune*, produced at Dorset Garden in the spring of 1679–80, when Sir Jolly cries out: "Gemini! What would become of me?" In *The Country-Wife*, Theatre Royal, January 1674–5, Mrs. Pinchwife exclaims: "O Jeminy!" Also *The London Cuckolds*, II, when Peggy, a silly young country girl, upon being told that all London cannot be seen in a week, exclaims: "O Leminy! not in a week, Aunt."

p. 108. *quops.* "To quop" is a later form of "to quap"=to throb, flutter, palpitate. This is one of Dryden's favourite words. Cf. *The Kind Keeper; or, Mr. Limberham*, produced at Dorset Garden, March, 1677–8, Act III, where Mrs. Saintly cries: "Oh, my Eyes grow dim! My Heart quops and my Back aketh!" Also Act IV: *Mrs. Termagant*. What mads me most I carry a Bastard of the Rogue's in my Belly: And now he turns me off, and will not own it. *Mrs. Overdon*. Lord, how it quops! You are half a Year gone, Madam— [*Laying her Hand on her Belly.*] A ballad *Duke of Monmouth*, 1681, has:

His great Heart quops, his Courage fails.

p. 108. *Jacobus's.* Jacobus was the current but not official name of a gold coin struck in the reign of James I. Originally issued in 1603, it was a sovereign of value 20/–, but in 1604 the Unite was issued and the sovereign became worth 22/–

p. 109. *a Glass-Coach, and six Flanders Mares.* No doubt Pope remembered this when he wrote:

> The gods to curse *Pamela* with her prayers,
> Gave the gilt coach and dappled *Flanders* Mares.
> *Moral Essays.* Epistle IX (to Martha Blunt), 49, 50.

p. 109. *had into the dark and cur'd.* On 25 November, 1786, there was produced at Drury Lane a comedy by Mrs. Hannah Cowley (1743–1809) *A School for Greybeards; or, The Mourning Bride* (4to, 1786 and 1787). The best things in it are borrowed from Mrs. Behn's excellent *The Luckey Chance; or, An Alderman's Bargain.* The audience took needless exception to Mrs. Cowley's harmless play, and certain expressions were altered on the second night. In Act V, 4, Alexis says to Viola: "As for you, Madam, bread and water, and a dark chamber shall be your lot——" But Sebastian (Bannister, jun.), who has married Viola, breaks in, crying: "No, Sir,—I am the arbiter of her lot; however, I confirm half your punishment; and a dark chamber she shall certainly have." Which seems an echo of Dryden. To this speech in the quarto Mrs. Cowley appends the following note: "This is the expression, I am told, which had nearly prov'd fatal to the Comedy. I should not have printed it, but from the resolution I have religiously kept, of restoring every thing that was objected to." So occult is the obscenity that myself by no exercise of imagination can I grasp it.

p. 109. *brace of Angels.* The Angel was a gold coin stamped with a device of S. Michael piercing the dragon. It was last coined by Charles I. It varied in value, but usually stood at about 10s. There are innumerable allusions and puns.

p. 109. *Canonical hour.* Cf. *The Country-Wife*, IV, 1, where Sparkish says to Alithea: "Come, my dearest, pray let us go to Church before the Canonical hour is past": and later, "Come, Madam, 'tis e'ne twelve a Clock, and my Mother charg'd me never to be married out of the Canonical hours." Also *The Way of the World,* I: *Mirabell. Betty*, what says your Clock? *Betty.* Turn'd of the last Canonical Hour, Sir. *Mirabell.* How pertinently the Jade answers me! Ha! almost one a Clock!

p. 110. *Braines enough, if they were butter'd.* Cf. *The Merry Wives of Windsor*, III, 5: "Well, if I be served such another trick, I'll have my brains ta'en out, and buttered, and give them to a dog for a new year's gift."

p. 110. *Busk.* A Busk is "a strip of wood, whalebone, steel or other rigid material passed down the front of a corset and used to stiffen and support it." O.E.D., which quotes, *inter alia*, 1688, R. Holme, *Armoury*, III, 94/2: "A Busk . . . is a strong piece of Wood, or Whalebone thrust down the middle of the Stomacker." A poem,

On a Juniper-Tree, cut down to make Busks, is found in the Antwerpen edition of Rochester, 1680, and in the various reprints. It is also printed amongst Mrs. Behn's Poems. See the edition by the present writer, vol. VI, p. 148, and notes, p. 422.

p. 110. *these Hangings*. The tapestries with which the stage was hung. This passage indicates the nature of the theatre where *The Wild Gallant* was originally produced, *i.e.* Vere Street, a "platform" stage. See the quotation from Dr. W. J. Lawrence's *The Origin of the English Picture-Stage*.

p. 111. *a man with Childe*. See the Introduction.

p. 112. *the party that own'd the Water was with Child*. Cf. *Henry IV*, Part II, I, 2: "He said, sir, the water itself was a good healthy water, but, for the party that owned it, he might have more diseases than he knew for."

p. 113. *bleak*. Pale and sickly. Forby, *Norfolk and Suffolk Words* (1840), says: "*Bleak* is still used in Norfolk to signify pale and sickly."

p. 113. *look*. Expect (to be delivered).

p. 113. *Directory . . . Scotch Kivenant*. *The Directory of Worship*, compiled by the Westminster Assembly of Divines, was drawn up to replace *The Book of Common Prayer*, forbidden during the years of the Great Rebellion.

The Solemn League and Covenant was initiated by Knox, and subscribed in December, 1557, for the express purpose of the overthrow of the Catholic Faith in Scotland. In the spring of 1638, following upon the riots which broke out at the introduction of the new Service Book in Edinburgh, the National Covenant was prepared and signed to bind all to the Reformed Kirk, that is to say Presbyterianism.

p. 115. *bowl must be well byassed*. The bias is the construction or form of the bowl imparting an oblique motion, and a well bias'd bowl is one thus perfectly constructed. The rub is "an obstacle or impediment by which a bowl is hindered in, or diverted from its proper course." These metaphors from bowls are exceedingly common. Cf. *The Old Batchelour*, acted January, 1693, I, 1, where Bellmour says: "Business is the rub of Life, perverts our Aim, casts off the Bias, and leaves us wide and short of the intended Mark."

p. 117. *promis'd him golden Mountains*. Cf. Terence, *Phormio*, 68, "modo non montis auri pollicens." S. Jerome adversum Rufinum, III, 39, has: "cum montes aureos pollicitus fueris." A German proverb, "Einene goldene Berge versprechen," is quoted by A. Otto, *Sprichwörter . . . der Römer*.

p. 117. *tantivy*. As an adverb=at full gallop; headlong. Grose, *Dictionary Vulgar Tongue* has: "Away they went tantwivy; away they went at full speed." Cf. Brome, *A Joviall Crew*, acted at the Cockpit, Drury Lane, in 1641, IV, 1, where Randall says: "Skife out this away, and skife out that away (He's no *Snayle* I assure you). And *Tantivy* all the country over."

p. 119. *scow'ring*. The word is here used in a double sense. To scour was to rampage the streets, breaking windows, assaulting passers-by, beating the watch, etc. This is a very early use. Shadwell has an excellent comedy, *The Scowrers*, produced at Drury Lane in the late winter of 1690, 4to, 1691, which gives a most realistic picture of these blackguardly fellows.

To scour has another sense, glanced at here=*futuere*.

p. 119. *Tiffany*. A kind of thin silk gauze. Cf. Philemon Holland's *Plinie*, XI, 22: "The invention of that fine silke, tiffanie, sarcenet, and cypres, which instead of apparell to cover and hide, shew women naked through them." In Mrs. Behn's *The Forc'd Marriage*, Lincoln's Inn Fields, December, 1670; 4to, 1671; we have, IV, 8: "*Enter* Erminia *veil'd with a thin Tiffany*."

p. 120. *turn her Girdle too on t'other side?* To turn one's girdle is to find a harmless outlet for anger or baffled revenge. Cf. *Much Ado About Nothing*, V, 1, 1599: *Prince*. I thinke he be angrie indeede. *Claudio*. If he be, he knowes how to turne his girdle. Ray, *Proverbs*, has: "If you be angry, you may turn the buckle of your girdle behind you."

p. 120. *Hans en Kelder*. Literally Jack-in-the-Cellar, *i.e.*, the unborn babe in the womb. The expression is a favourite with Dryden, and is not uncommon elsewhere. Cf. *A Westminster Wedding . . . Feb.* 17, 1679 (*Poems on State Affairs*, III, 1704, p. 193):

> There's somewhat more that *George* has got,
> (For *Trevor* left him who knows what)
> A Teeming Lady-Wife, nay more,
> A *Hansenkelder* got before.

p. 120. *Tympany*. A tympany is a tumour, or more generally any morbid swelling. The word was in common use from the sixteenth to the eighteenth century, and is often employed figuratively of being puffed up with pride.

p. 122. *the hairy Woman*. Anna Macallame, born in the Orkneys in 1615. This woman in October, 1662, was brought to London, and shown at Court to the King. An engraved portrait of her was published about the same time. She is represented in a fur cap and a man's gown; her beard is very large and flowing like that of an old man. Under the picture are the lines:

> Tho' my portraicture seemes to be
> A man's, my sex denies me so,
> Nature has still variety
> To make the world her wisdom know.

See further Granger's *Biographical History*, ed. 1824, Vol. VI, p. 23.

Another "hairy Woman" who was exhibited in London and much talked of as a curiosity at this period was Barbara Vanbeck.

This unfortunate female was born at Augsburg in 1629, being the daughter of Balthasar and Anna Urselerin. Her face, not unlike that of a monkey, and her hands were covered with hair, and her chin was decked with a very long and loosely spreading beard. One Michael Vanbeck married her in order that he might exhibit her throughout the chief cities of Europe. They were in London for many years, and perhaps remained there permanently. At any rate her "lively portraicture" was published in 1653, *Isaac Buen del et sculp*, and this was re-issued in 1658. She is represented as playing upon a harpsichord. Upon an extant example of the 1658 portrait is inscribed: "This woman I sawe in Ratcliffe Highway in the yeare 1668 and was satisfied she was a woman. John Bulfinch."

p. 122. *a stone-Priest.* This combination is usually of an animal, *e.g.* stone-ram, stone-ass, stone-colt, and meaning "not gelt," since the stones =the testicles. And so "lasciviously rampant." Cf. *The Merry Devil of Edmonton* (1608), IV, 1: "The stone Priest steales more venisonthan half the county." In*Bartholomew Fair* (acted in 1614), III, 2, Knock-hum cries: "Fine ambling Hypocrites! and a Stone-Puritan."

p. 122. *panck.* A dialect word: here, to heave. The *English Dialect Dictionary* has a number of quotations from local glossaries where pank=pant, heave. "How that old dog panks under the table"; "Jist heark how he do pank and blow."

p. 123. *in Diana's Grove.* The allusion is to Suckling's play *Aglaura*, produced at the Blackfriars in the Christmas of 1637, and shortly afterwards at Court; folio, 1638. This commences, Actus I. Scœna 1. *Enter* Iolas, Iolina.

> *Iolas.* Married! and in Diana's grove.
> *Iolina.* So was th'appointment, or my senses deceived me.
> *Iolas.* Married!
> Now by those powers that tie those pretty knots,
> Tis very fine: good faith, 'tis wondrous fine.
> . . . .
> Diana's grove?
> *Iolina.* Yes, Diana's grove.

The point of Isabelle's quotation is that in *Aglaura* Prince Thersames and Aglaura are secretly married in the grove during a royal hunting-party, whilst all others are engaged in their venery.

p. 124. *a trick to catch the old one.* A proverbial expression, which Middleton has used as the title of a capital comedy, *A Trick to Catch the Old One*, 4to, 1608. Cf. Day's *Isle of Gulls*, 4to, 1606, II: "We are in the way to catch the Old One."

p. 124. *Vintners feed.* To feed is a technical term meaning to give body to a liquor. O.E.D. quotes *London and Country Review*, 1742: "Receipts for feeding, fining, and preserving Malt-Liquor."

p. 126. *Leanders Destiny.* Leander was drowned on a stormy night in the Hellespont as he was swimming from Abydos to Sestus where his mistress Hero lived.

p. 127. *Salvages.* This obsolete form of Savage is found in Gower, and persisted for several centuries. Thus in Tate and Brady's version (1696) of the *Psalms*, vii, 2, we have:

> " Lest, like a salvage Lion he
> My helpless Soul devour."

p. 127. *writ of ease.* A certificate of discharge from employment. Cf. the Epilogue to *All for Love; or, The World well Lost,* 4to, 1678:

> *He does his best; and if he cannot please,*
> *Wou'd quietly sue out his* Writ of Ease.

p. 127. *like Vests.* On Monday, 8 October, 1666, Pepys notes: "The King hath yesterday in Council declared his resolution of setting a fashion for clothes, which he will never alter. It will be a vest, I know not well how." On the following Saturday, 13 October, the diarist saw the Duke of York "dress himself and try on his vest, which is the King's new fashion, and will be in it for good and all on Monday next, and the whole Court." Under 18 October, Evelyn writes: "To Court. It being the first time his Majesty put himself solemnly into the Eastern fashion of vest, changing doublet, stiff collar, bands and cloak, into a comely dress, after the Persian mode . . . resolving never to alter it, and to leave the French mode, which had hitherto obtained to our great expense and reproach. I had some time before presented an invective against that unconstancy, and one so much affecting the French fashion, to his Majesty, in which I took occasion to describe the comeliness and usefulness of the Persian clothing, in the very manner his Majesty now clad himself. This pamphlet I entitled *Tyrannus, or the Mode*, and gave it to the King to read." *Tyrannus, or the Mode; in a Discourse of Sumptuary Laws* was published 8vo, 1661.

Pepys, 15 October, 1666, describes the King's vest as "a very fine and handsome garment." Two days later he notes "The Court is all full of vests." It was said that Louis XIV "in defiance to the King of England, caused all his footmen to be put into vests, and that the noblemen of France will do the like." In *The Character of a Trimmer* ("Miscellanies by the Marquis of Halifax," 1704, p. 164) it is stated "that one of the instructions Madame brought along with her was to laugh us out of those vests, which she performed so effectually, that in a moment, like so many footmen who had quitted their master's livery, we all took it again, and returned to our old service" the French mode. Henrietta, Duchess of Orleans, was at Dover in May, 1670.

EXPLANATORY NOTES

THE RIVAL LADIES

p. 129. *Nos haec novimus esse nihil.* Martial XIII, ii, 8. Andrew Amos in his *Martial and the Moderns* (Cambridge, 1858, p. 39), points out that "the expression *nos haec novimus esse nihil* has been urged by several modern writers by way of a modest apology for the trivial nature of some of their compositions." He mentions that it is the motto of *Spectator* No. 158 (by Steele) and of Paul Whitehead's poem on boxing, the *Gymnasiad* (1744).

p. 133. *Roger Earl of Orrery.* 1621–79. Baron Broghill, third son of Richard Boyle, first Earl of Cork. Much of his life was spent in Ireland. Having helped to promote the Restoration and to secure Ireland for the King, he was created Earl of Orrery on 5 September, 1660. He resided in Ireland as Lord President of Munster until 1668, when he resigned all active duties owing to a quarrel with the Lord-Lieutenant, the Duke of Ormonde. An interesting figure in literature, he is best remembered by his heroic plays, *Henry V*, *Mustapha*, *The Black Prince.* His also is a brocaded romance of the school of Madeleine de Scudéry, *Parthenissa*, folio, 1654. "'Tis handsome language," said Dorothy Osborne, "you would know it to be writ by a person of good quality though you were not told it."

p. 134. *Xenophon.* It is true that the *Cyropaedia* (Κυροπαιδεία) of Xenophon the Athenian might be termed a political romance, the basis of which is a panegyric of Cyrus, founder of the Persian monarchy, but it has no historical authority. The allusion here, however, is rather to the *Ephesiaca, or the Loves of Anthia and Abrocomas*, 'Εφεσιακὰ τα κατα 'Ανθίαν καὶ 'Αβροκόμην, of Xenophon the Ephesian. The Greek original was first printed in 1726, but it had long been known. Poliziano in his *Liber Miscellaneorum*, LI, "Cur in Ephesiae Dianae templo molles appellati honores a Martiale," has several references: "Possumus item ad pompam referre, de qua Xenophon Ephesius in primo Ephesiacorum scribit. . . . Sic utique Xenophon scribit, non quidem Atheniensis ille, sed alter eo non insuavior Ephesius."

For Augustus Caesar see Suetonius, *Caesar Augustus*, 85: Unus liber exstat scriptus ab eo [Augusto] hexametris versibus . . . Exstat alter aeque modicus *Epigrammatum*, quae fere tempore balnei meditabatur. Nam tragoediam magno impetu exorsus, non succedenti stilo, abolevit: quaerentibusque amicis quidnam Aiax ageret? respondit Aiacem suum in spongiam incubuisse."

p. 134. *fit of the Gout.* In the *State Letters of the Earl of Orrery*, folio, 1742, is a Memoir of Orrery, by his chaplain Morrice, who has occasion to mention a letter directed to the Earl in Ireland by King Charles.

Morrice says that he himself had seen this letter, "and in the conclusion his majesty lets him know, he was very well pleased with that part of the Black Prince he had sent him, and conjured his lordship to go on and complete it, which if he could not do, until he had a fit of the gout, he wished him a fit presently, that he might the sooner finish it," (p. 39). In the Preface to Orrery's collected *Dramatic Works*, 2 vols., 1739, there is a reference to his scenes written when he was "labouring under the Torments and Anguish of the Gout."

p. 134. *and in Torment*. Plutarch, *De Defectu Oraculorum*, LI, tells of the agony and death of one of the Delphic Sibyls: "Κατέβη μεν εἰς τὸ μαντεῖον ὥς φασιν ἄκουσα καὶ ἀπρόθυμος, εὐθὺς δὲ περὶ τὰς πρώτας ἀποκρίσεις ἦν καταφανὴς τῇ τραχύτητι τῆς φωνῆς οὐκ ἀναφέρουσα δίκην νεὼς ἐπειγομένης ἀλάλου καὶ κακοῦ πνεύματος οὖσα πλήρης· τέλος δὲ παντάπασιν ἐκταραχθεῖσα καὶ μετὰ κραυγῆς ἀσήμου καὶ φοβιρᾶς φερομένη πρὸς τὴν ἔξοδον ἔρριψεν ἑαυτήν, ὥστε φυγεῖν μὴ μόνον τους θεοπρόπους ἀλλὰ καὶ τὸν προφήτην Νίκανδρον καὶ τοὺς παρόντας τῶν ὁσίων. ἀνείλοντο μέντοι μετὰ μικρὸν αὐτὴν εἰσελθόντες ἔμφρονα καὶ διεβίωσεν ὀλίγας ἡμεράς." Dryden probably had in mind Vergil's description of the inspired Sibyl, Æneid, VI, 77–80:

> At Phoebi nondum patiens immanis in antro
> bacchatur vates, magnum si pectore possit
> excusisse deum: tanto magis ille fatigat
> os rabidum, fera corda domans, fingitque premendo.

For further details see the special treatises on the Delphic oracle, such as H. Piotrowski, *De gravitate Oraculi Delphici*, Lipsiae, 1829; W. Götte, *Das Delphische Orakel*, &c., Leipzig, 1839; A. Mommsen, *Delphica*, Leipzig, 1878, and many other particular monographs.

p. 135. *That miserable Rhetorician . . . who solemnly Declaim'd before Hannibal of the Conduct of Armies, and the Art of War*. Phormio, a peripatetic philosopher. When Hannibal, after being driven from Carthage, came to King Antiochus at Ephesus, he was induced to attend a lecture by Phormio, who held forth for several hours on the subject of the duties of a commander-in-chief and the art of war. At the end Hannibal was asked what he thought of the philosopher, and said that he had seen many old dotards, but none who doted worse than Phormio.

The story is in Cicero's *De Oratore*, ii, 18, 75.

Catulus, one of the speakers in the dialogue, is saying that he has no need for some learned Greek who has never seen a law-court to give him stock precepts on rhetoric:

. . "ut Peripateticus ille dicitur Phormio, cum Hannibal Carthagine expulsus Ephesum ad Antiochum venisset exsul proque eo, quod eius nomen erat magna apud omnis gloria, invitatus esset ab hospitibus suis, ut eum quem dixi, si vellet, audiret; cumque is se non nolle dixisset, locutus esse dicitur homo copiosus aliquot horas de imperatoris officio et de re militari. Tum, cum ceteri, qui illum audierant, vehementer essent delectati, quaerebant ab Hannibale, quidnam ipse de illo philosopho iudicaret: hic Poenus non optime Graece, sed tamen libere respondisse fertur, multos se deliros senes saepe vidisse, sed qui magis, quam Phormio deliraret, vidisse neminem."

A. S. Wilkins in a note on this passage in his edition of the *De Oratore* writes, "Nothing further is known of this man [Phormio]" and mentions that Stobaeus, *Florilegium*, 54, tells a similar story, that Hannibal heard a stoic maintaining that the wise man [=the ideal stoic sage] alone had a knowledge of generalship, and burst out laughing, as he thought that no man could have knowledge of such matters if he had no practical experience of them.

James Howell, *Familiar Letters*, Bk. IV (1st published 1655), xxxix, has: "But why do I write to you of patience & courage? In doing this, I do no otherwise then *Phormio* did when he discours'd of War before *Hannibal*."

The anecdote was very popular, and occurs in several places in modern literature.

p. 135. *not Body enough.* It is well known that many wines cannot endure to travel, and if imported lose much of their flavour and bouquet. Most Italian wines, Chianti, Capri, Lacrima Christi, not to mention Orvieto and Montepulciano, are quite another thing when drunk in England, and far inferior to precisely the same vintages and quality drunk in their native land.

p. 135. *an Academy.* The French Academy, *l'Académie française*, was established by order of the King in 1635. In its original form it had been in existence some four or five years earlier. Under the patronage of Cardinal Richelieu, at whose request Louis XIII granted Letters Patent on 29 January, 1635, the Academy at once assumed an authoritative position of immense importance. Article XXIV of the original statutes lays down that "The principal function of the Academy shall be to labour with all care and diligence to give certain rules to our language, and to render it pure, eloquent and capable of treating the arts and sciences." Louis XIV showed the Academy great favour. It was actually in 1639 that the Academy commenced work upon their famous French Dictionary.

p. 135. *Leave to borrow Words.* In spite of his precept Dryden himself, especially in his earlier days, was wont to convey pretty freely from the French. E.g. *To His Sacred Majesty, A Panegyrick*, 1661:

> Hither in Summer ev'nings you repair
> To take the fraischeur of the purer air.

It must be remembered that in the character of Melantha, *Marriage-a-la-Mode*, produced in 1672, Dryden amply satirizes the craze for a Frenchified vocabulary. Alexandre Beljame's thesis, *Quae e Gallicis Verbis in Anglicam Linguam Johannes Dryden Introduxerit*, Paris, 1881, is useful but by no means altogether accurate. It is pedantic rather than scholarly.

p. 136. *Queen Gorboduc. Gorboduc*, the first regular tragedy in English, was performed on 18 January, 1562, as part of a "grand Christmasse" in the Inner Temple, London, and "after shewed before her Majestie." An unauthorized text appeared in 1565, and a genuine impression as *Ferrex and Porrex* in 1570. The unauthorized issue, *Gorboduc*, was reprinted in 1569, 1571, and 1590. The editions of 1565 and 1590 state that the first three acts of the play were written by Thomas Norton. The rest of the drama is from the pen of Thomas Sackville, Lord Buckhurst and Earl of Dorset, with whose name the main authorship of the work is traditionally associated. Gorboduc, King of Britain, divides his realm in his lifetime between his two sons Ferrex and Porrex. Dissensions arise; there is a fatal fraticidal rivalry, and the whole realm is thrown into anarchical confusion. The name of the Queen is Videna.

Oldham, *Horace his Art of Poetry*, has:

> At first the Musick of our Stage was rude,
> Whilst in the *Cock-pit* and *Black-Friars* it stood:
> And this might please enough in former Reigns,
> A thrifty, thin, and bashful Audience:
> When *Bussy d'Ambois* and his Fustian took,
> And men were ravish'd with Queen *Gordobuck*.

p. 136. *pronouncing Latin.* The question of the English pronunciation of Latin is still being discussed even to-day. It is said that in England a native pronunciation of Latin was adopted at the Reformation to emphasize yet more in detail the secession from the Catholic Church. However that may be, a very ugly, eccentric, and etymologically impossible method came into vogue, was generally used, and taught throughout the land. Of recent years other pronunciations, each more capricious and whimsical than the last, have been suggested by solemn conclaves of ushers and pedants. There is, of course, but one correct pronunciation of Latin, the so-called Italian pronunciation, which has been preserved without a break in the Benedictine family from the days when Latin was commonly spoken in the fifth century.

p. 136. *Angli suos ac sua omnia.* From the *Icon Animorum.* The passage occurs on pages 74–75 of the 1st edition (London, 1614), not quite one-third through Chapter IV. The earlier editions do not divide the chapters into sections, but in that of 1733 (Dresden and Leipzig) it is §36.

"Anglis ut plurimùm gravis animus, & in se velut ad consilium seductus; seipsos, & suae gentis mores, ingenia, animos, eximiè mirantur: Dum salutant, aut scribunt, descendere ad verba imaginariae servitutis quae istorum seculorum blandicies invênit, nisi fortè externis moribus imbuti, non sustinent."

It will be noticed that Dryden considerably departs from the words of his source.

p. 136. *invented . . . Blanck Verse.* It is hardly necessary to point out that Dryden here is completely mistaken, and that blank verse had been used in the drama by Shakespeare's predecessors.

p. 136. *Whipt at Westminster.* Under Dr. Busby.

p. 137. *Sir John Denham.* 1615–1669. His famous *Cooper's Hill* was published London, 1642, although said to have been written two years earlier. The influence of this poem was immense and enduring, so that we find Swift in *Apollo's Edict* advising:

> Nor let my votaries show their skill
> In aping lines from *Cooper's Hill,*
> For know I cannot bear to hear
> The mimicry of deep and clear.

p. 137. *The Siege of Rhodes. The Siege of Rhodes Made a Representation by the Art of Prospective in Scenes, And the Story sung in Recitative Musick*, performed at Rutland House, September, 1656. A second part was added, and the two parts were frequently acted at Lincoln's Inn Fields. *The Siege of Rhodes* is by no means so regular as the heroic tragedies of Dryden's school, since varying lyric measures are employed, and the choruses plainly mark an operatic origin.

p. 137 *defence of Poesie.* Under the two several titles *An Apologie for Poetrie* and *A Defence of Poesie* two separate editions of Sir Philip Sidney's work were printed in 1595. It must, however, have been written before 1583.

p. 137. *Ignobiliore materiâ depressus.* Julius Caesar Scaliger (della Scala), *Poetices libri octo*, Lyons, 1561, lib. VI: "Maximus poeta Claudianus solo argumento ignobiliore oppressus addit de ingenio quantum deest materiae." It will be noted that Dryden's quotation, although giving the sense of the criticism, is not strictly accurate.

p. 138. *They blow out Candles.* A hackneyed device upon the English and French stages at that period. In Thomas Corneille's *Le Feint Astrologue* (1648), III, 7, when Don Juan enters Jacinte utters a cry, "laissant tomber la lumière qu'elle porte." She hides herself, and a little later "se retirant avec violence de dessous la table qu'elle fait tomber avec la lumière qui s'estient" she runs away screaming "A l'aide, je suis morte." It is only fair to say that this scene is very effective, and has yet more effectively been reproduced by Dryden in *An Evening's Love.* In *She Wou'd if She Cou'd*, produced 6 February, 1667–8 at the Duke's House, V, Sentry runs away with the candle and leaves Sir Oliver and Lady Cockwood in the dark. Often natural and indeed necessary, such business with candles became trite and often forced and foisted in, so Shadwell in *A True Widow*, produced at Dorset Garden in the spring of 1678–9, Act IV, the

Playhouse scene, laughs at these stale tricks in the conduct of a comedy:

Enter Husband.

Wife. *O Gad! my Husband!*
1 Lover. *'Sdeath! what shall we do?*
Young Maggot. Now it thickens; an admirable Plot!
Husb. *O my Shins, my Shins!*
[The Husband falls over a Form, and breaks his Shins, and puts out the Candle.
Wife. *'Tis as we wish'd.*
Young Maggot. There's a Turn! Who would expect that? As great a Turn as can be, from Darkness to Light: Can any thing be greater?
[Husband takes up the Candle and blows it in again.
1 Lover. *Now we are undone again.*

So in *Wit for Money: or, Poet Stutter. A Dialogue between Smith, Johnson, and Poet Stutter*, 1691, which is a skit upon D'Urfey, more especially upon *Love for Money*, Poet Stutter (D'Urfey) cries: "As for *Plot*, Sir, I'll not yield it to any Poet or Politician; and there's my *Plotting Sisters* for one, which I'll match, with any Play in *Europe:* Either *She wou'd if she cou'd, Squire of Alsatia, Soldiers Fortune*, or any other——" when Smith, accusing him of reproducing *ad nauseam* for the hundredth time the old threadbare devices, interrupts tartly with "So you may indeed, the putting out of Candles, changing of Gowns; Tables and Traps are well enough imagined."

p. 138. *Fight till they Dye.* Cf. *The Rehearsal.* Actus II. Scaena V:

Enter four men at one door, and four at another, with their Swords drawn.

1 *Soldier.* Stand. Who goes there?
2 *Sol.* A Friend.
1 *Sol.* What Friend?
2 *Sol.* A Friend to the House.
1 *Sol.* Fall on. [*They all kill one another. Music strikes.*
Bayes. Hold, hold. [*To the Music. It ceaseth.*
Now here's an odd surprize: all these dead men you shall see rise up presently, at a certain Note that I have made in *Effaut flat*, and fall a Dancing. Do you hear, dead men? Remember your note in *Effaut flat.* Play on. [*To the Music.* Now, now, now. O Lord, O Lord! *The music play his Note, and the dead men rise, but cannot get in order.*

p. 139. *Slighted Maids.* Not without a glance at Sir Robert Stapylton's *The Slighted Maid*, produced at Lincoln's Inn Fields, early in 1662–3, a play upon which Dryden has some pretty severe strictures.

p. 140. *Honoria.* Malone, *Life of Dryden* (*Works*, Vol. I, Part I, 1800; p. 24), who somewhat exaggerates a complimentary letter of Dryden written (1655) to his cousin Honor Driden into a courtship of that lady, writes: "Perhaps the name of *Honoria*, in one of his earliest plays (*The Rival Ladies*), was adopted in consequence of his attachment to this inexorable beauty." A pretty conceit.

p. 142. [*The Scene draws.* Literally the flats drew open, and showed the deeper stage.

p. 142. *Hippolito bound to a Tree.* Thus in Rotrou's *Les Deux Pucelles*, III, 2, we have: "Léocadie, seule vêtue en homme et attachée à un arbre." The lady has a soliloquy of thirty-eight lines, which commences:

> Qu'un instable pouvoir gouverne nos destins!
> Combien de vilains jours suivent de beaux matins!

p. 143. *Picarons.* Pirates; corsairs. Cf. *Fryke's Voyage to the East Indies*, 1700: "The Streight of Sunda was very much infested with Pickaroons."

p. 147. *Canonique hours.* The canonical hours during which period of the day marriages may ordinarily be solemnized in a parish church. The canonical hours are now between 8 o'clock and 3 o'clock. Dryden transfers an English use to Spain.

p. 152. *A door opens.* One of the permanent proscenium doors.

p. 152. *by the Moon-shine.* The moon was regularly simulated as a scenic effect upon the Restoration stage, and there was certainly some such presentation of moonlight here. In Tuke's *The Adventures of Five Hours*, produced at Lincoln's Inn Fields, January, 1663, Act III, the garden scene, we have a stage direction "*The Rising Moon appears in the scene.*" There has been some scuffling and fighting in the dark, but Octavio cries:

> 'twill not be long,
> Now that the Rising Moon lends us some light.

In Mrs. Behn's posthumous play *The Widdow Ranter; or, The History of Bacon in Virginia*, Theatre Royal, winter of 1689, the Fifth Act opens with "*The* Sevana *in sight of the Camp; the Moon rises.*" In Mountfort's *Greenwich-Park*, Theatre Royal, 1691, Act III commences: "Scene 1. *The Park. The Moon: Enter* Dorinda *and* Aunt." Presently Young Reveller staggers in pretty well foxed, and exclaims: "'Tis a fine moon-shine Night."

There were moon-light effects on the court-masque of earlier days as in Jonson's masque of *Oberon*, 1611, when the moon was seen rising and discovered the satyr by her silver beams. Whether upon the ordinary platform-stage there was a scenic effect of the moon cannot perhaps be so confidently asserted, but the evidence points to something more than imaginary moon-light, and to me at any rate it seems plain that the moon was regularly simulated even in the public playhouses before the Restoration.

p. 153. *sculk in forms*. A form is the nest or lair where a hare croucheth. Thus Chaucer, *The Shipmannes Tale*, 103–104:

> As been thise wedded men, that lye and dare
> As in a forme sit a wery hare.

p. 160. *Eastern Quarries*. Of diamonds. Western mines, of gold.

p. 162. *Plate-fleet*. A convoy and vessels carrying precious metals and treasure.

p. 166. *a Serene*. An obsolete form of "Siren."

p. 167. *Poetry of the foot*. Every opportunity was seized to interlard a play with dances. In *The Cruelty of the Spaniards in Peru* (1658), one of the earliest representations after the closing of the theatre, Davenant utilized dancing, for a group of Indians enter "*and, gazing on the face of the Scene, fall into a Mimick Dance in which they express the Argument of the Prospect*."

In the Preface to *The Womens Conquest*, 4to, 1671, Edward Howard complains that "serious Plays" now rely not on their own themes or merits, but on their "Scenes, Machines, Habits, Jiggs, and Dances." Again, in the Preface to his *The Six days Adventure* he reiterates: "Scenes, Habits, Dancing, or perhaps an Actress take more with Spectators than the best Dramatick Wit." *The Rehearsal* very wittily burlesques the craze for the impertinent introduction of dances into a drama. "My Fancy," cries Bayes, "in this Play, is to end every Act with a Dance." When the two right Kings of Brentford descend from the Clouds, we have:

> 1 *King*. Come, now to serious counsel we'l advance.
> 2 *King*. I do agree; but first, let's have a Dance.

p. 168. *Ceres drawn by Dragons*. The masque is suggested by Claudian, *De Raptu Proserpinae*. Cf. I, 178–184:

> Hic ubi servandum mater fidissima pignus
> Abdidit, ad Phrygios tendit secura penates,
> Turrigeramque petit Cybelen, sinuosa draconum
> Membra regens, volucri qui pervia nubila tractu
> Signant, et placidis humectant frena venenis.
> Frontem crista tegit: pingunt maculosa virentes
> Terga notae: rutilum squamis intermicat aurum.

p. 170. *Hercules his Shirt*. When Nessus attempted to carry away Deianira Hercules pierced him with an arrow dipped in the venom of the hydra. The dying centaur bade Deianira collect his blood as this would ensure her husband's affection. In later years she became jealous of Iole, and when Hercules sent for his white sacrificial robe she steeped this in the blood of Nessus. The hero donned the garment, and as he grew warm the poison entered his pores causing excruciating pangs.

> Nec mora; letiferam conatur scindere vestem:
> Qua trahitur, trahit illa cutem; foedumque relatu,

Aut haeret membris frustra tentata revelli;
Aut laceros artus, et grandia detegit ossa.
Ipse cruor, gelido ceu quondam lamina candens
Tincta lacu, stridit, coquiturque ardente veneno.

Ovid, *Metamorphoseon*, IX, 166–171, a passage which it seems clear Dryden had in mind.

p. 171. *A Murd'rers touch.* "As in a secret murther, if the deade carcase be at any time thereafter handled by the murtherer, it will gush out of bloud, as if the blud were crying to the heauen for reuenge of the murtherer, God hauing appoynted that secret super-naturall signe, for tryall of that secrete vnnaturall crime, so it appeares that God hath appoynted (for a super-naturall signe of the monstruous impietie of the Witches) that the water shal refuse to receiue them in her bosom, that haue shaken off them the sacred Water of Baptisme." King James I, *Dæmonologie* (1597), Third Booke, chap. vi. Cf. Chapman's *The Widow's Tears*, 4to, 1612, V, 3 (ed. Parrott): "The Captain will assay an old conclusion, often approved, that at the murtherer's sight the blood revives again, and boils afresh; and every wound has a condemning voice to cry out guilty gainst the murtherer." There are very frequent references to this old belief.

p. 187. *Carrack.* A large ship of burden also fitted for warfare. A mighty galleon.

p. 191. *Scene the Third.* As has already been pointed out, the suggestions as to escape from the ship owe something to Petronius, *e.g.* one may compare Amideo's speech, "Here are Bundles . . ." and Hippolito's retort commencing, "Pithily spoken! . . ." with the Latin: "Ego vos in duas iam pelles coniciam vinctosque loris inter vestimenta pro sarcinis habebo, apertis scilicet aliquatenus labris, quibus et spiritum recipere possitis et cibum. conclamabo deinde nocte servos poenam graviorem timentes praecipitasse in mare. deinde cum ventum fuerit in portum, sine ulla suspicione pro sarcinis vos efferam." "ita vero" inquam ego "tanquam solidos alligaturus, quibus non soleat venter iniuriam facere? an tanquam eos qui sternutare non soleamus nec stertere?" *Petronii Satirae*, p. 70, ed. Franciscus Buecheler, Berolini, 1895.

p. 197. *Hulling.* To hull is to be driven about; to float aimlessly (as here). Cf. W. Toweson (1558) apud Hakluyt's *Voyages* (1589): "We lost our maine saile, foresaile, and spreetsaile, and were forced to lye a hulling."

p. 199. [*Exeunt.* No epilogue has been printed, and it was apparently lost. A similar accident occurred in the case of Mrs. Behn's comedy *The Dutch Lover*, 4to, 1673, when the Prologue was mislaid and could not be recovered for the press.

THE INDIAN-QUEEN

p. 207. *Ynca.* Inca or Inga, the Emperor or King of Peru. Dryden and Howard spell *Ynca*, but in the translation of *Polexandre*, folio, 1647, William Browne prefers *Inca* (pp. 36, 37, etc.). Garcilasso de Vega in his *Commentarios Reales* (1609), I, xxiv, says that Inca or Inga was sometimes more widely used to signify a "man of the blood royal" whilst the monarch was distinguished as Capa Inca. The epithet *Yupanqui*, "rich in all virtues," was often added to this title.

p. 207. *Montezuma.* Montecuzoma. The character as he appears in *The Indian-Queen* and *The Indian Emperour* is, of course, entirely unhistorical. Montezuma II, Lord of the Aztecs, was born about 1466, and succeeded to the headship, which had been previously held by his grandfather and uncle, in 1502. He was a warlike chief, who also gave much thought to the improvement of his capital. In later years he alienated his subjects by the heavy taxation necessary to support his ostentatious splendour. In April, 1519, Hernando Cortés landed at Vera Cruz, then an uninhabited beach. Led by the belief that Montezuma was a supreme ruler, the Emperor of Mexico, and not merely, as was in fact the case, the head war-chief of a number of confederate tribes, Cortés seized his person, conceiving that thus the pivot of the state was a prisoner, and that therefore the Mexican tribes could be controlled through the captive. Cortés did not realize that Montezuma was an elected officer who could be replaced without any serious trouble, and that the tribal council, supported by the medicine-men, was the real head of the confederacy. Montezuma died, broken in mind and body, 30 June, 1520, refusing to the last, it is said, to abjure the religion of his forefathers.

p. 207. *the Curtain rises.* This Prologue is very exceptional. It was the usual rule for the Prologue to be spoken by the actor or actors upon the apron before the rise of the curtain, and variations such as the present are extremely rare. One example is when Killigrew's company opened temporarily at Lincoln's Inn Fields with *Wit without Money* and Dryden furnished the Prologue which is printed in *Covent Garden Drollery*, and also in *Westminster Drollery*, the Second Part, 1672. In the British Museum (Sloane 4455. f. 20*b*) is a MS. of this Prologue: "The Prologue of a Play entitled Witt without Money—Spoken at the Dukes old Theatre (after the Kings was burnt) by the Kings players, Feb. 26, 1671. The Curtaine being drawne up all the Actors were discover'd on the stage in Melancholick postures, & Moone advancing before the rest speaks as follows, addressing himself chiefly to ye King then p^r^sent."

p. 207. *ancient Prophesies*. Songs and prophecies had actually existed among the Indians of Peru and Mexico, foretelling the arrival of a conquering race from over the seas. In ancient Mexico there was a universal tradition that Quetzalcoatl (Bright Shining Serpent), the bearded white man who in the halcyon days of their era had taught the Toltecs the use of metals, industry, skill and culture, before he had mysteriously disappeared from their midst prophesied that one day white men, bearded as he, would sail from over the seas, take possession of Mexico, and destroy the temples with their gods. See further the Franciscan Bernardino de Sahagun's *Historia Universal de Nueva España*, lib. III; cc. 3, 4, 13 and 14; Torquemada's *Monarquia Indiana*, Seville, 1615, lib. VI, c. 24; and Francisco Lopez de Gomara, *Crónica de la Nueva España*, cap. 222, apud Barcia *Historiadores Primitivos de las Indias Occidentales*, Madrid, 1749, tom. II.

In Yucatan, long before the Spaniards appeared, the poet Patzin-Yaxun-Chun had sung of the worshippers of a true God who would destroy the idols of the Itzalanos. The high priest of Tixcacayon, Cauch, said: "Your father comes, O Itzalanos! your brother comes, O Itzalanos! receive your bearded guests from the East, who come to bring the sign of God. God it is who comes to us, God meek and holy."

Among the Peruvian Indians legend spoke of certain white and bearded men, who, advancing from the shores of Lake Titicaca, established an ascendancy over the natives, and imparted to them the blessings of civilization. The Peruvian traditions may be found in the works of Christoval de Molina and the Indian Salcamayhua, which have been translated by Markham. The same or similar traditions are reported by authorities contemporary with the conquest of Peru, Ondegardo *Relacion Segunda* (MS.): Sarmiento *Relacion*, cap. 1 (MS. Escorial): Cieza de Leon, *Cronica*, cap. 105 (Anvers, 1554): *Conquista i Poblacion del Piru* (MS.): *Declaracion de los Presidente é Oydores de la Audiencia Reale del Peru* (MS.).

p. 209. *Thrice have the Mexicans before us fled*. Prescott, *History of the Conquest of Peru*, Book I, c. 1, speaking of Peru and Mexico says: "There is no trace of any communication with, or even knowledge of, each other to be found in the two nations."

p. 210. *Thou glorious Sun*. The Peruvian legend relates that the Sun, the great luminary and parent of mankind, sent two of his children, Manco Capac and Mama Oello Huaco, brother and sister, husband and wife, to teach the rude aborigines culture and civilization. They settled in the valley of Cuzco, initiated the simple folk into the arts of agriculture, weaving and spinning, and from this celestial pair was directly descended the Peruvian monarchy. Garcilasso de la Vega, *Commentarios Reales* (Lisboa, 1609), discusses the legend and is inclined to believe that Manco Capac was an early chief who in order to win greater respect gave out that he and his wife were children of the Sun, sent by their father from Heaven. "The belief in the fable of the Ynca's origin would be confirmed by the benefits and privileges he conferred on the Indians, until at last they firmly believed that he was the Child of the Sun, come from Heaven." (Markham's translation.) When an Inca died he was said to have been "called home to the mansions of his father, the Sun."

p. 212. *invades my ears*. Parodied in *The Rehearsal*, produced at the Theatre Royal, 7 December, 1671, V, 1:

King Usher. But stay, what sound is this invades our ears?

One may compare Davenant's *The Siege of Rhodes*, The First Entry:

Alphonso. What various noises do mine ears invade?
And have a consort of confusion made?

p. 214. *God of Vengance*. "The terrible Huitzilopochtli, the Mexican Mars; although it is doing injustice to the heroic war-god of antiquity to identify him with the sanguinary monster. This was the patron deity of the nation. His fantastic image was loaded with costly ornaments. His temples were the most stately and august of the public edifices; and his altars reeked with the blood of human hecatombs in every city of the empire." Prescott, *The Conquest of Mexico*, Book I, chapter 3.

p. 214. *Dy'd with their blood*. Human sacrifice was a prominent feature of the worship of nearly all the tribes of the Mexican confederacy, and greatly practised among the Aztecs in their vast teocalli, or temple, at Tenochtitlan. The Aztecs, indeed, kept up a continuous warfare against their neighbours, not with the intention of extending their empire, but rather for the avowed purpose of securing victims for their sacrifices. In battle their idea was not so much to kill as to take their enemies prisoners. Father Motolinia, in his letter of 2 January, 1553, to the Emperor Charles V, speaking of the human sacrifices with which the Emperor Ahuitzotl (1486–1502) celebrated the opening of a famous temple in Mexico, writes: "In a sacrificial service lasting three or four days 80,400 men were sacrificed. They were brought through four streets walking single file until they reached the idols." Father Durán, also, speaking of the same holocaust, says that the number of victims was incredible. The Vatican and Tellerian MSS. give the number of sacrifices as 20,000; and this seems more probable. Yet the time for the sacrifices was 13 hours, from sunrise to sunset; victims were slain simultaneously in no less than fourteen temples, whilst in the chief teocalli there were four groups of sacrifices. Each victim occupied less than five minutes.

p. 216. *gaulless Dove*. Dryden probably remembered Cowley's *Ode Upon His Majesty's Restoration and Return*:

Ah! mild and gaulless *Dove*,
Which dost the *pure* and *candid* Dwellings love.

The Whole Duty of Man, XVII, 19, Ed. 1658 (p. 147), speaks a "A Dove, a meek and gall-less creature,"

p. 224. *successive Monarchs*. Legitimate, as in the direct succession. The word is frequent in this sense. Cf. Creech's *Lucretius*, Second Edition, Oxford, 1683, Notes, p. 52: "Every *King* whether *Elective* or *Successive*, Rules by the *same* Authority."

p. 227. *You twice Ten Hundred*. Purcell composed the music for a revival of *The Indian-Queen*, but apparently did not complete the score owing to his death. His setting of the opening of Ismeron's solo has been described by Burney as "the best piece of recitative in our language." Professor Dent observes: "The whole solo is well planned for dramatic effect; opening with this magnificent piece of declamation it proceeds to a fantastic air in which the violins are well employed to enhance the interpretative power of the voice part; then after the remarkable dramatic passage to the words

From thy sleepy Mansion rise,
And open thy unwilling Eyes,

which leads to a climax on the dominant of the key, the whole character of the song changes to a gentle lulling melody, which prepares well for the appearance of the god himself. He rises to the accompaniment of two hautboys . . ."

p. 228. *Earthy Dun*. Dun is still used in some rural districts to signify a puddock; a toad. Saintsbury with wonted perspicacity informs us that dun is "an unintelligible substantive," and ventures on "a slight conjectural emendation." To crown this nonsense he adds: "Dun is certainly the name of a devil."

p. 228. *God of Dreams*. It does not appear that there was a special God of Dreams in Mexico. Tezcatlipoca, the sky-god, was supposed to be sender of terrible phantoms and night-visions, so perhaps he might be regarded as such, and, if Dryden had any particular deity in view, is here intended.

p. 230. *Act IV. Scene* 1. *The Scene opens*. The scene-plot of *The Indian-Queen* is remarkably well constructed from a technical point of view. Act III, Scene 1, the Triumph of Zempoalla occupies the whole depth of the Stage. Ismeron's cell closes over this, and the Conjurer is discovered in an inset. The God of Dreams rises and descends and there is a Song sung by Spirits, but no elaborate dance or masque, as for instance in *Tyrannick Love*, IV, since this is a front scene. The cell scene then opens upon the Prison, which requires the whole depth of the stage, and has been set during the previous dialogue. At "None can deceive me while I trust in this," *Exeunt omnes*, a front scene closes over the prison, and Orazia with the rest enter well down stage. At the end of Act IV this front scene opens to discover the Temple of the Sun for which the whole stage would be required. It must be remembered that the curtain was not drawn between the acts. The end of an act was denoted by an empty stage. For the front scenes the apron afforded ample convenience.

p. 230. *Fact*. Deed. A not uncommon use which persisted until the nineteenth century. Cf. Peter Woodhouse, *The Flea*, 1605 (ed. Grosart, 1877), 13:

The minde doth make the fact, or good or ill.

p. 231. *publick Heart*. There is a sarcastic play of words here upon the various shades of meaning implied by "publick." "Your publick Love" is your apparent or unconcealed passion; whilst "your publick Heart" touches upon the meaning "devoted to the general welfare." Clarendon, *History of the Rebellion*, 1647, VI, 246, has "publick-heartedness" in the latter sense.

p. 237. *Temple of the Sun*. The Sun was the especial deity of an order called the Eagles. It is supposed that the earliest temples raised by the Toltecs were dedicated to the Sun. The chroniclers Bernal Diaz, Oviedo, Gomara, and others speak of a vast gold disc "as large as a carriage-wheel," engraved with plants and animals, thirty palms in circumference and valued at twenty thousand *pesos de oro* which represented the Sun. (The *peso de oro* is calculated to be equivalent to £2 12s. 6d. of English money.) Boturini says in his *Idea de una Nueva Historia General de la América Septentrional*, Madrid, 1746, that the summit of the great pyramid of Teotihucan was crowned by a vast temple in which stood a colossal statue of the presiding deity, the Sun, made of one entire block of stone and facing the east. The breast of this monolithic idol was protected by a targe of burnished gold and silver whereon the first rays of the rising sun glinted and gleamed. An antiquary, writing in the earlier decades of the eighteenth century, speaks of having seen some huge fragments of the fallen statue, which was demolished by the holy zeal of the first Bishop of Mexico, the Franciscan Juan de Zumárraga. The remains of the figure had entirely disappeared in 1757 when Don Mariano Veytia visited the spot, as he relates in his *Historia Antigua de Méjico*.

In *Polexandre* (English translation, folio, 1647, p. 75) is described "an Altar, on which was an Idoll of gold, which held a Javilin in his hand; many great basons of gold round about the Altar."

p. 237. *ready for Sacrifice*. The Eagles were wont to offer human victims to the Sun upon a huge stone, the Stone of Tizoc, which was called "the drinking-cup of the Eagles."

It has been justly observed that human sacrifices have never been practised by any nation on a scale to be compared with the holocausts in ancient Mexico. The temples were mere shambles, swimming in blood. Bishop Juan de Zumárraga, in a letter written a few years after the Conquest, states that twenty thousand victims were yearly slaughtered in the capital. Antonio de Herrera, in his *Historia General de las Indias Occidentales*, says that throughout the kingdom on one particular feast each year twenty thousand victims were slain on the altars of the demons they worshipped. The chief object, indeed, of war with the Aztecs was not so much to extend their empire as to collect prisoners for sacrifice, and an enemy was never slain in battle if he could be taken alive. At the dedication of the great temple of Huitzilopochtli in 1486 the captives, who for several years had been reserved to that end, were ranged in files extending nearly two miles in length. The ceremonies occupied many days, and it is computed that there fell seventy thousand. The victims were decked with coronals of plumes and swiftly stretched one after another upon the great stone of sacrifice. The priest cut asunder the ribs with his sharp razor of *itztli*, and thrusting his hand into the reeking wound, tore away the heart which was deposited hot and bloody on the golden censer before the idol. The body was then thrown down the steep stairs of the pyramid. "The stench was more intolerable than that of the slaughter-houses in Castile," and well might Toribio designate these foul shrines as "Hell." See further Bernal Diaz del Castillo in his *Historia Verdadera de la Conquista de la Nueva España*, which sixty years after its composition was published at Madrid in 1632 under the auspices of the learned Mercedarian, Alonso Remon.

p. 242. *ere it be too late*. Saintsbury, in error, reads "or it be too late," and adds a note: "Probably one of of the latest uses of 'or' for 'ere' " ! The reading "or" does not occur.

p. 243. *he made a God*. The Aztecs believed that the souls of monarchs and warriors who fell in battle went with jubilee and radiant dances to accompany the Sun in his bright progress through the heavens. After an interval of time they then passed to a most delicious paradise.

p. 243. *Ounce*. Some vaguely identified medium-sized feline beast; most generally the lynx.

p. 246. *the Painters too. The Indian-Queen* was produced at the Theatre Royal in Bridges Street early in January, 1663–4, with long-studied and most unwonted magnificence. "For show, they say, [it] exceeds 'Henry the Eighth'," wrote Pepys. At the end of the second or early in the third week of December, 1663, *Henry VIII* had been put on by Davenant at Lincoln's Inn Fields with special scenery, new costumes, crowds, shows and processions, and general effects. Nearly ten years after in *The Rehearsal*, Theatre Royal, 7 December, 1671, Bayes showing "the greatest Scene that ever *England* saw . . . for state, shew, and magnificence" cries: "In fine, I'll justifie it to be as grand to the eye every whit, I gad, as that great Scene in *Harry* the Eight, and grander too, I gad."

THE INDIAN EMPEROUR

p. 248. *Dum relego.* Ovid, *Epistoiarum ex Ponto*, I, v, 15–16.

p. 255. *A Defence of an Essay.* This is only found in the Second Quarto of *The Indian Emperour*, 1668, and it was not re-issued during Dryden's lifetime. On Sunday, 20 September, 1668, Pepys, disappointed of the company of Henry Harris and Shadwell at dinner, ate his meal alone, "having since church heard the boy read over Dryden's reply to Sir R. Howard's Answer, about his Essay of Poesy, and a letter in answer to that; the last whereof is mighty silly, in behalf of Howard." The title of this tract runs: "A Letter from a Gentleman to the *Honourable* Ed. Howard, Esq.; Occasioned By a *Civiliz'd Epistle* of Mr. Dryden's Before his Second Edition of his *Indian Emperour.*" In the Savoy, Printed by Thomas Newcomb, 1668, 4to, eight leaves. This is an abusive attack upon Dryden, written by one "R.F." In an article in *The Gentleman's Magazine*, December, 1850, Peter Cunningham attributes this Letter to Richard Flecknoe, and suggests that here we have the reason for Dryden's animosity. Beyond the identity of initials, however, there seems to be no evidence that Flecknoe was the author.

p. 255. *The Great Favourite.* By Sir Robert Howard, produced at the Theatre Royal, Thursday, 20 February, 1667–8, and published 4to, 1668.

p. 255. *Dimock.* The hereditary Champion of England, as lord of the manor of Scrivelsby. In a letter to the *Spectator* (Feb. 23, 1901) advocating the retention or revival of the "Services of Grand Serjeantry," Mr. L. W. Vernon Harcourt writes:

"The service of *King's Champion* belongs to the Dymoke family, the representative of the ancient house of Marmion, and it appertains to the manor of Scrivelsby. Documentary evidence of this service dates back to 20 Edward I; but tradition makes it a Norman service. The earliest account of the ceremony is given by a chronicler of Richard II's coronation. The great estates of the Marmions had then become dispersed. Tanfield was in the hands of the Fitz-Hughes, Tamworth belonged to Baldwin Freville, while Scrivelsby had come to the Dymokes. Accordingly, several claimants for the service presented themselves, but the Court of Claims decided for Scrivelsby.

p. 256. *understanding all things.* Sir Robert Howard was notorious for his pretensions to universal knowledge. Evelyn, 16 February, 1685, writes: "I dined at Sir Robert Howard's, Auditor of the Exchequer, a gentleman pretending to all manner of arts and sciences, for which he had been the subject of comedy, under the name of Sir Positive; not ill-natured, but insufferably boasting. He was son to the late Earl of Berkshire."

Shadwell in his comedy *The Sullen Lovers*, produced at Lincoln's Inn Fields, Saturday, 2 May, 1668, had presented Sir Robert Howard as Sir Positive At-all, "A foolish Knight, that pretends to understand every thing in the World, and will suffer no Man to understand any thing in his Company; so foolishly Positive, that he will never be convinced of an Error, though never so grosse," and the caricature was amply recognized and laughed at by the whole town.

p. 256. *the Philosopher*. See Spartianus, *Vita Hadriani*, 15: "Et Favorinus quidem, cum verbum eius quondam ab Hadriano reprehensum esset atque ille cessisset, arguentibus amicis quod idonei auctores usurpassent, risum iucundissimum movit. Ait enim, 'Non recte suadetis, familiares, qui non patimini me illum doctiorem omnibus credere qui habet triginta legiones.' "

p. 256. *Repulse upon repulse*. *The Great Favourite*. Act I. Scene 1. *Enter* Lerma, *Alone*. The play commences with the lines Dryden here quotes.

p. 256. *borrowed from the observations of others*. Dryden is more than modest. The line of thought and arguments in the *Essay* have all the originality of genius. Martin Clifford, taking this hint, thus wantonly attacks Dryden: "I was about six years since a little acquainted with a Name-sake and Countreyman of yours, who pilfered out of Monsieur Hedelin, Mesnardiere, and Corneille, an Essay of Dramatick Poetry, wherein he tells us another tale." This seems to have been written in 1674. Martin Clifford's *Notes upon Mr. Dryden's Poems in Four Letters*, p. 8, 1687. (Clifford died in 1677.)

Monsieur Hedelin is François Hédelin, Abbé d'Aubignac, a famous critic and champion of the theatre. He was born at Paris, 4 August, 1604. Among his best-known works are: *Térence justifié*, 4to, 1646, Paris, an attack on Menage; *La Practique du théâtre*, 4to, 1669, Paris; and *Dissertations concernant le pöeme dramatique en forme de remarques sur les deux tragédies de M. Corneille, intitulées* Sophonisbe et Sutorius, 12mo, 1663, Paris. He died at Nemours, 27 July, 1676. Mrs. Behn in the Dedication to *The Luckey Chance*, 4to, 1687, quotes "The Abbot of *Aubignac*," as she quaintly terms him.

Hippolyte-Jules Pilet De La Mesnardière, born 1610, at Loudun, died 4 June, 1663, at Paris, was a well-known poet and critic. Bussy terms him "un *virtuose* qui a fort bien écrit de toutes les manières." He has left some dozen works, tragedies (*La Pucelle d'Orleans*, 1642; *Alinde*, 1643); poems, both French and Latin; historical "relations"; a panegyric on Trajan (paraphrased from Pliny); a *Traité de la Melancholie;* and miscellanea. His *La Poétique*, Paris, 4to, 1640, to which reference is here made, was left unfinished owing to the death of Richelieu who had inspired this theme. "Il donne," says Niceron, "des préceptes et des exemples sur la tragédie et l'élégie. Les préceptes sont empruntés des anciens, et il les expose non pas avec une brièveté didactique, mais souvent avec un faste oratoire; pour les exemples, il les tire quelquefois de son propre fonds." In 1640 (4to, Paris) De La Mesnardière published *Le Caractère élégiaque*, suite de *La Poëtique*.

p. 257. *what Gentleman.* Sir Robert Howard, "To the Reader," prefacing *The Great Favourite*, writes: "*But I have heard that a Gentleman in* Parliament, *going to speak twice, and being interrupted by another* Member, *as against the Orders of the* House, *he was excused by a Third, assuring the* House *he had not yet spoken to the Question.*"

p. 258. *Ut pictura. Ars Poetica*, 361.

p. 258. *Hæc amat. Ars Poetica*, 363–4:

> haec amat obscurum, volet haec sub luce videri,
> iudicis argutum quae non formidat acumen.

It will be noted that Dryden has "vult" for the correct "volet." "Velit" and "volet" are found in inferior MSS., but not "vult."

p. 258. *Et quae. Ars Poetica*, 149–50.

p. 259. *My conversation.* See Johnson's *Life of Dryden:* "Congreve represents him as ready to advise and instruct; but there is reason to believe that his communication was rather useful than entertaining. He declares of himself that he was saturnine, and not one of those whose sprightly sayings diverted company; and one of his censurers makes him say:

> Nor wine nor love could ever see me gay;
> To writing bred, I knew not what to say.

. . . Of Dryden's sluggishness in conversation it is vain to search or to guess the cause. He certainly wanted neither sentiments nor language: his intellectual treasures were great, though they were locked up from his own use. 'His thoughts,' when he wrote, 'flowed in upon him so fast, that his only care was which to choose, and which to reject.' Such rapidity of composition naturally promises a flow of talk; yet we must be content to believe what an enemy says of him, when he likewise says it of himself."

p. 259. *Reserate Clusos. Hippolytus*, l. 863.

p. 259. *Delectus verborum.* Cicero in his *Brutus*, LXXIII, quotes this as a maxim laid down by Caesar in his work "on the method of speaking in Latin," to which the title *De Analogia* was given.

p. 259. *instead of shutting.* But "shutting" remains uncorrected in "To the Reader" prefacing *The Great Favourite*, folio, 1692.

p. 260. *Barach.* "Barach" in Hebrew means *bless*, with the antithetical meaning of *curse*, the idea being that the blessing was overdone, and so really a curse, as in vulgar English as well as in the Semitic cognates. See Driver's *Gesenius* (1893), with references to 1 Kings xxi. 10, 13; Job i. 5, 11, and ii. 5, 9; and Psalm x. 3. See especially Psalm x. 3 and Job ii. 9. In the former passage the Authorized Version reads: "For the wicked . . . blesseth the covetous whom the Lord abhorreth," while the Revised Version has: "And the covetous renounceth, yea contemneth the Lord," and in the margin suggests as an alternative: "Or *blesseth the covetous, but contemneth*," &c. In Job ii. 9 the famous "curse God and die," becomes in the Revised Version "Renounce God and die."

p. 260. *Notions politick and grave*. In *The Sullen Lovers* Sir Positive At-all discourses at length upon politics. "I have found out such a Way for them to preserve *Flanders* from the *French* . . .," he cries, "if he will let me divide the Government with him I'll do it; otherwise if *Flanders* be lost, 'tis none of my Fault." At another juncture when Cardinal Mazarine is mentioned Sir Positive asserts: "Cardinal *Mazarine* a States-man? well, I will say nothing of myself for that . . . I may be at this Instant chief minister of State in *Russia;* but the Truth on't is, *Stanford*, I expect that nearer Home."

p. 261. *instruction of Princes, and reformation of States*. Perhaps in allusion to *The Great Favourite*. According to Pepys it was understood to be a satire on the Court. Thursday, 20 February, 1667–8: "By one o'clock to the King's house; a new play 'The Duke of Lerma,' of Sir Robert Howard's: where the King and Court was; . . . The play designed to reproach our King with his mistresses, that I was troubled for it, and expected it should be interrupted; but it ended all well, which salved all. The play a well-writ and good play, only its design I did not like of reproaching the King, but altogether a very good and most serious play."

p. 261. *now fettered in business*. From "To The Reader" prefacing *The Great Favourite*. An ardent Royalist, Sir Robert Howard, at the Restoration, was returned to Parliament for Stockbridge, Hants; he was made a Knight of the Bath, and became Secretary to the Commissioners of the Treasury. Later, in 1677, he was appointed Auditor of the Exchequer, which lucrative post he held until his death in 1698.

p. 261. *nullos habitura triumphos*. Lucan, *Pharsalia*, I, 12.

p. 261. *Sancho Pança's Doctor*. Doctor Pedro Rezio de Aguero, a purposely fantastic name. The doctor prescribed for Sancho "a hundred of small wafers, and a few thin slices of marmalade." *Don Quixote*, Part II, XLVII. (trans. Motteux).

p. 261. *my Lord L*. Malone notes: "I suppose, Lord Lauderdale. He was not created a duke until 1672."

p. 262. *Ficta voluptatis*. Horace, *Ars Poetica*, 338.

p. 262. *Sir John Berkenhead*. 1616—4 December, 1679. A staunch Royalist, Fellow of All Souls, M.P. for Wilton. In his poem, *In Memory of Mr. Cartwright*, he wrote that his deceased friend

> Knew the right mark of things, saw how to choose,
> For the great Wit's great work is to *Refuse*.

p. 263. Στῆ δ' ἄρ' ὑπ' Αἴαντος. *Iliad*, VIII, 267.

p. 266. *we are all mortal*. In allusion to Shadwell's quip in *The Sullen Lovers*, I, where Sir Positive At-all (Sir Robert Howard) with great solemnity informs Stanford: "I have thought of nothing else but Mankind this Month: . . . but betwixt you and I, let me tell you, we are all Mortal." The shaft is aimed at Howard's poem *Against the Fear of Death*.

p. 266. *Herculean Argument*. Power, 1664, has: "The first, which is the main and Herculean argument." *Herculanus* (Herculaneus) is a favourite adjective in Latin authors. Seneca has: "Unus tibi nodus, sed Herculaneus restat." *Epist*. 83, 23. Pseudo-Apuleius speaks of a "Herculanea nymphaea" (water-lily). *Herbarium*, 67.

p. 268. *the favour of the Duke of Lerma*. Francisco de Rojas y Sandoral, Marquis of Denia, was made Duke of Lerma immediately upon the accession of Philip III in 1598. For years the great favourite ruled with supreme authority. In 1618 he was compelled to resign all his offices, having been supplanted in the king's graces.

p. 271. *Anne*. Anne Scott, heiress of the Scotts, barons and earls of Buccleuch, upon the death of the elder sister, Lady Mary, in 1662, succeeded in her own right as Countess of Buccleuch. 20 April, 1663, she was married at Whitehall, "in the King's chamber," to the Duke of Monmouth. The newly wedded pair were created Duke and Duchess of Buccleuch. After the execution of her husband, Anne became the wife of Charles, third Lord Cornwallis, 6 May, 1688. She died, aged 81, 6 February, 1731–2. Perhaps Buckingham in *The Rehearsal*, I, 2, is having a backdoor hit at the Duchess when Bayes (I, 2) declares: "Were it not for the sake of some ingenious persons, and choice female spirits, that have a value for me, I would see 'em all hang'd, I gad, before I would e'er more set pen to papyr."

p. 273. *written with more Flame then Art*. This expression is burlesqued in *The Rehearsal*, I, 2, when Bayes says: "I write for some persons of Quality, and peculiar friends of mine, that understand what Flame and Power in writing is: and they do me the right, Sir, to approve of what I do."

p. 273. *Connexion of the Indian Emperour*. There is a bob at this in *The Rehearsal*, I, 2, as little Bayes boasts: "Sir, I have printed above a hundred sheets of papyr, to insinuate the Plot into the Boxes."

p. 274. *Alibech*. This name is from de Scudéry's *L'Illustre Bassa*, in which romance Alibech is the daughter of the pirate Arsalon.

p. 274. *The Scenes are old*. The scenery and dresses of *The Indian Emperour* were with some additions the same as those used in the production of *The Indian Queen*. Thus Act I, scene 2, "*The Temple*" was no doubt "*The Temple of the Sun*" of the earlier play (Act V, scene 1); "*The Magician's Cave*," Act II, scene 1, the cave of Ismeron (*The Indian Queen*, Act III, scene 2); "*Mexico*," Act III, scene 4, "*Mexico*" (*The Indian Queen*, Act I, scene 2); "*A Prison*," Act IV, scenes 1 and 4, Act V, scene 2, Montezuma's prison (*The Indian Queen*, Act IV, scene 1); whilst probably the "*Pleasant* Indian *Country*," Act I, scene 1, and Act II, scene 3, and "*The Camp*," Act III, scene 2, had also been used in the former drama. "*The*

Chamber Royal," Act III, scene 1, Act IV, scene 2, Act V, scene 1, and the "*pleasant Grotto*," Act IV, scene 3, were most likely new.

p. 277. *As if our old world.* These lines are laughed at in the famous *Timon, a Satyr upon several new Plays*, by Buckingham (?) and Rochester:

> Mine Host, who had said nothing in an hour,
> Rose up, and prais'd the *Indian* Emperour,
> *As if our Old World modestly withdrew,*
> *And here in private had brought forth a new.*
> There are two Lines! who but he durst presume
> To make the old World a withdrawing Room,
> Where of another World she's brought to Bed!
> What a brave Midwife is a *Laureat's* Head!

p. 278. *four hundred foot.* Actually the strength of the first armament of Cortés was one hundred and ten mariners; five hundred and fifty-three soldiers, including thirty-two cross-bow-men and thirteen arquebusiers; besides two hundred Indians of Havana, and a few Indian women for menial offices. He was provided with ten heavy guns, four light pieces called falconets, and plentiful ammunition. He had, besides, sixteen horses. The horse in the islands was of immense value.

There is some discrepancy among authorities as to actual numbers. Dryden seems to have followed the Letter from Vera Cruz, *Carta de Vera Cruz*, which speaks in round terms of four hundred soldiers. The above detailed estimate is that of Bernal Diaz. Diego Velasquez puts the numbers at a total of six hundred.

p. 278. *Taxallan.* Rather Tlascalan. Tlascala was a little republic lying midway between the Mexican Valley and the coast. The Tlascalans were the traditional enemies of the Aztecs against whom they had long maintained their independence. They early formed an alliance with Cortés and rendered him signal service.

p. 278. *broad Caus-way.* A great causeway stretching some four or five miles in length divided lake Chalco from Xochicalco on the west. It was a lance in breadth at the narrowest part, and in some places wide enough for eight horsemen to ride abreast. It was a solid structure of stones and lime, running directly through the lake and was declared by the Spaniards to be one of the most remarkable works they had seen in the new country.

p. 278. *bloody Sacrifice.* See note *Dyed with their Blood* to *The Indian-Queen*, *supra*.

p. 282. *Old Prophecies.* It is said that in the time of Montezuma there seems to have been a general feeling that the predicted hour of the return of Quetzalcoatl and the end of the Aztec dominion had come. When the Spaniards landed they were by many thought to be supernatural visitors, the "sons of destiny," whom it was useless or even profane to withstand. The Indian priests had preserved for untold years a verbal tradition that Mexico would be subdued by the race which came over the sea in floating palaces.

p. 284. *O mercy, mercy.* Congreve amusingly inserts this couplet in his Prologue "written for Jo. Haines and spoken by him at a new Comedy of Mr. Powel's," *A Very Good Wife*, produced at Drury Lane in the autumn of 1693.

> Mean time then, let me beg that you'd forbear
> Your Cat-calls, and the Instruments of War.
> *For Mercy, Mercy, at your Feet we fall,*
> *Before your roaring Gods destroy us all.*

p. 284. *cruel god.* The Aztec god of war and carnage, Huitzilopochtli, whose altars reeked with the blood of human hecatombs in every city, and to whom prisoners were sacrificed in vast numbers.

p. 285. *mild and gentle god.* Quetzalcoatl, the beneficent culture-hero, a Toltec divinity inherited by the Aztec, to whom no human sacrifices were offered. During his legendary reign on earth was the *aurea aetas* of Mexico. Quetzalcoatl was described as majestic and tall, having a white skin, long dark hair, a flowing beard. At last he embarked on his wizard skiff, and saying he would come again in the years to be, retired to the mystic land Tlapallan. The Mexicans ever looked for him and his following, and to this belief no little of the success of the Spaniards when they landed was due. The white strangers were the "men of destiny."

p. 291. *early Cocks.* Cf. Prudentius: *Liber Cathemerinon; Hymus ad Gallicinium;* 37–40.

> Ferunt, vagantes Dæmonas
> Lætos tenebras noctium,
> Gallo canente exterritos
> Sparsim timere, et cedere.

p. 291. *dusky Vallies.* Dryden has in mind Vergil, *Æneid* VI, 440–474.

p. 295. *I kill'd a double Man.* The Indians supposed a rider and his horse to be one and the same. "Equites," says Paolo Giovio, "unum integrum Centaurorum specie animal esse existimarent." *Elogia Virorum Illustrium*, Basil, 1696, VI, p. 229. This line is absurdly quoted by Loveby in Crowne's *The Married Beau; or, The Curious Impertinent*, produced at Drury Lane early in 1694, II:

> Virtue and fury flung her in a swoon.
> I might have said with Guyomar, one half lay
> Dead on the ground, the other ran away.

But it is Odmar not Guyomar who speaks thus.

p. 299. *Succesless.* This form was long popular. Cf. Miss Cuthbertson's *Forest of Montalbano*, 1810, vol. II, (p. 211): "This attempt to amuse the duca . . . proved successless."

p. 306. *This early Famine.* Actually, during the prolonged siege of Tenochtitlan, the Aztec capital, in 1521, the Indians suffered an extremity of starvation. All ordinary means of sustenance were exhausted, and men gnawed the bark of trees, ate grass, and even sought to stay the pangs of hunger with the most loathsome offal. Their only drink was the brackish water of the soil, saturated with the salt lake. Naturally disease raged hideously throughout the populace. Sahagun in his *Historia de Nueva España*, XII, 39 writes: "No tenian agua dulce para beber, ni para de ninguna manera de comer: bebian del agua salada y hedionda, comian ratones y lagartijas, y cortezas de árboles, y otras cosas no comestibles; y de esta causa enfermáron muchos, y muriéron muchos."

p. 326. *Guy. Friendship with him.* It is said that Quin once standing in the wings at a performance of *The Indian Emperour* thus jokingly parodied this couplet:

> Friendship with him whose Hand did *Odmar* kill!
> Tho' he was odd, yet thou art odder still.

p. 327. *a Christian Priest.* There were in the ranks of the Spaniards several priests, notably Fray Bartolomé de Olmedo, a Mercedarian of saintly life, and that holy secular Juan Díaz, who was martyred by the natives in Quechula near Tepeaca for having overthrown their demoniac idols. Little, however, could be done during the first stormy years of conquest, but when warfare had ceased a number of Franciscan missionaries went forth to evangelize the country. Dryden's fanatic has no place in history.

p. 327. *discover'd all thy store.* The racking of Montezuma is purely fictional. After the fall of the Aztec capital, Tenochtitlan, on 13 August, 1521, Cuauhtemotzin, the nephew of Montezuma, was captured, and as he refused to reveal where the royal treasures were hid the soldiers demanded that he should be put to the torture. This Cortés refused to sanction, until Julian de Alderete accused him of having come to a secret understanding with the captive prince and thus plotting to defraud the Spanish sovereigns and his army. Cortés then handed over Cuauhtemotzin to be questioned by the sworn tormentors. The Mexican brave could not be compelled to speak, and when his companion, the cacique of Tacuba, who was put to the torture with him, was unable to restrain his anguished groans, Cuauhtemotzin coldly rebuked him by exclaiming, "And do you think I, then, am taking sweet pleasure in my bath?" "¿ Estoi yo en algun deleite, ó baño?" Francisco Lopez de Gomara, *Crónica*, *c.* 145. This speech is traditionally rendered, "And do you think I am stretched on a bed of flowers?" It will be noticed that Dryden puts these phrases into Montezuma's mouth. Shortly Cortés rescued the Mexican princes from their suffering. They were, it proved, presently to be hanged for fomenting a conspiracy which aimed at a general massacre of the Spaniards. They died good Christians, however, being shriven by a Franciscan father before their execution.

p. 332. *Zoty.* Azotea (*Spanish*), a flat roof. The word, which is said to be of Moorish derivation, is still in common use in Spain and Mexico. The second quarto reads "balcone," and later editions have "Balcony." Cydaria, of course, appeared in one of the fixed balconies over the permanent proscenium doors. So in *Sr Martin Mar-all*, V, Mrs. Millisent and Rose enter "above"; a little later Sir Martin "*appears at the adverse Window.*" These terms "Window" and "above" both indicate the balconies. See the passage in *Sr Martin Mar-all* with explanatory note.